The Bloomsbury Companion to Modernist Literature

Also published by Bloomsbury

The Bloomsbury Companion to Holocaust Literature, edited by Jenni Adams
Modernism and Its Media, Chris Forster
Modernism and the Law, Robert Spoo
Modernist Lives, Claire Battershill
Modernism's Print Cultures, Faye Hammill and Mark Hussey
Modernism, Science, and Technology, Mark S. Morrisson

The Bloomsbury Companion to Modernist Literature

Edited by

Ulrika Maude and Mark Nixon

BLOOMSBURY ACADEMIC
LONDON • NEW YORK • OXFORD • NEW DELHI • SYDNEY

BLOOMSBURY ACADEMIC
Bloomsbury Publishing Plc
50 Bedford Square, London, WC1B 3DP, UK
1385 Broadway, New York, NY 10018, USA

BLOOMSBURY, BLOOMSBURY ACADEMIC and the Diana logo are trademarks of
Bloomsbury Publishing Plc

First published in Great Britain 2018

Cover design: Eleanor Rose
Cover image © Holger Leue / Lonely Planet Images / Getty Images

A catalogue record for this book is available from the British Library.

Library of Congress Cataloging-in-Publication Data
Names: Maude, Ulrika, editor. | Nixon, Mark, editor.
Title: The Bloomsbury companion to Modernist literature /
edited by Ulrika Maude and Mark Nixon.
Description: London ; New York : Bloomsbury Publishing, 2018. |
Series: Bloomsbury companions | Includes bibliographical references and index. |
Identifiers: LCCN 2018019126 (print) | LCCN 2018019358 (ebook) |
ISBN 9781780936550 (ePub) | ISBN 9781780935003 (ePDF) |
ISBN 9781780936413 (hardback)
Subjects: LCSH: Modernism (Literature)
Classification: LCC PN56.M54 (ebook) | LCC PN56.M54 B57 2018 (print) |
DDC 809/.9112–dc23
LC record available at https://lccn.loc.gov/2018019126

ISBN: HB: 978-1-7809-3641-3
        ePDF: 978-1-7809-3500-3
        eBook: 978-1-7809-3655-0

Series: Bloomsbury Companions

Typeset by Integra Software Services Pvt. Ltd.
Printed and bound in Great Britain

To find out more about our authors and books visit www.bloomsbury.com
and sign up for our newsletters.

Contents

List of Figures

Acknowledgements

The editors wish to thank the contributors for their good grace, their patience and their superb, insightful chapters. Warm thanks are also due to our press editor, David Avital, and Assistant Editor, Clara Herberg, who have offered unstinting support throughout the inception of this collection. Ulrika Maude would like to acknowledge that part of the work for this volume was undertaken during a one-year research fellowship (2015–2016) at the Helsinki Collegium for Advanced Studies in Finland. She wishes to thank Sari Kivistö, Director of HCAS at the time; Sami Pihlström, the former Director; co-Fellows Leszek Koczanowicz and Josephine Hoegaerts; and artists Päivi Maunu and Ilari Kähönen for many happy hours spent on Harakka Island and other favourite haunts in Helsinki. She would also like to thank Svetlana Kirichenko and Maija Väätämöinen for research assistance at the Collegium. Her deepest gratitude goes to Andrew Bennett for his support, intelligence and wit.

List of Contributors

Tim Armstrong's research interests include modernism and modernity, American literature and culture, literature and technology, and the poetry of Thomas Hardy. His publications include *The Logic of Slavery: Debt, Technology and Pain in American Literature* (Cambridge, 2012), *Modernism, Technology and the Body: A Cultural Study* (Cambridge, 1998) and *Modernism: A Cultural History* (Polity, 2005), as well as various edited collections. He has edited *Poems of Thomas Hardy* (Longman, 1993) and published a study of Hardy's poetry, *Haunted Hardy: Poetry, History, Memory* (Palgrave, 2000). He is general editor of the EUP series, Edinburgh Critical Studies in Modernist Culture, and is currently working on a project on modernist localism and deconstruction, *Micromodernism*.

Michael Bell is Fellow of the British Academy, Professor Emeritus in the Department of English and Comparative Literary Studies at the University of Warwick, and Associate Fellow of the Centre for Research in Philosophy, Literature and the Arts. He has written mainly on literary and philosophical themes from the European Enlightenment to modernity. His book-length publications include *Primitivism* (1973), *The Sentiment of Reality: Truth of Feeling in the European Novel* (1983), *F. R. Leavis* (1988), *D. H. Lawrence: Language and Being* (1992), *Gabriel García Márquez: Solitude and Solidarity* (1994), *Literature, Modernism and Myth: Belief and Responsibility in the Twentieth Century* (1997), *Sentimentalism, Ethics and the Culture of Feeling* (2001), *Open Secrets: Literature, Education and Authority from J-J. Rousseau to J. M. Coetzee* (Oxford, 2007) and *The Cambridge Companion to European Novelists* (ed.) (Cambridge, 2012).

Faith Binckes is Senior Lecturer in Modern and Contemporary Literature at Bath Spa University. She is the author of *Modernism, Magazines, and the British Avant-Garde: Reading Rhythm* (Oxford, 2010), articles on periodical culture, and on modernist authors such as Katherine Mansfield and Wyndham Lewis. Her monograph on the Irish writer Hannah Lynch, written with Dr Kathryn Laing, is in preparation. She is currently editing, with Dr Carey Snyder, a volume on women, periodicals and the modernist period. She will edit the volume of Wyndham Lewis's post-1930 art writing for the OUP edition of Lewis's *Collected Works*.

Conor Carville is Associate Professor of English at Reading University. His book on Irish cultural theory, *The Ends of Ireland: Criticism, History, Subjectivity*, was published by Manchester University Press in 2012. *Samuel Beckett and the Visual* was published by Cambridge University Press in 2018. Other recent publications include essays on Beckett's early poetry and on his novels *Watt* and *Murphy*. He is currently carrying out research in the Northern Irish poetry archives at Emory University and the Arts Council Northern Ireland Archives, as part of his British Academy–funded *Room to Rhyme* project. His book of poems, *Harm's Way* (2013), was published by Dedalus Press.

Jana Funke is Senior Lecturer in Medical Humanities and a Wellcome Trust Investigator based in the English Department at the University of Exeter. Her research focuses on modernist literature and culture, the history of sexuality, sexual science and medicine, and feminist studies and queer theory. Books include *The World and Other Unpublished Works by Radclyffe Hall* (Manchester, 2016), and the co-edited volumes *Sex, Gender and Time in Fiction and Culture* (with Ben Davies; Palgrave, 2011) and *Sculpture, Sexuality and History: Encounters in Literature, Culture and the Arts* (with Jen Grove; Palgrave, 2018).

Emily Hayman is Professor of Literature at Bard Early College in Baltimore. She received her PhD in English and Comparative Literature from Columbia University, and is currently revising a manuscript on British modernism and multilingualism.

Alexander Howard teaches modern and contemporary literature at the University of Sydney. He is the author of *Charles Henri Ford: Between Modernism and Postmodernism* (2017). His recent work has appeared in *Modernism/ Modernity*, *Affirmations: Of the Modern* and the *Journal of Modern Periodical Studies*. His research is also forthcoming in *Angelaki: Journal of Theoretical Humanities*.

Pericles Lewis is Professor of Comparative Literature, Vice President for Global Strategy, and Deputy Provost for International Affairs at Yale University. He is the author or editor of six books on twentieth-century literature, including *The Cambridge Introduction to Modernism* (2007).

Laura Marcus is Goldsmiths' Professor of English Literature at the University of Oxford. She has published widely on nineteenth- and twentieth-century literature and culture, with a particular focus on modernism. Her work on film and literature includes her monographs *Dreams of Modernity: Psychoanalysis, Literature, Cinema* (Cambridge, 2014) and *The Tenth Muse: Writing about Cinema in the Modernist Period* (Oxford, 2007), as well as essays on topics including early film theory, documentary cinema, and literature and film in the 1930s. Her current research projects include collaborative work on scholarly editions of Dorothy Richardson and on Virginia Woolf's short fiction, and a study of the concept of 'rhythm' in the late nineteenth and early twentieth centuries, in a range of disciplinary contexts.

Kirsty Martin is Senior Lecturer in English Literature at the University of Exeter. Her first book, *Modernism and the Rhythms of Sympathy*, was published by Oxford University Press in 2013. She is currently writing about literature and happiness.

Ulrika Maude is Reader in Modernism and Twentieth-Century Literature at the University of Bristol. She is the author of *Beckett, Technology and the Body* (Cambridge, 2009) and *Samuel Beckett and Medicine* (Cambridge, 2019). She is co-editor of *The Cambridge Companion to the Body in Literature* (Cambridge, 2015), *Beckett and Phenomenology* (Continuum, 2009), and *The Body and the Arts* (Palgrave Macmillan 2009). She is writing a book on modernist literature and medicine and working on a critical edition of Virginia Woolf's *Mrs. Dalloway* for the new Bloomsbury Editions series (Bloomsbury).

Tyrus Miller is Vice Provost, Dean of Graduate Studies and Professor of Literature at the University of California at Santa Cruz. He is the author of *Late Modernism: Politics, Fiction, and the Arts between the World Wars* (California, 1999), *Singular Examples: Artistic Politics and the Neo-Avant-Garde* (Northwestern, 2009), *Time Images: Alternative Temporalities in 20th-Century Theory, History, and Art* (Cambridge Scholars Publishing, 2009), and *Modernism and the Frankfurt School* (Edinburgh, 2014). He is the editor of *Given World and Time: Temporalities in Context* (Central European UP, 2008) and *A Cambridge Companion to Wyndham Lewis* (Cambridge, 2016). He is the translator/editor of György Lukács, *The Culture of People's Democracy: Hungarian Essays on Literature, Art, and Democratic Transition* (Brill, 2012) and series co-editor of Brill's Lukács Library series.

Julian Murphet is Scientia Professor in English and Film Studies in the School of the Arts and Media, UNSW, where he directs the Centre for Modernism Studies in Australia. He is the author of *Multimedia Modernism* (Cambridge, 2009) and *Faulkner's Media Romance* (Oxford, 2017). He edits the OHP journal *Affirmations: of the Modern*.

Mark Nixon is Associate Professor in Modern Literature at the University of Reading, where he is also Co-Director of the Beckett International Foundation. With Dirk Van Hulle, he is editor-in-chief of the *Journal of Beckett Studies* and Co-Director of the Beckett Digital Manuscript Project. He is also an editor of *Samuel Beckett Today/Aujourd'hui* and a former President of the Samuel Beckett Society. He has published widely on Beckett's work; his recent books include *Samuel Beckett's Library* (Cambridge, 2013 with Dirk Van Hulle) and the critical edition of Beckett's short story 'Echo's Bones' (Faber, 2014). He is currently preparing a critical edition of Beckett's 'German Diaries' (with Oliver Lubrich; Suhrkamp, 2019).

Benita Parry is Emerita Professor at the University of Warwick. She has written on the Literature of Empire, Peripheral Modernisms and Postcolonial Studies. Her monographs include *Delusions and Discoveries: Studies on India in the British Imagination* (Verso, 1972, 1998), *Conrad and Imperialism: Ideological Boundaries and Visionary Frontiers* (Palgrave, 1984) and *Postcolonial Studies: A Materialist Critique* (Routledge, 2004).

Alex Pestell completed his doctoral studies at the University of Sussex. His research interests include modernism, contemporary poetry, philosophy and the avant-garde. He is the author of *Geoffrey Hill: The Drama of Reason* (Peter Lang, 2016).

Sean Pryor is Senior Lecturer in English at The University of New South Wales. He recently published a new book, *Poetry, Modernism, and an Imperfect World* (Cambridge, 2017). He is co-editor, with David Trotter, of *Writing, Medium, Machine: Modern Technographies* (Open Humanities Press, 2016).

Lawrence Rainey is the author of many books on modernism, including *Ezra Pound and the Monument of Culture* (Chicago, 1991) and *Institutions of Modernism: Literary Elites and Popular Culture* (Yale, 1998). He founded the journal *Modernism/modernity*, which he edited for many years.

Laura Salisbury is Associate Professor in Medicine and English Literature. She has published widely on literary modernism and in the medical humanities – particularly on relationship between modernism and neurological accounts of language. She is the author of *Samuel Beckett: Laughing Matters, Comic Timing* (Edinburgh, 2012), and is co-editor of *Other Becketts* (Florida, 2002), *Neurology and Modernity* (Palgrave, 2010) and *Kittler Now* (Polity, 2015). With Lisa Baraitser, she is Principal Investigator on a Wellcome Trust Collaborative Award entitled 'Waiting Times'. As part of this research, she will be writing a cultural history of waiting. At the University of Exeter, she is based in the English Department and in the University's Wellcome Trust Centre for the Cultures and Environments of Health.

Ronald Schleifer is George Lynn Cross Research Professor of English and Adjunct Professor in Medicine at the University of Oklahoma. He has written or edited more than twenty books, the most recent of which are *Pain and Suffering* (Routledge, 2014) and *The Chief Concern of Medicine: The Integration of the Medical Humanities and Narrative Knowledge into Medical Practices* (co-authored with Dr Jerry Vannatta, Michigan, 2013). He has also published a number of books focused on what he calls cultural modernism. These include *Modernism and Time: The Logic of Abundance in Literature, Science, and Culture 1880–1940* (Cambridge, 2000), *Modernism and Popular Music* (Cambridge, 2011) and *A Political Economy of Modernism: Literature, Post-Classical Economics, and the Lower Middle Class* (Cambridge, 2018).

Paul Sheehan is Associate Professor at Macquarie University. He is the author of *Modernism, Narrative and Humanism* (Cambridge, 2002) and *Modernism and the Aesthetics of Violence* (Cambridge, 2013). He is editor of *Becoming Human: New Perspectives on the Inhuman Condition* (Westport, 2003) and of a special issue of *Textual Practice* 26:4 (2012), 'On the Uses of Anachronism'. He is currently writing a monograph on 'Continental Theory and the Rapture of Poetry'.

Andrew Thacker is Professor of Twentieth-Century Literature at Nottingham Trent University. He is the author or editor of several books on modernism, including the three volumes of *The Oxford Critical and Cultural History of Modernist Magazines* (Oxford, 2009–13), *Geographies of Modernism* (Routledge, 2005), and *Moving Through Modernity: Space and Geography in Modernism* (Manchester, 2003). He was a founder member and the first Chair of the

British Association for Modernist Studies and is an editor of the long-running interdisciplinary journal *Literature & History*.

Dirk Van Hulle, Professor of English Literature at the University of Antwerp and Director of the Centre for Manuscript Genetics, edited the new *Cambridge Companion to Samuel Beckett* (Cambridge, 2015). With Mark Nixon, he is co-director of the *Beckett Digital Manuscript Project* (www.beckettarchive.org) and editor-in-chief of the *Journal of Beckett Studies*. His publications include *Textual Awareness* (U of Michigan P, 2004), *Modern Manuscripts* (Bloomsbury, 2014), *Samuel Beckett's Library* (Cambridge, 2013, with Mark Nixon), *James Joyce's Work in Progress* (Routledge, 2016) and several genetic editions in the *Beckett Digital Manuscript Project*, including *Krapp's Last Tape/La Dernière Bande*, *Molloy* (with Magessa O'Reilly and Pim Verhulst), *L'Innommable/The Unnamable* (with Shane Weller) and the *Beckett Digital Library*.

Shane Weller is Professor of Comparative Literature and Co-Director of the Centre for Modern European Literature at the University of Kent. He has published on a range of modern European writers, including Franz Kafka, Samuel Beckett, Maurice Blanchot and Paul Celan. His monographs include *Beckett, Literature and the Ethics of Alterity* (Palgrave, 2006), *Modernism and Nihilism* (Palgrave, 2011) and *The Making of Samuel Beckett's L'Innommable/The Unnamable* (Bloomsbury, 2014, with Dirk Van Hulle).

Introduction:
Modernism, Experimentation and Form

Ulrika Maude

Literary modernism is characterized by dazzling experimentation, perplexing narrative and poetic form, and often by contradictory aesthetic and ideological tendencies. The desire to 'make it new' is combined with a nostalgic yearning for a lost and at times primitive past; the admiration for technology and science is paired with a suspicion of their dehumanizing threat; and although modernist writing can often be radically progressive and even revolutionary in political and sexual terms, it also frequently expresses a fascination with and allegiance to far-right traditionalist and even totalitarian ideologies.[1] The temporal and geographical parameters of literary modernism are similarly difficult to pin down. While modernism is often considered to begin in the late nineteenth century and to end around the 1940s or 1950s with so-called late modernism, there has always been controversy about the movement's temporal reach, and advocates of the so-called new modernist studies argue both that modernist literature continues to be written in the contemporary period and that it extends well beyond the geographical parameters of the Anglo-American world.[2] Despite considerable efforts to establish modernism as a historical category, with specific cultural, national and thematic boundaries, therefore, the movement continues to defy easy categorization and maintains a vital relevance in the twenty-first century.

In this sense, modernism has often been considered a stylistic rather than a temporal movement, and one of its most striking features is its salient formal experimentation. The experimental, anti-narrative structure of modernist writing is one of its crucial signifying features. The gaps, omissions and ellipses that tend to characterize modernist discourse and the overt challenge to narrative cohesion and closure that typifies the modernist novel, short story and drama are carefully considered, meticulously wrought traits of such writing. This lack of a traditional, cohesive structure in which the different actions, events and tropes of a narrative are made to appear purposive is problematized not only on the level of plot but also in the manner in which the various events portrayed relate to one another – or indeed fail to do just that. There are a number of reasons for this breakdown in structure and form. Charles Darwin's work on evolution, for instance, 'took narrative out of nature', as Paul Sheehan puts it (35), foregrounding, instead, the chance and randomness of contingent cell mutations that cast radical doubt over the purposiveness and design implicit in the biblical theory of creation, which had firmly placed humankind at the centre of the natural world. Medical discoveries, such as those in neurology, radically questioned the principles of free will and agency by which the idea of selfhood is conventionally understood, by demonstrating that many of the functions of the human body operate independently from the conscious mind and are governed by the autonomous nervous system, with consciousness a mere by-product of vital bodily functions. And studies in aphasia and Tourette's syndrome in the second half of the nineteenth century revealed that even language itself frequently escapes intention and often seems to speak itself. A parallel but rather different model of the human psyche was introduced by Sigmund Freud, who himself began his career as a neurologist and only later redirected his attention to developing the 'talking cure' for which he is famous. Psychoanalysis split the self into two by introducing what, in *Studies on Hysteria* (1895), Freud calls a 'second consciousness'. In this theory, the 'unconscious', as he came to refer to it, operates alongside the conscious mind, which, however, as a result of repression fails to recognize the subject's true desires. These desires and 'drives' are said to reside in the unconscious mind and to express themselves through various forms of body language – including tics and nervous symptoms, hysterical convulsions and slips of the tongue. This fundamental split in the self renders us strangers to ourselves and condemns us to a life of perpetual frustration and dissatisfaction, as Freud famously argued in *Civilization and Its Discontents* (1930).

As this might begin to suggest, modernism disrupts and disavows some of the fundamental conceptions of what it means to be human. In this sense, modernism doesn't necessarily make for comfortable or easy reading. As Frank Kermode argues in an influential book from 1967, there is something inherently consoling about the sense of an ending that conventional narratives present. Classical tragedy, for instance, is ultimately affirmative and reassuring: by presenting narratives structured around Aristotelian notions of peripeteia and anagnorisis (reversal and recognition), catharsis (release or purgation) and resolution, tragedy (and conventional narrative form more generally) offers a comforting return to what Tzvetan Todorov calls a 'new equilibrium'. The disrupted, aleatory or contingent, seemingly inconsequential, often fragmentary and fragmented narratives that characterize modernist writing, by contrast, are far more disquieting and disturbing than any story matter might be, for they upset precisely our sense of purposiveness, order and even ultimately signification.

One way to think about the disturbance and fragmentation of form, structure and meaning in modernist literature is to consider the Euclidean figure of the *gnomon* that famously features in the opening paragraph of 'The Sisters', the first story of James Joyce's *Dubliners* (1914). In geometry, a *gnomon* is the incomplete parallelogram that remains after a smaller but identically shaped figure has been removed from it, or as Bernard Benstock put it, 'a nonappearance suggesting a presence made palpable only by the concept of its absence'. (520) In *Dubliners*, the *gnomon* becomes a figure for the short story sequence itself, with each of the stories featuring striking absences or missing parts. In 'The Sisters', which stages the death of Father Flynn, the *gnomon* makes its appearance in old Cotter's insinuating but 'unfinished sentences': 'No, I wouldn't say he was exactly ... but there was something queer ... there was something uncanny about him. I'll tell you my opinion ... ', he says, in a way that specifically avoids presenting what should be the essential content of his sentences (Joyce, 2000, 3). It also appears in the boy-narrator's inability to make sense of what he sees and hears, including, indeed, what old Cotter has to say: 'I puzzled my head to extract meaning from his unfinished sentences', the boy remarks, in a way that seems to reflect the reader's own predicament (4). And it is prominently apparent in the failure of religious (and by implication literary) symbolism, including especially the 'idle chalice', which Father Flynn breaks but which is anyway empty: 'It was that chalice he broke ... That was the beginning of it', one of the titular sisters comments; 'Of course, they say it was all right, that it contained nothing, I mean. But still', she goes on, ambiguously (10, 9). In 'Eveline', the story of a young woman who contemplates leaving Dublin with her suitor, Frank, for a life in Argentina, the word 'home' is repeated ten times within the space of the story's five pages. As Eveline dusts her home, 'wondering where on earth all the dust came from', she takes note of a familiar object: 'And yet during all those years she had never found out the name of the priest whose yellowing photograph hung on the wall above the broken harmonium' (25). Eveline's apparent alienation from the objects in her home – including her ignorance of the priest's name – constitutes a *gnomon*, but it also points to an even starker missing element in the story. Eveline's physically and emotionally abusive father, who fails to provide the duty of care that he should to Eveline and his other children, renders him a 'father' only in name. Her home, therefore, offers none of the comfort, shelter and security that are conventionally associated with the concept; it, too, is a 'home' only in name. The fact that the priest in the picture is himself now in Melbourne constitutes another *gnomon*, for the reader is never informed *why* he left. His 'yellowing' picture is suggestive of decadence and decay, and may indicate that he left Ireland in disgrace, which seems to link him with Father Flynn in 'The Sisters', whose company, as old Cotter puts it, was 'bad for children' (4).[3] Frank, Eveline's suitor, who tells her 'stories of the terrible Patagonians' – mythical giants whose existence was known to be a tall tale – is himself 'frank' in name only, for as Katherine Mullin has revealed in her striking reading of the story, he is likely to be taking Eveline to a brothel rather than to be his wife in 'Buenos Ayres' (27).[4] But Dublin does not have much to offer a woman of Eveline's social class and background either, and the 'pitiful vision' of her mother on her deathbed 'laid its spell on the very quick of her being – that life of commonplace sacrifices closing in final craziness' (28). What the reader is shown in the disturbing image of the deranged mother is Eveline's future, should she decide not to leave Ireland. The narrative points to the deficiencies of 'home' as a national, domestic and gendered space: home has little to offer its working-class female protagonist. Although modernism has come under criticism for advancing a negative and ultimately disempowered aesthetic response to social reality, *Dubliners* attests to its early and persistent engagement in subtle but incisive social critique.

Another way in which the *gnomon* makes its appearance in *Dubliners*, as we have seen briefly in relation to the chalice in 'The Sisters', is through Joyce's deconstruction of conventional symbolism. 'Clay' focuses on Maria, who works in a Dublin laundry. She is described as having a 'very long nose and a very long chin', and it is noted three times that when she laughed, 'the tip of her nose nearly met the tip of her chin' (76, 77). The story is set on Hallows' Eve (Halloween), which reinforces the supernatural connotations of Maria's witch-like appearance. And yet, disjunctively and somewhat perplexingly, she is named after the Virgin Mary and is known as (and seems to pride herself on being known as) a 'peace-maker' (76). To further complicate matters, Maria works in the '*Dublin by Lamplight* laundry', a 'Magdalen's home' or 'reform institution' for former prostitutes and women who have had children out of wedlock (based in Ballsbridge, Dublin, at the time Joyce was writing 'Clay') (77, 239). Nothing quite adds up in the story, or for Maria – who is 'nice' and a 'peacemaker' but who seems to rub people up the wrong way; who is probably cheated by the 'stout gentleman' who 'has a drop taken' but who is charming to her on the tram; and who signally fails to end the deadly, permanent feud between Joe and his brother Alphy (78, 79). The story, in other words, is heavy with symbolism, which invites the reader to approach it as a coded message containing the key (the *clé*, as it were) to its own enigmas. And yet, try as one may to crack the code, the symbolism Joyce uses intentionally fails to add up. There is no key, or *clé*, in 'Clay', in other words, and even the title word is notable for its enigmatic non-appearance within the story itself.

Samuel Beckett, who was profoundly influenced by Joyce, does something similar with the hermeneutics of symbolism in his most famous work, *Waiting for Godot* (1953). The play is notably sparse in props and scenery, which makes the dead tree of Act I seem particularly significant. At the beginning of Act II, the tree has sprouted leaves, in what is seemingly a symbol of hope, regeneration and resolution. But Godot fails to arrive. The tree's sprouting is profoundly misleading if the audience seeks to read it as a symbol denoting epiphany, annunciation or resolution. As Daniel Albright puts it, rather than being an 'asymbolic' play (one that would be uninterested in or indifferent to symbolic meaning) *Waiting for Godot* is an 'anti-symbolic' play, one in which Beckett encourages us to interpret words, actions and props as symbols only to frustrate us in our hermeneutic urge; he exposes our 'proficiency' as readers and spectators as precisely the thing that will prevent us from properly attending to his play (53). Instead of offering us purposiveness, in other words, the play foregrounds chance, randomness and contingency – or indeed, as Beckett himself affirmed, the mere passing of time.

But we might discern a similar undoing of 'symbolic' meaning in Joseph Conrad's great novella *Heart of Darkness* (1899) – a work written half a century earlier, as modernism is just beginning to emerge as a dominant cultural force. The anonymous and shadowy narrator who reports to us the telling of Marlow's story warns us early that Marlow is not 'typical', because

> to him the meaning of an episode was not inside like a kernel but outside, enveloping the tale which brought it out only as a glow brings out a haze, in the likeness of one of these misty halos that sometimes are made visible by the spectral illumination of moonshine. (Conrad, 18)

Meaning in the story, as the narrator warns the reader, does not reside at the heart of the narrative, like a kernel, but is there only as something vague and indistinct, like a haze, mist or vapour; it merely *ghosts* the narrative, like a spectre. And yet, even for the experienced reader, it is nevertheless difficult not to expect that Kurtz, who is the goal and purpose of the journey that the narrative recounts, will provide answers to the numerous enigmas and ethical questions that the story presents. Once we finally encounter the elusive Kurtz, after three near-misses, he turns out to be nothing like the impressive figure we are led to expect (in this respect, at least, resembling that other early-modernist anti-hero, the Wizard of Oz, the titular character in a famous children's novel first published in the following year). As Peter Brooks has persuasively argued, in spite of our expectations of narrative closure and hermeneutic disclosure, Kurtz's final words, 'The horror! The horror!' (Conrad, 118), make a mockery of meaning, for they are 'minimal language, language [...] on the verge of a fall from language' (250).

Modernist poetry is similarly governed by what we might see as a centrifugal rather than centripetal aesthetic. One of the most striking examples can be found in Yeats's 'The Second Coming' (1919) and especially in the resonantly apocalyptic lines, 'Things fall apart; the centre cannot hold; / Mere anarchy is loosed upon the world' (ll. 3–4). Yeats is writing in the immediate aftermath of the First World War, which, with all its devastation, had wiped out the sense of optimism that the rapid technological and scientific advances of the nineteenth century had seemed to offer.[5] Responding also to a world turned upside down by the Russian Revolution, and to the troubles and incipient civil war in Ireland as the nation shook off its colonial chains, Yeats can furthermore be said to be anticipating the rise of fascism – which, as his poem seems to prophesy, would ultimately lead to the Second World War.

A similar anxiety and bewilderment over the breakdown of old ordering systems is signally present in *The Waste Land* (1922), where it is brought to the fore most strikingly in the apparently autobiographical lines, 'On Margate Sands. / I can connect / Nothing with nothing' (ll. 300–2). Eliot suffered a breakdown in 1921, and the lines are a reference to his personal circumstances and the time he spent recovering in Margate. But they also function as a more impersonal comment on the poem itself, in all its perplexing imagery, ventriloquized voices and often wantonly obscure references, citations and allusions. These and other modernist texts embody and perform the condition of modernity in their disparate, disjunctive, fragmented and often incongruently despairing formal qualities – a sense of ruination articulated in 'What the Thunder Said', the final section of *The Waste Land*, when the speaker talks of propping up the now-tenuous if not untenable notion of a self with 'fragments I have shored against my ruins' (l. 431).

An analogy can be found in certain visual artworks of the early twentieth century. The salient fragmentation of a high Cubist painting such as Georges Braque's *Woman Playing a Guitar* (1913) (Figure 1.1) can be read in terms of the constellated fragments of an image seen from various vantage points. This, in turn, can be interpreted in light of the philosophical doctrine of relativism, which proposes that rather than universal 'truths' we have different, conflicting, but equally valid perspectives on 'reality', embodied in the fractured image on the canvas. Another way of thinking about such paintings – which typically represent fragments of a face, a foot, a few fingers and perhaps a pipe, newspaper or a musical instrument, such as here, the guitar – is that the canvases self-consciously invite the spectator to piece together the fragments in order to allow the full picture to emerge. But no matter how long the observer spends looking at one of these dazzlingly beautiful paintings, the missing elements fail to appear: the only code that the observer cracks is that there is no code to crack – that 'meaning' is infinitely deferred.[6]

The fragmentation that, in a writer such as Eliot, is represented as a source of deep anxiety can, however, present itself as a source of exultation in other writers. One such is Virginia Woolf, who, in *Mrs Dalloway* (1925), stages Clarissa's sense of the unboundedness of the self in often ecstatic, jubilatory terms: 'sitting on the bus going up Shaftsbury Avenue, she felt herself everywhere, not "here, here, here"; and she tapped on the back of the seat; but everywhere' (2015, 136). At the florist's, where Clarissa buys flowers for her party, she muses that

> somehow in the streets of London, on the ebb and flow of things, here, there, she survived, Peter survived, lived in each other, she being part, she was positive, of the trees at home; of the house there, ugly, rambling all to bits and pieces as it was; part of people she had never met; being laid out like a mist between the people she knew best, who lifted her on their branches as she had seen the trees lift the mist, but it spread ever so far, her life, herself. (Woolf, 2015, 8)

The self that the novel presents to the reader is not the singular, masculine 'I' that Woolf condemned in *A Room of One's Own* (1929) – because, she wrote, 'in the shadow of the letter "I" all is shapeless as mist' – but rather a multiple and fluid self that is reflected in the prose and in the novel's overall structure (2000, 90).[7] Clarissa inhales the fragrance of the flowers at the florist's and through their scent intermingles with them, just as she feels herself intermingling with the trees, with her house, even with people she has never met. Woolf's prominent use of free indirect discourse – the peculiar osmosis of third-person narrator and individual character-focalizers – while not a modernist invention, itself offers an example of the most intense form of intersubjectivity. In free indirect discourse, character and narrator coalesce without, however, quite collapsing into one.

Figure 1.1 Georges Braque (1882–1963), *Woman Playing a Guitar*, oil on canvas, 130 × 73, 1913. Courtesy of Musée National d'Art Moderne, Centre Pompidou, Paris, France / Bridgeman Images. ©ADAGP, Paris and DACS, London, 2018.

The most prominent example of 'being part of people' Clarissa 'had never met' is her mysterious connection with Septimus Smith. The two never do meet, but an intimate connection is nonetheless established between them, for instance through the theme of illness. For while Septimus suffers from war-induced psychosis, we learn that Clarissa Dalloway, too, has been seriously ill with influenza and heart trouble. Septimus's suicide, which constitutes the main event – indeed the only real event, the climax – of the novel, is represented with compassion, understanding and, most strikingly, identification. It is never condemned as an act in Clarissa's mind but, instead, enigmatically commended: 'She felt glad that he had done it; thrown it away while they went on living' (2015, 167). In the three-page 'Introduction' Woolf wrote to the second, 1928 American edition of the novel – the only introduction she ever composed to any of her fictional works – she revealed that 'in the first version Septimus, who later is intended to be [Clarissa's] double, had no existence; and that Mrs. Dalloway was originally to kill herself, or perhaps merely to die at the end of the party' (2015, 357). The American edition of the novel has, since its first impression, contained an additional sentence, which Woolf omitted from the English edition: 'He made her feel the beauty; made her feel the fun' (2005, 182). The sense of beauty and jubilation Clarissa feels at Septimus's suicide is left ambiguous, but while it is perhaps precisely his inability to reconnect with ordinary, everyday life that leads to his suicide – since his psychosis knows only heightened, hyperbolic experience – his death paradoxically helps Clarissa to do just that. It brings her back to 'this life, to be lived to the end, to be walked with serenely' (2015, 165). In the novel, in other words, it is precisely the ordinary, the everyday, and Clarissa's intimate feeling of being as much part of her surroundings as they are of her, that functions as a locus of value and as a stay against the eroding, at times destructive passing of time.[8]

In the novels of the Anglo-Irish writer Elizabeth Bowen, the self is similarly far from the insular and arguably masculine immunity from one's surroundings. In *Death of the Heart* (1938), for instance, the novel's protagonist, Portia, whose early life has been spent on the Continent in hotels 'before the season, when the funicular was not working yet' (34) and who has more recently been living at Windsor Terrace in London in her half-brother's house, finds herself on holiday in Seale on the Sea, on the Kent coast. Reminiscing of Windsor Terrace, she observes, '*I am not there*':

> She began to go round, in little circles, things that at least her senses had loved –
> her bed, with the lamp turned on on winter mornings, the rug in Thomas's
> study, the chest carved with angels out there on the landing, the waxen oilcloth

down there in Matchett's room. Only in a house one has learnt to be lonely does one have this solicitude for *things*. One's relation to them, the daily seeing or touching, begins to become love, and to lay one open to pain. (1998a, 139)

The memory of Windsor Terrace seems to reside in the eyes and the skin, in 'the daily seeing or touching', in pre-reflective experiences that dissolve any clear demarcation between object and self. In her essay 'Bowen's Court' (1958), Bowen writes of a similar experience of her own, observing about the eighteenth-century big house that belonged to her family that 'between those who were here and me there is a physical link, forged of touch and sight – a matter of handling the same door knobs, mounting the same stairs, looking out at the same scene through the same windows' (2008, 148). Habit here transgresses individual experience and acquires a historical dimension. It becomes a transgenerational tie that in its effect seems to exceed both blood and heritage. Experience is encoded in the nerve endings of each generation through shared sensuous experience; it is transmitted through tactile objects or visual impressions afforded by the house itself. In *Heat of the Day* (1949), something like the reverse of this situation occurs when Roderick visits his mother Stella in her rented flat, with its alien-seeming furniture. Roderick acknowledges that it 'did not look like home' (47), but realizes nevertheless that 'somewhere between these chairs and tables must run the spoor of habit, could one but pick it up' (1998b, 52). The sofa he sits on, for instance, seems to be 'without environment' and the visit is made uneasy by the very 'absence of every inanimate thing they had in common'. The surrounding objects afford 'no benevolence' to the meeting, and the narrator goes on to say that 'love dreads being isolated, being left to speak in a void' (1998b, 55). Bowen's characters project their fears and desires onto objects, as Elizabeth Inglesby has argued (312–3), but the objects also have a hold over these emotions, as if they had scarred the characters, leaving their own inscriptions on the nerves and the senses. Bowen's writing seems to suggest that we bury our intentions in objects, which in turn arouse in us volitions, thoughts or emotions.

Katherine Mansfield's writing often exhibits a similar undoing of the singular, coherent self. In her stories, the energy flows and affects of the characters are typically driven by the surrounding landscapes and by the force field of other characters. Together with the writings of Woolf and Bowen, Mansfield's short stories indicate that female modernists often find value in the undoing of a selfhood that for male writers tends to function as an ambivalent locus of power and autonomy, as well as of insecurity and anxiety. And yet one can also find the dispersal of the self celebrated in the work of an anti-rationalist male writer such as D. H. Lawrence, whose characters seem most at ease when they no longer feel themselves to be 'persons' or selves. In his short story 'Sun', written in 1925, for example, Juliet has been sent from New York to the Mediterranean to take the sun cure (a popular form of treatment in the period, also known as heliotherapy) in order to recover from 'her silent, awful hostility' and the irritation her young child arouses in her, for whom she feels 'so horridly, ghastly responsible' (20). The urban Juliet is presented as 'pale' and curiously disembodied, a 'menacing ghost woman [...] spectral and vengeful' (35). As a result of living in New York, we learn, 'iron' has entered Juliet's 'soul' (19). When she first arrives at the Italian villa, she feels no affinity with her surroundings: 'She saw it all, and in a measure it was soothing. But it was all external. She didn't really care about it' (20). Juliet, however, has been advised by the doctor to 'lie in the sun' (20), which gradually, little by little, almost body-part by body-part – 'her breasts and her face, her throat, her tired belly, her knees, her thighs and her feet' (21) – transforms the 'nervous New York woman' into something or someone that is 'no longer a person, but a fleet sun-strong body, soulless and alluring as a nymph' (33). As Juliet's body becomes increasingly 'sun-tanned, wind-stroked' (33), her maternal and sexual instincts are revived. When, for instance, her child staggers among prickly thorns, she is 'quick as a serpent, leaping to him, when he was going to fall against the prickles. It surprised even herself. – "What a wild cat I am really!" she said to herself' (26). Upon visiting Juliet, her husband, Maurice, finds his wife transformed: 'the voice of the abrupt, personal American woman had died out, and he heard the voice of the woman of flesh, the sun-ripe body' (34). The anxious little boy, too, has been healed by the sun: 'The child fluttered around in silence, like a young animal absorbed in life' (28). The new Juliet has 'ceased to care about anything' (26), 'would take no thought for the morrow' (28) and now resembles a creature of pure animal instinct: 'She herself, her conscious self, was secondary, a secondary person, almost an onlooker' (26).

This book explores the central formal and thematic questions raised by modernist literature. The twenty-one chapters of Part I are divided into four sections that reflect major research areas in contemporary modernist studies: 'The Modernist Everyday', 'The Arts and Cultures of Modernism', 'The Sciences and Technologies of Modernism' and 'The Geopolitics and Economics of Modernism'. Part II features a 'Resources' section, offering a substantial 'A to Z of Key Words', an annotated bibliography of vital books on modernist literature and a chronology of key dates.

The opening section of Part I, 'The Modernist Everyday', explores the interest modernist writers took in representing ordinary, commonplace experience: it focuses on their concern to defamiliarize the everyday by giving it the kind of attention we often fail to because of what Virginia Woolf calls the 'cotton wool' of everyday experience (1985, 72). Habits, as Woolf implies in her autobiographical essay 'A Sketch of the Past', are performed only semi-consciously. They constitute part of what Woolf refers to as 'non-being' in that they are almost too familiar for us to spot, too liminal even, and difficult because of their familiarity to render into language. Eventfulness is easy to write about by comparison. But as Joyce commented to Djuna Barnes in 1919, a writer 'should never write about the extraordinary': 'That is for the journalist', he opines (Ellmann, 1983, 457). The ordinary and the everyday is almost infinitely elusive and presents the kind of challenge to representation that fascinated modernist writers.

The five chapters of the first section, then, approach the everyday from their own unique perspectives. The opening chapter, by Scott McCracken, concerns urban modernity and focuses on the everyday through the *leitmotif* of a bar of soap, a familiar daily object that, in the writing of Joyce and Dorothy Richardson, reveals the hidden depths of the quotidian. McCraken approaches the everyday through its paradoxicality, for it can entail both the ordinary and the extraordinary, routine actions and heightened or intense experiences, deep significance masked by apparent insignificance. The second chapter, 'Geographies of Modernism', focuses on the places, spaces and landscapes of modernist writing, which, as Andrew Thacker argues, have often been too narrowly conceived. Thacker begins by considering the work of cultural geographers and spatial theorists in reconfiguring our understanding of social spaces, before moving on to address the global and transnational reach of modernist literature and its wider implications for modernist studies. Shane Weller's focus, in turn, is on late nineteenth-century language scepticism, which plays a decisive part in shaping the formal and stylistic features of literary modernism. As Weller persuasively demonstrates, language scepticism triggers a desire in high modernist writers for linguistic renewal, which in late modernism evolves into an enactment of linguistic negativism. Kirsty Martin's chapter in turn questions the critical consensus of modernism as a 'cold' mode of writing, focusing on more difficult-to-articulate feelings in the work of Woolf, Lawrence and Eliot. The work of modernist writers, her chapter suggests, explores how profoundly the shape of a tree or the hue of a particular colour, a gesture or an encounter with one's own racing heart can affect the subject. Drawing from psychoanalysis, nerve theory and aesthetics, Martin's chapter maps modernism's new emotional range. In the concluding chapter of this section, Michael Bell turns his attention to modernism's relation to religion and to what anthropologists unmasked as both its origin and substitute, myth. Through a consideration of its pervasive focus on myth, Bell's chapter unveils the residual persistence of religious impulses in literary modernism.

The second section, 'The Arts and Cultures of Modernism', considers the ways in which music, the visual arts, film and popular culture shaped modernist writing and examines the inception and dissemination of writing through so-called 'little magazines' and modernism's manuscript culture. Modernist literature developed in part in reaction to formal innovations in music and the visual arts, as well as to the new medium of film, which was itself profoundly indebted to literature from its inception (symbolized by the public screening in Paris of films by the Lumière brothers in 1895). High modernist literary experimentation is in fact a relatively late development by comparison with the earlier radical formal experimentation in music and the visual arts – a point that Samuel Beckett makes in a letter to Axel Kaun in 1937. In this letter, Beckett pointedly questions whether 'literature alone [is] to remain behind in the old lazy ways that have so long ago been abandoned by music and painting?' (1983, 172). As Tim Armstrong argues in his chapter, although modernist literature tends to be engaged in 'a multi-media mapping of the senses', music nonetheless occupies a privileged role because of its affinity with language, for both entail 'inbuilt codes and expectations'. However, unlike language, music escapes conceptual thought and operates as 'the direct carrier of feeling', and as Schopenhauer argued, it offers the listener an intensely embodied experience. In his chapter on the visual arts, Conor Carville similarly foregrounds aesthetic embodiment in his analysis of the implications of Henri Bergson's notion of the fusion of subject and object, spectator and artwork. But modernist aesthetic theory also drew from neo-Kantian ideas of the autonomy of the artwork, and Carville traces theories of the visual through Beckett's abiding interest in the visual arts and their reflection in philosophical discourse. Laura Marcus's chapter examines the 'two-way relationship' between literary modernism and the new medium of film, offering a succinct overview of the ways in which this relationship has been perceived and conceptualized by critics, before turning to examine the influence of film and early film theory on the work of Woolf, Joyce, Gertrude Stein, Wyndham Lewis and Beckett.

Lawrence Rainey's chapter redresses a common misconception of modernism as constitutively hostile to popular culture through close readings of two high modernist works, *Ulysses* and *The Waste Land*. Rainey pays particular attention to the discourses of pantomime and cross-dressing in Joyce's novel, and reads Eliot's poem as focused on the typist's violation of conventions surrounding pre-marital sex and the treatment of the 'fallen woman'. Both works, as Rainey demonstrates, engage productively and prolifically with the mass culture of their time. Faith Binckes's chapter turns its attention to the modernist little magazines that played so central a role in the literary and aesthetic culture of the early twentieth century. Her focus is on the relation of periodical texts to typography and design, as well as on the political significance of modernist magazines. While many of the magazines accepted and advocated a high modernist male canon, others identified strongly with the vanguard of political thought, including the emerging discourses and movements of anarchism and feminism. In the last chapter in this section, Dirk Van Hulle attends to the many preserved notes and manuscripts that survive their authors, in what has come to be known as 'the golden age of the literary manuscript'. In Van Hulle's reading, the notes and manuscripts reflect a significant shift in interest from reality to the perception of reality and the workings of the mind; manuscripts, that is to say, offer a record precisely of this process. The study of literary manuscripts affords an understanding of the inception of the work, which in turn helps the reader to assess the intricacies of the finished poem, novel or play.

Modernism develops in the wake of critical developments in nineteenth-century scientific materialism, which entailed a number of paradigm-shifting discoveries, including evolutionary theory, neuron theory and Einstein's theory of relativity. Such discoveries triggered fundamental and often unnerving shifts in our understanding of the world and our place in it. It is therefore not surprising that 'The Sciences and Technologies of Modernism' constitutes a major area of research in contemporary modernist studies. The section opens with Paul Sheehan's chapter on the conceptual affiliations between Einstein's theory of relativity and the counter-realist aesthetics of modernism. The American poetic context of the 1920 and 1930s, Sheehan argues, accorded Einstein's theories a positive and constructive reception, while the Anglo-Irish response veered between ambivalence and affirmation. Jana Funke's chapter, in turn, argues that literary modernism was driven by an urge to find new modes of expression for the gender and sexual configurations, allegiances and identities opened up by the emerging sciences of sexuality, including psychiatry, psychology, psychoanalysis and sexology. These played an important role in the production of fluid or queer conceptions of gender and sexuality that have come to be seen as markers of literary modernism itself. Maude, in turn, analyses the ways in which modernist literature develops out of the intrinsic tension between scientific empiricism – the understanding of the world through observation and experimentation – and hermeneutics – the close analysis of signs, language and meaning. Developing the idea that Sigmund Freud can productively be read as a modernist writer and thinker, her chapter examines his modernist tendencies from the perspective of the tensions that emerge out of the origins of his clinical work in nineteenth-century science, on the one hand, and the hermeneutic method that forms the foundation of psychoanalysis, on the other. Maude proposes that this tension is also endemic to literature and that it appears in a dazzlingly heightened and intensified form in literary modernism. Salisbury's chapter focuses on modernist writers' engagement with theories of consciousness and perception, alongside their interest in psychopathological states of mind. She argues that only by placing new psychological theories of mind in dialogue with the philosophical and technological conditions of modernity can one make sense of the 'inward turn' that preoccupied so many modernist writers. Julian Murphet's chapter on modernism and technology concludes this section by focusing on the feelings of alienation and depersonalization afforded by omnipresent mechanization, which enabled natural objects, including human beings, to be stored as what Heidegger calls 'standing reserve'. Technology, Murphet proposes, channels desire and, in doing so, substitutes for it. Human beings become more machine-like as machines themselves assume increasingly human qualities. Technology's reach also affects literature itself, which is forced to update and modernize its means of production.

The final section, 'The Geopolitics and Economics of Modernism', responds to the central concerns raised by new modernist studies in its call for an urgent reassessment of the temporal and geographical parameters of modernism and a reconsideration of its Anglo-American bias. With this in mind, Emily Hayman and Pericles Lewis address the question of global modernism by focusing on the feeling of isolation, on conflicts of identity and on the resistance to existing social and political paradigms in a period of rapid cultural and generational change. Their chapter traces modernist themes from Singapore to Istanbul and from there to Buenos Aires, and finds a common thread in global modernism's need to break out of old artistic paradigms that fail to acknowledge or fully to incorporate the complications and contradictions of the modern world. Benita Parry's chapter, by contrast, identifies a departure from modernism in the stylistic strategies of what she calls 'peripheral literatures'. She argues that critics have favoured those forms of writing that have exhibited a penchant for formal experimentation at the expense of the continuing dynamism of realism. Tyrus Miller's chapter on modernist literature and politics, in turn, engages with the radical potential of avant-garde form, in its analysis of the relationship between formal experimentation and political meanings. Miller suggests that modernist writing highlights the gap between literary representation and the existing political situation, but argues that by doing so it imagines new possibilities for the political in the present and future. Closing the volume, Ronald Schleifer focuses on modernist economics, examining twentieth-century literature in relation to the transformations in economic practices and understanding at the turn of the century.

Notes

1 The slogan is the title of Pound's collection of essays *Make It New*, published in 1934. The phrase also occurs in block capitals in Pound's Canto LIII (265), published the same year.

2 New modernist studies was inaugurated by an influential article written by Douglas Mao and Rebecca Walkowitz in 2008, 'The New Modernist Studies', *PMLA*, 123, (3), 737–48.

3 The fact that one of the young boys in 'An Encounter', the second story in *Dubliners*, refers to the pervert that the boys meet as a 'queer old josser' adds credibility to this reading: 'josser' is nineteenth-century Australian slang for a clergyman.

4 See Katherine Mullin's *James Joyce, Sexuality and Social Purity*, 56–82.

5 As Santanu Das puts it, the First World War was 'the world's first industrial war' in which human ingenuity and modern technology were used on a mass scale for the brutalization and destruction rather than the betterment of humankind (Das, 136).

6 For a stunning political reading of high Cubism, see T. J. Clark, *Farewell to an Idea: Episodes from a History of Modernism*, 169–223.

7 See Vanessa Ryan, *The Vanishing Subject*, 190–8.

8 See Liesl Olson's reading of the novel in *Modernism and the Ordinary*, 66–77.

Bibliography

Albright, D. (2003), *Beckett and Aesthetics*. Cambridge: Cambridge University Press.

Beckett, S. (1983), *Disjecta: Miscellaneous Writings and a Dramatic Fragment*, R. Cohn (ed.). London: Calder.

Beckett, S. (2010), *Waiting for Godot*. London: Faber.

Benstock, B. (1988), 'The Gnomonics of Dubliners'. *Modern Fiction Studies*, 34, (4), 519–39.

Bowen, E. (1998a), *The Death of the Heart*. London: Vintage.

Bowen, E. (1998b), *The Heat of the Day*. London: Vintage.

Bowen, E. (2008), *People, Places, Things*, A. Hepburn (ed.). Edinburgh: Edinburgh University Press.

Brooks, P. (1984), *Reading for the Plot: Design and Intention in Narrative*. Oxford: Clarendon Press.

Clark, T. J. (1999), *Farewell to an Idea: Episodes from a History of Modernism*. New Haven and London: Yale University Press.

Conrad, J. (1995), *Heart of Darkness*. London: Penguin.

Das, S. (2003), *Touch and Intimacy in First World War Literature*. Cambridge: Cambridge University Press.

Eliot, T. S. (2015), *The Poems of T. S. Eliot: Collected and Uncollected Poems*, Christopher Ricks and Jim McCue (ed. and annot.). London: Faber.

Ellmann, R. (1983), *James Joyce*. Oxford: Oxford University Press.

Freud, S. (1974), *Studies on Hysteria*. The Pelican Freud Library 3. J. and A. Strachey (transl.). Harmondsworth: Penguin.

Freud, S. (1991), *Civilization, Society and Religion: Group Psychology, Civilization and Its Discontents and Other Works*, The Penguin Freud Library 12. J. Strachey (transl.), A. Dickson (transl.). London: Penguin.

Inglesby, E. C. (2007), '"Expressive Objects": Elizabeth Bowen's Narrative Materializes'. *Modern Fiction Studies*, 52, (2), 306–33.

'Josser', n. 1, (1989), *Oxford English Dictionary*, 2nd edn. Oxford: Oxford University Press.

Joyce, J. (2000), *Dubliners*, J. Johnson (ed., introd., and notes). Oxford World's Classics. Oxford: Oxford University Press.

Kermode, F. (1967), *The Sense of an Ending*. New York: Oxford University Press.

Lawrence, D. H. (2002), *The Woman Who Rode Away and Other Stories*, Dieter Mehl and Christa Jansohn (eds). The Cambridge Edition of the Works of D. H. Lawrence. Cambridge: Cambridge University Press.

Mao, D. and Walkowitz, R. (2008), 'The New Modernist Studies'. *PMLA*, 123, (3), 737–48.

Mullin, K. (2003), *James Joyce, Sexuality and Social Purity*. Cambridge: Cambridge University Press.

Olson, L. (2009), *Modernism and the Ordinary*. Oxford: Oxford University Press.

Pound, E. (1934), *Make It New*. London: Faber.

Pound, E. (1981), *The Cantos*. London: Faber.

Ryan, V. (1991), *The Vanishing Subject: Early Psychology and Literary Modernism*. Chicago: University of Chicago Press.

Sheehan, P. (2002), *Modernism, Narrative and Humanism*. Cambridge: Cambridge University Press.

Woolf, V. (1985), *Moments of Being: A Collection of Autobiographical Writing*, Jeanne Schulkind (ed.). San Diego and New York: Harcourt.

Woolf, V. (2000), *A Room of One's Own/Three Guineas*, M. Barrett (ed.). London: Penguin.

Woolf, V. (2005), *Mrs Dalloway*. Orlando, FL: Harcourt.

Woolf, V. (2015), *Mrs Dalloway*, A. E. Fernald (ed. and introd.). The Cambridge Edition of the Works of Virginia Woolf. Cambridge: Cambridge University Press.

Yeats, W. B. (2001), *The Major Works*, E. Larissy (ed.). Oxford World's Classics. Oxford: Oxford University Press.

Part One

Defining the Field and Research Issues

The Modernist Everyday

2

Anything but a Clean Relationship: Modernism and the Everyday

Scott McCracken

Introduction

The concept of the everyday can mean both everything and nothing.[1] It extends to every aspect of our lives, including those that go unnoticed. A concept with many names – the ordinary, the banal, the mundane, the quotidian, the habitual – it can be stretched to the point where it leaves no area of experience untouched.[2] Yet this comprehensiveness means it also includes those aspects of experience that are taken for granted or remain forever buried in our unconscious. The everyday represents a paradox or, as this chapter will suggest, a series of paradoxes. It can refer to both the ordinary and the extraordinary. Daily activities we hardly notice, such as washing our hands or eating breakfast, are everyday, but so too are states of heightened consciousness or intense experience, falling in love, intoxication, extreme physical pain or grief (Felski, 1999–2000, 29). Significance is often masked by insignificance. As Sigmund Freud documented in *The Psychopathology of Everyday Life* (1901), everyday slips of the tongue or lapses in memory can be the portals to unacknowledged fears and desires. As for art, everyday life is usually seen as its antithesis, yet Henri Lefebvre writes about an 'art of living', where life itself becomes a form of artistic expression (2008, 1: 199).

It was not so much the concept itself as these paradoxes that make the everyday so important in critical discussions of modernism.[3] The idea of the

I would like to thank Bryony Randall for her insightful comments and suggestions about an early draft of this chapter.

everyday as that which is there, but does not signify, implicates it in some of the key aesthetic questions of modernism: the relationship between art and the real; the relationship between art and the ordinary rhythms of daily life; the relationship between art and the unconscious; the relationship between art and the commodity. However, before exploring these questions in the work of T. S. Eliot, Dorothy Richardson, and Walter Benjamin, a discussion of one everyday object in James Joyce's experimental novel *Ulysses* (1922) will help to set the scene.

Leopold Bloom and the Bar of Lemon Soap

Ulysses takes place in Dublin, Ireland, on a single ordinary day, 16 June 1904. Just after eleven o'clock in the morning, the novel's anti-hero, Leopold Bloom, is travelling to the funeral of a close acquaintance, Paddy Dignam, when he is discomforted by a bar of lemon soap in his pocket, which is sticking into his behind. The obvious thing to do would be to move it to more suitable pocket, but Bloom is unwilling to draw attention to himself. Reluctant to interrupt the solemn atmosphere in the cab with a matter that might seem trivial in the face of Dignam's sudden death, he waits until the carriage stops at the graveyard before seizing his opportunity to act as his fellow passengers get out:

> Change that soap now. Mr Bloom's hand unbuttoned his hip pocket swiftly and transferred the paperstuck soap to his inner handkerchief pocket. He stepped out of the carriage, replacing the newspaper his other hand still held. (Joyce, 1993, 83)

A bar of lemon soap is an everyday object and for most of the day Bloom forgets that he has bought it. When he moves the soap, his actions are discreet and unobserved. Yet Joyce chooses to document not just Bloom's movements across Dublin but also those of the soap: from its purchase at Sweny's Chemist in Lincoln Place to its use in a public bath to its final destination in Bloom's home. The points in the day when it re-enters Bloom's conscious thoughts are always noted and its constant presence in his unconscious is signalled by hints and allusions. In the novel's more surreal episodes, such as the dream-like 'Circe', set in Dublin's red-light district, the soap even achieves the power of speech.

In an earlier, realist, novel, the soap might have functioned as what Roland Barthes calls a 'reality effect' (1989, 141–8). In the work of nineteenth-century novelists, such as Honoré de Balzac and Charles Dickens, everyday objects, the contents of a cupboard or a description of furniture, create a sense of the real. They anchor the narrative in a recognizable world, distinguishing it from fictions of fantasy or magic. Such objects may also serve to locate the social position of their owners. They represent distinctions of class and status, locating a character in relation to residual, dominant or emerging social orders. In Joyce's text the soap plays its part in establishing Bloom as an ordinary Dubliner, an 'everyman',[4] who performs his daily ablutions like everybody else; but, as the narrative proceeds, the object starts to exceed the limits of realism, intruding into a surreal realm, much as it sticks into Bloom's buttock, interrupting the narrative and disturbing the reader's comfort. For example, it makes an unexpected and disconcerting appearance in one of the imaginary newspaper headlines that punctuate the 'Aeolus' episode, set in the offices of the *Freeman's Journal*:

ONLY ONCE MORE THAT SOAP

Alerted once again to its presence by the smell of lemon on his handkerchief, Bloom moves the soap back to its original position in his hip pocket (Joyce, 1993, 101).

During the day, through use and friction, the bar gradually degrades in his pocket, becoming sticky and shaping itself to his body. It adheres not just to the paper it is wrapped in but also to the focal points of anxiety in Bloom's psyche. Just as the physical presence of the bar of soap returns through nudges and traces (its smell, the sensation of its melting surface), so feelings of guilt, inferiority and jealousy he associates with the soap seep into Bloom's conscious mind. As he tries to avoid his wife's lover, Blazes Boylan, he searches for it desperately just before he ducks in through the gate of the National Museum:

I am looking for that. Yes, that. Try all pockets. Handker. *Freeman.*
Where did I? Ah, yes. Trousers. Potato. Purse. Where?
Hurry. Walk quietly. Moment more. My heart.
His hand looking for the where did I put found in his hip pocket soap lotion have to call tepid paper stuck. Ah soap there I yes. Gate.
Safe! (150)

Each of the surprising variety of everyday objects he finds in his pockets indicates something about his life, but some of them assume a wider significance. The potato, which he carries for luck, for example, seems to allude to an Irish identity rooted in the famine of the nineteenth century. The soap, however, is a reminder of debt and guilt, specifically the fact that the soap and a lotion he has ordered from the chemist remain unpaid for, but it is also a signifier for some of Bloom's deeper anxieties.

It is not surprising, then, that the soap makes its presence known again after he masturbates on the beach while gazing at a young woman, Gerty McDowell. As he reflects while enjoying the lingering sensations of his own pleasure, he mistakes the scent of the soap for the smell of his own sperm:

> Source of life. And its extremely curious the smell. Celery sauce. Let me.
>   Mr Bloom inserted his nose. Hm. Into the. Hm. Opening of his waistcoat.
> Almonds or. No. Lemons it is. Ah no, that's the soap. (307)

In the novel's 'Circe' episode, the soap makes a surreal entrance, 'diffusing light and perfume', as it 'arises' like the sun over the scene:

THE SOAP

> We're a capital couple are Bloom and I.
> He brightens the earth. I polish the sky. (360)

If the soap's apparently autonomous existence can be partly accounted for by the role it plays in Bloom's unconscious, it also relates to its participation in a larger political economy. Soap was a widely advertised commodity at the turn of the twentieth century. Both soap and Bloom are indeed a 'capital couple', each playing a role in capitalist relations. Bloom is a copywriter, who composes advertisements that encourage the public to consume manufactured products such as soap or tinned meat. The bar of soap is not just a useful item but also a commodity, subject to the laws of economic exchange. It achieves an illusory autonomy through what Karl Marx called commodity fetishism, the process whereby the contradictions in social relations appear as relationships between things:

> The form of wood, for instance, is altered by making a table out of it. Yet, for all that, the table continues to be that common every-day thing wood. But, so soon as it steps forth as a commodity, it is changed into something transcendent. It not only stands with its feet on the ground, but in relation to other commodities, it stands on its head, and devolves out of its wooden brain grotesque ideas, far more wonderful than 'table turning' ever was. (Marx, 1954, 76)

The soap, like Marx's table, also achieves a lively life of its own, not least because it has not been paid for. Its ownership and value exist in an abstract rather than a concrete realm, playing a role in Dublin's complex economy of credit and debt. This overlaps with Bloom's sense of his personal morality. He leaves Sweny's chemist's, promising to pay for the soap when he returns later that day to pick up a lotion he has ordered. He never does, but the debt lodges itself in his unconscious, becoming associated with a more general sense of guilt that returns at critical moments, such as his escape from Boylan, when the word 'lotion' follows that of 'soap' (Joyce, 1993, 150). As the soap rises in 'Circe', the 'freckled face of Sweny, the druggist appears in the disc of the soapsun' demanding payment:

SWENY

Three and a penny, please.

The soap by this time has come to represent the process Freud in *The Interpretation of Dreams* (1900) calls 'condensation': where one object or image stands for a nexus of associations and ideas (Freud, 2001, 279–304). If guilt connects these associations, they nonetheless represent a wide range of hopes and desires, indicating the whole of Bloom's life experience. All of which contributes to how he apprehends even the slightest mundane incident. The bar of lemon soap represents both the daily in *Ulysses* and the extraordinary complexity of the social relations that produce the ordinary, including Bloom's personal sense of morality and the unseen role of the economy in structuring the everyday.

If the history of Bloom and the lemon soap seems to highlight the awkwardness of Bloom's fit with Dublin's daily life, then this is deliberate. Part of Joyce's artistic project was to create an Irish art that was international rather than inward looking and narrowly nationalist. He did not want to represent the daily as unproblematic. Another of the lemon soap's manifold roles in the novel is to mark out Bloom's difference, the otherness he experiences as the son of a Jewish father living in Irish Catholic Dublin. In 'Circe', a chorus of 'Sisters of Erin' sing of 'wandering soap' (Joyce, 1993, 407), linking the soap to Bloom's correspondence with the figure of the 'wandering Jew'. An element of Bloom's discomfort in the carriage relates to the anti-Semitism expressed by his fellow travellers. It doesn't help that their prejudice coalesces around the stereotype of the Jewish moneylender, an image that makes Bloom's small debt to Sweny assume a larger symbolic importance.

Similarly, the physical discomfort caused by the lemon is both an example of everyday discomfort and a metaphor for the social awkwardness Bloom feels and tries to cover up by trying, and failing, to tell an anecdote that reinforces anti-Semitic stereotypes. In fact, once established, it is possible to trace an association between the soap and Bloom's ambivalent relationship to Jewishness back to an earlier moment in the text, a visit to a local (non-kosher) Jewish butcher to buy pork kidneys for breakfast. There he sees a leaflet for a Zionist community inviting investment in a farm in Palestine, and he imagines holding a lemon: 'Nice to hold, cool waxen fruit, hold in the hand, lift it to the nostrils and smell the perfume' (49). In the light of that desire, the purchase of the lemon soap is not just an everyday act, but it also signifies a utopian (and, Bloom realizes, illusory) longing for a community in which not only would Bloom belong, but the production and consumption of goods would be visible and common to all.

The example of the lemon soap demonstrates the hidden dimensions of the everyday. If we remind ourselves of the four aspects of the everyday with which this chapter started – the real, the daily, the unconscious and the commodity – we can see that the lemon soap first works to anchor the narrative in a believable version of the real. Second, as an everyday object that plays a part in Bloom's daily routine, it helps to signify his ordinariness, his status as an everyman. Third, the lemon soap represents aspects of Bloom's unconscious psychic life: his uncertainties about his cultural identity, his sense of guilt, his ambivalent feelings about his wife's affair. Fourth, the bar of soap as commodity indicates that Bloom's ordinariness is positioned in relation to social and economic structures that are far more powerful than he is. Bloom's role as modern hero, a twentieth-century version of the ancient Greek hero Odysseus (whose name in Latin is Ulysses), is realized through his struggle to attain some agency in the face of those structures.

The Real

In these respects, the real is a problem, not a given, for the modernist text. Rather than 'reflecting' that which already exists, the modernist text presents itself as epistemological form, that is, a new way of knowing the real. If, at an earlier stage in the development of the novel, the soap might have acted as one of Roland Barthes's 'reality effects', an index of reality, embedding Bloom in a 'real' world, modernism is a response to the rapidly changing world described by Karl Marx and Friedrich Engels in the *Communist Manifesto*, where far from there being a stable reality, 'all that is solid melts into air'.[5] The response of the artistic avant-gardes of the early twentieth century was to emphasize the impermanence of any illusory sense of reality in a world that might change at any second. In this context, the bar of soap acts as a dialectical image, in the sense used by the critic Walter Benjamin.[6] On the one hand, it signifies the ordinary, daily rhythms of life. On the other, it reveals the extent to which dailiness is governed and regulated by forces that are much larger and more powerful than what can be perceived within the narrow horizon of individual experience. As a dialectical image, the soap halts and condenses for a moment the rapid flux of modernity, drawing attention to the thresholds, boundaries and fractures that structure reality and exposing the contradictions that produce it. Modernism uses a number of formal techniques to draw attention to these contradictions, which suggest the world is itself a work in process rather than a finished entity.

Modernist Techniques

The most important technique used to defamiliarize the everyday in modernist artworks is 'montage': the art of composition by the superimposition or juxtaposition of miscellaneous elements. It is not uncommon for objects to appear enchanted in some of the great nineteenth-century realists, notably Dickens (see Carey, 1973), but for the most part nineteenth-century realism keeps the discourse of the fantastic carefully within the bounds of a realist narrative. Modernist texts are far more likely to permit the unconscious to seep into our experience of the everyday. 'Stream of consciousness', surrealism and works of montage constructed using *objets trouvés* (found objects) are all defamiliarizing techniques that work to upset the social and aesthetic conventions that define our sense of the real.

Both 'stream of consciousness' and surrealism bring to representation the influence of the unconscious mind on our apprehension of the real. The rearrangement of conventional forms, the body or the face in Cubist painting for example, provokes new ways of seeing the world and of seeing things in the world. The juxtaposition of apparently unrelated pieces of text and objects as 'collage' or 'montage' in modernist artworks opens up the possibility of new conventions, both aesthetic and social. In Joyce's *Ulysses*, different styles – popular journalism, the mock-heroic, scholasticism, romance – are juxtaposed and parodied. In T. S. Eliot's poem, *The Waste Land* (1922), fragments of text are carefully edited together to produce a disorientating effect on the reader:

'On Margate Sands.
I can connect
Nothing with nothing.
The broken fingernails of dirty hands.
My people humble people who expect
Nothing.'
                    la la

To Carthage then I came

Burning burning burning burning
O Lord Thou pluckest me out
O Lord Thou pluckest

burning. (Eliot, 1974, 74)

One way of thinking about such passages is that modernism simply mimics the processes of urban modernity. The experience of the industrial city is an assault on the senses. It becomes impossible to comprehend its totality. Instead, it is only possible to apprehend impressions or fragments (see McCracken, 2010). But to see the modernist aesthetic of fragmentation as just mimetic is to overlook the extent to which it pushes its audience to reflect on the process it represents. In this respect, the significant thing about the modernist artwork is not its experimental form per se, but that it prompts us to think about everyday social processes towards which we would otherwise become blasé or habituated (see Simmel, 1974). In this respect, modernism, if not actively resistant, at least questioned the logic of modernization in capitalist societies.

Mass Culture

Sometimes modernist references to the everyday are explicit, as in Eliot's fragments of urban detritus in Section III of *The Waste Land*:

[…] empty bottles, sandwich papers,
Silk handkerchiefs, cardboxes, cigarette ends
Or other testimony of summer nights. (Eliot, 1974, 70)

More often the everyday object is an implicit referent around which our knowledge of the world can be reconfigured. In each case, modernism has a contradictory relationship to the mass society created by industrialization. In modernist art and literature, the industrial products that feed mass culture, such as Bloom's bar of soap or Eliot's list of discarded items in *The Waste Land*, often figure as a referent of the real. Yet, as Raymond Williams points out in his essay 'When Was Modernism?' (1989), the movements that produced modernist texts and artworks were not themselves mass movements. They were composed of small coteries and circles in metropolitan centres such as Paris, London and New York. The work they produced often set itself against mass culture. It was difficult, it had a small circulation, and most modernisms could justifiably be accused of elitism. It is then not surprising that historians such as Eric Hobsbawm argue that the new industrial technologies of mass entertainment, such as cinema and radio, played a greater role in changing culture than avant-garde and modernist art (1994, 178–98).

However, a balanced view of the relationship between modernism and mass culture needs to weigh the historian's justifiable concern with the culture of the majority and modernism's influence, by 1930, as what Fredric Jameson describes as a 'cultural dominant' (1991, 6). A closer look at the culture of the period suggests that the relationship between mass and elite cultures was more of a two-way process than a binary divide suggests. Modernism influenced popular culture, from high fashion to the fitted kitchen. In the 1920s, glossy magazines such as *Vogue* and *Vanity Fair* published articles that explained modernism for readers who wanted to understand the latest cultural trends. Modernism did impinge on everyday life. Clothes, book covers and domestic interiors were influenced by modernist design.

The relationship worked the other way as well. Cinema had an enormous impact on modernist writers.[7] The films of Charlie Chaplin were highly popular and influential on avant-garde dramatists such as Bertolt Brecht. By the 1930s, modernism had started to creep into the popular design of everyday household items, from crockery to paperback book covers. Modernist aesthetics became the cultural dominant not in the sense that most culture was modernist, but in the sense that modernism became the measure against which earlier and newer forms were judged. In mass culture this dominant could act as a signifier for elitism, as it does in the hard-boiled detective novels of Raymond Chandler, whose style was admired by leading modernists such as T. S. Eliot, or as a mark of distinction, as it did in magazines of high fashion.

The Everyday and Mood

Nonetheless, where this positions modernism in relation to the everyday is a matter of dispute. Critics of modernism, such as Rita Felski, argue that twentieth-century theories of the everyday have taken their cue from modernism, valuing the extraordinary over the ordinary. She quotes Samuel Beckett's epigram, 'habit is the ballast that chains the dog to its vomit', as a typical example (Felski, 1999–2000, 26),[8] an attitude she associates with a gendered contempt for routine dailiness. Felski recruits feminist theorists of the everyday, such as Agnes Heller (*Everyday Life*, 1984), in a bid to revalue ordinariness. However, arguably it was modernist women writers, such as Dorothy Richardson and Virginia Woolf, who initiated a gendered critique of dailiness (see Randall, 2007). Both writers focused on the daily work performed by women in the home. Dorothy Richardson even suggested this amounts to a form of art in itself. In *Revolving Lights* (1923), the seventh 'chapter-volume' of her long modernist novel *Pilgrimage*, the novel's heroine, Miriam Henderson, develops a theory in an argument with the character Hypo Wilson (based on the author H. G. Wells) that women's art is the art of making 'atmospheres':

> Women are emancipated [...] Through their pre-eminence in an art. The art of making atmospheres. It's as big an art as any other. Most women can exercise it, for reasons, by fits and starts. The best women work at it the whole of the time. Not one man in a million is aware of it. It's like air within air. It may be deadly. Cramping and awful, or simply destructive, so that no life is possible within it. So is the bad art of men. At its best it is absolutely life-giving. And not soft. Very hard and stern and austere in its beauty. And like mountain air. And you can't get behind it, or in any way divide it up. Just as with 'Art.' Men live in it and from it all their lives without knowing [...] the thing I mean goes through everything. A woman's way of 'being' can be discovered in the way she pours out tea. (Richardson, 1979, 3: 257)

Although Miriam's insights appear to support Felski's argument for a revaluation of the everyday, they also suggest that such a revaluation cannot escape the paradoxes that lie at the heart of the quotidian. While her concept of art as 'atmosphere' is created out of the everyday, its ability to break out of the limitations of its surroundings is not guaranteed: 'It may be deadly. Cramping and awful.' At 'its best it is absolutely life-giving', but it is not immediately clear whether this is because it fulfils the potential of the conditions of its making or because it transcends them, becoming something else. In other words, the question is: Does Richardson's female artist allow her audience, knowingly and unknowingly, to appreciate the everyday for what it is, or does she open their eyes to a realm of experience beyond their immediate (daily, habitual) environment?

To explore this question further, it is necessary to interrogate Richardson's concept of 'atmosphere'. Richardson knew German well, so it seems likely she was thinking of a concept from German aesthetics, *Stimmung*, which translates as 'atmosphere' or 'mood'.[9] She would have been aware that the etymology of *Stimmung* comes from the German word for 'voice', *Stimme*. Another translation is attunement, a concept which accords with the female artists' ability to orchestrate a relationship between people and things in a domestic space, bringing them into harmony. In other episodes in *Pilgrimage* Miriam manages to create an atmosphere/mood/sense of attunement in a room directly through music, for example by playing a Beethoven piano sonata (1: 56; 4: 638).

Although best known in the twentieth century through the work of the German philosopher Martin Heidegger, the concept of *Stimmung* has a long history in the philosophy of aesthetics. David Wellbery suggests that this history includes three aspects. First, the power of mood/atmosphere/attunement stems from the fact that it is a 'total quality' nonetheless experienced as an 'individual encounter': the mood meets 'the subject's state of self, making apparent how one is and how one will become' (Wellbery, 2003, 704). Second, moods are 'not only modes of our psychic inner life, but also atmospheres, which surround us'. They consist of

> an interaction of many elements, which is felt collectively. Moods have an integrative function with regard to objects and their properties. They combine into self-contained wholes, without specifying the rules for this synthesis. (705)

Finally, moods have a communicative dimension. The communication of a mood proceeds

> through suggestion, it is infectious; but it operates below the threshold of rational explanation (so is deniable, easy to repudiate), resulting in a common field of orientations, attitudes, dispositions, which is nevertheless unstable, because not secured by expressly symbolised norms. (705)

Although difficult to quantify, the notion of mood is a useful one, putting the concept of the everyday in a different light. It suggests that our relationship with everyday objects is conditioned by a complex set of relationships between people and things. Like the everyday, our experience of mood is paradoxical: we experience it subjectively, yet it has an undefinable, but unmistakeably objective existence, which allows it to be shared and communicated. Our experience of the everyday depends on mood, which is produced by a particular cultural moment or constellation that is experienced both subjectively and collectively. In this respect, modernist techniques of defamiliarization are designed to shock us out of a comfortable mood and to (re)instate a sense of agency (our agency or the agency of others) in the process of mood creation.

However, these techniques of defamiliarization work in different ways in different works of art. The German dramatist Bertolt Brecht used the *Verfremdungseffekt* ('distancing' or 'alienation' effect) in his theatre to interrupt the creation of all-absorbing (in Richardson's terms) 'cramping and awful' moods that would prevent his audience from thinking critically; he was, however, well aware that his theatre had to first create those moods before it could break them (see Brecht, 1964). For Richardson, women's art involves a careful tending to people and objects, an arrangement that, if got right, will expand rather than stifle consciousness. Despite their differences, both Brecht and Richardson use formal techniques to provoke new forms of consciousness in their audiences in order to set the relationship between art and the everyday into a new light. Arrangement and rearrangement are, as it turns out, at the heart of modernism's concern with the everyday. Modernist art is concerned with the arrangement of things and people *as they are*, but also *as they might be*. The mood or atmosphere produced by the former is usually unconscious. Modernist art rearranges in order to create a critical distance from the everyday, but also to seek the possibilities that exist within it: new moods, new atmospheres.

Arrangement

If this project appears relatively straightforward in relation to the fixed space of an interior or a theatre, the modern city presents a different set of problems. It is less easy to capture the diversity and complexity of the urban everyday, which is as much about rapid change and movement through the city as it is about fixed structures or stasis (McCracken, 2010). The modern city is experienced as fragmented, and urban experience itself becomes a series of intensities, punctuated by boredom. Modernism often also responds with an aesthetic of fragmentation, reflecting the subject's experience of the city, but modernist art is never entirely random, even where an element of chance or unpredictability is built into its form.

One uncategorizable example of modernism (uncategorizable in the sense that it is at one and the same time a work of art, and of criticism, and of history and of philosophy) that responds to fragmentations through the technique of montage is Walter Benjamin's *The Arcades Project*. An unfinished commentary composed between 1927 and 1940 in multiple strands on the history of the city that became the capital of modernism, nineteenth-century Paris, *The Arcades Project* can be compared with some of the avant-garde novels of the early twentieth century:

Joyce's *Ulysses*, Alfred Döblin's *Berlin Alexanderplatz* (1929), John Dos Passos's *U.S.A.* (1930–36) or E. E. Cumming's *EIMI* (1933). Benjamin wrote that he wanted to create a text composed entirely of quotations. The version of *The Arcades Project* that he left when he died is not quite that. It is largely made up of citations from other texts, but it also includes short commentaries by Benjamin, which add an extra dimension to his juxtapositions.

Using sources from newspapers, history, philosophy and literature, Benjamin builds up a composite representation of nineteenth-century Paris. Part of Benjamin's argument is that it is the very obsolescence of the arcades that opens them up for historical analysis: 'to become obsolete means: to grow strange' (1999, 336). Their decaying structures and out-of-date business practices reveal the processes through which the everyday is produced. In a sense, Benjamin performs a similar act of enforced degradation on his sources: breaking them up into fragments and reassembling them in such a way that they provoke new meanings.

Because Benjamin committed suicide rather than fall into the hands of the Nazis in 1940, the exact arrangement of the fragments that make up the Arcades Project will never be known. However, Benjamin gave a number of indications as to his method. Not only is the project an exercise in the aesthetics of montage, but the content is also preoccupied with the arrangement of things. Benjamin is fascinated by both interior and exterior spaces, and even more drawn to the thresholds between the private and public. He writes about the traces left by the human body on the soft furnishings of the bourgeois home, making it the perfect location for a murder mystery (1999, 20), and the semi-mystical function of the objects that mark urban boundaries and thresholds, which persist into modernity:

> At the entrance to the skating rink, to the pub, to the tennis court: *penates*.[10]
> The hen that lays the golden praline-eggs, the machine that stamps our names on nameplates, slot machines, fortunetelling devices, and above all weighing devices (the Delphic *gnōthi seauton*[11] of our day) – these guard the threshold [...] Of course, this same magic prevails more covertly in the interior of the bourgeois dwelling. Chairs beside an entrance, photographs flanking a doorway, are fallen household deities, and the violence they must appease grips our hearts even today at the ringing of the doorbell. (Benjamin, 1999, 214)

In a similar vein, Benjamin explores the histories of the underground passages and catacombs that honeycomb subterranean Paris, documenting their use during periods of civil unrest and revolution.[12] His use of montage juxtaposes the ordinary life of the city with those aspects of urban life that are either invisible or taken for granted. Influenced by but not wholly in sympathy with the surrealists, he employs their methods of shock and defamiliarization to provoke a new look at city spaces. He asks us to look at pavement slabs through new eyes, as if we were homeless and were looking for the most comfortable place to bed down on them:

> For what do we know of streetcorners, curb-stones, the architecture of the pavement – we who have never felt heat, filth, and the edges of the stone beneath our naked soles, and have never scrutinized the uneven placement of the paving stones with an eye toward bedding down on them. (P1, 10; Benjamin, 1999, 517)

Cities, for Benjamin, are replete with dreams and nightmares: 'arcades, winter gardens, panoramas, factories, wax museums, casinos, railway stations' are all '[d]ream houses of the collective' (405); but Benjamin is most interested in the points at which dreaming and waking meet: the uncertain point when the sleeper is not sure whether she is awake or asleep, but has still access to her dreaming as well as her waking worlds (see Buse et al., 2006, 105–12). The city, he suggests, is criss-crossed with thresholds and boundaries where dreamworlds and real worlds meet. Thus, for Benjamin, the everyday is poised on the threshold between *what is* and *what might be* (see McCracken, 2002). A modernist aesthetics of the city requires an appreciation of all its dimensions, all its real and surreal forms of consciousness.

However, one consequence of wanting to appreciate everything can be a loss of form, leading to incoherence or just boredom. In a continuation of their dispute in Richardson's *Revolving Lights*, Hypo accuses Miriam of being 'scattered': 'You're too omnivorous, Miriam. You get the hang of too many things. You're scattered' (1979, 3: 377). Critics have been divided about whether *Pilgrimage* represents an aesthetic of accumulation or whether there is a design behind its form.[13] It lacks the mythic structure of Joyce's *Ulysses* but where some critics have, like Hypo, seen it as superficial, extending to touch everything, but penetrating nothing in depth, others have seen a careful design in its structures of growing awareness and repetition, which allow Miriam's first impressions, which are indeed unformed and untested, to be reconsidered and reordered into meaningful experience.

Walter Benjamin's *Arcades Project* could be read as an analogous response to urban modernity. Its fragmented, citational structure reflects the scattered experience of the modern city. However, there is a design to its arrangement. The citations are carefully juxtaposed. Arrangement is key. The method borrows from that of the 'collector', who 'takes up the struggle against dispersion' (Benjamin, 1999, 211) and, as Benjamin describes it, makes his concern the transfiguration of things. To him falls the Sisyphean task of divesting things of their commodity character by taking possession of them. But he bestows upon them only a connoisseur value, rather than use value. The collector dreams his way not only into a distant or bygone world but also into a better one – one in which, to be sure, human beings are no better provided with what they need than in the everyday world, but in which things are freed from the drudgery of being useful. (9)

Modernism responds to the everyday by selecting, revaluing and rearranging. It is not the case that modernisms are contemptuous of the everyday. Unlike Beckett's dog, they are fascinated by rather than chained to the forms habit takes and the new forms thrown up by the cultures of capitalism, such as the commodity.

Port Sunlight

Another literary bar of soap illustrates this. Entering a shop in Switzerland in *Oberland* (1927), the ninth 'chapter-volume' of *Pilgrimage*, Miriam Henderson is struck by the international nature of the goods, many of them British, including Huntley and Palmer biscuits and, in a (possibly deliberate) echo of *Ulysses*, soap:

As if from the bright intense sunlight all about her, a ray of thought had fallen upon the mystery of her passion for soap [...] It was not only the appeal of varying shape and colour or even of the many perfumes each with its power of evoking images: the heavy voluptuous scents suggesting brunette adventuresses, Turkish cigarettes and luxurious idleness; the elusive, delicate, that could bring spring-time into a winter bedroom darkened by snow-clouds. The secret of its power was in the way it pervaded one's best realisations of everyday life. No wonder Beethoven worked at his themes washing and re-washing his hands. And even in merely washing with an empty mind there is a *charm*; though it is an empty charm, the illusion of beginning, as soon as you have finished, all over again as a different person. But all great days had soap, impressing its qualities upon you, during your most intense moments of anticipation, as a prelude. And the realisation of a good day past, coming with the early morning hour, is accompanied by soap. Soap is with you when you are in that state of feeling life at first hand that makes even the best things that can happen important not so much in themselves as in the way they make you conscious of life, and of yourself living. Every day, even those that are called ordinary days, with its miracle of return from sleep, is heralded by soap, summoning its retinue of companion days.

> To buy a new cake of soap is to buy a fresh stretch of days. Its little weight,
> treasure, minutely heavy in the hand, is life, past present and future compactly
> welded. (Richardson, 1979, 4: 62–3)

As in *Ulysses* the bar of soap is a dialectical image, where the object halts and condenses the larger structures that produce the everyday in modernity. In her study *Modernism, Daily Time and Everyday Life*, Bryony Randall writes that the 'mystery of [Miriam's] passion for soap' (2007, 76) reveals three imbricated aspects of dailiness: first, the way in which, although each day is different, it mirrors or contains all that have gone before, 'past present and future compactly welded'; second, soap was (as we have already seen in James Joyce's *Ulysses*) like Huntley and Palmer biscuits, part of an increasingly commodified daily life. The connection between sunlight and soap in the passage is partly a tongue-in-cheek reference to Sunlight, the widely advertised, mass-produced soap, which was made at Port Sunlight (named after the product) near Liverpool by Lever & Co. The bar of soap Miriam buys is almost certainly Sunlight soap, which was sold in Europe and America as well as throughout the British Empire using the phantasmagoric and narcotic imagery of advertising alluded to in the passage: 'voluptuous scents [...] brunette adventuresses, Turkish cigarettes and luxurious idleness'. Finally, the selection of soap takes it out of the obscurity of ordinariness and draws attention to the shared 'art of living' (Randall, 2007, 77–8). Randall borrows this phrase from Henri Lefebvre's imagined utopian future for the everyday, in his *Critique of Everyday Life*:

> In the future the art of living will become a genuine art, based like all art upon
> the vital need to expand [...] which will go beyond its own conditions in an
> attempt to see itself not just as a means but as an end. (Lefebvre, 2008, 1: 199)

She argues that Richardson continues this art, which Lefebvre sees as prefigured in earlier writers. Far from expressing contempt for the ordinary, Richardson sees the daily as an end in itself, attending not so much to 'things that can happen' as 'the way they make you conscious of life, and of yourself living' (Richardson, 1979, 4: 63).

It is noticeable that the paradoxes associated with the everyday continue in Randall's comprehensive definitions. Becoming conscious of life as that which already is and of living as daily existence requires an initial shock of strangeness, produced in modernisms by a sense of things being temporally or spatially out of place. The shock of illumination may come from the content of the artwork, for example the strangeness of seeing familiar commodities, like British biscuits, in the Swiss Alps. More commonly, as in *Ulysses*, *The Waste Land* or *Pilgrimage*, this content is combined with formal innovation and it is the form itself that initiates the experience of estrangement.

Conclusion

If we return to the original questions with which this chapter began – about the relationships between art and the real, art and the daily rhythms of life, art and the unconscious, and art and the commodity – we can see that while different modernists had quite different political visions of the world, what they shared was a rejection of the world as something fixed, as something that could be taken for granted. Modernist works of art propose a model of how we might come to know (albeit imperfectly) a world that is in the process of rapid change, where the rhythms of daily life are just one beat in a plurality of different temporalities, some of which are so powerful that they threaten to crush and break the illusion of individual subjectivity. Modernism's interest in that which escapes notice stems from its quest for an epistemology – a way of knowing – that is able to grasp the moment, even as it goes beyond it, to embrace the unconscious thoughts or discarded objects that are also a part of modernity. Modernism's paradoxical embrace of and critique of commodity culture can be understood as both a recognition of the power of the commodity form in capitalism and the recognition that what it represents is a concentration of power relations and desires which needs to be slowly unpicked using new artistic techniques appropriate to a new age. That these techniques produce an art that often seems remote from ordinary life should not fool us into thinking that the everyday is not at the heart of modernism's concerns. Modernism's legacy is both a fascination with the world as it is and a sense of dissatisfaction that it is not what it might be. Modernist artworks are shot through with the utopian desire for something different, something better. It is because that desire is still with us that they still mean something today.

Notes

1   For an overview of theories of the everyday, see Highmore (2002). For an overview of modernist literature and the everyday, see Randall (2010).

2   For Bryony Randall's definition of the everyday as a temporal and psychological phenomenon, opposed to the 'ordinary', see Randall (2015, 180–90, n.7).

3   It is more accurate to write of 'modernisms' in order to register the diversity of modernist artworks, but as a shorthand I use 'modernism' throughout this chapter.
4   Although true to the paradoxical nature of the everyday, John Xiros Cooper writes that he could also be described as an 'anyman' (2004, 165).
5   'All fixed, fast frozen relations, with their train of ancient and venerable prejudices and opinions, are swept away, all new-formed ones become antiquated before they can ossify. All that is solid melts into air, all that is holy is profaned, and man is at last compelled to face with sober senses his real conditions of life and his relations with his kind' (Marx and Engels, 1983, 207). See also Berman (1983).
6   For the best account of Benjamin's use of the dialectical image, see Tiedemann (1999).
7   See Laura Marcus's chapter in this volume.
8   The quotation comes from Samuel Beckett's *Proust and Three Dialogues* (1965, 19).
9   For a suggestive account of how mood analysis might work in cultural studies, see Highmore (2013).
10 Roman household gods.
11 Greek: 'know thyself'.
12 See Convolute C., 'Ancient Paris, Catacombs, Demolitions, Decline of Paris' (Benjamin, 1999, 82–100).
13 On Richardson's aesthetic as one of accumulation, see Mansfield (1919) and Watts (2013–14).

Bibliography

Barthes, R. (1989), 'The Reality Effect', in R. Howard (transl.), *The Rustle of Language*. Berkeley: University of California Press, pp. 141–8.
Beckett, S. (1965), *Proust and Three Dialogues*. London: John Calder.
Benjamin, W. (1999), *The Arcades Project*, H. Eiland and K. McLaughlin (transl.). Cambridge, MA and London: The Belknap Press of Harvard University Press.
Berman, M. (1983), *All That Is Solid Melts into Air: The Experience of Modernity*. London: Verso.
Brecht, B. (1964) *Brecht on Theatre*, John Willett (ed. and transl.). London: Methuen.
Buse, P., Hirschkop, K., McCracken, S. and Taithe, B. (2006), *Benjamin's Arcades: An Unguided Tour*. Manchester: Manchester University Press.
Carey, C. (1973), *The Violent Effigy: A Study of Dickens' Imagination*. London: Faber and Faber.
Cooper, J. X. (2004), *Modernism and Market Society*. Cambridge: Cambridge University Press.

Eliot, T. S. (1974), *The Waste Land,* in *Collected Poems 1909–1962.* London: Faber and Faber.

Felski, R. (1999–2000), 'The Invention of Everyday Life'. *New Formations: A Journal of Culture/Theory/Politics,* 39, (Winter), 13–31.

Freud, S. (1976), *The Psychopathology of Everyday Life.* Harmondsworth: Penguin.

Freud, S. (2001), *The Interpretation of Dreams,* Part 1, in *The Standard Edition of the Complete Psychological Works of Sigmund Freud,* Vol. IV. London: Vintage, pp. 279–304.

Heller, A. (1984), *Everyday Life.* London: Routledge and Kegan Paul.

Highmore, B. (2002), *Everyday Life and Cultural Theory: An Introduction.* London, New York: Routledge.

Highmore, B. (2013), 'Feeling Our Way: Mood in Cultural Studies'. *Communication and Critical/Cultural Studies,* 10, (4), (December), 427–38.

Hobsbawm, E. (1994), *The Age of Extremes: The Short Twentieth Century 1914–1991.* London: Michael Joseph.

Jameson, F. (1991), *Postmodernism, or, the Cultural Logic of Late Capitalism.* London: Verso.

Joyce, J. (1993), *Ulysses.* London: The Bodley Head.

Lefebvre, H. (2008), *Critique of Everyday Life,* 3 vols., John Moore (transl.). London: Verso.

Mansfield, K. (1919), 'Three Women Novelists'. *The Athenaeum,* 4640, (4 April), 140–1.

Marx, K. (1954), *Capital,* vol. 1. London: Lawrence and Wishart.

Marx, K. and Engels, F. (1983), 'Manifesto of the Communist Party', in E. Kamenka (ed.), *The Portable Karl Marx.* Harmondsworth: Penguin.

McCracken, S. (2002), 'The Completion of Old Work: Walter Benjamin and the Everyday'. *Cultural Critique,* 52, (1), 145–66.

McCracken, S. (2010), 'Imagining the Modernist City', in P. Brooker et al. (eds), *The Oxford Handbook of Modernisms.* Oxford: Oxford University Press, pp. 637–54.

Randall, B. (2007), *Modernism, Daily Time and Everyday Life.* Cambridge: Cambridge University Press.

Randall, B. (2010), 'Modernist Literature and the Everyday'. *Literature Compass,* 7, (9), 824–35.

Randall, B. (2015), 'Virginia Woolf's The Waves and the Everyday'. *Literature Interpretation Theory,* 26, (3), 173–93.

Richardson, D. (1979), *Pilgrimage.* London: Virago.

Simmel, G. (1974), 'The Metropolis and Mental Life', in D. Levine (ed.), *Individuality and Social Forms.* Chicago: University of Chicago Press.

Tiedemann, R. (1999), 'Dialectics at a Standstill', in Walter Benjamin, *The Arcades Project,* H. Eiland and K. McLaughlin (transl.). Cambridge, MA and London: The Belknap Press of Harvard University Press, pp. 929–45.

Watts, K. (2013–14), 'Miriam's Waste Paper Basket: Reading Economies in Pilgrimage'. *Pilgrimages: A Journal of Dorothy Richardson Studies,* 6, 46–62.

Wellbery, D. (2003), 'Stimmung', in K. Barck, M. Fontius, D. Schlenstedt, B. Steinwachs and F. Wolfzettel (eds), *Ästhetische Grundbegriffe. Historisches Wörterbuch: Postmoderne - Synästhesie.* Stuttgart, Weimar: Metzler. (An English translation is forthcoming in *New Formations: A Journal of Culture/Theory/Politics.*)

Williams, R. (1989), 'When Was Modernism?' in T. Pinkney (ed.), *The Politics of Modernism: Against the New Conformists.* London: Verso, pp. 33–5.

3

Geographies of Modernism

Andrew Thacker

Modernism is a cultural and aesthetic category with deep links to geography, but for many years criticism tended to overlook its affiliations with spatiality in favour of exclusively temporal and/or historical theorizations. It is true, of course, that in such formulations critics were influenced by the semantics of the term itself, as 'modernism' clearly implies a temporality, of being 'modern' rather than 'ancient', 'new' rather than 'old', and of having an awareness of being uneasily located within an unfolding history.[1] Discussion of modernism's relationship to the *avant-garde* and, more recently, the *arrière-garde* continues to foreground temporality as the key to understanding the theoretical landscape.[2]

However, if we consider one of the canonical texts of modernist criticism from the 1970s, Malcolm Bradbury and Alan McFarlane's *Modernisms: A Guide to European Literature 1890–1930* (1976), we discover that one of the strongest sections of the book is entitled 'A Geography of Modernism'. It contains seven chapters locating modernist art and literature across Germany, France, Russia, England and the United States (despite the 'European' subtitle of the volume). Many of these chapters are stimulating and of continuing relevance today, with a profound stress upon the urban character of modernism. In the 1970s, metropolitan modernism was mainly understood as an aspect of the movement's internationalism, in which cultural formations and 'isms' such as surrealism or futurism arose and then were shared across major cities in Europe and America. Today's geographical conception of modernism would be more likely to revise the notion of internationalism by also discussing globalization and transnationalism, terms rarely in critical usage forty years ago. Equally, the urban quality of modernism would also be supplemented by other geographical features: by analysis, for instance, of the role of pastoral spaces in modernism or of modernism at the seaside.[3] To take account of such developments, we would need to revise Bradbury and McFarlane's 'A Geography of Modernism' to stress a more plural notion of 'Geographies of Modernism' (Brooker and Thacker, 2005), just as Peter Nicholls's *Modernisms* (1995) signalled that the many movements of modernism contained perhaps as many differences as similarities.

Recent critical work has thus sought to expand our understanding of the complex ways in which modernism was located in particular places, how such locations inflected the nature of the modernism encountered there and how forms of modernism migrated to different locations. Did, for example, American writers such as Gertrude Stein, T. S. Eliot, Ezra Pound, Ernest Hemingway and Djuna Barnes, who were located in Europe for much of their lives, produce a different form of modernism from those American writers who stayed at home? Was the American artistic avant-garde of New York Dada itself formed from European visitors such as Marcel Duchamp? How did modernist writers imagine different locations within the cities they inhabited and wrote about? Did they produce metaphorical versions of the material spaces of cities such as London, Berlin or Paris? How was Irish modernism, in writers such as Yeats and Joyce, distinctive because of the colonial situation of Ireland in relation to Britain? What happened when modernist styles and attitudes travelled away from the metropolitan capitals (London, Paris, New York) discussed by Bradbury and McFarlane, and were reworked and reimagined in India, China, Japan or the diverse countries of Africa? In what sense can we talk of an African modernism (Woods, 2010) or an Indian modernism (Chadhuri, 2010; Mitter, 2007)? An overview of geographies of modernism would thus distinguish between two broad, and often overlapping, approaches to the topic. The first builds upon the work of cultural geographers and spatial theorists of modernism and modernity, such as Henri Lefebvre, Walter Benjamin, David Harvey, Michel de Certeau and Michel Foucault. This work attempts to explore the multiple ways in which modernist writing represents and engages with social space in, for instance, the depiction of cities, landscapes or architecture. A second tendency, often influenced by postcolonial studies or world literary studies, has been to consider the global and transnational spread of modernism as a cultural phenomenon, questioning the stylistic and historical parameters of what is defined as modernism. Key figures and ideas here include Susan Stanford Friedman and her concept of 'planetary modernism' (Friedman, 2010), Laura Doyle and Laura Winkiel's notion of 'geomodernism' (2005) and Jahan Ramazani's analysis of 'transnational poetics' (2006). This chapter thus outlines some of the main features of these different trajectories, discusses what they have in common and where they diverge, and explores the implications of the two approaches for future work in modernist studies. The remainder of the chapter briefly examines work by three modernist writers in the light of this understanding of geographies of modernism.

Spatial Theory and Modernism

The early twentieth century was not only the period in which modernist writers started to explore questions of geography and spatiality, but also the time when several key thinkers in the discipline of geography reinvented the subject along more 'modern' lines, shifting the focus from deterministic evolutionary and racialist categories to new notions of the complex interactions between human beings and their multiple landscapes. As Jessica Berman has noted, there is considerable similarity between the questions addressed by geographers, such as Halford Mackinder, Ellen Churchill Semple and Paul Vidal de la Blache, and the geographical frameworks utilized by many modernist writers at the start of the twentieth century: 'In the high modernist fiction of the years between 1910 and World War II, we encounter everywhere the same concerns about location, mapping, center and periphery, and race and its relationship to identity that also dominated the cultural geography of Semple, Mackinder, and Vidal de la Blache' (Berman, 2005, 285).

Recent critics have also interpreted modernist writing by drawing analogies with contemporary geographers, such as Jon Hegglund's reading of modernist fiction in the light of Mackinder's notions of 'spatial self-consciousness and imaginative projection' (2012, 14) or Chris GoGwilt's work on modernism and geopolitics (1993, 2000, 2010). However, other critics have also begun to develop theoretical approaches to literary texts, in modernism and other fields, which explicitly foreground issues of geography and spatiality and which draw upon more contemporary geographical thinkers. Robert J. Tally's work, for instance, has pioneered an approach he calls 'geocriticism', which focuses upon the dynamic relationships between space, place and literature (2013, 2014); the term itself is derived from a volume by the French critic, Bertrand Westphal, *Geocriticism: Real and Fictional Spaces* (2011). For Westphal this approach explores the relationships between actual and imagined geographies, shifting attention from 'the writer to the place', making the 'spatial referent' found in the texts the focus for critical analysis rather than, for instance, biographical information about the author (2011, 112–13). From a different perspective, Franco Moretti's work on the novel, as found in his *Atlas of the European Novel* (1998) and his short text

Graphs, Maps, Trees (2005), pioneers an approach he calls 'distant reading', in which he systematically maps the rise and diffusion of the novel in a form of literary cartography. Moretti's approach is guided by the idea that geography is 'not an inert container [...] but an active force, that pervades the literary field and shapes it in depth' (1998, 3). While Westphal's approach is textually focused, analysing literary texts in a relatively traditional way, Moretti's controversially eschews 'close reading' of the actual text in favour of plotting where novels were read, published or borrowed from libraries in a series of maps and diagrams.

Moretti's claim that space is not an 'inert container' but an 'active force' is indebted to one of the key figures in spatial theory in the twentieth century, Henri Lefebvre, who, in his magisterial work, *The Production of Space* (1991), outlined how geographical space is never simply a blank background on which social activity takes place, but is rather both produced by human activity and is an active force in shaping human societies. Lefebvre's work has not only influenced later geographical theorists such as Derek Gregory, David Harvey, Doreen Massey, Edward Soja and Neil Smith, but also proved influential for many literary critics whose work has centred on the geographies of modernism, such as Eric Bulson (2007), Hegglund (2012), Thacker (2003), and many of the contributors to the edited volumes, *Geographies of Modernism* (Brooker and Thacker, 2005) and *Regional Modernism* (Alexander and Moran, 2013). This critical work explicitly borrows various concepts and theories from cultural geographers and spatial theorists, adapting their usage in various ways to interpret literary texts. The volume, *Regional Modernism*, for instance, explores the geographical notion of *scale*, analysing how modernist writers engaged with more localized geographies than merely that of the nation-state, while Eric Bulson's *Novels, Maps, Modernity* (2007) analyses the role of maps, (dis)orientation, and placement in a range of modern writers, demonstrating how the cartographic imagination was of crucial significance to many novelists in this period.

Another significant example is the conceptual opposition between *space* and *place* which is often employed to understand how modernist writers engage with urban landscapes, broadly distinguishing between an alienating sense of the city as an abstract space and a more attached belonging to particular places within cities, such as rooms, cafes or restaurants. De Certeau's distinction between the tour and the map is a refinement of this space/place binary, and a key part of his notion of 'spatial stories', which links together Lefebvre's notion of social space and literary style; for de Certeau 'every story is a travel story – a spatial practice' and all stories 'traverse and organise places; they select and link them together; they make sentences and itineraries out of them' (1984, 115). Spatial stories always oscillate between discourses of the *map* and those of the *tour*, between a mapping of place that stresses stability and fixity, and a tour discourse that foregrounds how spaces are associated with movement and lived experience. Much modernist fiction contains examples of both of these discourses: writers explore the attempt to map and control urban space as well as employing tour discourses that subvert this, often in narratives about the *flâneur*, a key figure of modernity who wanders aimlessly through the city streets, first identified by Charles Baudelaire. Robert Hampson, for example, illustrates how James Joyce and Joseph Conrad produce fiction (in *Ulysses* and in *The Secret Agent*) in which the 'homogeneous, abstract space of the map' is displaced by the 'heterogeneous lived spaces of the journey' (2005, 63).

Much of this work on the geographies of modernism is historicist and materialist in orientation, exploring how specific spaces and geographies (such as nations, regions, cities, streets and buildings) were represented by modernist writers. These physical locations are then often linked to more metaphorical or imagined geographies, which examine how modernist writing did not simply aim for cartographic verisimilitude, but instead probed and revised how space and place were experienced in social and cultural modernity. Central to this approach is the question of spatiality: modernist writers live, leave or travel through specific places that mark their perception of the world, and many texts represent distinct places, spaces, cities, nations and islands directly; in addition, every text is written, published and read in a specific place. Thinking through the impact of these environments upon texts, in ways that can enhance existing social and historical modes of interpretation, is clearly one way of advancing the development of a specific 'geocriticism' or 'critical literary geography' of modernism.

Transnational and Global Modernisms

The second framework for a geography of modernism is, to an extent, influenced less by debates in cultural geography and spatial theory than by work in postcolonial studies and, more recently, world literary studies. For several decades, work in postcolonial studies has drawn attention to modernist practices in locations beyond Anglo-American and European traditions, such as in the Caribbean and Africa (see Emery, 2007; Gikandi, 1992; Ker, 1997; Ramazani, 2001). One of the key influences for this focus upon how the material spaces of imperial and colonial geography infuse cultural texts has been that of Edward

Said. In *Culture and Imperialism* (1993), Said noted that his project in this book was 'a kind of geographical inquiry into historical experience' and that just 'as none of us is outside or beyond geography, none of us is completely free from the struggle over geography' that is at the basis of imperialism and colonialism: this struggle, suggests Said, 'is not only about soldiers and cannons but also about ideas, about forms, about images and imaginings' (Said, 1993, 6). Given that the rise of European modernism coincided with the apex of European imperialism, it is hardly surprising that Said's reminder about geographical 'struggle' has been so influential on geographies of modernism.

More recent discussions, however, have developed Said's points by foregrounding globalization and transnationalism, as in many of the essays in *The Oxford Handbook of Global Modernisms* (2012). In this volume, the editors argue for an approach that moves beyond the postcolonial work pioneered by Said and others, since 'a global conception of modernism requires more than the geographical addition of previously ignored or marginalized traditions' (Wollaeger and Eatough, 2012, 4). A globalized understanding of modernism therefore attempts to move beyond existing national traditions (a French modernism, a Chinese modernism) by focusing upon the transnational, which 'presupposes the crossing of national borders' and which switches between a micro- and macro-level geographical focus, or what the editors call 'local complexity and large-scale visions' (5). One impetus for the shift to a transnational approach is thus to try to capture more geographical precision when discussing modernism, as many earlier critics had tended to discuss modernism as an *international* movement, arguably eliding 'local complexity'. Thus, Hugh Kenner's 1984 article on 'The Making of the Modernist Canon' suggested that works by a very limited number of writers such as Joyce, Eliot and Pound were 'best located in a supranational movement called International Modernism' (53). In Kenner's conception, this is a modernism that is 'located' in a vacuum in terms of material geographical space. Recent proponents of a transnational approach have, therefore, critiqued the 'international paradigm' developed by Kenner and other earlier critics because, in Ramazani's words, its 'internationalism was not always particularized, its Eurocentricism made scant room for the developing world, and its supposed universalism tended to de-ethnicize writers' (Ramazani, 2006, 350).[4]

The ramifications of a geographical framework that stresses the global and the transnational are profound for, as Susan Stanford Friedman argues in an important article on this topic, 'the new geography of modernism needs to locate many centers of modernity across the globe, to focus on the cultural traffic linking them, and to interpret the circuits of reciprocal influence and transformation that take place within highly unequal state relations' (Friedman, 2006, 429). Two important consequences of Friedman's argument are that she wishes to abandon 'the ahistorical designation of modernism as a collection of identifiable aesthetic styles' as well as 'the notion of modernism as an aesthetic period' with a single start and end point (432). If we now look for 'multiple modernisms' that can be located across the globe, then we are looking not at a singular modernist epoch, but different regimes of modernism, all engaged in encountering forms of social, economic and political modernity, some of which interconnect with others and some of which operate under a different time schema entirely.[5] Thus, we might argue that an 'Indian modernism' is composed of a number of different elements: indigenous aesthetic and cultural practices that continued throughout the conventional period of Anglo-American modernism; the importation of European modernist styles, often by writers who travelled abroad and then returned (the great Bengali poet, Rabindranath Tagore, met and was admired by many Anglo-American modernists, such as Yeats and Pound, while Mulk Raj Anand associated with members of the Bloomsbury Group); and the adoption of complex notions of being 'modern' by writers and artists operating after Anglo-American modernism is said to have finished – the contemporary novelist Amitav Ghosh might thus be said to typify Indian modernism (see Freedman, 2005). Friedman's argument, along with other such work, offers a profound challenge to many researching and teaching modernism, since it expands greatly the range of material that could come under the umbrella term of 'modernism'; indeed, this might be seen as one of the problems of this kind of spatializing of modernism, that it runs the risk of losing focus entirely and turning all twentieth- and twenty-first-century literature into some form of modernism.

Another question here involves the difficulties in moving beyond Western definitions of modernism to capture the specificities of multiple global modernisms. Friedman writes that a 'planetary modernist poetics must be plural, opening up the concept of formal ruptures to a wide array of representational engagements with modernity' (2010, 489). However, ruptures in form and representation have long been terms used to describe the aesthetic strategies of Western modernism. The difficulties of identifying non-Western modernisms without using Western modernist categories is something that Friedman is acutely aware of (480) but, as Andreas Huyssens comments, 'it may well turn out that, despite the best of intentions, [the] de-Westernization of

Modernism/modernity will remain limited because of the Western genealogy of the concepts themselves' (Huyssens, 2005, 13).

Arguably, the differences between a geography of modernism as understood by proponents of spatial theory and one by critics of transnational and global modernism are partly that of method and partly of emphasis. Hegglund's work, for instance, draws on ideas from globalization and transnational studies but he frames his approach in the following way: 'Rather than looking at modernism's spaces within a particular geography of imperialism and globalization, I examine modernism and political globalization as related events in a history of spatiality' (2012, 18). Hegglund thus understands 'modernism and globalization through the lens of spatiality' (19), while transnational criticism could be said to view the spaces of modernism through the lens of globalization.

Geography and Some Modernists

The current interest in geographies of modernism, wherever located, arguably has its origins in the intrinsic interest in space and geography to be found in many of the canonical texts of late nineteenth- and early twentieth-century Anglo-American modernism. To give a flavour of some of these geographies of modernism, I will discuss briefly Joseph Conrad, James Joyce and Virginia Woolf.

Conrad's travels as a seaman not only fed into novels such as *Lord Jim* (1900), *Nostromo* (1904) and *Heart of Darkness* (1899), but also sharpened his interest in space and geography as categories for shaping narrative. Maps, for example, often figure in his texts at key moments, such as Marlowe's invocation of the map of Africa at the start of *Heart of Darkness*, which he laments now lacks the 'blank spaces' of his youth due to imperial expansion by European powers: 'It had got filled since my boyhood with rivers and lakes and names. It had ceased to be a blank space of delightful mystery [...]. It had become a place of darkness' (Conrad, 1988, 11). In one sense, *Heart of Darkness* sets out to explore the implications of the story this map tells, while also attempting to reinscribe 'blankness' and mystery – but not of the 'delightful' kind – onto the map in the form of the incomprehensible behaviour of Kurtz in the jungle. A further meditation upon the nature of maps can be found in a much-cited essay written by Conrad in 1924, outlining the history of geography, 'Geography and Some Explorers', and first published in the mainstream magazine, *National Geographic Magazine*. In this essay Conrad outlined three phases of Western geography, praised exploratory geographical travels or what he terms 'geography militant' (Conrad, 1924, 243), and focused upon the limitations of cartography. As in *Heart of Darkness*, Conrad lamented the fact that the modern world now lacked unmapped spaces and recalled how, as a schoolboy, he put his finger 'on a spot in the very middle of the then white heart of Africa' and 'declared that some day I would go there' (271). When, some eighteen years later, Conrad found himself in the African Congo and thought he was standing on the spot he imagined as a child, his feeling was of disappointment and disenchantment with 'geography militant': 'A great melancholy descended upon me. Yes; this was the very spot'; the overwhelming sensation was of 'the distasteful knowledge of the vilest scramble for loot that ever disfigured the history of human conscience and geographical exploration' (272). Drawing upon de Certeau's theories of the tour and the map, Robert Hampson notes that Conrad was 'probably more involved with maps and mapping than any other major nineteenth- or twentieth-century British novelists' and because of this involvement he 'resists the map's colonization of space' and uses his fiction to uncover the historical practices, including the 'vilest scramble for loot' of imperialism, that gave rise to such cartographic projects (Hampson, 2005, 56).

While Conrad's texts of overseas travel offer the most obvious encounter with the many geographies of modernism, we can also analyse a novel such as *The Secret Agent* (1907) from the perspective of geographical and spatial theory. *The Secret Agent* explores London as a world city populated with immigrants, an experience drawing on Conrad's own background as one of the most deracinated of modern writers: born in Russian-controlled Poland he travelled the world as a merchant seaman for fifteen years before finally settling in Britain in 1896. With a plot concerning foreign anarchists pitted against the bourgeois British state, *The Secret Agent* offers a fascinating perspective on the cosmopolitan geography of particular areas of central London. At one point Verloc, the secret agent of the title, is said to be 'cosmopolitan enough not to be deceived by London's topographical mysteries' (Conrad, 1986, 53), a description that points to Conrad's awareness of how the modernist city requires a certain urban consciousness or cognitive map in order for the characters to find their way in the urban landscape. Conrad, in a later Preface to the novel, noted that its genesis lay in a revelation of London as a world city: 'the vision of an enormous town presented itself, of a monstrous town more populous than some continents and in its man-made might as if indifferent to heaven's frowns and smiles [...] Irresistibly the town became the background for the ensuing period of deep and tentative meditations' (41). The central story of Winnie

Verloc and her family, wrote Conrad, 'had to be disengaged from its obscurity in that immense town' and he had 'to fight to keep at arm's length the memories of my solitary and nocturnal walks all over London in my early days, lest they should rush in and overwhelm each page of the story' (Conrad, 1986, 41). In a sense Conrad, as an exile turned cosmopolitan author, struggles to keep the monster that is London as a 'background' rather than to have its 'topographical mysteries' obscure the story of the tragic death of Winnie Verloc's brother Stevie, and of her revenge upon her husband for perpetrating that death.

In this respect, Conrad's fears that the city will 'overwhelm' his narrative parallels the way that many characters in the story struggle once they leave the internal space of rooms for the streets of this monstrous town. London streets are represented in an acutely physical and palpable fashion – fog, mud, smells and sounds frequently force their presence upon the characters in the novel making the inorganic city into a kind of living entity. One street is like 'a wet, muddy trench' (141), shops are 'steamy' and 'greasy' and 'smell of fried fish' (162), and when Winnie flees her house after the murder of her husband, 'a slimy dampness enveloped her, entered her nostrils, clung to her hair' (239). The city always exerts a tactile hold upon its citizens as when Verloc, at home, leans against the window and feels that only the glass separates him from 'the enormity of cold, black, wet, muddy, inhospitable accumulation of bricks, slates, and stones' and considers 'the latent unfriendliness of all out of doors with a force approaching to positive bodily anguish' (84).

Yet the cosmopolitan citizen must struggle to find a place in this hostile world of matter, and one of the most interesting incidents occurs when the Assistant Commissioner visits a Soho restaurant. Leaving his office for the city streets is memorably compared to 'the descent into a slimy aquarium from which the water has been run off' and now a 'murky, gloomy dampness enveloped him' (150). As he enters the Strand by Charing Cross Station 'the genius of the locality assimilated him' and he is compared to one of the 'queer foreign fish' that frequent this location in the evening (151). The imagery of the street as an aquarium is a brilliant continuation of the idea of the city as an alien physical environment: humans here are literally like fish out of water. The location itself, suggests Conrad, acts upon an individual's identity, transforming the Assistant Commissioner from a 'native' to a 'queer foreign fish'. 'Assimilation' here is a process which reverses the normal understanding of the term: here the native inhabitant is assimilated to the uncanny and 'foreign' quality of the *genius loci* itself.

Conrad's meditation upon place, belonging and national identity here is continued when the Assistant Commissioner takes a hansom cab to 'a little Italian restaurant' in Soho, near to the Brett Street location of Verloc's shop. James McLaughlin provides a brilliant analysis of this episode in his account of how Conrad's novel 'constructs the modernist metropolis as a site of social anarchy' (2000, 23). For McLaughlin, the restaurant is a location in which 'identity is lost by being rendered blank and meaningless' (24): in it, one eats food that is other to one's sense of identity, rather than a cuisine that affirms one's national heritage. Soho, by the early twentieth century, had become a cosmopolitan quarter of European and non-European migrants, and a newspaper report of 1900 described it as 'more continental than it is English' (cited McLaughlin, 2000, 136). It was also, as McLaughlin and Judith Walkowitz argue, perceived as an area rife with political anarchists and sexual depravity, a reputation that gave this West End area the feel that the demonized East End of London possessed in the late nineteenth century (McLaughlin and Walkowitz, 2012). Much is made in the novel of the Soho location in terms of the spatiality of social class in London. Winnie, for example, is acutely aware that she has moved from a Belgravia address, where her mother kept apartments for rent, to a shop in Soho: towards the novel's end she is described as 'the respectable girl of the Belgravian mansion' (McLaughlin and Walkowitz, 2012, 253), an ironic epithet given she has just murdered her husband in the far from respectable location of Soho.

Walkowitz has traced in detail the cultural history of Soho from the later nineteenth century, showing the different stages in its development as a zone of cosmopolitan cultural activity, described in 1887 as 'the foreign quarter of the metropolis' (Walkowitz, 2012, 22). One key marker of this 'foreignness' was the establishment of French, then Italian restaurants in the area, such as the one visited by the Assistant Commissioner. Walkowitz traces how the rather negative associations of cosmopolitan Soho in the late nineteenth century changed in the first decade of the twentieth century: now Soho became a crucial part of a topography that was styled as *Bohemia in London*, as Arthur Ransome's popular book of 1907 described it. This bohemia self-consciously aped its Parisian antecedents in the development of a cafe society, with restaurants whose Frenchified names signalled their cosmopolitan tendencies. Sites such as the Café Royal, the Tour Eiffel and the Mont Blanc all attracted writers and artists, and became important locations of emerging modernist formations (see Brooker, 2004).

As McLoughlin notes, then, Conrad's negative depiction of the Italian restaurant as a place of 'fraudulent cooking mocking an abject mankind'

(2000, 151) is linked to the ironic distancing of his narrative voice, a style that Conrad had made his own in his earlier text, *Heart of Darkness*. Conrad was quite clearly one of the 'queer foreign fish' that inhabit London and its cosmopolitan restaurants, but he was equally determined to developed an identity as a 'native' English author. The complexities of this dialectic between home and abroad for the migrant writer become crystallized in the scene in the restaurant for, as McLaughlin writes, 'Conrad is attempting to flee a Soho that powerfully calls him (home)' (McLaughlin, 2000, 148). In the restaurant the Assistant Commissioner 'seemed to lose some more of his identity' and, catching himself in the mirror, is 'struck by his foreign appearance' (Conrad, 1986, 151). As he leaves he reflects upon how patrons of the restaurant lose their national characteristics, just as the dishes of food are also 'denationalized' due to being fraudulent. The Italian restaurant, writes Conrad, with delicious irony, 'is such a peculiarly British institution' (152). The social space of this Soho is not, therefore, seen as a site of cosmopolitan freedom, but a location for becoming, in Conrad's revealing term, 'unplaced' (152). Conrad's novel can thus be interrogated for its engagement with specific geographies of London, showing how social space, as understood by Lefebvre, affects class, national identity and belonging in the city. *The Secret Agent* does not offer us a cartographic representation of London so much as a demonstration of the ways in which certain geographies 'unplace' individuals in the modernist city.

Conrad's interest in travel, mapping and the ways in which social space structures our identities is also found in a writer such as James Joyce, another modernist who displays a profoundly cartographic imagination. Joyce, for instance, regularly showed an interest in mapping and its effects in his fiction: the first piece of writing we read by Stephen Dedalus, in *A Portrait of the Artist as a Young Man* (1916), is written in his geography primer and contains a child's mapping of his location in the world:

Stephen Dedalus

Class of Elements

Conglowes Wood College

Sallins

County Kildare

Ireland

Europe

The World

The Universe

(Joyce, 2000, 12)

The young Stephen is thus trying to locate himself in his world and the run of familiar geographical categories of scale (school, town, county, nation, etc.) is an attempt to turn abstract social space into a place of belonging. This dialectic between space and place can also be found throughout *Ulysses* (1922), which demonstrates how Joyce critically engaged with maps and mapping in his fiction. In *Ulysses*, we encounter a text which exemplifies and has at its core the modernist exploration of the relations between space, place and modernity. The novel seems to typify David Harvey's assessment of how modernism 'explored the dialectic of place versus space, of present versus past, in a variety of ways' and that while 'celebrating universality and the collapse of spatial barriers, it also explored new meanings for space and place in ways that tacitly reinforced local identity' (Harvey, 1989, 273). Joyce himself appeared well aware of this particular dialectic: 'For myself, I always write about Dublin, because if I can get to the heart of Dublin I can get to the heart of all the cities of the world. In the particular is contained the universal' (cited in Ellmann, 1976, 505). However, *Ulysses* does not reinforce the 'local identity' of place but instead interrogates the spatial politics of particular sites in Dublin, much as Conrad examined Soho in London. Joyce's overall conception of place, however, appears closer to Doreen Massey's definition of place as 'numerous social relationships stretched over space' (Massey, 1995, 69). In other words, *Ulysses* does interrogate the dialectic of place versus space, but the effect is to show how space and what Bloom calls 'joggerfry' (geography) (Joyce, 1993, 56) are always informed by social and political relationships, in particular those between Britain and Ireland.

Among the many guides to Dublin that Joyce used when composing *Ulysses* was a miniature map of the city, taken from the Ordnance Survey map of Ireland, and included in the Thom's Directory for 1904/5. Frank Budgen reports that 'Joyce wrote the "Wandering Rocks" [an episode in *Ulysses*] with a map of Dublin before him on which were traced in red ink the paths of the Earl of Dudley and Father Conmee. He calculated to a minute the time necessary for his characters to cover a given distance of the city' (1960, 122–3). However, much like Conrad, Joyce was also sceptical of the claims of cartography to capture the spatial and geographical nature of everyday experience in the city of Dublin, and several critics have noted how Joyce contests the spatial power embodied in Ireland's geographical status as part of the British Empire (see Gibbons, 2011; Howes, 2000). For example, 'Wandering Rocks' contains multiple journeys by Dublin citizens criss-crossing the streets of Dublin, following the 'technic', in Joyce's (Gilbert) schema for the novel, of the labyrinth. However, this picture of the bustling streets of the Dublin metropolis closes with a viceregal procession by the Governor General, the representative of the British crown in Ireland. The viceregal parade in one sense illustrates how the social space of Dublin is, ultimately, ruled by British imperial powers. While some citizens pause to acknowledge the procession, others offer forms of resistance to this imperial spatial power: thus, the viceroy is 'unsaluted by Mr Dudley White' (Joyce, 1993, 242) and ignored by John Wyse Nolan and the brother of the disgraced Irish nationalist leader, Charles Stewart Parnell. Joyce even encodes resistance in the actual material spaces of the city, as when the River Poddle, a tributary of the main river Liffey, displays 'in fealty a tongue of liquid sewage' (242) to the parade. Joyce also refers to the conflicted spatial history of Dublin in several references to sites along the route of the parade, which passes the place where one Irish nationalist leader, Robert Emmett, was hanged (230–1) and another where a planned statue for Wolfe Tone was never erected (220). This is in marked contrast to the many statues of military heroes loyal to the British Crown, such as Lord Nelson and the Duke of Wellington, which Joyce depicts in other places in the novel. As Eric Bulson notes, we can thus 'rewrite Budgen's vignette to say that Joyce "traced in red ink the paths" of his characters *over an Ordnance Survey map of Dublin*', and thus 'the map Joyce left in Ulysses [...] was an act of reappropriation, a way to imagine Ireland as an independent nation in the not so distant future with a colonial past' (Bulson, 2007, 81). To draw upon de Certeau, then, we can argue that Joyce's spatial story of Dublin offers us a 'tour discourse' that resists the imperialist map of the city.

The novels of Virginia Woolf also display a considerable interest in space and geography, and while Woolf's texts are less obviously engaged with colonial space than those of Joyce, the politics of spatiality is also central to her concerns. As Anna Snaith and Michael Whitworth argue, in Woolf's fictional and non-fictional texts 'the interrelationships she creates between real and imagined spaces' demonstrate her interest in 'the politics of spaces: national spaces, civic spaces, private spaces or the textual spaces of the writer/printer' (Snaith and Whitworth, 2007, 1). The relationship between 'real and imagined spaces' is noted in one of Woolf's earliest published pieces of writing, a review for the *Times Literary Supplement* of 1905, entitled 'Literary Geography'. The review considers two books in a series of illustrated guides to the places represented in the work of specific writers. Woolf discusses how certain writers, such as Scott or the Brontës, vividly evoke a country and its inhabitants but then goes on to note how we should distinguish between 'houses in the brain' and external geographies:

A writer's country is a territory within his own brain; and we run the risk of disillusionment if we try to turn such phantom cities into tangible brick and mortar [...]. No city indeed is so real as this that we make for ourselves and people to our liking; and to insist that it has any counterpoint in the cities of the earth is to rob it of half its charm. (Woolf, 1986, 35)

Much of Woolf's fiction is, arguably, dominated by this division between inner and outer space, between 'houses in the brain' and cities of bricks and mortar. Woolf thus refines this early statement upon literary geography, constructing a fiction that shows how material spaces rely upon imaginative conceptualization and how the territory of the mind is informed by an interaction with external spaces and places. In *Jacob's Room* (1992a), Woolf summarized these two spaces: 'The streets of London have their map; but our passions are uncharted' (Woolf, 1992a, 82). And contemplating how to construct *The Waves* in 1928, Woolf mused, 'what is my own position towards the inner & the outer? I think a kind of ease & dash are good; – yes: I think even externality is good; some combination of them ought to be possible' (Woolf, 1982, 209). Woolf does not reject externally mapped spaces, as 'Literary Geography' might seem to suggest, rather she charts psychic life via her use of stream of consciousness, criss-crossing the liminal regions of inner and outer with 'ease and dash' to reveal how this division itself is somewhat false. In her work, it is the interaction between inner and outer spaces that dominates, showing how Woolf's texts continue to interrogate the external geographies of modernity.

In particular her writings often explore the geography of London, in novels such as *Jacob's Room* and *Mrs Dalloway* (1925), and in essays such as 'The Docks of London' in *The London Scene* (1931–2), which examines the relationship between the capital and imperial space. *Mrs Dalloway*, for example, is often taken as a key instance of Woolf's interest in the 'dark places of psychology', as the narrative relies heavily on representations of the thoughts of its central characters. But the novel is equally interested in the geography of London and how external spaces interact with the interior lives of its characters; as Gillian Beer notes, in *Mrs Dalloway*, Woolf 'sets out the topography of London as precisely as does Defoe' and the 'accounts of walks and of districts register the characters' social space as well as their separations' (Beer, 1996, 52–3). An example of this depiction of social space is found if we consider the locations depicted in *Mrs Dalloway*. These are very circumscribed, as the novel is mainly set in Westminster and Mayfair, areas of power, wealth and influence, as would befit Clarissa Dalloway, wife of a Conservative MP. Thus, the novel explores the areas of London most associated with traditional forms of aristocratic prestige, rather than with cultural power (such as Bloomsbury, associated with Woolf's own life and only briefly mentioned in the novel) or financial power (the City, towards which Elizabeth Dalloway peers, but does not go). Woolf is thus very astute in her use of representations of space to indicate power and status. Inner city suburbs are mentioned, such as the 'poor mothers of Pimlico' (Woolf, 1992b, 21) waiting to see the Queen outside Buckingham Palace, but Pimlico is itself close to the Houses of Parliament where Richard Dalloway works, although it is not explored in detail in the novel. In a number of essays in the late 1920s and early 1930s, Woolf described the pleasure she took in exploring London, including areas such as the East End docks in *The London Scene*. In a diary entry of November 1923, Woolf daydreamed of wandering the city streets, 'walking say to Wapping' (Woolf, 1982, 272), a location in the much poorer East End of the city. So the lack of a more socially panoramic picture of the city in *Mrs Dalloway* is, then, a clear indication of Clarissa Dalloway's own circumscribed social space.

This brief discussion of Conrad, Joyce and Woolf has aimed to demonstrate some of the rich potential for understanding modernism through its multiple geographies. Future work in this area might include more of a rapprochement between the two strands of criticism outlined in this chapter, bringing a richer and more nuanced spatial and geographical vocabulary into dialogue with the more over-arching concepts influencing transnational and global modernist studies. Such work would continue to exemplify the idea that geography, in Moretti's words, is not 'an inert container' in which modernism occurs, but is rather 'an active force' that continues to shape how we understand modernist culture and its diverse locations.

Notes

1 For a classic analysis of the relationship between the modern and the historical, see De Man, 1970, 386.

2 On the *arrière-garde*, see Marx, 2009.

3 For such approaches, see Harris, 2010, and Feigel and Harris, 2011.

4 See also Jessica Berman's *Imagining World Literatures: Modernism and Comparative Literature* (2009). Berman argues that 'comparative modernist studies must at last kill that old bogey, "international modernism", along with its homogenizing impulses and its insistence on a singular universal sphere of readership' (Berman, 2009, 68–9).

5 Friedman's project, with its claim that a 'planetary modernist poetics must be plural', thus sets itself firmly against those interpretations of modernity and modernism that align themselves with Frederic Jameson's notion of a 'singular modernity'. For

Jameson this 'singular modernity' is to be identified with worldwide capitalism, with 'central' and 'peripheral' forms of modernist practice that are homologous with the uneven spread of capitalist development across the globe (see Jameson, 2002).

Bibliography

Alexander, N. and Moran, J. (eds) (2013), *Regional Modernism*. Edinburgh: Edinburgh University Press.

Beer, G. (1996), *Virginia Woolf: The Common Ground*. Edinburgh: Edinburgh University Press.

Berman, J. (2005), 'Modernism's Possible Geographies', in L. Doyle and L. Winkiel (eds), *Geomodernisms: Race, Modernism, Modernity*. Bloomington: Indiana University Press, pp. 281–96.

Berman, J. (2009), 'Imagining World Literatures: Modernism and Comparative Literature', in P. Caughie (ed.), *Disciplining Modernism*. New York: Palgrave Macmillan, pp. 53–71.

Bradbury M. and McFarlane, J. (eds) (1976), *Modernism 1890–1930*. Harmondsworth: Penguin.

Brooker, P. (2004), *Bohemia in London: The Social Scene of Early Modernism*. Basingstoke: Palgrave Macmillan.

Brooker, P., Gasiorek, A., Longworth, D. and Thacker, A. (eds) (2010), *The Oxford Handbook of Modernisms*. Oxford: Oxford University Press.

Brooker, P. and Thacker, A. (eds) (2005), *Geographies of Modernism*. London: Routledge.

Budgen, F. (1960), *James Joyce and the Making of Ulysses*. Bloomington: Indiana University Press.

Bulson, E. (2007), *Novels, Maps, Modernity: The Spatial Imaginary, 1850–2000*. New York: Routledge.

Chaudhuri, S. (2010), 'Modernisms in India', in P. Brooker, A. Gasiorek, D. Longworth and A. Thacker (eds), *The Oxford Handbook of Modernisms*. Oxford: Oxford University Press, pp. 942–60.

Conrad, J. (1924), 'Geography and Some Explorers'. *National Geographic Magazine*, XLV, (3), (March), 241–74.

Conrad, J. (1986), *The Secret Agent*. Harmondsworth: Penguin.

Conrad, J. (1988), *Heart of Darkness*, R. Kimbrough (ed.). New York: Norton.

De Certeau, M. (1984), *The Practice of Everyday Life*. Berkeley: University of California Press.

De Man, P. (1970), 'Literary History and Literary Modernity'. *Daedalus*, 99, (2), Spring, 384–404.

Doyle, L. and Winkiel, L. (eds) (2005), *Geomodernisms: Race, Modernism, Modernity*. Bloomington: Indiana University Press.

Ellmann, R. (1976), *James Joyce*. Oxford: Oxford University Press.

Emery, M. L. (2007), *Modernism, the Visual, and Caribbean Culture*. Cambridge: Cambridge University Press.

Feigel, L. and Harris, A. (eds) (2011), *Modernism-on-Sea: Art and Culture at the British Seaside*. Bern: Peter Lang.

Freedman, A. (2005), 'On the Ganges Side of Modernism: Raghubir Singh, Amitav Ghosh, and the Postcolonial Modern', in L. Doyle and L. Winkiel (eds), *Geomodernisms: Race, Modernism, Modernity*. Bloomington: Indiana University Press, pp. 114–29.

Friedman, S. S. (2006), 'Periodizing Modernism: Postcolonial Modernities and the Space/Time Borders of Modernist Studies'. *Modernism/modernity*, 13, (3), 425–43.

Friedman, S. S. (2010), 'Planetarity: Musing Modernist Studies'. *Modernism/modernity*, 17, (3), 471–99.

Gibbons, L. (2011), 'Text and the City: Joyce, Dublin, and Colonial Modernity', in V. Bénéjam and J. Bishop (eds), *Making Space in the Works of James Joyce*. New York: Routledge, pp. 69–90.

Gikandi, S. (1992), *Writing in Limbo: Modernism and Caribbean Literature*. Ithaca: Cornell University Press.

GoGwilt, C. (1993), *The Invention of the West: Joseph Conrad and the Double-Mapping of Empire*. Stanford: Stanford University Press.

GoGwilt, C. (2000), *The Fiction of Geopolitics: Afterimages of Culture from Wilkie Collins to Alfred Hitchcock*. Stanford: Stanford University Press.

GoGwilt, C. (2010), *The Passage of Literature: Genealogies of Modernism in Conrad, Rhys, and Pramoedya*. Oxford: Oxford University Press.

Hampson, R. (2005), 'Spatial Stories' in P. Brooker and A. Thacker (eds), *Geographies of Modernism*. London: Routledge, pp. 54–64.

Harris, A. (2010), *Romantic Moderns: English Writers, Artists and the Imagination from Virginia Woolf to John Piper*. London: Thames and Hudson.

Harvey, D. (1989), *The Condition of Postmodernity: An Enquiry into the Conditions of Cultural Change*. Oxford: Blackwell.

Hegglund, J. (2012), *World Views: Metageographies of Modernist Fiction*. New York and London: Oxford University Press.

Howes, M. (2000), '"Goodbye Ireland I'm going to Gort": Geography, Scale and Narrating the Nation', in D. Attridge and M. Howes (eds), *Semicolonial Joyce*. Cambridge: Cambridge University Press, pp. 58–77.

Huyssens, A. (2005), 'Geographies of Modernism in a Globalising World', in P. Brooker and A. Thacker (eds), *Geographies of Modernism*. London: Routledge, pp. 6–18.

Jameson, F. (2002), *A Singular Modernity*. London: Verso.

Joyce, J. (1993), *Ulysses*, J. Johnson (ed.). Oxford: Oxford University Press.

Joyce, J. (2000), *A Portrait of the Artist as Young Man*, J. Johnson (ed.). Oxford: Oxford University Press.

Kenner, H. (1984), 'The Making of the Modernist Canon'. *Chicago Review*, 34, (2), 49–61.

Ker, D. I. (1997), *The African Novel and the Modernist Tradition*. Bern: Peter Lang.

Lefebvre, H. (1991), *The Production of Space*. Oxford: Blackwell.

Marx, W. (2009), 'The 20th Century: Century of the Arrière-gardes?', in S. Bru, J. Baetens, B. Hjartarson, P. Nicholls, T. Orum and H. Van Den Berg (eds), *Europa! Europa?: The Avant-Garde, Modernism and the Fate of a Continent*. Berlin: De Gruyter, pp. 59–71.

Massey, D. (1995), 'The Conceptualisation of Place', in D. Massey and P. Jess (eds), *A Place in the World? Places, Cultures and Globalization*. Oxford: Oxford University Press, pp. 45–88.

McLaughlin, J. (2000), *Writing the Urban Jungle: Reading Empire in London from Doyle to Eliot*. Charlottesville: University Press of Virginia.

Mitter, P. (2007), *The Triumph of Modernism: India's Artists and the Avant-Garde, 1922–1947*. London: Reaktion.

Moretti, F. (1998), *Atlas of the European Novel, 1800–1900*. London: Verso.

Moretti, F. (2005), *Graphs, Maps, Trees: Abstract Models for a Literary History*. London: Verso.

Nicholls, P. (1995), *Modernisms: A Literary Guide*. Basingstoke: Macmillan.

Ramazani, J. (2001), *The Hybrid Muse: Postcolonial Poetry in English*. Chicago: Chicago University Press.

Ramazani, J. (2006), 'A Transnational Poetics'. *American Literary History*, 18, (2), 332–59.

Said, E. W. (1993), *Culture and Imperialism*. London: Vintage.

Snaith, A. and Whitworth, M. (eds) (2007), *Locating Woolf: The Politics of Space and Place*. Basingstoke: Palgrave Macmillan.

Tally, R. T. Jr. (2013), *Spatiality*. London: Routledge.

Tally, R. T. Jr. (ed.) (2014), *Geocritical Explorations: Space, Place, and Mapping in Literary and Cultural Studies*. New York: Palgrave Macmillan.

Thacker, A. (2003), *Moving Through Modernity: Space and Geography in Modernism*. Manchester: Manchester University Press.

Walkowitz, J. (2012), *Nights Out: Life in Cosmopolitan London*. New Haven: Yale University Press.

Westphal, B. (2011), *Geocriticism: Real and Fictional Spaces*. New York: Palgrave Macmillan.

Wollaeger, M. and Eatough, M. (eds) (2012), *The Oxford Handbook of Global Modernisms*. New York: Oxford University Press.

Woods, T. (2010), 'Modernism and African Literature', in P. Brooker, A. Gasiorek, D. Longworth and A. Thacker (eds), *The Oxford Handbook of Modernisms*. Oxford: Oxford University Press, pp. 926–41.

Woolf, V. (1982), *The Diary of Virginia Woolf*, 5 vols. A. O. Bell and A. McNeillie (eds). London: Penguin.

Woolf, V. (1986), 'Literary Geography', in A. McNeillie (ed.), *The Essays of Virginia Woolf*, 6 vols., Vol. 1: 1904–1912. London: The Hogarth Press.

Woolf, V. (1992a), *Jacob's Room*, S. Roe (ed.). London: Penguin.

Woolf, V. (1992b), *Mrs Dalloway*, S. McNichol (ed.). London: Penguin.

4

Modernism and Language Scepticism

Shane Weller

The history of the West has been marked by a recurrent sense that, in the face of certain thoughts, feelings, objects or experiences, words fail us. For Plato, the Ideas that constitute the real (of which human beings can capture only the shadows on the cave wall) may be described, but they remain in a more profound sense beyond the grasp of language. Similarly, the long tradition of negative theology – which insists that God can be expressed linguistically only in terms of what he is not, any positive articulation of his essence being at best a reduction, if not a distortion, of that essence – bears witness to a profound sense of the limited power of language. And yet, while the notion of the ineffable has been an abiding one in Western culture, the modern age has been distinguished in no small measure by a far more radical sense that language as such cannot capture reality, that there is an unbridgeable divide between word and world, and that, far from being a means to articulate both the inner and the outer realms, language is in fact precisely that which prevents such an articulation. According to George Steiner, for instance, modernity – which he sees as commencing in the 1870s – is the time of the 'after-Word', an epoch defined principally by the breaking of the contract between language and reality upon which Western culture was established (see Steiner, 1989, 93; cf. Noble, 1978). Alongside the widely held belief that language shapes rather than simply reflects or represents our world, the modern period is also marked by the conviction that the only hope of making contact with reality, be that reality objective or subjective, lies in a vigilant distrust of language, a distrust that can lead either to an attempted renewal of the word or to a commitment to its destruction.

Evidence to support the claim that a new and far more thoroughgoing scepticism towards language arises in Europe in the second half of the nineteenth century is to be found in both the literary and the philosophical discourses of the period. The realist aesthetic underpinning the works of the great nineteenth-century European novelists from Balzac to Tolstoy assumes, for the most part, that the inner world of consciousness, as well as the natural and cultural realms within which that consciousness is located, can be articulated in a shared language, even if there is also an increasing sense of the historicity of languages and the importance of dialectal variations. In short, for nineteenth-century realism the language of literature tends to be a refined or polished version of everyday language. Along with this there prevails a consensual relation between writer and reader, for both of whom language has an unproblematic referential function.

With the emergence of the Symbolist movement in France in the late nineteenth century, however, this easy confidence in what Stéphane Mallarmé describes in the poem 'The Tomb of Edgar Poe' (1876) as the 'words of the tribe' (*mots de la tribu*) (Mallarmé, 1982, 51) is placed in question. A decade later, in 'Crisis of Verse' (1886), Mallarmé declares that all languages are 'imperfect insofar as they are many; the absolute one is lacking [...]; the diversity, on earth, of idioms prevents anyone from proffering words that would otherwise be, when made uniquely, the material truth' (2007, 205). Mallarmé then goes on to anticipate the Swiss linguist Ferdinand de Saussure's notion of the arbitrariness of the linguistic sign – that is, the non-natural, non-mimetic relation between signifier and signified, or, in Mallarmé's case, between word and thing – by asserting that 'discourse fails to express objects by touches corresponding to them in shading or bearing [...]. Beside *ombre* [shade], which is opaque, *ténèbres* [shadows] is not very dark; what a disappointment, in front of the perversity that makes *jour* [day] and *nuit* [night], contradictorily, sound dark in the former and light in the latter' (205).

Crucially, however, Mallarmé claims that poetry 'makes up for language's deficiencies', it being a form of language that is 'essential', in contrast to the 'brute and immediate' language of everyday use. Poetry, for Mallarmé, is 'essential' language precisely because it overcomes the arbitrariness of the relation between word and world, the result being that in the poem 'the object named is bathed in a brand new atmosphere' (Mallarmé, 2007, 211). For Mallarmé, then, as subsequently for T. S. Eliot and many of the other high modernists, not least Ezra Pound, Djuna Barnes, James Joyce, Rainer Maria Rilke and Osip Mandelstam, the writer's task is precisely to 'purify the dialect of the tribe' (Eliot, 1969, 194), to renew language in a manner that goes far beyond the refining aims of the realist. In his radical spatialization of language in the poem 'A Throw of the Dice' (1897), Mallarmé sets the standard for the modernist revolution of the word, a revolution predicated on the sense that everyday language lacks the power to communicate or even to gesture effectively towards the real, which is itself reconceived by many writers as something deeply subjective and thus multiple. The reader of 'A Throw of the Dice' is faced with a language that has been spatialized and syntactically fragmented, and in which the materiality of the word is emphasized through dramatic typographical variations. Mallarmé's preferred image for this 'tampering' with verse is the constellation.

Like most neat distinctions within the field of literary history and aesthetics, the one between realist and Symbolist aesthetic tends to lose something of its purchase upon closer scrutiny. Three decades before Mallarmé's claims concerning the deficiency of all languages, his compatriot Gustave Flaubert is to be found in *Madame Bovary* (1857) questioning the power of the word. Flaubert has Emma's lover, Rodolphe, compare 'human language' (*la parole humaine*) to a 'cracked kettledrum on which we beat out tunes for bears to dance to, when what we long to do is make music that will move the stars to pity' (Flaubert, 2004, 170). According to Roland Barthes, it is precisely with Flaubert that literature's entire concern becomes the 'problematics of language' (Barthes, 1967, 9). It would be fair to say, however, that Mallarmé's operations on language in 'A Throw of the Dice' and his late sonnets are considerably more radical than Flaubert's in later novels such as *Salammbô* (1862) and *Bouvard and Pécuchet* (1881). In Mallarmé's poems of the 1890s, any simple correspondence between word and world disappears; in these works, language operates not so much referentially as in a manner akin to music, by way of evocation rather than description. This move away from the semantic to the affective takes up Schopenhauer's privileging of music above literature as the 'most powerful of the arts' (see Schopenhauer, 1966, 2: 448).

Barthes tells only part of the story, then, when he claims that Mallarmé's aim is the 'destruction of language, with Literature reduced, so to speak, to being its carcass' (Barthes, 1967, 11). For it is possible to see the Symbolist poetic rather differently, relating it back to Kant's conception of poetry in *The Critique of Judgement* (1790), where the German philosopher argues that poetry is the highest of the arts precisely because it offers us forms that accord with concepts in a manner that 'couples with the presentation of the concept a wealth of thought to which no verbal expression is completely adequate' (Kant, 1952, 190). Poetry for Kant, then, necessarily reminds us of the limits of language, but it does so in a manner that evokes that which remains unnamable. The limits of language would thus be both the precondition for and the justification of poetry.

If Mallarmé's intervention in the literary field can be read in at least two ways, so can the classic literary expression of the broken contract between word and world in Hugo von Hofmannsthal's 'Ein Brief' (1902), generally known in the English-speaking world as the 'Lord Chandos Letter'. This fictional missive from Lord Chandos to the philosopher Francis Bacon, a founding figure of the empirical natural sciences, records the former's sudden and devastating experience of the world as resistant to conceptualization – and thus to adequate linguistic articulation:

> Everything fell into pieces in front of me, the pieces into more pieces, and nothing could be contained in a single concept any more. Individual words swam around me: they melted into eyes, which stared at me, and which I had to stare back at: they are like whirlpools, it gives me vertigo to look down at them, they turn without cease, and transport you into nothingness. (Hofmannsthal, 1995, 11)

For Lord Chandos, then, the referential function of language has been lost. Language has become a screen or veil, wholly inadequate to map the real. This experience is essentially that of radical nominalism. When the habitual mode of apprehending the world breaks down, there emerge radical singularities that cannot, without distortion, be grasped by conceptual thinking – and thus cannot be captured by language. From such a nominalist perspective, to use the word 'tree' is simply a nonsense, since it captures nothing of trees in their diversity and mutability. All words suffer this fate. In the story 'Funes, the Memorious' (1942), Jorge Luis Borges's narrator claims that 'To think is to forget a difference, to generalize, to abstract' (Borges, 1993, 90). Similarly, the language crisis of Hofmannsthal's Lord Chandos is owing to his realization that to use language is to forget differences and, in so doing, to fail to grasp reality.

In philosophical discourse, a similar argument lies at the heart of a work published at the same time and in the same country (Austria): Fritz Mauthner's three-volume *Beiträge zu einer Kritik der Sprache* (Contributions to a Critique of Language, 1901–3). According to Mauthner, the entire history of Western philosophy has been afflicted by what he terms 'word superstition' or 'word fetishism', that is, the mistaking of the word for the reality. That said, Mauthner identifies a series of valiant attempts to achieve a philosophical critique of language. In medieval nominalism, one finds 'the first attempt at the real self-decomposition of metaphorical thinking'. If this attempt failed, it was because the nominalists could not free themselves from that 'supreme metaphor', God (Mauthner, 1923, 2: 474). In Mauthner's history of language critique, the next important step was taken by Kant, in the *Critique of Pure Reason* (1781), with its insistence that we can have no knowledge of the 'noumenal', or things in themselves (2: 476). Like the nominalists before him, however, Kant fails to carry his wholly justified 'negative thinking' through to its necessary conclusion, instead settling upon a new supreme metaphor: 'pure reason' (2: 477). While with Hegel, the 'old word superstition indulges in the wildest orgies' (2: 478), with Schopenhauer philosophy once again 'shakes often and strongly at the gates of the critique of language', only to lapse back into word superstition through the privileging of the concept of will (2: 478). As for Nietzsche, he remains, for all his critical energy, a victim of 'word fetishism', too enamoured by the power of his own rhetoric to achieve a genuine critique of language.

In his dismissal of Nietzsche, Mauthner makes no mention of the former's essay 'On Truth and Lying in a Non-Moral Sense', written in 1873, but only published posthumously. There, Nietzsche anticipates Mauthner's critique of metaphorical thinking by famously claiming that truth itself is nothing but a 'mobile army of metaphors, metonymies, anthropomorphisms' (Nietzsche, 1999, 146). Just as Mauthner summarily dismisses Nietzsche, so he in his turn would be dismissed by Wittgenstein, who, in the *Tractatus Logico-Philosophicus* (1921), endorses his fellow Austrian's view that philosophy should be a 'critique of language', only to qualify this with the phrase 'but not at all in Mauthner's sense' (Wittgenstein, 1981, 63). Mauthner champions the 'Nichtwort', or 'not-word' (Mauthner, 1923, 1: 83), as the ultimate means to overcome 'word superstition'. This 'not-word' is something other than silence, however, the latter being 'still a word', according to Mauthner. In contrast, the 'not-word' is a form of self-negating word, a form of language use that does away with itself as language. While being no less suspicious of language, Wittgenstein takes a different approach in his *Tractatus*, where he argues both that '*The limits of my language mean the limits of my world*' (Wittgenstein, 1981, 149) and that 'Whereof one cannot speak, thereof one must be silent' (189). For the philosopher, the only things that can be said are the 'propositions of natural science. *i.e.* something that has nothing to do with philosophy'. That which lies beyond language – as the 'inexpressible' (*Unaussprechliches*) – is the 'mystical', and this, Wittgenstein argues, '*shows* itself' (187).

In proposing the 'Nichtwort' as the means to free thinking from word superstition, Mauthner might seem to chime with Hofmannsthal's Lord Chandos, who informs his addressee that he is to abandon writing altogether, since linguistic expression will always miss the real. That this abandonment of the literary should be articulated with such rhetorical power is more than a mere paradox: it bespeaks a valorization of literature akin to both Kant's and

Mallarmé's championing of poetry, as that form of language ('essential' rather than 'brute and immediate') which alone can chart the limits of language. Mauthner's *Beiträge* contains a similar valorization of the literary, for he identifies a particular literary style as the means to break free of word superstition, namely an ironic use of language in the manner of Goethe's *Poetry and Truth* (1808–31). In this autobiographical work, Mauthner argues, Goethe 'really appears, more than any other writer before or after him, to rise above all possible limits of language, because he uses words to a certain extent ironically, in an inimitable way, that is to say with the clearly betrayed complaint that he must simply follow linguistic usage' (Mauthner, 1923, 2: 506). Goethe displays a 'superior manner of using words as mere words' (2: 507), and, in so doing, reminds the reader at every step of the gap between word and world. Mauthner's championing of Goethe is telling, since it reveals his (decidedly modernist) belief that a certain form of literary practice is capable of implementing a critique of language that remains unachieved in the history of philosophy.

Before we reflect on the consequences of these forms of late nineteenth- and turn-of-the-century language scepticism for the high modernism of the 1920s, it is important to consider what the reasons might have been for the emergence of such language scepticism at that particular historical moment. George Steiner is arguably right to claim that in part this loss of faith in the power of the word is owing to the rise of the sciences – physics, biology, chemistry – and the shift to non-linguistic ways of representing the world (see Steiner, 1967). As a result, a sense began to emerge that words are not the most effective means by which to comprehend the world. Mallarmé renders language pictorial as well as musical. Rhythm and image become as important as semantic charge. His emphasis upon 'Number' in 'A Throw of the Dice' might be read as reflecting an awareness of this shift away from language as the primary means of articulating reality.

In addition, one may point to a political transformation: the erosion of the sense of the bourgeoisie as a progressive class. Increasingly, artists came to see themselves as set in opposition to the very class to which so many of them belonged. In Mallarmé's idea of the 'words of the tribe', later taken up by T. S. Eliot in *Four Quartets*, one can certainly detect a class element. With the rise of mass culture, this sense of difference – and of artistic distinction – was only exacerbated. For an example, one need only look to the violently satirical reaction of the Austrian writer Karl Kraus to what he saw as, in Steiner's words, 'the lexical and grammatical decay of literary, journalistic, political, legal discourse' (Steiner, 1989, 112). In Kraus, the critique of language is, then, not so much philosophical as political. It is a form of ideology critique. More generally, the ever-increasing commodification to which Marx and his followers draw attention may be seen to extend to language itself, with the result being that writers (along with some philosophers, especially Martin Heidegger) came to see their task as the creation of a new, revivified language. Heidegger's neologistic philosophical lexicon is distinctly modernist precisely in its Mallarméan commitment to a language beyond the 'brute' language of the everyday.

This new sense of the writer's task forms part of the more general 'linguistic turn' in the twentieth century, in which language itself becomes the model or metaphor by which all experience is to be grasped (see, for example, Bell, 1999, 18). Rather than reflecting reality, language came to be seen as shaping or even producing it. In his posthumously published *Course in General Linguistics* (1916), Saussure describes language and thought (or signifier and signified) as being like two sides of a sheet of paper; to cut into one side is necessarily to cut into the other. The possibility of thought without or beyond language is simply dismissed. Another highly influential version of the argument that language has a shaping rather than a reflecting or descriptive role is to be found in Wittgenstein's *Tractatus*, in the claim that the '*The limits of my language* mean the limits of my world'. If my language is, in Mallarmé's words, 'brute', then so too will be my experience of the world. Upon the renewal of language would therefore depend the renewal of the world. Far from being a merely aesthetic affair, the modernist revolution of the word is nothing less than an attempt to change the world.

As a reaction to language scepticism, this attempted renewal came in various forms. That the Enlightenment project, embodied in the bourgeoisie, should have led not, as anticipated, to universal peace but to world war and millions of deaths more than justified the reaction against this project, and against the class that was supposed to carry it through to completion. This insight drives the most radical of the avant-garde movements: Dada. In the art of Dadaists such as Hugo Ball and Raoul Hausmann, language is subjected to the most extreme violence (see, for instance, Schaffner, 2007, 63–87). Words are dissected, and the shared language of Mallarmé's 'tribe' is replaced by sound-words with no clearly identifiable shared meaning. Hugo Ball's sound poem 'Karawane' (1917), for instance, begins: 'jolifanto bambla ô falli bambla/*grossiga m'pfa habla horem*' (qtd. in Schaffner, 2007, 73). Conventional language is replaced by new and unique 'words' that are highly suggestive, but in a manner that will differ from reader to reader. The sheer materiality of language is also emphasized, not least through varying typefaces and font sizes. No longer is language conceived as a window onto the world. Rather, the word itself takes on the materiality of the world. To read becomes an immersion in this linguistic material. This emphasis upon the radical materiality of the word is part of a highly politicized language scepticism: for Dadaists such as Ball and Hausmann, language was ideologically soiled. Rather than some imaginary purification (in the manner of a Mallarmé), the Dadaists sought to exhibit the necessarily ideological nature of all languages, not least poetic language.

In the modernist poetry that takes its inspiration from Rimbaud and Mallarmé, Roland Barthes detects the destruction of the 'spontaneously functional nature of language' (Barthes, 1967, 52). Words become more like things, and as a result their instrumental (referential) function is impeded or even negated. Gertrude Stein's *Tender Buttons* (1914) is an example of just such a frustration of the referential function. Discourse is concretized, atomized, even reified. It is in this kind of literary response to turn-of-the-century language scepticism that the Russian Formalists such as Victor Shklovsky and Roman Jakobson find what they take to be the defining characteristic of the literary, namely a defamiliarizing thickening of language. The word is no longer conceived as a medium; rather, it is a form of embodiment or enactment. Herein can be seen an ambiguity at the heart of the modernist revolution of the word in response to turn-of-the-century language scepticism. *On the one hand*, language has to be at one with its object; the distance between word and world is to be collapsed. *On the other hand*, language is impeding or interruptive; as word enacts world, so the word comes to replace world. It is but the shortest of steps from Mauthner's call for the 'not-word' (*Nichtwort*) to the claim that there is nothing but language – in short, that reality as such is essentially discursive.

In the wake of the Dada revolution of the word, Surrealism's commitment to automatic writing in the 1920s constitutes another response to language scepticism that is very much in line with Mallarmé's call for an 'essential' language in contradistinction to the 'brute' language of everyday life. The language of conscious construction is to be abandoned in favour of a language shaped by the unconscious. Freud's preoccupation with parapraxes, and with metonymic displacements and metaphorical condensations, lies behind the modernist commitment to ambiguity and polyvalency. This move is part of a more general trend in modernism to produce a language that, as Louis Sass argues, resembles the discourse of the schizophrenic (see Sass, 1992).

Just as the Dadaists engaged in acts of violence against language, breaking up words and creating entirely new ones, on the grounds that existing languages had become so ideologically tainted that the most radical form of intervention was called for, even at the risk of destroying language altogether, so the highest of the high modernists, James Joyce, would undertake what Eugene Jolas was the first to describe as a language 'revolution' (Jolas, 1962; cf. Leavis, 1982, MacCabe, 1978). According to Jolas, 'Modern life with its changed mythos and transmuted concepts of beauty makes it imperative that words be given new compositions and relationships' (Jolas, 1962, 80). He identifies various attempts made to achieve this by the German Expressionists and the Surrealists, as well as by Gertrude Stein, before turning to Joyce, in whose 'Work in Progress' (later *Finnegans Wake* (1939)) language is 'born anew before our eyes'. For Jolas, this rebirth is achieved through giving words 'odors and sounds that conventional language does not know' (Jolas, 1962, 89). In short, language is rendered material, sensuous. Samuel Beckett makes a similar point in his 1929 essay on Joyce's 'Work in Progress': 'Here is the savage economy of hieroglyphics. Here words are not the polite contortions of 20th century printer's ink. They are alive' (Beckett, 1962, 15–16).

Joyce's commitment to a sensuous language that can overcome the shortcomings of everyday language by wedding signifier and signified is in line with the Mallarméan commitment to an 'essential' language that operates at a level below the semantic. As Julia Kristeva argues, through the importance that it gives to rhythm and sound, to echolalias, this modernist strand (which she sees as commencing with Lautréamont and Mallarmé) prioritizes the 'semiotic' over the symbolic function of language (see Kristeva, 1984). This commitment to the semiotic lies at the heart of the modernist attempt to achieve linguistic renewal in the face of a loss of faith in 'everyday' language and stands as a heroic alternative to Rimbaud's retreat into poetic silence.

While driven, then, by a sense that language was failing – in the 1930s, while working on what would become *Finnegans Wake*, he took an interest in Mauthner's work – Joyce sought to renew it. In *Ulysses* (1922), this renewal entails the adoption of a range of styles and registers, each selected for its appropriateness to a particular scene. In the 'Oxen of the Sun' episode, Joyce maps the history of literary styles onto the growth of a foetus. On the one hand, this suggests that language is natural and that it 'grows' in a manner akin to the growth of the organic. On the other hand – and here a language-sceptical note is sounded – there is a parodic dimension to Joyce's procedure, recalling that of Flaubert's *Bouvard and Pécuchet*. The shifting from one style to another inevitably suggests the arbitrary nature of all styles. There is no 'natural' or 'pure' language – no *reine Sprache* of the kind evoked by Walter Benjamin in his landmark essay 'The Task of the Translator' (1923). If *Ulysses* reminds the reader ever more forcefully of linguistic and stylistic diversity, in *Finnegans Wake* Joyce responds differently to language scepticism, seeking to generate a new (sound) language out of a wide range of historical languages, with the underlying (unifying) principle being punning. Rather than a range of styles, words in *Finnegans Wake* signify in multiple directions simultaneously. This novel's difficulty is the result of this synchronic multiplicity. The sound of the 'fall' of 'a once wallstrait oldparr' that lies at the origin of the story 'retaled' in *Finnegans Wake* can be articulated, but only in a word that appears in no single dictionary, a 100-letter word unlike any other:

> bababadalgharaghtakamminarronnkonnbronntonnerronntuonnthunntrovarr hounawnskawntoohoohoordenenthurnuk! (Joyce, 2000, 3)

Alongside Joyce, the other high modernist to exhibit the most radical linguistic operation in response to language scepticism is Ezra Pound, whose *Cantos* (1917–69) draws from numerous languages (not only Western), although without blending these together in the manner of Joyce. In the *Cantos*, fragmentation tends to prevail, along with juxtaposition, although the spatialization remains far less adventurous than Mallarmé's in 'A Throw of the Dice'.

Other high modernists were considerably less extreme than Joyce and Pound in their attempts to find a new language, although the sense that the writer could not simply accept everyday language lay at the heart of their work, too. On the one hand, Proust's *In Search of Lost Time* (1913–27) is characterized not only by a convoluted syntax designed to capture the very movement of time as Bergsonian duration (*durée*), with its accretions and modifications, but also by a metaphoricity that never allows the reader to forget that the relation between mind and word is a highly mediated one. Samuel Beckett picks up on this when he asserts (in 1931) that 'The rhetorical equivalent of the Proustian real is the chain-figure of the metaphor' and that Proust's style is characterized by 'the crest and break of metaphor after metaphor' (Beckett, 1987, 88). The description of memory at the end of the first part of 'Combray', in *Swann's Way* (1913), is among the most celebrated of such metaphors, arising as it does out of a syntax of breath-defying sinuosity:

> And as in the game wherein the Japanese amuse themselves by filling a porcelain bowl with water and steeping in it little pieces of paper which until then are without character or form, but, the moment they become wet, stretch and twist and take on colour and distinctive shape, become flowers or houses or people, solid and recognisable, so in that moment all the flowers in our garden and in M. Swann's park, and the water-lilies on the Vivonne and the good folk of the village and their little dwellings and the parish church and the whole of Combray and its surroundings, taking shape and solidity, sprang into being, town and gardens alike, from my cup of tea. (Proust, 1992, 54–5)

On the other hand, in *Death on Credit* (1936), Louis-Ferdinand Céline adopts extreme parataxis, in stark counterpoint to Proustian hypotaxis. Céline's novel begins: 'Here we are, alone again. It's all so slow, so heavy, so sad … I'll be old soon. Then at last it will be over. So many people have come into my room. They've gone away. They've grown old, wretched, sluggish, each in some corner of the world' (Céline, 1989, 15). This atomized syntax becomes the form for a demotic language that exposes T. S. Eliot's attempts at the demotic in Part II of *The Waste Land* (1922) as little more than caricature.

The various – often very different – linguistic audacities of the high modernists are undertaken with the aim of finding a language in which the articulated meaning is incarnate in the materiality of the text. This pursuit of incarnated or enacted meaning arguably reaches its most extreme form in *Finnegans Wake*, characterized as that work is by a new and unique language, in which, as Beckett observed as early as 1929, the writing is 'not about something; *it is that something itself*' (Beckett, 1962, 14). The radicality of Joyce's 'revolution of language' can be understood only in the context of a no less radical language scepticism, against which it constitutes the most extreme reaction. *Finnegans Wake*, then, constitutes the *ne plus ultra* of the modernist reaction against language scepticism. That it should have been published in the year that the Second World War broke out is telling. No less telling is that another major work of high modernism, Hermann Broch's *The Death of Virgil*, should have been published in 1945, when Europe was in ruins, and that it should end with a gesture towards that which lies 'beyond language' (*jenseits der Sprache*) (Broch, 1995, 454), returning the reader to the very language scepticism against which high modernism sought so strenuously to define itself.

The failure of the high modernist attempt to achieve lasting cultural renewal through linguistic/aesthetic renewal became increasingly evident in the course of the 1930s, with the coming to power of the Nazis in Germany, Franco's defeat of the republican forces in Spain and Stalin's 'show trials' in the Soviet Union. With the outbreak of the Second World War, all hope of European regeneration in the wake of the First World War seemed to many to have been extinguished. The implications for the modernist engagement with language were considerable. It is no coincidence that one of the principal champions of *Finnegans Wake*, Samuel Beckett, should emerge as a major figure in late modernism, in which one finds a new response to the wave of language scepticism in the late nineteenth century. If late modernism may be distinguished from high modernism, then it is not least in the former's retreat from the word, a retreat that takes the form not of silence but of linguistic negativism, or what might, following Beckett, be described as 'unwording'. In a letter written in July 1937, Beckett set out the principles for a new kind of writing, a literature of the 'unword' or 'non-word' (*Unwort*) as opposed to what he describes as Joyce's 'apotheosis of the word' (Beckett, 2009a, 519). The first step towards the achievement of such a literature of the unword lay, according to Beckett, in a breaking down of the materiality of language, that very materiality which is so characteristic of high modernist literature. For the Beckett of 1937, language is a 'veil' or carapace, something to be rent asunder or bored into, in order to reach the reality behind it, a reality that, according to Beckett, may well be a 'nothingness' (Beckett, 2009a, 518). That it might be impossible to achieve such a rending of the language veil is suggested in *Watt*, the novel that Beckett wrote shortly after his reading of Mauthner and which he completed in 1945. As he puts it in that work: 'what we know partakes in no small measure of the nature of what has so happily been called the unutterable or ineffable, so that any attempt to utter or eff it is doomed to fail, doomed, doomed to fail' (Beckett, 2009b, 52–3).

That both Joyce and Beckett should have taken considerable interest in Mauthner's *Beiträge* in the 1930s, and that this interest should have led on the one hand to *Finnegans Wake* and on the other to *The Unnamable* (1953), reveals the two, very different ways in which language scepticism impacted on modernism. Unlike Joyce, Beckett took to heart the philosopher's idea of the 'not-word' and sought in his post–Second World War works to achieve a highly paradoxical writing of this 'not-word'. In the 1949 *Three Dialogues*, with Georges Duthuit, Beckett presents art's underlying principle as 'The expression that there is nothing to express, nothing with which to express, nothing from which to express, no power to express, no desire to express, together with the obligation to express' (Beckett, 1987, 103). In *The Unnamable*, he explores from the inside the impossible situation created by such a guiding principle: a speaker seeking to describe where, who and when he is, and, in Mauthnerian fashion, rejecting each and every self-identification as nothing but a metaphor. Beckett's narrator is trapped in words; seeking to go beyond words in order to grasp the reality of who, where and when he is, he finds himself obliged to rely on language. The paradox that is latent in Hofmannsthal's 'Lord Chandos Letter' – with its astonishingly eloquent condemnation of language – becomes in late modernism a cause for tortured linguistic negativism. Writing to undo language in order to reach that what lies beyond it, Beckett found himself committed to the impossible. This impossibility is reflected in the aporetic nature of *The Unnamable*, the narrator of which vacillates between antithetical positions on his nature with regard to language. On the one hand, he is nothing but words; on the other, something else entirely, something that no word can capture:

> I'm in words, made of words, others' words [...] I'm all these words, all these strangers, this dust of words, with no ground for their settling, no sky for their dispersal, coming together to say, fleeing one another to say, that I am they, all of them, those that merge, those that part, those that never meet, and nothing else, yes, something else, that I'm something quite different, a quite different thing, a wordless thing in an empty place (Beckett, 2010, 104)

That there is a distinctly new form of engagement with language scepticism in late modernism is suggested by the remarkable similarity between Beckett's articulation of the artist's predicament in the *Three Dialogues* and that of the French writer Maurice Blanchot in his first collection of critical essays, *Faux Pas* (1943). For Blanchot, 'The writer finds himself in the increasingly ludicrous condition of having nothing to write, of having no means with which to write it, and of being constrained by the utter necessity of always writing it' (Blanchot, 2001, 3). No less than Beckett's *Unnamable*, so Blanchot's first novel, *Thomas the Obscure* (1941), is characterized by unremitting linguistic negativism, with negative modifiers such as 'inexpressible', 'unsayable', 'indefinable', 'untransmissible' and 'ineffable' serving again and again to mark the limits of language.

Other post-war writers whose work may be seen as late modernist on account of such linguistic negativism include the poets Paul Celan and Geoffrey Hill. The shadow cast over language for each of these writers is the 'unspeakable' nature of the Holocaust. In an essay published in 1951, Theodor Adorno famously claimed that 'To write poetry after Auschwitz is barbaric' (Adorno, 1981, 34). He later found himself compelled to modify this assertion, in no small part on account of his reading of Beckett and Celan. What remains clear, however, is that the post-Holocaust world is one in which language scepticism takes on a far darker hue. In the poem 'Tübingen, January', from his 1963 volume *The Rose of No One*, for instance, Celan evokes Friedrich Hölderlin, whose own work from the period shortly before the darkening of his mind in 1804–5 anticipates (as both Benjamin and Adorno were among the first to note) the paratactic, fragmentary, dislocated language of late modernism. In Celan's poem, the only language that can begin to articulate post-Holocaust reality is a stammering, fragmented, repetitive language that is scarcely language at all: 'Should,/should a man,/should a man come into the world, today, with/the shining beard of the/

patriarchs: he could,/if he spoke of this/time, he/could/only babble and babble/ over, over/againagain.//("Pallaksh. Pallaksh.")' (Celan, 1988, 177).

The language revolution that is so characteristic of the European avant-garde (especially Expressionism and Dada) and of certain strands of high modernism (especially the later work of Joyce and Pound) stands in dialectical counterpoint to language scepticism, a response to this scepticism guided by the Mallarméan conviction that a radical renewal of language is both necessary and possible. Late modernism, in contrast, revisits turn-of-the-century language scepticism, haunted by a historically informed sense that it is not the renewal of the word that is required, but rather its negation, an insistence upon that which exceeds expression, that which is *unspeakable* in both senses of the word. Late modernists such as Beckett, Blanchot and Celan develop forms of linguistic negativism as what they take to be the only aesthetically and ethically justifiable response to a modernity perceived as catastrophic.

While remaining committed to the high modernist ideal that art must take its critical distance from modernity, the work of the late modernists is characterized by a far more pessimistic view of the power of art to transform society, and of the power of language to communicate either the experience of modernity or the possibility of any alternative to it. High modernism tends to turn to myth in order to make sense of, and to bestow order and coherence upon, what T. S. Eliot famously describes (in his 1923 essay on Joyce's *Ulysses*) as 'the immense panorama of futility and anarchy which is contemporary history' (Eliot, 1975, 177). In contrast, late modernism, with its painful awareness of the political uses to which myth was put by the totalitarian regimes of the 1930s and 1940s, has no such faith in any clear alternative to instrumental reason. Instead, late modernism finds itself obliged to take refuge in the negative. In this, it is forcefully anticipated by certain language-sceptical tendencies in high modernism. In *The Counterfeiters* (1925), for instance, André Gide includes a violent attack not just on literature as the most disgusting of all 'nauseating human emanations' but also on 'those promissory notes which go by the name of *words*' (Gide, 1966, 291). More influential upon late modernist language scepticism is Franz Kafka, who in what are now generally known as the 'Zürau Aphorisms' (1917–18) declares that 'To perform the negative is what is still required of us, the positive is already ours' (Kafka, 1994, 8). Kafka's own work forcefully anticipates late modernist language scepticism. As early as 1910, in a letter to Max Brod, he can be found declaring: 'My whole body warns me against every word; every word, before it lets me write it down, first looks around in all directions. The sentences literally crumble before me; I see their insides and then have to stop quickly'

(Kafka, 1978, 70). This anxiety about language develops in Kafka's later works into almost unremitting linguistic negativism. In his rewriting of the Greek myth of the sirens, Kafka asserts that their dangerous power lies not in their singing but in their silence. And in 'Josephine the Singer, or the Mouse Folk', a story about a singing mouse written in the last year of his life (1924), Kafka's narrator first questions whether the sound produced by Josephine is singing at all, and not merely 'piping' (Kafka, 1993, 234), and then concludes his narrative by recording her eventual disappearance: 'she will not sing' (250). This story captures a retreat from the word that is powerfully proleptic of late modernist language scepticism.

In the late modernism of a Beckett or a Celan, the performance of the negative takes the form of an 'unwording' in which language is turned back against itself, not in order to achieve an 'essential' language of the kind sought by Mallarmé and the high modernists, a language purged of the 'brute', but rather with the highly paradoxical aim of achieving a 'literature of the unword' that might disclose an image of what Beckett in 1945 describes as 'humanity in ruins' (Beckett, 1995, 278). In late modernism, then, late nineteenth- and turn-of-the-century language scepticism feeds into a conception not just of language (and its limits), or even of literature (and its limits), but of *the human and its limits*, which by the second half of the 1940s were revealed to be such as scarcely anyone in 1900 could have begun to imagine. The language scepticism that characterizes late modernism is thus rooted in a profound scepticism about humanity as such.

Bibliography

Adorno, T. W. (1981), 'Cultural Criticism and Society', in S. and S. Weber (transl.), *Prisms*. Cambridge, MA: The MIT Press, pp. 17–34.

Barthes, R. (1967), *Writing Degree Zero*, A. Lavers and C. Smith (transl.). London: Jonathan Cape.

Beckett, S. (1962), 'Dante . . . Bruno . Vico . . Joyce', in S. Beckett et al. (eds), *Our Exagmination Round His Factification for Incamination of Work in Progress*. New York: New Directions, pp. 1–22.

Beckett, S. (1987), *Proust and Three Dialogues*. London: John Calder.

Beckett, S. (1995), 'The Capital of the Ruins', in S. E. Gontarski (ed.), *The Complete Shorter Prose 1929–1989*. New York: Grove Weidenfeld, pp. 275–8.

Beckett, S. (2009a), *The Letters of Samuel Beckett, Volume I: 1929–1940*, M. D. Fehsenfeld and L. M. Overbeck (eds). Cambridge: Cambridge University Press.

Beckett, S. (2009b), *Watt*, C. J. Ackerley (ed.). London: Faber and Faber.

Beckett, S. (2010), *The Unnamable*, S. Connor (ed.). London: Faber and Faber.

Bell, M. (1999), 'The Metaphysics of Modernism', in M. Levenson (ed.), *The Cambridge Companion to Modernism*. Cambridge: Cambridge University Press, pp. 9–32.

Benjamin, W. (1992), 'The Task of the Translator: An Introduction to the Translation of Baudelaire's *Tableaux parisiens*', in H. Arendt (ed.), H. Zohn (transl.), *Illuminations*. London: Fontana, pp. 70–82.

Blanchot, M. (2001), *Faux Pas*, C. Mandell (transl.). Stanford: Stanford University Press.

Blanchot, M. (2005), *Thomas l'obscur. Première version, 1941*. Paris: Gallimard.

Borges, J. L. (1993), *Ficciones*, A. Kerrigan et al. (transl.). New York: Alfred A. Knopf.

Broch, H. (1995), *Der Tod des Vergil*. Frankfurt am Main: Suhrkamp.

Budick, S. and Iser, W. (eds) (1987), *Languages of the Unsayable: The Play of Negativity in Literature and Literary Theory*. Stanford: Stanford University Press.

Celan, P. (1988), *Poems of Paul Celan*, M. Hamburger (transl.). London: Anvil Press Poetry.

Céline, L.-F. (1989), *Death on Credit*, R. Manheim (transl.). London: John Calder.

Eliot, T. S. (1969), *The Complete Poems and Plays*. London: Faber and Faber.

Eliot, T. S. (1975), *Selected Prose of T. S. Eliot*, F. Kermode (ed.). London: Faber and Faber.

Flaubert, G. (2004), *Madame Bovary: Provincial Manners*, M. Mauldon (transl.). Oxford: Oxford University Press.

Gide, A. (1966), *The Counterfeiters*, D. Bussy (transl.). Harmondsworth: Penguin.

Göttsche, D. (1987), *Die Produktivität der Sprachkrise in der modernen Prosa*. Frankfurt am Main: Athenäum.

Hofmannsthal, H. von (1995), *The Lord Chandos Letter*, M. Hofmann (transl.). London: Syrens.

Jolas, E. (1962), 'The Revolution of Language and James Joyce', in S. Beckett et al. (eds), *Our Exagmination Round His Factification for Incamination of Work in Progress*. New York: New Directions, pp. 77–92.

Joyce, J. (2000), *Finnegans Wake*. Harmondsworth: Penguin.

Kafka, F. (1978), *Letters to Friends, Family, and Editors*, R. and C. Winston (transl.). London: John Calder.

Kafka, F. (1993), *Collected Stories*, G. Josipovici (ed.), W. and E. Muir et al. (transl.). New York: Alfred A. Knopf.

Kafka, F. (1994), *The Collected Aphorisms*, M. Pasley (transl.). London: Syrens.

Kant, I. (1952), *The Critique of Judgement*, J. C. Meredith (transl.). Oxford: Clarendon Press.

Kristeva, J. (1984), *Revolution in Poetic Language*, M. Waller (transl.). New York: Columbia University Press.

Leavis, F. R. (1982), 'Joyce and the "Revolution of the Word"', in G. Singh (ed.), *The Critic as Anti-Philosopher: Essays & Papers*. London: Chatto & Windus, pp. 121–8.

Levenson, M. (1999), *The Cambridge Companion to Modernism*. Cambridge: Cambridge University Press.

MacCabe, C. (1978), *James Joyce and the Revolution of the Word*. Basingstoke: Macmillan.

MacCabe, C. (2002), *James Joyce and the Revolution of the Word*, 2nd edn. Basingstoke: Palgrave Macmillan.

Mallarmé, S. (1982), *Selected Poetry and Prose*, M. A. Caws (ed.). New York: New Directions.

Mallarmé, S. (2007), *Divagations*, B. Johnson (transl.). Cambridge, MA: The Belknap Press of Harvard University Press.

Mauthner, F. (1923), *Beiträge zu einer Kritik der Sprache*, 3 vols. Leipzig: Felix Meiner.

Nietzsche, F. (1999), 'On Truth and Lying in a Non-Moral Sense', in R. Guess and R. Spiers (eds), R. Spiers (transl.), *The Birth of Tragedy and Other Writings*. Cambridge: Cambridge University Press, pp. 139–53.

Noble, C. A. M. (1978), *Sprachskepsis: über Dichtung der Moderne*. Munich: Text & Kritik.

Proust, M. (1992), *In Search of Lost Time, Vol. I: Swann's Way*, C. K. Scott Moncrieff and Terence Kilmartin (transl.), revised by D. J. Enright. London: Chatto & Windus.

Sass, L. A. (1992), *Modernism and Madness: Insanity in the Light of Modern Art, Literature and Thought*. New York: Basic Books.

Saussure, F. de (1983), *Course in General Linguistics*, C. Bally and A. Sechehaye (eds), with the collaboration of A. Riedlinger, R. Harris (transl.). London: Duckworth.

Schaffner, A. K. (2007), *Sprachzerlegung in historischer Avantgardelyrik und konkreter Poesie*. Berlin: ECA.

Schopenhauer, A. (1966), *The World as Will and Representation*, E. F. J. Payne (transl.), 2 vols. New York: Dover.

Sheppard, R. (1991), 'The Crisis of Language', in M. Bradbury and J. McFarlane (eds), *Modernism: A Guide to European Literature, 1890–1930*. Harmondsworth: Penguin, pp. 323–36.

Steiner, G. (1967), *Language and Silence: Essays 1958–1966*. London: Faber and Faber.

Steiner, G. (1989), *Real Presences: Is There Anything in What We Say?* London: Faber and Faber.

Van Hulle, D. (1999), 'Beckett – Mauthner – Zimmer – Joyce', in T. F. Staley (ed.), *Joyce Studies Annual 1999*. Austin: University of Texas Press, pp. 143–83.

Van Hulle, D. (2002), '"Out of Metaphor": Mauthner, Richards and the Development of Wakese', in D. Van Hulle (ed.), *James Joyce: The Study of Languages. New Comparative Poetics 6*. Brussels: Peter Lang, pp. 91–118.

Van Hulle, D. (2005), '"Nichtsnichtsundnichts": Beckett's and Joyce's Transtextual Undoings', in C. Jaurretche (ed.), *Beckett, Joyce and the Art of the Negative*. Amsterdam and New York: Rodopi, pp. 52–61.

Wittgenstein, L. (1981), *Tractatus Logico-Philosophicus*, C. K. Ogden (transl.). London and New York: Routledge.

5

Modernism and Emotion

Kirsty Martin

In his essay 'The Painter of Modern Life' (1859–60), Charles Baudelaire suggests that to express and appreciate the experience of modernity we should try to imagine the perspective of a child or of someone recovered from an illness, who suddenly sees everything afresh and with new vigour:

> Let us go back, if we can, by a retrospective effort of the imagination, towards our most youthful, our earliest, impressions, and we will recognize that they had a strange kinship with those brightly coloured impressions which we were later to receive in the aftermath of a physical illness [...] The child sees everything in a state of newness [...] Nothing more resembles what we call inspiration than the delight with which a child absorbs form and colour [...] genius is nothing more nor less than *childhood recovered* at will. (Baudelaire, 1964, 8–9)

What the child and the convalescent share is a sense of heightened perception and feeling. Baudelaire proceeds to suggest that artistic success is born of 'curiosity':

> It is by this deep and joyful curiosity that we may explain the fixed and animally ecstatic gaze of a child confronted with something new, whatever it be, whether a face or a landscape, gilding, colours, shimmering stuffs, or the magic of physical beauty assisted by the cosmetic art. A friend of mine once told me that when he was quite a small child, he used to be present when his father dressed in the mornings, and that it was with a mixture of amazement and delight that he used to study the muscles of his arms, the gradual transitions of pink and yellow in his skin, and the bluish network of his veins [...] Need I add that today that child is a well-known painter? (Baudelaire, 1964, 8)

Baudelaire imagines modernism and modernity as consisting in a rich attention to newness: a type of responsiveness to everything, 'whether a face or a landscape, gilding, colours, shimmering stuffs', and a joy in things that might previously have been missed, 'the muscles of his arms [...] the bluish network of his veins'. Modern art is linked repeatedly to emotional response: 'delight', 'deep and joyful curiosity' and 'amazement and delight'. It is defined here by feeling and by the capacity for being moved afresh by the world: it is defined by being able to feel that things are new and being able to respond emotionally to newness.

In recent years, an appreciation of modernism's central concern with emotion has come ever more to the fore, from Suzanne Clark's exploration of *Sentimental Modernism* (1991) to more recent discussions of modernism, affect and emotion by critics including Charles Altieri, Michael Bell, Anthony Cuda, Kirsty Martin, Sophie Ratcliffe and Julie Taylor.[1] Such work has sought to overturn previous critical accounts of modernism that, far from seeing it as driven by curiosity and delight, argued that modernist literature defined itself by resisting emotion. Modernism, the argument went, defined itself in opposition to Victorian and Romantic sentimentality, adopting instead a stance of 'ironic detachment' (Whitworth, 2007, 14).[2]

It is possible to find some support for this traditional sense of modernism as privileging irony and coldness, and opposing sentiment.[3] There are frequent denunciations of feeling in modernist texts – such as, to give just one example, T. E. Hulme's attempt to attack and banish sentimentality in his essay 'Romanticism and Classicism' (1914). In this essay, Hulme criticizes tendencies to see literary merit as defined by literature's ability to produce sympathetic feeling:

> I object to the sloppiness which doesn't consider that a poem is a poem unless it is moaning or whining about something or other [...] The thing has got so bad now that a poem which is all dry and hard, a properly classical poem, would not be considered poetry at all. How many people now can lay their hands on their hearts and say they like either Horace or Pope? They feel a kind of chill when they read them. (Hulme, 1924, 126)

Hulme attacks the 'sloppiness' that defines poetry by emotional expression: 'moaning or whining'. By contrast, he suggests that poetry in the future will be distinguished by this 'kind of chill' – he predicts a future consisting of just this kind of 'dry, hard, classical verse' (Hulme, 1924, 133).

The stark contrast between on the one hand a critical tradition suggesting that modernism might be defined by its lack of emotion, supported by statements of the need for 'cold, hard verse', and on the other hand the recent proliferation of literature focusing on modernism's capacity for feeling can partly be explained by thinking about what modernism sought to do with emotion. Baudelaire's 'The Painter of Modern Life' describes viewing everything with curiosity, seeing everything as new and strange. And one of the possible reasons that, until recently, modernism's interest in emotion tended to be neglected is that modernist writers were attempting to see emotion itself in new ways and were interested in forms of emotion we might struggle to recognize or understand. D. H. Lawrence, in his essay 'The Novel and the Feelings' (1925), even specifically disowned the term 'emotion':

> I say feelings, not emotions. Emotions are things we more or less recognise. We see love, like a woolly lamb, or like a decorative decadent panther in Paris clothes: according as it is sacred or profane. (Lawrence, 1985, 202)

What Lawrence is rejecting with the word 'emotion' is something 'recognizable' – he is rejecting what we think we know about emotions and rejecting comforting images of emotions: 'like a woolly lamb'. The term 'feelings', Lawrence continues, allows one to discuss emotions which we might know less about, emotions which are written into our bodies in unsettling ways and which might disrupt the stability of our sense of self.

It is this interest in what is less known and recognized about emotion that is central to modernism. Current interest in modernism and emotion has coincided with a revaluing of emotion taking place across philosophy, neuroscience and psychology. In discussing emotion in modernism, there have been attempts to show how modernism might illuminate questions about emotion that continue to be debated today: how close is emotion to thought? Might feeling itself be a type of thinking? How far can we understand emotion as embodied – is empathy, for instance, all due to 'mirror neurons'?[4] Modernism's determination to show us feeling afresh suggests the possibility of looking again at what emotion might be. In this chapter, I will focus on three key modernist writers – Virginia Woolf, D. H. Lawrence and T. S. Eliot – and consider how their work illuminates some intricate and troubling aspects of emotion.

Virginia Woolf, Sensuousness and Abstraction: The Feeling of Seeing the Sea

In her essay 'Poetry, Fiction, and the Future' (1927), Virginia Woolf argued that writers should extend the emotional range of their novels:

> For under the dominion of the novel we have scrutinized one part of the mind closely and left another unexplored. We have come to forget that a large and important part of life consists in our emotions towards such things as roses and

nightingales, the dawn, the sunset, life, death, and fate; we forget that we spend much time sleeping, dreaming, thinking, reading, alone; we are not entirely occupied in personal relations; all our energies are not absorbed in making our livings. The psychological novelist has been too prone to limit psychology to the psychology of personal intercourse; we long sometimes to escape from the incessant, the remorseless analysis of falling in love or falling out of love, of what Tom feels for Judith and Judith does or does not altogether feel for Tom. (Woolf, 1994b, 435–6)

With this statement Woolf dismisses much of the staple subject matter of Victorian novels, discarding both the marriage plot, 'the remorseless analysis of falling in love or falling out of love', and the emphasis on what she calls in 'Modern Fiction' (1925) the 'materialist' tendency to focus on material and social context, on 'making our livings' (Woolf, 1994a, 159). In contrast, she is interested in things we experience by ourselves – in attention not to other people and relationships but to concepts, 'life, death, and fate', and to the non-human, 'the dawn, the sunset'. She argues that what the modern novelist might try to capture is influences that are hard to explain: 'the power of music, the stimulus of sight, the effect on us of the shape of trees or the play of colour, the emotions bred in us by crowds, the obscure terrors and hatreds which come so irrationally in certain places or from certain people, the delight of movement, the intoxication of wine' (Woolf, 1994b, 439).

Focusing on such things, Woolf isolates for her attention obscure forms of feeling. Exploring 'the effect on us of the shape of trees or the play of colour', she seems interested in how our emotions are prompted and shaped all the time by everyday things, but in ways which might seem hard to understand, by influences which might barely have been noticed before. In previous literature, there had been attempts to think about such forms of response – one might think for instance of Wordsworth's interest in the pleasure to be derived from the shapes and colours taken of the landscape, from 'silver wreaths/Of curling mist' (ll.564–5), to 'the level plain/Of waters coloured by impending clouds' (ll.565–6) (Wordsworth, 1979, 61). But what 'Poetry, Fiction, and the Future' argues for is a redirection of our attention to such subtle and complex feelings, suggesting that we need to look more closely at these forms of reaction.

How this might work can be thought about by turning to Woolf's novel *To the Lighthouse* (1927). This is a novel that leaves much out. While the Victorian novel might carefully have described slow changes and developments over time, in this novel swathes of time are passed over. Where in the Victorian novel there might have been pages of mourning and grief at the death of central characters, in this novel key characters (Mrs Ramsay, Prue Ramsay, cherished son Andrew Ramsay) die with only bracketed explanations.[5] Instead of focusing on the emotions that previous novels might have considered central, Woolf's novel redirects its attention.

In particular, it redirects its attention onto subtle responses to things and situations that are difficult to describe. This is evident throughout the novel, but might be illustrated through the descriptions of the interactions of the artist Lily Briscoe and Mr William Bankes. Mrs Ramsay watches these two together and considers them the stuff of a love plot: 'an admirable idea had flashed upon her this very second – William and Lily should marry' (Woolf, 2008, 25). But in *To the Lighthouse* the marriage plot, and the emphasis on 'falling in love and falling out of love', is resisted by Lily, who imagines pleading with Mrs Ramsay: 'she would urge her own exemption from the universal law [...] she liked to be alone; she liked to be herself' (43).

And Woolf's novel echoes Lily's protest: instead of focusing on developing Lily and William's relationship, Woolf lavishes time on other stories and emotions. One form of emotion that receives much attention is the feeling provoked by looking at the sea, the response one has to suddenly seeing expanses of water. Lily Briscoe and William Bankes are impelled by such emotion, as they suddenly decide to walk down to the sea:

> 'It suddenly gets cold. The sun seems to give less heat', she said, looking about her, for it was bright enough, the grass still a soft deep green, the house starred in its greenery with purple passion flowers, and rooks dropping cool cries from the high blue. But something moved, flashed, turned a silver wing in the air. It was September after all, the middle of September, and past six in the evening. So off they strolled down the garden in the usual direction, past the tennis lawn, past the pampas grass, to that break in the thick hedge, guarded by red-hot pokers like brasiers of clear burning coal, between which the blue waters of the bay looked bluer than ever.
>
> They came there regularly every evening drawn by some need. It was as if the water floated off and set sailing thoughts which had grown stagnant on dry land, and gave to their bodies even some sort of physical relief. First, the pulse of colour flooded the bay with blue, and the heart expanded with it and the body swam, only the next instant to be checked and chilled by the prickly blackness on the ruffled waves. Then, up behind the great black rock, almost every evening spurted irregularly, so that one had to watch for it and it was a delight when it came, a fountain of white water; and then, while one waited for that, one watched, on the pale semi-circular beach, wave after wave shedding again and again smoothly a film of mother-of-pearl. (Woolf, 2008, 19–20)

This passage describes, as Woolf puts it in 'Poetry, Fiction, and the Future', 'those influences which play so large a part in life, yet have so far escaped the novelist' (Woolf, 1994b, 439). Lily is attentive to the play of colour around her, the grass a 'soft deep green', 'the purple passion flowers'. And then her responsiveness to such things becomes deepened as she watches the sea. The sea seems to separate out parts of Lily and William's cognitive life: 'set sailing thoughts which had grown stagnant'. Their bodies are aligned with the sea – it itself seems like a heart, with a 'pulse of colour', and in turn their hearts 'expanded with it'. Lily and William seem to travel emotionally across the water, to be given over to it: 'only the next instant to be checked and chilled by the prickly blackness on the ruffled waves'.

There is an absorbed oddity to this moment in *To the Lighthouse*. Woolf is suggesting one might be propelled by minute adjustments of feeling of which one is barely conscious. It is not clear why Lily and William feel impelled to move towards the sea, with the non sequitur 'It was September after all [...] So off they strolled', and later Woolf refers vaguely to what brings them to the sea, describing them as 'drawn by some need'. There is an oddity to the entire scene – Lily's initial words 'It suddenly gets cold' are a strangely unnatural form of speech, with a reflective quality which seems almost to suggest she is beginning to narrate the novel herself. And there's something uncanny about William and Lily's uniformity – as they move towards the sea they both feel the same things and seem unified in their responses: 'They came there [...] gave to their bodies'. Their uniformity escalates to the point at which they seem merely figures for a generalized emotional response, with the anonymized phrase: 'the heart expanded with it'.

Woolf is intent on exploring forms of emotional response which are difficult fully to understand, and throughout the novel she is interested in questions of how we respond to things like pure colour and shape and to the sudden movement of waves. These questions are thought through in the novel in terms of visual art. Lily defends her painting of Mrs Ramsay and James from the accusation that 'no one could tell it for a human shape' by arguing that 'There were other senses, too, in which one might reverence them. By a shadow here and a light there, for instance' (Woolf, 2008, 45). In this suggestion that arrangements of shadow and light might express one's feelings for another person and constitute a type of reverence, Lily has been seen as partly expressing the Post-Impressionist ideas of art explored by Woolf's sister Vanessa Bell and by Woolf's friends Roger Fry and Duncan Grant.[6] Contemporary theories of Impressionist and Post-Impressionist art sought to explore how we respond to mere pure shape, pure colour or 'rhythm'. Roger Fry argued that:

> Particular rhythms of line and particular harmonies of colour have their spiritual correspondences, and tend to arouse now one set of feelings, now another. The artist plays upon us by the rhythm of line, by colour, by abstract form, and by the quality of the matter he employs. (Fry, 1996, 105)

Fry's account of our response to art touches on elements of emotional response that are difficult to understand – raising questions of why we might respond to things as abstract as the 'rhythm of line […] colour […] form'. His allusion to 'spiritual correspondences' reaches after the reasons for such responses, grasping for some transcendent explanation for why we would respond in particular ways to different colours and patterns. The difficulty of thinking about how we understand response to 'rhythm […] colour […] abstract form' still prompts questions today. Christopher Butler discusses the issue in thinking about the pleasure of painting:

> Much of the turn from representation to abstraction in the history of painting […] depends on our learning to derive a pleasurable emotional response from what becomes simple or geometric or irregular shape or 'pure colour' in many later paintings. But how can such non-representational elements and their colour combinations alone cause within us emotions which give us pleasure? They do not engage us in a drama; they are not representations of objects or situations […] For abstraction in art […] by definition plays with and denies us our wish to rationalize our responses by naming and analysing situations and natural objects. (Butler, 2004, 122–3)

This question 'how can such non-representational elements and their colour combinations alone cause within us emotions which give us pleasure?' suggests ongoing concern about why we would respond to things that are purely abstract, or purely sensuous, and suggests how such emotions still deny us 'our wish to rationalize our responses'.

Woolf's novel persistently focuses attention to these types of ungraspable emotions. She redirects attention from some of the mainstays of Victorian fiction onto sudden moments of rapture, prompted by things like colour, light and movement. Her work echoes Baudelaire's depiction of how one might be moved by anything: 'whether a face or a landscape, gilding, colours, shimmering stuffs' (Baudelaire, 1964, 8). Her work also continually suggests that such responses might be difficult to explain. It remains unclear why Lily and William should be impelled by the change of light over the sea or the expansiveness of the water, and Lily struggles to explain how her relationship to Mrs Ramsay might best be captured by a light here and a shade there. But while Woolf does reach for a language and form for such emotions, her novel also just emphasizes their importance. Woolf returns repeatedly to how the heart might expand on seeing an expanse of water – as when Mrs Ramsay sees the sea on walking into town with Charles Tansley:

> but here, the houses falling away on both sides, they came out on the quay and the whole bay spread before them and Mrs Ramsay could not help exclaiming, 'Oh, how beautiful!' For the great plateful of blue water was before her; the hoary Lighthouse distant, austere, in the midst; and on the right, as far as the eye could see, fading and falling, in soft low pleats, the green sand dunes with the wild flowing grasses on them, which always seemed to be running away into some moon country, uninhabited of men. (Woolf, 2008, 14)

There is a sudden instant responsiveness to the sea here and a sense again of an intense, obscure response. Mrs Ramsay is impelled by something – 'Mrs Ramsay could not help exclaiming' – and Woolf's mode of explaining her response is just to show us the scene: 'For the great plateful of blue water was before her.' The sea itself seems to move away from human understanding, and such emotions in Woolf's work move away constantly from our own full comprehension: they 'always seemed to be running away'.

Gestures and Emotion

In turning away from the habitual focus points of emotion in the novel and exploring instead things like responses to colour and light, Woolf's work suggests a further way in which modernist writers thought afresh about feeling. Modernist writers not only deflected emotions onto the non-human, but also explored the possibilities of making discussion of emotion less explicit, more focused on subtle and fleeting moments. In *To the Lighthouse*, as mentioned above, key characters' deaths are recorded only in brackets. Most notably, the death of the central character, Mrs Ramsay, is recorded thus: '[Mr Ramsay stumbling along a passage stretched his arms out one dark morning, but Mrs Ramsay having died rather suddenly the night before he stretched his arms out. They remained empty.]' (Woolf, 2008, 105). Grief, here, is presented through the eeriness of outstretched, empty arms – gesture and movement stand in for a full and direct account of emotion.

This way of presenting emotion, through fleeting gestures, through movement, is something that runs throughout Woolf's work. It has been picked up most recently by Abbie Garrington's work on *Haptic Modernism*, which focuses on *The Years* as a 'peculiarly gestural novel' (Garrington, 2013, 119).

Garrington suggests that Woolf's intense interest in gesture can be understood in the context of then-current thinking about the significance of body language, and she draws attention in particular to Charlotte Wolff, a psychoanalyst and palm reader whom Woolf herself consulted (despite the disapproval of Leonard Woolf) (2013, 125–6).[7] Charlotte Wolff, in her work *A Psychology of Gesture*, detailed the emotional import of bodily movement: 'The way in which a woman opens and shuts the door, how she walks, gives you her hand, takes a chair, remains seated, gets up, the way she lights a cigarette, tears up a letter, turns the pages of a book, arranges flowers – all these things contribute to a picture of her personality' (Wolff, 1945, 5).

In modernist works, gesture often seems central: both embodying and expressing the emotions and personality of an individual, and prompting emotion in the observer. This is apparent throughout Woolf's work, but is perhaps most clear in the work of D. H. Lawrence. Lawrence today is perhaps best known for his sexually explicit writing and for his banned novel, *Lady Chatterley's Lover* (1928). Yet his work is also notable for the significance he allots to the inexplicit, to the ways in which feeling might be enfolded in the smallest things, in gesture and in movement. Lawrence's attention to gesture is evident from his early novel, *Sons and Lovers* (1913). This novel pays exceptional attention to first impressions. As Paul Morel meets Miriam, he watches her intently:

> Miriam was moving about preparing dinner. Paul watched everything that happened. His face was pale and thin, but his eyes were quick and bright with life as ever. He watched the strange, almost rhapsodic way in which the girl moved about, carrying a great stew-jar to the oven, or looking in the saucepan. The atmosphere was different from that of his own home, where everything seemed so ordinary. When Mr Leivers called loudly outside to the horse, that was reaching over to feed on the rose bushes in the garden, the girl started, looking round with dark eyes, as if something had come breaking in on her world. There was a sense of silence inside the house and out. Miriam seemed as in some dreamy tale, a maiden in bondage, her spirit dreaming in a land far away and magical. (Lawrence, 1992, 176)

Here, personality is expressed by the most everyday things – so that Miriam's way of 'looking in the saucepan' might in a mysterious way express her personality. The narrative contemplates what Miriam's way of moving might mean, with the language becoming gesturative in its attempt to describe the 'strange, almost rhapsodic' way she moves. Paul constantly guesses at the significance of her movements, with the language of conjecture, moving into simile 'as if something had come breaking in on her world'.

This focus on detail is not in itself modernist – indeed it is a characteristic of the Victorian novel – but the way in which gestures, movements, seem to stand in for other and more explicit descriptions of the characters' emotions does come to be characteristic of Lawrence's writing and of the modernist novel more generally.[8] When Paul later meets Clara, he is again captivated by movement, especially her manner of shaking hands, which is highly suggestive: she seems 'at once to keep him at a distance, and yet to fling something to him' (Lawrence, 1992, 270).

Such descriptions of gesture transfer attention from the conscious aspects of the relationship to something unvoiced, and below the surface of ordinary communication. And attention to gesture in this way suggests a form of feeling that is intricately embodied. Lawrence considered this further in his essay 'The Novel and the Feelings', as he wrote about

> listening-in to the voices of the honorable beasts that call in the dark paths of the veins of our body, from the God in the heart. Listening inwards, inwards, not for words nor for inspiration, but to the lowing of the innermost beasts, the feelings, that roam in the forest of the blood, from the feet of God within the red, dark heart. (Lawrence, 1985, 205)

Feeling for gesture in Lawrence's work suggests this 'listening-in'. It also suggests the complexity of the relationship between emotion and the body. In Lawrence's description of how one listens in for the 'feelings that roam in the forest of the blood', emotions become animalistic, and the blood forms forests.

In Lawrence's descriptions of gesture and Woolf's discussions of responding to shape, colour and movement, the body is intricately involved. There is a giving over of the body in *To the Lighthouse* as Lily and Mr Bankes watch the sea and 'the heart expanded with it and the body swam', and there is a sense of emotion being infolded into gesture in Lawrence's work, of feeling situated in the 'dark paths of the veins of our body [...] within the red, dark heart'. Part of modernism's curiosity about emotions, and part of the modernist reimagining of emotion, is related to the way in which then-contemporary ideas of feeling and thought suggested the need to rethink the relationship between emotion, the body and the self.

Modernist Emotion and the Body: The Red Dark Heart

The intricate relationship between emotion, the body and the self in the modernist novel can be seen especially clearly by turning again to Woolf, and in particular *The Waves* (1931). In this novel, the character Jinny runs through the garden as a child:

> 'I was running,' said Jinny, 'after breakfast. I saw leaves moving in a hole in the hedge. I thought "That is a bird on its nest". I parted them and looked; but there was no bird on a nest. The leaves went on moving. I was frightened. I ran past Susan, past Rhoda, and Neville and Bernard in the tool-house talking. I cried as I ran, faster and faster. What moved the leaves? What moves my heart, my legs? And I dashed in here, seeing you green as a bush, like a branch, very still, Louis, with your eyes fixed. "Is he dead?" I thought, and kissed you, with my heart jumping under my pink frock like the leaves, which go on moving, though there is nothing to move them.' (Woolf, 2011, 8)

Jinny's emotions are aligned, unsettlingly, with the movements of her body. As Woolf describes how she 'cried as [she] ran, faster and faster', the word 'as' suggests at once simultaneity, that she cries while she runs, and also that her tears are somehow like her running, and indeed that they are running out of control. Jinny's emotions, and her movements, seem oddly to be compelled, like the way in which the leaves are moved. What alarms her about the leaves moving is that nothing seems to move them: 'there was no bird on a nest. The leaves went on moving', and her running and sobbing seem also to be without cause or control, and thus like the leaves: 'What moved the leaves? What moves my heart, my legs?' As she kisses Louis 'with my heart jumping under my pink frock like the leaves', Jinny's emotions seem at once intimate to her person, something she inhabits and moves within, and yet foreign to her.

This awareness that emotion might depend on the body in ways that are beyond our control, and which remain insufficiently understood, is something that runs through modernist literature, from Woolf's *The Waves*, to Lawrence's discussions of bodies, emotions and sexuality, to moments such as that in Ford Madox Ford's *Parade's End* (1924–28) where Valentine notes that the whole of her love affair with Tietjens so far has depended on bodily subtlety, that it had 'passed without any mention of the word "love"; it passed in impulses; warmths; rigors of the skin' (Ford, 1982, 267). And concern about the embodiment of emotion and such things as 'impulses; warmths' is especially evident when one turns to the way in which modernism thinks about feeling in relation to the heart. The heart is traditionally linked with thinking about emotion and love – yet modernist accounts of the heart often emphasize a strange disconnection between feeling and the heart, or a sense that the heart registers emotions which we do not consciously recognize. In Thomas Mann's *The Magic Mountain* (1924), Hans Castorp is shocked by how his racing heart suggests an emotional excitement that he does not feel and later seems almost relieved to fall in love – as then his emotion falls in line with his bodily symptoms. He reflects that this meant that 'he felt within himself the emotion proper to his heart beats' and no longer has to feel his emotions and body as strange to himself: 'For now he need not feel that it so beat of its own accord, without sense or reason or any reference to his non-corporeal part' (Mann, 1999, 138–9). In his sense of the problematic relationship between feeling and the body, and his anxiety that the heart 'might beat so of its own accord', Mann is touching on contemporary debate about whether emotions might take us over in this way, whether they might seem to possess us 'without sense or reason or any reference to his non-corporeal part'.

This is a concern that is not peculiar to modernism. Kirstie Blair has noted that images of the heart in Victorian poetry are often highly fraught with anxieties about affect, because the heart is both 'active and passive; the most intimate part of an individual yet the most detached, in the sense that its actions cannot necessarily be controlled' (Blair, 2006, 4). Yet the complexity of the perceived relationship between the body and emotion in the early twentieth century was also shaped by pressures specific to the modernist moment. As Sally Shuttleworth and Jenny Bourne Taylor have shown, the nineteenth and early twentieth centuries saw ongoing debate about 'the complex relationship between the mind and the body', about whether feeling was the property of some immaterial part of the person, a type of immortal soul, or whether it could all be explained with reference to the material properties of the body (Shuttleworth and Bourne Taylor, 1998, xiii). In the early twentieth century, advances in neuroscientific understanding seemed to suggest that all of our emotions might be explained with reference to our nervous system – but the heart was never displaced entirely as a centre of emotion, and in thinking about the interplay of the heart and the nerves there was particular concern about how emotion was embodied.[9] In *The Science of Life* (1931), H. G. Wells, Julian Huxley and J. P. Wells suggested that there was ongoing uncertainty over how much of feeling might depend on the heart and the blood, and how much on the nerves:

> Twenty or thirty years ago it was thought that the co-operation of part with part was ensured through the nervous system alone, either consciously through the brain or unconsciously by the subordinate systems of nervous communication [...] nowadays we are beginning to realize that a very large part of the harmonizing task is done through substances emitted by one organ and reaching another by way of the blood. (Wells et al., 1931, 35)

There is a sense in this book of the uncertainty about how feeling and impulse travel about the body, and how different parts of the body seem to harmonize. This passage suggests that the transport of feelings in the body depends on both the heart and the nerves, but the book also gives a sense of a constantly colliding flurry of feeling, arguing that: 'If we could see the whole living web of the nervous system laid out before us, and if a nervous impulse was a visible thing, we should get a picture of continual thrilling and rippling activity' (Wells et al., 1931, 71).

The ongoing uncertainty about the workings of emotion in the body, coupled with a perception of feeling as 'continual thrilling and rippling', is reflected in moments in modernist literature where the energies of the body create emotions that run beyond a character's control or even their conscious perception. Throughout *The Waves*, hearts beat faster and beyond control. As Neville reaches London at the end of a train journey, he feels that 'as we approach London, the centre [...] my heart draws out too, in fear, in exultation' (Woolf, 2011, 55); Louis feels 'impulses wilder than the wildest birds strike from my wild heart' (45); Jinny senses her heart pounding and her blood 'bright red, whipped up, slapping against my ribs' (34). As the characters in *The Waves* sit together at lunch, they seem to be possessed of one heart, 'Comfort steals over us. Gold runs in our blood. One, two; one, two; the heart beats in serenity, in confidence, in some trance of well-being' (107), and then the hearts and nerves seem again to suggest the extent to which emotion disturbs and shapes the modernist novel: 'The nerves thrill in their thighs. Their hearts pound and churn in their sides' (112).

T. S. Eliot and a 'Moment's Surrender'

This essay began with the acknowledgement that modernism's engagement with emotion had at one stage been neglected because so many modernist writers seem to go out of their way to disown expressions of unfettered emotion or sentimentality. Of all modernism's protestations against emotion, it is probably T. S. Eliot's which is most often quoted. In 'Tradition and the Individual Talent' (1919), T.S. Eliot wrote that '[p]oetry is not a turning loose of emotion, but an escape from emotion; it is not the expression of personality, but an escape from personality' (Eliot, 1975, 43). Critics seeking to restore an awareness of emotion's centrality to modernism have argued that this statement is far from straightforward: as I have argued elsewhere, Eliot's poetic practice 'mitigates this principle'; Taylor has noted that the lines are 'notoriously vexed and ambiguous'; Michael Bell has noted that 'his phrasing revealed an emotional subtext, a fear or condescension towards feeling, underlying the general literary principle' (Martin, 2013, 13; Taylor, 2012, 6; Bell, 2000, 162).[10] Eliot's work suggests the complications inherent in modernism's attitude to emotion and reveals how what might seem to be a rejection of emotion reveals instead its intricate revaluing.

Eliot's statement that poetry provides an 'escape from emotion' can be complicated by turning to almost any examples of his own work. To give just one, towards the end of *The Waste Land* (1922) there is a famous question-and-answer section:

> *Damyata*: The boat responded
> Gaily, to the hand expert with sail and oar
> The sea was calm, your heart would have responded
> Gaily, when invited, beating obedient
> To controlling hands. (Eliot, 1969, ll.418–22)

These lines, like Woolf's *To the Lighthouse*, suggest how one might respond to things like colour, light and expansiveness. In the declaration, 'The sea was calm, your heart would have responded', emotional response seems to be guided by the expanse of water but also by things beyond one: 'the hand expert with sail and oar'. The body seems to be moved without the control of a mind: 'your heart would have responded'. And the reference to this form of emotional response is at once wistfully conjectural and absolutely definite. As A. D. Moody has emphasized that this response is only hypothetical, that while '[t]he form of the verse implies a parallel', the words '"*would have* responded" make the second statement nearly the opposite of the first' (Moody, 1979, 103). Yet while 'would have' is *nearly* the opposite of the first, it is also importantly not quite the opposite. While the line is in the conditional tense, it nevertheless evinces a surety about this form of emotional response – there's a certainty that it *would* have taken place.

Michael Bell has argued that '[t]here is no alternative within a self-conscious modernity to the primordiality of feeling', and Eliot's poetic practice chimes with this statement (Bell, 2000, 207). Despite all of modernism's disavowals of particular types of emotion, feeling remains central to modernism – and indeed seems to provide modernist literature's driving impulse. Modernist literature and art is shaped by an interest in feeling for the slightest things, by approaching emotions at new angles and revealing new aspects of experience. As intimated in Baudelaire's predictions concerning modernity, modernist literature offered ways of considering how we might respond emotionally to light, colour and gesture – and it also explored how such emotions troubled the idea of human autonomy, suggesting that we were controlled by our bodies in ways that we might still struggle to understand.

Emotion in the modernist novel sometimes seems displaced – focused not on direct discussions of relationships or events, but on things like the changing light, fleeting gestures and intricate bodily mappings. Yet even while emotion might be focused onto small things, or small moments, it seems finally that the intensity of modernist literature's engagement with emotion means that such moments override all its famous protestations against emotion. The moments of feeling seem to matter more than all the moments of restraint. An idea akin to this is explored in *The Waste Land*, again with reference to the heart:

> *Datta*: what have we given?
> My friend, blood shaking my heart
> The awful daring of a moment's surrender
> Which an age of prudence can never retract. (Eliot, 1969, ll.401–4)

This is a description of being given over to emotion – with the heart in control, 'blood shaking my heart'. As the description of this 'moment's surrender' proceeds, the lines from *The Waste Land* indicate how we might view moments of emotional intensity within a modernism often concerned with defending itself against emotional excess. Such moments, Eliot suggests, count for more than any amount of moderation – they provide something that 'an age of prudence can never retract'.

Notes

1   See Clark, 1991; Altieri, 2004; Bell, 2000, especially 160–204; Cuda, 2010; Martin, 2013; Ratcliffe, 2008, especially Chapters 3 and 4; and Taylor, 2012, which discusses modernism and emotion primarily in the light of 'affect theory', arguing for the value of the word 'affect' rather than 'emotion' (Taylor, 2012, 18–20). An essay collection, *Modernism and Affect* (Taylor, 2015), further pursues the interpretation of modernism in the light of affect theory.

2   For other examples of critics downplaying the importance of emotion to modernism, see David Trotter's focus on a 'will-to-abstraction' in *Paranoid Modernism* (2001, 3), and the opening of Peter Nicholls's *Modernism: A Literary Guide* which emphasizes 'ironic distance' (1995, 3). For discussion of these and other examples, see *Modernism and the Rhythms of Sympathy* (Martin, 2013, 10–14).

3   See, for instance, Jessica Burstein's *Cold Modernism*, which identifies a strand
    of modernism which 'dispenses with' '[p]sychology [...] the unconscious', and
    dispenses with 'emotion, with its emphasis on affect and binding relations to the
    world' (2012, 12).

4   For a discussion of such questions in relation to modernist literature, see
    Martin, *Modernism and the Rhythms of Sympathy* (2013, 14–23 and *passim*),
    as well as Ratcliffe, *On Sympathy* (2008, 13–16 and Chapters 3 and 4). For a
    discussion of developments in thinking about emotion across disciplines and
    their relevance to literature, see Suzanne Keen, *Empathy and the Novel* (2007,
    passim).

5   For further discussion, see Alan Warren Friedman's *Fictional Death and the
    Modernist Enterprise* which discusses Victorian deathbed scenes (Friedman,
    1995, 74–7), and how in contrast in *To the Lighthouse*, 'in a sense, Mrs. Ramsay's
    death [...] never happens' (224). Friedman's argument is extended to consider the
    treatment of death and corpses in modernist literature in David Sherman, *In a
    Strange Room* (2014).

6   See, for instance, Jane Goldman's discussion of *The Feminist Aesthetics of
    Virginia Woolf: Modernism, Post-Impressionism and the Politics of the Visual*
    (1998).

7   For further discussion of Woolf and Charlotte Wolff, see Hermione Lee, *Virginia
    Woolf* (1997, 667–8).

8   See Lowe's chapter on 'Other People's Shoes: Realism, Imagination and Sympathy'
    in *Victorian Fiction and the Insights of Sympathy: An Alternative to the Hermeneutics
    of Suspicion* (Lowe, 2007, 61–121), for a discussion of detail and emotion in the
    Victorian novel.

9   Laura Salisbury and Andrew Shail show that 'neurological conceptions of
    the self were primary components of the ways in which "modernity" [...]
    conceptualized itself and its subjects' (2010, 1). For a discussion of the
    competing roles of the nerves and the heart in understanding emotion, see
    John Gordon, 'T.S. Eliot's Head and Heart', *English Literary History* (1995,
    979–1000).

10 For another discussion of Eliot and emotion, see Taylor, *Modernism and Affect*
    (2015, 3–5).

Bibliography

Altieri, C. (2004), *The Particulars of Rapture: An Aesthetics of the Affects*. Ithaca: Cornell
    University Press.
Baudelaire, C. (1964), 'The Painter of Modern Life (1859–60)', in J. Mayne (transl. and
    ed.), *The Painter of Modern Life and Other Essays*. London: Phaidon Press, pp. 1–41.

Bell, M. (2000), *Sentimentalism, Ethics, and the Culture of Feeling*. Houndmills: Basingstoke.

Blair, K. (2006), *Victorian Poetry and the Culture of the Heart*. Oxford: Oxford University Press.

Burstein, J. (2012), *Cold Modernism: Literature, Fashion, Art*. Pennsylvania: The Pennsylvania State University Press.

Butler, C. (2004), *Pleasure and the Arts: Enjoying Literature, Painting, and Music*. Oxford: Oxford University Press.

Clark, S. (1991), *Sentimental Modernism: Women Writers and the Revolution of the Word*. Bloomington: Indiana University Press.

Cuda, A. (2010), *The Passions of Modernism: Eliot, Yeats, Woolf, and Mann*. Columbia: University of South Carolina Press.

Eliot, T. S. (1969), 'The Waste Land' (1922), in *The Complete Poems and Plays of T. S. Eliot*. London: Faber and Faber, pp. 61–80.

Eliot, T. S. (1975), 'Tradition and the Individual Talent', in F. Kermode (ed.), *Selected Prose of T. S. Eliot*. London: Faber and Faber, pp. 37–44.

Ford, F. M. (1982), *Some Do Not …*, in J. Barnes (introd.), *Parade's End*. London: Penguin.

Friedman, A. W. (1995), *Fictional Death and the Modernist Enterprise*. Cambridge: Cambridge University Press.

Fry, R. (1996), 'Post-Impressionism', in C. Reed (ed.), *A Roger Fry Reader*. Chicago: University of Chicago Press, pp. 99–110.

Garrington, A. (2013), *Haptic Modernism: Touch and the Tactile in Modernist Writing*. Edinburgh: Edinburgh University Press.

Goldman, J. (1998), *The Feminist Aesthetics of Virginia Woolf: Modernism, Post-Impressionism and the Politics of the Visual*. Cambridge: Cambridge University Press.

Gordon, J. (1995), 'T.S. Eliot's Head and Heart'. *English Literary History*, 62, (4), (Winter), 979–1000.

Hulme, T. E. (1924), 'Romanticism and Classicism', (1914), in H. Read (ed.), *Speculations: Essays on Humanism and the Philosophy of Art*. London: Kegan Paul, Trench, Trubner and Co.

Keen, S. (2007), *Empathy and the Novel*. Oxford: Oxford University Press.

Lawrence, D. H. (1985), 'The Novel and the Feelings', in B. Steele (ed.), *The Study of Thomas Hardy and Other Late Essays*. Cambridge: Cambridge University Press, pp. 200–5.

Lawrence, D. H. (1992), *Sons and Lovers*, H. Baron and C. Baron (eds). Cambridge: Cambridge University Press.

Lee, H. (1997), *Virginia Woolf*. London: Vintage.

Lowe, B. (2007), 'Other People's Shoes: Realism, Imagination and Sympathy', in *Victorian Fiction and the Insights of Sympathy: An Alternative to the Hermeneutics of Suspicion*. London: Anthem Press, pp. 61–121.

Mann, T. (1999), *The Magic Mountain*, H. T. Lowe-Porter (transl.). London: Vintage Books.

Martin, K. (2013), *Modernism and the Rhythms of Sympathy*, Vernon Lee, Virginia Woolf and D. H. Lawrence (eds). Oxford: Oxford University Press.

Moody, A. D. (1979), *Thomas Stearns Eliot: Poet*. Cambridge: Cambridge University Press.

Nicholls, P. (1995), *Modernism: A Literary Guide*. Basingstoke: Macmillan Press.

Ratcliffe, S. (2008), *On Sympathy*. Oxford: Oxford University Press.

Salisbury, L. and Shail, A. (2010), 'Introduction', in L. Salisbury and A. Shail (eds), *Neurology and Modernity: A Cultural History of Nervous Systems, 1800–1950*. Basingstoke: Palgrave Macmillan, pp. 1–40.

Sherman, D. (2014), *In a Strange Room: Modernism's Corpses and Mortal Obligation*. Oxford: Oxford University Press.

Shuttleworth, S. and Bourne Taylor, J. (1998), 'Introduction', in S. Shuttleworth and J. Bourne Taylor (eds), *Embodied Selves: An Anthology of Psychological Texts 1830–1890*. Oxford: Clarendon Press, pp. xiii–xviii.

Taylor, J. (2012), *Djuna Barnes and Affective Modernism*. Edinburgh: Edinburgh University Press.

Taylor, J. (2015), 'Introduction', in J. Taylor (ed.), *Modernism and Affect*. Edinburgh: Edinburgh University Press, pp. 1–19.

Trotter, D. (2001), *Paranoid Modernism: Literary Experiment, Psychosis, and the Professionalization of English Society*. Oxford: Oxford University Press.

Wells, H. G., Huxley, J., and Wells, G. P. (1931), *The Science of Life*. London: Cassell and Company Ltd.

Whitworth, M. H. (2007), 'Introduction', in M. H. Whitworth (ed.), *Modernism*. Malden, MA: Blackwell, pp. 3–60.

Wolff, C. (1945), *A Psychology of Gesture*, A. Tennant (transl.). London: Methuen & Co. Ltd.

Woolf, V. (1994a), 'Modern Fiction', in A. McNeillie (ed.), *The Essays of Virginia Woolf, Vol. IV*. London: Hogarth Press, pp. 157–65.

Woolf, V. (1994b), 'Poetry, Fiction, and the Future', in A. McNeillie (ed.), *The Essays of Virginia Woolf, Vol. IV*. London: Hogarth Press, pp. 428–41.

Woolf, V. (2008), *To the Lighthouse*, D. Bradshaw (ed.). Oxford: Oxford University Press.

Woolf, V. (2011), *The Waves*, M. Herbert and S. Sellers (eds). Cambridge: Cambridge University Press.

Wordsworth, W. (1979), 'The Prelude', in J. Wordsworth, M. H. Abrams, and S. Gill (eds), *The Prelude 1799, 1805, 1850*. New York: W. W. Norton.

6

Myth and Religion in Modernist Literature

Michael Bell

The grand cultural narratives often define modernity as the decay of religious belief, although the jury is likely to be out for a long time before there can be any final judgement on the ultimate fate of religion. Nonetheless, a widespread waning of belief is the inevitable context for considering it in the period generally thought of as modernist and the process is a complex one. In the lives of individuals, the shedding of religious faith can be experienced in a variety of ways, from painful and frightening loss to joyous liberation, with all of these perhaps occurring in stages to the same individual. Something analogous happens in the life of a culture, and early twentieth-century literature in the European and Anglophone worlds reflects a particular phase in the gradual displacement of religious belief by a secular world view. Moreover, cultural change is not only slow but uneven, and the tension between critical consciousness and institutional forms, for example, is caught in the fact that Sir James Frazer, whose monumental study *The Golden Bough* (1890–1915) effectively showed Christ to be only another seasonal god from the ages of superstition, was obliged in his capacity as university professor to subscribe to the Christian faith. At the same time, of course, religion, which has by no means died out, and may never do so, is internally affected by changing conditions, above all by its no longer being the assumed norm.

Myth and/or Religion

In so far as what is at stake in loss of faith are psychological shifts affecting a whole view of the world, these are perhaps most intimately articulated in works of imaginative literature. This significance is by no means confined to those self-consciously avant-garde writers we have come to call 'modernist', but these writers do collectively represent a range of classic responses inscribed within the intellectual landscape of the time, including such features as the rising prestige of science, the shock of the Great War, the questioning of empire and the emergence of modern anthropology. Most significantly, many of these writers shared, albeit in quite different ways, a very relevant interest in myth, and not just at the level of thematic content but as a structuring principle and a mode of response to the world.

Religion in the nineteenth century had undergone critique from the twin powers of scientific reason and historical scholarship, both of which were invincible within their own terms. But myth had emerged as a crucial category in which these terms were themselves thrown into question. Hence the ambivalent relation of religion and myth: although reduction to merely mythic status was religion's most damaging possibility, it could nonetheless affirm against these corrosive critiques its intrinsic authority as myth. On the one hand, to be revealed as myth was a more essential threat to traditional religious belief than is posed by scientific reason because science is not ultimately addressed to religious questions. Yet on the other hand, myth was the category that could most effectively underwrite religion in the context of modernity. This can be seen by listing some of the important discursive texts which chart changing conceptions of religion in the period. These include Friedrich Nietzsche, *The Birth of Tragedy* (1872); Matthew Arnold, *Literature and Dogma* (1873); William James, *The Varieties of Religious Experience* (1902); Emile Durkheim, *The Elementary Forms of the Religious Life* (1915); and Sigmund Freud, *The Future of an Illusion* (1927). James's study catches a cultural moment in that it surveys the extreme forms of religious belief and conduct, such as self-punitive asceticism, and assumes that the reader, like him, will view these no longer as high points of spiritual attainment but as psychological curiosities. Yet James remains respectful of the religious impulse as such and in so far as he approaches the different kinds of faith as inarguable products of temperament and world view, it can be said that he, along with all of these other writers, considers religion as a form of myth, and all of them, apart from Freud, respect it as a fundamental motive in human existence. Only Freud treats it in a spirit of scientific positivism as an empty and damaging illusion to be overcome.

In the Anglophone tradition, Matthew Arnold's *Literature and Dogma* represented the important transition inherited by the modernist generation. He argued that the biblical story was to be understood not as revealed truth but as the epic record of the Jewish people's profound exploration of the ethical impulse and with a significance, therefore, for humanity at large. Far from evacuating the truth value of Christianity, Arnold accorded it a newly intrinsic power, the power of the literary imagination. But this was also to enhance the significance of literature itself which was now understood not as simply reflecting truths available by other means but as in itself the primary producer of moral values and understanding. The best word for imaginative forms bearing such a burden of meaning is 'myth', and this was the force of the term as taken up by a number of early twentieth-century writers. The dominant spirit of Victorian anthropology, as in Edward B. Tylor and James Frazer, had been a demystifying explanation of primitive superstition but, as John B. Vickery (1973) has explicated at length, the modernist readers of *The Golden Bough* were entranced by the mythic wealth it had revealed. And this ironic turn on the value of myth may be applied more generally to the question of religion in modernity. For in the eyes of some of the more acute observers, the evident decline of religion threw its underlying cultural function and importance into relief, albeit under the sign of myth rather than that of metaphysical doctrine or historical belief.

At the same time, modernist literary mythopoeia was typically different from the archaic forms examined by contemporary anthropologists because of its artistic self-consciousness. It is a truism that, in secularized modernity, art replaces religion and Arnold's concern for the moral and civilizing impact of literature makes him a significant example of this claim. But the claim can be understood at varying levels of cultural generality or philosophical specificity. The German philosophical tradition, stemming from Immanuel Kant and passing through Friedrich Schiller, had long accorded a special significance not just to the moral impact of works of art, but more specifically to the domain of the aesthetic considered as a metaphysical definition. Nietzsche's *The Birth of Tragedy* is the primary link between this tradition and modernist writers.

Nietzsche argued that ancient Greek tragedy evolved from Dionysian orgiastic festivals in which the community periodically underwent a necessary, life-affirming participation in the destructive, pre-civilized, pre-individualized, pre-moral realm of nature. Significantly, the mythic figure of Dionysos was not a moral idea, he had no allegorical equivalence, and he therefore presided over a complex psychological action whose meaning could remain largely unconscious or inarticulate. The wildness of the Dionysian revels was always controlled by their prescribed time and place but, in a crucial shift emphasized by Nietzsche, they acquired a more subtly internal form of control: they were gradually transposed by the Greeks from a literal activity into a mode of artistic representation. The community now participated in the psychological function of the festival through a structured dream enacted for them on the stage. Nietzsche's name for this organized and impersonalized dream, designed to enact necessary processes forbidden in everyday life, was the aesthetic. Nietzsche might as well have entitled his book the birth of culture, or of the aesthetic, and in post-Nietzschean modernism the aesthetic proves to be the modern *equivalent* of archaic myth. That is to say, although the old relation to myth is not possible for a modern sensibility, the aesthetic provides a comparable function.[1]

The notion of art as a self-conscious equivalent for the psychological function performed by archaic myth also has a broader philosophical import. One definition of modernity might be the awareness that the world, as world, is a human creation. Human beings do not create world out of nothing and they are not responsible for existence, but world as the meaningful order they inhabit is a human creation – most notably by virtue of language. What is sometimes called 'the linguistic turn' is the modern recognition that, instead of a given world of objects named by Adam, it is language that creates the discrimination of objects by which a world is formed. Language precedes world. Hence, whereas archaic man is believed to have unwittingly projected his conceptions and emotions on to the world as magic and gods, and more developed Cartesian man came apparently to understand the demarcation of self and world, so modern post-Kantian man recognized his inescapable implication in the formation of world. What archaic man did unwittingly, modern man does self-consciously. Giambattista Vico's *The New Science* (1744), one of James Joyce's sacred books, came fully into its own with the recognition that poetic creation is the primordial act by which man creates culture, creates world, creates himself. In the beginning, indeed, was not the Word, but the word. In 1800, Friedrich Schlegel and Friedrich W. J. Schelling both independently desiderated a 'new mythology' on which to base a poetry to rival that of the classical world, but several of the modernist generation recognized that mythology does not need to precede poetry because poetry is itself mythopoeic, or world-creating. Yet there is a further aspect still in the philosophical turn to myth.

Part of the modern turn from Victorian anthropology lay in the question of what is meant by the primordial conditions of culture. The Victorian generation tended to suppose that the early stages of human evolution were, or should be, left in the past and were therefore of mainly historical interest. Or if they were still with us they should be extirpated. The moderns, by contrast, were likely to insist that they were a permanently necessary condition, beneath rather than behind us so to speak, and for that very reason largely unconscious. Like the ground we stand on, they are necessary but invisible or unregarded. It was in this spirit that Nietzsche had raised the question of value. The primary concern of Western philosophy had been epistemological: What do we know, how do we know it, and how do we know we know it? What value we put on what we know seemed a secondary question but Nietzsche argued that we only seek to know in the first place what it interests us to know. The question of value is unconsciously prior to the question of knowledge and this is a permanently necessary priority rather than a simply evolutionary one. In the twentieth century, Martin Heidegger sought to go a step further in the same spirit. He argued that prior to the question of value was the question of Being, which is even more unregarded.

Heidegger saw the history of Western thought and culture, at least since the time of Socrates, as a progressive loss of Being. His translators capitalize Being to distinguish it from individual beings. The sense is that our habitual instrumental relations with the beings that surround us has led to a progressive incapacity to respond to the primary mystery of their presence as such, the Being of these beings. Like Nietzsche, then, he prized the mythopoeic sensibility he saw in the pre-Platonic world and also rejected the Christian tradition for its dualism, dogmatism and degeneracy, but he thought Nietzsche had neglected something more radical, attention to Being, the recognition of which was the true *proprium* of myth and of art. Heidegger's more contemplative model suggests a quasi-religious piety towards the world and if the supersession of religion by art is part of the story of modern religious consciousness then the list of discursive texts outlined above should include Heidegger's lectures 'On the Origin of the Work of Art' (1950). The non-instrumental concentration of the artwork, he argues, focuses a non-transcendental but reverential sense of Being. Once again, as in the earlier texts, religion is evacuated of its other-worldly significance and understood as a more profound mode of response to this world.

The thinkers enumerated so far provide an analytic frame through which to understand a range of mythopoeic and religious standpoints in modernist literature, with myth itself remaining an ambiguous category, either exploding religion or preserving it under another name. It would be impossible to survey all the possible figures encompassed by this theme, but what follows delineates an analytic spectrum by considering in turn a traditionally religious writer; a writer who explicitly replaces religion with a Nietzschean conception of the aesthetic; several writers for whom the loss of belief is a powerfully felt absence; and finally some writers who find their own forms of religious relation to the world.

Religion in Modernism

T. S. Eliot is a generally acknowledged modernist who reveals with special clarity the tension between myth and religion in the period. His well-known allusion to the Fisher King legend in *The Waste Land* (1922) has made him an apparently prime instance of modernist mythopoeia, although on closer inspection it shows the reverse. In a review of James Joyce's *Ulysses* (1922), he praised its 'use' of the 'mythic method' which makes the 'modern world' with all its 'futility and anarchy' possible for 'art' (Eliot, 1923, 483). The formulation is actually ambiguous and the plangency of his description is truly appropriate not to Joyce but to Eliot's own *The Waste Land*, where the fertility myth is a nostalgic and satiric background to the contemporary world rather than a mythopoeic transformation of it. Indeed, to put the point more critically and substantively, the fertility that is ostensibly celebrated in the myth is belied by the pervasive sexual distaste and snobbery in the poem. Actually, Eliot creates a compelling, but highly personal, vision of modernity which became for a large readership the classic definition of it. That was the truly mythopoeic power of the poem. Meanwhile, a properly mythopoeic writer, in the sense to which Eliot was gesturing, would not think of myth as a 'method' to be 'used'. Myth does not serve a vision attained by other means; it *is* the vision.

Yet Eliot was right from his point of view to resist a truly mythopoeic posture in that sense because his underlying commitment was to religious belief, even if this was not fully available to him at the time of composing *The Waste Land*. In retrospect, his use of myth in that poem can be seen as a placeholder for the religious faith so memorably explored in *Ash Wednesday* (1930) and *Four Quartets* (1935–42). The *Four Quartets* are poems of spiritual struggle and quest rather than expressions of secure faith, and by the same token an appreciation of them is not contingent on the reader's belief. They share the methods, and the great themes, of other modernist literature while giving them a religious inflection. As meditations on the overcoming of time, and the meaning of history, they invoke Augustinian intuitions of the eternal to define their version of the mythic spatializing of time explicated by Joseph Frank (1963) in a classic essay on spatial form as a defining feature of modernism. They also invoke artistic creation, and poetry in particular, for insight into spiritual transcendence. Eliot's poems, in other words, share the imaginative means and preoccupations of his mythopoeic contemporaries, yet these are always in the service of keeping open the possibility of a religious vision, and there is a firm principle at stake, not merely a rhetorical extravagance, in the line from 'East Coker', 'The poetry does not matter' (Eliot,

1930, 125). Eliot always rejected the humanism and aestheticism from which, in complex transformations, the mythopoeia of other modernists, such as James Joyce, Thomas Mann or the later W. B. Yeats, was derived.

Modernism after Religion

As has already been suggested, Joyce's *Ulysses*, perhaps the classic work of European modernism, did adopt, in as ostentatious a manner as could be imagined, a mythopoeic posture on the Nietzschean aesthetic model. Despite its rich elements of satire, and of sober realism, it is a secular celebration of man as the linguistic and cultural animal. In doing so, it sees the contemporary world through a lens of timelessly mythic values and concerns. The impact of the Homeric parallel, as a ghostly presence to the reader rather than a literal reality to the characters, is to focus, within the apparently random passage of their single modern day, a transhistorical pattern in their lives. Most importantly for the present theme, however, Joyce articulated his understanding of the aesthetic by using traditionally theological terms to which he gave newly secular meanings. Once again, while this might seem simply to downgrade the religious tradition, it also honours it in so far as theological tradition is recognized as the historical form in which spiritual experience has been most subtly and intimately mapped. And so the Joycean artist, as defined in *A Portrait of the Artist as a Young Man* (1916), is the 'priest of the eternal imagination' (Joyce, 1964, 221) who presents the world not *sub specie aeternitatis* (from the point of view of eternity) but from the standpoint *temporis nostri* (of our own time). Joyce makes very explicit the supersession of religion by art.

Yet the slow death of religion can take a variety of forms. It may be that the infrastructure of social and rhetorical conventions stays in place while the faith itself is almost unconsciously abandoned. Hence the predicament of the Anglican church in modern Britain as it maintains its established status in an increasingly secular, humanist, inclusive and quasi-democratic social order to which it has largely accommodated. More darkly, the ostensible belief may be a way of granting authority to social order so that religion is not only, as in Marx's phrase, the 'opiate of the people' but also the alibi of the powerful.[2] Nietzsche, again anticipating a central modernist theme, thought that power was a primary, if largely unacknowledged, motive of human action and that the central problem of modernity was its implicit and *de facto* nihilism. The mischief of this condition lay partly in its being so unconscious, or actively denied. He is famously associated with the declaration that 'God is dead' but in *The Gay Science* this statement is attributed to a madman who appears in the marketplace in the bright morning hours with a lantern (Nietzsche, 1974, 181). The image suggests a momentous recognition that cannot be communicated to those who cannot, or will not, hear. We cannot tell, moreover, whether the man is really mad or is only perceived as such by the incomprehending populace. And if he is mad, is this the result of being the solitary bearer of such a shattering truth, a truth which is deranging rather than deranged? The image renders at once a seismic shift in world view and the general unconsciousness with which ordinary life goes on.

The God-shaped Hole

A comparable duality can manifest itself as a temporal process in the lives of individuals. Loss of faith is often an immensely painful and anxious process, and especially so for those who have personal and spiritual gravitas, yet when it is finally over it may come to seem entirely inconsequential. The great metaphysical drama dwindles to a trite illusion. But this may take some time and the period from the late nineteenth to the late twentieth century enacts this protracted process on a cultural, historical scale. Fyodor Dostoevsky's novel *The Brothers Karamazov* (1880) is a classic expression of the abyssal recognition faced by Nietzsche's madman. For the profoundly thoughtful Ivan Karamazov it is horrifying to acknowledge that, without God, 'All is permitted', that there are no moral restraints, while his illegitimate, and intellectually trivial, half-brother enacts quite literally the nihilism which for Ivan would remain only in the realm of philosophical speculation. As in Nietzsche, the culture is practically infected by nihilism even though those who really recognize it are very few, and they are likely to be the least dangerous in themselves yet with incalculable effects on others. In that respect, Ivan's influence is an image of the uses to which Nietzsche's own thought was to be put in the twentieth century. *The Brothers Karamazov* is an epochal book, registering a shock which is hard to imagine occurring with the same force in the twentieth century. Individuals still lose their faith, but their stories are unlikely to have a comparably tragic and representative resonance for their readers. Twentieth-century writing is more typically the exploration of aftermath, whether by nostalgia for filling what Salman Rushdie has called the 'god-shaped hole' or by exploring the new moral landscape that is revealed.[3]

The desire to fill the 'god-shaped hole' was evident in the immense late nineteenth-century interest in theosophical and hermetic tradition, and in the approach to the supernatural by extra-religious means such as séances, ghosts or automatic writing. W. B. Yeats, who came to maturity in this period, is a striking instance of a major modern poet deeply committed to all these interests. More particularly, as in the Society for Psychical Research, founded in 1882, there was a desire to bring such putative experience of the supernatural within scientific protocols. Examining instances of mediumship or photographs of supernatural beings may have had the mixed motives of exposure and vindication, but both intentions acknowledged the authority of science. Conversely, August Comte, in promoting the secular and scientific social order of Positivism, thought it would need the ceremonial forms and imagery of religion to make it popularly acceptable. Meanwhile, the new products of scientific advance, such as the radio and the phonograph, had initially an aura of the supernatural about them in making it possible to hear the voices of the absent or the dead. Rudyard Kipling's story 'Wireless' (1902) catches the spirit of this. But people adjust readily enough to new technologies and the dominant spirit of the modernist generation was an astringent critique of such religiose nostalgias. Joyce mocks the hermetic fashion of his elders in the 'Scylla and Charybdis' episode of *Ulysses*, while Hans Castorp's distaste for a séance in Thomas Mann's *The Magic Mountain* (1924) has a similarly epochal resonance. But while the late nineteenth century exemplifies a number of what may reasonably be interpreted as substitutions for religious beliefs or comforts, the twentieth century shows more subtle, or at least less obvious, modes of continuance. What this phase of modernity often struggles to maintain is not a religious content but the god-shaped hole itself.

For the serious believer, loss of faith is a great metaphysical drama in which eternity is at stake. Pascal's wager and Dostoevsky's anguished characters are notable instances. But when religious faith departs it eventually takes with it the sense of high tragic drama surrounding the question. That is another way of explaining the turn to myth at this time, as a dramatic necessity rather than a philosophical posture. In *The Waste Land*, as much as in *Ulysses*, D. H. Lawrence's *The Rainbow*, Yeats's Irish legends or Marcel Proust's lost paradise, the myth provides a context of cosmic drama within which the, often quite everyday, action is played out. Hence, in some highly secular writers, there is a nostalgia, not for religious belief, but for the order of significance that belief once enabled. The classic and influential example of this for the modernist generation was Gustave Flaubert.

Flaubert was a nihilist, but also a romantic imbued with immortal longings. In Augustinian tradition man was created with a desire for the infinite which could only be satisfied by God. Flaubert was the great exponent, and analyst, of that form of romanticism in which this psychological structure persists but without belief in the divine, the one object by which the desire for the infinite could be assuaged. At the same time, as a romantic, he saw that this longing, albeit illusory, gave dignity to a human existence. The saving feature of Emma Bovary, however deluded, is that, in contrast to almost everyone around her, she feels this longing. Moreover, Flaubert, like Joyce later, recognized that in European tradition this predicament of unassuageable desire found its most profound and lucid definition in religious terms. Like a number of subsequent writers in the twentieth century, or like Pier Paolo Pasolini's film of *The Gospel of St Matthew* (1964), his tale of 'St Julien l'hospitalier' (1877) tells the miraculous and redemptive story of the saint in a factual way that leads the reader to participate in the emotions of faith without subscribing to the faith itself. The modern reader enters the tale's world of medieval belief through an evidently aesthetic suspension of disbelief, for Flaubert is a further example of art superseding religion except that in his case it is not redemptive. The extraordinary ending of the tale, in which the saint is gathered into eternity in Christ's embrace, is so moving precisely because of the incredibility of the world view it invokes. Flaubert's art constructs its complex and elegant structures of meaning only to define and intensify the nihilism of which they ultimately speak.

In the twentieth century, the atheistical invocation of cosmic drama is perhaps most striking in the existentialist writings of Albert Camus and Jean-Paul Sartre. Camus was a great admirer of Dostoevsky, and works such as *The Myth of Sisyphus* (1942) and *The Rebel* (1951) turn on a sense of man as victim of injustice for which a divine perpetrator is required. He draws on classical and mythic figures such as Sisyphus but the underlying emotional structure is surely that of a reversed Christianity inherited through the medium of Dostoevsky. Camus's cosmic revolt appealed especially to the young as it takes a while to notice how much it depends on what Raymond Williams would call a 'structure of feeling' ultimately derived from a religious loss. If in Camus these lines of inheritance are relatively clear, in Sartre they are more complexly involved with formal philosophical argument, but the essential structure of Flaubertian post-religious tradition can be seen in a novel such as *Nausea* (1938). The central character, Roquentin, contemplates a chestnut tree root which, unlike Yeats's 'great-rooted blossomer', gives him a vision of complete absence of meaning and purpose until he is transformed in some measure, albeit a little unconvincingly perhaps, by listening to a black woman jazz singer. The book is powered by a mood and, along with the specific psychological condition of Roquentin and the general historical context of post-war France, the novel's underlying world view surely reflects a phase in the loss of religious significance. Matthew Arnold in his poem 'Dover Beach' (1867) had predicted the slow ebbing of the tide of belief and in Roquentin that ebb can be felt in its horrified revelation of pure matter bereft of meaning.

But if the cosmic drama of the existentialist generation depends on the residual power of a religion which is ostensibly being denied, Samuel Beckett, particularly in the plays and novels which first made his name iconic of a presumed world view, offers a more self-conscious and ironic handling of the conflict between these two necessities: he keeps a sense of the cosmic drama associated with religious belief while undercutting the melodrama from which its loss is virtually inseparable. This has, however, made his tone or implication elusive and ambiguous. In *Endgame* (1957), Hamm says of God 'The bastard! He does not exist' (Beckett, 1958, 55). The remark is finely poised between invoking the cosmic significance invested in the notion of God, which is a necessity of the piece, while stripping His stated non-existence of its tragic overtones. The danger here is of reading such moments too much in the existentialist tragic mode of Camus, who maintains such a divine opponent for the purpose of his humane rebellion. When Beckett first became well known in the 1960s, and was given the Nobel Prize, there was a widespread tendency to read through the pessimistic foreground of his works and to praise the spirit of humane endurance in such formulations as 'You must go on. I can't go on, I'll go on' (Beckett, 1959, 418). The urge to find a recuperative or redemptive reading is irrepressible. But in his case the underlying dynamic is perhaps the other way round. All the grand cosmic attitudes are parodied and rejected but they have to be invoked in order to achieve that purpose. The continuing artistic struggle, therefore, is rather for a mode of resistance to the redemptive sentiment for which he found himself being celebrated. He is a striking instance of the maintenance of the god-shaped hole for essentially dramatic purposes, almost as a stage property. There may be an inescapable double bind here, however, in that the affirmative reading can never be completely excluded. Maybe that is a contributory reason for his turn to increasingly abstract and minimalist forms in his later years.

Religion Rediscovered

As was suggested in relation to William James, an ironic by-product of general secularization is sometimes to throw a searching, and eventually positive, light on the significance of religion in human life. As well as those, like Eliot, who turn to a traditional form of religion, there are others who, while rejecting inherited religious belief, rediscover an essentially religious relation to the world. They affirm a primordial mode of feeling and response which may be the ancestor of the religion they reject. Most importantly, such a conception generally rejects any idea of the supernatural in order to understand religion as a mode of relation to the natural world. At this point the category of religion begins, analytically speaking, to merge with that of myth but it makes sense to speak of it as religious in so far as it underwrites a form of life centred on a sense of reverence. If for a writer like Arnold, in his summative and analytic mode, we could say that religion rests on myth, for these other writers, with their intense concentration on the mystery of Being, we might say that myth rests on religion. We read them not for any general idea or philosophy that could be drawn from them, but for their exemplary responsiveness to the world. Two notable instances are Rainer Maria Rilke and D. H. Lawrence.

Rilke's *Duino Elegies* (1912–22), like Eliot's *Four Quartets*, are an extraordinary expression of religious consciousness in modernity although, unlike Eliot, Rilke seeks only a this-worldly understanding. Hence, in his case, the poetry really does matter. For him, as for many modern writers, poetry is not, as Alexander Pope put it, merely the dress of thought but its body.[4] That is to say, there is no pre-existing idea or reality that the language of poetry expresses and which could be encountered by other means; it is itself the process of exploration through concrete metaphors which is the nearest we can come to the kind of insight that is in question. Hence, for example, the knowledge of mortality and providing ways of facing it constitute a significant part of religion. Rilke's tenth elegy speaks of a 'City of Pain' populated by those who have died. It has echoes of the classical Greek and Roman underworlds, which help to locate its significance while keeping it remote from Christian habits of thought and feeling. Yet neither does it quite fit the classical world view either for it is evidently focused on a modification of sensibility for living in this world rather than imagining another. Indeed, it is always the case, when a culture's view of the afterlife is considered in an anthropological spirit, that it unconsciously reveals the values and assumptions of this-worldly life in the culture concerned. Rilke quite consciously uses the image of the afterlife in this spirit. Susan Sontag's *Illness as Metaphor* (1978), itself a critique of modern secular attitudes to mortality, argues that all human beings carry two passports, one for the land of the well and the other for the land of the sick. She meant that even quite a short period of debilitating illness or pain places one as if in a different world in which the well are strangely defamiliarized precisely in their unconsciousness of being so. Likewise, Rilke's 'City of Pain' is not a statement about the afterlife but, like a photographic negative, it sees the present world in an unfamiliar way, evacuated of its usual substance, and yet, as one begins to realize with a gradual adjustment of vision, it is in some sense an equally true record.

The philosopher Martin Heidegger sought contemporaneously to articulate a comparable sense of Being, and with a revealing sense of struggle. For his philosophical discourse is notoriously difficult and controversial, such that even sympathetic readers can flicker between acknowledging him as the major philosopher of the twentieth century and dismissing him as an unwitting charlatan buoyed up by his own obfuscatory jargon. In his later years he wrote remarkable essays on poetry, language and thought in which he drew on passages of poetry, most notably from Friedrich Hölderlin and Georg Trakl, to instantiate his meditations on Being; and his own mode of thought in these essays was poetic as much as rational, drawing insight from the associations and derivations of words. He also drew on Rilke, whose poetry could well be adduced in forming a judgement about Heidegger's own ultimate substance and significance.[5] Heidegger and Rilke share a response to the world which is just as remote and incomprehensible from modern, secular, instrumental positivism as is the traditional religion it confidently rejects. Or otherwise expressed, the overlap between Rilke and Heidegger invokes a lengthy poetic and philosophical tradition which critiques the optimistic rationality of Enlightenment by reconstituting a form of religious consciousness.

D. H. Lawrence shared much of the sense of Being exemplified in Rilke or articulated in Heidegger but was more explicit in defining his outlook as religious. Having been quite pious in his boyhood and youth, he grew out of his Christian faith but continued to see himself as 'a passionately religious man' (Lawrence, 1981, 165). *The Rainbow* (1915) was the first novel to express his fully mature world view and, not incidentally perhaps, it encompasses a philosophical and psychological analysis of the place of religion in modern life. As a family saga covering more than three generations of the Brangwens, its narrative extends from the late eighteenth century to the beginning of the twentieth century. But it also invokes a much longer span of time with a continuing impact within this historical period. With its central image of the rainbow and its setting in Marsh farm, the novel places its history within two rival myths of origin, the biblical and the Darwinian. The story of the fall and loss of Eden is in tension with the progressive vision commonly associated with Darwinian evolution. The blend of biblical and evolutionary discourse throughout the novel corresponds for Lawrence to the two major psychological impulses felt, in varying proportions, by all his characters. In the opening movement of the novel, the Brangwen men are exhausted but largely fulfilled by the daily and seasonal round of farming life, while the women look to a larger world of education and culture. It soon becomes clear, however, that this apparently gendered contrast points to the double motive in all the characters as they struggle to develop as individuals without losing a sense of rootedness and relatedness. In the final generation, the central character, Ursula Brangwen, who has been deeply affected by her pious father from whom she has gradually distanced herself, has a vision of the rainbow. She is now completely secular but retains the religious impulse of her ancestors as an intuitive trust in life.[6]

In this respect, *The Rainbow* is an instructive contrast to Emile Durkheim's *The Elementary Forms of the Religious Life*, also published in 1915. As the title suggests, Durkheim, a French social anthropologist, was likewise concerned to penetrate beneath the complex cultural forms of religion to discern its essential nature and concluded that it is the symbolic expression of the social instinct. The etymological derivation of the word 'religion' suggests a binding or linking and for Durkheim it is what binds human beings together; it is the ligaments, so to speak, of the social body. In Lawrence, the primary connection is of the individual to the natural world and the cosmos, with the social dimension accorded a secondary and problematic status in the order of human values. For Lawrence, to experience 'true relatedness' was the supreme goal of a human life, and it included relation to other human beings, but only as part of a relation to the world and to the myriad other beings with which we share it. Relationship, for him, was not closeness, but respect for difference, which was why he invoked the imagined lives of animals and even plants. It was not because he thought he could understand these other beings but precisely to experience their irreducible strangeness. Yet they are our *fellow* creatures, for difference can only be experienced in relationship just as meaningful relationship is founded on difference. It was such a sense of difference that he thought lacking in contemporary human relations and it was likely to be achieved only as part of a proper relation to the world and its creatures. Like Ursula's father, Will Brangwen, the inherited religion projects a mystery on to the supernatural, while for Lawrence there is mystery enough in every creature encountered on the earth. Religion for him is the mystery of Being which he called 'the fourth dimension' (Lawrence, 1988, 361).

During his last five years, Lawrence was terminally ill and, despite his refusal to acknowledge this in his daily life, his poetry records a preparation for death which can be placed alongside the *Four Quartets* and the *Duino Elegies* as a supreme instance of modern religious expression. He visited the Etruscan tombs and was deeply impressed by an early form of life very different from the ancient Mexican religion he had imagined being revived in *The Plumed Serpent* (1926). Having returned to Europe, and specifically to Italy, he was horrified by its turn to fascism. Lawrence, the greatest modern primitivist in the sense of drawing from archaic and tribal cultures, gestures in his writing towards what is still primordial and necessary in human life. For the same reason, however, he was the most significant critic of modern primitivism as a sentimental indulgence. Fascism was such an *ersatz* primitivist religion, invoking the ancient Roman state which, as Lawrence pointed out, had wiped out the Etruscan civilization which was its superior in living responsiveness. If the vision of the afterlife is most truly a revelation of this-worldly values in a culture, then the tombs of the Etruscans showed their instinct for a delicately vital relation to the world and to each other.

Lawrence drew on his encounter with the Etruscan tombs in poems contemplating his own death which he approached as the last great experience, and responsibility, of life. In the ages of faith a good death was the culmination of a good life and it could acquire the value of a willed act by the dying person's spiritual preparation. In 'Bavarian Gentians' and 'Ship of Death', composed shortly before his death in 1930, Lawrence imagined actively descending into the darkness or being carried away on a vessel of his own construction. As in Rilke, there is no transcendence into a supernatural domain, only a set of images irradiated by an intense psychological quest and the acceptance of imminent dissolution within a reverential trust in life.

Conclusion?

As might already be deduced from Freud's *The Future of an Illusion*, the perdurance of religion in modernity, at least for non-believers who do not accept the simpler explanations, is a mystery in itself. It may be that religion is destined slowly to disappear. But it may also be that modernity will come to recognize the religious deficit hinted at by some of the great early twentieth-century writers. The contemporary problem of environmental damage and climate change, for example, can be approached in purely technical terms or it can be seen as the symptom of a radically unhealthy mode of being in the world. Heidegger and Lawrence would say that, even if the effects could be moderated to a point of sustainability, the most essential damage is already done by having an attitude of instrumental rapacity towards the world.

Likewise, if art has in some sense moved into the place of religion this is by creating an especially intense and privileged interpersonal arena for the realization and critique of fundamental values. But the extent to which it can create such values is open to question and the relatively increased prestige of art may have served to obfuscate the underlying religious deficit. Hence, while the Punch and Judy show of atheists versus bishops will doubtless continue its long and popular run in public life, the true action is likely to be elsewhere. It may become apparent, for example, that some sense of reverence is a moral necessity for individual and collective human life; and atheists should after all treat the Deity with some respect since the invention of God is an important step towards the invention of the human. In Goethe's late novel *Wilhelm Meister's Years of Travel* (1829), a work that was already modernist before its time, Wilhelm's son attends a Pedagogical Province in which the pupils make not the sign of the cross, but a three-stage gesture indicating in turn reverence for what is above them, for the earth beneath them and for the social realm before them. Each boy acknowledges, as Lawrence said of the early Brangwen farmer, 'something standing above him and beyond him in the distance' (Lawrence, 1989, 9). The religious gesture is at once centrally important and yet deliberately indeterminate with respect to any particular belief. So too, just as literary modernism took a while to catch up formally with Goethe's novel, it may be that modernity will eventually come to acknowledge a mode of being that accommodates the religious impulse, not just as a tolerated anachronism but as a living necessity.

Notes

1   This complex subject is treated at length in Michael Bell, *Literature, Modernism and Myth: Belief and Responsibility in the Twentieth Century* (1997).
2   The phrase is used in Marx's Introduction to his *Contribution to Critique of Hegel's Philosophy of Right* (1843).
3   The meaning of this expression is developed in the opening chapter of Salman Rushdie's *Midnight's Children* (1982, 10–23), although the actual phrase is not used on this occasion.
4   '*True Wit* is *Nature*, to Advantage drest, / What oft was *Thought* but ne'er so well *Exprest*'. *Essay in Criticism* (1714), ll. 297–8 (Pope, 1961, 272–3).
5   See especially Heidegger's 'What Are Poets For?' (1971).
6   For a fuller treatment of this aspect of *The Rainbow*, see Bell (1992, 51–96).

Bibliography

Beckett, S. (1958), *Endgame*. New York, Grove Press.

Beckett, S. (1959), *Molloy, Malone Dies, The Unnamable*. London: Calder and Boyars.

Bell, M. (1992), *D. H. Lawrence: Language and Being*. Cambridge: Cambridge University Press.

Bell, M. (1997), *Literature, Modernism and Myth: Belief and Responsibility in the Twentieth Century*. Cambridge: Cambridge University Press.

Eliot, T. S. (1923), 'Ulysses, Order and Myth'. *Dial*, 75, 483.

Eliot, T. S. (1930), *The Complete Poems and Plays of T. S. Eliot*. New York: Harcourt, Brace and World.

Frank, J. (1963), 'Spatial Form in Modern Literature', in *The Widening Gyre, Crisis and Mastery in Modern Literature*. New Brunswick, NJ: Rutgers University Press.

Heidegger, M. (1971), 'What Are Poets For?', in A. Hofstadter (transl.), *Poetry, Language, Thought*. New York: Harper & Row.

Joyce, J. (1964), *A Portrait of the Artist as a Young Man*. New York: Viking Press.

Lawrence, D. H. (1981), *The Letters of D. H. Lawrence*, G. J. Zytaruk and J. T. Boulton (eds). Cambridge: Cambridge University Press.

Lawrence, D. H. (1988), *Reflections of the Death of a Porcupine and Other Essays*, M. Herbert (ed.). Cambridge: Cambridge University Press.

Lawrence, D. H. (1989), *The Rainbow*, Mark Kinkead-Weekes (ed.). Cambridge: Cambridge University Press.

Nietzsche, F. (1974), *The Gay Science*, Walter Kaufmann (transl.). New York: Random House.

Pope, A. (1961), 'Essays in Criticism' (1714), in E. Audra and Aubrey Williams (eds), *Pastoral Poetry and An Essay on Criticism (The Twickenham Edition of the Poems of Alexander Pope, Vol. I)*. London: Methuen and New Haven: Yale University Press.

Rushdie, S. (1982), *Midnight's Children*. London: Picador.

Schelling, F. W. J. (1993 [1800]), *System of Transcendental Idealism*. Charlottesville, VA: University of Virginia Press.

Schlegel, F. (1968 [1800]), *Dialogue on Poetry and Literary Aphorisms*, E. Behler and R. Struc (transl.). Philadelphia, PA: Pennsylvania State University Press.

Vickery, J. B. (1973), *The Literary Impact of the Golden Bough*. Princeton, NJ: Princeton University Press.

The Arts and Cultures of
Modernism

7

Modernism and Music

Tim Armstrong

Music has often been a privileged vehicle for understandings of modernism. Important moments of rupture were frequently musical: the shock of the first performance of *Rite of Spring* in Paris in 1913, with its savage strummings and rapid shifts in time signature; the raucous Futurist sound machines, the *intonarumori*, on the stage of the Coliseum in London in 1914; the scandal of Jean Cocteau's ballet *Parade* in Paris in 1917, with its music by Eric Satie and designs by Picasso; the megaphonic chanting of Edith Sitwell's near-nonsense to William Walton's eccentric orchestra in *Façade* in1923; jazz as 'noise emancipated' – Walter Benjamin's term – an emblem of the nervous polyrhythms of the modern world, carried from America to Europe (Benjamin, 1999, 862).

The reasons for this prominence are twofold. First, with its stress on formal development across the centuries, and particularly in its internalized notions of development in sonata form, and its reliance on explicit codes of expression, music provides a place where breaks in form are easily marked. Musical modernism shifts away from melody and the tonic-dominant system, either towards the distributed, abstract mathematical values of the twelve-note system or even more disruptively towards noise itself, sound rather than notes. Second, the sonic world's status as inescapable impulse – we absorb it with our bodies; we cannot turn away or shut our ears to it (see Connor, 1996) – reflects the modernist preoccupation with embodied aesthetics. This allies music to modernism's depiction of somatic experience and streams of consciousness, and at times to its recourse to primitivism.

In terms of the relations between literature and music, the situation is of course more complex: music provides both an external point of reference and an aesthetic; it can appear within the work's reality or inform its modes of writing and representation. Rather than language aspiring to the condition of music, as in the tradition which descends from Walter Pater and Stephane Mallarmé, modernism often reaches towards a dynamic multimedia mapping of the senses in the tradition of Richard Wagner's *Gesamkunstwerk*; or equally their aggressive juxtaposition, sound and sight clashing, as in Sergei Eisenstein's understanding of montage and sound film (for a general account, see Halliday, 2013). But within that sensory paradigm, music nonetheless has a privileged role because of its ambiguous status, at once close to or 'like' a language – a highly formal one with inbuilt codes and expectations – but also the direct carrier of feeling. To that can be added a further complication: in the twentieth century music becomes increasingly bound to the productive and reproductive technologies which epitomize modernity: to the player-piano, gramophone, radio, and cinema. Modernist performance often demanded new technologies: *Façade*, the piece with music by William Walton set to chanted poems by Edith Sitwell, first performed in 1922, employed a Sengerphone (a papier-mâché megaphone that also covered the nasal cavities, producing a more natural tone). Igor Stravinsky and later the American composer Conlon Nancarrow used the player-piano to produce music so fast that no human player could readily play it; Bohuslav Martinů, Oliver Messiaen and others used the Theremin, an early electronic instrument with toneless gradations.

For Theodor Adorno in 'Music, Language and Composition' (1956), music transcends the tension between expression and form because it aspires to a directness of communication which distances it from language while remaining related to it (Adorno, 2002, 113–26). It is for similar reasons that modern artworks have often found in music a model for an organized synthesis of motifs which seem disparate, intermittent or even baffling. The drift of music, in Satie, Arnold Schoenberg, Alban Berg and Anton Webern, towards atonality, dissonance or sparseness and silence (Satie's 'white ballet') mirrors modernism's suspicion of representation and expression. In his 'German letter' to Axel Kaun of 1937, Samuel Beckett describes music as an avant-garde that, in this respect, literature has failed to match:

> As we cannot eliminate language all at once, we should at least leave nothing undone that might contribute to its falling into disrepute. To bore one hole after another in it, until what lurks behind it – be it something or nothing – begins to seep through; I cannot imagine a higher goal for a writer today. Or is literature alone to remain behind in the old lazy ways that have been so long ago abandoned by music and painting? [...] Is there any reason why that terrible materiality of the word surface should not be capable of being dissolved, like for example the sound surface, torn by enormous pauses, of Beethoven's seventh

Symphony, so that through whole pages we can perceive nothing but a path of sounds suspended in giddy heights, linking unfathomable abysses of silence? (Beckett, 1983, 172)

For similar reasons, for Adorno music emblematizes the general problem of the continuation of the avant-garde: in his 1955 essay 'The Aging of the New Music', he attacks Schoenberg's followers in the use of twelve-tone technique for its decline into 'abstract negation' (Adorno, 2002, 187), an arid formalism in which its innovations no longer shock; no longer demonstrate a dialectical relation to the social milieu which produces them.

The Question of the Avant-Garde

At the beginning of the modernist experiment in London, at least, the question of what music would have to contribute to the avant-garde was less certain than it later was for Adorno, given the power of art as a point of reference. In *Antheil and the Treatise on Harmony* (1924), Ezra Pound notes that 'The Vorticist Manifestos of 1913–14 left a blank space for music; there was in contemporary music, at that date, nothing corresponding to the work of Wyndham Lewis, Pablo Picasso, or Gaudier-Brzeska' (Pound, 1927, 37). Pound, whose output as a music critic is considerable, became interested in music as modernist practice largely in the period after 1920. His definition of the chord as a 'complex of sound' (40) and his talk of George Antheil's '"decomposition" of the musical atom' (148) bring music into a general alignment with Vorticism, but Pound also insists that poetry must learn from music a multisensory rhythmic complexity so that it 'becomes not only aware of that given form, but more sensitive to other forms, rhythms, defined planes, or masses. It is a scaling of eye-balls, a castigating or purging of aural cortices; a sharpening of verbal apperceptions' (44). Pound's theory of the 'Great Bass' asserts a connection between pitch and rhythm which unifies notions of structure in different analytic frames:

> Down below the lowest note synthesized by the ear and 'heard' there are slower vibrations. The ratio between these frequencies and those written to be executed by instruments is OBVIOUS in mathematics. The whole question of tempo, and of a main base in all musical structure resides in use of these frequencies. (Pound, 1966, 73)

The drive here is towards a synthesis of different senses and artistic modes. As Brad Bucknell argues, this parallels the Vorticist stress on relations between elements rather than things in themselves (Bucknell, 2001, 74), but also between differently scaled modes of analysis like the *Cantos* considered as locally related fragments on the one hand and the overall structure of the poem on the other hand.

Pound was careful to rule out both Stravinsky and the Italian Futurists from his account of modernist music. Nevertheless, the Futurists, seeking to reform all areas of art, were (as Douglas Kahn [1999] and others have argued) part of a crucial musical shift away from music towards the values of noise, of a liberation from the restrictions of the chromatic scale. In 'The Art of Noises: Futurist Manifesto' (1913, rev. 1916), Luigi Russolo proposes a new music for two reasons: first, a boredom with the values of traditional classical music, and a restless search for new stimulation; second because noise represents the 'clamour' of a technological society, 'the throbbing of valves, the pounding of pistons, the screeching of gears, the clatter of streetcars' (Albright, 2004, 180). Because noise is attached to the life process, it 'is familiar to our ears and has the power to remind us immediately of life itself' in its irregularity; it is not detached from life as music is (81). In a similar manner, the American Henry Cowell and the Australian Percy Grainger advocated the use of tone rows and glissandi (what Grainger called 'free music') detached from the musical scale, and later composers like Anteil incorporated noisemakers into their output.

The composer and pianist who often represented modernity in popular imagination was not Russolo, Stravinsky or even Antheil, but the largely forgotten Leo Ornstein, an emigrant from the Ukraine to the United States. His American recitals were packed; 1914 London performances of work by Busoni, himself and others, pioneering the use of tone clusters (a large block of adjacent notes played at once), were described as 'Futurist'; his reputation reached as far as Australia. Works like 'Wild Men's Dance' and 'Suicide in an Airplane', all composed before 1920, influenced later composers like Cowell, Antheil and Nancarrow – although Ornstein himself burned out and faded in the early twenties. The tone cluster had some European progenitors, in the main being used to register the dissonance of battle. But as it developed more systematically it was associated especially with Americans: Charles Ives, Scott Joplin, Cowell and later Lou Harrison. Its layering of slabs of almost inevitably dissonant sound (adjacent notes hit in groups, sometimes with padded bars) signals rupture of the kind that Beckett celebrated, but also a return to nature: roars; cliffs of sounds; primitive blows. Once again it represented a break with musical tradition, especially in relation to the tradition of melody and counterpoint and the values associated with the single note and the selective action of the hand in its trained interaction with the complexity of the piano.

While it is not possible to translate the values of such musical revolution directly into literature, one can see in the general modernist stress on rhythm, noise, and the word as impulse some suggestive parallels. Blocks of sound, layers of words rather than metrical development, are intrinsic to the methodology of Pound, Marianne Moore, William Carlos Williams and the poets who follow them; the layered noise of language in *Finnegans Wake* (1939) – a work full of both natural music, onomatopoeic thunder, and reference to opera and other musical forms – is, Joyce asserted, 'pure music' (Prieto, 2002, 63).

Many manifestos of modernist music also share the modernist suspicion of genre and indeed of the parameters of established music: harmony and counterpoint; the scale itself, attacked in compositions which use micro-scales or, like Russolo's Futurist scores, graphed as continuous frequency maps of tonal shifts rather than steps and intervals. Commentators on jazz often insisted that standard musical notation could not deal with its melodic and rhythmic complexity, noting the use of rubato (shifts in tempo), syncopation, glissandi and melisma to bend the standards which were at the core of the repertoire (see, for example, Ernest Ansermet, 'On a Negro Orchestra' [1919], in Albright, 2004, 368–73). As Sam Halliday notes, modernism in music encompasses a range of features: tonality and the chromatic scale, pitch, rhythm and instrumentation were all involved (Halliday, 2013, 134). The musical collage and layering of composers like Charles Ives – who literally figures the collision of different kinds of music in his work – the incorporation of ragtime and jazz in the work of Claude Debussy, Ernst Krenek, Dmitri Shostakovich and others; such qualities link music to modernist aesthetics in the visual field.

There is less space here for other aspects of music in the period which should nevertheless be noted. One is the relation between music and the market – fostering, Mark Katz suggests, a stress on trademark style and difference in performances of classical music, a version of the genius as publicist also present in modernist literature (Katz, 2004; Rainey, 1998). In Adorno's view, music that exists outside the developmental logic of the Western tradition is barely worthy of attention. But the globalization which is a central aspect of the modern world brings a variety of musical traditions into Western tradition, whether the American Spirituals used by Antonín Dvořák or the gamelan used by Debussy, Poulenc and Hindemith. Styles swirl and mix: to take one small example, the steel guitar developed in Hawaii around the turn of the century and later transferred to the American mainland may have been inspired by a combination of Portuguese and Indian immigrants using the steel-slide technique of Indian instruments like the *gottuvadyam*. Modernism incorporates these elements, at times, under the heading of primitivism, but because notes are not marked as quotations in the way that literary interpolations are, one might argue that music more quickly develops a dialogue with the forms it imports – as indeed do poly-vocal texts which operate under the sign of music, like *Finnegans Wake*.

Schopenhauer and the Stream of Consciousness

We can pursue a particular aspect of music, its linkage to embodied experience. For Arthur Schopenhauer (1788–1860) in *The World as Will and Idea* (1819), music offers a privileged access to the individual will, the true source of knowledge of the Will which is the fundamental truth of existence. Music carries the pulse of the Will, not as a representation but as a direct transcription of being itself:

> Music is as direct an objectification and copy of the whole will as the world itself, nay, even as the Ideas, whose multiplied manifestation constitutes the world of individual things. Music is thus by no means like the other arts, the copy of the Ideas, but the *copy of the will itself*, whose objectivity the Ideas are. This is why the effect of music is so much more powerful and penetrating than that of the other arts, for they speak only of shadows, but it speaks of the thing itself. (Schopenhauer, 1909, I 333)

Schopenhauer's thinking on music – on the status of the soprano, tenor and bass parts, on the reconciliation of harmony and melody – is complex, especially when he returns to the subject in Chapter 39 of the third volume of his study 'On the Metaphysics of Music', and elaborates on the alternation of mood and form in music as they relate to the Will:

> Thus, in general, music consists of a constant succession of more or less disquieting chords, i.e., chords which excite longing, and more or less quieting and satisfying chords; just as the life of the heart (the will) is a constant succession of greater or less disquietude through desire and aversion, and just as various degrees of relief. Accordingly the harmonious sequence of chords consists of the correct alternation of dissonance and consonance. A succession of merely consonant chords would be satiating, wearisome, and empty, like the languor produced by the satisfaction of all wishes. Therefore dissonances must be introduced, although they disquiet us and affect us almost painfully, but only in order to be resolved again in consonances with proper preparation.

Indeed, in the whole of music there are really only two fundamental chords, the dissonant chord of the seventh and the consonant triad, to which all chords that occur can be referred. This just corresponds to the fact, that for the will there are at bottom only dissatisfaction and satisfaction, under however many forms they may present themselves. And as there are two general fundamental moods of the mind, serenity, or at least healthiness, and sadness, or even oppression, so music has two general keys, the major and the minor (Schopenhauer, 1909, III 243)

Music here, when the listener opens her mind to it, is a schooling in the possibilities of existence (and in some senses in the ethics of accommodation), as well as the representation of the particular struggles of the composer. Schopenhauer writes that the individual will is itself like a musical responder, 'the trembling string that is stretched and twanged' (Schopenhauer, 1909, III 237).

Schopenhauer's thought on music reached English readers via interpreters such as Francis Heuffer (father of Ford Madox Ford) and H. R. Haweis, informing the 'Wagner mania' of the late 1870s and 1880s. But a more potent influence for the novel, I would argue, is the link between his vitalism and accounts of the stream of consciousness: if we seek to represent a flow of experience in which the world is perceived in terms of the various embodied intensities of perception and memory, music as conceived by Schopenhauer provides a model. Indeed, as Eric Prieto argues, the reception of Schopenhauer's thinking in Wagner influences developing ideas of interior monologue, most importantly in Edouard Dujardin's description of the method of his 1888 novel *Les lauriers sont coupés*, which was in turn a crucial influence on Joyce:

> Dujardin bases his analogy between the Wagnerian leitmotiv and the interior-monologue technique on a simple empirical observation: the substance of thought is, like the sound stream of a melody, unidirectional (i.e., running continuously in time), but the content of thought is full of motivic recurrences [...] Joyce, building on Dujardin's theory of the interior monologue, also equates music with thought processes when he invokes the model of musical counterpoint for the 'Sirens' chapter of *Ulysses*. The counterpoint analogy, like Dujardin's leitmotiv analogy, depends on a basic empirical observation, that of the mind's ability to operate on several stimuli at the same time. (Prieto, 2002, 62)

I will return to this topic shortly, but it is worth noticing that Schopenhauer's thinking can also influence accounts of poetry as a kind of pure experience. Wallace Stevens read Schopenhauer with approval as a young man, returning to his philosophy in his essay 'A Collect of Philosophy' (1951). He refers to music again and again in his poetry: as a marker of the sounds of existence, and as a human making which responds to that natural music. The following passage from 'Description without Place' (Stevens's 1945 Phi Beta Kappa poem at Harvard), in which he meditates on the recent war, is a deep response to Schopenhauer's understanding of music as an account of will:

> There are potential seemings, arrogant
> To be, as on the youngest poet's page,
>
> Or in the dark musician, listening
> To hear more brightly the contriving chords.
>
> There are potential seemings turbulent
> In the death of a soldier, like the utmost will,
>
> The more than human commonplace of blood,
> The breath that gushes upward and is gone,
>
> And another breath emerging out of death,
> That speaks for him such seemings as death gives.
>
> There might be, too, a change immenser than
> A poet's metaphors in which being would
>
> Come true, a point in the fire of music where
> Dazzle yields to a clarity and we observe,
>
> And observing is completing and we are content,
> In a world that shrinks to an immediate whole,
>
> That we do not need to understand, complete
> Without secret arrangements of it in the mind.   (Stevens, 1997, 298)

Schopenhauer says 'the will is warmth, the intellect is light'. 'Dazzle' signals the limitations of vision and of metaphor's perspectivism; music is the human world unmediated, as Stevens suggested a few years later in his essay 'The Whole Man: Perspectives, Horizons' (1954): 'The principle of music would be an addition to humanity if it were not humanity itself, in other than human form' (Stevens, 1997, 875). It is interesting, too, that in this poem we move from the 'contriving' of the musician – often Stevens's focus in his early work – to music as a pure listening, untouched by the discursive, as in Schopenhauer's account. Indeed, the technicalities of making music, a traditional figure for *poesis*, are often supplanted in modernist accounts by the notion of music as an absolute experience.

Stevens references recorded music on a number of occasions (see Armstrong, 2007). If music offers a transcription of being, it is one mediated by the performers of any piece; the listener hears two overlayered accounts, two histories. Recorded music, on the other hand, preserves an original historical moment and transmits it to another time. Recorded music enters modernist literature through a variety of routes: through allusions to and representations of the player-piano or gramophone, but also through tropes in which the recording of music captures the sense of a particular ineffable moment – part of an overall shift of modernism towards the conception of writing as media rather than self-expression (see Murphet, 2009).

Music and the Bildungsroman

Schoenberg and his school epitomize a musical modernity in which the narrative as exemplified by sonata form and the valuing of the tonic (associated above all with Beethoven) is abandoned, along with melody. Because of this eschewing of the developmental logic which reaches a kind of climax in the self-consciously ironic gestures of Richard Strauss's *Ein Heldenleben* (*A Hero's Life*, 1898), the relation between music and the *Bildungsroman* becomes a particularly interesting one. This is an issue on which I will focus the remainder of this chapter, using four examples of the subgenre (if it can be called that) of the music novel: in chronological order, Henry Handel Richardson's neglected 1906 masterpiece *Maurice Guest*; James Weldon Johnson's *The Autobiography of an Ex-Colored Man* (1912); Dorothy Richardson's sequence *Pilgrimage* (begun in 1915 and completed in 1935); and Thomas Mann's study of the end of modernism, *Doctor Faustus* (1947). In each case, the developmental narrative of the novel outstrips or clashes with the intensities incarnated in music, resulting in narratives of death or apocalypse, or at least a flight from musical life. Music in this sense represents one of the defining contradictions of modernism, skewed between an absolute drive towards formal innovation and a desire to derive the energies for that movement from the life process, from a vitalism whose link to the avant-garde is in fact intermittent and ultimately in tension with its historicity. This is Mann's narrator in *Doctor Faustus*, discussing the *Apocalypse*, the masterpiece of his doomed composer-friend Leverkühn, in eminently dialectical fashion:

How often has this intimidating work, in its urge to reveal in the language of music the most hidden things, the beast in man as well as his sublimest stirrings, incurred the reproach both of blood-boltered barbarism and of bloodless intellectuality! I say incurred; for its idea, in a way, is to take in the life-history of music, from its pre-musical, magic, rhythmical, elementary stage to its most complex consummation; and thus it does perhaps expose itself to such reproaches not only in part but as a whole. (Mann, 1968, 359)

'Blood-bolted barbarism' in Mann's novel is placed in historical terms outside its musical story; it takes over when the music ends, as we will shortly see.

The connection between music and passion is central to what could be described as one of the most Wagnerian novels written in English, the Australian Henry Handel Richardson's (nom de plume for Ethel Richardson's) *Maurice Guest*. Set in the world of international music students in Leipzig, *Maurice Guest* carries in the rhythms of its musical subject matter and its three movements the tempestuous *Totentanz* of its protagonists. The novel is less interested in character in the traditional sense – it cannot easily be called a Bildungsroman, and deals with a central character who in many ways remains blank, deliberately detached from his origins in an English small town, and with musical ambitions which begin strongly but carry him nowhere, abandoned in the wake of his obsession with the *femme fatale* Louise, who is in turn in love with the egoistical violinist Schilsky. Where the musical avant-garde appears in the novel, it is in the work of the bloodless and detached Schilsky, who writes apocalyptic 'Symphonic poems' in the new style: 'Zarathustra' and 'Über die letzten Dinge' (titles borrowed from Nietzsche and Otto Weininger, respectively). What drives the novel forward is less music than the play of passions and the 'values' associated with particular positions and relations, rather than with character itself, carried in a prose that often aspires to the rhythms of music. This is Maurice overhearing Louise, who is talking to Schilsky:

What she said was inaudible to him; but it was enough to be able to listen, unseen, to her voice. Hearing it like this, as something existing for itself, he was amazed at its depth and clearness; he felt that her personal presence had, until now, hindered him from appreciating a beautiful but immaterial thing at its true worth. At first, like a cadence that repeats itself, its tones rose and fell, but with more subtle inflections than the ordinary voice has: there was a note in it that might have belonged to a child's voice; another, more primitive, that betrayed feeling with as little reserve as the cry of an animal. Then it sank, and went on in a monotone, like a Hebrew prayer, as if reiterating things worn threadbare by repetition, and already said too often. Gradually, it died away in the surrounding silence. (Richardson, 1908, 150)

Maurice Guest makes the life of music less a matter of an avant-garde than it is an expression of embodied existence. Stylistically, the novel is characterized by repetition of a few set motifs – triangulated and frustrated desire, ambition, the approval of teachers – and by a setting which could almost be that of an opera – a few rooms, the cafe, the park and the concert hall. The narrative ends with a climax in which its opening motifs are echoed as the despairing and abandoned Maurice shoots himself in the breast – a walk in the woods on a raw spring day, a vision of passing clouds – and moves immediately to a coda, itself echoing and recapitulating earlier scenes in which Louise is seen from outside. This is an orchestration in which struggle is described – for long passages pain and obsession dominate, 'worn threadbare by repetition' – and only resolved in death.

Maurice Guest is an important text in relation to the link, discussed above, between stream of consciousness and an understanding of music derived from Schopenhauer and Wagner. Henry Handel Richardson's namesake Dorothy Richardson similarly uses music to carry certain values – intimacy, the pulse of being and its communication – strongly associated with her own style. *Pointed Roofs* (1915), the first volume of *Pilgrimage*, like *Maurice Guest* makes Germany the exemplary *Kulturnation*, a place of a musical seriousness and passion unknown in the protagonist's English upbringing. Miriam finds her attitudes challenged:

> Miriam's uneasiness changed insensibly to the conviction that these girls were learning in Germany not to be ashamed of 'playing with expression'. All the things she had heard Mr. Strood – who had, as the school prospectus declared, been 'educated in Leipzig' – preach and implore, 'style,' 'expression,' 'phrasing,' 'light and shade,' these girls were learning, picking up from these wonderful Germans. They did not do it quite like them though. They did not think only about the music, they thought about themselves too. Miriam believed she could do it as the Germans did. She wanted to get her own music and play it as she had always dimly known it ought to be played and hardly ever dared. (Richardson, 1979, I 45)

Later in the same chapter, she achieves just this, a moment of performance freed from self-consciousness:

> She held the chord for its full term ... Should she play any more? ... She had confessed herself ... just that minor chord ... anyone hearing it would know more than she could ever tell them ... her whole being beat out the rhythm as she waited for the end of the phrase to insist on what already had been said. As it came, she found herself sitting back, slackening the muscles of her arms

and of her whole body, and ready to swing forward into the rising storm of her page. She did not need to follow the notes on the music stand. Her fingers knew them. Grave and happy she sat with unseeing eyes, listening, for the first time. (Richardson, 1979, I 57)

That finding underlies *Pilgrimage* as a record not simply of the stream of consciousness, but of a more general opening of the novel to the rhythm of being. Listening involves an abandonment of self-consciousness akin to this 'German' service to music. But we also discover, as Miriam's pilgrimage continues, that felt life in its mundane heterogeneity is more important to her than the stricter logic of musical development – the celebration of technique, of production. Even at the very end of the sequence, music signals 'the strangeness of the adventure of being, of the fact of the existence, anywhere, of anything at all' (IV 638), rather than any consummation. The sequence has no cadenza; Miriam's life achieves no firm pattern of upward struggle, of conflict and resolution, but it does offer a confrontation of experience and, as Angela Frattarola argues, the communication of that experience, often expressed with a Schopenhauerian stoicism. At the end of *Honeycomb* (1917), the third novel of *Pilgrimage*, nursing her dying mother, Miriam dreams of her school-mate Lilla playing the piano: 'It shocked her that Lilla should know so deeply and express her lonely knowledge so ardently. Her gold-flecked brow eyes, that commonly laughed at everything, except the problem of free-will, and refused questions, had as much sorrow and certainty as she had herself. She and Lilla were one person, the same person. Deep down in everyone was sorrow and certainty' (Richardson, 1979, I 484).

James Weldon Johnson's *The Autobiography of an Ex-Colored Man* also shapes the ambitions of its unnamed musician-writer in his engagement with musical tradition. But music has a curious role in the novel, signalling the ambiguity of racial culture. The narrator is an outsider to 'race', raised without explicit knowledge of his origins, which are nevertheless signalled by various clues including his mother's emotional singing style ('largo'). He learns ragtime piano as an abstract accomplishment: 'I had the name at that time of being the best ragtime player in New York. I brought all my knowledge of classical music to bear and, in so doing, achieved some novelties which pleased and even astonished my listeners' (Johnson, 1995, 99). This sense of music as a kind of deracialized and commoditized communication is confirmed when he takes ragtime to Europe with his white sponsor, where he plays to German musicians one of whom, to his astonishment, immediately picks it up and reworks its modes according to a sophisticated musical understanding – mirroring modernist composers like

Stravinsky. 'I had been turning classical music into ragtime, a comparatively easy task and this man had taken ragtime and made it classical. The thought came across me like a flash – It can be done, why can't I do it?' (Johnson, 1995, 123). It is this moment which drives him towards a more racialized understanding of black music, closer to Johnson's own; he returns to the United States in order to investigate the passionate traditions of Southern music-making (largely the 'old slave songs', the Spirituals) and to make them part of a universal art, like an American version of the black British composer, Samuel Coleridge Taylor.

The narrator's white sponsor, with a certain justice, describes this task as one of 'making a Negro out of yourself' (Johnson, 1995, 125), and indeed as a 'researcher' of black life rather than an organic part of it, he worries whether his aim is 'to help my people' or 'distinguish myself'; this is 'a question I have never definitively answered' (127). The spectre or reverse passing in the novel, that is to say, is framed by music as a mode of exchange. And while the narrator's journey to the South yields material and inspiration (here he briefly refers to his possible 'genius' rather than seeing himself as a musical journeyman), his catastrophic encounter with the spectacle of a lynching inevitably contrasts the local violence of racism with the supposedly universal exchanges involved in music. He is driven away from the humiliation of racial identification, passing as white, and consigned to a secondariness which makes him a reproducer rather than producer of folk tradition – indeed he has been described as 'gramophonic' in his status as a vehicle of the sounds of others (Biers, 2013, 128ff). Music is consigned to the domestic sphere and to the 'secret' account of his life – to the Chopin he plays to woo his wife, to the parlour rather than the public stage. In that sense, the possibilities of *Bildung* and communication carried by music are denied, again by a 'barbarism' which freezes the self into immobility.

The last of my examples, Thomas Mann's *Doctor Faustus* (1947), is a novel concerned with the modernist end-game; with a German apocalypse which is both historical and musical, its narrator Zeitblom writing the life of his friend the composer Adrian Leverkühn between May 1943 and the last days of the war in 1945, with Germany burning around him. He tells the story of Leverkühn's career and its climax in a fit in 1930, after which Leverkühn, like Nietzsche, lives ten more years in a state of near-catatonia – through the period of Nazi hegemony. At the centre of the narrative is Zeitblom's transcription of Leverkühn's own journal, purporting to describe a dialogue and pact with the devil made in Italy in 1912.

Clearly, Mann wished his novel to be sensitive to musical historiography: he read Adorno's *Philosophy of the New Music* in manuscript and consulted with him on the musical elements of the novel. Leverkühn is partially modelled on Schoenberg and Krenek, as well as on Nietzsche, whose composition, the 'Manfred Meditation', Hans von Bülow described as a product of brain fever or a parodic and catachrestic attempt at the 'music of the future' (Ross, 2011). Leverkühn's teacher, the musician and lecturer Kretschmar, is the vehicle for musical thinking, lecturing on the philosophy of music, the artlessness of Beethoven's late style and so on. Like Mann's (he edited Schopenhauer in 1948), Kretschmar's thinking converges at times with that of Schopenhauer: speaking of Wagner, he notes that music celebrates a 'cosmic aptitude for allegory: for those elements that were, as it were, the first and simplest materials of the world' (Mann, 1968, 64) – the idea of music as allegorical in its relation to the Will was central to Schopenhauer's teaching. Leverkühn's own musical development is meticulously presented by the narrator: his progress through the opera *Love's Labours Lost*; settings of Blake, Keats and Klopstock; the oratorio *Marvels of the Universe*; the *Apocalypse*; and his final work, *The Lamentation of Doctor Faustus*. *The Lamentation* is itself involved (in Zeitblom's analysis) in a 'dialectical process' of development, subsuming centuries of musical tradition (Mann, 1968, 466).

But against that background, we have a narrative which is disrupted in its temporality, drawing out the tensions in a philosophical tradition in which music is at once nature and culture (despite his understanding of music as involving a hierarchy from nature – allegorically the bass – to the civilized, the soprano part, Schopenhauer had no strong account of musical history itself). Zeitblom insists that the work is the expression of a perennial alienation: 'the *Lamentation* is expression itself; one may boldly state that all expressivism is really lament [...] The echo, the giving back of the human voice as nature-sound, and the revelation of it *as* nature-sound, is essentially a lament' (Mann, 1968, 466). But the complexity of the novel's narration is, as we have noted, located in a layered history where the music that Leverkühn produces is supposed to allegorize the barbarism that follows its production. Leverkühn's 1912 confession is transcribed by Zeitblom in all its asynchronic register (he writes and often speaks in 'a sort of elder German' [475]). The devil himself – whether we take his presence as 'real' or a symptom of Leverkühn's madness – places himself and his interruption of time – his delaying of the effects of syphilis to give the composer the creative period *entre deux guerres* – at the centre of the notion of the avant-garde. This is the temptation he offers:

> Know, then, we pledge you the success of that which with your help you will accomplish. You will lead the way, you will strike up the march of the future, the lads will swear by your name who thanks to your madness will no longer need

to be mad [...] Not only will you break through the paralyzing difficulties of the time – you will break through time itself, by which I mean the cultural epoch and its cult, and dare to be barbaric, twice barbaric indeed, because of coming after the humane (Mann, 1968, 236)

The 'barbaric' is central to the avant-garde's interruption of history, this says, a dark anticipation of the Third Reich imagining itself as violently seizing history and producing its own millennium. Implicitly, it is this fantasy which places Nazi Germany outside history for Mann, as a catastrophic negation of the inheritance of the West. But because the music *precedes* the history (and even precedes in its diabolic origins in 1912 the horrors of the First World War), it can only stand in an allegorical and implicitly timeless relation to history; it is not so much a record of history as an expression of the logic of its coming into being. We are back with Schopenhauer. Narrative, however, must juggle these different times and developments; it must deal with the life of Germany after 1930 and with Zeiltblom's struggle to sustain his narrative in 1945, beyond the musical frame; his struggle to write rather than compose.

In each of these novels, competing logics attached to the idea of music are enacted. Music within the Western tradition promises development, communication, and the notion of a perfected expressive technique; it parallels, in its nineteenth-century inheritance, the *Bildungsroman*. But when confronted by atavistic forces – desire, racism, tyranny – its formal discipline is abandoned; its closeness to language collapses; it is either abandoned or reaches towards the 'twice barbaric' sounds of rupture. A tension emerges, that is to say, between the values of music and those of discourse. What Stevens called 'The more than human commonplace of blood,/The breath that gushes upward and is gone' does involve a gesture towards an absolute music, but not anything easily realized in the novel, which remains tied to a developmental narrative that fails as modernism's non-narrative monstrosity is revealed. But what the idea of music nevertheless also allows is a writing which bears the trace of will in Schopenhauer's sense, a recording of the rhythms of individual experience and desire. In that sense at least, Zeitblom remains the most faithful listener of Mann's novel, recording the suffering of his friend, and of his nation, beyond the catastrophic end of music.

Bibliography

Adorno, T. W. (2002), *Essays on Music*, R. Leppert (ed.), S. H. Gillespie (transl.). Berkeley: University of California Press.

Albright, D. (2000), *Untwisting the Serpent: Modernism in Music, Literature, and the Visual Arts*. Chicago: University of Chicago Press.

Albright, D. (ed.) (2004), *Modernism and Music: An Anthology of Sources*. Chicago: University of Chicago Press.

Armstrong, T. (2007), 'Player Piano: Poetry and Sonic Modernity'. *Modernism/ modernity*, 14, 1–19.

Beckett, S. (1983), *Disjecta: Miscellaneous Writings and a Dramatic Fragment*, R. Cohn (ed.). London: John Calder.

Benjamin, W. (1999), *The Arcades Project*, H. Eiland and K. McLaughlin (transl.). Cambridge, MA: Belknap Press.

Biers, K. (2013), *Virtual Modernism: Writing and Technology in the Virtual Era*. Minneapolis: University of Minnesota Press.

Bucknell, B. (2001), *Literary Modernism and Musical Aesthetics: Pater, Pound, Joyce and Stein*. Cambridge: Cambridge University Press.

Connor, S. (1996), 'The Modern Auditory I', in R. Porter (ed.), *Rewriting the Self: Histories from the Renaissance to the Present*. London and New York: Routledge, pp. 203–23.

Frattarola, A. (2001), 'Auditory Narrative in the Modernist Novel: Prosody, Music, and the Subversion of Vision in Dorothy Richardson's Pilgrimage'. *Genre*, 44, (1), 5–27.

Halliday, S. (2013), *Sonic Modernity: Representing Sound in Literature, Culture and the Arts*. Edinburgh: Edinburgh University Press.

Johnson, J. W. (1995), *Autobiography of an Ex-Colored Man*. London: X Press.

Kahn, D. (1999), *Noise, Water, Meat: A History of Sound in the Arts*. Cambridge, MA: MIT Press.

Katz, M. (2004), *Capturing Sound: How Technology Has Changed Music*. Berkeley: University of California Press.

Mann, T. (1968), *Doctor Faustus*, H. T. Lowe-Porter (transl.). Harmondsworth: Penguin.

Murphet, J. (2009), *Multimedia Modernism: Literature and the Anglo-American Avant-Garde*. Cambridge: Cambridge University Press.

Pound, E. (1927), *Antheil, and the Treatise on Harmony, with Supplementary Notes*. Chicago: Pascal Covici.

Pound, E. (1966), *Guide to Kulchur*. London: Peter Owen.

Prieto, E. (2002), *Listening in: Music, Mind and the Modernist Narrative*. Lincoln: University of Nebraska Press.

Rainey, L. (1998), *Institutions of Modernism: Literary Elites and Public Culture*. New Haven: Yale University Press.

Richardson, D. (1979), *Pilgrimage*, 4 vols. London: Virago.

Richardson, H. H. (1908), *Maurice Guest*. London: Heinemann.

Ross, A. (2011), 'Bülow on Nietzsche', The Rest Is Noise: Books, Articles, and a Blog by the Music Critic of *The New Yorker*, 10 May 2011, http://www.therestisnoise. com/2011/05/b%C3%BClow-on-nietzsche-more.html (accessed December 2014).

Schopenhauer, A. (1909), *The World as Will and Idea*, 3 vols. R. B. Haldane and J. Kemp (transl.), 7th edn. London: Kegan Paul, Trench, Trübner.

Shockley, A. (2009), *Music in the Words: Musical Form and Counterpoint in the Twentieth Century Novel*. Farnham: Ashgate.

Stevens, W. (1997), 'The Whole Man: Perspectives, Horizons', in F. Kermode and J. Richardson (eds), *Collected Poetry and Prose*. New York: Library of America, pp. 872–7.

Woolf, W. (1999), *The Musicalization of Fiction: A Study in the Theory and History of Intermediality*. Amsterdam: Rodopi.

8

Modernism and the Visual Arts:
Kant, Bergson, Beckett

Conor Carville

The issue of how the human experience of light and sound waves is cognitively organized into stable images, how sensation becomes perception, and the relation of this process to temporality is one of the great philosophical problems of modernism. In the France of the 1920s and early 1930s, it was especially contentious as a central point of disagreement between the two dominant philosophical currents of the time: neo-Kantianism and Bergsonism. In the cultural and critical realm, it was in the arena of painting that the debate was played out in its most radical forms. This is most obvious when we consider the reception of Cubism, where the neo-Kantian approaches of critics like Daniel-Henry Kahnweiler and Maurice Reynal responded to, and for a long time obscured, the Bergsonian analyses of Albert Gleizes and Jean Metzinger. It is not too much to say that, right across Europe, painting became a key means of testing epistemological thought. The question of the correlation between painting and beholder was conceived in terms of the relationship between subject and object, with particular attention paid to the possibility of direct, unmediated access to the object.

Samuel Beckett's lifelong concern with the aesthetics of the subject–object relation must be seen in this context. Yet Beckett's relationship with such debates must also be placed in a wider, more properly literary context. A sensitivity to painting is a tendency that he shares with many modernist writers. Walter Pater, for example, is a figure with an immense influence on modernist literature and one who, in the essays on Leonardo da Vinci and Giorgione, made important aesthetic advances through the consideration of painting. Pater often described the imagination in terms of intensity of visual perception and argued that great poetry depends upon 'perfect fidelity to one's own inner presentations, to the precise features of the *picture* within'. In *The Renaissance*, meanwhile, he claimed that art is 'always striving to be independent of the mere intelligence, to become a matter of *pure perception*' (Pater, 1919, 138; my italics). We also find the latter phrase prominently in Beckett's 1931 essay *Proust*. It may be that both Beckett and Pater discovered the phrase independently in Arthur Schopenhauer, but the coincidence, if such it is, demonstrates at the very least Beckett's early interest in the unmediated visual image, a concept that stretches right back to modernism's first stirrings. It is most probably through Joyce that Pater makes an impact on Beckett's early accounts of the image. In 'Dante . . . Bruno . Vico . . Joyce' (1929), Beckett describes Joyce's *Work in Progress* in terms of 'a sensuous untidy art of intellection', a phrase which is then qualified slightly: 'perhaps "apprehension" is the most satisfactory English word' (Beckett, 1961, 10). Significantly, Beckett goes on to quote Stephen Dedalus's modernist description of the ideal, autonomous image in Joyce's *A Portrait of the Artist as a Young Man* (1916):

> the esthetic image is first luminously apprehended as selfbounded and selfcontained upon the immeasurable background of space or time which is not it. You apprehended it as *one* thing. You see it as one whole. You apprehend its wholeness. (Beckett, 1961, 10)

Stephen's account is of course highly idiosyncratic, but it is also a product of its moment. Although its terms are taken from Aristotle and Aquinas, it owes much to Pater. When the latter argues that in artistic creation 'all depends upon the original unity, the vital wholeness and identity of the initiatory apprehension' (Pater, 1910, 22), he anticipates Joyce's description of 'the instant wherein [...] the aesthetic image, is apprehended luminously by the mind which has been arrested by its wholeness' (Joyce, 1992, 231). But Pater also supplies another important ingredient of pure perception when he sees 'a sort of thought in sense' as the goal of art (1910, 48). This anticipates the desire of a wide range of modernists for a writing that can mobilize conceptual thought without losing its grasp on the particular. Such a notion of apprehension as a comportment towards the aesthetic object that is immediate, sensuous and yet not limited to somatic response is strongly present in T. S. Eliot, for example. If the Beckett of the Vico essay thinks 'apprehension' is the best word to describe how *Work in Progress* might be grasped, he is thus situating himself in an established tradition.

The high-modernist, largely formalist position suggested by these influences is, however, constantly traversed and interrupted by another current in contemporary aesthetics that accompanies the Pater, Eliot, Joyce lineage. This is a materialist, avant-garde account of the visual image, one that draws on contemporary science and in particular optics, neurology and experimental psychology. Thus, for example, in 1917 Arthur Symons argues that literature depends upon 'the sensation flashed through the brain, the image on the mental retina'. He goes on to describe this as 'the painter's method, a selection made almost visually: the method of the painter who accumulates detail on detail' (1917, 346). When Ezra Pound later introduces the term *phanopoeia* to describe the poetic use of visual metaphors, he alludes to Symons by defining it as 'the throwing of an image on the mind's retina', again locating the image within the new physiological understanding of cognition (2010, 52). T. E. Hulme also drew deeply on contemporary continental philosophy, experimental psychology and art history to ground his poetics in the materiality of the body. Henri Bergson was of course important here. But Hulme was also interested in now lesser-known French figures such as the psychologist Théodule Ribot and the anti-Kantian philosopher Jules de Gaultier. As Wallace Martin has pointed out, Ribot argued that 'immediate impressions or images are closer to reality and therefore more distinct, more reliable than ideas' (1970, 196). Here, we can see an elevation of the image over the concept that parallels the one that underpins the more philosophical notion of apprehension. Martin goes on to say, rightly, that it was in Ribot's approach that 'early twentieth century writers found a scientific sanction for an aesthetic of the image' (200). What is more, Ribot, like Hulme, associated such mental images primarily with the eye, as is apparent from his use of the term 'plastic' to describe the process that creates them:

> By 'plastic imagination' I understand that which has for its special character clearness and precision of form; more explicitly those forms whose materials are clear images (whatever be their nature) [...] giving the impression of reality. (Ribot, 1906, 184)

This use of the term 'plastic' here is derived directly from modernist art criticism. We will be returning to it at several points, as it plays an important role in Beckett's aesthetic thought. He might have encountered the idea first in the pages of *transition*. As is well known, this journal was a crucial testing ground for Beckett's literary aspirations in the very early years of his career. It is also however a vital resource in tracking the commerce between the visual and other arts in the period. In the pages of *transition* painting, cinema and photography were regularly appealed to as models for artistic practice. This is evident above all in the regular use of the term 'plastic' to describe the ideal work of art. Hence, for example, in November 1929, the magazine's founder and editor Eugene Jolas dismisses Surrealist montage and lauds Charles Sheeler's 'plastic objectivity', arguing that 'his camera gives us the finest imaginative possibilities through light and dark arrangements which approach the abstract and crystal purity of poetry' (Jolas, 1929, 123). In the same issue, Stuart Gilbert's essay 'The Function of Words' argues that in what he and Jolas called 'the revolution of the word':

> Words are treated as plastic media; their forms and colours may be blended according to the instinctive treatment of the artist, and insofar as he has apprehended and can express the racial affective values of the signs he employs, he will enable the readers of his work to share his emotion. (Gilbert, 1929a, 204)

Finally, in 'The Novel Is Dead, Long Live the Novel', a manifesto signed by Jolas, Gilbert and others, we have a clear summary of the modernist goal of direct intimacy between self and world, with the plastic as catalyst: 'The novel of the future will be a plastic encyclopedia of the fusion of subjective and objective reality' (Gilbert, 1929b, 239).

Beckett, too, employed the 'plastic' as a term of aesthetic approbation. The *transition* aesthetic is present in his novel *Dream of Fair to Middling Women* (completed 1932, published 1992), for example, when Belacqua cherishes the 'scraps of German' that play in his mind as 'grand, old, plastic words', emphasizing the material quality of the unfamiliar language (Beckett, 1992, 191). It is through the term 'plastic' that I want to explore the way Beckett attempts to accommodate the two strands of thinking about the visual that I have been associating with modernism and the avant-garde.

The first declaration of Beckett's visual aesthetic occurs in 'Dante . . . Bruno . Vico . . Joyce'. Here, Beckett, referring to what would become *Finnegans Wake* (1939), writes that 'we are presented with a statement of the particular' and explicitly associates such a statement with painting (1961, 11). That Joyce's 'system of Poetics' attends to the particular rather than the universal is a central contention of the essay on *Work in Progress*, and Beckett's account of Vico's thought clearly sees the latter as authorizing the Joycean procedure. For our purposes, it is important that Beckett's earliest programmatic aesthetic examines a figure who anticipates some of the key concerns of modernist visual aesthetics, in particular the notion of art's relation to non-conceptual understanding, and the problem of the empathic relation between painting and beholder. Both issues are fundamental to the evolution of Beckett's work.

In Beckett's brief summary, Vico's account of the historical development of poetry depicts 'primitive' peoples as incapable of conceptual thinking or 'of receiving anything more abstract than the plain record of objectivity' (1961, 9).

As a result, their poetry, language and myths are characterized by aversion to abstraction and investment in the immediate. Their poetry 'is all passion and feeling', attending to sensation rather than the concept, while their language is limited to the strongly visual codes of gesture and hieroglyphics which, in their identity of form and content, are an example of what Beckett calls 'direct expression'. Finally, primitive myth is not allegorical but 'a statement of fact' for 'the actual creators of these myths gave full credence to their face-value. Jove was no symbol: he was terribly real' (9). Principles of bodily and affective immediacy, and a lack of mediation by transcendental or symbolic frameworks thus connect 'primitive' poetry, language, myth and art. Beckett's reading of Vico, in other words, deploys an avant-garde rhetoric of pure direct unmediated perception. And this is how Beckett often sees *Work in Progress* too, for when he turns to Joyce's text proper he deploys the same terminology he used to describe primitive poetry: 'Here is direct expression – pages and pages of it' (9).

'Direct expression' is Beckett's phrase for language that impacts directly on the reader, drawing on passion and affect rather than being filtered through the intellect. Hence, his essay's celebrated description of Joyce's language as an object in the world, with the same potentialities and forms of agency as such objects, rather than a system of reference to them. As with primitive language, the content of *Work in Progress* is organic to its form, with the latter conceived dynamically, in terms of physical action and sensation: 'when the sense is sleep the words go to sleep [...] When the sense is dancing the words dance' (Beckett, 1961, 10). Beckett glosses this description with a series of examples of such affective, bodily writing: Shakespeare's 'greasy words that express corruption', or 'the ooze squelching' in Dickens's descriptions of the Thames (10). This then is what Beckett admiringly calls, using T. S. Eliot's terminology from the essay on the Metaphysicals, a 'sensuous untidy art of intellection' (10).

From this essay to the letter to Axel Kaun of July 1937 and beyond, Beckett's comments on aesthetics often see writing in terms of a surface, a fabric which bears an image: a sheet or a veil or curtain. That is to say, the text or image is identified with its material support: page, canvas, brain, retina, body. An early example, which John Pilling dates to August 1931, is the poem 'Alba', in particular the second stanza:

Whose beauty shall be a sheet before me
A statement of itself drawn across the tempest of emblems
So that there is no sun and no unveiling

And no host
Only I and then the sheet
And bulk dead. (Beckett, 2012, 10)

Beckett also uses elements of this description in *Dream of Fair to Middling Women*, and the two passages, when taken together, throw considerable light on each other. The occasion in the novel is one of those sudden, longed-for subtractions from the phenomenal world that are experienced by the main character, Belacqua, sometimes voluntarily and sometimes not. Beckett describes this curious mental state in a prose that owes a great deal to the sacerdotal, Paterian cadences of the aesthetic epiphanies in Joyce's *Portrait*, and the passage also partakes of Stephen's prized sense of the 'self-bounded and self-contained' nature of the 'aesthetic image':

> Plane of white music, warpless music expunging the tempest of emblems, calm womb of dawn whelping no sun [...] still flat white music, alb of timeless light. It is a blade before me, it is a sail of bleached silk on a shore, impassive statement of itself drawn across the strata and symbols, lamina of peace for my eyes and my brain slave of my eyes [...] the mysteries of bulk banished and the mind swathed in the music and candour of the dawn-foil, facts of surface. The layers of Damask fused and drawn to the uppermost layer, silken blade. Blind and my mind blade of silk, blind and music and whiteness facts in the fact of my mind. (Beckett, 1992, 181–2)

Although this is an account of some form of vision, however, the prose description relies even more overtly than the poem on images of material support of various kinds. The plane, parapet, alb, sail, lamina and fused 'layers of Damask' are all 'facts of surface', as the passage puts it. Although the repeated references to whiteness, blindness and bleaching suggest erasure, there is a simultaneous emphasis on the persistence of a material presence. If, as the poem puts it, 'bulk' is 'dead', surface is not, and it is the insistence of the latter that seems to supply the 'facts' that inhere in 'the fact of my mind' with which the quotation ends. There is a strong suggestion that the image is a kind of tympanum or communicating membrane where world and self are contiguous. Belacqua summons an autonomous, white surface, where a complete communion of mind and world takes place beyond mere 'emblems'. The reference to 'my brain slave of my eyes' situates all of this within the discourse of experimental psychology, as does the general conception of the image as a coincidence of the facts of the world and the facts of mind. And yet all this is in tension with the transcendental, formalist quality that is also undeniably present.

If we keep in mind this conflict between a formalist, transcendental impulse and a materialist, bodily one, we can perhaps begin to take the measure of Beckett's contradictory and exasperating *Proust*. Throughout this essay, Beckett is scathing about the ways in which conceptual thought works to conceal the real. Thus, Beckett approves 'when the object is perceived as particular and unique and not merely the member of a family, when it appears independent of any general notion and detached from the sanity of a cause, isolated and inexplicable in the light of ignorance, then and only then may it be a source of enchantment' (1965, 22). This, and particularly the notion of isolation, is clearly derived from Schopenhauer, who argues for an aesthetic that rests on 'secure contemplation of the presented object removed from all context' (Schopenhauer, 1969, I 264). In more explicitly Kantian language, for Beckett such an object 'resists the propositions of [the] team of syntheses' or, again alluding to Kant, stimulates 'the free play of every faculty' (Beckett, 1965, 23). This combination of Kant and Schopenhauer is also reflected in a repeated reference to 'disinterest' as the core quality of the aesthetic object (30).

Beckett started reading Schopenhauer in July 1930, and it is here perhaps that the most important proximate source for the tensions between formalism and materialism in his visual aesthetics can be found (see Beckett, 2009, 32–3). It is true that, drawing on Locke, Schopenhauer held out the possibility of a non-Kantian, intuitive direct perception between subject and object. It is also true that he relied heavily on physiology, early brain science and optics in his account of the senses. Yet there is, in Schopenhauer, an obscurity about the intuitive perception he opposes to Kantian concepts. On the one hand, it is not simply a question of the body's physiological registration of sense data. As he puts it: 'the objective world [...] cannot just step into our head from without, already cut and dried, through the senses' (Schopenhauer, 1974, 78). Rather, it needs the aid of the understanding which, while not conceptual, is still an organizing force, subjecting sensation to the minimal categories of time, space and causality to produce a viable representation. On the other hand, however, Schopenhauer often returns to sheer bodily materiality as the ground of experience. In this respect, the following is typical: 'all thinking is a physiological function of the brain, just as digestion is of the stomach' (2000, I 46).

As a result, it is simply not clear in the German philosopher's work what the relation is between an intuitive cognition, the production of a representation, and pure sensation as datum. And things become even more unclear where the relationship between body, brain and nervous system and the aesthetic image is concerned. Yet there are several moments, in *Dream*, where Beckett strongly suggests that all three of these elements can simply be elided, for example the description, quoted earlier, of beauty as 'music and whiteness facts in the fact of my mind'.

What is more, when we turn to Schopenhauer's proposals for a specifically aesthetic perception, it is the *absence* of emotion and affect, the detachment from worldly suffering, that is famously key. In such circumstances, we 'discard entirely our own personality for a time, in order to remain *pure knowing subject*, the clear eye of the world' (Schopenhauer, 1969, 185–6; my italics). Beckett asserts an almost identical 'pure perception of a pure subject' towards the end of *Proust*, which contrasts with what he now calls 'the caricature furnished by direct perception', or again 'the abject and indigestible husks of direct contact with the material and concrete' (1965, 89, 65). There is a clear shift here from the 'direct expression' of 'Dante … Bruno. Vico… Joyce'. Directness and immediacy are not now valued in the same physical, bodily terms as before. The aspiration is towards something much more rarified and, as Beckett puts it more than once, 'immaterial'. This is further borne out in the essay when 'the joys and sorrows of the body' are dismissed as mere 'superfoetations', as compared to 'the only world that has reality and significance, the world of our own latent consciousness' (Beckett, 1965, 13). Or the even more stark rejection of affect and the 'vegetable' body at the end of the essay, when Beckett returns approvingly to Proust's pure 'transcendental apperception' (90). This he describes as 'contemplative, a pure act of understanding, will-less', as distinct from the 'still, almost breathless passion' of the youth in Giorgione's *Concerto*, where 'the spirit [is] shattered in corruption, damp and rotting' (91). In the latter case, and in the examples from Keats and d'Annunzio which Beckett also supplies, there is a continuity between the sensuous body and the temporal flow of the material world, but it is given a strongly negative, entropic inflection. All of this suggests the persistence of a high-modernist, neo-Kantian, transcendental aesthetic.

And yet, despite all this it remains true that often in *Proust* we find a notion of perception and the aesthetic that emphasizes both the physiological and the emotional as much as it does dispassion and the impersonal. Why might this be so? One clue comes as the essay is dismissing the habitual and inauthentic nature of voluntary memory. Here, Beckett writes that 'the images it chooses are as arbitrary as those chosen by imagination, *and are equally remote from reality*' (1965, 32). Voluntary memory and the imagination are thus equated, and both found wanting for their distance from reality. This is likely a reaction to Breton's recent claim that 'the imagination [...] alone causes real things' (1972, ix). It is this anti-Surrealist suspicion of the imagination, repeated on a number of occasions, that accounts for Beckett's contrary tropism towards the material, empirical body, even as he regularly extols the virtues of the timeless, impassive Idea. Thus, at one point aesthetic experience is described as dependent upon the 'tense and provisional lucidity of the nervous system' (Beckett, 1965, 21). Similarly, involuntary memory – which is consistently elided with authentic aesthetic experience in the essay – is seen as material inscription: 'we can only remember what has been registered by our extreme inattention and stored in that ultimate and inaccessible dungeon of our being to which Habit does not possess the key' (31). Here again, there returns a familiar sense of material, 'direct' continuity between body and world that ballasts any recourse to the sublations of the Surrealist imagination.

If we turn to Beckett's analysis of one of Proust's characters in particular, we can clearly see him working through these contradictory concerns with the formal and the material, the ideal and the somatic, and arriving at a kind of solution. The narrator's first glimpse of Albertine, a 'pure act of understanding-intuition', as Beckett later describes it in classic Schopenhauerian terms, relies on what we now think of as familiar modernist notions of the artwork as timeless, opaque and disinterested (1965, 61). Thus, she is 'ineffable and inaccessible', and, with specific reference to painting, as 'eternally and hermetically exclusive as a frieze or a frescoed cortege' (45–6).

Slightly later, however, Beckett introduces two further modes of the visual image, comparing two depictions of Albertine in terms of an opposition between an arbitrary, superficial 'realist' image and one that is 'inward'. This contrast is explicitly thematized in terms of a distinction between a 'pictorial multiplicity' and 'a plastic and moral multiplicity'. Note the approving use of the term 'plastic' in the latter, which is privileged as:

> no longer a mere *superficies* and an effect of the observer's angle of approach rather than the expression of an *inward and active* variety, but a *multiplicity in depth*, a turmoil of objective and immanent contradictions over which the subject has no control. (Beckett, 1965, 47; my italics)

Here, we have Beckett grappling explicitly with his contradictory tendencies towards the formal and the material. Although both aspects of Albertine are conceived in terms of temporal unfolding, there is a clear preference. While *pictorial* multiplicity is the mere 'effect' of many subjective points of view on an object, the *plastic* is an 'expression' of something more profound, a faint echo of the 'direct expression' of Vico and *Work in Progress*. In the case of the pictorial, it is evident that Beckett is speaking of the 'superficial' account of

Albertine's changing visual appearance at different points in the novel. These are the moments in Proust's narrative where Albertine is seen from the outside, so to speak: familiar 'realist' visual images that register changes in perspective on the object. This recalls Bergson's critique of what he termed 'cinematographic thinking': 'Instead of attaching ourselves to the inner becoming of things, we place ourselves outside them in order to recompose their becoming artificially. We take snapshots, as it were, of the passing reality' (Bergson, 1922, 322). The pictorial qualities of Albertine, and by extension of Proust's novel as a whole, are thus assimilated to a writing that foregrounds the contingent outward transformation of appearance and gesture. This is the pure surface of images that Beckett constantly describes in terms of 'impenetrability', 'impermeability' and resistance to interpretation.

Plastic multiplicity, by contrast, while also temporal, is *inward*. Beckett describes it in terms of depth, a movement below or behind the surface, referring to the 'immanent contradictions' of the 'multiplicity in depth' – and evoking both the experimental psychologist Wilhelm Wundt and Kant as he does so – arguing that 'the multiple aspects (read Blickpunkt for this miserable word) [do] not bind into any positive synthesis' (1965, 65). The dismissal of synthesis here is crucial, in that it confirms that Beckett is contrasting a transcendental dualism that successfully synthesizes intuition and understanding, with something rather more (though not completely) Bergsonian. This is what Beckett calls, in a vital phrase right at the start of *Proust*, a 'dualism in multiplicity'. For it is with this paradoxical term that Beckett acknowledges the tension in his essay between two forms of the modernist image: one is the autonomous, timeless image, drawing on the dualism of Kant and Schopenhauer; the other is the more vitalist, positivist and directly perceived image, drawing on Bergson and contemporary psychological and scientific discourses. The plastic image incorporates both, and Beckett understands it primarily in terms of painting.

In the mid-1930s, Beckett moves away from the quasi-Bergsonian position that he adopted at key moments in *Proust*, so that a modernist formalism again has the upper hand, although Beckett's position also becomes more idiosyncratic, more recognizably his own. The distance from Bergson is evident most of all in a suspicion of vitalism, animism and 'life' itself, and a turn towards a rhetoric of the inorganic and the petrified. Here, the painter Cézanne is the catalyst:

> What a relief the Mont St Victoire after all the anthropomorphised landscape –
> van Goyen, Avercamp, the Ruysdaels, Hobbema, even Claude, Wilson and Crome
> Yellow Esq., or paranthropomorphised by Watteau [...] or hyperanthropomorphized
> by Rubens [...] Cézanne seems to have been the first to see landscape and state it as

material of a strictly peculiar order, incommensurable with all human expressions whatsoever. Atomistic landscape with no velleities of vitalism. (Beckett, 2009, 222)

Beckett then returns to these themes in his next letter. He is writing here of the *Self-Portrait of 1880*:

I do not see any possibility of relationship, friendly or unfriendly with the unintelligible, and what I feel in Cézanne is precisely the absence of a rapport that was all right for Rosa or Ruysdael for whom the animising mode was valid, but would have been false for him, because he had the sense of his incommensurability not only with life of such a different order as landscape but even with life of his own order, even with the life – one feels looking at the self-portrait in the Tate [...] operative in himself. (Beckett, 2009, 227)

Henceforth, Beckett's notion of the plastic will always be associated with the inhuman, the radically material and the evacuation of human meaning. All vestiges of a Bergsonian 'life force' are removed, and the artwork is understood in terms of its formalist resistance and hermeticism. Ten years later, as he is writing *Watt* (1953), the term 'plastic' appears again. Watt is attempting to describe his memory of the visit of the Galls to Mr Knott's house:

it was not ended when it was past, but continued to unfold, in Watt's head, from beginning to end, over and over again, the complex connection of its lights and shadows, the passing from silence to sounds and from sound to silence, the stillness before the movement and the stillness after, the quickening and retarding, the approaches and the separations, all the shifting detail of its march and ordinance, according to the irrevocable caprice of its taking place. It resembled them in the vigour with which it developed a purely plastic content, and gradually lost, in the nice processes of its light, its sound, its impacts and its rhythm, all meaning, even the most literal. (Beckett, 1998, 69)

This is the first of the scenes 'of great formal brilliance and indeterminate purport' that will haunt Watt during the remainder of his stay in Mr Knott's house. Here, conventional perception is not replaced by authentic sensuous experience: 'formal brilliance' suggests something rather more austere and reserved than the erotics of the image implied in Eliot, or the hortatory immediacy of Hulme and Pound. Similarly, the 'indeterminate purport' of Watt's images is rather more equivocal than the modernist norm. What we are left with is what the narrator calls a 'purely plastic content'. As mentioned above, with reference to Ribot and his literary followers, plastic is a term that migrated from the visual arts into experimental psychology and from there into literary discourse. In its conventional, art-critical use, it is associated in particular with the preeminent art critic of the interwar period in both Britain and France, Roger Fry. Beckett's resort to the term in *Watt* thus draws attention both to the profoundly visual nature of his poetics of the image and to the antecedents of that heritage in pre-war modernism. But what I want to emphasize here is the way that, in the passage above, the plastic does not refer to that fusion of subject and object that, in various ways, attracted Pater, Pound, Eliot and the *transition* circle. Rather than that, the description of the memory emphasizes the negativity and loss that is now central to Beckett.

The next moment that I want to consider comes from a slightly later short story, 'First Love', written in the late 1940s. There the narrator is describing, or trying to describe, the face of a prostitute who has accosted him:

> As to whether it was beautiful, the face, or had once been beautiful, or could conceivably become beautiful, I confess I could form no opinion. I had seen faces in photographs I might have found beautiful, had I known even vaguely in what beauty was supposed to consist. And my Father's face, on his death bolster, had seemed to hint at some form of aesthetics relevant to man. But the faces of the living, all grimace and flush, can they be described as objects? (Beckett, 1980, 22–3)

Beauty is introduced here primarily in terms of visual sensation, but again it is an experience that the narrator has little or no knowledge of. Or, more accurately, not enough to make an aesthetic judgement. There is a 'hint' that such an exercise of judgement might become possible at the moment of death, or in a photograph, however. In other words, there is the implication that it is only at the point where the face, in death, achieves the status of autonomous object, definitively displaced from human experience, that aesthetic judgement is possible. 'First Love's' meditation on the beautiful thus both conforms to and challenges the Kantian account of aesthetic judgement. Kant's sense of the difficult questions the aesthetic object poses for the beholder is present in the narrator's concern to categorize what he sees. Yet, for Beckett, such questions also raise issues of temporality, affect, the body, the everyday. In other words, the Bergsonian, avant-garde inheritance is still here. In the passage from 'First Love', temporality is present first through the narrator's claim that the prostitute's face might once have been, or might become, beautiful, and second through the highly visual account of the changeability, affects and sensations of the living face at the description's end. When the narrator wonders whether the faces of the living can be described as objects, and so be understood as art, he emphasizes the excess of sensation over concept and the time-bound nature of the human experience of the world. In this way, the narrator's relation to beauty does not conform to the Kantian model, as for the latter art stages the process whereby the understanding organizes sense-experience into intelligible form, without ever concluding it. Contrary to this, Beckett suggests the possibility of a strictly non-Kantian process: the experience of pure sensation without the mediation of the concept.

And yet, although there is a departure from the transcendental aesthetic and its associated notions of apperception, there also seems to be a latent attraction to a formalism that is ultimately securely Kantian. The suggestion that the static photograph and the impassive face of the corpse might be the ideal aesthetic objects is in keeping with the mocking, disenchanted tone of the story. Despite this, something serious is afoot alongside the irony, as becomes particularly evident when the extract is considered in relation to the many undead, 'petrified' bodies and faces of Beckett's later work. The mechanical objectivity of the photograph and the absolute desubjectification of the corpse both, in their different ways, accord to the idea of an autonomous object, subtracted from the everyday, replete and self-communing. In this sense, the passage from 'First Love' reads like a version, or perversion, of a mode of visual aesthetics, heavily indebted to Kant, that will become highly influential in twentieth-century visual culture. The twentieth-century displacement of Kantian formalism from the activity of the 'disinterested' beholding subject to the material art object itself, epitomized by Clement Greenberg's work, bears a marked affinity to the 'aesthetics relevant to man' that Beckett sketches in 'First Love'. Having said this, Beckett's rueful, paradoxical association of such a 'human' aesthetics with the corpse brings to this nexus of ideas something that is wholly his own.

Beckett's distance from modernist aesthetics of the Greenberg type is apparent from the final piece I want to consider: 'La Peinture des van Velde, ou le Monde et le Pantalon' (1945), published in *Cahiers d'Art*. Here, an unidentified voice declares: 'Everything is an object for painting, not excluding states of the soul, dreams, and even nightmares, on the condition that their transcription is made with plastic means.' Beckett then abandons his ventriloquism to comment:

> Would it be by any chance the use or the non-use of these devices that would decide the presence or absence of a given painting on the prescribed line [i.e. the line of French painting]?
>
> In any case it would be useful, interesting even, to know what is meant by plastic means. Yet no one will ever know. Only the initiated can pick up the scent. (Beckett, 1983, 121; my translation)

Clearly, the voice that Beckett mimics in his essay is a member of this initiate. Despite himself using the term in *Watt* and elsewhere, Beckett now describes the term 'plastic' as a kind of shibboleth used to reinforce the professional status of an elite circle.

Beckett's target here is likely to be the contemporary critic and curator Bertrand Dorival, who writes, to take one example, that 'at the heart of this conviction that a pictorial work is before anything a plastic work how can we not detect the French spirit of logic?' (Dorival, 1946, 322). Although Beckett laments the plastic's lack of definition in contemporary criticism, Dorival does go on to give an example of what he means, referring to the way painters like Pignon, Gischia, and others require of their pens and pencils 'all they are able to give, but do not try to make them do anything that is not in their nature', so that if there is 'a game of light and shadow' when charcoal is used, for example, 'it is because it is of the essence of these tools to create chiaroscuro and model a sculptural form' (322). There is a version of a Greenbergian notion of truth to materials here, a sense of the emphasis Dorival and others place not on subjective expression, but the exploration of formal problems internal and exclusive to painting as a medium.

Such a definition of painting presupposes skill, experience, and a strong sense of aesthetic decorum, that is to say the ability to identify and exploit only those modes of mark-making inherent to the 'genius' of a particular tool, a procedure that is by no means as obvious as it initially seems. The master of such techniques, according to critics such as Dorival, was Georges Braque. It is significant then that Beckett uses a comparison with Braque to clarify the specific differences between Bram van Velde and the painting to which he is opposed. According to the essay 'certain canvasses by Braque' *seem* to be 'plastic meditations' on the same kind of techniques that Bram uses. But these are only the tentative investigations of a 'hypothesis'. Beckett goes on: 'His [Bram's] means have the specificity of a speculum, existing only in relation to their function. He doesn't take enough interest in them to doubt them. He only interests himself in what they reflect' (Beckett, 1983, 127). In other words, this painting is not one which is entranced with its own operations and conditions, with formal investigations of problems internal to the history of painting. Indeed, Beckett will insist that the distinguishing mark of Bram's work is its refusal to conform to the kind of elegant, sophisticated plastic painting of which Dorival approves. Thus, he asks: 'But suppose the definition was to be acquired [and] any gummyeyed fool before a given painting could shout: "It's good, the means are plastic," [...] *What would be said, then, of the artist who would renounce it?*' (121–2; my italics).

Hence, Beckett's emphasis on what seem to be lapses in taste or technique in Van Velde's work, elements that are at odds with the consummate skill of someone like Braque. This is what he calls 'everything unreasonable, ingenuous, uncoordinated, badly-executed this painting presents' or again 'the categorial negligence that [...] translates the urgency and primacy of the interior vision so well' (Beckett, 1983, 129). Both of these descriptions are clearly an extension of what Beckett had earlier approvingly called a 'willed creative mismaking' (122). Bram's interior vision necessitates a practice that will break out of the overly aestheticized, formal procedures of French modernism as it was being promoted at the time, and this is carried out through the deliberate abuse of materials rather than a loving fidelity to their supposed essence.

Instead, as Beckett explains it, the task of the painter is to work so that 'the fundamental invisibility of exterior things ... itself becomes a thing, *not a simple consciousness of limit*, but a *thing* that we can see and make seen, and make, not in the head [...] but on the canvas' (1983, 130; my italics). A painting 'in the head' is premised on the performance of a successful act of judgement, as the beholder tests the free play of their own cognition before the image. We saw Beckett disagree with this orthodox Kantianism as far back as *Proust* (though now the target is more likely phenomenology). Van Velde's 'mixture of mastery and boredom' realizes instead a sense of the artwork as an autonomous thing that materializes an otherwise indiscernable truth: 'the thing one sees there is no longer represented merely as *suspended*, but strictly as it is, really frozen' (127). Beckett's anti-vitalism makes itself felt here again. It is not that painting suspends time, but supersedes it, like the face of the dead Father. In this way, Van Velde detaches himself from Braque and 'a whole school of painting' by which Beckett means Bazaine, Tal-Coat, and the other members of the so-called Nouvelle École. And through his description of this process, Beckett finally detaches himself from modernism.

Bibliography

Beckett, S. (1961), 'Dante . . . Bruno . Vico . . Joyce', in *Our Exagmination Round His Factification for Incamination of Work in Progress*. London: Faber, pp. 5–13.
Beckett, S. (1965), *Proust and Three Dialogues*. London: Calder.
Beckett, S. (1980), *The Expelled and Other Novellas*. London: Penguin.
Beckett, S. (1983), *Disjecta*, Ruby Cohn (ed.). London: Calder.
Beckett, S. (1992), *Dream of Fair to Middling Women*. Dublin: Black Cat.
Beckett, S. (1998), *Watt*. London: Calder.

Beckett, S. (2009), *The Letters of Samuel Beckett, Vol. 1: 1929–1940*, M. Fehsenfeld and L. M. Overbeck (eds). Cambridge: Cambridge University Press.

Beckett, S. (2012), *The Collected Poems of Samuel Beckett*, S. Lawlor and J. Pilling (eds). London: Faber.

Bergson, H. (1922), *Creative Evolution*, A. Mitchell (transl.). London: Macmillan.

Breton, A. (1972), *Manifestoes of Surrealism*, R. Seaver (transl.). Ann Arbor: University of Michigan Press.

Dorival, B. (1946), *Les Étapes de la Peinture Française Contemporaine, III*. Paris: Gallimard.

Gilbert, S. (1929a), 'The Function of Words'. *transition*, 18, (November), 203–6.

Gilbert, S. (1929b), 'Novel Is Dead, Long Live the Novel'. *transition*, 18, (November), 239.

Jolas, E. (1929), *transition*, 18, (November), 123.

Joyce, J. (1992), *A Portrait of the Artist as a Young Man*. London: Penguin.

Martin, W. (1970), 'The Sources of the Imagist Aesthetic'. *PMLA*, 85, (2), (March), 196–204.

Pater, W. (1910), *Appreciations, with an Essay on Style*. London: Macmillan.

Pater, W. (1919), *The Renaissance*. London: Macmillan.

Pound, E. (2010), *ABC of Reading*. New York: New Directions.

Ribot, T. (1906), *Essay on the Creative Imagination*. London: Routledge and Kegan Paul.

Schopenhauer, A. (1969), *The World as Will and Representation*, E. F. J. Payne (transl.). New York: Dover.

Schopenhauer, A. (1974), *Fourfold Root of the Principle of Sufficient Reason*, E. F. J. Payne (transl.). La Salle, IL: Open Court.

Schopenhauer, A. (2000), *Parerga and Paralipomena*, E. F. J. Payne (transl.). Oxford: Oxford University Press.

Symons, A. (1917), *Figures of Several Centuries*. London: Constable.

9

Modernist Literature and Film

Laura Marcus

The close and complex relationships between modernist literature and film have become central topics in the last two decades, driven in part by a concern with the interactions between technology and the arts. There is an understanding of both writing and film as dimensions of a broader 'media ecology' (a 'multimedia modernism', in Julian Murphet's phrase) which includes different modes of representation, mediation and communication – photographic, graphic, telephonic and, more recently, digital – interacting in various and different degrees. There is also a desire to understand how film, as it emerged in the final years of the nineteenth century, contributed to the shaping of a modernist literature whose beginnings, though the dating is not uncontested, are frequently situated towards that century's close. Nor is the influence from film to literature one way: film, from its early years onwards, sought narrative form and its stories were frequently drawn from plays, poems and novels. Early accounts of film as a medium, and then as an art, turned to the topic of literary adaptation, as well as the question of cinema's particular modes of visual storytelling. There were explorations, too, of the ways in which writers were responding to the threat, and the promise, of the new medium.

The recent focus on the centrality of film to modernist literature and culture has, to a certain extent, occluded not only discussions from the first decades of the twentieth century but also the extensive critical writings in this area published in the 1960s and 1970s. Texts by, among others, Keith Cohen, Alan Spiegel and Claude-Edmonde Magny looked, in particular, at the ways in which film form had shaped works of high modernism (including those by William Faulkner, James Joyce and Virginia Woolf) and American literature. Magny's *The Age of the American Novel: The Film Aesthetic of Fiction between the Two Wars* (published in French in 1948, but not translated into English until 1972) explored the idea that the changes that had taken place in both the American and the French novel, and the 'evolution of novelistic technique' evident in both national literatures, might have a common source in 'the imitation, conscious or unconscious, of the techniques of the film' (Magny, 1972, 3). Her film examples were largely drawn from the mid-twentieth century, and she focused on the increased use of first-person narrative in film (taken to its limit in the use of subjective camera in *The Lady in the Lake*, 1947), depth of field (as in Orson Welles's *Citizen Kane*, 1941) and the use of ellipsis, in film and fiction. Both Spiegel, in his *Fiction and the Camera Eye* (1976), and Cohen, in *Film and Fiction: The Dynamics of Exchange* (1979), concentrated more fully on questions of vision and motion. Spiegel, tracing a line of development from Flaubert to Joyce, developed an account of 'ocular loneliness' in Joyce's writings: 'a kind of spiritual separateness that begins with a passive, affectless eye and will never permit the observer total rapport with his visual field' (Spiegel, 1976, 67).

Cohen extended Magny's concerns with ellipses and partial views, and Spiegel's with the advent of film as an event in the history of perception, to make the argument that cinema was the epitome of twentieth-century relativism, cutting up and reordering reality in ways that had a profound impact on the modernist novel. His objective, he wrote, was 'to trace this exchange of energies from the movies […] to the modern novel, whose major innovations will be seen as closely patterned after those of the cinema'. The movies created a crisis for the novel, Cohen claimed, which 'the innovative novelist […] was to exploit to his or her own advantage', by using 'the techniques of fragmented vision and discontinuity peculiar to the movies' (1979, 6). Cohen's central argument was that 'the contours of modern narrative would not be what they are without the precedents set by the movies' (10) and, indeed, that the very survival of the novel as a literary genre, as well as the particular innovations to be found in modernist fiction, had been dependent upon novelists' readiness to model their narratives on film form and film expression.

Accounts of the cinema in Cohen's and in related texts sought to define the essence of film's identity, in particular through its relations of space and time, as well as its blending of technology and art, of mimesis (film's doubling of reality) and montage (its cutting and reordering of its materials), of presence and absence effects and of the levelling of subject (or self) and object. Such a focus looks back to earlier writings on film aesthetics, in which time-space relations, the animations of the object world and the conditions of movement and motion were perceived to define the medium: many of these works appeared in the 1920s and 1930s, authored by writers and aestheticians including Rudolf Arnheim,

Herbert Read and Erwin Panofsky. The approach of Cohen and others also drew on film theories more nearly contemporary, including the film writings of André Bazin and of Siegfried Kracauer, whose *Theory of Film: The Redemption of Physical Reality* was published in 1960, though it drew on earlier materials. The philosopher Stanley Cavell's *The World Viewed: Reflections on the Ontology of Film* (1971) was, like the work of Bazin and Kracauer, concerned with a filmic ontology, including the relations between presence and absence which Cavell perceived to be both definitional of cinema's identity as a medium and indicative of the conditions of existence in modernity. Finally, we can perceive the influence of theories informing the 'nouveau roman' and the 'nouvelle vague' in France in the post-war years, in which film and novel were brought into the same conceptual frameworks, and in which debates revolved around such issues as the 'cleansing' of the perceiving eye of sentiment and habit and the workings, and narrative representations, of chance and contingency.

There was less writing on film and modernist literature in the years following the 1970s. While this was the period in which film studies was becoming fully established as an academic discipline and while there was significant conversion between 'structuralist' approaches to film and literary narratives, film's claims to disciplinary status entailed, in substantial part, taking a distance from literary studies. The strongly textualist approaches (focused on the play of language and writing) taken by much literary and critical theory in this period rendered visuality and visual culture less prominent. It was not until the 1990s, as an aspect of developments in 'modernist studies' and a 'visual turn' in literary studies more generally, that critical enquiries into the relationship between modernism and film again began to proliferate. Many of the seemingly new approaches, as I shall show, gathered up the preoccupations of earlier writers on the topic, but there has, in recent years, been a strong perception that the determining influence of cinema on modernist literature and culture has been largely overlooked and that it is only now becoming visible to us.

One important dimension of this new visibility, or at least for the perception of its newness, has been the radical reappraisal of early film history. The shift from a view of cinema in its first years as the 'primitive' prehistory of film to an apprehension of it as a representational form in its own right has been particularly significant. The highly influential concept of the 'cinema of attractions', theorized by the film historians Tom Gunning and André Gaudreault in relation to early cinema, denotes an understanding of film in its first years as a form of spectacle, marked by the display of its own technical powers and possibilities. The focus on the 'performativity' of early cinema has, more recently, been extended by a concern with modernism, performance and embodiment. Studies such as those of Anthony Paraskeva and Carrie Preston have explored the importance of the performing and gestural body in modernist literature, film, dance and theatre, taking in writers including Joyce, Wyndham Lewis, H. D. and Samuel Beckett. Susan McCabe has connected the focus on the 'hysterical body' at the turn of the century with the avant-garde cinema of the early twentieth century and the film poetry of writers including H. D., T. S. Eliot, William Carlos Williams and Marianne Moore. The centrality of Charlie Chaplin, viewed as exemplary of the performative body, the 'shocked' body of the modern subject and the body–machine nexus in modernity, has (as I discuss below) become a major preoccupation in a number of recent studies.[1]

Absolute distinctions between film and theatre (which were frequently upheld in early writings on cinema, as film sought to establish itself as an autonomous artistic form) have thus begun to cede to a sense of the profound connections between the two. Renewed attention to the film–theatre relationship has led not only to a return to the writings of Bertolt Brecht on this topic but, in a different context, to research into the ways in which theatrical performances mediated between novels and their film adaptations in the early years of narrative cinema, including the films of D. W. Griffith. Furthermore, while the novel remains central to an understanding of film–literature relationships in the modernist period, poetry, in addition to drama, has entered the frame in much more substantial ways. In Julian Murphet's account, 'it was the writers of the Anglo-American literary avant-garde who first and most illustriously "absorbed" the technical world of the second industrial revolution into their formal labors with language' (2009, 37): his examples include not only Gertrude Stein and Wyndham Lewis but the poets Ezra Pound and Louis Zukofsky.

A further context has been the intense focus in modernist studies on coteries, networks and publishing history – the 'institutions of modernism', to borrow Lawrence Rainey's phrase – which has led to a much greater concentration on early twentieth-century film cultures as an aspect of modernism. This has taken in dimensions such as the place of cinema in the journals and little magazines of the period, the work of the film societies that were founded in the late 1910s and 1920s, and the circumstances of film exhibition and spectatorship (see Marcus, 2007). These historically based aspects are barely present in studies such as Cohen's and Spiegel's, in which film, despite the naming of certain filmic examples, has a largely abstract form. David Trotter's study *Cinema and Modernism* (2007) sets new terms for our understanding of modernist film and literature, and pits itself against generalized concepts of the 'cinematic' or 'cinematographic' in literary works. The arguments of *Cinema and Modernism* are based on what writers could have known of the cinema, and the particular stage of its developments, at the time they were writing. The felt importance of writers' actual knowledge of, and contact with, the cinema is also seen in recent work on topics such as James Joyce's role in setting up the *Volta* cinema in Dublin in 1909 (arguably the first dedicated cinema space in Ireland) and Virginia Woolf's engagements with the film medium, exemplified in her 1926 essay 'The Cinema'.

Before turning to such encounters and representations, I want to raise the question of film and literature in relation to debates about modernism, modernity and their interconnections. The interest in cinema and modernism in recent decades has arisen in the context of broader theories of modernity and modern experience and an understanding of cinema's central role in the culture of modernity. As Tom Gunning writes, 'Given its striking appeal to popular sentiment, its mechanical force and play, its enlivening and contradictory tension between picturing and moving, cinema metaphorised modernity' (2006, 302). The work of Walter Benjamin, including his model of film as the embodiment of the modern experience of 'shock' and as the revelation of aspects of phenomenal experience unavailable to the human eye, has been central in this context.[2] Recent literary critics have proposed models of modernist literature running directly counter to those earlier critiques and accounts which defined modernism as a reaction against cultural modernity (critiques concerned, for example, with valorizations of private as against public/mass experience and with modernist literature's resistances to machine culture). The identification of modernist writing with, and not against, the cultures of modernity has found some of its strongest support in the allying of literature with cinema which, as Gunning suggests, has come to represent modernity *tout court*.

There has also been a blurring of boundaries (in literary studies and in critical theory) between concepts of modernism and avant-gardism (previously upheld, for example, in Peter Bürger's influential work), and between modernism and mass culture (the 'great divide' described by Andreas Huyssen). Cinema again plays a central role in these new conceptual formations. While the avant-garde cinema of the early twentieth century adopted strategies which were in accord with the experimental art and literature of the same period (as, for example, in the case of Cubism), there was also an avant-garde of viewing which did not seek to differentiate between avant-garde and popular cinema, but found in all films the potential for a radical and subversive anti-aesthetic. Thus, in France, a practice of Surrealist film-spectatorship developed which entailed moving from cinema to cinema (during the years of 'continuous performance') to create the experience of a composite film which would be all and none of the film fragments that had actually been perceived during the cinema-crawl. Film's particular techniques and modes of representation were celebrated as new forms of visual experience: the French film theorist and film-maker Jean Epstein, to take one example, would write of the film close-up as simultaneously creating new modes of proximity and of estrangement.[3] His contemporary Philippe Soupault, a poet and novelist who wrote extensively on the early cinema and was particularly absorbed by Chaplin, wrote enthusiastically of American film, recalling in 1930 that 'it brought to light all the beauty of our epoch, and all the mystery of modern mechanics [...]. The American picture-producers understood the drama that lay hidden in a lock, in a hand, in a drop of water'. 'All French poetry', he claimed, 'submitted profoundly to its imprint' (Soupault, 1930, 17). The so-called 'Americanization of culture' was by no means universally celebrated at this time, but the axes of European-American culture were constructed across, or in defiance of, the terms of high and popular culture.

Such configurations were also central to some of the most significant 'little magazines' of the early twentieth century, including *The Little Review, transition* and *Broom*. All three journals played a crucial role in sustaining the dialogue between American and European modernisms, in which the machine culture of modernity and of visual culture were central concerns. *Broom: An International Magazine of the Arts* ran from 1921 to 1924; its assistant editor was the young American writer, Matthew Josephson (who went on to become a successful critic, historian and journalist). Josephson was introduced to the Parisian Dadaists by Man Ray and used the pages of *Broom* to proclaim an American Dada and 'the Age of the Machine': 'A new art and new literature spring sturdily from the machine civilization', an advertisement in the journal pronounced.[4] As Dickran Tashjian has noted, Josephson in the 1920s 'pulled together a machine age manifesto in the process of development by many artists and writers', putting illustrations and photographs by Joseph Stella and Paul Strand in the journal, and publishing essays by Jean Epstein and others on the machine-self (Tashjian, 1986, 224). Other contributors included the artist Moholy-Nagy (on 'Light: A Medium of Plastic Expression'), Blaise Cendrars, Paul Strand and Philippe Soupault. The journal drew much of its energy from the Parisian Dadaists' and, subsequently, the Surrealists' passion for all things American, and it is here that film, and visual culture more generally, played a central role.

The British film journal *Close Up*, which ran from 1927 to 1933, has also been central to an understanding of the close connections between modernist literature and film (see Donald, Friedberg, and Marcus, 1988). Co-edited from Switzerland by the artist Kenneth Macpherson and the writer Bryher (Winifred Ellerman), the magazine published numerous articles by the poet and novelist H. D. (who also acted in three of the four films directed by Macpherson in this period, including *Borderline*, in which Paul Robeson played the central role) and the writer Dorothy Richardson, author of the multivolumed autobiographical novel *Pilgrimage*. The reach of *Close Up* into the international contexts of film-making and film culture was near-unparalleled (the journal, for example, was deeply entwined with Berlin film culture and published the first English-language versions of a number of articles by the Soviet director and film theorist Sergei Eisenstein). The journal also retained a strong commitment to the literary in rendering 'writing about film' as an artistic or avant-garde practice in its own right. Macpherson's editorials, as well as articles by H. D., Dorothy Richardson and, though they were less frequent contributors, Gertrude Stein and Marianne Moore, sought to represent the actuality of film-spectatorship, exploring in their prose (and, on occasion, their poetry) the relations between the immediacy of visual experience and the temporal dimensions of narrative, filmic and discursive.

Traversing the years of the transition to sound, *Close Up* also opens up the intense debates in the period over the coming of sound to film, which transformed not only the institutional and economic contexts of film-making but also the very nature of film aesthetics, formed and predicated on the silent cinema (as they would often continue to be in film aesthetics, many years after the transition) and on visuality as the defining quality and essence of the medium. *Close Up* reveals a gradual accommodation to 'the talkies', supported by the Soviet directors' model of 'contrapuntal sound' or 'sound montage' as a way of countermanding the staginess and static qualities of synchronized sound film in its early years. The two writers for the journal who did not make this accommodation were H. D. and Dorothy Richardson, and this is suggestive of a gendered dimension to the resistance to sound, and to the perceived intrusions of the voice into (as H. D. conceived it) the world of half-lights and dreams.

More broadly, recent research has made clear the centrality of cinema and film-going to women audiences, the important roles played by women film critics in the early years of cinema and the importance of film to women modernist writers. These included, in Anglo-American contexts, not only those already mentioned – H. D., Bryher, Richardson, Woolf, Stein and Moore – but also Djuna Barnes (who wrote on cinema for the journal *Theatre Guild Monthly* and whose journalism in the first decades of the twentieth century frequently invoked the spectacle and narrative conditions of the new film medium), Mina Loy (whose poems engage with many aspects of mass culture, including film), Iris Barry (an aspiring poet and one-time companion of both Pound and Wyndham Lewis who became best known for her film criticism and for her central role in the formation of the Film Library at New York's Museum of Modern Art) and the novelist Elizabeth Bowen. Their writings on film, regular or occasional, anticipated or continued the focus in *Close Up* on the experience of film-viewing, taking in the space of the cinema auditorium, the paradoxes of solitary viewing within the collective sphere of the cinema (including the implications of this for concepts of aesthetic experience as individual or communal) and the impact of dimensions such as light, sound and music in the cinema space. This attention to sensory experience, which could be understood as 'phenomenological' or 'haptic' (to be defined as a form of 'touching with the eye'), is neither essentially gendered nor limited to women's experience (it plays a significant role, for example, in Kenneth Macpherson's writings on film). It is, however, more marked in the work of women modernists, and this is reflected in the greater proportion of essays by women writers representing film-spectatorship, including Woolf's 'The Cinema' and Elizabeth Bowen's 'Why I Go to the Cinema', published a decade later (1938).

'The Cinema' is one of the most significant meditations on film to have been produced by a modernist writer and has generated significant critical discussion. The essay first appeared in *Arts* (New York) in June 1926: a variant version was published in the *Nation and Athenaeum* on 3 July 1926 and (without Woolf's consent) as 'The Movies and Reality' in the *New Republic* of 4 August 1926. Two unpublished typescript drafts also exist: they, like the published essays, reveal both Woolf's sense of the essentially speculative nature of any commentary on the cinema, in a context in which its future development could only be surmised, and the consistency of her particular interests in film. She saw in the cinema a means of capturing sensations and emotions too circumstantial, fleeting or abstract to be the subjects of the established arts. The earliest draft refers to the sensations we experience (which might be fear or excitement) 'in a garden where the wind blows a feather pirouetting before us' or with 'the emergence of an unexpected shadow'.[5]

Film would thus appear to be closer to nature than to art, and Woolf saw in it the potential for a comprehension of 'reality' at once entirely new and 'archaic' or 'primitive': the essay in all its versions comes back repeatedly to an image of 'the savages of the twentieth century watching the pictures' (Woolf, 1994, 348). While a number of commentators have interpreted this as Woolf's negative response to film, such a reading reduces and simplifies the complexities of her response. Woolf was by no means alone in understanding film as a medium at once absolutely modern and yet reaching back to the earliest forms of human expression, as in modes of picture-writing, and to the fundamentals of human emotion (Fear, Pain, Rage, Anger, Joy). Any aversion to film Woolf felt was centred on its 'development' into the adaptation of literary texts, and in particular novels: her responses to adaptations of *Anna Karenina* and (as discussed in the draft version of her essay) *Vanity Fair* are entirely negative. Film-makers had moved away, she noted, from early documentary films, or *actualités*, and in so doing had left behind the most powerful dimension of the cinema: its power to body forth the world as it is. The future cinema she envisaged would represent both the world of dreams (in which relations of time and space are subject to no known laws) and present reality in its contingency, detail and, it could be argued, modernity. As she wrote towards the close of the variant version of the published essay, 'How all this is to be attempted, much less achieved, no one at the moment could tell us. We get intimations only in the chaos of the streets, perhaps, when some momentary assembly of colour, sound, movement, suggests that here is a scene waiting a new art to be transfixed' (Woolf, 1994, 595). The representation of the city was, as I discuss below, a crucial forum for the encounter between literature and film in modernist culture.

As Woolf worked on 'The Cinema' essay, she was also writing the central section of her novel *To the Lighthouse* (1927), 'Time Passes', which presents the world of matter through time and in the absence (or near-absence) of a human observer: Woolf described it as 'eyeless' writing. The ghostly presences of Mr and Mrs Ramsay – the one absent, the other now dead – appear on the walls of the decaying house in the form of projected film: '(and faint and flickering, like a yellow beam or the circle at the end of a telescope, a lady in a grey cloak, stooping over her flowers, went wandering over the bedroom wall, up the dressing-table, across the wash-stand [...])' (Woolf, 1992, 149). The passage of ten years between the first and third parts of the novel (though it is also condensed into one night, during which the world tosses and turns in the nightmare of history) has its mirror in the gap of ten years alluded to in 'The Cinema'. These come between the present in which the early films are being viewed and the past of the realities they record. In the variant version of the essay, Woolf writes, 'We are beholding a world which has gone between the waves [...] The war sprung its chasm at the foot of all this innocence and ignorance, but it was thus that we danced and pirouetted, toiled and desired, thus that the sun shone and the clouds scudded up to the very end' (1994, 592).

Both 'The Cinema' and *To the Lighthouse* record the abundant energies of the moment (as in the first section of the novel, 'The Window') and the workings of time and death on living matter. The earliest commentaries on the cinema defined the medium as embodying the presence of an absence, a relation which informs Woolf's essay and novel, and which underlies the work of film theorists such as Christian Metz and Stanley Cavell. Georg Lukács, writing in 1913, constructed the distinction between theatre and film as one between the 'absolute *present*' of the stage and the 'lack of this "present" [which] is the primary characteristic of the "cinema" […] cinematic images, equal in their essences to nature, are no less organic and alive than those images of the stage. Only they maintain a life of a completely different kind' (Lukács, 2001, 13–14). It is unlikely that Woolf would have known Lukács' essay, but her approach to film is similar in many respects: it includes the belief that the cinema represents, in Lukács' words, 'a new *beauty*' which should not be defined on the basis of the existing arts but 'is precisely a beauty worthy of its own *aesthetic* evaluation and determination' (13).

The issue of the ways in which novelistic techniques changed and altered as a response to film is a complex and vexed one. We can never know how the writing of Woolf, or any other modernist writer, might have developed without an awareness of film and film technique. We can, however, speculate, with a high degree of confidence, that film made its impact both on Woolf's approaches to aesthetic questions and on her formal solutions to issues of narrative construction. Thus her way of representing 'simultaneity' in 'The Lighthouse', the third and final section of the novel, was almost certainly inflected by a familiarity with cinematic strategies. These include parallel editing (or cross-cutting) as a means to depict events taking place at the same moment but in different spaces, as well as the shot-reverse-shot structure of continuity editing which has its literary correlative in the novel in the views from shore to sea and back from sea to shore. In 'The Cinema', Woolf wrote of a future cinema in which 'we should have the continuity of human life kept before us by the representation of some object common to both lives' (1994, 352): her novel *The Years* (1937) represents this continuity through various objects – a painting, a chair, a walrus-brush – which survive the years and changes in place and circumstance.

James Joyce's relationship to the cinema is rather more diffuse than that of Woolf. Explorations of the topic have addressed the impact on his writing, in particular *Ulysses* (1922), of pre-cinematic technologies (such as the Mutoscope, referred to by Leopold Bloom in the 'Nausicaa' episode of the text in conjunction with 'Peeping Tom') and early cinema (see, for example, Mullin, 2003). This history is book-ended by Joyce's meeting, in the 1930s, with Sergei Eisenstein, who had described *Ulysses* as the most important event in the history of cinema (rather than literature). The founding of the *Volta* cinema in Dublin in 1909, by Joyce and three businessmen with experience of running cinemas whom he had met in Trieste, adds a further dimension. The films screened during the six months of the venture were almost entirely French and Italian, and included 'art' films and theatrical adaptations as well as comedies and non-fiction films. Luke McKernan, who has extensively researched the *Volta* programming, suggests that it is in its multifariousness that 'we may most profitably look for the Joycean connection' (2010, 27). The ludic dimensions of early film, and early film performance, were perhaps particularly influential. The fascination with metamorphoses and with the animation of objects central to the films of George Méliès, magician turned film-maker in cinema's first years, as well as the quick-change artistry of the performer Leopoldi Fregoli, have been seen as shaping forces on the 'Circe' or 'Night-town' episode of *Ulysses*, with its transformations of bodies between sexes and species and its animated objects: Bloom's singing bar of soap, the brothel-madam Bella's erotic talking fan.

The 'Wandering Rocks' section of the novel evokes rather different dimensions of the cinema, in its representation of motion and transport around Dublin. In an exemplary reading of the episode, David Trotter notes the ways in which the fact of the city brings Dubliners into relation with each other – losing the two central protagonists, Stephen and Bloom, in the crowd – 'beyond the reach of montage' (2007, 91). Trotter is arguing here, as throughout his study, against the assumption that 'montage' should be understood as the central mediating term between modernist literature and film. He finds in 'Wandering Rocks' the forms of movement, 'automatism' (the neutrality of the camera-eye) and 'intercutting' at work in the *actualités* of film's earliest years, a cinema which included numerous films of Dublin's daily life and of public events in the city. Such spectacles would seem to be parodied in the closing part of 'Wandering Rocks', with its representation of a cavalcade in which all the figures who have appeared in earlier scenes are presented and named in the narrative.

To this one might add Joyce's depiction, throughout the episode, of part-objects and persons: 'The blind of the window was drawn aside. A card *Unfurnished Apartments* slipped from the sash and fell. A plump bare generous arm shone, was seen, held forth from a white petticoat bodice and taut shiftstraps. A woman's hand flung forth a coin over the area railings. It fell on the path' (Joyce, 1993, 216). This 'sectional vision', and the fragmentation of bodies and objects, seems closer to a rather later cinema. It could be suggested (as in Eisenstein's claim for the importance of *Ulysses* in the history of cinema) that the relationship between

Joyce's writing and the cinema was one of mutual influence, mediated by, and embodied in, modern urban experience. For the German writer Alfred Döblin, author of *Berlin Alexanderplatz* (1929), a novel much influenced by *Ulysses*, Joyce's novel had shown the extent to which cinema had 'penetrated the sphere of literature [...] To the experiential image of a person today also belongs the streets, the scenes changing by the second, the signboards, automobile traffic [...] the fleeting quality, the restlessness' (Döblin, 1994, 514).

In recent work on film and modernism, the figures of Gertrude Stein, Wyndham Lewis and Samuel Beckett have become prominent. Stein has in the past been more fully associated with modernist painting than with film – she and her brother Leo were prominent art collectors in the Paris of the 1920s and 1930s – but the close relationship, and at times shared identity, between avant-garde artists and film-makers at this time contributed to the cinematic contexts for her work. As she wrote in her essay 'Portraits and Repetition':

> I was doing what the cinema was doing, I was making a continuous statement of what that person was until I had not many things but one thing [...] I, of course did not think of it in terms of the cinema, in fact I doubt whether at that time I had ever seen a cinema but, and I cannot repeat this too often any one is of one's period and this our period was undoubtedly the period of the cinema. (Stein, 2004, 106)[6]

The 'continuous present' of Stein's prose could also be understood as the 'tense' of cinema, while her deployment of repetition and/with difference has its corollary in film's putting into motion, at the level of projection, a series of still frames whose differentiations mark the flow of time in fractions of a second.

For the avant-garde film-makers, artists and writers of the early twentieth century, Charlie Chaplin (or 'Charlot', as he was known in France) came to stand for the film medium itself. Fernand Léger's 'Dadaist' film *Ballet mécanique* (1924) is composed of machine imagery, the movements of everyday objects and the repetitive movements of human figures, opening and closing with a fractured and recomposed representation of the figure of Chaplin. Chaplin's walk – the defining dimension of the figure of the Tramp – and his gestural screen-life more generally became a focus for the complex and contested understanding of the human being as organic or mechanical/automatic creature. For Walter Benjamin, Chaplin's unique significance was that 'in his work, the human being is integrated into the film image by way of his gestures [...] The innovation of Chaplin's gestures is that he dissects the expressive movements of human beings into a series of minute innervations' (2002b, 94). In his autobiography, Chaplin recorded a conversation he had with Gertrude Stein when they met in America: 'She theorized about cinema plots: "They are too hackneyed, complicated and contrived." She would like to see me in a movie just walking up the street and turning a corner, then another corner, and another' (1964, 302).

Wyndham Lewis wrote disparagingly of the 'infant-cult' in his account of Chaplin in *Time and Western Man* (1924), linking Chaplin, 'child-man', to the personae and work of Anita Loos (a highly successful cinema screenwriter and author of the comic 'Hollywood' novel *Gentlemen Prefer Blondes*, 1925) and Gertrude Stein, whose prose he defined as similarly *faux-naif* and infantilized. Lewis's critique of Chaplin, and in particular the Tramp persona, is extended (even as the figure energizes) in the novel *The Childermass* (1928), in which the two central characters, Pullman and Satters, are reunited in the afterlife (both having died in the First World War) as, in Anthony Paraskeva's phrase, 'animated stiffs' (2013, 100). The despotic Bailiff, who at times appears in the guise of Chaplin, requires that they enact routines from Chaplin's films. Paraskeva observes that 'Lewis effects a total separation between movement and volition by writing his two leads as the dried shells of cinematic automata, screen personas detached from their point of origin and hardened into mechanised cliché' (101). Here the animus would seem to be directed against film's automatic life, as well as the forms of imitative behaviour and crowd response connected to the Chaplin figure and to cinema as mass culture in general. Yet there are inconsistencies and paradoxes both in Lewis's cultural critiques and in his models of comedy. Michael North notes of his writing: 'Laughter and machinelike behaviour are intimately connected, but it is not at all clear how the hard, machinelike laughter of the scoffer is to be distinguished from the mechanical behaviour it is supposed to explode' (2009, 117). Lewis's critiques, moreover, are often at their fiercest when their objects come closest to his own ideas: this is almost certainly true of his relationship to Chaplin's early films.

In later works, including *The Revenge for Love* (1937), Lewis explored literary character in relation to the Hollywood screen image and the face in close-up, as in references to his central protagonist Victor Stamp smiling his 'Clark Gable smile – one side of his face all sardonic half-mirth, the scalp muscles ploughing up the forehead to make it all go careworn, so as to embitter the onesided smile down below still more' (Lewis, 1972, 90). The intense focus on physiognomy and facial gesture is characteristic of Lewis, but the representation of modern subjects who model themselves on, or are made by, the personae of the Hollywood dream factory occurs frequently in the writing of the period. It is central, for example, to the work of Graham Greene, who was deeply involved with film culture. On emerging from a cinema, the protagonists of *Brighton Rock* pass by 'a blonde with Garbo cheeks [who] paused to powder on the steps up to the Norfolk bar' (Greene, 2004, 196): the boundary between the film world and the real world has thinned to transparency.

Writers in the 1930s were engaging with film as a talking medium, but for many the lure of the silent film remained strong. Chaplin famously held out against sound cinema for a decade after the arrival of the 'talkies' and his 'conversion to sound' was only ever a partial one. Samuel Beckett's absorption in film was also closely tied to the silent era. In a letter written to Thomas McGreevy at the beginning of 1936, Beckett wrote of seeing '*Becky Sharp* in colour' and observed that the film, while a success in London, had been a 'complete flop' in Dublin. This gave him hope, he wrote, that 'the industrial film will become so completely naturalistic, in stereoscopic colour & gramophonic sound, that a back water may be created for the two dimensional silent film that had barely emerged from its rudiments when it was swamped'. Silent and sound film could then become 'two separate things and not question of a fight between them or rather of a rout' (Beckett, 2009, 311). The hope that silent film could continue as a separate art to that of sound film had indeed been quite widely entertained a few years earlier, and had been expressed in the pages of *Close Up*, back numbers of which Beckett was reading at this time. The reference to the 'back water' of the silent film indeed closely echoes a *Close Up* article by Dorothy Richardson, published in 1930, in which she lamented the passing of silent cinema, but celebrated the discovery, in 'a neglected central backwater' in London, of a cinema showing silent films in 'continuous performance', including Chaplin's *The Gold Rush*: 'We were seeing these films with new eyes. They stood the test. These new [sound] films, we said, may be the companions, they can never be the rivals of the silent film.' The 'essential potency', she concludes, 'of any kind of silent film, "work of art" or other, remains untouched' (Richardson, qtd. in Donald, Friedberg and Marcus, 1998, 200).

In 1936, as Beckett worked on his novel *Murphy* (1938), his interest in film was at its height. He wrote to Eisenstein at this time, 'to ask to be considered for admission to the Moscow State School of Cinematography', noting that he was most interested 'in the scenario and editing end of the subject' (Beckett, 2009, 317). He received no reply. Other letters of this period show him engaging with the writings, and films, of Eisenstein and Pudovkin, and expressing interest in the principles of Soviet 'montage' (see Antoine-Dunne, 2002, 2003). The depth and breadth of film's influence on Beckett (to include not only the Soviet and the German Expressionist cinema of the 1920s and 1930s but film in its earliest years) can be observed in his silent *Film* (1965). Here the silent film actor Buster Keaton is both subject and object of scenes of looking and looking away, and repeated visual references to *Battleship Potemkin* emerge. Beckett replicates Eisenstein's transfer of an eyeglass between figures on the screen and stages a sequence in which a woman, holding a lorgnette to her eye, opens her mouth in an expression of horror which mirrors that of Eisenstein's wounded schoolteacher, her mouth held open in a scream, on the Odessa steps. As with the artist Francis Bacon's *Study for the Nurse in the Film 'Battleship Potemkin'* (1957), the forms and images of silent film, and of the cinema of the modernist period more generally, continued to reverberate in works of literature and art.

The question of the relationship between modernist literature and film, and indeed literature and film more generally, also remains an open and active one. We can never fully comprehend the impact of the new medium of film on its early viewers and commentators: we look back from the perspectives of those who have grown up in a film age and, most recently, in a digital age. Insights into the ways in which cinema impacted on literary representations nonetheless continue to be developed. At the present time, they run in a number of particularly strong directions. These include substantial work on film history and film culture and a greater knowledge of the specificities of the films that were viewed and that made their mark; modes of 'close reading' of both film and literary texts, and their shared and differing engagements with time, space and narrative form; and a broader understanding of 'media ecologies', in which film shares a platform with other technologically mediated forms of communication, including literary texts. The issues remain as alive and as complex today as they were a century ago.

Notes

1   See Gordon (2001), McCabe (2005), Trotter (2007), North (2009), Seed (2009), Preston (2011) and Paraskeva (2013).
2   See, in particular, Benjamin's 'The Work of Art in the Age of Its Technological Reproducibility' (2002a) [1936].
3   See, for example, Epstein's 'On Certain Characteristics of *Photogénie*' (2012) [1926].
4   See back inside cover of *Broom*, 5, no. 1 (August 1923).
5   Woolf, Virginia, Draft 1 of 'The Movies', 135. Held in the Henry W. and Albert A. Berg Collection of English and American Literature, The New York Public Library.
6   Stein (2004, 106).

Bibliography

Antoine-Dunne, J. (2002), 'Beckett and Eisenstein on Light and Contrapuntal Montage'. *Samuel Beckett Today/Aujourd'hui*, 11, 315–23.

Antoine-Dunne, J. (2003), 'Beckett, Eisenstein and the Image: Making an Inside an Outside'. *Critical Studies*, 21, (1), 193–213.

Beckett, S. (2009), *The Letters of Samuel Beckett, Vol. 1: 1929–1940*, M. L. Fehsenfeld and L. M. Overbeck (eds). Cambridge: Cambridge University Press.

Benjamin, W. (2002a), 'The Work of Art in the Age of Its Technological Reproducibility', in H. Eiland and M. W. Jennings (eds), *Walter Benjamin: Selected Writings*, vol. 3. Cambridge, MA: Harvard University Press, pp. 101–33.

Benjamin, W. (2002b), 'The Formula in Which the Dialectical Structure of Film Finds Expression', in H. Eiland and M. W. Jennings (eds), *Walter Benjamin: Selected Writings*, vol. 3. Cambridge, MA: Harvard University Press, pp. 94–5.

Bowen, E. (1938), 'Why I Go to the Cinema', in C. Davy (ed.), *Footnotes to the Films*. London: Lovat Dickson, pp. 205–20.

Bürger, P. (1984), *Theory of the Avant-Garde*. Minneapolis: University of Minnesota Press.

Cavell, S. (1979 [1971]), *The World Viewed: Reflections on the Ontology of Film*, enlarged edn. Cambridge, MA: Harvard University Press.

Chaplin, C. (1964), *My Autobiography*. London: Bodley Head.

Cohen, K. (1979), *Film and Fiction: The Dynamics of Exchange*. New Haven and London: Yale University Press.

Döblin, A. (1994 [1928]), '*Ulysses* by Joyce', in A. Kaes, M. Jay and E. Dimendberg (eds), *The Weimar Republic Sourcebook*. Berkeley and Los Angeles: University of California Press.

Donald, J., Friedberg, A. and Marcus, L. (eds) (1998), *Close Up: Cinema and Modernism 1927–1933*. London: Cassell.

Epstein, J. (2012 [1926]), 'On Certain Characteristics of *Photogénie*', in T. Milne (transl.), S. Keller and J. N. Paul (eds), *Jean Epstein: Critical Essays and New Translations*. Amsterdam: Amsterdam University Press, pp. 292–6.

Gordon, R. B. (2001), *Why the French Love Jerry Lewis: From Cabaret to Early Cinema*. Stanford, CA: Stanford University Press.

Greene, G. (2004 [1938]), *Brighton Rock*. London: Vintage.

Gunning, T. (2006), 'Modernity and Cinema: A Culture of Shocks and Flows', in M. Pomerance (ed.), *Cinema and Modernity*. New Brunswick, NJ: Rutgers University Press.

Huyssen, Andreas (1987), *After the Great Divide: Modernism, Mass Culture, Postmodernism*. Bloomington: Indiana University Press.

Joyce, J. (1993 [1922]), *Ulysses*. Oxford: Oxford University Press.

Lewis, W. (1972 [1937]), *The Revenge for Love*. Harmondsworth: Penguin.

Lukács, G. (2001 [1913]), 'Thoughts toward an Aesthetic of the Cinema', in J. Blankenship (transl.), *Polygraph: International Journal of Culture and Politics*, 13, 13–18.

Magny, C. E. (1972), *The Age of the American Novel: The Film Aesthetic of Fiction between the Two Wars*, Eleanor Hochman (transl.). New York: Frederick Ungar.

Marcus, L. (2007), *The Tenth Muse: Writing about Cinema in the Modernist Period.* Oxford: Oxford University Press.

McCabe, S. (2005), *Cinematic Modernism: Modernist Poetry and Film.* Cambridge: Cambridge University Press.

McKernan, L. (2010), 'James Joyce and the Volta Programme', in J. McCourt (ed.), *Roll Away the Reel World: James Joyce and Cinema.* Cork: Cork University Press, pp. 15–27.

Mullin, K. (2003), *James Joyce, Sexuality and Social Purity.* Cambridge: Cambridge University Press.

Murphet, J. (2009), *Multimedia Modernism: Literature and the Anglo-American Avant-Garde.* Cambridge: Cambridge University Press.

North, M. (2009), *Machine-Age Comedy.* Oxford: Oxford University Press.

Paraskeva, A. (2013), *The Speech-Gesture Complex: Modernism, Theatre, Cinema.* Edinburgh: Edinburgh University Press.

Preston, C. (2011), *Modernism's Mythic Pose: Gender, Genre, Solo Performance.* Oxford: Oxford University Press.

Seed, D. (2009), *Cinematic Fictions: The Impact of the Cinema on the American Novel up to the Second World War.* Liverpool: Liverpool University Press.

Soupault, P. (1930), *The American Influence in France*, B. Hughes and G. Hughes (transl.). Seattle: University of Washington Bookstore.

Spiegel, A. (1976), *Fiction and the Camera Eye: Visual Consciousness in Film and the Modern Novel.* Charlottesville: University Press of Virginia.

Stein, G. (2004), 'Portraits and Repetitions', in Patricia Meyorowitz (ed.), *Look at Me Now and Here I Am: Writings and Lectures 1911–1945.* Harmondsworth: Penguin.

Tashjian, D. (1986), 'Engineering a New Art', in Richard Guy Wilson, Dianne H. Pilgrim, Dickran Tashjian (eds), *The Machine Age in America, 1918–1941.* New York: Brooklyn Museum of Art, in association with Harry N. Abrams, pp. 205–68.

Trotter, D. (2007), *Cinema and Modernism.* Oxford: Blackwell.

Woolf, V. (1992 [1925]), Draft 1 of 'The Movies'. Virginia Woolf Collection of Papers, Henry W. and Albert A. Berg Collection of English and American Literature, New York Public Library. [Articles, essays, fiction, and reviews], vol. 2, May 1922, 1925 (Part II of 1925), pp. 135–51.

Woolf, V. (1992 [1927]), *To the Lighthouse.* Harmondsworth: Penguin.

Woolf, V. (1994 [1926]), 'The Cinema', in A. McNeillie (ed.), *The Essays of Virginia Woolf, Vol. 4: 1925–1928.* London: Hogarth Press.

10

Modernism and Popular Culture

Lawrence Rainey

Almost thirty years have elapsed since Andreas Huyssen published *After the Great Divide: Modernism, Mass Culture, Postmodernism*. Although the issues he addresses in that book are now constellated in very different ways, his formulations achieved a schematic clarity that made them beguiling and worthwhile revisiting. For Huyssen, building on earlier work by Peter Bürger (1984), a sharp distinction was to be drawn between modernism and the avant-garde. Modernism was typified by its hostility to mass or popular culture. 'Mass culture has always been the hidden subtext of the modernist project', Huyssen urged, a project in which popular culture is construed as a threat of encroaching formlessness, gendered as female, and held at bay by reaffirming and refortifying the boundaries that divide authentic art and inauthentic mass culture (Huyssen, 1986, 47, 53).

Hostility to mass or popular culture not only defined modernism's essence, but it differentiated it from the avant-garde (Dada, constructivism, futurism, surrealism and the New Objectivity of the Weimar Republic [*Neue Sachlichkeit*]). While modernism seeks to reaffirm the boundaries of traditional art, the avant-garde 'attempts to subvert art's autonomy, its artificial separation from life, and its institutionalization as "high art,"' an impulse that also accounts for its 'urge to validate other, formerly neglected or ostracized forms of cultural expression', chief among them popular culture (Huyssen, 1986, 61).

The third term contributing to this constellation, after modernism and the avant-garde, was postmodernism, a term endowed with breathtaking elasticity. It could take 'the form of happenings, pop vernacular, psychedelic art, acid rock, alternative and street theater', though it could also embrace 'Kerouac, Ginsberg and the Beats, Burroughs and Barthelme' (Huyssen, 1986, 193, 188).

Architecture presented a special problem: yes, there was 'something patently absurd' about Robert Venturi's claims that the vernacular style of the Caesars Palace casino, in Las Vegas, offered the blueprint for a renewal of contemporary architecture; nevertheless, such claims forced us 'to acknowledge the power they mustered to explode the reified dogmas of modernism' (Huyssen, 1986, 188). More importantly, the case of Venturi exemplified a much wider phenomenon: 'Pop in the broadest sense was the context in which a notion of the postmodern first took shape, and from the beginning until today [1985], the most significant trends within postmodernism have challenged modernism's relentless hostility to mass culture' (Huyssen, 1986, 188). In short, postmodernism was aligned with the historical avant-garde in its acceptance of the popular and the vernacular; modernism, instead, was a reactionary, perhaps paranoid attempt to roll back the tide of mass or popular culture. This cluster of ideas has become sufficiently influential that one recent book can simply refer to 'the Great Divide theory' – tersely echoing the title of Huyssen's book (Goldstone, 2013, 22).

There were many problems with Huyssen's arguments. One was his troubling distinction between modernism and the avant-garde. Huyssen kept illustrating the distinction with increasing desperation, if not always success: 'It makes little sense to lump Thomas Mann together with Dada, Proust with André Breton, or Rilke with Russian constructivism' (Huyssen, 1986, 163).

Fair enough. But is Rilke, with his many images of roses and angels, best thought of as a modernist? Or is he one more variant of late nineteenth-century decadence, overlaid with a Grecian veneer? And why shouldn't one collate Breton with Proust? After all, when working for the French publisher Gallimard in 1920, Breton went daily to Proust's flat and read aloud the proofs for *The Guermantes Way*. As for the opposition between Thomas Mann and Dada, it glosses over the immense gap in their literary quality. Consider the opening to Raoul Hausmann's 'Pamphlet against the Weimar Republic's Conception of Life', which begins:

> I announce the Dadaistic world!
> I laugh at science and culture, these ailing safeguards of a society condemned to death.[1]
>
> (Hausmann, 1977, 49)

Laudable sentiments, perhaps, but expressed with a crudity at some remove from the delicate ironies found everywhere in Mann. Indeed, one may wonder whether the adolescent posing of Dada merits equivalence with the musings of Gustav von Aschenbach or the subtle acerbities of Serenus Zeitblom.

Another problem resides in the aesthetic parameters that Huyssen ascribes to postmodernism. He insists that it includes 'Kerouac, Ginsberg and the Beats, Burroughs and Barthelme', but then goes on to include the architects Robert Venturi, Michael Graves and Philip Johnson, albeit with reservations. But for most observers there is a difference between the cultivation of sincerity and spontaneity promulgated by the Beats and the arch and knowing wit of postmodernist architecture. Perhaps both do have their origins in the popular, as Huyssen asserts; but there is a big difference between the popular and 'the popular', a difference that resides in irony, a quality notable only for its absence in the writings of Ginsberg, Kerouac and the Beats. As defined by Huyssen, the postmodern yokes together, under a single rubric, aesthetics that are deeply incompatible, if not downright inimical to one another.

Nor is it self-evident that his principal thesis, that modernism was relentlessly hostile to popular culture, even has much hold in the English-language world, at least not if we take Joyce's *Ulysses* as a representative text. After all, when Simon Dedalus and Ben Dollard sing their renditions of 'When First I Saw' and 'The Croppy Boy' (in the 'Sirens' episode), they are simply restaging a ritual of middle-class parlour life, public singing, a mode of conjuring sociability that remained part of popular life until it was slowly decimated by the onslaught of recorded song after 1918. And their choice of tunes is revealing: 'The Croppy Boy' was a perennial Irish favourite well into the 1960s, while 'When First I Saw' was essentially a parlour song, one that has since dropped out of any musical repertoire except in its earlier Italian form, 'M'apparì'. (It continues to appear in every tenor's collection of greatest arias only because the high notes at the end offer an occasion for vocal display.) The opera in which it first appeared, *Martha* (1847), though performed in 1906 and subsequent seasons at the New York Metropolitan Opera, has entirely vanished from the modern repertory, dismissed as too light, too French, too middlebrow.

Even the few quotations of Latin that take place in *Ulysses* only reinforce the book's dialogue with popular culture. For every Latin quotation comes from the Catholic mass, universally performed in Latin until 1962, when the Second Vatican Council authorized the vernacular masses still in use today. Pointedly, *Ulysses* never quotes from Vergil, Cicero or Tacitus, benchmarks of classical Latin, but only from the ecclesiastical Latin known to every churchgoer.

Every reader of *Ulysses* swiftly discerns that the book has an elastic, mobile relationship with both the *Odyssey* and Mozart's most popular opera, *Don Giovanni*. Molly Bloom, we learn early on, will be singing the opera's duet 'Là ci darem la mano' with Blazes Boylan at a forthcoming concert, hinting at the love triangle that forms a central plot thread. But most readers will be disconcerted by the novel's repeated references to *Turko the Terrible*. The first appears in 'Telemachus', when Stephen Dedalus ponders the events his mother once recollected:

> She heard Royce sing in the pantomime of *Turko the Terrible* and laughed with others when he sang:
> I am the boy
> That can enjoy
> Invisibility.

> (Joyce, 1984, 1.257–62)

The second occurs a bit later when Leopold Bloom, walking in the morning towards the butcher's shop, imagines himself somewhere in the Far East:

> Wander through awned streets. Turbaned faces going by. Dark caves of carpet shops, big man, Turko the terrible, seated crosslegged, smoking a coiled pipe.
> (Joyce, 1984, 4.88–90)

The third occurs in 'Circe', when Bloom sees a phantasmagoric vision of his wife's late father, Major Tweedy:

> *Major Tweedy, moustached like Turko the terrible, in bearskin cap with hackleplume and accoutrements, with epaulettes, gilt chevrons and sabretaches, his breast bright with medals, toes the line.*
> (Joyce, 1984, 15.4612–15)

It is possible that Stephen also sees this hallucination, since the text, at this point, no longer obeys the logical-causal coordination of realism. But what are we to make of it?

Turko the Terrible was a Christmas pantomime that premiered at the Gaiety Theatre in Dublin in December 1873, that theatre's first-ever pantomime. It was written by the Irish author Edwin Hamilton (1849–1919), though it was also repeatedly updated and revised as it moved into subsequent years. Further, Hamilton was merely adapting or rewriting an earlier pantomime by William Brough, an 'extravaganza' that was at first, in 1868, titled *Turko the Terrible; or, The Fairy Roses*, and later, in 1876, retitled *Turko the Terrible; or, the Great Princess Show* (Thornton, 1961, 17).[2] In the 1873 Gaiety production, the role of Turko was played by Edward E. Royce, and we know that he sang 'Invisibility'. But thanks to the impressive research of Cheryl Herr, we also know that Royce had already performed the same song a year earlier in a burlesque called *Amy*

Robsart (Eldred's Company, 1872, Gaiety), where he achieved a 'striking success' (Herr, 1986, 120). The song, in short, was simply lifted from the burlesque (*Amy Robsart*, 1872) and inserted into the pantomime (*Turko*, 1873) that was an adaptation of an extravaganza (another *Turko*, 1868). Still more, Royce returned to Dublin in 1892, again at the Gaiety Theatre where, in homage to his earlier success, he played the role of Captain M'Turco in that year's 'Grand Christmas Pantomime', *Sindbad the Sailor*. Did he reprise 'Invisibility' yet again? We do not know. We do know, however, that this 1892 production, alongside *Sindbad the Sailor*, featured characters named Tindbad (the tailor) and Whinbad (the whaler).[3] Famously, as Bloom falls asleep at the end of the 'Ithaca' episode, he recalls that he is weary because he has travelled so far during the course of the day. The text then asks the simple question, 'With?' Which begets the answer:

> Sinbad the Sailor and Tinbad the Tailor and Jinbad the Jailer and Whinbad the Whaler and Ninbad the Nailer and Finbad the Failer and Binbad the Bailer and Pinbad the Pailer and Minbad the Mailer and Hinbad the Hailer and Rinbad the Railer and Dinbad the Kailer and Vinbad the Quailer and Linbad the Yailer and Xinbad the Phthailer.
>
> (Joyce, 1984, 17.2321–26)

Joyce, in other words, adopts and adapts the principles that drive the energies of popular pantomime, turning them into a machine that generates his very text. Such simple devices of repetition and variation are exploited again and again. When viewed against the backdrop of Mozart's *Don Giovanni*, for example, Bloom is both Leporello (in relation to Molly) and Don Giovanni (in relation to Martha Clifford, or whoever stands behind that name). But he is also simultaneously Lionel (in the opera *Martha*), a role also momentarily assumed by Simon Dedalus when he sings 'When First I Saw', the aria sung by Lionel in *Martha*. To suggest this heady fusion of the opera character Lionel with Simon Dedalus and Leopold Bloom, Joyce exuberantly conjures a single word: Siopold! (Joyce, 1984, 11.752). Identity is no longer a fixed or given status, but an amalgam of any number of roles within any number of popular fictions.

Nowhere does Joyce adopt popular cultural forms more vigorously than in the 'Circe' episode. It begins when Stephen Dedalus and his friend Lynch enter into 'nighttown', Joyce's name for a Dublin slum notorious for harbouring houses of ill repute. While they walk and talk, Stephen repeatedly interrupts their conversation with snatches of song, evidently in Latin. A reader who assembles these snatches will discover that Stephen is singing lines from the Catholic mass, specifically the second chant that precedes the blessing of the altar in the mass that is sung in the Paschal or Lenten season, the period of roughly four Sundays preceding Easter:

Vidi aquam – Introit for Paschal (Lent)		**Translation: I saw water**
Vidi aquam egredientem de templo a		I saw water pouring forth from the temple from
latere dextro. Alleluia.	(77)	its right side. Alleluia.
Et omnes ad quos pervenit aqua ista	(84)	And all those to whom that water came
Salvi facti sunt	(98)	Have been redeemed.

(Joyce, 1984, 15.77, 84, 98)

With these words, the text signals one of the two forms most crucial for structuring 'Circe', the Catholic mass of the Easter period. 'Circe', in effect, will register the metaphorical or fantastic death and resurrection of its two unheroic protagonists, Leopold Bloom and Stephen Dedalus. But what is the second form?

Noticing the presence of the mass should not blind us to another popular form no less powerfully present in 'Circe'. A hint about it comes only a few lines farther down, when Lynch asks Stephen, 'Where are we going?' Stephen replies: 'Lecherous Lynx, to *la belle dame sans merci*, Georgina Johnson, *ad deam qui laetificat iuventutem meam*' (Joyce, 1984, 15.121–122). It's the last phrase, *ad deam qui laetificat iuventutem meam*, that seizes our attention, because it invokes the second line of the same 'Introit' earlier invoked by Buck Mulligan in the book's first spoken speech, when he carries his shaving bowl to the top of the Martello tower and intones the chant that a priest would utter when approaching the altar before communion, 'Introibo ad altare Dei':

Introibo ad altare	**Translation: I shall enter into the altar**
Introibo ad altare Dei	I shall enter into the altar of God,
Ad Deum qui laetificat iuventutem meam.	Towards God, who has made glad my youth.

But Joyce seizes on these well-known phrases to introduce a slight alteration in the wording, changing only a single letter: the 'u' in the word 'deum', meaning 'God', has been replaced with an 'a', turning it into 'deam' or 'goddess'. His alteration encapsulates a broader transformation in the mass's form, one related to the role of gender in a competing popular form. Not much later, it makes its appearance when Leopold Bloom is enchanted by the sudden apparition of his dead mother, Ellen:

ELLEN BLOOM

(in pantomime dame's stringed mobcap, widow Twankey's crinoline and bustle, blouse with muttonleg sleeves buttoned behind, grey mittens and cameo brooch, her hair pleated in a crispine net, appears ...) (Joyce, 1984, 15.282–85)

Widow Twankey is a female character in the Christmas pantomime *Aladdin*, but she is played by a 'pantomime dame', the term applied to a man who plays a female role and is a comic foil to the 'principal boy', Aladdin, played by an actress. Indeed, we know a celebrated Widow Twankey of Joyce's day, Dan Leno.

Pantomime dames are played either in an extremely camp style or else by men acting 'butch' in women's clothing, wearing big make-up and big hair, having exaggerated physical features and performing in a melodramatic style. Joyce, in short, is invoking the sensational theatricality and cross-dressing of British pantomime as a counterweight to the solemnity of the Roman Catholic mass, and the explosive mixture of these genres gives 'Circe' its wild, comical, hypnotic power.

When, later in 'Circe', the brothel owner or 'whoremistress' Bella Cohen makes her appearance (15.2742–48), she speaks only a single line in propria voce ('My word! I'm all of a mucksweat' [15.2750]) before being transformed, via a single letter, from Bella into Bello:

BLOOM

(mumbles) Awaiting your further orders we remain, gentlemen ...

BELLO

(with a hard basilisk stare, in a baritone voice) Hound of dishonour!

BLOOM

(infatuated) Empress!

BELLO

(his heavy cheekchops sagging) Adorer of the adulterous rump!

BLOOM

(plaintively) Hugeness!

BELLO

Dungdevourer!

BLOOM

(with sinews semiflexed) Magmagnificence!

BELLO

Down! *(he taps her on the shoulder with his fan)* Incline feet forward. Slide left foot one pace back! You will fall. You are falling. On the hands down!

(Joyce, 1984, 15.2832–49)

Figure 10.1 The Widow Twankey, played by Dan Leno (1860–1904). Cheryl Herr remarks: 'The coy curtsey emphasizes the message embroidered on the satin panel, "No Reasonable Offer Refused."' Courtesy of Mander and Mitchenson/University of Bristol/ArenaPAL.

This initial dialogue establishes the tone for everything that follows. Bloom has been transformed into a woman, just as Bella has been turned into Bello, a man who dominates and orders him about. Bloom, in other words, experiences the everyday degradations experienced by women, degradation that even extends to small items of clothing as Bella promptly orders that he be 'laced with cruel force into vicelike corsets of soft dove coutille with whalebone busk' (15.2975), and, perhaps more importantly, demands that he confess his sins:

> Say! What was the most revolting piece of obscenity in all your career or crime?
> Go the whole hog. Puke it out! Be candid for once. (Joyce, 1984, 15.3041–42)

Bloom, heeding her command, confesses that he once sniffed his wife's underwear, but that doesn't suffice and, angrily, Bella offers Bloom for auction:

> BELLO
>
> What offers? (*he points*) For that lot. Trained by owner to fetch and carry basket in mouth. (*he bares his arm and plunges it elbowdeep in Bloom's vulva*) There's fine depth for you! What, boys? That give you a hardon? (Joyce, 1984, 15.3088–90)

Does Bello's query, 'What offers?' echo the 'No Reasonable Offer Refused' embroidered into Dan Leno's costume? Whatever the case, Bloom has now been turned into a prostitute who will be sold to the highest bidder, a variant of Bella/Bello Cohen herself. This portion of the text, in other words, becomes an inverted microcosm of the entire episode, with its male-dominated world in which the women of 'nighttown' are oppressed in exactly this manner. He experiences first-hand the forms of exploitation that are sexual relationships as constituted in the novel's present day. But he can do so only because the novel so explicitly invokes the gender-bending properties of British pantomime, in which the 'pantomime dame' is a man and the 'principal boy' a woman. Popular culture isn't being held at bay here, as Huyssen asserts; it is being welcomed, adopted as the motor that drives the book's central action.

Further, we must add an important qualification. For pantomime is a distinctly British institution, a phenomenon wholly unknown to American, German, French, Italian or other audiences. Yet that is also telling: for Huyssen consistently treats popular culture as though it were a monolithic and homogeneous whole, a solid and unchanging block. But it was only after 1920 that popular culture, under the impress of the Hollywood cinema that swept through Europe in the 1920s, began to assume something like its modern form, and then only fitfully. That change, in turn, precipitated the decline of British music hall, so deeply admired by T. S. Eliot and so liberally quoted throughout *Ulysses* (most notably

'Those Seaside Girls' and 'My Girl's a Yorkshire Girl'), a decline that would leave it a ruin by the outbreak of the Second World War. In 1927, meanwhile, Britain passed the Cinematograph Films Act, requiring that a certain percentage of the films shown on British screens be produced in Britain, but that merely led to 'quota quickies', inferior films that audiences disliked. Instead, what did most to revive the British film industry was the influx of (mostly Jewish) refugees from Nazi Germany after 1933. Popular culture, even within a single country such as Britain, was a complex and ever-changing field in which a constellation of competing forms competed, thrived – and sometimes died. British pantomime survived; British music hall died; while British cinema has had a more complex history. But Huyssen flattens everything into a monolithic block that strips popular culture of every particularity. Just as he addresses modernism without ever adducing a single passage from a modernist text, so he conjures a blank and largely empty popular culture that may never have existed. What masquerades as a historical genealogy turns out to be a species of legerdemain, a shell game with historically empty shells.

Consider another modernist masterpiece, *The Waste Land*. There are many ways to approach it, and one common reading emphasizes the relationship between the cards dealt out by Madame Sosostris in Part I and the title of Part IV, emphasizing the poem's unity. Famously, at line 55, Madame Sosostris tells her listener (who is a figure for the reader): 'Fear death by water'. And just as plainly, the title of Part IV reads 'Death by Water'. We have, in other words, a use of repetition, a likeness. As one critic has observed of Madame Sosostris: 'She must provide the dots that the rest of the poem must connect into a semblance of plot' (Bedient, 1986, 56).

This is perceptive, provided we understand that its keyword is really 'semblance', to be taken in the strong sense as 'an assumed or unreal appearance of something: mere show'. *The Waste Land* has neither a plot nor narrative coherence, but the semblance of a plot, the likeness of a plot that swiftly dissolves into illusion. For it requires only a moment to recall that Madame Sosostris is a charlatan or that the drowned Phoenician sailor isn't even a card in the traditional Tarot pack. And when she discloses the drowned Phoenician card:

> Here, said she,
> Is your card, the drowned Phoenician sailor,

The text swiftly divorces itself from straightforward narrative, intruding cruelly:

> (Those are pearls that were his eyes. Look!)

Phlebas the Phoenician, whose reappearance (read: repetition) at first promises narrative connectedness between the first and later parts of the poems, turns out to be another figure in the poem's grim histrionics of non-relationship. *The Waste Land* doesn't have a narrative; instead, it has the scent of a narrative that hovers in the air, like the perfume of a woman who has just left the room.

If there is a single moment in the poem where we can see that grim histrionics of non-relationship enacted, and a moment as well where the conjunction of narrative and repetition is restaged with ferocity, it is the encounter between the unnamed typist and the (equally unnamed) young man carbuncular, an encounter that takes place in the middle of the poem's Part III or in the middle of the five-part work. It is a long passage stretching over forty-two lines (from line 215 to line 256); it presents a continuous story that is punctuated by three interruptions/repetitions from Tiresias, the prophetic figure who has experienced life in both sexes.

In taking up a typist as subject matter in a serious poem, Eliot was doing something unprecedented. Before *The Waste Land*, typists had figured only in light verse that was humorous or satirical.[4] To be sure, typists had long been a subject matter for novels: between 1893 and 1922, sixty-five novels had been published in which the principal protagonist, the heroine, had been a typist. But of these, only eight specifically took up the subject taken up here, a typist who engages in what we would now call premarital consensual sex.[5] The typical age of the typist was twenty-two, and it was a ubiquitous convention of these novels that they were orphans, stemming from middle-class families that had precipitously fallen on hard times. Often, the novels elaborated on commonplaces of contemporary journalism about typists, which highlighted stories about the poor food they consumed, the cramped lodgings they inhabited, which often meant that a bed would double as a divan, or even the threadbare lingerie they wore.[6] Eliot succinctly revisits these topoi (starting at line 220):

> At the violet hour, the evening hour that strives   220
> Homeward, and brings the sailor home from sea,
> The typist home at teatime, clears her breakfast, lights
> Her stove, and lays out food in tins.
> Out of the window perilously spread
> Her drying combinations touched by the sun's last rays,   225
> On the divan are piled (at night her bed)
> Stockings, slippers, camisoles, and stays.

But the passage is doing more than recycling realistic details in the poem. For beginning at line 224, a quatrain slowly emerges into view, and by its end it lies spread before us as neatly as 'Stockings, slippers, camisoles, and stays'. Well, perhaps a bit less neatly: for the metre of this passage is marked by deep uncertainty – it shifts uneasily between four and five stresses per line, and ranges between nine and thirteen syllables in length – uncertainty that turns it into a sign of poetry's flimsiness, its fragility in the face of the modern world, or that tacitly asks a question: can poetry's traditional resources, rhythm and rhyme, suffice for what the modern world can throw in its path? A typist, her room, a scene of urban squalor.

A similar uncertainty is evident in the point of view that is adopted from the very moment the typist appears on the scene (line 215):

> At the violet hour, when the eyes and back
> Turn upward from the desk, when the human engine waits
> Like a taxi throbbing waiting

For what perspective can enable us to see, at the same time, 'the eyes and back' of that 'human engine', unless a very contorted or abnormal one? And these difficulties in meter and perspective find a counterpart in syntactical complications that require the reader to readjust and reconsider. Consider this passage (line 218):

> I Tiresias, though blind, throbbing between two lives,
> Old man with wrinkled female breasts, can see
> At the violet hour, the evening hour that strives   220
> Homeward, and brings the sailor home from sea,
> The typist home at teatime, clears her breakfast, lights
> Her stove, and lays out food in tins.

At line 222, the phrase 'the typist home at teatime' is made to perform three different grammatical functions. On the one hand, it may be the grammatical object of the verb 'see' (line 219); on the other, it may be the grammatical object of the verb 'brings' (line 221), which in turn is governed by the noun phrase 'the evening hour' (back in line 220):

> [...] the evening hour that strives
> Homeward, and brings the sailor home from sea,
> The typist home at teatime,

At the same time, however, 'the typist' is simultaneously not just a grammatical object, but also a grammatical subject that governs the verb 'clears' in line 222:

The typist home at teatime, clears her breakfast, lights
Her stove, and lays out food in tins.

Nor is this case of syntactic uncertainty an isolated aberration. At line 237, the verb 'endeavours' (in 'Endeavours to engage her in caresses') lacks any grammatical subject to govern it, and the same thing happens again at line 247 with the verb 'bestows' (in the line 'Bestows one final patronising kiss'), which again lacks a grammatical subject to govern it.

This syntactic uncertainty makes what happens next still more startling. For when the poem returns to the scene, the principal actress disappears (beginning at line 231):

He, the young man carbuncular, arrives,
A small house agent's clerk, with one bold stare,
One of the low on whom assurance sits
As a silk hat on a Bradford millionaire.
The time is now propitious, as he guesses,   235
The meal is ended, she is bored and tired,
Endeavours to engage her in caresses
Which are unreproved, if undesired.
Flushed and decided, he assaults at once;
Exploring hands encounter no defence;   240
His vanity requires no response,
And makes a welcome of indifference.
[...]
Bestows one final patronising kiss,   247
And gropes his way, finding the stair unlit ...

In this tableau, the typist vanishes as an autonomous agent. She exists only through the thoughts of the young man carbuncular, reduced to a present-tense variant of free indirect discourse, as at line 235 ('as he guesses ... she is bored and tired') or into the pronominal object of his gropings, as at line 237 ('Endeavours to engage her ... '). Further on, she dissolves into a series of negations at once ghastly and ghostly:

'unreproved'   line 238
'undesired'   line 239
'no defence'   line 240
'no response'   line 241
'indifference'   line 242

Their horror is amplified because four of the negations occur in the emphatic position of ending a line of verse, reverberating with each other (thus, 'no defence' in line 240 rhymes with 'indifference' in line 242) or with other rhyme words ('undesired' with 'tired' at lines 238 and 236; or 'no response' with 'at once', in lines 241 and 239). Words such as 'unreproved', 'undesired' or 'indifference' are said to have privative prefixes, because the prefix deprives a word of its original force. But the same term appears in the cognate word 'privation', and that is certainly what we have here: inexplicable, unbearable privation.

Not only the typist disappears in the course of this central tableau. The young man carbuncular, as soon as he 'assaults at once' (line 239), is displaced with synechdoche ('Exploring hands encounter ... ' in line 240) and then vanishes under personification ('His vanity requires no response' in line 241). Even his 'final patronising kiss' has nobody or nothing that serves as a grammatical subject to bestow it; we must infer that 'bestows' is governed – but is anything being 'governed' here? – by the subject of the preceding clause, 'His vanity'. Vanity is a cognate of the term 'vanishing' that we have used to describe the typist's disappearance: both stem from the Latin word *vanus*, meaning 'empty', or to cite a fuller definition: '1, *that contains nothing, empty, void, vacant*; 2, *empty* as to purport or result, *idle, null, groundless, unmeaning, fruitless, vain*' (Lewis and Short, 1980, s. v. *vanus*). But is that all there is at the end? Void and vacant, groundless and unmeaning. Or does it convey 'that sense of universal and hysterical negation so characteristic of the avant-garde', as Matei Calinescu notes in a passage quoted approvingly by Huyssen? (Huyssen, 1986, 163).

That final kiss is horrific, rehearsing a convention of popular fiction, in which the novel makes a kiss into the climax of a scene, a chapter, even a whole work. Eliot, instead, turns it into a gratuitous anti-climax. Then he turns to the coda, the aftermath.

Eliot was not the first author to portray a young woman in the aftermath of a sexual liaison. Beginning in 1908, some eight novelists took up secretaries who engage in what we would now call premarital consensual sex, using it to revisit the conventions of the 'fallen woman novel' that had been codified in the Victorian period.[7] One such book is *The Questing Beast*, by Ivy Low, a leftist and feminist, first published in 1914; after the heroine, Rachel Cohen, has her first sexual experience, this is how she reacts:

> She wondered if she had not plumbed the limits of disgust. She could not believe that life would ever hold zest for her again. A very plain person, who had never seen his face in a glass and had had to form an opinion of

his features from his natural vanity and the features of other people, might have felt, on being suddenly presented with a mirror, something of the shock and horror that Rachel now felt. Exactly the question that this person would most naturally ask was constantly in Rachel's mind: 'Am I like *that*?' ... Rachel, hitherto triumphant over other people's weakness, now thought, in her bitter humiliation, that none was so fallen that she was not sister to. Again and again the memory of her pride in being 'not that sort of girl' stung her to fresh writhings. (Low, 1914, 157)

Consider an analogous scene from a novel serialized in numerous newspapers throughout the United States, all those belonging to the Hearst news syndicate, with some fifty million readers; it was called *Chickie* and appeared just a year after *The Waste Land*'s publication:

> In her mind was a black spot of terror. It grew large – a stark live thing, shaking her pulse with dread. It was the memory of the night.
>
> She shrank from it. It pressed down and seized her heart. It was a dark, heavy beast crouching on her chest. She tried to beat it off. It came nearer and blew warm, sickening breaths in her nostrils. Fighting, she had to draw them down. Again and again ...
>
> She hid from it – oh, she would get away – push off this thing of horror weighing so heavily on her breast. Be free – be light again.
>
> She hated herself. (Meherin, 1925, 272–3)[8]

Both books were written by feminists who were tacitly urging a more tolerant approach to premarital consensual sex. But the guilty histrionics that ensue are double-edged; they make it seem as if their heroines have participated in something unspeakably sordid, something genuinely meriting condemnation, if only because the heroine herself has issued such a judgement. Disgust, shock, horror, bitter humiliation, terror, dread, memories that sting, seize the heart, or weigh heavily: here is the lexicon of the contemporary, popular novel when treating a post-coital scene.

The text of *The Waste Land* is more restrained:

> She turns and looks a moment in the glass,
> Hardly aware of her departed lover;   250
> Her brain allows one half-formed thought to pass:
> 'Well now that's done: and I'm glad it's over.'
> When lovely woman stoops to folly and
> Paces about her room again, alone,
> She smoothes her hair with automatic hand   255
> And puts a record on the gramophone.

More than any other passage in the poem, this one attracted the ire of conservative critics, damned as a desecration of an earlier poem by Oliver Goldsmith, which begins:

> When lovely woman stoops to folly
> And finds too late that men betray,
> What charm can sooth her melancholy,
> What art can wash her guilt away?

Eliot's aesthetic, by contrast, is aloof, austere, evincing icy neutrality. He shuns both the easy moralizing of Goldsmith and the guilty histrionics typical of the contemporary novel, replacing them with the mute, and yet eloquent, gesture of playing a popular song to fill the silent void: *empty* as to purport or result, *idle, null, groundless, unmeaning, fruitless, vain*.

Two points in Eliot's final two lines are arresting. One is that 'automatic hand'. For in Western philosophy from Aristotle to Heidegger, the hand has been invoked to signal the critical difference between the human and the animal, at once the instrument of reason and its material counterpart.[9] Yet the typist's gesture blurs precisely that boundary between wilful human action and the helplessness of automatism. At the same time, it also invokes what might be called a lyrical temporality and effect: for it interrupts, shocks and freezes the scene. Gesture, here, is being summoned to substitute for speech, assigned a total expressivity. Tellingly, Eliot himself urges that the hand performs an analogous function in the Jacobean play, *The Duchess of Malfi*. Reviewing a recent performance of it in 1920, he singles out the notorious scene in which the Duchess, trapped in a darkened chamber, is deceived into kissing a severed hand, one which she is told is that of her lover Antonio. It was 'extraordinarily fine', Eliot says, for 'here the actors were held in check by violent situations which nothing in their previous repertory could teach'. What Eliot calls 'the scene of the severed hand' has an uncanny effect: it prevents the actors from acting. The dead hand, contracted in the clutch of rigor mortis, dispenses with all mediation, which can only 'distort', and is transformed into an eerie paradox: it is a trope of not troping and, at the same time, is pure, unmediated communication. 'Here', writes Eliot, 'the play itself got through, magnificently, unique' (Eliot, 1920, 37).

Another resides in the name of the machine that the typist cranks up: rhyming with 'alone', it is the gramophone. It comes with an etymology that Eliot knew well: the first part of the word, 'gramo-', derives from the ancient Greek word *gramma*, meaning a 'letter' or an 'inscription'; while the second part, '-phone', is the ancient Greek word for 'voice'. Inscribing voices is of course just what *The*

Waste Land has been doing, both in its lavish use of quotation and in its brisk modulations through numerous voices. It has become a machine for replaying them, a species of dictaphone. And that, after all, is one of the fundamental activities performed by a typist in this period, taking dictation, inscribing the voice of someone else onto paper. Her final action is a microcosm of the poem – and is all the more haunting for just that reason.

In the long scene that occupies the middle of the poem, competing rhetorics reach an impasse. The trope of repetition, uttered insistently by Tiresias, is cancelled out by the shards of narrative that culminate only in still more repetition – an 'automatic hand', a 'record on the gramophone'. The two rhetorical modes restage a grim histrionics of non-relationship, itself a recapitulation of the grisly puppet show that is the encounter between the typist and the young man carbuncular.

What was the poem's relationship to contemporary popular culture? Just one year after the poem appeared, the novel *Chickie* came out in newspapers belonging to the Hearst syndicate, running from 26 November 1923 to 28 February 1924. It told the story of a young typist who engages in premarital consensual sex, and the ensuing complications. Ten months later, on 13 January 1925, shooting for the film version began at the First National studio in New York; it starred Dorothy Mackail (1903– 1990), and was produced by Earl Hudson (1892–1959) and John Francis Dillon (1884–1934). Dillon, at the time, was celebrated for one work, *Flaming Youth* (November 1923), a film that had turned Colleen Moore into a superstar and made her 'the first to establish the screen archetype of the flapper' (Konzarski, 1994, 307). Single-handedly, *Flaming Youth* 'launched the flapper cycle' of films that were produced over the next six years and remained a constant 'reference point for later flapper films' (Ross, 2001, 422, n8). Moore herself replayed the role six months later (in May 1924) in *The Perfect Flapper*, also produced by Hudson and directed by Dillon, and would do so a third time in *We Moderns* (November 1925), again directed by Dillon.

Dillon, plainly, adhered to a successful formula, and when he began *Chickie*, he elected to turn it, too, into a flapper film. But to turn a domestic melodrama, the book, into a flapper film was no easy feat, and the resulting film, released in April 1925 (it ran for the next three months), showed the scars of that process. As a biting review in the *Los Angeles Times* put it: 'Of all the stupid, tiresome, badly acted, inartistic, long drawn-out, badly cut, uninterestingly photographed, moronic pictures, *Chickie* takes the medal.' But, the same reviewer noted, 'It is breaking local records – its local box-office being almost without precedent' (Carr, 1925, C2).[10]

Alas, when *Chickie* finally made it to Britain, a year later in June 1926, it entirely lacked the pop-cultural hinterland that might have made it comprehensible. Because there were no Hearst newspapers in Britain, the novel had enjoyed a much reduced readership. Further, because Dorothy Mackail happened to be the best friend of cinematic comedienne Marion Davies, William Randolph Heart's mistress, Hearst-owned newspapers lavished *Chickie* with favourable reviews. But that was no help in Britain, where it flopped.

In short, *The Waste Land*'s potential dialogue with popular culture went unnoticed: the poem and *Chickie*, as well as *The Questing Beast*, shared overlapping concerns that can prove mutually illuminating. But the two novels also moved within economies of popular culture that were separated by deep and unbridgeable differences. There was never, at this time, a single popular culture that encompassed both. *The Questing Beast* was never published in the United States, and *Chickie* remained an almost exclusively American phenomenon.

Andreas Huyssen's examination of modernism and popular culture offered schematic clarity, but achieved it at the price of all historical and textual complexity.[11] Its defence of postmodern architecture was also measured but unhelpful. But in the present day, the postmodern is now as remote as the Grizzly Bear Dance, and probably just about as popular. The sterile attempt to lay claim to the postmodern and the popular, at the expense of demonizing modernism, now seems very *vieux jeu*. It's time to start over.

Notes

1	The translation is mine.
2	The later edition (London: R. K. Burt & Co.), from 1876, is reported by the British Library.
3	Herr reproduces the pantomime programme for *Sindbad the Sailor* (1986, 122).
4	Examples include Crosland, 1902, 30–2; Miner, 1904; Kiser, 1907; and Lang, 1923, 179–80. A serious, and hence rare, poem about a typist is *Interlude: Eurydice* by Arthur Henry Adams (1906, 34–6).
5	The eight novels are listed here. Four are British: *Sally Bishop: A Romance* (Temple Thurston, 1908); *The Questing Beast* (Low, 1914); *Latchkey Ladies* (Grant, 1921); and *Lilian* (Bennett, 1922). For a discussion of these four, see *From the Fallen Woman to the Fallen Typist* (Rainey, 2009, 273–97). The other four are American: *The Winning Chance* (Dejeans, 1909); *Gloria Gray, Love Pirate* (Doles Bell, 1914); *The Dwelling-Place of Light* (Churchill, 1917); and *Chickie: A Hidden, Tragic*

Chapter from the Life of a Girl of This Strange 'Today' (Meherin, 1925). This latter edition was published as a movie tie-in; the book's real first edition appeared serially in all the newspapers belonging to the legendary Hearst empire, between 26 November 1923 and 28 February 1924.

6   On the topos that typists ate poorly, see 'Five O'Clock Tea talk; A Woman's Restaurant', ('Frances', 1903, 918); *Suffragette Secretaries: A Report on Office Life 60 Years Ago* (Anonymous, 1979, 19–29); *The Questing Beast* (Low, 1914, 42–3); and *Money Isn't Everything* (Cole, 1923, 24–5). On their poor and cramped housing, see *The Girl behind the Keys* (Gallon, [1903] 2005, 5); and on the bed/divan, see *The Grain of Dust* (Philips, [1911] 1912, 300). On the shabby underclothes, see *The Questing Beast* (Low, 1914, 9) and *The Grain of Dust* (Philips, 1912 [1911], 326).

7   The category of the 'fallen woman' conflated three forms of sexual activity later deemed quite distinct: premarital consensual sex, extramarital sex and prostitution. The best overviews of Victorian sexuality remain Michael Mason's two volumes, *The Making of Victorian Sexual Attitudes* (1994a) and *The Making of Victorian Sexuality* (1994b). On the fallen woman, with reference only to prostitution, see *Tainted Souls and Painted Faces: The Rhetoric of Fallenness in Victorian Culture* (Anderson, 1993). On the theme in the English novel, see *The Fallen Woman in the Nineteenth-Century English Novel* (Watt, 1984); on it in drama, see 'The Fallen Woman on Stage: Maidens, Magdalens, and the Emancipated Female' (Eltis, 2004, 222–36).

8   On this novel and its filmic adaptation, see 'Popular Literature, Silent Film, and the Perils of Genre: Chickie (1923–1925)' (Rainey, 2010, 277–88).

9   See *The Complete Works of Aristotle, Parts of Animals* (Barnes, 1984, vol. 1, 1071–72); for Heidegger, see the terms 'presence-at-hand' and 'ready-to-hand' which recur through his *Being and Time* (Heidegger, 1961).

10 My discussion here abridges many complications; see the fuller treatment in 'Popular Literature, Silent Film, and the Perils of Genre: Chickie (1923–1925)' (Rainey, 2010, 277–88).

11 For Huyssen's later defence of his book, see his 'High/Low in an Expanded Field' (2002, 363–74). For a later assessment that offers a broad context, see 'Exploring the Great Divide: High and Low, Left and Right' (Scholes, 2003, 245–69).

Bibliography

Adams, A. H. (1906), *London Streets*. London: T. N. Flouris.

Anderson, A. (1993), *Tainted Souls and Painted Faces: The Rhetoric of Fallenness in Victorian Culture*. Ithaca: Cornell University Press.

Anon. (1979), 'Suffragette Secretaries: A Report on Office Life 60 Years Ago', in *Survey of Secretarial and Clerical Salaries: Alfred Marks Bureau, Statistical Series Division*, October, 19–29.

Barnes, J. (ed.) (1984), *The Complete Works of Aristotle*. Princeton: Princeton University Press.

Bedient, C. (1986), *He Do the Police in Different Voices: 'The Waste Land and Its Protagonist'*. Chicago: University of Chicago Press.

Bennett, A. (1922), *Lilian*. London: Cassell.

Bürger, P. (1984), *Theory of the Avant-garde*. Minneapolis: University of Minnesota Press.

Carr, H. (1925), 'Harry Carr's Page'. *Los Angeles Times*, 17 June, C2.

Churchill, W. (1917), *The Dwelling-Place of Light*. New York: Macmillan.

Cole, S. (1923), *Money Isn't Everything*. London: Mills and Boon.

Crosland, T. W. H. (1902), 'To the American Invader', in *Outlook Odes*. London: At the Unicorn.

Dejeans, E. (1909), *The Winning Chance*. Philadelphia: J. B. Lippincott.

Doles Bell, P. (1914), *Gloria Gray, Love Pirate*. Chicago: Robert & Co.

Eliot, T. S. (1920 [1919]), '"The Duchess of Malfi" at the Lyric; and Poetic Drama'. *Art and Letters*, 3, (1), (Winter), 36–39.

Eltis, S. (2004), 'The Fallen Woman on Stage: Maidens, Magdalens, and the Emancipated Female', in K. Powell (ed.), *The Cambridge Companion to Victorian and Edwardian Theatre*. Cambridge: Cambridge University Press, pp. 222–36.

'Frances' (1903), 'Five O'Clock Tea talk; A Woman's Restaurant', *T. P.'s Weekly*, 11 December 1903, 918.

Gallon, T. (2005), *The Girl behind the Keys*. Ed. Arlene Young. Ontario: Broadview Press.

Goldstone, A. (2013), *Fictions of Autonomy*. Oxford: Oxford University Press.

Grant, M. (1921), *Latchkey Ladies*. London: William Heinemann.

Hausman, R. (1977), 'Pamphlet gegen die Weimarische Lebensauffassung', in K. Riha and H. Bergius (eds), *Dada Berlin: Texte, Manifeste, Aktionen*. Stuttgart: Reclam.

Heidegger, M. (1961), *Being and Time*, J. Macquarrie and E. Robinson (transl.). New York: Harper & Row.

Herr, C. (1986), *Joyce's Anatomy of Culture*. Urbana: University of Illinois Press.

Huyssen, A. (1986), *After the Great Divide: Modernism, Mass Culture, Postmodernism*. Bloomington: Indiana University Press.

Huyssen, A. (2002), 'High/Low in an Expanded Field'. *Modernism/modernity*, 9, (3), 363–74.

Joyce, J. (1984), *Ulysses*, W. Gabler (ed.). New York: Vintage.

Kiser, S. E. (1907), *Love Sonnets of an Office Boy*. Chicago: Forbes.

Konzarski, R. (1994), *An Evening's Entertainment: The Age of the Silent Feature Picture, 1915–1928*. Berkeley: University of California Press.

Lang, A. (1923), 'Matrimony', in L. Lance (ed.), *The Poetical Works of Andrew Lang*. London: Longmans, pp. 179–80.

Lewis, C. and Short, C. (1980), *A Latin Dictionary*. Oxford: Oxford University Press.

Low, I. (1914), *The Questing Beast*. London: Martin Secker.

Mason, M. (1994a), *The Making of Victorian Sexual Attitudes*. Oxford: Oxford University Press.

Mason, M. (1994b), *The Making of Victorian Sexuality*. Oxford: Oxford University Press.

Meherin, E. (1925), *Chickie: A Hidden, Tragic Chapter from the Life of a Girl of This Strange 'Today'*. New York: Grosset & Dunlap.

Miner, E. (ed.) (1904), *Our Phonographic Poets: Written by Stenographers and Typists upon Subjects Pertaining to Their Arts, Compiled by 'Topsy Typist'*. New York: Popular Publishing.

Philips, D. G. (1912), *The Grain of Dust*. New York: D. Appleton and Co.

Rainey, L. (2009), 'From the Fallen Woman to the Fallen Typist'. *English Literature in Transition, 1880–1920*, 52, (3), 273–97.

Rainey, L. (2010), 'Popular Literature, Silent Film, and the Perils of Genre: Chickie (1923–1925)'. *Literature/Film Quarterly*, 38, (4), 277–88.

Ross, S. (2001), ' "Good Little Bad Girls": Controversy and the Flapper Comedienne'. *Film History*, 13, 409–23.

Scholes, R. (2003), 'Exploring the Great Divide: High and Low, Left and Right'. *Narrative*, 11, (3), 245–69.

Temple Thurston, E. (1908), *Sally Bishop: A Romance*. London: Chapman & Hall.

Thornton, W. (1961), *Allusions in Ulysses*. Chapel Hill: University of North Carolina Press.

Watt, G. (1984), *The Fallen Woman in the Nineteenth-Century English Novel. Croon Helm*. Totowa: Barnes & Noble.

11

Modernist Magazines

Faith Binckes

In April 1911, a 21-year-old John Middleton Murry wrote to a friend, sharing his interpretation of 'modernism' and outlining his plans for an artistic and literary magazine that could be used to promote it:

> Modernism means, when I use it, Bergsonism in Philosophy [...] Bergsonism stands for Post-Impressionism in its essential meaning – and not in the sense of the Grafton Exhibition. [The magazine] is to be kept absolutely cosmopolitan [...] We will have no Shavianism or False Aestheticism ... But still we want more younger men from England – young men in London; who have not gone thro' the unenthusiastic aesthetic atmosphere of Oxford: How to get them is the problem?
>
> We are arranging to have the paper distributed in Edinburgh, Glasgow, Manchester, London, Oxford, Cambridge, Paris, New York, and Munich and all over the world by subscription. (Murry to Philip Landon, qtd. in Lea, 1959, 24)

Murry's youthful naiveté was apparent here, not least in his vision of the 'paper' effortlessly winging its way to a global network of subscribers. Nevertheless, we can still recognize 'modernism' through the distinguishing elements on Murry's projected contents list. 'Modernism' should be the preserve of the 'young'. It should also be 'absolutely cosmopolitan'. As Murry knew from his recent visits to Paris, 'Bergsonism in Philosophy' united a range of diverse contemporary movements in art and literature on or around 1910.[1] But Murry was equally clear that the modernism his magazine would present would be distinctive from this field, as well as participating in it. Most obviously, Murry's version of Post-Impressionism was offered as an alternative to the version on show at Roger Fry's exhibition of the previous year.[2] Moreover, his confidence in the fact that his publication would represent this artistic movement in its 'essential meaning' demonstrated that he did not consider Fry's version of Post-Impressionism to have either priority, or authority, over his own. When the magazine, eventually called *Rhythm*, first appeared in the summer of 1911, it held true to these tenets.

This early outline of *Rhythm* is just one example of the long-acknowledged role periodical publications played in the emergence and development of modernism. These magazines came in a huge variety of forms, reflecting and embodying the complexity and richness of the modernist field. They also represented the forces of competition and collaboration that shaped that field from the ground up. So, on one hand, Murry's assertion that 'modernism' indicated a certain set of things 'when I use it' registered a distinctive editorial perspective, taking ownership of the definition. On another, his statement acknowledged that other definitions were equally possible. As composite texts that thrived on shared traditions but also on their difference from one another, magazines generated a modernism that could not exist either as a single or as a static category. As his list also makes plain, the composite format of magazines encouraged associations and juxtapositions, often between different areas of related aesthetic production. For this reason, certain publications were particularly effective – and have become particularly well known – as vehicles for groups whose members worked across the arts. This was the case for *Lacerba* for the Futurists, *BLAST* for the Vorticists, *DADA* for the Dadaists or for any number of later Surrealist publications. But the story of modernist magazines is also populated with periodicals that operated far less exclusionary editorial policies. A good example would be *The New Age*, the first periodical to be reproduced on the landmark digital resource The Modernist Journals Project. This magazine was revived by Holbrook Jackson and A. R. Orage, the latter taking full editorial control in 1908. *The New Age* resembled a newspaper more than an illustrated magazine like *Rhythm* or *BLAST*. It contained coverage of politics and current events, but it also hosted writing on modern art and literature by the likes of Ezra Pound, T. E. Hulme and Murry himself, thriving on clashes of ideas and opinions. In a 1964 article on the twentieth-century periodical scene, Cyril Connolly divided magazines into two camps to reflect these supposedly opposing editorial strategies. 'Little magazines are of two kinds, dynamic and eclectic', he stated: 'Some flourish on what they put in, others by whom they keep out' (1964, 95–6). In fact, appealing as this neat distinction might be, the lines between the 'dynamic' and the 'eclectic' were very frequently blurred. By virtue of their format and their periodicity, all magazines are in a certain sense 'eclectic', and the dynamism of even group-orientated little magazines was generally reflected in their combustibility as much as it was in their coherence. On the latter score, modernist magazines have an extremely colourful history

– part fact, part folklore – that includes more than its fair share of verbal and physical dust-ups. But, equally important, magazines could be the site of unlikely yet productive alliances. Adam McKible's account of *The Liberator*, a New York magazine with a strong Marxist ethos, provides a particularly good example. In one number for 1922, editor Mike Gold described Elsa von Freytag-Loringhoven loudly reciting Dadaist poetry to fellow poet and co-editor Claude McKay, best known as an author of the Harlem Renaissance. McKible enquires 'What was Freytag-Loringhoven – a prominent contributor to the avant-garde *Little Review* and sometimes an outspoken racist and anti-Semite – doing in the office of *The Liberator* with a black Jamaican and a Jew from Manhattan's Lower East Side?' (McKible, 2007, 198). Although this artistic triangulation was brief, as the Gold–McKay partnership lasted less than a year, McKible's article serves as a reminder that the myriad components of artistic production – social, textual, sexual, financial, aesthetic – collide within the material confines of a magazine and within the spaces inhabited by its makers.

The shifting configurations of this primary modernist scene have been echoed by ongoing revisions to modernism in the critical canon. A closer look at the fortunes of *Rhythm*, and of those whose work appeared regularly in it, is a good case in point. The magazine played an important role in the early careers of Murry, Katherine Mansfield and (to a lesser extent) D. H. Lawrence. It also published artwork, including images by Picasso, Henri Gaudier-Brzeska, André Dunoyer de Segonzac and the Russian modernist Natalia Gontcharova. The prime mover behind the artistic content, and one of its major contributors, was Scottish modernist J. D. Fergusson. Murry had become friends with Fergusson while in Paris, and the older man acted as Art Editor until December 1912. *Rhythm* also included regular illustrations from women artists from Fergusson's expatriate circle: Americans Anne Estelle Rice and Marguerite Thompson, and the British artist and poet Jessica Dismorr. Some of these names have been written into histories of modernism throughout the twentieth century – Picasso being the most obvious. But most others have enjoyed a more uncertain position. Now viewed as a major female modernist, in spite of early recognition Mansfield was 'nearly erased [...] from the history of the movement' and it is still unclear where (and how) Murry himself should be placed (Kaplan, 1991, 1). Despite the pioneering work of its female members, the artists, who exhibited as 'the Rhythmists' or 'the Rhythm Group', are generally sidelined in histories of the period. However, as one of the leaders of the 'Scottish Colourists' – a term coined in the 1940s – Fergusson has always been recognized as a key figure in Scottish art history.[3]

The increasing availability of modernist magazines in digital editions has been part of this ongoing, if uneven, process of rediscovery and reappraisal.[4] This has both assisted, and been assisted by, the emphasis on temporal and geographical expansion that has characterized the 'New Modernist Studies' (Mao and Walkowitz, 2008, 737). As we have seen, even in 1911 Murry was insistent that his magazine should be 'absolutely cosmopolitan' and imagined that it might find readers 'all over the world'. In the twenty-first century, interest has grown both in the terms under which a global modernism might be theorized – as 'cosmopolitan', 'international' or 'transnational' – and in the specifics of its forms.[5] This has also prompted a consideration of the role of magazines in an integral but apparently opposing drive, as 'scholars have been drawn to analysing the historical avant-garde's contrapuntal focus on localism – the specificities of place, time, nationality, region, and milieu – that emerged as a component of (rather than as a trend opposed to) the transnationalism generally taken to characterise literary modernism' (White, 2013, 1). These co-existing alternatives look paradoxical when articulated in critical prose. But within a magazine, multiple 'periodical codes' always operate simultaneously, bringing multiple contexts to bear on any content.[6] Plainly, these contexts explode further when we consider magazines as a 'world form', whose study is confined more by logistics – disciplinary and institutional – than by their own significance or contribution to modernism. As Eric Bulson observes, the lines of inheritance that link, for example, the distinctive 'little magazine' culture of mid-twentieth-century Africa to the European modernist magazines of the 1920s are only one element in an infinitely larger cross-pollination of style and of print form (2012, 267–8). In formal terms, then, magazines collapse the apparent distance between the 'global' and the 'local', as they do the divides between literary periods. As such, periodical texts can be said to represent not only an expansion but a parallel concentration of the modernist field.

A further aspect of this 'expansion' has been the increasing attention paid to the presence of modernism in periodicals Connolly would have placed on the outer perimeter of 'eclecticism'. This includes fashion magazines such as *Vogue*, which demonstrated a general interest in modernist art and literature, and which in its British edition led to contributions by writers such as Virginia Woolf and Elizabeth Bowen.[7] More challenging still to earlier notions of the 'modernist magazine' are so-called 'middlebrow' publications such as *Good Housekeeping* or *Charm: A Magazine of New Jersey Home Interests* (Wood, 2010, 12–24). The latter, published by Bamberger's Department Store in the mid-1920s, was the venue for one of Mina Loy's only critical essays on contemporary poetry, and Djuna

Barnes also appeared in print there under a pseudonym.[8] Later, public-service-orientated reviews like BBC magazine *The Listener*, which published criticism by the likes of Herbert Read and Wyndham Lewis, provoke additional questions about the temporal boundaries of modernism, as well as its institutionalization in the second half of the twentieth century.[9] And yet, even magazines that seem to issue from what has been designated as the 'centre' – temporally, generically and geographically – can present definitional questions. One example is the British magazine *Coterie*. It was first published in May 1919, ran until the number for Winter 1920/21, and was relaunched as *New Coterie* in 1925.[10] Andrew Thacker has noted that although *Coterie* published numerous writers and artists closely associated with distinct pre-war 'schools' – not only Vorticists but Imagists and Georgians – the magazine contained no mention of any of these groups. Thacker connects this to the time in which *Coterie* was published and to a post-war context in which the artistic landscape had irrevocably changed (2009, 478). Certainly Lewis's attempts to revive Vorticism after the war – attempts that were still visible in his magazine *The Tyro*, which shared contributors with *Coterie* – were never sustained. It is therefore possible to see *Coterie* as representative of a sea change in modernist literary history, affected not only by the passing of time and modernism's ongoing investment in the 'new' but by a move away from a pre-war group-orientated avant-garde. However, *Coterie*'s interest in the miscellaneous can also be seen as something of a magazine tradition, which had informed modernist magazines from the outset. As early as 1896, *The Savoy*, labelled by Connolly as a 'dynamic' magazine, disavowed a group identity in favour of a pragmatic emphasis on quality.[11] Rather than choosing between these two interpretations, it is more accurate to say that *Coterie* participated in both.

This reworking of tradition, via the links magazines maintained with their periodical heritage, can be understood as part of a drive that was central to modernism's formal preoccupations across the board. In the light of this, Murry's promise that *Rhythm* would avoid 'False Aestheticism' is less anachronistic than it initially appears. In *Rhythm* Murry had attacked Wilde outright, accusing him of distorting the legacy of later nineteenth-century French authors, principally Baudelaire (Murry, 1913, xxvii). But elsewhere in the magazine, while sticking to the language of reinvigoration common to much early twentieth-century discourse, he gave credit to the influence of a movement that he clearly did not consider 'false'.[12] There were many reasons to point out how much modernism owed to aestheticism and to figures such as Arthur Symons and Holbrook Jackson, who bridged the gap between the two generations. We could think of T. S. Eliot carefully annotating his copy of Symons's *The Symbolist Movement in*

Literature, underlining its striking descriptions of the poetry of Jules Laforgue.[13] Periodicals could express this engagement more directly still. In the November 1917 number of the British modernist magazine *The Egoist*, Symons's work was printed alongside that of Eliot, Lewis and Pound.[14] But for editors of early twentieth-century little magazines, the most obvious debt was the example set by *The Yellow Book* (1894–97) and *The Savoy* (1896). These texts – the latter jointly edited by Symons – were far from being the only high-profile magazines of the 1890s, but their combination of a series of visual, textual and promotional elements set the tone for a range of similar modernist publications. Aubrey Beardsley was closely associated with both, initially co-editing *The Yellow Book* before becoming Symons's co-editor on *The Savoy*, and his graphics remain their most immediately identifiable signature. These designs compacted influences from William Morris and Japanese woodcuts with a sinuous and striking monochrome borrowed from contemporary poster design and influenced by eighteenth-century caricature. The originality that sprang from this hybridity was visible more generally in the magazines. *The Yellow Book* was happy to cross generational borders. It secured high-profile contributions from the likes of Henry James and Lord Frederick Leighton, but it also promoted the work of young and challenging writers. Prominent among these were female authors such as Vernon Lee, Charlotte Mew and Ada Leverson.[15] National boundaries and their associated publishing conventions were traversed too. Henry James appeared largely due to the efforts of American editor Henry Harland, although James later sought to distance himself from the innovations of more popular magazine culture that Harland also used in *The Yellow Book*. If anything, *The Savoy* went further. It published Beardsley's erotic, macabre lyric 'The Ballad of a Barber' and the tale of a marriage wrecked by a wife's alcoholism, 'A Mere Man'. It included writing about, and some writing by, Zola, Verlaine and Mallarmé. Alongside a series of pieces by Yeats, *The Savoy* published Havelock Ellis's essays on Nietzsche and morality in literature, and an essay by Edward Carpenter on 'The Simplification of Life'. Both magazines harnessed the controversy stirred up by Decadence to underline their significance to the movement, publishing not only the positive but also the negative reviews that they received. Despite taking advantage of popular modern print outlets – the prospectuses for *The Yellow Book* announced that it would be available not only from bookshops and libraries but also from 'railway bookstalls' – they also conveyed an impression of exclusivity, claiming an advanced cultural perspective that rejected the majority view ([Anon.], 1894 ii). The latter position was underscored when both were forced to close as a result of some form of moral controversy.[16]

The English-speaking magazines of the early twentieth century were anxious about their status – particularly when compared to the vibrant Continental scene. Publications such as the *Mercure de France*, or Munich's graphic and literary magazine *Jugend*, seemed to possess a combination of aesthetic modernity and popularity that eluded comparable English-language ventures. In this atmosphere, the notoriety and physical presence of *The Yellow Book* made it particularly attractive to editors. Murry was certainly not alone in his ambition to make *Rhythm* 'the *Yellow Book* for the modern movement' (1935, 275). Ford Madox Ford claimed a similar ambition for his far more sober-seeming *The English Review*, which he initiated in December 1908 and continued to edit until February 1910.[17] In this magazine, which was more obviously influenced by the *Mercure de France*, Ford juxtaposed figures such as James and Joseph Conrad (who also acted as an assistant editor) with Wyndham Lewis and D. H. Lawrence, whose first publications appeared in the magazine (Morrisson, 2001, 32–9). Wyndham Lewis's *BLAST*, which appeared just twice in 1914 and 1915, was, like *The Yellow Book*, published by John Lane and Co. and carried an advert for its predecessor in the back of its first number. Lewis returned Ford's favour by publishing the first instalment of 'The Saddest Story' (better known as *The Good Soldier*, the title of its completed novel form) in the first of its two numbers. In her autobiography, Margaret Anderson named *The Yellow Book* as both inspiration and warning when she was planning *The Little Review*. Concerned friends had reminded her of its collapse, she recalled, while she had reminded them of its status as a 'precious possession' on the library shelves of book-lovers (Anderson, 1930, 44). *The Little Review*, which Anderson went on to edit with Jane Heap, would, in its turn, become a precious possession, not least for its publication of twenty-three instalments of James Joyce's *Ulysses*, prior to its suppression.

To mention The *Yellow Book, The Savoy* and *Ulysses* in close succession inevitably draws attention back to the confrontation between modernist magazines as vehicles for challenging or transgressive content and those who policed the boundaries of public decency. For these publications, as for their predecessors, the censorship of a text or image could sometimes work in a magazine's favour, allowing it to advertise its radical stance. Murry publicly noted his printers' refusal to include certain pieces in *Rhythm*, for instance.[18] The first number of *BLAST* did include Pound's risqué satirical poem 'Fratres Minores', but with several (badly) redacted lines (Pound, 1914, 48). As 'Fratres Minores' was a criticism of poets whose verse was too caught up with sex, these visible but partial deletions allowed *BLAST* both to mark its difference from, and to participate in, a popular mode of modernist taboo breaking. In other cases, the desire to challenge existing norms would cause history to repeat itself. *The Freewoman* suffered an identical fate to *The Savoy* when W. H. Smith's withdrew it from sale, not because of any supposed obscenity, but because it found the editor Dora Marsden's language unsuitably violent (see Glendinning, 1987, 39). Unsurprisingly, then, as both Joyce and the *Little Review* were already on the radar of the authorities, the excisions Pound made in the 'Calypso' instalment of *Ulysses* – which detailed Leopold Bloom's bowel movements – prior to its appearance in *The Little Review* reflected his aesthetic and his pragmatic concerns. 'In the thing as it stands you will lose effectiveness', Pound wrote: 'The excrements will prevent people from noticing the quality of things contrasted' (letter to Joyce, [29 March] 1918; qtd. in Pound and Joyce, 1968, 131).

These engagements with legal and editorial authority, as with numerous other material concerns, point to some of the ways in which magazines participate in the wider publishing field. This holds true for magazines owned by a publisher, as well as for those affiliated with a specific printer or being published entirely independently. Modernist magazines were intimately connected with the revolutions in book and typographical design of the early twentieth century – the header for *The New Age* was designed by Eric Gill, for instance – although this element has not played as significant a role in recent periodical scholarship as we might expect. Sometimes magazines were backed by publishers with progressive reputations, as was the case for *BLAST* and John Lane. More rarely, magazines became progressive publishers in their own turn. The Egoist Press, which emerged from *The Egoist* magazine, was funded by its editor Harriet Shaw Weaver and published books by Joyce, Lewis, Dora Marsden, Robert McAlmon and Marianne Moore. The company that magazines kept is an important element when trying to understand how modernist periodicals were located within what are commonly known as 'communications circuits' – that is, the complex processes of production and transmission that are fundamental to reception and interpretation.[19] This could involve connections forged between magazines that shared a publisher or direct relationships that form the basis of what Lucy Delap has called 'periodical communities', whose shared interests sometimes defy expectation (2000, 233–76). It was common for magazines to carry announcements for books and for other periodicals, even when they resisted more obviously commercial forms of advertisement, and many modernist magazines published regular reviews of other recent magazine publications. Clearly, such reviews contribute to reception history, but they also present a way in which the identity of the magazine that published them was shaped, for instance through the promotion of a 'periodical community'.

But it was also true that these reviews could draw attention to the difference between the magazine in which they were published and those under review. Pound's lengthy series 'Studies in Contemporary Mentality', which ran in *The New Age* between August 1917 and January 1918, is an extended example of the latter.[20] Pound's acute and highly irreverent readings of a range of popular magazines dissected, paraphrased and occasionally imitated their content and its arrangement. The hilarious analysis in September 1917 of *The Strand*, and of its patriotic Sherlock Holmes story 'His Last Bow: Sherlock Holmes Outwits a German Spy', also contained serious points regarding Pound's own aesthetic commitments and, perhaps, the values circulating at a time of war: 'Whenever art gets beyond itself, and laps up too great a public, it at once degenerates into religion. Sherlock is on the way to religion, a modern worship of efficiency, acumen, inhumanity' (Scholes and Wulfman, 2010, 245). The end of his next contribution, on the illustrated weekly *The Sphere*, shared some similarities with Joyce's satirical use of newspaper discourse and layout in the 'Aeolus' chapter of *Ulysses*, but opened with more general 'Reflections on Letter-Press'. This critique of the more popular magazine field allowed not only Pound, writing tongue-in-cheek as a 'simple-hearted anthropologist', but also *The New Age* to position themselves by implication (248).

This awareness of periodical texts – and sometimes 'periodical communities' – as participants in a wider publishing culture provides an invaluable sense of modernism's embeddedness in the financial and material conditions of its production. But it is equally important to note that those periodicals were distinctive within that culture. This is not just a matter of the distinctiveness individual publications carved out for themselves – the sort that Murry claimed for *Rhythm* or that Pound generated for *The New Age* in the examples given above. The versions of modernist texts that appear in magazines are typically distinctive, first of all because they have a different context from those published in, or as, books. For instance, there are several reasons why reading Jean Rhys's first publication 'Vienne', as the story initially appeared in Ford Madox Ford's Paris-based *the transatlantic review* in 1924, is a different experience to reading it in her Jonathan Cape collection *The Left Bank and Other Stories* (1927). The magazine's table of contents for that number shows Rhys in the company of familiar expatriate American modernists, many of whom had clear 'localist' modernist affiliations. 'Vienne' was preceded by Hemingway's 'Cross-Country Snow' and was followed by Robert McAlmon's 'The Village' and an instalment of Gertrude Stein's 'The Making of Americans'. The number featured other young and less well-known authors who shared an interest in the MidWest. Elma Taylor's story 'Calico' focused on a woman who, having dreamt of moving into town for years, finds herself lost and dislocated once there. The magazine also included Amabel Williams-Ellis's 'London Night' and a portion of Ford's 'Joseph Conrad: A Portrait'. The 1927 collection shared some elements of this context. Ford remained a significant presence in both publications, and the thematic organization of the collection emphasized Paris as a location. Nonetheless, following Christopher GoGwilt, one could argue that the absence of Ford's recollections of Conrad removed a significant intertext for Rhys's writing, one that drew attention to the colonial experiences of modernity beyond the obvious Franco-transatlantic modernism promoted by the magazine (GoGwilt, 2011, 82–4). One could also explore a line of similarity in the shared themes of unsettled geographical and gendered identity that surface in Rhys's fractured account of a post-war former imperial capital, and the various meditations on gender, narrative and place that run through the stories of Hemingway, Taylor, Stein and Williams-Ellis listed above. This first appearance of 'Vienne' illustrates another of the notable aspects of magazine publication – that of actual textual variance. Rhys revised and expanded 'Vienne' prior to its book publication in 1927 (and would do so again prior to publication in the 1968 collection *Tigers Are Better Looking*). The narrative was significantly smoothed out. The sharp discontinuity GoGwilt notes between the French 'Vienne' and the English 'Vienna' – a discontinuity that hints at the marks left on Caribbean speech by these two languages, as much as it does the suppression of German – was played down by the removal of the French from the opening sentence of the story.[21]

Modernist magazines, and the texts published in them, must therefore be understood as sharing a number of convergences that operate on multiple levels. The richness of this textual and referential layering, and its often surprising combinations of forces, underlines the capacity of the form to 'make new' even the established contours of its own canon. As many of the examples given above show, magazines can be said to conform to an accepted, even a conservative, high modernist canon that includes Joyce, Pound, Eliot, Yeats, Lewis and Ford. The publications in which these authors appeared – *The Savoy, The Little Review, BLAST, The Egoist, The English Review, the transatlantic review* – were listed in early institutionalizing accounts of modernist magazines by the likes of Hugh Kenner and Malcolm Bradbury. This canon opens a little with the inclusion of *Rhythm* and *Coterie*, and opens still further with the addition of a North American political publication like *The Liberator*. But if the study of magazines has changed the way we think about modernism more generally, rather than simply adding more publications to its repertoire, what, we might ask, are the most important areas of revision?

There are a range of answers to this question, but one of the most salient ones is the revisioning of the role politics played in modernism, both in the specific and in the general senses of the term. The notion that modernism generally separated the aesthetic from the political – and when it didn't tended to affiliate itself with sometimes extreme right-wing ideologies – has been thoroughly revised by the study of periodicals and magazines over the last two decades. Although it thrived on controversy and was famous for hosting debates between figures of different political orientations, *The New Age* was launched as an explicitly Socialist publication. Emma Goldman was a significant presence in the early issues of *The Little Review*, and she was also the subject of Anderson's provocative appreciation, titled 'The Challenge of Emma Goldman' (1914, 5–9).[22] The social upheavals of the first decades of the twentieth century and the dominating horror of the First World War all made themselves clearly felt on the pages of modernist magazines. Murry, Mansfield and Lawrence's short-lived *The Signature* (1916) was one example of an explicitly anti-war magazine staffed by well-known modernists. *BLAST*'s War Number reflected at length on the relationship between actual war and the aesthetic front it had attempted to open up, presenting a far more ambivalent, but equally powerful statement. Lewis's opening editorial and series of articles on the war, and Helen Saunders's poem 'A Vision of Mud' bracketed Henri Gaudier-Brzeska's 'Vortex Gaudier-Brzeska: Written from the Trenches'.[23] The first page provided a quick summary of Gaudier-Brzeska's combat history, moving swiftly on to his manifesto-style meditation upon mass conflict. When the reader turned the page, they were faced with a continuation of the manifesto, but also with a black-rimmed notice of Gaudier-Brzeska's time and place of death. Allan Antliff's study of anarchist publications with explicitly modernist aesthetic agendas – such as *Revolt* (1916) – demonstrates the attraction magazines held for those who were politically as well as artistically avant-garde. But in a wider sense, periodicals offer powerful testimony of publishing as an unavoidably political act and demonstrate modernism's commitment to remaking as a social as well as an aesthetic project. A figure such as Dora Marsden, who between 1911 and 1919 jointly edited *The Freewoman*, then *The New Freewoman* and then their successor *The Egoist*, illustrates the appeal of the periodical format for an individual uncomfortable with the majority of the templates available to her, including those of the Suffrage movement with which she initially aligned herself. In its exposition – but also exploration – of the multifaceted and transnational 'feminist' movement, *The*

Freewoman 'serves as an example of cross-national exchange within avant-garde movements and, specifically, within early twentieth-century feminism' (Delap, 2007, 79). But within this, Marsden's contributions to magazines exemplified the liberating potential of the periodical format, in terms of content, genre and mode of address. Her editorials were an example, as much as an examination, of what it meant to be a 'free woman', as they themselves ranged freely in style as well as in content. The November 1917 number of *The Egoist*, which we have touched upon with reference to Symons, contains a good example in Marsden's article, 'Lingual Psychology XII: A Detailed Moment of Consciousness'. In this extraordinary text, Marsden undertook a phenomenological self-analysis prompted by the face of a girl that appeared unbidden in her mind after an evening's work. The article pursued a recognizably modernist 'train of thought' as it uncoiled in Marsden's consciousness, allowing her to elaborate on questions of memory, temporality and 'imaginary images', but also to experiment with a variety of intersecting narrative techniques (Marsden, 1917, 147). The text was a psychological case study, divided up into discrete analytical paragraphs. But it was also filled with cross-cutting dialogue, juxtaposition and free indirect speech. The text was unavoidably engaged with gender and with unspoken currents of intellectual and bodily feeling. Marsden recalled first that the girl was a former pupil, then remembered aspects of her physicality and demeanour, bringing to the surface an incident when the girl's shy blushes provoked pleasurable recognition in two older women.[24] When, at the outset of the series, William Carlos Williams sent in a letter to *The Egoist*, protesting against Marsden's 'attempted destruction of masculine psychology', her response was crisp and unapologetic: 'Mr Williams's "criticism" will be more helpful when he makes it clearer what the distinction is which he draws between male and female psychology. Is it anything beyond the fact that one is written by a man, the other by a woman? If not, most of us will feel that we have not been helped very far.'[25]

Williams's negative interpretation of Marsden was wide of the mark. And yet, this encounter illustrated another vital component of modernism's engagement with gender politics and the tensions implicit in it – that is, the growing prominence and authority of women as editors of, as well as contributors to, magazines.[26] Marsden – and her more retiring initial co-editor Mary Gawthorpe – can be listed here not only with Mansfield, Weaver, Anderson and Heap, but with Harriet Monroe, Marianne Moore and Alice Corbin Henderson.[27] The latter three all participated in the running of *Poetry* (Chicago) at different times. Moore became Managing Editor of *The Dial* in 1925, following Alyse Gregory. Bryher financially supported and co-edited the cinematic review *Close Up* (1927–33) with Kenneth Macpherson, assisted by H.D. Other women – Beatrice Hastings of *The New Age*, to name one – vigorously defended their centrality to periodical publications that did not always recognize their financial or editorial contributions officially. Jayne Marek lists a series of women involved in editing the magazines of the Harlem Renaissance. These included Jessie Redmon Fauset, who worked as literary editor for *The Crisis*, and Gwendolyn Bennett and Zora Neale Hurston who were part of the 'editorial collective' behind *Fire!!* (Marek, 2007, 105). Marek's caution in using 'modernism' or 'Harlem Renaissance' as descriptive terms is important when analysing the role of magazines in a racially inflected modernist field, and yet, as we have noted throughout, any 'movement' read through the lens of periodical culture is always already refracted and made plural. Recent works on magazines such as *The Crisis* (1910–34), *Fire!!* (1926) and *Opportunity* (1923–42; 1949) have not only discussed their acknowledged significance as vehicles for distinctive African American literary modernisms but have also addressed the more unexplored significance of their visual and formal composition. For Rachel Farebrother, the 'collage aesthetic' visible in many modernist forms takes on a different historical resonance in African American print culture, concerned with making visible discontinuities, ruptures and erasures (2009, 11–12). While this supports GoGwilt's reading of Rhys's use of linguistic rupture in *the transatlantic review* (and asserts the significance of its later erasure), Farebrother also points out the ways in which the periodical form could be used recuperatively, to patch together a community of otherwise scattered and silenced voices.[28] Elsewhere, the incendiary single issue of *Fire!!* (November 1926) rejected discourses of racial uplift, presenting itself as a crucible for a radical new modernist aesthetic that broke sexual as well as formal rules. A good example would be Langston Hughes's poem 'Elevator Boy' contrasted with the more sonorous quality of an earlier *Crisis* poem like 'The Negro Speaks of Rivers' (June 1921). In 'Elevator Boy', the speech is not sonorous but slangy, the rhythm of the poem and its narrow confines on the page indicating not only a modern, jazzy, African American idiom but the routines of repetitious and alienated labour (White, 2013, 167).[29] In 'The Negro Speaks of Rivers', by contrast, the speaker alludes to a pan-African history that runs through black experience in the Euphrates, the Congo and the Mississippi: 'My soul has grown deep like the rivers'. Aaron Douglas's cover image of *Fire!!* referred directly to African roots, yet that heritage was configured very differently than in earlier magazines. Other legacies were also apparent. Bruce Nugent – an artist-writer who worked frequently in linear monochrome, not unlike Beardsley – returned to the Decadent signatures of *The Savoy* and *The Yellow Book* in his story 'Smoke, Lilies and Jade'.[30] Nugent's text self-consciously positions its narrator, Alex, as a young bohemian dandy. Almost entirely punctuated with ellipses, the text winds its way smokily through Alex's memories and daydreams, and themes such as interracial and bisexual desire, incorporating the first names of the young writers involved with the magazine just as it incorporated the totemic names of Wilde, Freud, Schnitzler and Gurdjieff. The story was a bravura act, not of 'passing' but of 'crossing'.[31] Its hybrid style and form recalibrated the legacy of those famous *fin-de-siècle* periodical texts, articulating the political impulses noted above with playful seriousness.

For all these reasons, then, it is increasingly difficult to reassess modernism without addressing the periodical texts in which it was made and constantly remade. Following Marek, it is even tempting to consider a move away from the descriptive phrase 'modernist magazines', with its always-problematic shorthand for a mercurial period and an even more mercurial form. A simple reversal produces 'magazine modernism'. This emphasizes 'modernism' as a set of practices unavoidably shaped by a medium with its own qualities and conventions – one that will continue to inform modernist studies in the second decade of the twenty-first century.

Notes

1   Henri Bergson (1859–1941), the French philosopher whose writings and lectures were enormously influential on early modernist conceptualizations of time and consciousness.

2   This was the first of two exhibitions organized by Roger Fry and held at the Grafton Galleries in 1910 and 1912, respectively. The first of these has been viewed as a watershed moment for modern art in Britain. However, as Murry's statement suggests, alternative perspectives on 'Post-Impressionism' were in circulation in Britain at this point.

3   John Duncan Fergusson (1874–1961), who lived and worked in Paris for many years, explored an idiom with stylistic connections to both Fauvism and Cubism. One of the other Colourists, Fergusson's friend S. J. Peploe, was also a regular contributor to *Rhythm*.

4   The best known of these are the Modernist Journals Project (MJP) based at Brown University and the University of Tulsa, the Modernist Magazines Project (MMP) based at De Montfort University and the University of Sussex, and The

Blue Mountain Project, which operates at Princeton University. Numerous other resources – for instance, Periodicals Archive Online – provide access to periodicals with identifiably modernist content, but do not focus specifically upon it.

5   See, in particular, the work of Susan Stanford Friedman (2006 and 2010).

6   'Periodical codes', a phrase derived from Jerome McGann's 'bibliographical codes', describe the multiple elements from which a magazine is composed. See Thacker and Brooker (2009, 5–9).

7   For an early perspective, see Jane Garrity's 'Selling Culture to the "Civilized": Bloomsbury, British *Vogue*, and the Marketing of National Identity' (1999); see also Jessica Burstein's more recent study *Cold Modernism: Literature, Fashion, Art* (2012, 123–50).

8   See Roger Conover's note on Loy's article, 'Modern Poetry'. Loy published in *Charm* in April 1925, and her work was reprinted in Mina Loy, *The Lost Lunar Baedecker* (1997, 217). See also O'Connor and Cummings (1984).

9   See, for example, the digital archive of Lewis's art criticism in *The Listener*, which provides a good overview of the magazine in the Wyndham Lewis Late Writing Project: http://www.unirioja.es/listenerartcriticism/index.htm

10   See Thacker (2009) and Tollers (1986).

11   'We are not Realists, or Romanticists, or Decadents. For us, all art is good which is good art' (Symons, qtd. in Beckson, 1987, 127).

12   'Aestheticism', he stated, 'has had its day and done its work' (Murry, 1911, 36).

13   See Soldo (1983).

14   Symons's 'Notes Taken in Constantinople and Sofia' was printed immediately after the final installment of Lewis's first novel *Tarr* and immediately before an essay on Elizabethan classicism by Pound. Eliot's 'Reflections on Contemporary Poetry' appeared in the same number.

15   See Ledger (2007) and also Krueger (2014).

16   The downfall of *The Yellow Book* was caused by the mistaken association between the magazine and Oscar Wilde during the period of his trial. In the case of *The Savoy* a seemingly innocuous instance of male nudity in one of William Blake's engravings, reprinted to accompany an essay by W. B. Yeats, caused W. H. Smith's to withdraw it from sale.

17   In 1921, Ford retrospectively described his aim of making *The English Review* an 'aube-de-siecle' *Yellow Book*; quoted in Peppis (2000, 23).

18   '… we regret that the state of public opinion in England should be such that it is impossible to obtain any degree of free expression for a serious work of art' (Murry, 1912, 34).

19   Robert Darnton's model, first used in his 'What Is the History of Books?' in 1982 and revisited in 2007, has become central to modern book history.

20   Pound's series has been described by Robert Scholes as a sort of originary example of periodical scholarship. See Scholes and Wulfman (2010).

21 This sort of versioning is far from unusual, of course. When it was republished in his collection *Personae*, Pound chose to restore 'Fratres Minores' to its unexpurgated form, while Joyce reinstated the passage Pound had deleted from 'Calypso' in the first edition of *Ulysses*.

22 Emma Goldman (1869–1940) was an American radical and feminist, one of the most influential anarchist activists and theorists of her era.

23 *BLAST* (1915), Lewis's 'Editorial' (5–6), 'War Notes' (9–16) and 'Artists and the War' (23), Saunders's 'A Vision of Mud' (73) and Gaudier Brzeska's 'Vortex (Written from the Trenches)' (33–4) were the most conspicuous engagements with the conflict.

24 'There is a slight shiver of contact as eye meets eye, followed by an interchange of glances which, without saying, mean: "How shy!" "Isn't it delicious!"' (Marsden, 1917, 150).

25 Editor [Marsden], 'Correspondence: The Great Sex Spiral', *The Egoist*, April 1917, 46.

26 Female editors did, of course, exist prior to the twentieth century. For a Victorian example, see Palmer (2011).

27 The key critical text here remains Jayne Marek's *Women Editing Modernism: 'Little' Magazines and Literary History* (1995).

28 Her discussion of editor W. E. B. DuBois's correspondence column, 'The Outer Pocket', which identified a global readership of men and women of colour and let them speak in their own words, points to the significance of this aspect of periodical format (Farebrother, 2009, 192–3).

29 The cover image was provided by Aaron Douglas.

30 Caroline Goeser's work on visuality and race in the period deals extensively with the strategies of African American artists, including Nugent. See, for example, Goeser (2006).

31 See Goeser (2007, 166) and White (2013, 164–7).

Bibliography

Anderson, M. (1914), 'The Challenge of Emma Goldman'. *The Little Review*, 1, (3), (May), 5–9.

Anderson, M. (1930), *My Thirty Years' War*. London: Alfred Knopf.

Anon. (1894), *The Yellow Book: An Illustrated Quarterly*. Prospectus to Volume 3, October. London: Elkin Mathews and John Lane.

Beckson, K. (1987), *Arthur Symons: A Life*. Oxford: Oxford University Press.

Bulson, E. (2012), 'Little Magazines, World Form', in Wollaeger, M. and Eatough, M. (eds), *The Oxford Handbook of Global Modernisms*. New York: Oxford University Press, pp. 267–8.

Burstein, J. (2012), *Cold Modernism: Literature, Fashion, Art*. University Park, PA: Penn State University Press.

Connolly, C. (1964), 'Fifty Years of Little Magazines'. *Art and Literature* (March), 95–6.

Darnton, R. (2007), '"What Is the History of Books?" Revisited'. *Modern Intellectual History*, 4, 495–508.

Delap, L. (2000), 'The Freewoman, Periodical Communities, and the Feminist Reading Public'. *Princeton University Library Chronicle*, 61, 233–76.

Delap, L. (2007), *The Feminist Avant-Garde*. Cambridge: Cambridge University Press.

Farebrother, R. (2009), *The Collage Aesthetic in the Harlem Renaissance*. Farnham: Ashgate.

Friedman, S. S. (2006), 'Periodizing Modernism: Postcolonial Modernities and the Space/Time Borders of Modernist Studies'. *Modernism/modernity*, 13, (3), 425–43.

Friedman, S. S. (2010), 'Planetarity: Musing Modernist Studies'. *Modernism/modernity*, 17, (3), 471–99.

Garrity, J. (1999), 'Selling Culture to the "Civilized": Bloomsbury, British *Vogue*, and the Marketing of National Identity'. *Modernism/modernity*, 6, (2), 29–58.

Glendinning, V. (1987), *Rebecca West: A Life*. London: Weidenfeld and Nicholson.

Goeser, C. (2006), *Picturing the New Negro: Harlem Renaissance Print Culture and Modern Black Identity*. Lawrence: University Press of Kansas.

Goeser, C. (2007), 'Black and Tan: Racial and Sexual Crossing in Ebony and Topaz', in Churchill, S. and McKible, A. (eds), *Little Magazines and Modernism: New Approaches*. Aldershot: Ashgate, pp. 151–75.

GoGwilt, C. (2011), *The Passage of Literature: Genealogies of Modernism in Conrad, Rhys, and Pramoedya*. New York: Oxford University Press.

Kaplan, S. J. (1991), *Katherine Mansfield and the Origins of Modernist Fiction*. Ithaca: Cornell University Press.

Krueger, K. (2014), *British Women Writers and the Short Story Reclaiming Social Space, 1850–1930*. London: Palgrave Macmillan.

Lea, F. A. (1959), *The Life of John Middleton Murry*. London: Methuen.

Ledger, S. (2007), 'Wilde Women and The Yellow Book: The Sexual Politics of Aestheticism and Decadence'. *English Literature in Transition*, 50, (1), 5–26.

Loy, M. (1997), *The Lost Lunar Baedecker*. Manchester: Carcanet Press.

Mao, D. and Walkowitz, R. (2008), 'The New Modernist Studies'. *PMLA*, 123, (3), 737–48.

Marek, J. (1995), *Women Editing Modernism: 'Little' Magazines and Literary History*. Kentucky: University Press of Kentucky.

Marek, J. (2007), 'Women Editors and Little Magazines in the Harlem Renaissance', in Churchill, S. and McKible, A. (eds), *Modernism and Little Magazines: New Approaches*. Aldershot: Ashgate, pp. 105–18.

Marsden, D. (1917), 'Lingual Psychology XII: A Detailed Moment of Consciousness'. *The Egoist*, 4, (10), (November), 145–50; 159.

Editor [Marsden] (1917), 'Correspondence: The Great Sex Spiral'. *The Egoist*, 4, (3), (April), 46.

McKible, A. (2007), 'Life Is Real and Life Is Earnest: Mike Gold, Claude McKay, and Elsa von Freytag-Loringhoven', in Churchill, S. and McKible, A. (eds), *Little Magazines and Modernism: New Approaches*. Aldershot: Ashgate, pp. 197–213.

Morrisson, M. S. (2001), *The Public Face of Modernism: Little Magazines, Audiences, and Reception, 1905–1920*. Madison: University of Wisconsin Press.

Murry, J. M. (1911), 'Aims and Ideals'. *Rhythm*, 1, (1), (Summer), 36.

Murry, J. M. (1912), 'Acknowledgements'. *Rhythm*, 1, (4), (Spring), 34.

Murry, J. M. (1913), 'The Influence of Baudelaire'. *Rhythm*, 2, (14), (March), Literary Supplement, xxvi–xxvii.

Murry, J. M. (1935), *Between Two Worlds: An Autobiography*. London: Jonathan Cape.

O'Connor, J. and C. Cummings (1984), 'Bamberger's Department Store, Charm Magazine, and the Culture of Consumption in New Jersey, 1924–1932'. *New Jersey History*, 102 (Fall-Winter), 1–33.

Palmer, B. (2011), *Women's Authorship and Editorship in Victorian Culture: Sensational Strategies*. Oxford: Oxford University Press.

Peppis, P. (2000), *Literature, Politics, and the English Avant-Garde: Nation and Empire, 1901–1918*. Cambridge: Cambridge University Press.

Pound, E. (1914), 'Fratres Minores'. *BLAST*, 48.

Pound, E. and Joyce, J. (1968), *Pound/Joyce: The Letters of Ezra Pound to James Joyce*. London: Faber and Faber.

Scholes. R. and Wulfman, C. (2010), *Modernism in the Magazines: An Introduction*. New Haven: Yale.

Soldo, J. (1983), 'T. S. Eliot and Jules Laforgue'. *American Literature*, 55, (2), (May), 137–50.

Thacker, A. (2009), 'Aftermath of War: Coterie, New Coterie, Robert Graves and The Owl', in Thacker, A. and Brooker, P. (eds), *Oxford Critical and Cultural History of Modernist Magazines: Volume 1*. Oxford: Oxford University Press, pp. 465–84.

Thacker, A. and Brooker, P. (2009), 'General Introduction', in *The Oxford Critical and Cultural History of Modernist Magazines: Volume 1*. Oxford: Oxford University Press, pp. 1–26.

Tollers, E. (1986), 'Coterie', in Sullivan, A. (ed.), *British Literary Magazines: The Modern Age*. New York: Greenwood Press, pp. 110–13.

White, E. B. (2013), *Transatlantic Avant-Gardes: Little Magazines and Localist Modernism*. Edinburgh: Edinburgh University Press.

Wood, A. (2010), 'Made to Measure: Virginia Woolf in Good Housekeeping'. *Prose Studies*, 32, 12–24.

12

Minding Manuscripts: Modernism, Genetic Criticism and Intertextual Cognition

Dirk Van Hulle

In disciplines such as the study of visual arts, there is a long tradition of examining the painting process to interpret the painted result. Applied to literary studies, this procedure involves at least two approaches, which Jonathan Culler has termed 'a basic distinction, too often neglected in literary studies': one approach starts from meanings and tries to find out how they come about; the other approach starts from forms and tries to find out what they mean. In literary studies, these two approaches are referred to as 'poetics' and 'hermeneutics': 'Poetics starts with attested meanings or effects and asks how they are achieved. [...] Hermeneutics, on the other hand, starts with texts and asks what they mean, seeking to discover new and better interpretations' (Culler, 2009, 84). These approaches are not mutually exclusive. In Culler's dichotomy, however, poetics is seen as an approach modelled on linguistics, examining, for instance, why a particular passage seems ironic, what makes us sympathize with a character or why a particular ending seems right, whereas another does not seem to 'work'. These effects are usually analysed on the basis of the published texts, but it is both possible and useful to add a temporal dimension to this approach. The making of a tale often involves numerous notes, plans, sketches and multiple drafts, which is the domain of genetic criticism. This branch of literary studies, focusing on writing processes, understands 'poetics' in its etymological sense, derived as it is from the Greek verb *poein*, 'to make'.

With reference to poetry in the realm of modernist literature in English, famous examples such as the facsimile edition of the *avant-texte* of T. S. Eliot's *The Waste Land* or Helen Gardner's genetic study of *The Composition of 'Four Quartets'* indicate the apparent use of manuscript research despite the author's repeated expressions of doubt as to the usefulness of genetic criticism. As for dramatic texts, the genesis of Samuel Beckett's theatrical works serves as an interesting paradigm, as it has been the subject both of critical studies (Gontarski, 1985; Pountney, 1988) and of annotated editions, including the author's theatrical notebooks (Beckett, 1992a,b, 1993). In terms of prose fiction in English, a particularly strong tradition of genetic research developed in Joyce studies. In other literatures, the manuscripts of modernist authors such as Franz Kafka, Thomas Mann and Marcel Proust have also been the subject of careful scrutiny. In this chapter, I would like to focus on the genre of prose fiction, because – as I will argue – there seems to be a connection between the preservation of manuscripts and a modernist interest in the workings of the mind, which is particularly noticeable in prose fiction.

When writers' interest gradually shifted from reality to the perception of reality, a process that was especially pronounced in the period of modernism, this development implied an increased focus on the mind. This shift coincided in the first half of the twentieth century with what Florence Callu has called 'the golden age of the literary manuscript' (1993, 65). The fact that so many writers from this period have preserved their notes and drafts could be a measure of the value they attached to these traces of the creative process, giving them a special status in their œuvre and enabling readers to apply 'poetics' in addition to 'hermeneutics'. My research hypothesis is that knowing how something was made can contribute to an understanding of how it works and that this also applies to literary texts.

The Process of Taletelling

There is more to the telling of a tale than meets the eye. Whether a story is published in print or online, the writing and telling of the tale is an art that deserves close scrutiny. This means that the writing process is regarded as an integral part of a rationale, a particular conception of, or view on, literature. It is remarkable how often the writing process is made thematic in modernist and late modernist writings. This is not a mere coincidence. The motif of the telling as part of the tale is indicative of the status of the writing process in the narrative composition.

This motif is also inextricably linked with the observation that writers in the beginning of the twentieth century were explicitly interested in the workings of the mind and with the observation that many of the characters in the literary writings of this period, such as K. in Kafka's works or Stephen Dedalus in Joyce's *A Portrait of the Artist as a Young Man* (1916), are modelled after their creators, not in an (auto)biographical but in an 'autographical' sense (see below). Metafictional references to the writing process may be understood as part of the literary evocations of the mind. The evocation of fictional minds constitutes one of at least six main facets of a narrative text (based on structuralist narratology as well as the more recent insights of post-classical narratology): (1) time and temporal ordering; (2) space and spatialization; (3) actions, events and emplotment; (4) characters and characterization; (5) focalization (perspective) and narration (voice); and (6) fictional minds (consciousness representation).

From the perspective of genetic criticism, Raymonde Debray Genette has shown how useful the combination of manuscript research with narratology can be, for instance in her genetic analysis of the excipit (the closing paragraphs) of Flaubert's story 'Un Cœur simple' (Debray Genette, 2004). This combination of genetic criticism and narratology is not unidirectional. In the past (though less in recent years), narratologists were not afraid of taking recourse to manuscript research to investigate one or other of the six facets mentioned earlier. As to aspect 5 (focalization and narration), for instance, a notable example is Dorrit Cohn's 1968 study of Kafka's *Das Schloss* (1926), 'K. enters *The Castle*'. The manuscript informs her examination of Kafka's narrative techniques in a rather spectacular way, since the famous 'K.' turns out to be a relatively late addition to the manuscript.

Originally, the first part of the manuscript had a first-person narrator. With only a few minimal replacements, Kafka changes the first-person narrator into 'K.' and refers to the experiencing self through third-person pronouns. The shift from first person to third person turns homodiegetic narration (with a narrator telling the story from within the fictional world) into heterodiegetic narration (with a narrator who does not take part in the plot) and yet maintains the fixed internal focalization (Bernaerts and Van Hulle, 2013), as the adverb 'today' in the following sentence illustrates: 'Das Schloβ [...], das ich *heute* noch zu erreichen gehofft hatte, entfernte sich wieder' ['The castle [...], which I had hoped to reach *today*, receded again'] (Ms./26, qtd. in Cohn, 1968, 31; emphasis added). In the published version, 'I' is replaced by 'K.' but 'today' (*heute*) remains unchanged. 'The logic of a first-person narrative determines [...] that the period of time lying between experience and recounting be known to the narrator' (Cohn, 1968, 32), but this logic is less self-evident if the narrating self is effaced.

In the manuscript version of Kafka's *The Castle*, with its first-person narrator, 'the narrating self remains effaced', since 'by shifting the focus entirely onto the experiencing self, the past situation loses its pastness and becomes a virtual present within the text' (Cohn, 1968, 31). Kafka's use of temporal adverbs such as 'today' (*heute*) or 'now' (*jetzt*) in combination with the past tense within the *erlebte Rede* [free indirect discourse, narrated monologue] are, according to Cohn, signals of what she calls 'the complete surrender of the narrator to his own earlier self' (33). It was possible and even relatively easy for Kafka to replace 'I' with 'K.' because of this surrender to the experiencing self. Another example is this series of three questions: 'Wo waren wir? Ging es nicht mehr weiter? Würde Barnabas mich verabschieden?' ['Where were we? Didn't it go any further? Would Barnabas take leave of me?'], which in the published version became 'Wo waren sie? Ging es nicht mehr weiter? Würde Barnabas K. verabschieden?' ['Where were they? Didn't it go any further? Would Barnabas take leave of K.?'] (qtd. in Cohn, 1978, 170). While past-tense first-person narratives 'cannot eliminate the temporal distance between the moment of narration and the narrated moment' (Cohn, 1968, 144), the past-tense third-person narrative has the advantage that it creates the illusion of immediacy. Thanks to the manuscript, Cohn's attention was drawn to *how* (in Culler's sense) Kafka created this effect, since the manuscript foregrounds the experiencing self (Cohn, 1978, 170; emphasis added).

This emphasis on the 'experiencing self' suggests an interesting avenue to study aspect 6 (the evocation of consciousness or fictional minds). Especially in this category, the combination of genetic criticism and narratology can break new ground in modernist studies. To examine this avenue in the following sections, the works of James Joyce and Samuel Beckett will serve as case studies.

Fictional Minds and Manuscripts

The evocation of consciousness and the emphasis on the experiencing self suggest a link with phenomenology and Husserl's technique of bracketing. The three questions from Kafka's manuscript ('Where were we? Didn't it go any further? Would Barnabas take leave of me?') express a form of narrative uncertainty that prefigures the three opening questions in Samuel Beckett's *The Unnamable* (1953): 'Where now? Who now? When now?' The order of these central narratological questions is different in the original French version: 'Où maintenant? Quand maintenant? Qui maintenant?' (see Beckett, 2013). In the second manuscript version (UoR MS 1227/7/9/1), there were initially only two questions; the third question ('Quand maintenant?') was added at a later stage, above the line. And in the earliest manuscript version (HRC MS SB 3–10, inside front cover) the two questions 'Où maintenant? Qui maintenant?' turn out to be a substitution for an even earlier incipit that reads as follows: 'Je ne saurais dire comment j'y suis arrivé. D'ailleurs quelle est cette situation?' ['I couldn't tell how arrived there. Moreover, what is this situation?'] (Beckett, 2013; HRC MS SB 3–10, 01r). By adding questions, Beckett thus created the effect of bracketing (in a phenomenological sense). In the initial opening sentence, the first person seemed to be a given; in the later versions, this first person was no longer taken for granted. Then, in the version with the two questions, one element at least seemed to be given: 'maintenant'. By adding the third question, even this temporal 'given' of the narrative situation became uncertain: 'Quand maintenant?'

This temporal dimension – perhaps even more than the spatial and personal dimensions – suggests the potential to transgress the borders of the storyworld.[1] Since *The Unnamable* is a first-person narrative, the other two questions can intuitively be completed: 'Where [am I] now? Who [am I] now?' But this is grammatically less evident with 'When [am I] now?' In combination with the question 'Who now?' the 'when' question at the very beginning of the story implies the suggestion that the narrator/narrated has a past. And later on in the story, this past will be connected to his 'avatars' – the protagonists in Beckett's preceding novels, such as Murphy, Watt, Mercier, Molloy, Malone. This metafictional and metaleptic[2] gesture relates to Beckett's notion that 'the individual is a succession of individuals', as he noted in his essay *Proust* (Beckett, 1999a, 19) – an idea that is most explicitly staged in his play *Krapp's Last Tape*. The transition from *Malone Dies* to *The Unnamable* is an interesting moment in the succession of narrators. For, on the one hand, Beckett seems to be pushing a Cartesian model of the mind to extremes, and, on the other hand, he implicitly prefigures a post-Cartesian model.

The caricature of the Cartesian model is what Daniel C. Dennett has dubbed the 'Cartesian theatre' or the so-called homunculus model, locating consciousness in the pineal gland or conarium, as if *The Unnamable*'s 'who' question could be solved by answering the 'where' question. Since the homunculus inside the brain would need a brain himself, with a smaller homunculus inside, etc., this series of conarium-within-conarium eventually becomes more and more infinitesimal until, not unlike Murphy's pineal gland, the 'conarium has shrunk to nothing' (Beckett 2009a, 6). The result is a Chinese boxes model that locates consciousness at an 'ideal core of the onion', to use another metaphor Beckett employed in his essay *Proust* (1931) (Beckett, 1999a, 29).

On the other hand, a post-Cartesian model seems to be intuitively prefigured in some modernist and late modernist works. Instead of looking for a 'core of the onion', this other model sees the workings of the mind in terms of a process. While Beckett's novels *Molloy* (1951), *Malone Dies* (1951) and *The Unnamable* push the homunculus model to extremes, they also hint at the possibility of such a post-Cartesian, processual approach to the study of the human mind. In *Malone Dies*, for instance, Malone literally *writes* his self, by means of an exercise book and a pencil. In this capacity, he is paradigmatic of the 'autograph' in the sense suggested by H. Porter Abbott, whose 'working distinction between autography and autobiography is that autography is the larger field comprehending all self-writing' (1996, 2).

The Autograph: Beyond 'Endogenesis'

Although Porter Abbott does not study manuscripts in his book *Beckett Writing Beckett*, the notion of the 'autograph' in his narratological context does not need to be separated from its original meaning in manuscript studies. In Medieval studies, the word 'autograph' is used to denote a manuscript in the hand of the text's author, as opposed to the vast majority of Medieval manuscripts that were written in the hand of a scribe. There is a reason why so many modernist authors kept their manuscripts or donated many of them to university libraries, as in Beckett's case. The autograph is a key concept in literary research into the human mind, which in turn is a central concern of modernist literature. The autograph in the sense that the self is 'written by itself' comes close to Dennett's notion of 'narrative selfhood' and his 'multiple drafts model' of consciousness – his alternative to the 'Cartesian theatre' (see below). Moreover, building on David Herman's work on cognitive narratology, the notion of the autograph can be connected to the notions of the 'extended mind' (Clark and Chalmers, 1998) and the 'extensive mind' (Hutto and Myin, 2013), to investigate how intertextuality functions as a model of the 'extended mind' at work; and how manuscript research plays a role in modernist writers' literary enquiries into the human mind. To examine this, my case study is James Joyce's use of Wyndham Lewis's critique of behaviourism and of 'telling from the inside' in *The Art of Being Ruled*.[3]

The controversy between Lewis (interested in the notion of space) and Joyce (who, according to Lewis, was too preoccupied with the notion of time) is reflected in the so-called 'dime-cash' problem in *Finnegans Wake* (Joyce, 1939,

149.11–150.14), considered from the point of view of a 'spatialist'. In the first draft, the 'dime' was originally spelled 'time': 'my disposals of the same time-cash problem elsewhere, *naturalistically*, of course, from the blinkpoint of a spatialist' (Joyce 1963, 99; emphasis added). In *The Art of Being Ruled* (1926), the 'spatialist' Wyndham Lewis had already criticized the 'considerable degree of *naturalism* aimed at' in *Ulysses*, suggesting a correspondence between Leopold Bloom's stream of consciousness and the conversation of Mr. Jingle in Charles Dickens's *The Pickwick Papers*. His conclusion was that Joyce made extensive use of 'a fashionable naturalist device – that usually described as "presenting the character from the *inside*"' (Lewis, 1989, 346).

This description corresponds with what early critics of modernism called the 'journey within' (Guerard, 2006, 326). Building on Herman's criticism of this 'critical commonplace' (Herman, 2011), I suggest that this inside-versus-outside image is an inexact metaphor, based on an obsolete Cartesian body/mind split, which to some extent is also recognizable in Raymonde Debray Genette's distinction between 'endogenesis' and 'exogenesis' (1979). 'Endogenesis' is everything that belongs as it were to the inside (Gr. *endo*) of the writer's 'own' writing project, whereas 'exogenesis' stands for the external source texts he or she makes use of during the writing process. I should immediately add that genetic criticism has always recognized that the border between endo- and exogenesis is indistinct (see de Biasi, 1996). But the point I want to make relates to the inside/outside, endo/exo metaphor, which may still be a remnant of our age-old bias towards an 'internalist' model of the mind, based on Descartes. Dennett's alternative to this 'Cartesian theatre' is his so-called 'multiple drafts model' of consciousness, which roughly corresponds with the multiple versions that typically characterize 'endogenesis'.

Dennett compares the workings of the conscious mind to a process of editorial revision, with various additions, emendations and overwritings (Dennett, 1991, 112). The resulting narrative sequences are, again, subject to continuous editing, to the extent that there is 'no single narrative that counts as the canonical version', because 'at any point in time there are multiple "drafts" of narrative fragments at various stages of editing in various places in the brain' (113). Especially to genetic critics and textual scholars, this may seem a plausible model of the mind, but I want to add two nuances.

First, this model is not new. In November 1929, Benjamin Crémieux wrote a review of 'Work in Progress', arguing that Joyce's purpose in distorting words was to escape from the abstract symbols they represented and to bring them closer to cognition. Joyce allowed the words 'to reproduce the hesitations, the errors, the drafts of cognition' ('de leur permettre de reproduire les hésitations, les erreurs, les ébauches de la pensée').[4] So, Crémieux already prefigured Dennett's metaphor of the multiple drafts model of cognition.

Second, Dennett employed this metaphor to explain consciousness, but in genetic criticism, this is not just a metaphor: these multiple drafts are real. They are the stuff that fiction is made of. In other words, the manuscripts are not just a record of but an integral part of the cognitive process. This *externalizes* Dennett's model and brings it closer to another recent paradigm in cognitive sciences, called enactivism, which has affinities with the extended mind theory. According to this theory, the mind is not limited to the brain, inside the skull; the mind is an interaction between an intelligent agent and his or her physical and cultural environment.

To study literary evocations of this 'extended mind' at work in modernism, an adequate starting point is the incipit of *Anna Livia Plurabelle* (first published as a separate book in 1928), which later became chapter 8 of *Finnegans Wake*: 'O/tell me all'. In his study of the making of *Anna Livia Plurabelle*, Fred Higginson described the pleasure that he took in *Finnegans Wake* as 'the pleasure of watching the mind at work' (1960, 14). Higginson was one of the first to analyse the *Wake* as a 'Work in Progress', taking its successive versions into account, watching the mind at work and choosing the river chapter as his subject. Evidently, the metaphor of stream of consciousness imposes itself. The text of *Anna Livia Plurabelle* is famous for the hundreds of river names that are woven into the text, but it can hardly be called a description of the river Liffey. It would be more precise to see the text in performative terms: it performs 'imagination', it enacts the workings of a mind. This performative rendition of the notion of 'stream of consciousness' adds a cognitive dimension to what A. Walton Litz called Joyce's '*rendering* [rather than description] of the river' (1964, 113).

This metaphor of the river also recurs in Dennett's view on consciousness. In his multiple drafts model, he considers the telling of tales to be a 'fundamental tactic of self-protection, self-control, and self-definition' (Dennett, 1991, 417). He therefore sees the 'self' in terms of 'narrative selfhood', consisting of what he calls 'streams of narrative':

> These streams of narrative issue forth *as if* from a single source – not just in the obvious physical sense of flowing from just one mouth, or one pencil or pen, but in a more subtle sense: their effect on any audience is to encourage them to (try to) posit a unified agent whose words they are, about whom they are: in short, to posit a *center of narrative gravity*. (418)

This positing of a centre of narrative gravity is exactly what happens in the opening of *Anna Livia Plurabelle*: the presentation of streams of narrative issuing forth *as if* from a single source.

Dennett, however, mixes this river metaphor with another powerful metaphor: that of the web. He suggests that

> our fundamental tactic of self-protection, self-control, and self-definiton is not spinning webs or building dams, but telling stories, and more particularly concocting and controlling the story we tell others – and ourselves – about who we are. […] Our tales are spun, but for the most part we don't spin them; they spin us. Our human consciousness, and our narrative selfhood, is their product, not their source. (418)

But Dennett also notes that 'Unlike a spider, an individual human doesn't just *exude* its web; more like a beaver, it works hard to gather the materials out of which it builds its protective fortress' (416).

The statement that a human being does not just 'exude its web' comes remarkably close to the age-old 'querelle des anciens et des modernes', notably to the fable of the spider and the bee in Jonathan Swift's *Battle of the Books* (1704). As a 'modern' writer, the spider may be under the illusion that it builds its web 'with [its] own hands, and the materials extracted altogether out of [its] own person', as Swift puts it (Swift, 1986, 112), but the Ancients point out that the spider also feeds on insects and the 'vermin of its age', otherwise it would not be able to make its web.[5] So, whereas the river metaphor corresponds well with the endogenetic process (as described, for instance, by Higginson), the web metaphor corresponds rather well with exogenetics.

Incorporating 'Exogenesis'

Applying Swift's terms to Joyce, it seems fair to say that he mainly worked according to the manner of the bee, and of the Ancients, gathering his 'verbal booty' – or 'butin verbal', as Samuel Beckett called it in a letter to Thomas MacGreevy (8 November 1931; Beckett, 1999b, xiv) – wherever he could find it. Wyndham Lewis accused him of lacking any special viewpoint of his own. In contrast, Lewis would probably have considered himself more of a spider, on the side of the moderns. Joyce, however, showed him that he was also feeding on the 'vermin of his age', to use Swift's terms.

A good example is Wyndham Lewis's criticism of behaviourism in his book *The Art of Being Ruled* (1926), where he starts railing at 'Professor Watson', 'the greatest exponent of behaviorism, and the king of testers' (Lewis, 1989, 339). Joyce took down the word 'tester' in his *Finnegans Wake* notebook VI.B.20 and a few other notes from Lewis's rant against behaviourism. Lewis ridicules Watson's way of explaining everything in terms of stimulus and response; he also ridicules Watson's argument that 'introspectist' psychology threw away the notion of the 'soul' only to replace it by the notion of a 'mind' that 'was to remain always hidden and difficult of access' (Watson, qtd. in Lewis, 1989, 339). As opposed to this 'introspectist' inward turn, some cognitive philosophers such as Louise Barrett only very recently suggested that there is something to say for Watson's behaviourist approach and that 'a stimulus-response mechanism is a legitimate "cognitive" process' (Barrett, 2011, 10).

Against this cognitive background, Joyce's reaction to Lewis is quite interesting: after reading Lewis's rant against behaviourism, Joyce responded 'behavioristically' in *transition* 6 (Joyce, 1927, 98), employing this adverb in the first draft of chapter 6, in which 'Professor Levis-Brueller' (99) tries to explain the 'dime-cash problem' and starts with the question '*Why am I not born like a Gentilman*' (99), alluding to Lewis's discussion of Bloom's 'gentleman-complex – the Is he or isn't he a gentleman? – the phantom index-finger of the old shabby-genteel' (Lewis, 1993, 105). But soon enough the Professor notices that his message is not coming across: 'As my explanations here are probably above your understandings I shall revert to a more expletive method which I frequently use when I have to sermo with muddleclass pupils' (Joyce, 1927, 100). To illustrate his point he tells the fable of 'The Mookse and the Gripes' (101).

In *transition* 6, this fable ends at the bottom of page 105 ('*I no canna stay!*'). Page 106 opens with the Professor's smug recapitulation ('As I have now successfully explained to you ... ') and on the next page (106a)[6] he reminds his audience:

> My heeders will recoil with a great leisure how at the outbreak before trespassing on the space question [...] I proved to mindself as to your sotisfiction how his abject all through [...] is nothing so much more than a mere cashdime however *genteel* he may want ours (106a; emphasis added)

Again, the word 'genteel' alludes to what Lewis called the 'gentleman-complex' of the 'shabby-genteel' (Lewis, 1993, 105).

In *transition* 6, the fable is followed by the Professor's second illustration, the Burrus and Caseous episode: 'Burrus, let us like to imagine, is a genuine prime, the real choice, full of natural greace [...] whereat Caseous is oversely the revise of him' (106a). Again, this episode is filled with 'exogenetic' fragments derived from Lewis's critique. In the chapter 'Hatred of Language and the Behaviorist "Word-Habit"' (in *The Art of Being Ruled*), just before discussing Watson's behaviourism, Lewis had argued that 'without the control of the intellect, words have tended to go over into music' (1989, 339). Joyce alludes to this theme on page 106d when he introduces 'Margareen': 'We now romp through a period of pure lyricism of shamebred music evidenced by such words in distress as *I cream for thee, Sweet Margareen*' (106d). Her intermediary position ('Margareena she's very fond of Burrus but, alick and alack! She velly fond of chee'; 106e) is appropriately presented as an intermezzo in the 'art of being rude' (106e-f). And finally, in *The Art of Being Ruled*, Lewis had made a link between Joyce's literary project and the 'exploitation of madness, of ticks, [and] *blephorospasms*, and eccentricities of the mechanism of the brain' (347; emphasis added), which Joyce alludes to on page 106f: 'a boosted blasted bleating blatant bloaten blasphorus blesporous idiot'.

Joyce's 'endogenetic' incorporation of references to Lewis's 'exogenetic' criticism is interesting in a cognitive context because it shows how Joyce managed to draw attention to the act of taletelling by turning the telling into the content of the tale. The point Joyce made, several decades before Dennett came up with the multiple drafts model, was that the telling of tales is constitutive of the human mind. And perhaps Joyce intuitively pushed the point even further than Dennett's theory of narrative selfhood by suggesting that this is not an exclusively internal affair, but that it involves the environment. As a consequence, a more enactive understanding of narrative selfhood provides a model of the mind that implies the undoing of the inside/outside, exo/endo split. As an alternative for this split in literary studies, it might be useful to understand (especially modernist) taletelling in terms of *intertextual cognition*.

Conclusion: Intertextual Cognition

In the past, genetic research into Joyce's notebooks has been derogatively called 'source hunting' or 'philological spadework'. I would argue that this derogatory attitude was a remnant of a view on modernism as an 'inward turn', which saw the mind in terms of an inside/outside metaphor, the equivalent of what Hutto and Myin call the 'Senior Partner Principle' (in the context of cognitive philosophy):

> To suppose that what is constitutive of mentality must reside in organisms or their brains alone is to endorse a Senior Partner Principle holding that, although a partnership with environmental factors may be causally necessary for cognition,

the organism's or system's brain 'wears the trousers' in the relationship; only brains bring mentality to the party. In the place of this, we promote the more even-handed Equal Partner Principle as the right way to understand basic mental activity. Accordingly, contributions of the brain are not prioritized over those of the environment. (Hutto and Myin, 2013, 137)

Exogenetic research should of course not be limited to detective work. But on the other hand, disparaging exogenetic research as 'source hunting' may imply a similar Senior Partner Principle, focusing too narrowly on what is alleged to derive directly from the author's 'brain': the endogenesis. I suggest modernist studies might benefit from a more integrative approach along the lines of the Equal Partner Principle, focusing on the interaction (rather than the distinction) between endogenesis and exogenesis.

This is not just a methodological issue and it does not apply only to genetic criticism, for this Equal Partner Principle reflects an enactive approach to what might be termed 'intertextual cognition'. Intertextuality differs from 'source hunting' in that it puts the emphasis on the reader rather than on the author. It is the reader who finds links between a text and other texts and thus establishes the intertext. Given this focus on *other* texts, it may seem hard – at first sight – to reconcile intertextuality with, for instance, Dennett's notion of 'narrative selfhood'. But if we apply this notion of 'narrative selfhood' (consisting of so-called 'streams of narrative') to fictional minds, the exogenetic dimension of so many modernist texts stresses the fact that what Dennett calls the 'streams of narrative' issue forth *as if* from a single source. The effect of these 'streams of narrative' on an audience (readers) is to encourage *them* to posit a *centre of narrative gravity* (Dennett, 1991, 418). The exploration of the mind, which is a preoccupation of so many modernists, therefore counts on the reader's 'positing' of this centre. And this positing is markedly intertextual. Manuscript research (especially exogenetic criticism) encourages such an intertextual reading. The enactments of the 'streams of narrative' that make up a fictional narrative selfhood in *Anna Livia Plurabelle* and the fable of the Mookse and the Gripes show the large extent to which this narrative selfhood consists of 'exogenetic' material. This observation leads us, first, to agree with David Herman's suggestion that modernism's investigations of the mind imply less of an 'inward turn' than the critical commonplace would have it; and secondly, to suggest that Dennett's 'multiple drafts model' might benefit from opening up its 'inward' focus to a more enactivist approach that sees consciousness in terms of the extended mind, which finds its literary equivalent in intertextuality and also relies on the mind of the reader.

A fictional character that could be said to personify this intertextual cognition is Lucky in Beckett's *Waiting for Godot*. In a sense, Lucky prefigures and 'performs' Dennett's idea that 'Our tales are spun, but for the most part we don't spin them; they spin us' and that 'Our human consciousness, and our narrative selfhood, is their product, not their source' (Dennett, 1991, 418). When Lucky is asked to dance, he responds 'naturally' to the impression of being caught in a web or a net: 'He thinks he's entangled in a net' (Beckett, 2009c, 37). And when he is asked to 'think', his mind seems to be similarly entangled in a net or a web of allusions and references. Since many modernists and late modernists were preoccupied with the attempt to evoke the workings of the human mind, it is not a coincidence that intertextuality plays such an important role in their writings. From a cognitive point of view, intertextuality functions as a model of the taletelling self as a narrative 'work in progress'. By revisiting Dennett's 'multiple drafts model' and 'narrative selfhood' from an enactive perspective and studying the extended mind at work in real (not just metaphorical) drafts, minding manuscripts reveals itself as a valuable way of examining the central modernist concern with the workings of human consciousness and cognition.

Notes

1   In narratology, metalepsis denotes the transgression of the boundaries between narrative levels. For an in-depth study of this phenomenon in Beckett's works, see Debra Malina, *Metalepsis and the Construction of the Subject* (Columbus, OH: The Ohio State University Press, 2002).

2   In the preceding novels, Beckett prepared the ground for this metaleptic transgression. In *Molloy*, the subject of the first question (where?) was the first 'given' in the narrative situation: 'I am in my mother's room' (Beckett, 2009b, 3). The 'when' question, however, was problematized in the closing lines: 'Then I went back into the house and wrote, It is midnight. The rain is beating on the windows. It was not midnight. It was not raining.' (184)

3   For a more detailed and extensive analysis of Joyce's incorporation of Lewis's critique as a form of the extended mind at work, see Van Hulle, 2016a; the case study from Joyce's work in this essay is a revised version of the proceedings of the 24th James Joyce Symposium in Utrecht (June 2014; see Van Hulle, 2016b).

4   'Ce que recherche l'auteur d'*Ulysses*, en créant ou en déformant les mots, c'est d'échapper au symbole abstrait qu'ils représentent, c'est de les rapprocher de la pensée, de leur permettre de reproduire les hésitations, les erreurs, les ébauches

de la pensée, de reproduire le courant ininterrompu de la pensée' (University at Buffalo, James Joyce Collection, clippings, envelope 33: 1018).

5   In this way, 'The spider's web appears as a proper part of [what Richard Dawkins called] the spider's extended phenotype', which Andy Clark compares to the extended mind (Clark, 2012, 287).

6   In *transition* 6, the fable was followed by the story of Burrus and Caseous. Joyce was extremely late with his lengthy addition for which the editors of *transition* even had to take apart the first four hundred copies of the review, which had already been stitched. The page numbering also had to be adapted.

Bibliography

Abbott, H. P. (1996), *Beckett Writing Beckett: The Author in the Autograph*. Ithaca: Cornell University Press.

Barrett, L. (2011), *Beyond the Brain: How Body and Environment Shape Animal and Human Minds*. Princeton and Oxford: Princeton University Press.

Beckett, S. (1992a), *The Theatrical Notebooks of Samuel Beckett. Volume Two: Endgame. With a Revised Text*, S. E. Gontarski (ed.). New York: Grove Press.

Beckett, S. (1992b), *The Theatrical Notebooks of Samuel Beckett. Volume Three: Krapp's Last Tape. With a Revised Text*, J. Knowlson (ed.). New York: Grove Press.

Beckett, S. (1993), *The Theatrical Notebooks of Samuel Beckett. Volume One: Waiting for Godot*. D. McMillan and J. Knowlson (eds), New York: Grove Press.

Beckett, S. (1999a), *Proust and Three Dialogues with Georges Duthuit*. London: John Calder.

Beckett, S. (1999b), '*Dream' Notebook*, J. Pilling (ed.). Reading: Whiteknights Press.

Beckett, S. (2009a), *Murphy*, J. C. C. Mays (ed.). London: Faber and Faber.

Beckett, S. (2009b), *Molloy*, S. Weller (ed.). London: Faber and Faber.

Beckett, S. (2009c), *Waiting for Godot*, M. Bryden (ed.). London: Faber and Faber.

Beckett, S. (2013), *L'Innommable/The Unnamable: A Digital Genetic Edition*, D. Van Hulle, S. Weller and V. Neyt (eds), Brussels: University Press of Antwerp, www.beckettarchive.org.

Bernaerts, L. and Van Hulle, D. (2013), 'Narrative across Versions: Narratology Meets Genetic Criticism'. *Poetics Today*, 34, (3), 281–326.

Callu, F. (1993), 'La Transmission des manuscrits', in A. Cadiot and C. Haffner (eds), *Les Manuscrits des écrivains*. Paris: CNRS editions/Hachette, pp. 54–66.

Clark, A. (2012), 'Embodied, Embedded, and Extended Cognition', in K. Frankish and W. M. Ramsey (eds), *The Cambridge Handbook of Cognitive Science*. Cambridge: Cambridge University Press, pp. 275–91.

Clark, A. and Chalmers, D. J. (1998), 'The Extended Mind'. *Analysis*, 58, 10–23.

Cohn, D. (1968), 'K. Enters the Castle. On the Change of Person in Kafka's Manuscript'. *Euphorion*, 62, 28–45.

Cohn, D. (1978), *Transparent Minds: Narrative Modes for Presenting Consciousness in Fiction*. Princeton: Princeton University Press.

Crémieux, B. (1929), 'Le Règne des Mots' (Candide, 14 November 1929), review among the University at Buffalo's uncatalogued newspaper clippings, James Joyce Collection (Poetry Collection), UBC 33: 1018.

Culler, J. (2009), *Literary Theory*. New York: Sterling.

De Biasi, P.-M. (1996), 'What Is a Literary Draft? Towards a Functional Typology of Genetic Documentation'. *Yale French Studies*, 89, 26–58.

Debray Genette, R. (1979), 'Génétique et poétique: le cas Flaubert', in *Essais de critique génétique*, Paris: Flammarion, pp. 21–67.

Debray Genette, R. (2004), 'Flaubert's "A Simple Heart", or How to Make an Ending', in J. Deppman, D. Ferrer and M. Groden (eds), *Genetic Criticism: Texts and Avant-Textes*. Philadelphia: University of Pennsylvania Press, pp. 69–95.

Dennett, D. C. (1991), *Consciousness Explained*. London: Penguin.

Gardner, H. (1978), *The Composition of 'Four Quartets'*. London: Faber and Faber.

Gontarski, S. E. (1985), *The Intent of Undoing in Samuel Beckett's Dramatic Texts*. Bloomington: Indiana University Press.

Guerard, A. J. (2006), 'The Journey Within', in P. B. Armstrong (ed.), *Joseph Conrad, Heart of Darkness*. New York and London: Norton Critical Editions, pp. 326–36.

Herman, D. (2011), 'Re-Minding Modernism', in D. Herman (ed.). *The Emergence of Mind: Representations of Consciousness in Narrative Discourse in English*. Lincoln: University of Nebraska Press, pp. 243–71.

Higginson, F. H. (1960), *Anna Livia Plurabelle: The Making of a Chapter*. Minneapolis: University of Minnesota Press.

Hutto, D. D. and Myin, E. (2013), *Radicalizing Enactivism: Basic Minds without Content*. Cambridge, MA: The MIT Press.

Joyce, J. (1927), 'Continuation of a Work in Progress'. *transition*, 6 (September), 87–106f.

Joyce, J. (1939), *Finnegans Wake*. London: Faber and Faber.

Joyce, J. (1963), *A First-Draft Version of 'Finnegans Wake'*, D. Hayman (ed.). Austin, TX: University of Texas Press.

Joyce, J. (1978–79), *The James Joyce Archive*, M. Groden et al. (eds). New York: Garland.

Kahler, E. von (1973), *The Inward Turn of Narrative*, R. and C. Winston (transl.). Princeton: Princeton University Press.

Lewis, W. (1989 [1926]), *The Art of Being Ruled*, R. W. Dasenbrock. Santa Rosa: Black Sparrow Press.

Lewis, W. (1993 [1927]), *Time and Western Man*, P. Edwards (ed.). Santa Rosa: Black Sparrow Press.

Litz, A. W. (1964), *The Art of James Joyce: Method and Design in Ulysses and Finnegans Wake*. Oxford: Oxford University Press.

Malina, D. (2002), *Metalepsis and the Construction of the Subject*. Columbus, OH: The Ohio State University Press.

Pountney, R. (1988), *Theatre of Shadows: Samuel Beckett's Drama 1956–76*. Gerrard's Cross: Colin Smythe.

Swift, J. (1986), *A Tale of a Tub and Other Works*, A. Ross and D. Woolley (eds with introd.). Oxford: Oxford University Press.

Van Hulle, D. (2016a), *James Joyce's 'Work in Progress': Pre-Book Publications of 'Finnegans Wake' Fragments*. London: Ashgate.

Van Hulle, D. (2016b), 'The Worldmaker's *Umwelt*: The Cognitive Space between a Writer's Library and the Publishing House'. *European Joyce Studies*, 24, 173–87.

The Sciences and
Technologies of Modernism

13

Einstein, Relativity and Literary Modernism

Paul Sheehan

On the face of it, the juxtaposition of modernism and science constitutes a fundamental mismatch. Whether the criterion be method (empirical testability), ideology (the belief in progress) or framework (systematic organizational schemas), the modern scientific world view seems irreconcilable with the principles of aesthetic modernism. Such a critical distancing can be seen in *Mrs Dalloway* (1925), with Virginia Woolf's satirical depiction of the medical establishment and its codes of conduct. When faced with a patient suffering from shell shock, that most modernist of nervous disorders, Woolf's physicians propose sedation and 'proportion' as treatments – with disastrous results. This is, however, only one part of a wider picture; as we will see, a short time after *Mrs Dalloway*, Woolf embraced a different kind of modern scientific paradigm, one derived from the new physics.

In addition, there were other modernist writers who had no misgivings about drawing freely on scientific metaphors, allusions and analogies in their works. Perhaps the most famous of the latter is T. S. Eliot's depiction of the poet's mind as a 'shred of platinum' (Eliot, 1932, 18). He uses this image to draw a parallel between a catalytic substance able to transform oxygen and sulphur dioxide into sulphurous acid and the poet's capacity to turn emotions and feelings into art. Along with Eliot's later praise of James Joyce's *Ulysses* (it has 'the importance of a scientific discovery') (Eliot, 1975, 177), it is apparent that modernism has a more complex and ambivalent relationship with the discourse of science than a superficial overview might suggest.

When it comes to the more specific question of modernism's relationship to Einstein and relativity, however, the reverse would appear to be the case. Covert affinities between the science of relativity and the principles of literary modernism are not hard to find: both tend to embrace paradox, rather than progress; both abjure universal chronometry, in favour of more diverse, polytemporal perspectives; and both press at, and move beyond, the limits of realism, whether scientific or literary. Yet even with these accordances, which have been widely acknowledged, there are evident difficulties in securing more concrete and nuanced links between the two. These difficulties might be summarized as too advanced, too abstruse and too recent.

Perhaps the least surmountable stumbling block is the disciplinary one. The new physics of the early twentieth century was based on mathematical proofs beyond the grasp of most, if not all, practitioners of literary modernism. This has led some critics to conclude that the latter possesses only the most cursory, incidental relationship to relativity theory (Sleigh, 2011, 156). Moreover, theoretical physics is at the 'hard' end of the science spectrum, where cultural ramifications are less easy to identify – unlike those of the life sciences (i.e. Darwin), mind science (Freud) or the so-called 'science of history' (Marx and others), all of which have been successfully incorporated into modernist studies. And then there is the problem of influence. Histories of literary modernism invariably cite as extra-disciplinary progenitors not only Darwin, Freud and Marx but also Schopenhauer, Nietzsche and Bergson – all thinkers who emerged out of nineteenth-century thought and who broke decisively with it. Einstein's cultural renown, by contrast, does not begin until the 1920s, by which time modernism was well into its 'high' phase of production.

Recognition of these difficulties has taken both positive and negative forms. The latter is evident in surveys of modernism and science, which tend to pass fairly briskly from the concerns of Victorian science – thermodynamics, entropy, the discovery of radiation – to (advanced) quantum physics and/ or information theory, bypassing Einstein altogether; or else referring to relativity theory only fleetingly, then moving quickly on.[1] In a more positive vein, scholars have attempted to alleviate the difficulties outlined earlier by introducing a mediating factor of some kind. Metaphor is the prime candidate here, as the go-between linking scientific concepts with literary invention. Daniel Albright, for example, in *Quantum Poetics: Yeats, Pound, Eliot, and the Science of Modernism* (1997), uses the language of waves and particles to find new ways of exploring the often contradictory tenets of modernist poetry. And in *Einstein's Wake: Relativity, Metaphor, and Modernist Literature* (2001), Michael Whitworth examines metaphors of form in literary periodicals, as a means of connecting scientific theories with modernist writing. But as productive as this method has been, I want to propose a different kind of rapprochement between relativity theory and modernism: a shared theoretical orientation that engages closely with the nature of the real and questions what this confrontation can yield.

As it is generally understood, the modern epoch is defined by instability, upheaval, incongruity and paradox, by the declamation that the centre cannot hold and, concomitantly, that the constituents of reality are out of joint. Modernism's response to the tumult of modernity is to seek upheavals in art – disturbances of form and remakings of tradition, necessitating radical forms of stylization. Allied to this is the uneasy awareness that the observable, empirically measureable world does not line up neatly with the new conceptual understandings of it; other movements and forces, below the threshold of the perceiving eye and the conscious mind, confound the disclosures of phenomenal reality. Or to put it another way: our experience of the modern is at sharp odds with the forms of representation available to embody it. If the science of relativity has much that seems to accord with the work of literary modernism, it is because of this mutual averment that the real has its own laws and dispositions, and that nature and art alike can only gain access to them obliquely.

How, then, do Einstein and modernism meet? Not mathematically, but conceptually – first by routing relativity through philosophy and then by (further) routing it through aesthetics. In terms of philosophical affiliations, modernism and relativity both explore, with some tenacity, different kinds of temporal anomaly. Indeed, many literary modernists saw time as a tyranny that needed to be overcome. Nineteenth-century temporal logic in particular had to be resisted, based as it was on the belief that time is linear, progressive and indomitable, the time of empire and industry, and of social conformity. Modernism responded to this unspoken authority by introducing discontinuity, heterogeneity and irregularity into the rhythms of nature (especially the circadian cycle) and technology (mechanical clock-time).[2] With relativity, then, Einstein further weakened the regimen of temporal consistency. He showed that different observers can measure different times for the same event – if they are moving relative to each other. Although measurable, these differences are often minute. But for objects moving at high (i.e. relativistic) speeds, time dilation is significant, and it has far-reaching implications.

The above example highlights what is perhaps the most difficult aspect of Einstein's theories: their radically *ahuman* quality. Insofar as human actants appear in these theories, they function simply as bodies – mere objects in the world of matter, representing vantage points or vessels falling through space, susceptible to particular forces and counter-forces exerted by fields of energy. Concomitantly, a significant part of modernism is more deliberately antihumanist. As Simon During notes, literary modernism's turn away from philosophical anthropology, and its consequent abandonment of the 'ideal of humanist progress', left it 'unable to affirm human substance' (During, 2013, 151, 158). For D. H. Lawrence, this meant that the 'old stable ego of the character' was no longer tenable (Lawrence, 1981, 183). Modernist 'subjects', therefore, are hollowed out and disaffected, fictional avatars for the hypothetical human agents that Einstein uses to demonstrate how relativity works. As we will see, this notion of a 'hollowed-out' subject is further complicated by the vicissitudes of modernist interiority.

The aesthetic dimensions of relativity theory are less evident than its philosophical implications, but the former can nonetheless be seen in Einstein's efforts to popularize his works – a move that greatly enhanced the worldwide fame he has enjoyed almost continuously since 1920. The first steps on this path, in the Anglophone world, were a short book entitled *Relativity: The Special and the General Theory* (1920), in which Einstein outlined his two seminal works for a general readership, and *The Meaning of Relativity* in 1922, a transcription of the high-profile lectures he gave the previous year at Princeton University. In addition to these self-penned works, a number of non-specialist elucidations appeared around the same time, from such luminaries as Arthur Eddington (*Space, Time and Gravitation: An Outline of the General Relativity Theory* [1920]) and Bertrand Russell (*ABC of Relativity* [1925]).

In his plain-language writings, Einstein famously exploited the *gedanken* or thought experiment, his favourite expository device. Consider, for example, one of the conclusions he draws in the original 'special relativity' paper of 1905:

> So we can see that we cannot attach any *absolute* signification to the concept of simultaneity, but that two events which, viewed from a system of co-ordinates, are simultaneous, can no longer be looked upon as simultaneous events when envisaged from a system which is in motion relatively to that system. (Lorentz, 1923, 42–3)

In *Relativity*, Einstein illustrates this counter-intuitive notion of simultaneity via the now-famous scenario of the man on the bank and the man on the train (Einstein, 2006, 26–8). Since each occupies a different reference frame (i.e. 'system of co-ordinates'), each will have a different sense of temporal order. The man on the bank sees two bolts of lightning strike the train, one at the back and the other at the front, simultaneously; the man on the train, however, who is in motion relative to the bank, will first see the bolt that strikes the front of the train (towards which he is moving) before he sees the bolt that strikes the back (away from which he is moving). According to Einstein, both views are correct. Like so much else in the observable world, simultaneity is dependent on the reference frame of the observer. Thus, Einstein did not just describe the 'relativity of simultaneity', in his popular account of it; he also, in a sense, 'staged' it for a mass audience, giving it the starkness and simplicity of a folk tale.

Einstein's works also contain more formal aesthetic qualities. Writing in the early 1960s, Thomas Kuhn notes that hard evidence is not all that is required for a new scientific paradigm to take hold: '[S]ometimes it is only personal and inarticulate aesthetic considerations that can do that. [...] Even today Einstein's general theory attracts men principally on aesthetic grounds, an appeal that few people outside of mathematics have been able to feel' (Kuhn, 1996, 158). Yet many people 'outside of mathematics' have responded to Einstein's celebrated formula, $E = mc^2$, in aesthetic ways. Its reputation as the world's most famous scientific equation is based to a large extent on the elegant simplicity of its shape: just three terms, bound in a relationship that conjoins an absolute (the speed of light) with two variables (energy and mass). The mutual convertibility of the two variables offers resources for the imagination, suggesting that matter is protean and unpredictable, rather than fixed and inviolate. Literary experimentation, as with conceptual understanding, cannot *prove* the play of relativity here, only offer instantiations of it; yet those instantiations can provide radical new contexts for Einstein's theories and augment the latter's connate aesthetic qualities.

A potential objection to the present argument might be, Why invoke Einstein and relativity at all? What can they offer to literary modernist studies that other theories of non-linear temporality elide or overlook? If a single thinker could be said to have produced a philosophy of modernist time, it is Henri Bergson. His belief in a time of lived experience, which he calls *durée*, or duration, emphasizes the power of intuition to gainsay relief from the pressures of causality and make human freedom a real possibility. In Bergson's view, the data given to consciousness are immediately and unavoidably temporal, and hence a riposte to the regimentation of clock-time (whose instruments of measurement, in any case, transpose the experience of *durée* into spatial representations). Einstein, too, challenges the absolute character of Newtonian time. However, he does not posit in its stead *subjective* time, as does Bergson, but *perspectival* time. Subjective time presupposes a more malleable, changeable and irregular alternative to objective or clock-time. If Einstein is, in the strictest sense, only really interested in clock-time, it is to show how *that time* is malleable, changeable and irregular. Rather than the observer's consciousness determining these changes, then, it is reality itself that is relativized. But if Einstein's theories are borne out by this practice of objective measurement, how does it accord with the principles of literary modernism?

At the heart of the modernist assault on the protocols of realism is an intensified subjectivity, conveyed through such technical devices as impressionism, interior monologue, stream of consciousness and the use of free indirect speech. But this so-called 'subjective turn' belies the fact that many literary modernists also seek to express new relationships with the objective world. A characteristic move is to moderate the radical subjectivity of a character's interior life by rendering it *from the inside out* – on its own terms, as it were, rather than from the outside in, as literary realism would have it. The effect of this move is to depersonalize the inner life of such a character, by presenting it through an 'objectivizing' lens. Charles Altieri suggests that something like this takes place in William Faulkner's *The Sound and the Fury* (1929), through the narration of the mute, mentally disabled Benjy. Altieri writes,

> In Benjy's world subjectivity and objectivity enter strange conjunctions. Of course the objectivity in Benjy's rendering of the world is severely reductive because it renders only sensations without articulate judgments. But [...] this absence of judgment becomes a strange and enticing freedom. There is no gulf between what Benjy registers and what is actually taking place. (Altieri, 2007, 76)

Faulkner picked up some of this technique from his reading of Joyce.[3] In *A Portrait of the Artist as a Young Man* (1916), the developing consciousness of the novel's protagonist, Stephen Dedalus, is presented in strikingly dispassionate ways. Language and form convey the phases of Stephen's mental maturation, the ontogenetic principle that engenders it confounding any easy distinction between internal and external. Moreover, the 'objective subjectivity' that results is also evident in other modernist undertakings: in T. S. Eliot's project to objectify emotion; in Wyndham Lewis's rendering of human anatomy in terms of hard surfaces and inanimate objects; in Ezra Pound's valourization of objectivity as the essence of imagist poetics; and in Ford Madox Ford's insistence that impressionism is actually a more reliable way of rendering the true conditions of the real.[4] These 'strange conjunctions' of subjective/objective attributes tally with the postulations of Einsteinian physics and its demonstration that measurements of time and material objects fluctuate under relativistic conditions. In the absence of a universal metric, relations between things – between observer and observed – assume new configurations for the literary-modernist outlook as much as for the science of relativity.

Reading Modernism Relativistically

The modernist novel, in its most exigent forms, is engaged in a constant struggle: to reshape the time-dependent nature of narrative, by finding new forms of periodicity. The modernist poem, by contrast, is not bound to this charter. Moreover, in being freed from having to resist the demands of temporal propriety, some of the resources it shares with the modernist novel can be seen more starkly. In particular, it reveals one of modernism's elemental literary figures: the arrested instant. Impression, image, symbol, moment and epiphany all constitute modes of instantaneity, in which the pressures of causal inference that underpin the burgeoning of event are suspended. For this reason, these techniques constitute the most valuable assets that the novel has to dilate time indefinitely or to stop it clean in its tracks.

Yet even as these poetic figurations have been successfully exploited by novelists, it is evident that modernist poets themselves have responded to relativity by bringing to the fore a wider range of concerns, from cosmology to prosody. In the early 1920s, for example, W. B. Yeats briefly took an interest in the science of relativity. After reading a primer on the subject, he considered accommodating Einstein's view of the cosmos into his occult system of gyres and spheres; a marginal reference to a 'four dimensional [*sic*] sphere' (Yeats, 1978, notes, 31) is all that survives of this plan. A number of American modernist poets, by contrast, zealously embraced and promoted what they took to be the essence of Einstein's scientific revolution.

William Carlos Williams is arguably the strongest poetic advocate of relativity – and the earliest. When Einstein visited America and lectured at Princeton University, in April 1921, Williams celebrated the historic occasion with a poem, 'St Francis Einstein of the Daffodils'. Somewhat eccentrically, Williams presents the already world-famous scientist as an embodiment of vitalist principles, attuned like St Francis to the natural environment and its seasonal variations:

> Einstein, tall as a violet
> in the lattice-arbor corner
> is tall as
> a blossomy peartree ...

> (Williams, 1951, 379)

The month of April is important (as it was for Eliot, in the same period, drafting what would become *The Waste Land*), with the coming of spring. Rebirth is thus presented as a kind of freedom, for the mind as much as for nature, heralded by the arrival of the scientific revolutionary in the new world.

Williams's early interest in Einstein deepens across the decades, culminating in a 1948 essay on 'The Poem as a Field of Action'. Brushing aside almost half a century of modernist experimentation, Williams avers that poetic structure – by which he means measure and foot, the 'accepted prosody' of the poem – has remained unchanged. He writes,

> How can we accept Einstein's theory of relativity, affecting our very conception of the heavens about us of which poets write so much, without incorporating its essential fact – the relativity of measurements – into our own category of activity: the poem. [...] Relativity applies to everything, like love, if it applies to anything in the world. (Williams, 1969, 283)

What Williams calls the 'relativity of measurements' must lead, he says, to a reinscription of 'prosodic values' (Williams, 1969, 286). The primary task of the post-war American poet is thus to develop new rhythmic structures capable of reflecting those values. Williams considered his own contribution to poetic relativity to be the 'variable foot', a method of using unconventional line-breaks that was, he believed, indubitably American.[5]

Williams's advocacy is paralleled by Louis Zukofsky's, who sought to establish a broader colloquy between poetry and science. His early interest in the physicist's life spurred him to undertake the English translation of Anton Reiser's *Albert Einstein: A Biographical Portrait* (1930). Among the many borrowings for Zukofsky's epic poem-sequence *A*, which he began around the same time, are details and anecdotes from Reiser's biography.[6] In terms of formal applications, concrete (if oblique) examples can be seen at the end of 'A'-8' and throughout 'A'-9'. Zukofsky composed these sections according to a mathematical formula that determined internal rhymes and (in 'A'-9') rearranged a handful of terms across the stanzas ('values', 'labor', 'things', 'use'). Exchange-value, that quintessentially Marxian concept, is shown still to be operating in a newly relativized universe: 'But see our centers do not show the changes/Of human labor our value estranges' (Zukofsky, 1978, 106).

A third instance of poetic relativity is expounded by Charles Olson, an American modernist inheritor. In his notion of open or projective verse – formulated after reading Einstein's 1934 collection of *Essays in Science* – Olson deems poetic energy to be both transformative and transferrable: 'A poem is energy transferred from where the poet got it [...] by way of the poem itself to [...] the reader'. There is, he says, an energy 'peculiar to verse alone', that is different from (but equivalent to) the energy that 'the reader, because he is a third term, will take away' (Olson, 1960, 387). In attempting to map Einsteinian physics onto the poetic imagination, Olson makes poetic creativity part of a dynamic process that does not stop at the printed page, with the word. Moreover, two years before developing these ideas Olson envisaged poetic time and space as unfixed, inconstant and radically inseparable ('Nor I nor Einstein would want to disentangle [time and space]') (Olson, 1974, 2). Projective verse thus facilitates poetic spacetime, binding ear, breath, syllable and line with the field of objects, including man and his relationship to the forces of nature.

As Olson's Einstein-inspired musings indicate, bringing modernism and relativity into productive alignment is a matter of reading practices as well as writing strategies. This means attending to those fictional/poetic moments when physical processes no longer conform to one's intuitions or expectations, when the distribution of matter creates ripples in the phenomenal world. If Newtonian mechanics regarded space as a rigid, homogeneous medium, susceptible neither to change nor to any conditional agencies, Einstein saw it as heterogeneous, as implicated in temporal irregularities and possessing 'a power to take part in physical events' (Hey and Walters, 1997, 188). Reading modernism relativistically is, therefore, not just a question of metaphorical appropriations or conceptual parallels but also of textual anomalies.

The American poets mentioned above stand out for the approbation and support they lend to Einsteinian relativity, affirming its applicability to modernist literary poetics. But if many English and Irish literary modernists reacted more coolly to the new physics, that did not preclude them from absorbing, on some level, its cardinal precepts. The remainder of this chapter focuses on two such pairs of writers, who present complementary attitudes to Einstein and relativity: one engaging with these subjects directly and explicitly, in light of the debates they have provoked; and the other proffering fictional examples of relativity that signify covert affiliations rather than mindful projections or applications. In the late 1910s and early 1920s, D. H. Lawrence and James Joyce form such a pair; and at the other end of the 1920s, a similar coupling can be seen with Wyndham Lewis and Virginia Woolf. Einstein's relationship to literary modernism can thus be gauged through these four exemplars, in the first decade of his ascendancy as a cultural figurehead.

D. H. Lawrence: The Politics of Relativity

Although in many ways the chief Anglo-modernist exemplar of relativity theory, D. H. Lawrence did not treat the subject with unbridled reverence. 'Einstein isn't so metaphysically marvellous', he tells a correspondent in 1921, after reading Einstein's popular account of his theories (Lawrence, 1987, 37). Despite this apparent dismissal, Lawrence declared his interest in relativity soon afterwards in *Fantasia of the Unconscious* (1922) – his philosophical treatise on social and individual identity – and in the semi-autobiographical novel *Kangaroo* (1923), an exposé of civil and political unrest in Australia. But Lawrence's clearest statement of approval is conveyed much later, in the poem 'Relativity' (1929):

> I like relativity and quantum theories
> because I don't understand them
> and they make me feel as if space shifted about like a swan that can't settle,
> refusing to sit still and be measured;
>
> (Lawrence, 1972, 210)

Even this apparently straightforward paean to relativity (and quantum physics) has political nuances. Lawrence presents the unsettled motion of the swan as a 'refusal', a rebuff to those scales of measurement on which modern science is so reliant. Unlike quantum theory, relativity science does not, of course, posit any such resistance, because objects, distances and temporal changes can still be measured; the results, however, will vary across reference frames. But in making this claim, Lawrence's speaker is depicting both relativity and quantum theories as anti-scientific – or, at least, as putting the scientific method in question.

In the earlier *Fantasia of the Unconscious*, Lawrence more openly brushes relativity theory against the grain. 'The universe isn't a spinning wheel', he writes, 'It is a cloud of bees' (Lawrence, 2004, 72). In other words, the 'clockwork universe' model bequeathed by Newton ignores the complexity and unpredictability of the cosmos. Lawrence then homes in on his subject: human beings resemble that cloud of bees, he writes, in that '[w]e have no one law that governs us'; and because of this encompassing truth, it follows that 'we are in sad need of a theory of human relativity'. But establishing that theory will not be easy, because for each human individual to enjoy a fullness of being means entering into a 'living dynamic relation' with his or her fellow creatures. The relation that Lawrence proposes will not be founded on love, brotherhood or equality. To the contrary, he writes,

> The next relation has got to be a relationship of men towards men in a spirit of unfathomable trust and responsibility, service and leadership, obedience and pure authority. Men have got to choose their leaders, and obey them to the death. And it must be a system of culminating aristocracy, society tapering like a pyramid to the supreme leader. (Lawrence, 2004, 191)

The principle of relativity, strictly adhered to, does not eradicate the need for authority. The swan that refuses 'to sit still and be measured' may be an avatar of freedom, but once relativity enters the domain of human relations, there must be social hierarchies. This hard-nosed realization is the stimulus for the novel that Lawrence begins soon afterwards, in June 1922, not long after his arrival in Australia.

The main purpose of that novel, *Kangaroo*, is to render more fully Lawrence's notion of a theory of human relativity. Scientific disputation is not the issue here; relativity, for Lawrence, is but a tool or instrument for prising open existential dilemmas about the self, democracy, power, violence and leadership. These are pressing issues for any writer attempting to diagnose the post-war malaise, as Lawrence does in *Kangaroo*; indeed, the long shadow of the Great War hangs over the novel's action as well as its debate. The latter is initiated by Benjamin 'Kangaroo' Cooley, a lawyer, ex-soldier and would-be social reformer, who represents (one version of) Lawrence's 'supreme leader' archetype.

In chapter 6, Cooley outlines to Richard Somers, the author's erstwhile alter-ego, his conception of the ideal polity. It would be, he says, a kind of benign tyranny: 'I want to keep *order*. I want to remove physical misery as far as possible. [...] And that you can only do by exerting strong, just *power* from above' (Lawrence, 1994, 111). Cooley sees this in terms of a proto-Nietzschean 'reverence for life' that eclipses petty human requisitions. 'The secret of all life', he declares, 'is in obedience: obedience to the urge that arises in the soul, the urge that is life itself [...] It is a subtle and conflicting urge away from the thing we already are' (112). But obedience is not merely an internal, self-liberating matter, says Cooley, because man 'needs to be relieved from this terrible responsibility of governing himself when he doesn't know what he wants, and has no aim towards which to govern himself' (113).

Somers clarifies and completes these thoughts in chapter 14 ('Bits'), which leads him to a partial repudiation of relativity. What Somers calls the 'history of relativity in man' is governed by a series of dialectical shifts. A man's naked being-in-the-world confers on him a kind of freedom, like the swan's; but that freedom can be suffocating, as he must submit his individuality to the clutches of a 'sympathetic humanity'. Somers, like Cooley, vehemently rejects the latter, because '[t]he bulk of mankind haven't got any central selves [...] They're all bits' (280). Later, he concludes a soul-searching monologue about 'relativity in dynamic living' with a reflection that might have come directly from 'Kangaroo' Cooley, showing the two men to be ideologically attuned: 'When the flow is power, might, majesty, glory, then it is a culminating flow towards one individual. [...] It is the grand obeisance before a master' (303). A crypto-fascist reordering of social relations, trading liberty for leadership: this is Lawrence's antidote to the calamity of the Great War and to the industrialized democracy that supposedly caused it. Somewhat adventitiously, Lawrence hews a kind of absolute from his politics of relativity, turning Einstein on his head and stretching his theory to breaking point.

James Joyce: Relativistic Mechanics

Where Lawrence treats relativity theory as pliable and suggestive, using it to lend scientific weight to his ideas about social reform, Joyce incorporates it into his web of puns and parodies. To that end, *Finnegans Wake* (1939) contains numerous allusions to Einstein and to 1920s debates on space and time. In a children's geometry lesson, for example, the scientist is referred to as 'Eyeinsteye', and oblique mention is made of 'his Noblett's surprize' (Joyce, 2012, 305–6); and Ein/stein is transfigured into the opposition elm/stone (an allusion to the physicist's birthplace of Ulm).[7] Earlier, however, Joyce had shown himself to be alert to the counter-realist possibilities of relativity physics, most notably in the 'Wandering Rocks' chapter of *Ulysses* (1922). First published in serial form in 1919, the chapter shows Joyce experimenting with synchroneity, as he fits the novel's entire cast of characters into nineteen vignettes of varying lengths.[8]

In section one, a near-anonymous 'onelegged sailor' is first glimpsed, 'swinging himself onward by lazy jerks of his crutches' (Joyce, 2000, 280). By section three he has made it around MacConnell's corner and is heading up Eccles Street, towards the Blooms' residence. And finally, thirteen sections later, the sailor arrives at 14 Nelson St. The geographical gap between Eccles St and Nelson St is less than 100 metres, yet Joyce has deviously inserted thirteen other sections into that gap. There is, then, no attempt to make time and space map onto each other, as realism would demand; instead, Joyce meticulously crafts a polylinear reality, a multi-form event-structure that implicitly exploits the potentialities of non-Euclidean space.

Molly Bloom's involvement in this episode reveals similar modifications of narrative logic, as she awaits a visit from her lover, 'Blazes' Boylan. Signalling her availability to Boylan, Molly puts a sign in the window that reads 'unfurnished apartments'. In section two, her 'generous white arm' (Joyce, 2000, 288) throws a coin down to the onelegged sailor. In the next section, the 'unfurnished apartments' card slips off the window sash; and the arm, or now the *hand*, throws the same coin to the same onelegged sailor. And finally, six vignettes later, the card is put back on the window sash – even though only a few seconds has elapsed since it fell from the sash. It is only at this point that we know it is number 7 Eccles St, the home of Molly and Leopold Bloom.

Reading Joyce realistically, 'Wandering Rocks' is a kind of mosaic, an accretion of diverse 'snapshots' of Dublin life that, taken together, signify a panoramic whole. The chapter has traditionally been read in such terms as the 'novel in miniature', a composite portrait of Joyce's Dublin in nineteen interlocking parts. Reading Joyce relativistically, by contrast, means suspending the desire for completeness, for a full and comprehensive picture. On the one hand, Joyce is demonstrating the 'relativity of simultaneity' that Einstein described in his special theory, by showing different time-flows across reference frames[9]; but on the other, he is also adducing the curvature of spacetime, the anti-Newtonian anomalies predicted by Einstein's general theory. In (re)presenting the same or adjacent moments, and applying different narrative rhythms to them – by changing a word, re-weighing an emphasis or adding/subtracting a detail – Joyce modulates the spatio-temporal pressures exerted on them. The role of matter then becomes fundamental, as spacetime gets pushed and pulled, stretched and warped, consonant with the wayward lives of Dublin's capricious citizens.

Wyndham Lewis: Einstein in the Flux

Although Einstein's theories break with Newtonian conceptions of (Euclidean) space and (absolute) time, they still possess some continuity with nineteenth-century science. The question of *energy*, in particular, was paramount from the mid-century on, with the discovery of electromagnetic waves and formulation of the second law of thermodynamics.[10] Energy is also crucial for Wyndham Lewis and Ezra Pound, who made it central to the Vorticist manifestoes they devised for the first issue of *Blast* in June 1914. Indeed, as regards Einstein's notion of mass-energy conversion, Daniel Albright sees Vorticism itself 'to some extent, [as] the application of this conversion-principle to poetry' (Albright, 1997, 168). But if energy was the Einsteinian concept that Lewis could embrace, *time* (or, more precisely, *spacetime*) was the one the most abhorred. A monumental polemic, *Time and Western Man* (1927), catalogues in some detail Lewis's objections to the 'time-cult' that, he was convinced, had crippled modern fiction, philosophy and science. Lewis's aim, then, was to rescue the self from the flux of becoming to which Bergson and his ostensive acolytes – Joyce, Proust, Gertrude Stein – had consigned it.

In performing this operation, Lewis argues that Einsteinian 'timelessness', that is, the loosening up of all fixed temporal coordinates, is of a piece with the 'time-obsessed' philosophizing of his arch-nemesis Bergson. Thus, Lewis finds it 'unlikely' that Einstein would not have read the work of Bergson; credits Einstein with inadvertently rehabilitating Bergsonian philosophy; and treats Duration and Relativity as a single conceptual entity (Lewis, 1928, 143, 86). As for the distinction made earlier in this chapter, between Bergson's subjective or intuitive theory of time and Einstein's objective, perspectival approach, Lewis will have none of it. For although Einsteinian theory, he writes, 'sets out to banish the mental factor altogether and to arrive at a purely physical truth, it nevertheless cannot prevent itself turning into a psychological or spiritual account of things, like Bergson's' (111). As if realizing that he is on shaky ground here, Lewis redirects his critical scorn at Einstein's biographer, Alexander Moszkowski, where he does score some hits.

As Lawrence did five years earlier, Lewis immediately followed up these animadversions on relativity with a narrative exposition of his views. The fruit of this attempt, *The Childermass* (1928), also resembles *Kangaroo* in that it is haunted by the devastation of the First World War. Two dead soldiers, Pullman and Satterthwaite, form a pseudo-couple and negotiate, as best they can, a camp known as the 'Time-Flats' – part of a limbo-like afterlife or 'afterworld', an uncanny dystopia that appears to be as tenuous and provisional as a film set. In this vaguely hostile environment, the 'timeless' and the 'time-obsessed' – or 'Duration and Relativity' – are made to seem compatible, thus legitimating the thesis that backfired in *Time and Western Man*. A metamorphic energy permeates both characters and locale, so that nothing is solid or stable, just as (Lewis says) Bergson's theory predicts. Moreover, although space and time are deliberately separated (the two men, or shades, 'get along splendidly with regard to space, but time is another matter'), the very notion of 'Time-Flats' belies this separation, providing a geo-temporal union that cannot but evoke four-dimensional spacetime (Lewis, 1965, 41). Objects, too, change size in accordance with their motion – a slowed-down, hallucinatory variation on the relativity-effect. And as Paul Edwards notes, a 'relativity of perspective' organizes certain scenes, indicating a deeper absorption of Einsteinian theory than Lewis himself would allow (Edwards, 2000, 327).

Virginia Woolf: The Velocities of Everyday Experience

Einstein is a marginal but insistent presence in Woolf's writings of the 1920s. Thus, he appears in *Mrs Dalloway* (1925) as no more than a thought, streamed through the consciousness of a bystander who watches the mysterious aeroplane depart (it is, he thinks, a symbol 'of man's soul [...] Einstein, speculation, mathematics, the Mendelian theory') (Woolf, 1992a, 30). In the same period, Woolf notes in her diary that if non-linear, Einsteinian time is true, then 'we shall be able to foretell our own lives' (Woolf, 1980, 68) – an idea she may have obtained from her Bloomsbury associate Bertrand Russell. And several years later, in *A Room of One's Own* (1929), Woolf reflects on 'sitting at our ease' and discussing certain topics of conversation: 'physics, the nature of the atom [...] [or] relativity' (Woolf, 2000, 23). But as keenly aware as she is of Einstein's wider cultural import, Woolf does not appear at this time to have had first-hand contact with any of his (or his explicators') work.[11]

Despite this limitation, even a cursory glance at Woolf's high-modernist novels, with their attempts to catch the ebb and flow of experience using alternate temporalities, suggests concordances with the new physics. *The Waves* (1931) is arguably the most intensively relativistic of these works. It stands as a book-length diagnosis of the problem that Lewis identifies in *Time and Western Man*: the fate of the self in a turbid, accelerating modernity. But from Woolf's perspective, relativity is the solution, not an exacerbation of the problem. Like Lawrence, she brings relativity into the realm of social being, applying Einsteinian tenets to the velocities of everyday experience.

Wave-forms disclose the relativity of human encounter for the six 'speakers' (to call them 'characters' would be imprudent) who narrate the novel. Woolf's waves function as patterns or oscillations that carry energy from one place to another, and also as forms of disturbance, as deformations of matter: '"When Miss Lambert passes," said Rhoda, "[...] everything changes and becomes luminous"'; '"There is Jinny," said Susan. "She seems to centre everything [...] all the rays ripple and flow and waver over us, bringing in new tides of sensation"' (Woolf, 1992b, 34, 99). About to meet with the group, Bernard feels internally dislocated: 'They have come together already. In a moment, when I have joined them, another arrangement will form, another pattern. [...] Already at fifty yards distance I feel the order of my being changed.' Louis puts it most succinctly: 'Meeting and parting, we assemble different forms, make different patterns.' (Woolf, 1992b, 175, 140–1) Life itself, for Woolf's speakers, unfolds as a kind of wave-pattern, a periodic figuration that can regulate, rearrange or discombobulate (244).

Trains and platforms, which appear intermittently throughout the novel, provide more specifically Einsteinian reference points. Woolf's speakers board and leave stationary trains, observe guards on platforms and view the world through train windows. As if narrativizing Einstein's man on the bank/man on the train thought experiment, Woolf makes Bernard relativity-conscious: 'Meanwhile as I stand looking from the train window, I feel strangely, persuasively, that [...] I am become part of this speed, this missile hurled at the city.' And as he later notes, '[W]hen I am leaving you and the train is going, you feel that it is not the train that is going, but I, Bernard' (Woolf, 1992b, 91, 109). Like *The Waves* as a whole, these reflections undercut Lewis's (earlier) claim, in *Time and Western Man*, that there is 'so far no outstanding exponent in literature or art of einsteinian physics' (Lewis, 1928, 87). Where Lewis and Joyce are reluctant relativists, in their attempts to both incarnate and disavow Einstein's theories, Woolf is that 'outstanding exponent' and a flag-bearer for a modernist aesthetics of relativity more broadly.

In the new century, a multi-purpose term has sprung up that rekindles a way of thinking prior to Einstein's scientific revolution. That neo-Newtonian term is 'real time', and it figures in medical imaging technologies, in stock-market reports and in both broadcast and social media. There is real-time computing, real-time tracking systems and real-time polling of public opinion. The term has come to be used as a shorthand definition of modern-day instantaneity. Real time means *no time*, no delay between an event and its legibility across space; hence, it annuls the need for competing or conflicting reference frames. As for the term's ubiquity, that can be ascribed to its entwinement with the ideology of globalization. Indeed, the dream of a globalized world is predicated on real time, on the annihilation of distance through technology. Real time is, then, a kind of wish-fulfillment fantasy, a collective delusion on the part of the post-industrial West.

The poetics of relativity formulated by Williams, Zukofsky and Olsen, and advanced by Lawrence, Joyce, Woolf and even Lewis – the awareness of irreducible temporal and spatial differentials – is an implicit riposte to the real-time credo and a reminder of just how fanciful and tendentious that dream is. It is through Einstein's contestation of Newtonian absolute time and homogeneous space that this poetics can be properly grasped. And by reading modernism relativistically, as we have seen, it is possible to discern how the paradoxes of the real can be mapped and probed by the exigencies of the word.

Notes

1   Gillian Beer's influential *Open Fields: Science in Cultural Encounter* (Beer, 1996), for example, has a chapter on the 'Rise of Literary Modernism', but it focuses on wave theory rather than relativity. Broader surveys of literature and science that neglect modernism and relativity include *One Culture: Essays in Science and Literature* (Levine and Rauch, 1987); *Beyond the Two Cultures: Essays on Science, Technology, and Literature* (Slade and Yaross Lee, 1990); *The Third Culture: Literature and Science* (Schaffer, 1998); *Science and Literature: Bridging the Two Cultures* (Wilson and Bowen, 2001); and *Literature and Science* (Sleigh, 2011). Conversely, there are good, albeit brief, accounts of relativity and modernism to be found in Peter Childs's *Modernism* (2000, 65–8); and T. Hugh Crawford's essay 'Modernism' in Bruce Clarke and Manuela Rossini (eds), *The Routledge Companion to Literature and Science* (2011, 510–11); and Stephen Kern, in *The Culture of Time and Space 1880–1919* (2003), addresses these subjects in a wider historical framework.

2   For recent studies of modernism's polytemporal fixations, see Ronald Schleifer, *Modernism and Time: The Logic of Abundance in Literature, Science, and Culture 1880–1930* (2000); and Bryony Randall, *Modernism, Daily Time and Everyday Life* (2007).

3   See, for example, John D. Sykes, Jr., 'What Faulkner (Might Have) Learned from Joyce' (2005).

4   See Eliot (1932); Lewis (1967, 307); Pound (1951, 45), and Ford (1964, 39).

5   There is still some uncertainty as to what Williams's method actually was, in terms of the 'variable foot'. The clearest examples of the latter can be found in Book II, Section 3, of *Paterson* (1992 [1948]) and throughout *The Desert Music, and Other Poems* (1954).

6   See Alan J. Friedman and Carol C. Donley, *Einstein as Myth and Muse* (1985, 75–7).

7   See Duszenko, 'The Relativity Theory in Finnegans Wake' (1994, 63).

8   Jeff Drouin describes 'Wandering Rocks' as 'a narrative experiment in relativistic mechanics', suggesting that Joyce's reading of *The Little Review* and *The Egoist* in 1918–19 gave him insights into the new physics. See Drouin, 'Early Sources for Joyce and the New Physics: The "Wandering Rocks" Manuscript, Dora Marsden, and Magazine Culture' (2009).

9   See Booker, 'Joyce, Planck, Einstein, and Heisenberg: A Relativistic Quantum Mechanical Discussion of Ulysses' (1990, 582).

10 See Armstrong 2005, 115–16.

11 This changed in 1937, when Woolf read *The Mysterious Universe* (1930), a popular account of the new physics by the British astrophysicist James Jeans. See *Virginia Woolf* (Whitworth, 2005, 184).

Bibliography

Albright, D. (1997), *Quantum Poetics: Yeats, Pound, Eliot, and the Science of Modernism.* Cambridge: Cambridge University Press.

Altieri, C. (2007), 'Modernist Innovations: A Legacy of the Constructed Reader', in A. Eysteinsson and V. Liska (eds), *Modernism, Vol. 1,* Amsterdam and Philadelphia: John Benjamins Publishing, pp. 67–86.

Armstrong, T. (2005), *Modernism: A Cultural History.* Cambridge: Polity Press.

Beer, G. (1996), *Open Fields: Science in Cultural Encounter.* Oxford: Clarendon Press.

Booker, M. K. (1990), 'Joyce, Planck, Einstein, and Heisenberg: A Relativistic Quantum Mechanical Discussion of Ulysses'. *James Joyce Quarterly,* 27, (3), 577–86.

Childs, P. (2000), *Modernism.* London and New York: Routledge.

Crawford, T. H. (2011), 'Modernism', in B. Clarke and M. Rossini (eds), *The Routledge Companion to Literature and Science.* London and New York: Routledge, pp. 510–11.

Drouin, J. (2009), 'Early Sources for Joyce and the New Physics: The "Wandering Rocks" Manuscript, Dora Marsden, and Magazine Culture'. *Genetic Joyce Studies,* 9, (Spring), Online: http://www.geneticjoycestudies.org/GJS9/GJS9_jdrouin.htm (accessed 12 June 2014).

During, S. (2013), 'Modernism in the Era of Human Rights'. *Affirmations: of the Modern,* 1, (1), (Autumn), 151, 158.

Duszenko, A. (1994), 'The Relativity Theory in Finnegans Wake'. *James Joyce Quarterly,* 32, (1), 61–70.

Edwards, P. (2000), *Wyndham Lewis: Painter and Writer.* New Haven: Yale University Press.

Einstein, A. (2006), *Relativity: The Special and the General Theory,* R. W. Lawson (transl.). London: Penguin.

Eliot, T. S. (1932), *Selected Essays.* London: Faber and Faber.

Eliot, T. S. (1975), *Selected Prose of T. S. Eliot,* F. Kermode (ed.). London: Faber and Faber.

Ford, F. M. (1964), *Critical Writings of Ford Madox Ford,* F. MacShane (ed). Lincoln: University of Nebraska Press.

Friedman, A. J. and Donley, C. C. (1985), *Einstein as Myth and Muse.* Cambridge: Cambridge University Press.

Hey, T. and Walters, P. (1997), *Einstein's Mirror.* Cambridge: Cambridge University Press.

Joyce, J. (2000), *Ulysses.* London: Penguin.

Joyce, J. (2012), *Finnegans Wake.* Oxford World's Classics. Oxford: Oxford University Press.

Kern, S. (2003), *The Culture of Time and Space 1880–1919.* Cambridge, MA: Harvard University Press.

Kuhn, T. (1996), *The Structure of Scientific Revolutions,* 3rd edn. Chicago and London: The University of Chicago Press.

Lawrence, D. H. (1972), *Selected Poems*, K. Sagar (ed.). Harmondsworth: Penguin.

Lawrence, D. H. (1981), *The Letters of D. H. Lawrence, Vol. II: 1913–16*, G. J. Zytaruk and J. T. Boulton (eds). Cambridge: Cambridge University Press.

Lawrence, D. H. (1987), *The Letters of D. H. Lawrence, Vol. IV: 1921–24*, W. Roberts, J. T. Boulton and E. Mansfield (eds). Cambridge: Cambridge University Press.

Lawrence, D. H. (1994), *Kangaroo*, B. Steele (ed.). Cambridge: Cambridge University Press.

Lawrence, D. H. (2004), *Fantasia of the Unconscious and Psychoanalysis of the Unconscious*, B. Steele (ed.). Cambridge: Cambridge University Press.

Levine, G. and Rauch, A. (eds) (1987), *One Culture: Essays in Science and Literature*. Madison: University of Wisconsin Press.

Lewis, W. (1928), *Time and Western Man*. New York: Harcourt, Brace and Company.

Lewis, W. (1965), *The Childermass*. London: John Calder.

Lewis, W. (1967), *Blasting and Bombardiering*. Berkeley and Los Angeles: University of California Press.

Lorentz, H. A. (1923), Albert Einstein et al. *The Principle of Relativity*. New York: Dover.

Olson, C. (1960), 'Charles Olson: Projective Verse', in D. Allen (ed.), *The New American Poetry 1945–1960*. Berkeley and Los Angeles: University of California Press, pp. 386–96.

Olson, C. (1974), 'Notes for the Proposition: Man Is Prospective'. *Boundary*, 2, (1/2), 1–6.

Pound, E. (1951), *The Letters of Ezra Pound 1907–1941*, D. D. Paige (ed.). London: Faber and Faber.

Randall, B. (2007), *Modernism, Daily Time and Everyday Life*. Cambridge: Cambridge University Press.

Schaffer, E. S. (ed.) (1998), *The Third Culture: Literature and Science*. Berlin and New York: W. de Gruyter.

Schleifter, R. (2000), *Modernism and Time: The Logic of Abundance in Literature, Science, and Culture 1880–1930*. Cambridge and New York: Cambridge University Press.

Slade, J. W. and Yaross Lee, J. (eds) (1990), *Beyond the Two Cultures: Essays on Science, Technology, and Literature*. Ames: Iowa State University Press.

Sleigh, C. (2011), *Literature and Science*. New York: Palgrave Macmillan.

Sykes, J. D. Jr. (2005), 'What Faulkner (Might Have) Learned from Joyce'. *Mississippi Quarterly*, 58, (3–4), 513–28.

Whitworth, M. (2005), *Virginia Woolf*. Oxford: Oxford University Press.

Williams, W. C. (1951), *Collected Earlier Poems*. New York: New Directions.

Williams, W. C. (1954), *The Desert Music, and Other Poems*. New York: Random House.

Williams, W. C. (1969), *Selected Essays*. New York: New Directions.

Williams, W. C. (1992), *Book II, Section 3, of Paterson*. New York: New Directions.

Wilson, D. L. and Bowen, Z. R. (eds) (2001), *Science and Literature: Bridging the Two Cultures*. Gainesville, FL: University Press of Florida.

Woolf, V. (1980), *The Diary of Virginia Woolf, Vol. III: 1925–1930*, A. Olivier Bell and A. McNeillie (eds). London: Hogarth Press.

Woolf, V. (1992a), *Mrs Dalloway*. Harmondsworth: Penguin.

Woolf, V. (1992b), *The Waves*. Oxford: Oxford World's Classics.

Woolf, V. (2000), *A Room of One's Own*. London: Penguin.

Yeats, W. B. (1978), *A Critical Edition of Yeats's A Vision*, G. M. Harper and W. K. Hood (eds). New York: Macmillan.

Zukofsky, L. (1978), *A*. Berkeley: University of California Press.

14

Modernism, Sexuality and Gender

Jana Funke

The emergence of modernism coincides historically with considerable shifts in social and cultural understandings of gender and sexuality. At the fin de siècle, the New Woman inspired debates about autonomous femininity, female sexuality (within and outside of marriage) and reproduction that continued to be rehearsed well into the twentieth century. Calls on behalf of some New Woman writers for the rise of a New Man were only one expression of ongoing and often anxiety-ridden negotiations of models of masculinity over the course of the late nineteenth and early twentieth centuries. The First World War has been read as a caesural moment of crisis with regard to gender roles in which masculine ideals were debunked and emancipatory possibilities opened up for women; whatever freedoms were yielded in this historical moment, strict attempts to regulate and police gender styles and forms of sexual expression persisted over the course of the late nineteenth and early twentieth centuries. At the same time, developing fields of knowledge, particularly anthropology, psychoanalysis and sexology, offered new understandings of gender and sexuality that were perceived as both liberating and regulatory; the same ambiguities apply to emerging social and political debates that centred on sexual behaviour and gender roles, including eugenic concerns about the 'health' of the nation and race, the suffrage movement, birth control campaigns, and homophile activism.

Modernist writers and artists drew inspiration from and, in turn, contributed to wider debates about masculinity and femininity, gender relations, sexual desire and sexual identification. However, modernism did not simply inform or shape ideas about gender and sexuality; gender and sexuality are also categories that are crucial to the ways in which modernism has been defined and understood. Gender, as a structuring category, has been central to the continuing feminist project of moving beyond a narrowly 'masculinist' modernist canon by including women writers and artists and by shedding light on the critical engagement with gender roles within their works (e.g. Garrity, 2013; Gilbert and Gubart, 1989; Harrison and Peterson, 1997; Scott, 1990, 2006). Sexuality, too, has been employed as a category to define and redefine modernism, as is evident in articulations of 'perverse' or 'queer modernisms' characterized by an interest in homoerotic and homosexual desire and sexual deviance and perversion more generally (e.g. Boone, 1998; Schaffner, 2011a; Schaffner and Weller, 2012). The delineation of 'Sapphic' or 'lesbian modernisms', which centre on articulations of female same-sex desire or female sexual autonomy in the works of women writers and artists, depends on categories of both gender and sexuality (e.g. Benstock, 1990; Collecott, 1999; Hackett, 2004; Jay, 1995; Winning, 2000).

Such attempts to define modernism in terms of femininity, queerness or lesbianism raise the question of the extent to which modernist literary and artistic production was itself driven and inspired by the wish to articulate a range of gendered and sexual possibilities. In other words, how did an interest in gender and sexuality that is characteristic of modernity more generally inspire the search for self-consciously new means of expression, some of which we recognize as 'modernist'? And how does our understanding and definition of modernism change once we begin to consider the constitutive role of gender and sexuality in producing new forms of knowledge and expression?

Modernism, in this view, forms part of a broader explosion of discourses about sexuality that has influentially been described by Michel Foucault in the first volume of *The History of Sexuality* (1976). Foucault's account focuses specifically on the sciences of sexuality that emerge over the course of the nineteenth century and that include the intersecting fields of psychiatry, psychology, psychoanalysis and sexology. These fields jointly constructed modern understandings of 'sexuality', elevating it to a category that was fundamental to an understanding of the human subject. According to Arnold Davidson, this discursive instalment of sexuality at the very core of human life meant that 'our existence became a sexistence, saturated with the promises and threats of sexuality' (Davidson, 2004, xiii). The modern subject was a sexual subject through and through; every thought and action was, in one way or another, linked to sexuality, and the individual could even be defined, classified and labelled on the basis of his or her sexual desires.

Henceforth, any exploration of the 'dark places of psychology' (Woolf, 2003, 152), to quote Virginia Woolf, crucially involved close attention to sexual desires and longings. As a result, elaborate 'fictions of interiority and sexuality' emerged (Boone, 1998, 5). These included Leopold and Molly Bloom's auto-erotic fantasies and dreams as well as Clarissa Dalloway's erotic moment of being: 'a match burning in a crocus; an inner meaning almost expressed' (Woolf, 2000, 27). Such well-known examples are often considered as indicative of the modernist turn away from external or 'material' reality and towards interiority. This turn towards the inner sexual life can also be traced within the sciences of sexuality, which calls into question any rigid divide between the literary and scientific sphere. Indeed, following Paul Peppis, such scientific discourses can usefully be considered as part of modernism in that they 'participate in the formation of modernism as a broad cultural movement encompassing a range of groups, practices, and disciplines and as a variety of linguistic, rhetorical, and stylistic innovations in response to modernity in its myriad manifestations' (Peppis, 2014, 11). Since such innovation was driven, in particular, by the desire to find a new language for sexuality, it is necessary to develop a nuanced understanding of 'sexual modernism' that encompasses forms of exchange and collaboration across disciplinary boundaries and literary and non-literary fields of expression and that is alive to the multiple and intersecting languages of sexuality invented and circulated at this time.

Scholarship to date has paid particular attention to the resonances between psychoanalysis and literary culture, including the shared interest in bringing into consciousness and also into language allegedly repressed and unconscious sexual desires, wishes and longings. The 'literary' quality of Freud's case studies has been widely noted, and scholars have also explored the influence of Freudian psychoanalysis on a wide range of writers including W. H. Auden, Samuel Beckett, André Breton, Bryher (Annie Winifred Ellerman), H. D. (Hilda Doolittle), James Joyce, D. H. Lawrence, Lytton Strachey and Rebecca West. The reception of psychoanalysis among such authors was often critical or at least sceptical. Woolf claimed she had not read Freud until 1939, which is doubtful to say the least, given that her very own Hogarth Press had begun to publish English translations of Freud's works in the early 1920s and was thus responsible for circulating Freudian ideas in the UK (Abel, 1989). Lawrence was introduced to (Freudian and Jungian) psychoanalytic ideas earlier and indirectly, particularly by his German wife Frieda Weekley, whom he had met in 1912, and by British psychoanalysts Barbara Low and David Eder. Lawrence would go on to denounce Freud as a 'psychiatric quack' (Lawrence, 1923, 9), and he vehemently rejected psychoanalytic attempts to rationalize sexuality by bringing it into the realm of the conscious mind. While Lawrence shared the psychoanalytic conviction that sexuality was at the heart of the human subject and that sexual desires needed to be expressed, he was also deeply suspicious of the regulatory force inherent in making sexual desire conscious in order to articulate it in and through language, of turning sexuality into an object of knowledge that could be submitted to rational analysis.

The encounter with psychoanalysis and other sexual sciences was also crucially gendered. H. D. was analysed by Freud himself over several months in Vienna in 1933 and, again, in 1934. She gave an account of her experiences in *Tribute to Freud* (written in 1942) and also in her posthumously published poem 'The Master' (written between 1934 and 1935). Such texts offer insights into the ways in which women writers struggled with and reworked psychoanalytic ideas about femininity. H. D. took issue with Freud's view of the female body as castrated, lacking and deficient; to counter such arguments, she affirmed that '*woman is perfect*' (H. D., 1981, 411; DuPlessis and Friedman, 1981). However, H. D., like other female writers, also experienced the engagement with psychoanalysis as empowering and revitalizing, in particular with regard to her sexuality – the fact that she desired men and women – and her self-perceived gender ambiguity. This indicates that it is imperative to move beyond antagonistic approaches that have pitted a 'male' sexual science against a 'female' form of literary expression (e.g. Jeffreys, 1985; Smith-Rosenberg, 1985), and to explore exchanges and communications across alleged binaries of literature, science and gender. It is important to question, for instance, to what extent female writers like H. D. and her partner, Bryher, and also authors such as Radclyffe Hall and Olive Schreiner felt they were themselves contributing to the 'scientific' project of writing about sexuality (Bauer, 2009).

An intersecting branch of sexual science that also explored the nexus of gender, physical sex and sexuality was sexology, itself a loosely defined and often explicitly cross-disciplinary field of knowledge that combined a range of medical and non-medical forms of knowledge, including psychiatry and neurology, psychology, anthropology and history (Bland and Doan, 1998; Fisher and Funke, 2015; Waters, 2006). Like psychoanalysis, sexology should be understood as a strongly 'literary' discourse (Bauer, 2009; Peppis, 2014; Schaffner, 2011a, b). The most eminent English sexologist Havelock Ellis, for instance, reviewed Thomas Hardy's work and wrote an introduction to J. K. Huysman's *À Rebours*, was friends with Arthur Symons, Schreiner, H. D. and Bryher, edited a series of unexpurgated Elizabethan plays, and wrote a utopian novel and a fictionalized travel memoir. In addition, literary sources were regularly used as evidence in sexological publications – Austro-German psychiatrist Richard von Krafft-Ebing, for instance, drew on works by the Marquis de Sade, Jean-Jacques

Rousseau, Charles Baudelaire and Théophile Gautier among others in his influential *Psychopathia Sexualis* (Schaffner, 2011b).

In addition, the pervasive use of patient case studies or case histories in sexological publications placed introspective and subjective narrative accounts of individual sexual experiences and desires at the very heart of the sexological project (Oosterhuis, 2000; Peppis, 2014). Indeed, there was an awareness on behalf of sexologists like German-Jewish physician Magnus Hirschfeld that literary experimentation with narrative was crucial in order to facilitate the expression and representation of the wide range of genders and sexualities sexologists were keen to explore (Funke, 2011). Sexology, then, offered more than rigid explanatory models of the origins and causes of sexual desire or encyclopaedic lists of newly coined identity categories such as 'the homosexual', 'the sexual invert', 'the transvestite', 'the sadist' or 'the masochist'. Moreover, the narratives of sexual formation and development presented in sexological publications did not always align neatly with the explanatory frameworks within which these narratives were presented (Crozier, 2000; Peppis, 2014). Instead, case histories often troubled any rigid or static notion of sexual identity or one-sided accounts of sexual desire as either inborn or acquired. Moreover, the case history emerged as an important tool that was used strategically by reform-oriented sexologists like Ellis or Hirschfeld to oppose pathologizing views of (particularly male) homosexuality that had been articulated in other sexological publications, and to affirm the health and social respectability of the male homosexual or sexual invert (Crozier, 2008). As such, sexology was a conflicted and multivalent discourse that created a rhetorical space within which complex narratives of the sexual self were constructed and circulated.

Literary writers occupied the same rhetorical space and were in direct dialogue with sexological attempts to write and narrate the sexual self. Novels like E. M. Forster's *Maurice* (written in 1913–14, but published posthumously in 1971), Edward Prime Stevenson's *Imre: A Memorandum* (published in a limited-edition imprint under the pseudonym Xavier Mayne in 1906) or Bryher's autobiographical novels, *Development* (1920) and *Two Selves* (1923), rework the *Bildungsroman* to depict the formation of the sexual subject. Bryher, who knew Ellis personally and travelled to Greece with him and H. D. in 1920, drew on psychoanalytic and sexological accounts to understand her cross-gender identification (her desire to be a boy) and her same-sex desire. Her autobiographical fiction deploys narrative methods to delay the developmental process of maturation that would result in the establishment of fixed or stable categories of sexual and gender identity, and champions an ongoing process of sexual and gendered development instead. Even Radclyffe Hall's *The Well of Loneliness* (1928), which famously drew on sexological terminology in labelling its female protagonist Stephen Gordon as a 'sexual invert', offers complicated and conflicted aetiologies of sexual identity and considers both congenital and hereditary factors as well as cultural and social influences (Dellamora, 2011; Green, 2003).

An understanding of the indeterminacy of the causes and origins of sexual desire and the instability of sexual identity categories was thus very much part of literary and sexological discourse. Indeed, even Woolf's *Orlando* (1928), which is often seen as a subversive and anti-sexological high modernist antidote to Hall's overtly realist *The Well of Loneliness*, does not necessarily have to be read as a novel opposed to sexology. Woolf's narrator decides to 'let biologists and psychologists determine' (Woolf, 1998, 134) the truth about Orlando's sex, showing no interest in doing so him or herself. Yet, the scientific discourses that are evoked here were not invested in static understandings of physical sex, sexual desire or gender identification. Edward Carpenter, Ellis, Hirschfeld and Otto Weininger, for instance, were all interested in 'sexual intermediacy', that is to say, forms of experience and subjectivity that worked across gender and sexual binaries. Indeed, Vita Sackville-West – the subject of Woolf's fictional biography – had herself studied the writings of Weininger and Carpenter and, on the basis of such reading, affirmed 'that cases of dual personality do exist, in which the feminine and the masculine elements alternately preponderate' (Sackville-West, 1973, 108). To be sure, *Orlando* can be read as a feminist critique of the problematic gendered assumptions underpinning sexological and psychoanalytic thought (Parkes, 1996, 144–79). At the same time, however, Woolf's creative exploration of the intersections of gender, sex and sexuality and of the indeterminacy and instability of the sexual self can also be seen as part of a broader sexual modernism that includes sexology, psychoanalysis and other sciences of sexuality.

This sexual modernism was united in assuming that the creation of self-consciously new narratives of sexuality signalled a decisive and transformative break with an allegedly 'repressed' past. Speaking openly about sexual desires and behaviours that might be seen as 'obscene' was viewed as a radical gesture that served to constitute and authorize as 'revolutionary' and 'new' different scientific and literary discourses. There was thus a shared sense that the open discussion of sexual matters and the forging of a new language of sexual experience was, as Woolf humorously stated, 'a great advance in civilisation' (Woolf, 1985, 196).

Indeed, following Rachel Potter, '[o]ne could go so far as to suggest that modernist texts, in their more liberatory guises, became identified with radical and obscene transgression' (Potter, 2013, 11). Certainly, literary writers joyfully depicted and celebrated 'transgressive' sexual acts, such as male and female masturbation in Joyce's work, lesbian cunnilingus in Djuna Barnes's *Ladies Almanack* (1928), or cross-class, extramarital and non-reproductive anal sex in Lawrence's *Lady Chatterley's Lover* (1928). This modernist fascination with transgression and obscenity was paradoxically facilitated by the fact that modernism emerged during a period of particularly strict regulation in the history of censorship. In Britain, it was only after the 1959 Obscene Publications Act that it became possible to defend literary works against charges of obscenity on the basis of their artistic merits and the author's intention. The Act was famously put to the test when Penguin was unsuccessfully prosecuted in 1960 for publishing a full and unexpurgated edition of *Lady Chatterley's Lover*, which had previously been available only in bowdlerized form.

The publication of Radclyffe Hall's lesbian novel, *The Well of Loneliness*, three decades earlier, in 1928, had brought about one of the most widely publicized obscenity trials in the history of British law. Hall's novel was banned as 'obscene' in Britain despite the fact that it was published with a prefatory note by Ellis, attesting to its 'notable psychological and sociological significance' (Ellis, 2001, 35). Moreover, a large group of literary experts, including Arnold Bennett, Vera Brittain and Woolf, had appeared in court to defend the book. Many of these writers were less than convinced of the book's literary merits, but came together to defend the right of authors like Hall to speak openly about sexual matters, including lesbianism. The *Well of Loneliness* trials and the support Hall received from the wider literary community indicate that the first decades of the twentieth century were a period in which literary and non-literary writers, editors and publishers were strongly aware of the very real possibility of state censorship and united in the struggle for free speech.

However, censorship was not only repressive. Hall's novel, for instance, which was subsequently published in the United States (where a censorship trial had failed), France and other European countries, gained a large readership precisely because of the scandal created by the trials. Exploring further the productive potential of censorship and repression, recent scholarship, focusing primarily on Britain and the United States, has demonstrated the extent to which modernism itself was shaped, if not paradoxically enabled, by actual, anticipated or imagined censorship (Bradshaw and Potter, 2013; Marshik, 2006; Pease, 2009; Potter, 2013). To some degree, modernist experimentation can be seen as a product of this climate of repression in which writers and artists were forced to develop strategic means of encoding or obscuring the representation of sexual experiences, desires and bodily processes that might otherwise be deemed as 'obscene'.

Indeed, overtly experimental novels like *Orlando* or Djuna Barnes's *Nightwood* (1936) did avoid censorship (although it has to be noted that Barnes' editor, T. S. Eliot, did remove several more explicit references to homosexuality from the novel and that Woolf had the freedom of self-publication with the Hogarth Press). *Ulysses*, however, was banned as obscene in the United States in 1921 after the 'Nausicaa' episode had appeared in the *Little Review*, forcing Joyce to publish the first full edition of the novel in France. Publishing abroad or privately were strategies used by many authors to avoid censorship and to circulate sexually explicit materials, but other texts, such as Gertrude Stein's autobiographical lesbian novel *Q.E.D.* (written in 1903) or Forster's *Maurice*, remained unpublished during the authors' lifetime due to self-censorship.

Concerns about the accessibility and potential impact of sexual material under state censorship were also debated in literature itself. Under the 1868 Hicklin Ruling, Lord Cockburn had defined obscenity as 'the tendency [...] to deprave and corrupt those whose minds are open to immoral influences and into whose hands the publication might fall' (cited in Potter, 2013, 17). Such fears were based on gender-, age-, class-, race- and ethnicity-related assumptions about readership and audience: women, the young, the working classes and racial or ethnic 'others' were considered to be at particular danger of being 'corrupted'. Literary works responded to such anxieties: in Oscar Wilde's *The Picture of Dorian Gray* (1891), Dorian's corruption is crucially linked to his reading of a 'poisonous book' – a thinly veiled reference to *À Rebours* (1998, 107). Similarly, Celia Marshik points out that Jean Rhys's *Voyage in the Dark* (1934) places another French novel, Émile Zola's controversial study of prostitution, *Nana* (1880), in the hands of eighteen-year-old Caribbean chorus girl, Anna, whose life soon enters a downward spiral (Marshik, 2006, 183). As such, these novels raised awareness of and also affirmed a potential link between the influence of literature and the moral corruption of 'vulnerable' readers.

Other authors reinforced the affirmative and liberating potential of sexual knowledge, particularly for women. In *The Well of Loneliness*, Stephen Gordon is able to understand herself as a 'sexual invert' when she discovers the sexological studies of Karl Heinrich Ulrichs and Krafft-Ebing in her father's library. It was not just the self-identified sexual invert who lacked access to information about sexuality, however. Lawrence described as 'monstrous' women's sexual ignorance in modern society: 'they know nothing, they can't think sexually at all, they are morons in this respect. It is better to give all young girls this book [*Lady Chatterley's Lover*], at the age of seventeen' (Lawrence, 1993, 309). Woolf also negotiated the question of how and when women learn about sexuality. Clarissa Dalloway remembers her sexual and political ignorance as a girl – 'She knew nothing about sex – nothing about social problems' – and it is Sally Seton who teaches Clarissa about sex and socialism by sharing the works of William Morris, which had to be 'wrapped in brown paper', and Plato and Shelley (Woolf, 2000, 28). Here and elsewhere, particularly in *A Room of One's Own* (1929), Woolf linked the exchange of secret or unofficial knowledge between women to potential sexual and political subversion that is always at danger of being censored or repressed. Like other women writers, she presented the experience of censorship not only as gendered, but also as both disabling and enabling; there was a sense of the liberating and subversive potential stemming from the difficulties of knowing and articulating women's experiences of sexuality and the body.

An awareness of the indeterminacy of sexual knowledges and languages and their dependence on factors of gender, class, economic status, age, race and ethnicity can also usefully inform the study of sexual modernism more broadly. Following Laura Doan, it is crucial to keep asking the question, 'Who knew what when?' (2001, 130). As we have already seen, scholarship has explored the ways in which sexological and psychoanalytic ideas and concepts were received and reworked by literary writers (although there has been a tendency to overlook the fact that the sexual sciences were more open-ended and conflicted in themselves and often offered indeterminate and fluid rather than rigid and static understandings of gender and sexuality). We know that writers like Barnes, Bryher, H. D., Eliot, William Faulkner, Forster, Langston Hughes, Christopher Isherwood, Joyce, Lawrence, Claude McKay, Radclyffe Hall, Dorothy Richardson, Vita Sackville-West and Woolf were familiar with sexology. Emerging scholarship on the transnational history and reception of Northern-European sexual science is also beginning to unveil important new sites of dialogue, such as Japanese writer Taruho's engagement with Krafft-Ebing in the 1920s (Angles, 2011), thus globally expanding the scope of sexual modernism. Nonetheless, it is important not to assume writers' and readers' familiarity with sexological thought, especially given that sexology was also affected by tightly controlled censorship regulations, particularly in Britain (Brady, 2005). Ellis and John Addington Symonds's *Sexual Inversion*, for instance, was itself banned as 'obscene' upon first publication in Britain in

1897, forcing Ellis to publish the remaining seven volumes of his *Studies in the Psychology of Sex* in the United States.

The resulting difficulties in accessing sexological writings raise challenging questions about literary production, reception and readership. Historians of sexuality have begun to show that sexological ideas were, at times, transmitted and mediated through popular culture, but did not reach broader audiences in the first decades of the twentieth century, with potential exceptions like the *Well of Loneliness* trials, which catapulted into public consciousness the figure of the 'sexual invert' (Doan, 2001; Oram, 2007; Sigel, 2012). How relevant and influential sexology really was in shaping authors' understanding of themselves and their desires, the manner in which they wrote about gender and sexuality, and the reception and understanding of their works thus remains an important field of investigation.

It is also crucial to move beyond sexology and psychoanalysis and to consider what other (sometimes overlapping) discourses and forms of knowledge were drawn upon to construct gender and sexuality in the modernist period. Decadence and aestheticism, for instance, need to be considered as constitutive languages of sexual modernism that continued to shape debates about gender and sexuality well into the twentieth century. In the nineteenth century, the decadent rejection of nature, reproduction and utilitarianism had found expression in the joint celebration both of art for art's sake and of sexualities that were considered non-reproductive and unnatural. As such, decadence situated the sexually deviant or perverse at the very heart of aesthetic debate and thus created a powerful legacy that shaped modernist production. The lesbian woman (as a potentially reproductive yet effectively sterile figure) came to embody a decadent ideal, which early twentieth-century writers would inherit and revise. Barnes's modernist manipulation of decadent aesthetics and radical subversion of the very distinction between natural and unnatural genders and sexualities offers one important example (Carlston, 1998; Caselli, 2009; Hardie, 2005). The figure of the dandy-aesthete was also reworked in the modernist period; in the 1920s, female artists and authors like Romaine Brooks, Claude Cahun and Radclyffe Hall reappropriated the figure of the dandy to challenge or, at least, renegotiate naturalized understandings of gender and sexuality (Blessing, 2001; Glick, 2009; Lucchesi, 2001). Recent work on black modernism and the Harlem Renaissance has also explored the queerness of the black dandy as a figure that disrupts conceptions of gender, sexuality, race and ethnicity and draws attention to the intersections and ultimate instability of such markers of identity (Miller, 2009).

A related discourse that emerged over the course of the nineteenth century and strongly influenced constructions of gender and sexuality in the modernist period is Victorian Hellenism. The homoerotic dimension of Victorian Hellenism, evident in the works of Oxford-educated fin-de-siècle authors like Walter Pater, Symonds and Wilde (Dowling, 1994), continued to find expression in the modernist period, for instance, in the work of Cambridge Apostles like Forster and Strachey (Ardis, 2007; Taddeo, 2002). In addition to *Maurice*, Forster's lesser-known first published short story, 'Albergo Empedocle' (1903), links Hellenism and homoeroticism by introducing the theme of reincarnation. Harold, the young male protagonist, visits Greece during his honeymoon, remembers his past life and escapes his unhappy marriage by losing himself in the Greek past. While doctors diagnose the young husband with 'mania' and refer him to an asylum, the male narrator, who professes his love for Harold, concludes: 'I firmly believe that he has been a Greek – nay, that he is a Greek, drawn by recollection back into a previous life' (Forster, 1971, 36). Ancient Greece also offered female modernists a means to articulate desires and identities that might otherwise be difficult or impossible to express, as H. D.'s creative engagement with the Classical and specifically Sapphic tradition indicates (Collecott, 1999; Gregory, 1997). Moreover, Hellenism became closely intertwined with sexological discourse and often offered reform-oriented writers like Ellis, Hirschfeld, Carpenter or Symonds a means to correct pathologizing views of homosexuality. Many of the autobiographical case studies that were included in sexological studies contain references to Ancient Greece and highlight the formative influence of thinkers like Plato on the individual's self-understanding. Earl Lind's *Autobiography of an Androgyne*, first published in the *Medico-Legal Journal* in 1918, and its sequel, *The Female Impersonators* (1922), are a particularly elaborate example of the creative reception of Classical culture in the service of modern articulations of gender and sexuality.

Religion, spirituality and the occult offered additional ways of thinking about and articulating conceptions of gender and sexuality. The esoteric philosophy of theosophy imported allegedly Eastern concepts and arguments that became integral to Western feminist political culture and also intersected with sexological discourse (Dixon, 1997, 2001). The spiritualist movement, which experienced a surge of renewed interest in the climate of mourning created by the First World War, was closely intertwined with debates about eugenics and reproduction (Ferguson, 2012). The different ways in which such religious, spiritual and occult discourses allowed writers like H. D., May Sinclair, Sylvia Townsend Warner, Rebecca West and W. B. Yeats to reconceptualize masculinity, femininity and sexuality have not yet been fully explored. The possibility that the individual could survive beyond death, experience reincarnation (as in Forster's 'Albergo Empedocle') or transcend telepathically the limitations of the individual subject located in time and space made it possible, for instance, to think of the self as possessing multiple sexes and genders and of experiencing different forms of relationality or seemingly incongruous forms of desire. Radclyffe Hall would combine in an unorthodox fashion Catholic, spiritualist and theosophical ideas to explore precisely these themes in texts like her comic reincarnation novel, *A Saturday Life* (1925), or the short story 'Miss Ogilvy Finds Herself' (1934) (Dellamora, 2011; Funke, 2016).

Decadence and aestheticism, Hellenism, and religion and spirituality are certainly not the only discourses that need to be taken into account (in addition to sexology and psychoanalysis) to renegotiate the scope and contours of sexual modernism. Indeed, one of the key characteristics of sexual modernism is its containment of multiple coinciding, intersecting and colliding forms of knowledge and expression that often work across the conventionally drawn boundaries of literature, science, religion and spirituality. Moreover, as we have seen, ignorance and silence need to be understood as integral components of sexual modernism that were indicative of forms of repression and inequality, which were themselves dependent on gender, class, race and age, but that could also offer enabling strategies of resistance. Thus, sexual modernism comprises a bewildering multiplicity of intersecting and overlapping means of conceptualizing sexuality and gender, but it is also made up of gaps and absences of knowledge and language. In addition to the self-conscious interest in transgression and subversion that many modernist writers shared, this fundamental indeterminacy of language and knowledge constitutes the fluid or queer conceptions of gender and sexuality that have come to be seen as a key marker of modernism itself.

Acknowledging the constitutive indeterminacy of sexual modernism also draws attention to the way in which categories and concepts of gender and sexuality have shaped scholarly interpretations of modernist texts. As Doan, who has posed this challenge to historians of sexuality, maintains: 'Negotiating the past in relation to gender and sexuality forces us to raise our tolerance for conceptual messiness as we engage in the pleasures of conjecturing about what may in the end prove unknowable and irresolvable' (2013, 104). The question of how literary modernist studies might contribute to the important project of exploring the 'disordered, mutable, incoherent, and indeterminate' experiences of the past without relying on overly rigid or static categories of gender and sexuality remains to be addressed (Doan, 2013).

One potential starting point is to consider critically the tendency (which is also, to some degree, expressed in this chapter) to understand sexuality primarily in terms of gender, that is, as attraction between two people of the same or opposite gender. In so doing, we are at risk of not fully theorizing how other categories of difference, such as class, age and race, crucially structured the experience of sexuality across any assumed divide between heterosexuality and homosexuality, which was not as prevalent during the modernist period as has been assumed (Brickell, 2006). To be sure, age, class and race played a crucial role in articulations of same-sex desire and opposite-sex desire in the late nineteenth and twentieth centuries; it is also worth asking how our understanding of sexual modernism might shift if we focused, for instance, on the depiction of age and ageing in texts like Townsend Warner's *Lolly Willowes: Or the Loving Huntsman* (1926) or on the erotics of age difference in Strachey's *Elizabeth and Essex* (1928), without assuming that these texts necessarily encode same-sex desire or that they can be understood by drawing on models of sexuality that privilege gender.

Even more challenging is the question of whether it is possible (or desirable) to reconsider the very centrality of deviance and perversion itself to our understanding of sexual modernism. Of course, as we have seen, modernism itself has been defined in terms of transgression, deviance and perversion and this has led to productive synergies, in particular, with queer theory. Yet, as historians of sexuality are beginning to point out, the queer focus on the deviant or abnormal has also restricted and arguably skewed the scope of historical and possibly literary investigation (Doan, 2013; Houlbrook, 2005). Many of the discourses that have been discussed over the course of this chapter, including sexology, did not, as has often been assumed, focus specifically on the deviant or perverse, but were also interested in understanding forms of gender presentation and sexual desire that might easily be dismissed as 'heteronormative' by queer scholars. Reproductive and marital sexualities, pregnancy, maternity and paternity were part of a broader repertoire of gendered and sexual experiences that were investigated, for instance, in the marital advice, birth control or sex education literature of the 1910s and 1920s, but that have not yet been explored fully with regard to the literary writing produced in the same period.

Overall, the point of such historically informed challenges to established readings of modernist sexualities and genders is neither to insist on more rigidly 'historicist' readings of the experiences and desires of the past nor to disavow the potential for literary works to resonate with the feelings and desires of readers in the present. Rather, the point of expanding sexual modernism in the way this chapter proposes – across various literary and non-literary forms of knowledge and expression, and beyond familiar ways of categorizing gender and sexuality – is to show that it is even more complicated, indeterminate, and, in this sense, even more queer than the sexual modernism we have come to know.

Bibliography

Abel, E. (1989), *Virginia Woolf and the Fictions of Psychoanalysis*. Chicago: University of Chicago Press.

Angles, J. (2011), *Writing the Love of Boys: Origins of Bishōnen Culture in Modernist Japanese Literature*. Minneapolis: University of Minnesota Press.

Ardis, A. L. (2007), 'Hellenism and the Lure of Italy', in D. Bradshaw (ed.), *The Cambridge Companion to E.M. Forster*. Cambridge: Cambridge University Press, pp. 62–76.

Bauer, H. (2009), *English Literary Sexology: Translations of Inversion, 1860–1930*. Basingstoke: Palgrave.

Benstock, S. (1990), 'Expatriate Sapphic Modernism: Entering Literary History', in K. Jay and J. Glasgow (eds), *Lesbian Texts and Contexts: Radical Revisions*. New York: New York University Press, pp. 183–203.

Bland, L. and Doan, L. (eds) (1998), *Sexology in Culture: Labelling Bodies and Desires*. Chicago: University of Chicago Press.

Blessing, J. (2001), 'Claude Cahun, Dandy Provocateuse', in S. Filin-Yeh (ed.), *Dandies: Fashion and Finesse in Art and Culture*. New York: New York University Press, pp. 185–203.

Boone, J. A. (1998), *Libidinal Currents: Sexuality and the Shaping of Modernism*. Chicago: University of Chicago Press.

Bradshaw, D. and Potter, R. (eds) (2013), *Prudes on the Prowl: Fiction and Obscenity in England, 1850 to the Present Day*. Oxford: Oxford University Press.

Brady, S. (2005), *Masculinity and Male Homosexuality in Britain, 1861–1913*. Basingstoke: Palgrave.

Brickell, C. (2006), 'Sexology, the Homo/hetero Binary, and the Complexities of Male Sexual History'. *Sexualities*, 9, (4), 423–47.

Carlston, E. G. (1998), *Thinking Fascism: Sapphic Modernism and Fascist Modernity*. Stanford: Stanford University Press.

Caselli, D. (2009), *Improper Modernism: Djuna Barnses's Bewildering Corpus*. Farnham: Ashgate.

Collecott, D. (1999), *H. D. and Sapphic Modernism*. Cambridge: Cambridge University Press.

Crozier, I. (2000), 'Havelock Ellis, Eonism and the Patient's Discourse; or, Writing a Book about Sex'. *History of Psychiatry*, 11, (42), 125–54.

Crozier, I. (2008), 'Introduction: Havelock Ellis, John Addington Symonds and the Construction of Sexual Inversion', in I. Crozier (ed.), *Sexual Inversion*. Basingstoke: Palgrave, pp. 1–86.

Davidson, A. I. (2004), *The Emergence of Sexuality: Historical Epistemology and the Formation of Concepts*. Cambridge: Harvard University Press.

Dellamora, R. (2011), *Radclyffe Hall: A Life in the Writing*. Philadelphia: University of Pennsylvania Press.

Dixon, J. (1997), 'Sexology and the Occult: Sexuality and Subjectivity in Theosophy's New Age'. *Journal of the History of Sexuality*, 7, (3), 409–33.

Dixon, J. (2001), *Divine Feminine: Theosophy and Feminism in England*. Baltimore: Johns Hopkins University Press.

Doan, L. (2001), *Fashioning Sapphism: The Origins of a Modern English Lesbian Culture*. New York: Columbia University Press.

Doan, L. (2013), *Disturbing Practices: History, Sexuality, and Women's Experience of Modern War*. Chicago: Chicago University Press.

Dowling, L. (1994), *Hellenism and Homosexuality in Victorian Oxford*. Ithaca: Cornell University Press.

DuPlessis, R. B. and Friedman, S. S. (1981), '"Woman Is Perfect": H. D.'s Debate with Freud'. *Feminist Studies*, 7, (3), 417–30.

Ellis, H. (2001), 'Commentary', in L. Doan and J. Prosser (eds), *Palatable Poison: Critical Perspectives on the Well of Loneliness*. New York: Columbia University Press, p. 35.

Ferguson, C. (2012), *Determined Spirits: Eugenics, Heredity and Racial Regeneration in Anglo-American Spiritualist Writing, 1848–1930*. Edinburgh: Edinburgh University Press.

Fisher, K. and Funke, J. (2015), 'British Sexual Science beyond the Medical: Cross-disciplinary, Cross-historical and Cross-cultural Translations', in H. Bauer (ed.), *Sexology in Translation*. Philadelphia: Temple University Press, pp. 95–114.

Forster, E. M. (1971), 'Albergo Empedocle', in G. H. Thomson (ed.), *Albergo Empedocle and Other Writings*. New York: Liveright, pp. 5–36.

Foucault, M. (1990), *The History of Sexuality. Volume 1: An Introduction*. New York: Vintage.

Funke, J. (2011), 'Narrating Uncertain Sex: The Case of Karl M.[artha] Baer', in B. Davies and J. Funke (eds), *Sex, Gender and Time in Fiction and Culture*. Basingstoke: Palgrave, pp. 132–53.

Funke, J. (ed.) (2016), *The World and Other Unpublished Works by Radclyffe Hall*. Manchester: Manchester University Press.

Garrity, J. (2013), 'Modernist Women's Writing: Beyond the Threshold of Obscolence'. *Literature Compass*, 10, (1), 15–29.

Gilbert, S. M. and Gubar, S. (1989), *No Man's Land: The Place of the Woman Writer in the Twentieth Century*. New Haven: Yale University Press.

Glick, E. (2009), *Materializing Queer Desire: Oscar Wilde to Andy Warhol*. Albany: State University of New York Press.

Green, L. (2003), 'Hall of Mirrors: Radclyffe Hall's *The Well of Loneliness* and Modernist Fictions of Identity'. *Twentieth Century Literature*, 49, (3), 277–97.

Gregory, E. (1997), *H. D. and Hellenism*. Cambridge: Cambridge University Press.

Hackett, R. (2004), *Sapphic Primitivism: Productions of Race, Class, and Sexuality in Key Works of Modern Fiction*. New Brunswick: Rutgers University Press.

Hardie, M. J. (2005), 'Repulsive Modernism: Djuna Barnes' *"The Book of Repulsive Women"'*. *Journal of Modern Literature*, 29, (1), 118–32.

Harrison, E. J. and Peterson, S. (1997), *Unmanning Modernism: Gendered Re-Readings*. Knoxville: University of Tennessee Press.

H. D. (1981), 'The Master'. *Feminist Studies*, 7, (3), 407–16.

Houlbrook, M. (2005), 'Sexing the History of Sexuality'. *History Workshop Journal*, 60, 216–22.

Jay, K. (1995), 'Lesbian Modernism: (Trans)forming the (C)anon', in G. Haggerty and B. Zimmerman (eds), *Professions of Desire: Lesbian and Gay Studies in Literature*. New York: MLA, pp. 73–7.

Jeffreys, S. (1985), *The Spinster and Her Enemies: Feminism and Sexuality 1880–1930*. London: Pandora.

Lawrence, D. H. (1923), *Psychoanalysis and the Unconscious*. London: Martin Secker.

Lawrence, D. H. (1993), *Lady Chatterley's Lover and A Propos of Lady Chatterley's Lover*. London: Penguin.

Lucchesi, J. (2001), '"The Dandy in Me": Romaine Brooks's 1923 Portraits', in S. Filin-Yeh (ed.), *Dandies: Fashion and Finesse in Art and Culture*. New York: New York University Press, pp. 153–84.

Marshik, C. (2006), *British Modernism and Censorship*. Cambridge: Cambridge University Press.

Miller, M. (2009), *Slaves to Fashion: Black Dandyism and the Styling of Black Diasporic Identity*. Durham: Duke University Press.

Oram, A. (2007), *Her Husband Was a Woman!: Women's Gender-Crossing in Modern British Popular Culture*. London: Routledge.

Oosterhuis, H. (2000), *Stepchildren of Nature: Krafft-Ebing, Psychiatry, and the Making of Sexual Identity*. Chicago: University of Chicago Press.

Parkes, A. (1996), *Modernism and the Theater of Censorship*. Oxford: Oxford University Press.

Pease, A. (2009), *Modernism, Mass Culture, and the Aesthetics of Obscenity*. Cambridge: Cambridge University Press.

Peppis, P. (2014), *Sciences of Modernism: Ethnography, Sexology, and Psychology*. Cambridge: Cambridge University Press.

Potter, R. (2013), *Obscene Modernism: Literary Censorship and Experiment 1900–1940*. Oxford: Oxford University Press.

Sackville-West, V. (1973), *Portrait of a Marriage*. London: Weidenfeld and Nicolson.

Schaffner, A. K. (2011a), *Modernism and Perversion: Sexual Deviance in Sexology and Literature, 1850–1930*. Basingstoke: Palgrave.

Schaffner, A. K. (2011b), 'Fiction as Evidence: On the Uses of Literature in Nineteenth-Century Sexological Discourse'. *Comparative Literature Studies*, 48, (2), 165–99.

Schaffner, A. K. and Weller, S. (eds) (2012), *Modernist Eroticisms: European Literature after Sexology*. Basingstoke: Palgrave.

Scott, B. K. (1990), *The Gender of Modernism: A Critical Anthology*. Bloomington: Indiana University Press.

Scott, B. K. (2006), *Gender in Modernism: New Geographies, Complex Intersections*. Urbana: University of Illinois Press.

Sigel, L. Z. (2012), *Making Modern Love: Sexual Narratives and Identities in Interwar Britain*. Philadelphia: Temple University Press.

Smith-Rosenberg, C. (1985), *Disorderly Conduct: Visions of Gender in Victorian America*. Oxford: Oxford University Press.

Taddeo, J. A. (2002), *Lytton Strachey and the Search for Modern Sexual Identity: The Last Eminent Victorian*. London: Routledge.

Waters, C. (2006), 'Sexology', in H. Cocks and M. Houlbrook (eds), *Palgrave Advances in the Modern History of Sexuality*. Basingstoke: Palgrave, pp. 41–63.

Wilde, O. (1998), *The Picture of Dorian Gray*. Oxford: Oxford University Press.

Winning, J. (2000), *The Pilgrimage of Dorothy Richardson*. Madison: University of Wisconsin Press.

Woolf, V. (1985), *Moments of Being: A Collection of Autobiographical Writing*. New York: Harcourt.

Woolf, V. (1998), *Orlando*. Oxford: Oxford University Press.

Woolf, V. (2000), *Mrs Dalloway*. Oxford: Oxford University Press.

Woolf, V. (2003), *The Common Reader. Volume 1*. London: Vintage.

15

Modernism, Neurology and the Invention of Psychoanalysis

Ulrika Maude

In this chapter, I want to consider the inception of psychoanalysis as it develops both from neurology, the empirical study of the material brain, and from what I will call hermeneutics, the close analysis and interpretation of text, of language. Like the idea of the embodied mind that informs this chapter, the confluence of neurology and hermeneutics might seem paradoxical if not antithetical, because while one examines the physiological workings of the brain without touching on the question of meaning, the other raises the question of meaning without being concerned with the physical mechanisms that allow meanings to be produced. I want to argue, however, that this tension or contradiction is also endemic to literature in general and to modernist literature in particular. Developing the idea put forward by certain critics that Sigmund Freud can productively be read as a modernist writer and thinker, I will examine his modernist tendencies from the perspective of the tensions that emerge out of the origins of his clinical work in nineteenth-century neurological science.

As is well known, Freud began his career as a 'poverty-stricken young physician', an empirical scientist who was also, however, deeply interested in literature and was said to have 'bought more books than he could afford and who read classic works into the night, deeply moved and no less deeply amused' (Gay, 1988, 45). Voracious in his intellectual appetites and uncertain of which direction to take in his medical career at the General Hospital in Vienna, Freud sampled, over a period of three years, a variety of medical specialties including 'surgery, internal medicine, psychiatry, dermatology, nervous diseases, and ophthalmology', before finally settling on nervous disorders (Gay, 1988, 41). In March 1885, Freud applied for a travel grant, which provided him with 'a meager stipend and a no less meager six months' leave of absence' (Gay, 1988, 47). Despite its meagreness, the stipend was to prove decisive, for Freud would use it to travel to Paris to study under Jean-Martin Charcot at the Salpêtrière Hospital. As Adam Phillips has argued, it was Charcot more than any of the other 'remarkable men' he encountered in Vienna, Paris or elsewhere who had 'the greatest influence on Freud's life and work' (2014, 84).

Appointed head physician at the Salpêtrière in 1862, Charcot established a neurology clinic at the hospital in 1882. It was the first of its kind in Europe, and in addition to Freud, Charcot's students at the Salpêtrière included such eminent figures as Joseph Babinski, Pierre Janet, William James and Georges Gilles de la Tourette. Together, these scientists and philosophers were instrumental in establishing the modern (and indeed modernist) disciplines and discourses of psychology and psychiatry. While Babinski was the first physician to separate hysteria from organic causes, Janet was the first to analyse the notion of trauma. Besides being responsible for inaugurating American pragmatism (along with Charles Sanders Peirce and John Dewey), William James can be said to have introduced the modern scientific study of psychology in the United States by establishing the first Department of Psychology at the University of Harvard and by publishing a still highly influential book, *Principles of Psychology* (1890). Gilles de la Tourette, in turn, is today known for his work on neurological disorders, especially the condition characterized by involuntary verbal and motor tics that carries his name, Tourette's syndrome.

As this might suggest, the late nineteenth century was a period of rapid and remarkable scientific advance during which various neurological conditions were observed and named. In addition to Tourette's syndrome, these included other involuntary movement disorders (so-called 'dyskinesias'), such as Parkinson's disease. Charcot's own research between 1868 and 1881 into what at the time was known as 'Shaking Palsy', after a well-known essay by the British surgeon James Parkinson from 1817, was groundbreaking. Tourette's syndrome was particularly significant: closely researched at the Salpêtrière Hospital as 'maladie des tics', the disorder was observed by both Charcot and Freud, but principally researched by Gilles de la Tourette – so much so that from the 1960s, the syndrome has carried his name. Its clinical delineation dates back to 1885, when Freud was a student at the Salpêtrière, and we know that he read Gilles de la Tourette's article on the disorder, and that he disagreed with its argument about the provenance and nature of the illness, an early indicator of a wider, albeit still-nascent difference between neurological and psychoanalytic understandings of the disorders studied at Charcot's clinic in Paris.[1] As is well known, Charcot had a particular interest in the aetiology of hysteria, which he understood as a neurological disorder and, although since its inception and 'by its very name a woman's complaint' (from the Greek *hystera* for 'womb'), hysteria was not for Charcot a condition restricted to female patients. In 1882, in order to pursue his interest in male hysteria, Charcot inaugurated the hospital's *service des hommes*, dedicated to 'the study and treatment of [male] subjects suffering from transient nervous and neurological disorders' (Micale, 1990, 372). During the 1880s, Charcot wrote sixty-one detailed case studies of male hysteria, took notes on thirty additional cases and treated numerous other male patients who suffered from what were categorized as hysterical symptoms (Micale, 1990, 371). The predisposing cause of hysteria, he argued, was heredity, in line with nineteenth-century ideas of degeneracy or 'bad stock' (Hacking, 2002, 22–3). However, for Charcot, the triggers of hysteria in the two sexes were different: 'moral causes could incite hysteria in women, but in men, unless the disorder appeared when the patient was very young, physical trauma, or shock, was the main predisposing cause' (Hacking, 2002, 33). Freud's obituary for the neurologist, published in September 1893, praises Charcot above all for treating hysteria in the last ten years of his life as a serious area of study; it would be precisely Freud's interest in this perplexing condition of dyskinesia and related symptoms that would instigate the psychoanalytic method. As if in recognition of Charcot's influence, a reproduction of André Brouillet's well-known painting, 'Une leçon clinique à la Salpêtrière' (1887), would hang above Freud's famous couch until his death and can still be seen at the Freud Museum, housed in his final home in London.

Knowledge of neurological discoveries rapidly entered popular consumption. In France, this was through the public 'performances' of hysterics on the stage of the Salpêtrière Hospital. In his famous Tuesday lectures, Charcot would 'exhibit one or more patients and develop their cases and their symptoms before the admiring eyes of a crowd' (Hacking, 2002, 35). Knowledge of neurological conditions was also disseminated through the journal *Nouvelle iconographie photographique de la Salpêtrière*, which distributed images of sufferers of hysteria, epilepsy and other neurological disorders, and which ran from 1888 to 1918 and had Gilles de la Tourette as one of its founders. Furthermore, as Mark Micale has suggested, at the end of the nineteenth century, 'the name of the Salpêtrière invaded even the popular magazines and newspapers' (1990, 198); according to Georges Didi-Huberman, 'hysteria was covertly identified with something like an art, close to theatre or painting' (2003, xi). Rae Beth Gordon, who has researched the influence of neurology on French performance culture, argues that 'The Parisian cabaret and café-concert between 1865 and 1907 were characterized by a convulsive body language made up of frenetic, angular, and "mechanical" movements accompanied by tics and grimaces.' She has shown that late nineteenth-century cabaret performances in Paris were notably influenced not only by the neurological work going on in the semi-public theatre-like lecture room of the Salpêtrière Hospital but also by the promulgation and popularization of such work in French newspapers and magazines of the day (Gordon, 2004, 100).

Charcot codified the movements of sufferers of hysteria as convulsive, whereas those who suffered from epilepsy, he argued, displayed so-called clownism: trembling, contractures, facial asymmetry, tics, grimaces and constant agitation. Akathisia, the inability to remain seated, and limping were other pathologies of movement associated with hysteria and epilepsy, and these symptoms entered the stage and later the screen through cabaret and music hall performers who went on to work in cinema and often had extremely successful careers in film. This was a common career trajectory for comedians such as Dranem and Louis-Jacques Boucot in France and Karl Valentin in Germany – the latter commonly referred to as 'the German Charlie Chaplin'. Indeed, the avant-garde film-maker Jean Epstein identified Charlie Chaplin's style as itself one of 'photogenic neurasthenia': his 'entire performance consists of the reflex actions of a nervous, tired person', Epstein commented (1998, 238). Chaplin began his career performing in London music halls in the mime troupe of Fred Karno, and as Gordon points out, 'one has only to compare Chaplin's gait to that of the psychiatric patients filmed at the Salpêtrière between 1910 and 1912' to spot the connection between Charcot and 'Charlot' – the French nickname for Chaplin (2004, 99). Epstein himself had studied medicine before becoming a film-maker and hence had a keen eye for its influences on the new art form. The Röntgen ray and the first Lumière film, after all, both appeared in 1895, and as is evidenced in Etienne-Jules Marey's stop-motion photographs (a precursor to film), the development of early cinema is closely entwined with medical culture. Early cinema is also replete with references to the discourse and practice of neurology and psychiatry. Robert Wiene's *Das Cabinet des Dr Caligari* (*The Cabinet of Dr Caligari*, 1920), as the final scenes of the film reveal, stages the life of the inmates of a mental asylum. Gordon argues that a prominent early motif of cinema, corporeal dislocations, 'reminded one of marionettes or automatons and thus evoked the mechanical, automatic life of the hysteric' (2004, 112). Thus, in a 1902 film by Georges Méliès entitled *Turn of the Century Surgeon*, a surgeon removes, and then replaces, each of his patient's limbs. This process is inverted in Ernst Lubitsch's 1919 film *Die Puppe* (*Doll*), in which Hilarius, a doll-maker, functions as a kind of physiologist who miraculously, limb by limb, assembles a doll so lifelike that it is impossible to tell it apart from its model (both model and doll being played by the same actress, Ossi Oswalda).

For what neurological conditions such as Parkinson's disease, Tourette's syndrome and epilepsy had in common, and what was seen as a source of black humour in cabaret and early cinema, was the body's seemingly mechanical capacity to act outside of the realm of conscious intention. Indeed, the influential study of humour by the French philosopher Henri Bergson, *Laughter: An Essay on the Meaning of the Comic* (1899), owed much to neurological discoveries and their impact on performance culture. Bergson argued that 'the attitudes, gestures and movements of the human body are laughable in exact proportion as that body reminds us of a mere machine' (1921, 29). Humour, Bergson stressed, arises from 'something mechanical encrusted on the living', for 'a comic character is generally comic in proportion to his ignorance of himself' (1921, 37, 16). This makes the subject appear as if deprived of his or her essential freedom. Bergson's work brings out the way in which the neurological disorders that informed the performance style of music hall, vaudeville, cabaret and film themselves questioned notions of agency and intentionality, thus casting serious doubt over received notions of subjectivity by suggesting that the mechanical, the automatic and the involuntary were integral to the self. These pathologies questioned the fundamental philosophical category of free will, which the Salpêtrians regarded as a mere metaphysical invention (see Harris, 1991, xvii).

The scientific and philosophical implications of these developments in the discourse of neurology had a profound impact on modernist literature, both thematically and in formal terms, and can be said to have been one of the instigators of the radical experimentation in style and form that modernism is known for. Hysteria in its day was considered a contagious disease, seen to be transmitted through imitation, and this is strikingly staged in T. S. Eliot's remarkable early prose-poem 'Hysteria', written and published in 1915. During his time in Paris from 1910 to 1911, Eliot had read Pierre Janet's work on hysteria and later referred to him, in the *Criterion*, as 'the great psychologist'.[2] In the same year, 1915, Eliot married Vivienne Haigh-Wood, his first wife, whom he had met in 1914 and who already had a history of mental instability. The speaker in Eliot's poem witnesses the onset of a hysterical attack in his female companion and traces the 'contagious' effects of the attack on his own soma: 'I was drawn in by short gasps, inhaled at each momentary recovery, lost finally in the dark caverns of her throat, bruised by the ripple of unseen muscles' (Eliot, 2015, 26). An earlier, similarly striking proto-modernist example of hysteria appears in Guy de Maupassant's short story 'Le Tic' (1884), translated into English as 'The Spasm'. The story stages the development of a 'violent spasmodic movement' in the hand of a father whose daughter has been buried alive – a recurrent fear and concern in the period. The narrator comments, in an example of what would come to be known as conversion hysteria, that each time the father 'wanted to reach an object, his hand made a hook-like movement, a sort of irregular zigzag, before it succeeded in touching what it was in search of' (Maupassant, 1903, 848–9). The zigzag pattern, Charcot argued, presented in the visual scotoma of hysterical patients, and it appears as a recurring trope for hysteria in a number of silent films, including *The Cabinet of Dr Caligari* and Lubitsch's *Doll*. Here one could also mention Louis Aragon and André Breton's 1928 essay 'The Fiftieth Anniversary of Hysteria', which advocated hysteria not as 'a pathological phenomenon' but as 'a supreme form of expression' (Aragon and Breton, 1978, 321). The essay was translated into English by Samuel Beckett.

Another even more crucial neurological development was the French neurologist Paul Broca's localization of language in the brain, in a landmark scientific paper from 1861. Where speech had previously been considered the immaterial performance of the soul, it was, after Broca's discoveries in aphasia – the partial or total loss of language – seen to be a fragile bodily function, subject to injury and impairment. Broca's most famous patient, a farmer named Leborgne, had suffered from epilepsy since childhood and at the age of thirty experienced the sudden onset of aphasia. By the time he was admitted to the Bicêtre Hospital in 1840, Leborgne was only able to utter the monosyllable 'tan', which he would repeat in response to any question posed to him. Broca subjected Leborgne, who came to be known as 'Tan', to a series of neurological and physiological tests that showed that his nervous system functioned normally and that he had at least the intellectual capacity required for speech, which proved that his aphasia had not been caused by lack of intelligence. When Tan died in 1861, Broca autopsied his brain. He found 'substantial damage from lesions to the second and third convolutions of the left frontal lobe', now known as Broca's area (Eagle, 2014, 5). Tan's medical history, test results and the findings of the autopsy enabled Broca to make the momentous announcement at the meeting of the Society of Anthropology of Paris that 'the lesion to the frontal lobe was the cause of the loss of speech' (Broca, 1861, 238).[3] In the two years that followed, Broca would find twelve additional cases of evidence for his theory of speech localization, which had first been proposed, in the 1790s, albeit without clinical proof, by Franz Joseph Gall's theory of brain localization.[4]

Before Broca's finding, language had been considered a faculty endowed upon us by divine powers. Speech, it was assumed, was a spiritual, metaphysical phenomenon, devoid of the messy materiality of embodiment. This conception of speech stemmed from a dualist understanding of the self and equated speech with the immateriality of thought. Broca's discovery of 1861 for the first time conclusively located language in the brain and rebutted the received understanding of speech as the transparent performance of the soul. Language, it turned out, was a fragile physiological function, easily impaired. Language disorders, that is to say, revealed the material and mechanical dimensions of language, which in turn questioned its status as the expression and fulcrum of the self. Language, it was now discovered, could escape the realm of intention and will – something that fundamentally challenged previous conceptions of speech and further consolidated nineteenth-century findings of nerve theory, which had paved the way to a non-agential self whose will and intention were at least in part conditioned by organic processes. The formal experimentation of modernist literature can in part be understood as a response to the paradigm shift in the understanding of how language, the medium of literature, functioned.

T. S. Eliot's high modernist works, especially *The Waste Land* (1922) and poems such as 'The Hollow Men' (1925), contain numerous seemingly dissociated, ventriloquized voices, whose origin is unclear to the reader. Lines such as 'Bin gar keine Russin, stamm' aus Litauen, echt deutsch' (l. 12 of 'The Burial of the Dead') or 'My nerves are bad tonight. Yes, bad. Stay with me. / Speak to me. Why do you never speak. Speak' (ll. 111–12, from 'The Game of Chess'), although containing meaning, seem devoid of any specific origin and do not seem to function propositionally within the context of the poem. In fact, they seem positively to flaunt their status as non-propositional speech. The lines appear seemingly out of nowhere, in the manner of what Broca's contemporary, the British neurologist John Hughlings Jackson, referred to as 'a reflex'. By contrast with propositional speech, which is volitional and requires mental effort, non-propositional clauses – what neurolinguists call 'ready-mades' – operate automatically. Hughlings Jackson made the discovery of non-propositional speech in 1864, in his research into cardiovascular disease, which he noted, was sometimes accompanied by the loss of the 'expression of ideas [...] as distinguished from the mere utterance of words by the lips, tongue and palate' (Hughlings Jackson, 1915, 30). This was a result of a blockage to a cerebral artery, which had caused damage to the ventroposterior region of the frontal lobes, Broca's area (the language-area in the brain). Such a blockage seemed to leave the mechanical production of speech intact, but affected the speaking subject's grasp of the semantic content of the utterance. Hughlings Jackson later, in 1879, added that 'phrases, which have a propositional structure, have in the mouths of speechless patients no propositional function' (Hughlings Jackson, 1932, 174). The utterance of 'ready-mades', such as greetings, oaths, curses and other interjections, nursery rhymes, proverbs and prayers, however, is also a prominent feature of all speech, everyone's speech, although under ordinary conditions, non-propositional speech appears only as a supplement to propositional utterances. In this category of utterance, Hughlings Jackson included swearing, which, he argued, is not 'strictly speaking [...] a part of language', but a habit that adds emotional force 'to the expression of ideas' (1915, 40). Interjections and other ejaculations, he added, belong to the same category of non-verbal utterances, for they 'have become easy of elaboration by long habit, and would require but slight stimulus for perfect execution'. For Hughlings Jackson, 'the explanation of the way in which these phrases are so to speak manufactured is that they are a reflex' (1915, 41). In showing how such reflexes underlie or inhabit all speech, he seems to suggest that they constitute the *other* of language production: both not-speech and the very substance itself *of* speech.

In *The Waste Land*, quotations from the high canon of (mostly but not exclusively) Western literature appear side by side with snatches of popular song and with ventriloquized, non-propositional lines from unheard conversations to demonstrate how in the waste land of contemporary culture, the literary tradition – what is conventionally taken to be our highest achievement in language – seems to have no greater status or significance than the habitual utterance of the voices we encounter in 'The Burial of the Dead' (l. 12) or in 'The Game of Chess', begging an absent interlocutor to 'speak' and to respond (l. 112). A case in point of the literary tradition itself being reduced to non-propositional utterance is 'Twit twit twit / Jug jug jug jug jug jug' (ll. 203–4 of 'The Fire Sermon'). The second line is a reference to John Lyly's comedy *Campaspe* (1584), but here, it has the appearance and effect of mere noise. In part V of 'The Hollow Men', the Lord's Prayer (*For Thine is the Kingdom*, ll. 10, 24) runs near-parallel to the nursery rhyme modelled on 'Here we go round the Mulberry Bush' (in Eliot's version, *'the prickly pear'*, ll. 1–3) and has itself been reduced to non-propositional speech, seeming to appear automatically, outside of any discernible context; it is even typographically placed in the actual margins of the poem. Something similar occurs in Samuel Beckett's late modernist play *Happy Days* (1961), in which the protagonist, Winnie, repeatedly quotes and misquotes her classics, so that 'moody Madness laughing wild / Amid severest woe' from Thomas Gray's 'Ode on a Distant Prospect of Eton College' (1747, ll.

79–80) becomes in Winnie's rendition 'laughing wild … something something laughing wild amid severest woe' (Beckett, 2010, 18). Gray's lines, now almost devoid of their semantic content, function non-propositionally and have here been reduced to rhythm and sound-pattern, and the merest snatches of sense.

Neurology, then, like the psychoanalytic method that Freud would go on to invent and inaugurate, has at its core an interest in the limitations of agency, intention and will: as Adam Phillips puts it, Freud's understanding of the human subject is 'a person with little autonomy' who is 'subjected to forces he [or she] can for the most part neither control nor understand' (2014, 30–1). There was no better place, in 1885, than the Salpêtrière to study this crisis of agency and autonomy, with its so-called hysterico-epileptics, and equally importantly, with its highly charismatic head physician, Jean-Martin Charcot, who provided Freud with a new model of what being a scientist could mean. As Freud points out in his obituary, Charcot had seen as a student 'all the wildness of paralyses, spasms, and convulsions' that had 'neither name nor understanding' and had premised his career on taking these conditions seriously. The hysteric, Freud explained, 'was no longer a malingerer, for Charcot had thrown the whole weight of his authority on the side of the genuineness and objectivity of hysterical phenomena'. For Freud, Charcot 'had the nature of an artist – he was, as he himself said, a *"visuel"*, a man who sees' (Freud, 1995, 49, 53, 49). As Phillips puts it, Charcot was that 'paradoxical person', a scientist who was also an artist, a 'great neurologist who could quote Dante or Virgil, a doctor whose work artists and writers were intrigued by' (2014, 87). However, the one decisive aspect of Charcot's work with which Freud categorically disagreed was the notion of degeneration. As he put it in his obituary: 'So greatly did Charcot over-estimate heredity as a causative agent that he left no room for the acquisition of nervous illness […] nor did he make a sufficiently sharp distinction between organic nervous affections and neuroses, either as regards their aetiology or in other respects' (Freud, 1995, 55). Charcot's understanding, in other words, left no room to consider the causes or symptoms of nervous disorders. An organic cause is as close to contingent as the theory of degeneration would permit: it puts an end to meaning and interpretation. Freud's version of hysteria, based on the concept of neuroses, opened the symptom up to interpretation and to signification. The symptoms of the neurotic, in other words, functioned as a text.

Freud, with his lifelong habit of immersing himself in the classics, was himself well-versed in hermeneutics, in the interpretation of texts, and even had literary ambitions of his own, as his own comparison of his case studies to short stories in *Studies on Hysteria* (1895) would reveal:

I have not always been a psychotherapist. Like other neuropathologists, I was trained to employ local diagnoses and electro-prognosis, and it still strikes me myself as strange that the case histories I write should read like short stories and that, as one might say, they lack the serious stamp of science. [...] The fact is that local diagnosis and electrical reactions lead nowhere in the study of hysteria, whereas a detailed description of mental processes such as we are accustomed to find in the work of imaginative writers enables me, with the use of a few psychological formulas, to obtain at least some kind of insight into the course of that affection. (Freud and Breuer, 1974, 231)

Freud was an interpreter of signs, a paradoxical medical empiricist in search of 'textual', narrative meaning. This tension in his work, Bruno Bettelheim has argued, is only accentuated by James Strachey's translation of Freudian terms into 'scientese' in order to 'reach an Anglo-American audience assumed to be looking for Freud-as-natural-scientist' (Weinstein, 2005, 274 n. 4). Bettelheim draws attention to the fact that the German *Seele* (soul), for instance, is almost invariably translated as 'mind' (1983, 70–2) and *Fehlleistung* (fail + achievement or accomplishment) as 'parapraxis' – 'a combination of Greek words to which the reader has no emotional response expect annoyance at being presented with a basically incomprehensible word', as he caustically remarks (1983, 87–8). 'To be interested in the psychological rather than the neurological', Adam Phillips comments, 'was patently to be interested in fictions as truths' (2014, 90). Neurophysiology was therefore to fall short for Freud, and the analytic session he would develop would emerge as an externalization of what happened inside the mind, for one cannot see thought by studying the brain: thinking was something that a neurological examination could not unveil. Freud would listen to his patients, let them speak for themselves rather than speak for them, and apply his literary skills to what he heard, and as Charcot recommended, to what he saw. In *The Question of Lay Analysis*, he makes his views on the shortcomings of a medical training clear and advocates instead the study of the humanities, including *Literaturwissenschaft* (Freud, 1950, 118). As Jean-Michel Rabaté has noted, *Literaturwissenschaft* 'conflates personal literary expertise and something like the "science" of literature, which may include criticism' (2014, 3). Freud's method was to be premised on a close (textual) analysis of symptoms as signs and symbols. For the early Freud, unlike for Charcot, a tic, convulsion, paralysis, slip of the tongue, even accident was restored to meaning, on the model of the classics. In his 'Preliminary Communication on the Psychical Mechanism of Hysterical Phenomena', written with Breuer in the same year as his obituary for Charcot (1893), Freud writes that in hysteria groups of ideas originating in hypnoid states are present and [...] these are cut off from associative connection with other ideas, but can be associated among themselves, and thus form the more or less highly organised rudiment of a second consciousness, a *condition seconde*. If this is so, a chronic hysterical symptom will correspond to the intrusion of this second state into the somatic innervation which is as a rule under the control of normal consciousness. (Freud and Breuer, 1974, 66–7)

Here we have, *avant la lettre*, the inception of the unconscious. Freud and Breuer also argue that a 'psychical trauma – or more precisely the memory of the trauma – acts like a foreign body which long after its entry must continue to be regarded as an agent that is still at work' (1974, 56–7). The agency of the conscious self has been taken over by this foreign body occupying a second consciousness, later to become the unconscious. Intentionality, albeit now of a much more provisional, tricky and unruly sort, has been restored. Another Freudian invention or discovery, the drive – *Trieb* – does something similar: Jean-Luc Nancy has argued that Freud 'wants to hear in it at once more than an utterly programmed "instinct" and less than a programmatic "intention" or "aim"' (Nancy, 2013, 102). The Freudian subject is caught between these two modalities.

Freud's method is poised between an elaborate, perhaps even overly elaborate theoretical framework – whose limitations he also frequently acknowledges – and a much more tentative practice. Freud writes that 'I learnt to restrain speculative tendencies and to follow the unforgettable advice of my master, Charcot: to look at the same things again and again until they themselves begin to speak' (2001, 22). 'Theory is good', Freud quotes Charcot as saying, 'but that doesn't prevent things from existing' (1995, 50). Freudian analysis, in other words, can be called 'idiographic': 'Idiographic sciences deal with events that never recur in the same form – that can be neither replicated nor predicted' (Bettelheim, 1983, 42). Michel de Certeau argues that 'every psychoanalytic treatment directly contradicts a first norm, a constituent part of scientific discourse, which argues that the truth of the utterance be independent of the speaking subject' (1986, 26). Because psychoanalysis, in other words, 'is also a clinical practice, [...] its operative concepts rely on (and relay) the singularity of each case', as Freud's own case studies so clearly attest, and each is tied specifically to the utterance of a speaking subject (Rabaté, 2014, 199). In much the same way, any reading of a literary text responds in the first place to the individual and singular arrangement of words that constitutes a poem, a novel or a play. It is for this reason that Jean-Luc Nancy calls Freudian psychoanalysis 'the most clearly and most resolutely non-religious of modern inventions' and therefore 'the least disposed to give itself over to any set of beliefs whatsoever': the specificity or the singularity of the psychoanalytic case can in principle challenge or disrupt the theoretical paradigm (Nancy, 2013, 99, 100). Psychoanalysis can therefore be said to operate in a state of perpetual self-revision, just as any totalizing or even thematic reading of a literary text can be undone by the formal and linguistic specificity of the work to which it refers.

The tension in psychoanalysis, which on the one hand develops from neurology and Charcot's reading of hysteria and other nervous disorders as contingent organic illnesses, and on the other from a hermeneutic method which reintroduces a certain agency, intentionality and ultimately meaning, however provisional, to the symptoms, is also the key tension in literature and in modernist literature in particular: a central principle in modernism is the vacillation between a materialist understanding of the self that puts an end to the symbolic and the opposing impulse towards interpretation, analysis and meaning. It is a tension that is apparent, for instance, in Woolf's observation, in 'On Being Ill' (1926, 1930), on literature's tendency to separate mind from body and to privilege the former (here she is referring to the literary tradition rather than to modernism): literature, she observes,

> does its best to maintain that its concern is with the mind; that the body is a sheet of plain glass through which the soul looks straight and clear, and, save for one or two passions such as desire and greed, is null, negligible and non-existent. On the contrary, the very opposite is true. All day, all night the body intervenes; blunts or sharpens, colours or discolours, turns to wax in the warmth of June, hardens to tallow in the murk of February. The creature within can only gaze through the pane – smudged or rosy; it cannot separate off from the body like the sheath of a knife or the pod of a pea for a single instant; it must go through the whole unending process of changes, heat and cold, comfort and discomfort, hunger and satisfaction, health and illness, until there comes the inevitable catastrophe; the body smashes itself to smithereens. (Woolf, 2008, 101)

For Woolf, there is no perception or thought that is not conditioned by bodily events, as the neuro-scientist Antonio Damasio would come to argue in his influential study *Descartes' Error* (1994), almost seventy years later. Woolf's own fiction stages this drama in Clarissa Dalloway's ageing, as it does in Septimus Smith's shell shock in *Mrs. Dalloway* (1925): 'He looked at people outside; happy they seemed, collecting in the middle of the street, shouting, laughing, squabbling over nothing. But he could not taste, he could not feel. In the teashop among the tables and chattering waiters the appalling fear came over him – he could not feel.'[5] (Woolf, 2015, 79) Septimus no longer has the ability to feel for others, or even himself. He suffers flashbacks and sensory loss – both symptoms of shell shock – and not only experiences anhedonia, the inability to feel pleasure, but apathy, the startling inability to feel at all, which strips the world of significance. This is evidenced in the terrifyingly matter-of-fact way in which he throws himself out of the window of his London apartment, to his death.

The Waves (1931), a novel which frequently foregrounds the mechanical and automatic reactions of its protagonists, culminates in Bernard's musings on 'the dart and flicker of the tongue':

> 'Pass' … I would say. 'Milk' … she might answer, or 'Mary's coming' … – simple words for those who have inherited the spoils of all the ages but not as said then, day after day, in the full tide of life, when one feels complete, entire, at breakfast. Muscles, nerves, intestines, blood-vessels, all that makes the coil and spring of our being, the unconscious hum of the engine, as well as the dart and flicker of the tongue, functioned superbly. Opening, shutting; shutting, opening; eating, drinking; sometimes speaking – the whole mechanism seemed to expand, to contract, like the mainspring of a clock. (Woolf, 2011, 209)

The passage foregrounds the complexity of 'the hum of the [human] engine', made of 'Muscles, nerves, intestines, blood-vessels, all that makes the coil and spring of our being', and the sense the ageing Bernard has of its seeming transparency in youth, when everything 'functioned superbly'. The mind itself, the narrator implies, is near-boundless 'in the full tide of life', merging with and becoming not merely other minds (as the novel indicates through the intense connection between its six protagonist-narrators) but even objects of the natural world, including inanimate things. Woolf stages the new, modernist conception of subjectivity, one which is determined by 'muscles, nerves, intestines, blood vessels', in other words by something that would frequently also appear in Freud's writing in addition to or as a supplement to or even a precondition for what we might call the 'hermeneutic drive', namely an organic intentionality staged perhaps most clearly and elegantly in 'Beyond the Pleasure Principle', from 1920. In this essay, which itself contains a number of neurological considerations, Freud advanced the striking claim that life is a tension, a mistake, and that each organism seeks to cancel itself out: 'the aim of all life is death', he provocatively and compellingly argued, following and echoing the nineteenth-century German philosopher Arthur Schopenhauer (1991, 311).[6]

I want to conclude, however, with a brief discussion of Samuel Beckett's late modernist play *Not I*, first written for the stage in 1972, with two 'characters' or rather players: Mouth and Auditor. Mouth, who habitually suffers from mutism, laughs, screams and spews out language, a 'sudden urge ... once or twice a year ... always winter some strange reason' and the urge, appropriately, takes place in the 'nearest lavatory' (Beckett, 2009, 92). Auditor, who remains silent throughout the play, gesticulates three times. His movements consist of 'simple sideways raising of arms from sides and their falling back, in a gesture of helpless compassion. It lessens with each recurrence till scarcely perceptible at third' (Beckett, 2009, 83). Mouth has been read as a hysteric, while the figure of Auditor evokes both the religious confession and what is sometimes called its secular form, psychoanalysis or psychotherapy, which Beckett himself underwent from 1933 to 1935, with Wilfred Bion at the Tavistock Clinic in London. The text, in true Beckettian fashion, is meticulously crafted, with every word and syllable carefully weighed. And yet, in performance it is rendered virtually incomprehensible by the rapid tempo Beckett required for the deliverance of Mouth's lines. In Beckett's own direction, the monologue was paced so fast with the help of a metronome that it turned into what we might see as the ultimate end-point of all literature: rhythm and sound pattern. Beckett wrote to Alan Schneider, the foremost American director of his plays, on 16 October 1972, that Mouth's speech was 'a purely buccal phenomenon, without mental control or understanding, only half heard. Function running away with organ'. Of Mouth's voice, he stated: 'I hear it breathless, urgent, feverish, rhythmic, panting along, without undue concern with intelligibility. Addressed less to the understanding than to the nerves of the audience, which should in a sense *share her bewilderment*' (Harmon, 1998, 283).

In 1975, Beckett rewrote the play for television. He now discarded the figure of Auditor in order to dedicate the full screen to Mouth, so that what was now at the forefront was the sheer physical labour of language production, the 'lips moving ... imagine! ... her lips moving! ... [...] and not alone the lips ... the cheeks ... the jaws ... the whole face ... all those– ... what? ... the tongue? ... yes ... the tongue in the mouth ... all those contortions without which ... no speech possible' (Beckett, 2009, 89). The focus of the play now seems to have shifted from a therapeutic encounter of some sort to the materiality of language itself, its almost sheer embodiedness, its mechanical nature as physiological function, as we witness Billie Whitelaw's tongue, teeth, lips and jaw at work in the visceral labour of language production, with specks of spittle caught on the spot-lit screen, 'and the whole brain begging ... something begging in the brain ... begging the mouth to stop ... pause a moment ... if only for a moment ... and no response' (Beckett, 2009, 90). As Beckett remarked in a letter to Alan Schneider, he was drawing a distinction 'between mind & voice' (Harmon, 1998, 283). There *is* a residual narrative of trauma that one can capture in the few words one can grasp. But the tension is precisely between the brute, near-scatological mechanism of language production and the spectator's attempt to make sense of the content of the words uttered. Mouth's monologue, with its broken syntax, is poised between meaning and its eradication, encapsulated in the play's refrain, 'all the time the buzzing ... dull roar ... in the skull' (Beckett, 2009, 91).

Freud's thinking and writing – which grows out of and resides between the empirical-materialist desire to understand physiology and the hermeneutic drive, if not rage for meaning – is modernist precisely in its vacillation between mechanism and function on the one hand and the symbolic and meaningful on the other. As is well known, modernist writers themselves tended to be suspicious, even hostile towards psychoanalysis, because it seeks to endow actions with meaning and because the modernist aesthetic is premised on the offer or suggestion of meaning but its ultimate withdrawal or holding back. While this may be said to be a feature of all literature (while it may be said indeed to *define* the literary), it is taken to its extremes in modernist literature, in which the hermeneutic code never finally yields to what Roland Barthes calls the proairetic code: the completion and closure of event and, by proxy, sense. In Jean-Luc Nancy's reading of Freud, the subject 'comes about through his narrative'. But for Nancy, this is not a 'speaking subject' but instead 'he who is placed in the world by word – word, or what could better be named significance, the opening of a possibility of sense' (104).

If we read Freud carefully, we find in his work a constant undoing of what is often called the system, theory or method of psychoanalysis. For although Freud frequently advanced hypotheses, he was also equally candid about their limitations: about the incomprehension and impossibility he often faced in his practice and about the often interminable nature of analysis itself (Freud, 2001). Freud's psychoanalysis develops precisely in relation to the modernist tension between the transcendental and the material, between the mind and the body, and between meaning and its ultimate undoing or eradication.

Notes

1   See Kushner (1998), who highlights Freud's familiarity with contemporary critiques of Gilles de la Tourette's typology of 'maladie des tics'. Georges Guinon, for instance, argued that hysteria and 'maladie des tics' were not distinct disorders, but rather

that the latter was an extreme form of hysteria. Kushner argues that 'Persuaded by Guinon, rather than by Gilles de la Tourette, Freud would use the term "convulsive tics" as a differential diagnosis for hysteria' (1998, 14), which also explains why, when he came to write the case study of Frau Emmy von N., he classified her disorder as hysteria rather than as 'maladie des tics de Gilles de la Tourette'. In 1980, Else Pappenheim proposed that 'Freud had at first believed that "Frau Emmy suffered from *tic convulsif* (Gilles de la Tourette's disease), but discarded the diagnosis in favour of hysteria, because he had uncovered the psychological meanings of her symptoms under hypnosis"' (Kushner, 1998, 2).

2   Eliot made this observation in the little magazine *Criterion*, in April 1934, 451–2. See Brugière (2007, 87–8 n.1) for a quotation of Eliot's entry. For a discussion of Janet's work, see the section entitled 'Pathologies of Perception' in Laura Salisbury's chapter in this volume.

3   French original: 'la lésion du lobe frontal a été la cause de la perte de la parole'. English translation by Christopher D. Green at http://psychclassics.yorku.ca/Broca/perte-e.htm. Accessed 22 October 2017.

4   Broca's aphasia is also known as productive aphasia, for it affects the production of speech on the level of grammar, syntax and the conflation of lexical items. In 1876, the research of the German psychiatrist and neuropathologist Carl Wernicke unveiled a different type of aphasia that affects language reception, now known as receptive aphasia or Wernicke's aphasia.

5   Although the term 'shell shock' is never used in direct reference to Septimus Smith in *Mrs. Dalloway*, we do, however, witness Sir William, Septimus's physician, talking about 'the deferred effects of shell shock' at Clarissa's party, after Septimus's suicide (Woolf, 2015, 164).

6   Freud writes, quoting Schopenhauer, that death is the 'true result and to that extent the purpose of life' (1991, 322).

Bibliography

Aragon, L. and Breton, A. (1978 [1928]), 'The Fiftieth Anniversary of Hysteria', in F. Rosemont (ed.), *What Is Surrealism? Selected Writings*. London: Pluto Press, pp. 50–1.

Beckett, S. (2009), *Krapp's Last Tape and Other Shorter Plays*, S. E. Gontarski (ed.). London: Faber.

Beckett, S. (2010), *Happy Days*, J. Knowlson (ed.). London: Faber.

Bergson, H. (1921 [1899]), *Laughter: An Essay on the Meaning of the Comic*, C. Brereton and F. Rothwell (transl.). New York: Macmillan.

Bettelheim, B. (1983), *Freud and Man's Soul*. New York: Knopf.

Breger, L. (2001), *Freud: Darkness in the Midst of Vision*. New York: Wiley.

Broca, P. P. (1861), 'Perte de la Parole, Ramollissement Chronique et Destruction Partielle du Lobe Antérieur Gauche du Cerveau'. *Bulletin de la Société Anthropologique*, 2, 235–8.

Brugière, B. (2007), 'French Influences and Echos in Tradition and the Individual Talent', in G. Cianci and J. Harding (eds), *T. S. Eliot and the Idea of Tradition*. Cambridge: Cambridge University Press, pp. 75–89.

Certeau, M. de (1986), *Heterologies: Discourse on the Other*, B. Massumi (transl.). Minneapolis: University of Minnesota Press.

Didi-Huberman, G. (2003), *Invention of Hysteria: Charcot and the Photographic Iconography of the Salpêtrière*, A. Hartz (transl.). Cambridge MA: The MIT Press.

Eagle, C. (2014), *Dysfluencies: On Speech Disorders in Modern Literature*. London: Bloomsbury.

Eliot, T. S. (2015), *The Poems of T. S. Eliot, Volume I*, C. Ricks and J. McCue (eds). London: Faber.

Epstein, J. (1998 [1921]), 'Magnification', in R. Abel (ed.), *French Film Theory and Criticism: A History/Anthology 1907–1939, Vol. I: 1907–1929*. Princeton: Princeton University Press, pp. 235–41.

Freud, S. (1950). *The Question of Lay Analysis*, N. Procter-Gregg (transl.). New York: W. W. Norton.

Freud, S. (1964 [1937]), 'Analysis Terminable and Interminable', in *The Standard Edition of the Complete Psychological Works of Sigmund Freud, Vol. XXIII*, J. Starchey and A. Freud (transl.). London: Hogarth Press and The Institute of Psychoanalysis, pp. 216–53.

Freud, S. (1991 [1920]), 'Beyond the Pleasure Principle', in A. Richards (ed.), *On Metapsychology: The Theory of Psychoanalysis*. The Penguin Freud Library, XI. Harmondsworth: Penguin, pp. 275–338.

Freud, S. (1995 [1893]), 'Charcot [Obituary]' in P. Gay (ed.), *The Freud Reader*. New York: W. W. Norton, pp. 48–55.

Freud, S. (2001 [1914]), 'On the History of the Psychoanalytic Movement', in *The Standard Edition of the Complete Psychological Works of Sigmund Freud, Vol. XIV*, J. Strachey and A. Freud (transl.). London: Vintage, pp. 7–66.

Freud, S. and Breuer, J. (1974 [1895]). *Studies on Hysteria*. The Pelican Freud Library 3. J. and A. Strachey (transl.). Harmondsworth: Penguin.

Gay, P. (1988), *Freud: A Life for Our Time*. New York and London: Norton.

Gordon, R. B. (2004), 'From Charcot to Charlot: Unconscious Imitation and Spectatorship in French Cabaret and Early Cinema', in M. S. Micale (ed.), *The Mind of Modernism: Medicine, Psychology, and the Cultural Arts in Europe and America, 1880–1940*. Stanford, CA: Stanford University Press, pp. 93–124.

Hacking, I. (2002), *Mad Travelers: Reflections on the Reality of Transient Mental Illnesses*. Cambridge, MA: Harvard University Press.

Harmon, M. (1998), *No Author Better Served: The Correspondence of Samuel Beckett and Alan Schneider*. Cambridge, MA: Harvard University Press.

Harris, R. (1991), 'Introduction', in J. M. Charcot (ed.), *Clinical Lectures on Diseases of the Nervous System*, R. Harris (ed.). London: Tavistock/Routledge, pp. ix–lxviii.

Hughlings Jackson, J. (1915 [1864]), 'Loss of Speech: Its Association with Valvular Disease of the Heart and with Hemiplegia on the Right Side', in 'Reprint of Some of Dr. Hughlings Jackson's Papers on Affections of Speech', *Brain*, 38, 28–42.

Hughlings Jackson, J. (1932 [1879]), 'On Affections of Speech from Disease of the Brain', in J. Taylor (ed.), *Selected Writings of John Hughlings Jackson, Volume Two*. London: Hodder and Stoughton, pp. 171–83.

Kushner, H. I. (1998), 'Freud and the diagnosis of Gilles de la Tourette's Illness'. *History of Psychiatry*, IX, 1–25.

Maupassant, G. de (1903), *The Complete Short Stories of Guy de Maupassant*, M. W. Dunne (transl.). New York: Blue Ribbon Books.

Micale, M. S. (1990), 'Charcot and the Idea of Hysteria in the Male: Gender, Mental Science, and Medical Diagnosis in Late Nineteenth-Century France', *Medical History*, 34, 363–411.

Nancy, J.-L. (2013), *Adoration: The Deconstruction of Christianity II*, J. McKeane (transl.). New York: Frodham University Press.

Phillips, A. (2014), *Becoming Freud: The Making of a Psychoanalyst*. Jewish Lives. New Haven and London: Yale University Press.

Rabaté, J.-M. (2014), *The Cambridge Introduction to Literature and Psychoanalysis*. New York: Cambridge University Press.

Weinstein, P. (2005), *Unknowing: The Work of Modernist Fiction*. Ithaca and London: Cornell University Press.

Woolf, V. (2008 [1930]), 'On Being Ill', in D. Bradshaw (ed.), *Virginia Woolf: Selected Essays*. Oxford World's Classics. Oxford: Oxford University Press, pp. 101–10.

Woolf, V. (2011 [1931]), *The Waves*, M. Herbert and S. Sellers (eds). The Cambridge Edition of the Works of Virginia Woolf. Cambridge: Cambridge University Press.

Woolf, V. (2015 [1925]), *Mrs. Dalloway*, A. E. Fernald (ed.). The Cambridge Edition of the Works of Virginia Woolf. Cambridge: Cambridge University Press.

16

Modernism, Psychoanalysis and Other Psychologies

Laura Salisbury

'[C]himney-sweeping'. This was Fräulein Anna O's joking description of the new treatment for hysterical symptoms she was undergoing in the 1880s with Dr Josef Breuer. In more serious moments and perhaps more memorably, she referred to the nascent practice of psychoanalysis as the 'talking cure' (Breuer, 1893, 29), thus underscoring psychoanalysis' insistent link to linguistic modes and representations. But as Breuer's collaborator, Sigmund Freud, was later to suggest, perhaps the joke reveals as much as the more sober account, given the comic's capacity to carve routes into material the mind cannot and will not face straight on. Though chimney-sweeping implies a rather routine operation – something like spring cleaning – condensed within the image is a much less homely, more *unheimlich*, or uncanny idea. If the house can be taken as an image of the self, the chimney is a hidden space that cuts through the core of the building. Though central to the functioning of the home, inside the house the chimney is only visible via contours and bulges. The chimney is necessary for the hearth's cosy warmth, but it is also clogged with the soot and smut that are the precipitates of a fire that might stand for civilization itself. Darker still, the chimney in the nineteenth century could have held for Anna O the ghost of a deathly space – a site of child labour and abuse. But there is a glimmer of the folk erotics and romance of the 'lucky' sweep, too, which perhaps prefigures Anna O's developing desires for her doctor. The unreasonable strength of these feelings would frighten Breuer away from psychoanalysis and into a second honeymoon with his wife, but for Freud they became the bedrock of psychoanalytic technique through the attempt to understand the patient's transference of earlier modes of relating on to their doctor.[1] As Stephen Frosh has it, psychoanalysis admits that '[s]omething lives at the heart of the human subject, outside the realms of normal egoic control, something not-I'; but what distinguishes the Freudian unconscious is its dynamic character – it is something '*present*, active, pushing for expression, motivating, causal' (2003, 118). A blockage in a chimney can burn down the whole edifice.

Of course, it would be impossible to unpick the metaphor of 'chimney-sweeping' in this way without the psychoanalytic processes of interpretation Anna O was beginning to name. And one of the reasons why psychoanalysis became the dominant accent in cultural accounts of the mind by the middle of the twentieth century, and why it has been the most significant way of using psychology to read literary modernism, is precisely Freud's emphasis on representation and interpretation. Freud's focus on representation has its root in the idea, expressed in *The Interpretation of Dreams* (1900; published in English in 1913) and brought back to the centre of psychoanalysis in Jacques Lacan's work in the 1950s, that the unconscious is structured like a language (Lacan, 2007). For Freud, the human organism desires the production of its own pleasure, and our instinctual drives are encoded into us in such a way that expressions of sexuality and extreme self-preservation, often figured as aggression, become the impulses from which we gain most pleasure. For society to function, however, we must order and control our instinctual drives, and so they are repressed, pushed down into the unconscious to which the conscious mind can have no direct access. But these repressed desires will always seek to express themselves, to irrupt into the consciousness. This may happen in jokes or in the famous Freudian slips of the tongue, but most significantly for the early Freud it happens in dreams, where the repressive function of the conscious mind is temporarily lifted. Still, the essential, or 'latent', content of the dream can only emerge by slipping past the repressive function of consciousness in disguised form. Repressed ideas thus undergo a form of condensation and displacement through modes akin to the production of metaphors and metonyms in literary creation, re-emerging as potently significant symbols that can be decoded. As Freud puts it, 'dream-content seems like a transcript of the dream-thoughts into another mode of expression, whose characters and syntactic laws it is our business to discover by comparing the original and the translation' (1900, 278). Psychoanalysis, which emerges coterminously with the major strands of literary modernism, seems, then, to offer a fundamentally literary heuristic through which to understand the mind and through which the mind is structured, and a new conduit into portions of experience related to irrationality and desire that exist beneath the embattled structures of social repression (see Marcus, Rabaté, Stonebridge).

Freud was not the first to posit the existence of unconscious aspects of mental life, however, nor to suggest that established ways of viewing the world and ourselves imposed a false coherence on to experience. As modernist scholarship from the 1990s onwards has shown, although psychoanalysis became dominant in cultural representations of the mind by the middle of the twentieth century, its theory and practice emerged from a network of other psychologies, neurological discourses and philosophical accounts of mental life in the late nineteenth century that were just as significant for literary modernism. This wider field includes those working in experimental and positivist modes, such as Wilhelm Wundt, who founded the first psychological laboratory in 1879, and who broke down the workings of the mind into their structural elements via experiments on reaction times, sensory perception and attention. Others like Franz Brentano opposed experimental methods, advocating introspection instead, to argue, in an empiricist mode, that there was no reality beyond that perceived by the senses. William James taught his first course in experimental psychology at Harvard in 1875–76, using methods learned from Herman von Helmholtz, who in 1867 famously 'clocked' the nervous impulse at between 35 and 45 metres per second (McKendrick, 1874, 7); but James's work also aimed to establish the philosophical underpinnings of psychology. As Judith Ryan has shown in *The Vanishing Subject: Early Psychology and Literary Modernism*, these diverse modes of anatomizing consciousness and sensory perception were deeply influential on early modernism. Although psychoanalysis's concentration on the question of representation, alongside desire and narrativization in the form of memory's after-shocks, resonates with literary modernism's central concerns, the extraordinary shape of the perceiving, sensing consciousness emerging from the broader field of psychology cuts as deeply to the core of the modernist project.

'Subject and Object and the Nature of Reality'

It has been a commonplace to speak of the modernist moment as defined by a 'turn inwards' to questions of mind and subjective experience. At one level, this hardly seems like a break from the past, for it is difficult to think of a more profound exploration of psychology of character, nor a more potent sense of layered inner life, than that which emerges from George Eliot's *Middlemarch* (1874). Still, where the modernist 'turn inwards' might be different is in its swerving away from the idea of a rich core of subjectivity existing in a finely detailed but essentially stable external world of objects. For throughout the nineteenth century, there was a developing sense that aesthetic modes that emphasized the wholeness and continuity of a perceiving self were no longer able to withstand the dismantling of the scaffolding on which such unified perceptions were based. Alongside the scientific challenges to narratives that framed the world according to religious modes, this period saw a persistent unpicking of the stability, in both philosophical and aesthetic terms, that had been drawn from Kant's transcendental idealism. In his *Critique of Pure Reason* (1781), Kant argues for synthetic *a priori* categories that consolidate disparate empirical sense experiences under a transcendental, cognitive unity. By this account, experience depends on 'necessary conditions' – *a priori* forms that structure, hold true for and transcend that world of experience. In Kant's terms, '[u]nity of synthesis according to empirical concepts would be altogether accidental, if the latter were not based on the transcendental ground of unity. Otherwise it would be possible for appearances to crowd in upon the soul' (1965, 14). But throughout the nineteenth century, the perceived wholeness of this world began to sheer away, as synthesis and the maintenance of the coherence of reality was divested of its transcendental elements and relocated within the self and its psychological capacities. As a consequence, as Jonathan Crary has shown, '[i]t became imperative for thinkers of all kinds to discover what faculties, operations, or organs produced or allowed the complex coherence of conscious thought' (1999, 15).

Crary suggests that, in philosophical terms, it was Schopenhauer's unifying principle of the subjective 'will' that offered to restabilize the system (1999, 15). But by anchoring unity to a faculty so susceptible to flickering in and out and to distraction from external elements, Schopenhauer was also implying a more subjective, contingent, intermittent possibility of coherence. The philosopher Henri Bergson used memory and projection into the future to synthesize immediate sensory perceptions, but one did not need a Freud to show that memory and desire were hard to hold to stable, objective formations. In 1890, William James offered ideas that emerged from both philosophical introspection and new experimental psychological methods to describe how a baby born into a world perceived as 'one great blooming, buzzing confusion' (1983, 462) comes to experience a continuous sense of itself. For James, consciousness is not adequately described as a string of associations; rather, sensations and perceptions are compounds:

> Consciousness [...] does not appear to itself chopped up in bits. Such words as 'chain' or 'train' do not describe it fitly as it presents itself in the first instance. It is nothing jointed; it flows. A 'river' or a 'stream' are the metaphors by which it is most naturally described. *In talking of it hereafter, let us call it the stream of thought, of consciousness, or of subjective life.* (James, 1983, 233)

Consciousness, as a flow, is determined neither by its constituent parts nor by its relation to transcendental categories; instead, it tracks the shapes of our subjective, intermittent attention and interest in the world.

For James, writing in both philosophical and scientific psychological mode, our psychic life necessarily has a subjective rhythm – of drifts and resting places, of 'flights and perchings' (1983, 236) – that is temporally extended. This account of psychological functioning remains physiological and material, but it is James's philosophical reflection on the human capacity to attend to the world, to form it into a pragmatically unified shape through a subjective capacity for interest, which has a traceable influence on literary modernism. Indeed, May Sinclair invokes James' 'stream of consciousness' in 1918 to describe Dorothy Richardson's extraordinarily extended account of Miriam Henderson's mind. Sinclair speaks of the need to 'throw off the philosophic cant of the nineteenth century' – 'the distinction between idealism and realism, between subjective and objective' (1918, 58) – as Richardson's work, by her account, connects the reader to '[a]ll that we know of reality at first hand' (57). For Sinclair, Richardson's radical narrative technique demonstrates that '[r]eality is thick and deep, too thick and deep, and at the same time too fluid to be cut with any convenient carving knife' (57) into the subjective and the objective.

In Virginia Woolf's *To the Lighthouse* (1927), although '[s]ubject and object and the nature of reality' (1964, 28) are Mr Ramsay's areas of professional, philosophical expertise, his idea of 'angular essences' is refused in favour of a multiplicity of perspective that flows in and out of the purview of the narration. When trying to finish her painting of Mrs Ramsay, Lily Briscoe indeed comes to know that '[f]ifty pairs of eyes were not enough to get round that one woman with' (1964, 224). The Ramsays' son James also finally realizes that the angular shape of the lighthouse and its tenebrous impression are both expressions of a truth: 'So that was the Lighthouse was it? No, the other was also the Lighthouse. For nothing was simply one thing' (211). What Woolf gives, and what Richardson gives, are the fragmentary glimpses and subjective conditions that, in fact, by Sinclair's account, 'life imposes on us all': 'It is just life going on and on. It is Miriam Henderson's stream of consciousness going on and on' (Sinclair, 1918, 59). And if our understanding of the world no longer matches the shapes of aesthetic realism, if the idea of a stable subject, fully present to and cognizant of itself and its experience, no longer seems tenable, then the structures of literary representation will also have to alter. Moving away from the idea that reality might be graspable through the atemporal unity of apperception, literary modernism's capturing of the flickering intermittence of perception and sensation that extends across time and a narration that no longer needs to offer 'any grossly discernible beginning or middle or end' (Sinclair, 1918, 59) becomes a potent way of miming a self understood as always in the process of becoming, rather than present as a unified being.

In his account of the modern artist in 1863, Charles Baudelaire similarly made clear that the notion of a stable, even stolid self had come unstuck in the transactions of Parisian modernity:

> [T]he lover of life, may also be described as a mirror, to a kaleidoscope endowed
> with consciousness, with which every one of its movements represents a pattern of
> life, in all its multiplicity [...] It is an ego athirst for a non-ego, and reflecting it
> at every moment in energies more vivid than life itself, always inconstant and
> fleeting. (Baudelaire, 1992, 400)

Here is a consciousness as shifting and crystalline as the reflections of a Paris of light and glass – a consciousness that takes on the qualities of objects glittering on the surface of the retina. And by the time Ford Madox Ford was writing *The Good Soldier* (1915), the subjective impressions of its narrator, Dowell, dominate its content, form and frame of understanding. There is no getting behind Dowell's impressions to the reality of a stable world. He admits how he likes

> being drawn through the green country [on a train] and looking at it through
> the clear glass of the great windows. Though, of course, the country isn't really
> green. The sun shines, the earth is blood red and purple and red and green and
> red. (Ford, 1972, 44)

Throughout the novel, the fictional environment's shape and mood track both the possibilities and limitations of a consciousness that comes to seem positively psychopathological in its inability to see beyond its projections and investments.

Writing of literary impressionism in 1913, Ford spoke of the need to render 'those queer effects of real life that are like so many views seen through bright glass':

> through glass so bright that whilst you perceive through it a landscape or a
> backyard, you are aware that, on its surface it reflects a face of a person behind
> you. For the whole of life is really like that; we are almost always in one place
> with our minds somewhere else. (Ford, 1964, 40–1)

Although Ford ends with an idea of a mind separable from an object world in which bodies take their place, he nevertheless implies that 'the whole of life' might admit a more complicated, more implicated structure of subject and object. For the metaphor of the pane of glass makes clear that one does not simply see *through* one's impressions to a stable scene beyond; one sees *with* one's impressions. Mental impressions become a material medium that enables a seeing through to what is beyond, but not without reflecting and refracting the object world according to its own material properties. Ford is not claiming that there is no world beyond subjective impressions; as Michael Levenson notes, 'Ford never denied that we ascend from perception to knowledge and from sensation to understanding' (1984, 380). But it is only through the impression – an impression understood as a medium – that we might access the world. Ford's aim was thus to find an aesthetic capable of registering 'the odd vibration that scenes in real life have' (1964, 42) – a 'vibration' found precisely by centring on the flickering, temporally extended processes of perception through which subject-world and object-world meet to form a representation of reality.

The idea that the 'real world' might be constructed in the transactions between the inner and outer will, of course, be particularly suggestive to writers, who necessarily use mediation – words and literary form – to structure their representations. Just as Ford focuses attention on the reflective, refractive materiality of glass to foreground its status as a medium, rather than a clear window on the real, many modernist writers worked to score and scuff up the transparency of their language. In a mode of both admiration and alarm, Woolf speaks in 'Character in Fiction' of Joyce's 'indecency', of his status as a 'desperate man who feels that in order to breathe he must break the windows' (1988, 434). But she goes on later to imagine in *A Room of One's Own* (1929) a new kind of writer who might have 'broke[n] the sentence' and 'broken the sequence', but 'has every right to do both these things if she does them not for the sake of breaking, but for the sake of creating' (2015, 61). The aim is no longer to allow the medium to recede in the impression of external reality, but to represent the mediation that takes place within consciousness and perception through new, extruding forms.

In another oft-quoted modernist articulation of how an 'ordinary mind on an ordinary day' might be rendered, there is a similar emphasis upon making clear the transactions between objects and subjects in any perception of reality. In Woolf's essay 'Modern Fiction' (1925), impressions of the fleeting object world press and score on subjective perception:

> The mind receives a myriad impressions – trivial, fantastic, evanescent, or engraved with the sharpness of steel. From all sides they come, an incessant shower of innumerable atoms [...] Life is not a series of gig lamps symmetrically arranged; life is a luminous halo, a semi-transparent envelope surrounding us from the beginning of consciousness to the end. Is it not the task of the novelist

to convey this varying, this unknown and uncircumscribed spirit, whatever aberration or complexity it may display […]? (Woolf, 1994, 161)

If, as Crary has noted in *Techniques of the Observer*, eighteenth-century philosophical accounts of mental activity were figured as working like a stamp to fix the constancy and consistency of objects, for Woolf, at least at this moment in 1925, a more fundamental permeability of subject and object world is admitted.

Woolf was to claim in 1924, rather knowingly, that '[o]n or about 1910, human character changed' (1988, 421). Her Essay 'Character in Fiction' implies a change in both literary and more general psychological terms, but Laura Marcus has suggested that Woolf uses the formulation of 'human character' rather than 'human nature' because 'character' is specifically connected to writing via the Greek *kharattein*, to engrave (2014, 11). From Aristotle onwards, 'character' has been distinguished from 'nature' by being formed rather than found, and by emphasizing the materiality of impressions on consciousness that are 'engraved with the sharpness of steel' Woolf figures character and consciousness as things that are worked on and moulded by the world, as much as they shape it through acts of perception and representation. 'Let us record the atoms as they fall upon the mind in the order in which they fall', Woolf thus writes in 'Modern Fiction': 'let us trace the pattern, however disconnected and incoherent in appearance, which each sight or incident *scores* upon the consciousness' (Woolf, 1994, 161; my emphasis). These same terms repeat in *To the Lighthouse*, as we hear of Lily's 'accumulated impressions', 'the intensity of her sensation' and her 'I respect you (she addressed him silently), in every atom' (Woolf, 1964, 29) on a single page. Within essay and novel, Woolf's work impresses on its reader how both the subject and object worlds are constituted of the same 'atoms'; and as perspective shifts from subject to object, oscillating from seemingly stable and unyielding definition to shifting plasticity, the novel seems formally to mime Woolf's understanding of reality itself. '[L]ife' is found neither inside nor outside, but in the 'semi-transparent envelope' in and through which our transactions with the world take place.

Pathologies of Perception

In the late nineteenth century, the production of unity in perception and consciousness was fundamentally relocated within the psyche's capacity to represent and synthesize disparate portions of experience; consequently, psychological dysfunction in the period was frequently framed as a disordering of this synthetic capacity. A host of newly described and culturally visible psycho-neurological disorders emerged, with hysteria, neurasthenia, aboulia and agnosia tracking the disintegration of the supposedly smooth relationship between consciousness and automatic behaviours, alongside the coherence of the subject's capacity to synthesize and represent their experiences to themselves. These new psychopathologies stretched the limits of how the human was imagined to function, putting the putatively rational self into often alarming contact with the automatic and the compulsive in ways that made clear that much of mental life occurred beyond the limits of conscious awareness.

As Henri Ellenberger has noted in his influential history of dynamic psychiatry, it was Pierre Janet, rather than Sigmund Freud, who was most influential in tracing the psychological elements within the epidemic of hysteria seizing patients in the late nineteenth century. He was appointed to the Salpêtrière Hospital in Paris by neurologist Jean-Martin Charcot in 1890, but soon began to pull away from his neurophysiological colleagues in insisting that he considered hysteria's 'physiological conditions as mere translations of the psychological ideas' (Janet, 1907, 322–3). Janet was interested in phenomena such as somnambulism, automatic writing, expressions of multiple personality and hallucinations, which had previously been left to the expertise of physiologists because they seemed to emerge automatically and were thus outside of the purview of the psyche. But Janet's early work brings such experiences back into the frame of psychology by attending to dissociation, and the 'désagrégation' of perceptual and cognitive modes that takes place in patients unable smoothly to synthesize their experience. Janet tracks in numerous patients the splitting of perception and cognition, which, through dissociation, become oddly autonomous in the psyche and are experienced in strangely intensified ways. In *L'Automatisme psychologique* (1889), Janet offers a comprehensive account of automatisms as forms of psychopathology that appear when the mind is able only to synthesize a limited number of phenomena. Because of 'the lack of power on the part of the feeble subject to gather, to condense, his psychological phenomena, and to assimilate them to his personality' (Janet, 1907, 501), there is a 'shrinking of the field of consciousness' and the production of activity in the 'subconscious' mind. In 1901, Janet frames a psychological theory that allows him to group such illnesses together into a single clinical category – *psychasthenia* (lack of mental strength). Janet concludes that the shrinking of the field of consciousness encountered in hysterical patients is frequently the result of traumatic experience that weakens the subject, causes dissociation, and then the formation of an *idée fixe* that has its own particular symbolic logic and chains of association. This *idée fixe* will then become a centre around which other psychological phenomena arrange themselves to become something akin to a distinct personality that sits below normal conscious awareness.

This emphasis on the weakening of the mind's ability to synthesize disparate elements into the contours of a seemingly smooth and coherent personality is nevertheless aligned with the notion that the dissociated portions of the psyche still work according to a logic. And this logic is symbolic – often oddly and rigidly so. In 1928, the Surrealist poets Louis Aragon and André Breton, both of whom had some medical training, trumpeted hysteria as 'the greatest poetic discovery of the nineteenth century' (1948, 9). Why? Because the work of Janet (and others) demonstrates that the sliding of the relationship between two things that takes place in symbolic formations is not simply the product of language or artistic representation; instead, the relationship between mind and body itself is the product of the human's functioning as a symbolic, representational animal. For Janet, hysterical symptoms are vivid physical manifestations of ideas and associations that express the wild, excessive logic of the *idée fixe*. By Janet's account, hysteria is an 'ensemble of maladies through representation' (Janet, 1901, 488) caused by a lack of psychological synthesis, in which shards of dissociated elements play themselves out across the body. Surrealism takes this new sense of the fragments, distortions of focus and excessive symbolic linkings that form the logic of what normative society deems to be madness, as a potent artistic possibility. It uses a logic that psychopathology has shown to be within the capacity of the human, while taking minds and bodies beyond social limits of propriety.

Djuna Barnes's novel *Nightwood* (1936) also uses psychopathology and drives to structure the narrative, but there is little characterization that produces recognizable selves; indeed, the text works precisely to undercut the notions of origin and continuity usually used to stabilize subjects. Felix Volkbein is obsessed with heredity and the culture of European aristocracy, but is cut through with a disowned Jewish heritage that cannot be papered over with Old Masters, aristocratic manners and the Catholic Church. Dr Matthew O'Connor remains uncategorizable in his sexual and gender identity, while his professional title turns out to be inauthentic – just another surface curlicue on a baroque text that thematically and formally proliferates surface while refusing depth.

The protagonist of *Nightwood*, Robin Vote, is first encountered in a hotel room, lying on a bed, and compared to a painting by 'the *douanier* Rousseau':

'she seemed to lie in a jungle trapped in drawing room [...] thrown in among the carnivorous flowers' (Barnes, 1950, 56). For reasons that are not given, she is a wanderer and an alcoholic, and yet the chapter that describes her is not 'L'Alcoholique'; it is called 'La Somnambule' (sleepwalker). Like Rousseau's *fin de siècle* primitivism, the anachronistic feathers she wears ('of the kind [Felix's] mother had worn' (66)) and her clothes of heavy brocade fabrics and 'phosphorous glowing' (56) that recall a decadent aesthetic, the reference to 'La Somnambule', also takes us back to the 1890s. For, lying in her bed, legs 'spread as in a dance', 'hands, long and beautiful, lay on either side of her face, the thick lacquered pumps looking too lively for the arrested step' (55), Robin resembles one of those theatricalized set-piece photographs of 'hysterics' in the paradoxically hyperkinetic paralysis of a grand mal seizure taken in Charcot's Salpêtrière of the 1890s.[2] She is, after all, described as lying in a 'set', though one more like a circus than a clinic (the Salpêtrière might sometimes have seemed more like that too, of course). Here described as someone who has 'the structure of the somnambule, who lives in two worlds' (56), there as displaying a 'stubborn cataleptic calm [...] strangely aware of some lost land in herself' (70), the novel reaches for images and vocabulary that evoke Janet's clinical environment to convey Robin's lack of ability to synthesize her personality – her life that 'held no volition for refusal' (67). And yet, it is certainly not the case that Robin's dissociations and désagrégations are meant to suggest a diagnosis, an aetiology of symptoms or indeed any answers. Instead, the image and vocabulary of something like the clinic, though not the Salpêtrière itself, perhaps suggest that the novel is interested in the chain of wild substitutions – those endless metaphorical slidings of hysteria – that evoke the refusal of the syncretic processes of coherent personality in favour of 'a woman who is beast turning human' (59) and back again. As Daniela Caselli has shown, *Nightwood* mostly refuses modernist free indirect discourse and the depths of consciousness it invokes (2009, 157–8); instead, words, images and people are constantly on the slide. Disaggregation and then the reformation of other meanings around a heightened *idée fixe* that has its own symbolic logic and chains of association but that, unlike in Janet's world, are always subject to the possibility of collapse mirror *Nightwood*'s mode and mood, but do not offer a key to its meaning. Instead, modernism and psychology reflect on each other to intimate how in *Nightwood* 'all needs to be made sense of, nothing simply is' (Caselli, 2009, 163). All syntheses seem too weak to hold, and the fixities present in the text come to feel more like fixations – fixations without any subject to anchor them.

Recording as They Fall

Returning once again to Woolf's 'Modern Fiction', there is another word that might capture our attention in the famous phrase: 'Let us record the atoms as they fall' – and that is 'record'. Much modernist literary criticism over the past two decades has been concerned with mapping the relationship between modernist literature and the new writing and recording technologies that emerged coextensively with it (see Armstrong, Trotter). As Friedrich Kittler's work has emphasized, one of the distinctive differences between the modes of representation that had been used for millennia and the new representational technologies that emerged in the latter half of the nineteenth century was the removal of human translation from the scene. Photosensitized paper or celluloid and wax cylinders were all able to record the data of the world directly, without a mediating consciousness. Without having to submit information through judgement, the new 'indexical' media of phonograph and film camera (invented in 1877 and 1888, respectively) registered the imprint of the real rather than representation. They recorded atoms literally as they fell, without distinction between random data and meaningful configurations, while meaning-making was reconceptualized as a process of filtering signal (intended information) from noise. Kittler forges a link between these writing and recording technologies, and a new account of mind in the work of scientists such as Gustav Fechner. Rejecting the Kantian philosophical orthodoxy that the mind could not be subjected to experiment or be quantified mathematically, in 1860 Fechner set up empirically reproducible experiments on sensation to which he gave the name psychophysics. He bridged the gap between the study of the mind and the methodologies of the physical sciences and physiology, testing the relationship between physical stimuli and the sensations and perceptions they affect through phenomena such as reaction times that precede conscious mentation. For Kittler, the mind subjected to these experiments is refigured accordingly as a recording machine that, as with a phonogram, is inscribed with both significant sound and noise without qualitative distinction (1990, 206–64). Kittler suggests that because psychophysics reads the mind as a *tabula rasa* onto which data is imprinted and then replayed, structures of meaning in the mind are once again figured as emergent and contingent rather than immanent.

The aspect of literary modernism that most interests Kittler is the transcription of nonsense and noise in Dada and Surrealism that mirrors the storage capacities of the new media and, he argues, reproduces the words and sounds that emerge from new psychological experimentation and come to visibility in the disorders of the aphasic, the psychotic, the hysteric. André Breton, who had worked with war-shattered soldiers on a neurological ward in Nantes, indeed recommends in 1924, via his reading of Janet and James, an artistic method that returns to the automatic writing experiments of William James' psychological laboratory of the 1880s:[3]

> Write quickly, without any preconceived subject, fast enough so that you will not remember that you are writing and be tempted to reread what you have written
> [...] Put your trust in the inexhaustible murmur. (Breton, 1972, 29–30)

Futurism mimics the mechanical sounds of the world of noise – zong-toomb-toomb – while Joyce's '*Ulysses*-gramophone' is interested in both sound and linguistic sense, recording the noise of the train in Molly's bedroom ('frseeeeeeee eeeeeeeeeeeefrong') (Joyce, 1992, 904) as well as the noise of her free associations from which background sounds can only imperfectly be differentiated.

In a famous description of psychoanalytic technique, Freud makes a link between new media and the unconscious mind by comparing the analyst to a telephone receiver. 'The doctor must put himself in a position to make use of everything he is told for the purposes of interpretation and of recognizing the concealed unconscious material without substituting a censorship of his own', he writes: 'To put it in a formula: he must turn his own unconscious like a receptive organ towards the transmitting unconscious of the patient. He must adjust himself to the patient as a telephone receiver is adjusted to the transmitting microphone' (1912, 114–15). Here, we find Freud turning to portions of the psyche and communications that lie both below and before the structuring, interpretative, selective aspects of the rational, conscious mind. All must be admitted – sense and nonsense, significant sound and noise – for new structures of meaning to reveal themselves to interpretation. But this overdetermined metaphor is also a useful figure for thinking through how literary modernism and psychology might relate to one another. For we see a technology of modernity – a seemingly objective mechanical ear – invoked in a process that cannot easily be submitted to empirical scientific method: the meeting of two unconscious minds. Freud's example indeed focuses attention precisely on the impossibility of separating modern objects and methods from sites of subjectivity and desire. David Trotter has recently brought literature and the cultural history of telephony into productive exchange by showing how each reveals in the other a complex negotiation of the 'transgressive erotics of connection' (2013, 57). What Freud's image of the telephone receiver might similarly offer is an intimation of just how entangled technological and scientific modernity is with elements that pull against its putative objectivity.

As Mark Micale notes, the late nineteenth-century understanding of the functioning of the mind and its relationship to a body is not easily matched with contemporary disciplinary formations. 'Distinct intellectual and disciplinary counterparts to early twenty-first-century psychiatry, neurology, psychology, and philosophy of mind did not exist', he writes. To complicate things further, late nineteenth-century psychological medicine also clearly emerged from contact with fields of enquiry now figured as determinedly unscientific: 'hypnosis, somnambulism, psychical research, magnetotherapy, metallotherapy, dream interpretation, mediumistic psychology, automatic writing, faith healing, and spiritualism' (Micale, 2004, 10). Janet spent considerable time tracking spiritualist modes of automatic writing alongside manifestations of hysteria in asylums. James investigated one Mrs Piper – a medium from Boston who had seemingly developed psychic abilities after a road accident damaged her neurological functioning – without, as Roger Luckhurst notes, ever being able really 'to decide whether her spirit guides and trance selves were psychological or supernatural phenomena' (2008, 41). To go back to the period between 1860 and 1940 is to find oneself in a field of rich and complex interactions where disciplinary borders had not yet hardened, and the borders between scientific and cultural spheres were particularly porous. Although one story the history of science and medicine likes to tell is an essentially Whiggish account of inevitable progression and improvement, with scientific psychology emancipating itself from past mistakes by purifying itself of its non-scientific elements, such a narrative is a particular distortion of the messy, noisy networks of association, influence and mutual constitution in this period of modernity. In fact, the psychology of the period precisely mirrors literary modernism's own paradoxical relationship with the complexity of the modern moment – its concern with both positivism and atavism, new technologies and the body's primal drives, scientized rationality and 'primitive' irrationality.

Psychoanalysis and the Night-Mind

On 17 June 1936, an elderly man who would soon have to flee the country of his birth received the gift of a letter published in *The New Republic*:

> Sir: The eightieth birthday of Sigmund Freud gives us the welcome opportunity of offering our congratulations and homage to the Master whose discoveries have opened up the way to a new and profounder understanding of mankind. He has made eminent contributions to medicine, psychology, philosophy and

art [...] The ideas he formulated and the terms he coined have become part of our daily life, and in every field of knowledge, in literature, art, research, history of religion, prehistory, mythology, folklore, pedagogy and, last but not least, in poetry, we can trace his influence. The most memorable achievement of our generation will be, beyond doubt, the psychological achievement of Sigmund Freud. [...] *Thomas Mann, Romain Rolland, Jules Romains, H.G. Wells, Virginia Woolf, Stefan Zweig.* (Mann et al., 1936)

Given that Woolf claimed she did not read Freud until 1939, though paradoxically suggested that she scanned his words while typesetting the *International Psychoanalytic Library* for the Hogarth Press in 1924, this underwriting of Freud's cultural authority seems positively ripe for a psychoanalytic reading in its lack of straightforwardness. When Woolf did admit to reading the work, three years later and only after his death, she owned in her diary of 8 December 1939 to 'gulping up Freud', seeming finally to allow herself to gorge on an influence that had been so defensively disowned in the 1920s.

Even though Woolf appeared keen to avoid reading Freud in the 1920s, Elizabeth Abel has described how she was embedded in a world profoundly conscious of psychoanalytic ideas. James and Alix Strachey, part of the Bloomsbury Group, were both analysed by Freud in 1920 and dominated the translation and dissemination of his ideas through the Hogarth Press. Woolf's brother Adrian Stephen and his wife Karin were enthusiastically converted to psychoanalysis and undertook trainings. Melanie Klein, who was to have such a profound influence on the development of theories of 'object relations' that are still the main accent of British psychoanalysis, came to 50 Gordon Square (the Stephens' home) in 1925 to deliver lectures to Ernest Jones' newly formed British Psycho-analytic Society. As Frosh points out, Klein's emphasis on understanding destructive impulses and moving towards the possibility of reparation may have seemed particularly compelling following the perceived irrationality of the slaughter of the Great War (2003, 116–7), and the hope in some modernist quarters that art might, in T. S. Eliot's terms, be a way of 'controlling, of ordering, of giving a shape and a significance to the immense panorama of futility and anarchy which is contemporary history' (1923, 483). Nevertheless, Woolf was explicitly hostile to psychoanalysis in the 1910s and 1920s (Jouve, 2000, 254–6), referring to the Freud she 'read' while typesetting as an expression of 'gull-eyed imbecility' (Woolf, 1977, 135). And yet, in 'A Sketch of the Past' (1939), she speaks of a cathartic process that resembles Freud's idea of 'remembering, repeating and working through' the traumatic loss of her parents. She indeed admits that after writing *To the Lighthouse*, she 'ceased to be obsessed by [her] mother, I no longer hear her voice. I do not see her. I suppose I did for myself what psychoanalysts do for their patients [...] And in expressing it I explained it and then laid it to rest' (1982, 94).

Woolf's hostility to undertaking a personal analysis may have been linked to a worry about undoing the knots from which her creative process was untangled; still, as can be seen in 'Modern Fiction', Woolf felt that '[f]or the Moderns, "that", the point of interest, lies very likely in the dark places of psychology' (1994, 161). As Michael Rustin has noted, one of the aims some literary modernisms and psychoanalysis shared was to 'extend the domain of reason to the sphere of the emotions, and of the residues of irrationality that were not readily comprehensible within rationalistic categories' (1999, 106). Of course, Surrealism and Dada were not interested in the extension of reason, but in hearing and recording the noise that emanated from the unconscious, and many literary modernists, like Freud himself, remained ambivalent about the wedge of unfathomable, motivating darkness at the core of subjectivity. At moments Freud aimed psychoanalysis at reclamation:

> The intention of psychoanalysis, is to strengthen the ego, to make it more independent of the super-ego, to widen its field of perception and enlarge its organization, so that it can appropriate fresh portions of the id. [...] Where id was there ego shall be. It is the work of culture – not unlike the draining of the Zuider Zee. (1933, 79)

Yet persistently, Freud suggested that the work of culture might have a more troubling place in the battle for expression between conscious and unconscious elements. Against the reclamation work of what came to be known as 'ego psychology', it was Jacques Lacan's 'return to Freud', and to the former's emphasis on the question of language, that reconfigured psychoanalysis not as a search for stable ground but as a place where more radically disruptive structures of self based on the slidings of signification could find their voice.

One of the earliest literary enthusiasts for Freud was D. H. Lawrence. In *Psychoanalysis and the Unconscious* (1921), he praises Freud's vitalism, stating:

> We must discover, if we can, the true unconscious, where our life bubbles up in us, prior to any mentality. The first bubbling life in us, which is innocent of any mental alteration, this is the unconscious. [...] It is the spontaneous origin from which it behooves us to live. (Lawrence, 1962, 13)

Lawrence, though, had less time for Freud's systematizing, and for a large strand of what might be called Romantic Modernism, it was Carl Jung's analytical psychology, rather than Freud's psychoanalysis that was always searching out scientific respectability, that offered greater creative possibilities. As is well known, Jung and Freud acrimoniously split in 1913, seemingly (though not completely) due to Jung's insistence that libido need not necessarily be sexual. Jung had worked as a psychiatrist with Bleuler at the Burghölzli Psychiatric Hospital in Zurich, and there began to outline a theory of complexes related to the psychogenesis of *dementia praecox* (later, schizophrenia), to show how delusional formations had their own difficult but explicable logic. Influenced by Freud, but unlike him in that he did not primarily see neurotic patients, Jung drew from the study of psychosis the idea that the psyche includes repressed personal material, as Freud insists, but that there is also unrepressed material in the unconscious – material that had never been known to consciousness. Jung's interest in this 'collective unconscious' meant that, like many modernists, he was drawn to Romantic accounts of creativity and to valorizing what was considered to be pre-modern or 'primitive' to trace the patterns of significance behind and beneath the crust of social modernity.

In the late 1920s and into the 1930s, it was through the writer and publisher Eugene Jolas that the most sustained relationship between modernism and Jung's work took place. Jolas was a multilingual American working in Paris, whose magazine *transition* aimed to explore how literary innovation – a 'Revolution of the Word' – might reshape the human subject, connecting people back to a primal, pre-modern unity. In *transition* 15, Jolas proclaims the need for a new language: 'We need the twentieth century word. We need the word of movement, the word expressive of the great new forces around us [...] The new vocabulary and the new syntax must help destroy the ideology of a rotting civilization' (Jolas, 1929, 13). In James Joyce's 'Work in Progress' (later to become *Finnegans Wake*) published in *transition*, Jolas thought he had found a mode of writing able to tap into a universal linguistic unconscious. And in *The Language of the Night* (1932), Jolas goes on to affirm that it is only the poet, as spiritual medium, who can bore down vertically into the primal elements of language: 'the poet in giving back to language its pre-logical function makes a spiritual revolution – the only revolution worth making today' (Jolas, 1932a, 60).

In 'Literature and the New Man' (1930), Jolas turns his aesthetic and spiritual project from the Freudian notion of the personal unconscious, which was too scientized, too in tune with what rationality wants, towards Jung:

> In the essay which *transition* is publishing in this issue ['Psychology and Poetry'], an epochal step forward has been made. Not only does the unconscious express the repressed elements of the personal life of the creator, says Dr Jung, but it is also the vessel containing elements that relate him to the collective life of

humanity [...] [T]he poet gathers these forces in him and presents them through his conscious act as a revivified condition of the personal-collective unconscious. [...] The creative imagination is not a priori a rational one. It proceeds from the primal, almost somnambulistic phase to that of intuition. Then the intelligence sets in. (Jolas, 1930, 17)

Jolas's Romantic Modernist manifesto 'Poetry Is Vertical' that appears in *transition* 21 (1930) follows this idea of the purpose of poetry:

> The transcendental 'I' with its multiple stratifications reaching back millions of years [...] is brought to the surface with the hallucinatory irruption of images in the dream, the daydream, the mystic-gnostic trance, and even the psychiatric condition.
>
> The final disintegration of the 'I' in the creative act is made possible by the use of language which is a mantic instrument. (Jolas et al., 1932, 148)

In 'Night-Mind and Day-Mind' (1932), Jolas affirms his commitment to language as a form of psychological, mystical connection: 'We have today means for investigating the night-mind and day-mind [...] Psychology has opened the gates of the chthonian world. It is a world within our reach' (Jolas, 1932b, 223). As will be clear, Jung and Jolas are representatives of a modernism that was never simply modern.

Joyce never consented to having an analysis with Jung,[4] though some artists took the opportunity of undergoing a practice felt by some to be 'the most memorable achievement of our generation' (Mann et al., 1936). Bryher, for example, arranged for her partner H.D. to have a three-month analysis with Freud in 1933, from which the compelling book *Tribute to Freud* (1956) emerged. But for most writers, psychoanalysis, like other psychologies, was encountered through a complex network of experiences of reading, conversing, living that can be hard to reduce to singular sources or lines of influence. Even when one has the notes Samuel Beckett typed up on psychoanalysis and psychology while having therapy with Wilfred Bion in the 1930s (see Feldman), such sources offer only a compelling start, rather than an end, to any analysis of the importance these accounts of the mind had for a modernist writer. The Beckett and Bion encounter is indeed instructively unproductive of any simple account of influence. For Beckett was struggling to get his writing going and published at that fraught moment, while Bion, who was later to become one of the most significant figures in the theory and practice of psychoanalysis in the British context, had not undergone a psychoanalytic training at the time he was working with Beckett. Beckett terminated the therapy early, though later averred that it had helped him; Bion never suggested that his experience with Beckett had been particularly significant for his theory and practice. Technical terms from psychoanalysis and other psychologies resonate throughout Beckett's work, but always in ambivalent, parodic ways, with the discourses looking askance at one another. Nevertheless, psychoanalysis does give literary critics some tools for thinking through the anxieties of influence, the unstable lines of power in the citation of authority, the inconsistencies of memory and the defences of both conformity and rebellion that saturate evocations of the modernist mind. Perhaps to understand the 'turn inwards', then, it is most important to have one's ear turned receptively outwards, to the complex lines of connection in the discursive networks where radical literary forms and new notions of mind come into charged contact.

Notes

1   Freud introduced the concept of transference to explain how patients frequently unconsciously remember and then repeat difficult past experiences with significant people (such as parents) with their analyst. By analysing this mode of relating rather than rejecting, judging or colluding with it, Freud suggests that psychoanalysis can unravel or 'work through' in the present the problems of the past.
2   See Didi-Huberman (2003) for these images and an analysis of their construction as theatrical 'set-pieces'.
3   See Armstrong (1998, 187–219).
4   For an illuminating account of the contact between Joyce and Jung, including the latter's rather bad-tempered essay on *Ulysses* and Jung's treatment of Joyce's daughter Lucia, see Rabaté (2014, 150–5).

Bibliography

Abel, E. (1989), *Virginia Woolf and the Fictions of Psychoanalysis*. Chicago and London: University of Chicago Press.

Aragon, L. and Breton, A. (1948), 'Le cinquantenaire de l'hystérie (1878–1928)', in M. Nadeau (ed.), *Histoire du Surréalisme: Documents surréaliste*. Paris: Seuil, p. 125.

Armstrong, T. (1998), *Modernism, Technology and the Body*. Cambridge: Cambridge University Press.

Barnes, D. (1950), *Nightwood*. London: Faber and Faber.

Baudelaire, C. (1992), 'The Painter of Modern Life', in P. E. Charvet (ed.), *Selected Writings on Art and Literature*. London: Penguin, pp. 390–435.

Breton, A. (1972), *Manifesto of Surrealism*, in *Manifestos of Surrealism*, R. Seaver and H. R. Lane (transl.). Ann Arbor MI: University of Michigan Press.

Breuer, J. (1893), 'Fräulein Anna O', in *Case Histories from Studies on Hysteria*. The Standard Edition of the Complete Psychological Works of Sigmund Freud, *Vol. II (1893–95)*. London: Hogarth Press, pp. 19–47.

Caselli, D. (2009), *Improper Modernism: Djuna Barnes's Bewildering Corpus*. Farnham: Ashgate.

Crary, J. (1990), *Techniques of the Observer: On Vision and Modernity in the Nineteenth Century*. Cambridge, MA: MIT Press.

Crary, J. (1999), *Suspensions of Perception: Attention, Spectacle, and Modern Culture*. Cambridge, MA: MIT Press.

Didi-Huberman, G. (2003), *The Invention of Hysteria: Charcot and the Photographic Imaginary of the Salpêtrière*, A. Hartz (transl.). Cambridge, MA: MIT Press.

Eliot, T. S. (1923), 'Ulysses, Order and Myth'. *The Dial*, 75 (November), 480–3.

Ellenberger, H. (1994), *The Discovery of the Unconscious*. London: Fontana.

Feldman, M. (2006), *Beckett's Books: A Cultural History of the Interwar Notes*. London: Continuum.

Ford, F. M. (1964), 'On Impressionism', in F. MacShane (ed.), *The Critical Writings of Ford Madox Ford*. Lincoln, NA: University of Nebraska Press, pp. 33–55.

Ford, F. M. (1972), *The Good Soldier: A Tale of Passion*. Harmondsworth, Penguin.

Freud, S. (1900), *The Interpretation of Dreams*, in *The Standard Edition of the Complete Psychological Works of Sigmund Freud, Vol. IV*. London: Hogarth Press, pp. ix–627.

Freud, S. (1912), 'Recommendations to Physicians Practising Psycho-Analysis', in *The Standard Edition of the Complete Psychological Works of Sigmund Freud, Vol. XII (1911–1913)*. London: Hogarth Press, pp. 109–20.

Freud, S. (1933), 'New Introductory Lectures on Psycho-Analysis', in *The Standard Edition of the Complete Psychological Works of Sigmund Freud, Vol. XXII (1932–1936)*. London: Hogarth Press, pp. 1–182.

Frosh, S. (2003), 'Psychoanalysis in Britain: "The Rituals of Destruction"', in D. Bradshaw (ed.), *A Concise Companion to Modernism*. Oxford: Blackwell.

H. D. (1974), *Tribute to Freud*. Boston: D. R. Godine.

James, W. (1983), *The Principles of Psychology*. Cambridge, MA: Harvard University Press.

Janet, P. (1901), *The Mental State of Hystericals: A Study of Mental Stigmata and Accidents*, C. Corson (transl.). New York: Putnam's.

Janet, P. (1907), *The Major Symptoms of Hysteria*. New York: Macmillan, 1907.

Jolas, E. (1929), 'Proclamation: The Revolution of the Word'. *transition*, 16, (17), 13.

Jolas, E. (1930), 'Literature and the New Man'. *transition*, 19/20, 13–19.

Jolas, E. (1932a), *The Language of the Night*. The Hague: Servire Press.

Jolas, E. (1932b), 'Night-Mind and Day-Mind'. *transition*, 21, 222–3.

Jolas, E. et al. (1932c), 'Poetry Is Vertical', *transition*, 21, 148–9.

Jouve, N. W. (2000), 'Woolf and Psychoanalysis', in S. Rogers and S. Sellers (eds), *Cambridge Companion to Virginia Woolf*, Cambridge: Cambridge University Press, pp. 245–72.

Joyce, J. (1992), *Ulysses: Annotated Students' Edition*. London: Penguin.

Kant, I. (1965), *Critique of Pure Reason*, N. K. Smith (transl.). New York: St Martin's Press.

Kittler, F. (1990), *Discourse Networks, 1800/1900*, M. Metteer, with C. Cullens (transl.). Stanford, CA: Stanford University Press.

Lacan, J. (2007), 'The Instance of the Letter in the Unconscious, or Reason since Freud', in *Ecrits: The First Complete Edition in English*, B. Fink (transl.). London: W. W. Norton and Co.

Lawrence, D. H. (1962), *Psychoanalysis and the Unconscious*. New York: Viking.

Levenson, M. (1984), 'Character in The Good Soldier'. *Twentieth Century Literature*, 30, (4), 373–87.

Luckhurst, R. (2008), *The Trauma Question*. London: Routledge.

Mann, T., Rolland, R., Romains, J., Wells, H. G., Woolf, V. and Zweig, S. (1936), 'For Sigmund Freud's 80th Birthday'. *The New Republic*, 17 June 1936.

Marcus, L. (2014), *Dreams of Modernity: Psychoanalysis, Literature, Cinema*. Cambridge: Cambridge University Press.

McKendrick, J. G. (1874), *A Review of Recent Researches on the Physiology of the Nervous System*. Edinburgh.

Micale, M. (2004), 'The Modernist Mind: A Map', in Mark Micale (ed.), *The Mind of Modernism: Medicine, Psychology, and the Cultural Arts in Europe and America, 1880–1940*. Stanford, CA: Stanford University Press, pp. 1–20.

Rabaté, J.-M. (2014), *The Cambridge Introduction to Literature and Psychoanalysis*. Cambridge: Cambridge University Press.

Rustin, M. (1999), 'Psychoanalysis: The Last Modernism?' in D. Bell (ed.), *Psychoanalysis and Culture*. London: Duckworth, pp. 105–21.

Ryan, J. (1991), *The Vanishing Subject: Early Psychology and Literary Modernism*. Chicago: University of Chicago Press.

Sinclair, M. (1918), 'The Novels of Dorothy Richardson'. *The Egoist*, (April), 57–9.

Stonebridge, L. (1998), *The Destructive Element: British Psychoanalysis and Modernism*. Basingstoke and London: Macmillan.

Trotter, D. (2013), *Literature in the First Media Age*. Cambridge, MA: Harvard University Press.

Woolf, V. (1964), *To the Lighthouse*. Harmondsworth: Penguin.

Woolf, V. (1977), *A Change of Perspective: The Letters of Virginia Woolf, Vol. 3*, N. Nicolson (ed.). London: Hogarth Press.

Woolf, V. (1982), *Moments of Being: Unpublished Autobiographical Writings*, J. Schulkind (ed.). London: Triad/Granada.

Woolf, V. (1988 [1924]), 'Character in Fiction', in A. McNeillie (ed.), *Essays of Virginia Woolf, Vol. 3*. London: Hogarth Press, pp. 420–38.

Woolf, V. (1994 [1925]), 'Modern Fiction', in A. McNeillie (ed.), *Essays of Virginia Woolf, Vol. 4*. London: Hogarth Press, pp. 157–65.

Woolf, V. (2015), *A Room of One's Own, and Three Guineas*. Oxford: Oxford University Press.

17

Modernism and Technology

Julian Murphet

At a critical point in his epic, 'A', Louis Zukofsky writes: 'Technology throws light upon mental conceptions' (1981, 58). He is adapting a footnote to 'the development of machinery' in *Capital*, Vol. 1, where Marx proposes that 'Technology reveals the active relation of man to nature, the direct process of the production of his life, and thereby it also lays bare the process of the production of the social relations of his life, and of the mental conceptions that flow from those relations' (1990, 494). Elaborating what he elsewhere calls the ineluctable 'metabolism' between human beings and their natural environments, Marx establishes technology as the chief organ of – and hermeneutical key to – that metabolism in the modern period. Technology's general interpretive function, its light-shedding quality, is second to none in the period of large-scale industry, during which articulated systems of automated machinery for the first time in history subordinated working people as so many 'conscious organs [...] of the automaton' (Marx, 1990, 544). Indeed, *Capital* can be read as one gargantuan projection of a cellular chiasmus in which people become things, and things assume the qualities of people, thanks to modern technology's assumption of the role of 'master' (549). And when, as Veblen remarked, 'the machine process makes use of the workman' (1922, 306), technology becomes invested with explosive explanatory power.

Critical theory's account of modern technology highlights the social basis of its application. Herbert Marcuse writes that 'Technology, as a mode of production, as the totality of instruments, devices and contrivances which characterise the machine age is thus at the same time a mode of organizing and perpetuating (or changing) social relationships, a manifestation of prevalent thought and behaviour patterns, an instrument for control and domination' (1982, 138–9). Technology is simultaneously a system of apparatuses and devices, and the set of social relations that makes them necessary. It is a *social logic*; it participates in the contradictions of the mode of production – capitalism – that assumes it. But for all that, in its physical form, it is capitalism *instantiated*, materialized. It is the social totality inscribing itself in space and regulating time; the exoskeleton of a self-conflicted socio-economic organism that, for a time, works, and then, overnight, is discarded like a cicada husk. The museum of technology is the fossil record of capitalism, encoding its dynamics and processes in legible material signatures. It is thus, in its own way, a cultural phenomenon, a system of signs.

Somewhat earlier in his poem, Zukofsky cites Marx's political antipode, Henry Ford:

> Industry itself is a part of culture.
> …
> We need beauty in everything, and culture
> Should be a thing of practice,
> Not something apart.
> Everything should be a thing of beauty,
> Well made and well thought out. (26)

This distinctively American response to the technologization of the lifeworld in modernity proposes that we strike out the constitutive difference between 'base' and 'superstructure'. Technology allows the commodification of culture, even as it permits the 'acculturation' of commodities. Thanks to technical design, everything is now cultural, even as everything is also economic, but the technological universalization of the aesthetic is also its demise. As Hugh Kenner once put it, 'Technology tended to engulf people gradually, coercing behaviour they were not aware of' (1987, 10). The diffusion of technocratic rationality, efficiency and conformity throughout the modern is not immediate. It consists in a pervasive radiation, through disparate media, of inbuilt presuppositions of value that gradually, but inevitably, displace and extinguish the 'principle of individualism' on which the bourgeois era had been ideologically predicated. The inevitable historical displacement of smaller manufacturing enterprises by large-scale, concentrated forms of economic organization bears strange cultural and ideological fruit. Technology 'characterises the pervasive mode of thought and even the manifold forms of protest and rebellion. This rationality establishes standards of judgement and fosters attitudes which make men ready to accept and even to introcept the dictates of the apparatus' (Marcuse, 1982, 141).

Modernism experienced the technological saturation of literary substance intimately. But it did so in two rather different ways: at the level of content and at the level of form. Cultural labour, or the aesthetic, has often been analysed in terms of a structuration of phenomenological and existential materials – a putting of 'raw' experiential content to work in 'cooked' formal apparatuses that have their own technical histories and laws of development. We must therefore think of literature's relation to the second machine age in a double sense: on the one hand, there is a profound alteration within the very raw material itself, the experiential phenomena in need of aesthetic organization; on the other hand, there is the contagious effect of the technological era on the 'laws of art' that make formalization possible in the first place. These distinct levels can be presented separately.

Technical Phenomena

In an important essay dating from the dawn of the Atomic Age, Martin Heidegger argues that the 'essence of technology' consists in its adversarial relationship to nature, a relationship defined by the constitutive challenge it poses: that nature stand forth and reveal itself as so much stored energy, what he calls 'standing-reserve'. This 'enframing' dictates 'that nature reports itself in some way or other that is identifiable through calculation and that it remains orderable as a system of information' (Heidegger, 1977, 23). The logic of quantification is an 'extreme danger', Heidegger remarks, since not only does it deny to us some more originary and authentic 'experience [of] the call of a more primal truth' (28), and thereby 'blocks *poiesis*', it takes us 'to the very brink of a precipitous fall; [man] comes to the point where he himself will have to be taken as standing reserve' (27). Just as Marx had shown that the business of modern large-scale industry was to reduce working people to so many interchangeable units of labour power, Heidegger cries out against technology's tendency to convert us into batteries of 'standing-reserve', to drive the machine system ever forward.

Literature's reflection on this dangerous 'enframing' begins in earnest with that great epic of the Reformation, Milton's *Paradise Lost*. One of the key moments takes place in the war in heaven and concerns Satan's sudden realization that heaven can itself be enframed as a standing-reserve. In his rebellious need for 'more valid Armes/Weapons more violent' (Milton, 1969, 329), Satan calls to mind a scene 'Deep under ground, [where] materials dark and crude,/Of spiritous and fierie spume' await release as so much combustible energy: 'pregnant with infernal flame' (330). It is a vision to grip the rebel army's imagination and incite their toil:

in a moment up they turnd
Wide the Celestial soile, and saw beneath
Th' originals of Nature in thir crude
Conception; Sulphurous and Nitrous Foame
They found, they mingl'd, and with suttle Art,
Concocted and adusted they reduc'd
To blackest grain, and into store convey'd:
Part hidd'n veins diggd up (nor hath this Earth
Entrails unlike) of Mineral and Stone,
Whereof to found thir Engins and thir Balls
Of missive ruin; part incentive reed
Provide, pernicious with one touch to fire. (Milton, 1969, 331)

Avant la lettre, Heidegger's notion of 'standing-reserve' has rarely been more precisely distilled into an aesthetic image. Milton attends, in the sinuous rolling-out of his blank-verse syntax, to the imbrication of spiritual, natural and bodily layers in the Satanic 'challenge' of technology to nature. The martial dream of conquest, the slumbering muscular powers of the diabolic legions and the subterranean elements themselves, all are woven into an incendiary figure for the technological itself: an army equipped with its obscene 'Engins'.

Goethe, in his *Faust*, could scarcely excel this almighty anticipation of the age of technology, although his hero's culminating task, at the end of Part II, is to force nature's 'elemental power unharnessed, purposeless' (Goethe, 1990, verse 10219) into grand development schemes. Marshall Berman sums up the alarming technological vision of capitalist modernity there vouchsafed:

> Suddenly the landscape around him metamorphoses into a site. He outlines great reclamation projects to harness the sea for human purposes: man-made harbours and canals that can move ships full of goods and men; dams for large-scale irrigation; green fields and forests, pastures and gardens, a vast and intensive agriculture; waterpower to attract and support emerging industries; thriving settlements, new towns and cities to come – and all this to be created out of a barren wasteland. (Berman, 1983, 62)

Once again the sublime literary image of a Satanic pact distils the 'essence of technology' into a vision of global transformation. The earth (the immemorial elements in their cosmic unity) is to be violently converted into a 'world', a humanized habitat, by virtue of the prodigious application of technical knowledge and regimented labour: 'Take up your tools, stir shovel now and spade!/What has been staked must at once be made' (Goethe, 1990, 463).

Literature anticipated and disclosed the modern technological age better than any other medium or format. Within 100 years of *Faust*, industrial reality had literally become Faustian, capable of gargantuan feats of transformation, such that literature itself was challenged at its core. Marx reflected wonderingly on this in the introduction to his *Grundrisse*:

> It is well known that Greek mythology is not only the arsenal of Greek art but also its foundation. Is the view of nature and of social relations on which the Greek imagination and hence Greek [mythology] is based possible with self-acting mule spindles and railways and locomotives and electrical telegraphs? What chance has Vulcan against Roberts and Co., Jupiter against the lightning-rod and Hermes against the Credit Mobilier? All mythology overcomes and dominates and shapes the forces of nature in the imagination and by the imagination; it therefore vanishes with the advent of real mastery over them. What becomes of Fama alongside Printing House Square? (Marx, 1993, 110)

The consequences of this line of thinking are staggering. Literature, an analogical system of information subsisting on chains of association and reference stretching back to mythological templates and figures, suddenly finds its substructure deracinated. The hereditary power of myth 'vanishes' at a stroke in the kingdom of technology, where (as Marx phrased it in the *Manifesto*)

> The bourgeoisie, during its rule of scarce one hundred years, has created more massive and more colossal productive forces than have all preceding generations together. Subjection of Nature's forces to man, machinery, application of chemistry to industry and agriculture, steam-navigation, railways, electric telegraphs, clearing of whole continents for cultivation, canalisation of rivers, whole populations conjured out of the ground – what earlier century had even a presentiment that such productive forces slumbered in the lap of social labour? (Marx and Engels, 1978, 477)

These actual Faustian powers, once unleashed as history, challenged the very forms in which Goethe and Milton had anticipated their arrival, for the epic and the dramatic poem lose their conventional bearings in a technically subjugated world.

Heidegger's deeper worry, as we saw, was what this portended for 'man' himself, exposed in this new horizon as so much manipulable stored energy. The modern genre of science fiction is where some of the more striking formal developments of that worry are made good. H. P. Lovecraft's story 'The Whisperer in Darkness' concerns the frustrated intercourse between two lonely, single men in New England, brought into virtual contact by way of a controversy in the local papers. Their disavowed homoerotic bond is displaced onto a fantastic race of beings from the interstellar wastes whose colossal, unsexed brains communicate via tech-free telepathy. The first part of the tale concerns the efforts of the older man to convince the younger that these beings exist, a task made possible only by technological mediation: photographs of the beings' clawprints and a phonograph recording of one of their inhuman voices – 'like the drone of some loathsome, gigantic insect ponderously shaped into the articulate speech of an alien species' (Lovecraft, 1984, 227). The second part reveals the nature of the beings' plans for the men they desire, which turns on an application of the phonographic principle to the central nervous system. Prefiguring our digital fantasies of neural downloads by eighty years or more, Lovecraft asks his reader to imagine

> a harmless way to extract a brain, and a way to keep the organic residue alive
> during its absence. The bare, compact cerebral matter was then immersed in an
> occasionally replenished fluid within an ether-tight cylinder of a metal mined
> in Yuggoth, certain electrodes reaching through and connecting at will with
> elaborate instruments capable of duplicating the three vital faculties of sight,
> hearing, and speech. (Lovecraft, 1984, 257)

Thus, the information-rich human 'soul' is reduced to its rudimentary biological essentials and made transportable: 'It was as simple as carrying a phonograph record about and playing it wherever a phonograph of corresponding make exists' (Lovecraft, 1984, 257–8). Man himself is here very literally 'taken as standing-reserve', just as Heidegger would caution: a battery of neural energy encased in electrified chambers of ether-proof metal, ready for exportation.

So it is that the 'relationships among men are increasingly mediated by the machine process. But the mechanical contrivances which facilitate intercourse among individuals also intercept and absorb their libido, thereby diverting it', as Marcuse observed (1982, 144). Just as the cylinders absorb whatever erotic energies subsisted between Wilmarth and Akeley in Lovecraft's tale, so too the gramophone seems to have arrogated to itself the sexual excitement conspicuously missing from the tryst between the typist and her 'young clerk carbuncular' in T. S. Eliot's 'Fire Sermon' section of *The Waste Land* (1969, 70). To be sure, as Juan Suárez puts it, 'the gramophone highlights the squalor of the scene and comes to stand for the vulgarity and disenchantment of contemporary existence' (Suárez, 2007, 124), but all the same, the nameless song her 'automatic hand' elicits from the machine presumably gives both voice and formulaic melodic shape to an affect, an intensity, that the typist was unable to feel during her actual intercourse. 'Well now that's done: and I'm glad it's over', she mutters to herself as he skulks off (Eliot, 1969, 70); glad presumably because she can now experience in a hit tune what she was unable to in the event. Constant Lambert casts a censorious light on this scene: 'second-rate mechanical music is the most suitable fate for those to whom musical experience is no more than a mere aural tickling, just as the prostitute provides the most suitable outlet for those to whom sexual experience is no more than the periodic removal of a recurring itch' (Lambert, 1934, 239). In the modern, technology does most of our perceiving and feeling for us – and we pay for it, in a kind of generalized techno-prostitution. At stake in this wholesale transference is the very status and meaning of that staple concept of Humanism, 'experience'.

Benjamin liked to muse on what he called the contemporary 'poverty of experience' in modernity (Benjamin, 1999, 732), while Adorno complained that 'the very possibility of experience is in jeopardy', thanks to the interposition of technological means between the human nervous system and the environment (Adorno, 1991, 55). Giorgio Agamben, dour inheritor of this line of thought, proposes that experience is 'no longer accessible to us. For just as modern man has been deprived of his biography, his experience has likewise been expropriated' (Agamben, 1993, 13). And the expropriator is above all technology itself. Kenneth Fearing's poem 'Radio Blues' plays with the conceit of turning a radio dial to find the missing existential key:

> 20, 25
> is that what you want, static and a speech and the
> > fragment of a waltz, is that just right
> or what do you want at twelve o'clock, with the visitors
> > gone, and the Scotch running low
> > 30, 35, 35 to 40 and 40 to 50
> free samples of cocoa, and the Better Beer Trio, and
> > hurricane effects for a shipwreck at sea
> but is that just right to match the feeling that you have
>
> > > > (Fearing, 2004, 85–6)

Radio 'turns all participants into listeners and authoritatively subjects them to broadcast programs which are all exactly the same' (Adorno and Horkheimer, 1997, 122), or, not quite, since the format of mass culture is repetition with variation. Fearing's insistent rhetorical question of a customer survey – 'is that what you want', 'is that just right' – seeks to align a narrow range of prefabricated, commercial materials with a mood or subjective disposition whose satisfaction would suddenly amount to the very thing itself, an 'experience'. Somewhere on the dial, the argument satirically proposes, it lies in waiting: that flood of phenomenological intensity flowing from finding exactly what you want without quite knowing what it is or having to work for it. What goes missing in this version of the Romantic formula is of course the very basis of any mood, the 'subject' itself. As the final lines grasp the matter:

> is that what you want to match the feeling that you have
> 9000, 10,000
> would you like to tune in upon your very own life, gone
> somewhere far away.   (Fearing, 2004, 87)

Technology alienates the subject from its own vitality and hardwires it to the apparatus as a biological servomechanism or appendage. The equipment does the experiencing; the human being consumes it.

One obvious corollary of this inversion is that technology, as the receptacle of alienated experience, becomes disproportionately desirable. Technophilia restores vitality to the alienated situation, but not in its wonted place. 'The machine that is adored is no longer dead matter but becomes something like a human being. And it gives back to man what it possesses: the life of the social apparatus to which it belongs', Marcuse adds (1982, 144). Marx's famous chiasmus of commodity fetishism attains here to a tragicomic apotheosis: the technological commodity, a social relation between persons become a thing, is now raised to the level of love object. This is played out in innumerable aesthetic sites of modernism, from Duchamp's 'The Bride Stripped Bare by Her Bachelors, Even' (1915–23), where the cut-out 'bachelors' direct their libidinal energies at a mechanical cross between a hills hoist and a churn, oblivious to the 'bride' herself who looms, unmolested, in an elevated panel chamber, to Eisenstein's legendary 'cream separator' sequence from *The General Line* (1929), to the erotic splicing of Kiki of Montparnasse and an abundance of shiny domestic appliances in Léger's *Ballet mécanique* (1923–24), and beyond. Literature's first fully fledged foray into these dynamics was Villiers de l'Isle-Adam's decadent novel, *L'Ève future* (c. 1886), a modern Pygmalion narrative in which Thomas Alva Edison builds an android with the physical characteristics of his nobleman friend's fiancée, but none of her vacuous psychology – a walking, talking machine with which the frustrated Lord Ewald is all-too ready to fall in love. Indeed, in this substitutive logic it is not just that it becomes possible to love technologically mediated 'things' in place of real women and men, but love itself today knows no other form: persons are always and already the sum total of the 'stuff' through which technology defines them:

I loved my love with a platform ticket,
>A jazz song,
A handbag, a pair of stockings of Paris Sand –
>I loved her long.
I loved her between the lines and against the clock,
>Not until death
But till life did us part I loved her with paper money
>And with whisky on the breath.
I loved her with peacock's eyes and the wares of Carthage,
>With glass and gloves and gold and a powder puff
With blasphemy, camaraderie, and bravado
>And lots of other stuff.
I loved my love with the wings of angels
>Dipped in henna, unearthly red,
With my office hours, with flowers and sirens,
>With my budget, my latchkey, and my daily bread.

>(MacNeice, 2007, 102–3)

In MacNeice's fine satire from 1939, the syntactical form of endless concatenations of mediating 'stuff' (arranged into jingling rhymes and the galloping metre of a 'jazz song') vitiates the love lyric at root by placing the more romantic values (camaraderie, the wares of Carthage, the wings of angels) in equivalent adjacency with the vulgar and mechanical detritus of everyday life. Technology, in making this deluge of libidinal mediation available, supplants the love object herself; for what is 'my love' here but the grey, palimpsestic figure of every stray product used to 'love her' with?

If the love object is 'technologized', so, irresistibly, is the subject itself and the field of their relations. In Dashiell Hammett's unsparing vision of life in a capitalist technocracy, *Red Harvest* (1929), the detective is reduced to a nameless operative, and his investigations into the criminal syndicate that runs the mining town Poisonville amount to an ironic counterpoint between two organizational systems: one institutional and bureaucratic, the other corporate and criminal (Hammett, 2010). The Continental Op's quest for epistemological exposure of the 'machine' that governs the small town thus reflects satiric light on the Continental organization itself, since the common element uniting their 'machineries' is violence: a pitiless and inhuman indifference to the cost in human life made current by a technocratic ascendancy. Cynicism is the appropriate lingua franca of a system in which there is no 'villain' as such, only a machine-like brutality akin to Marx's description of the large-scale industrial process: 'In the factory we have a lifeless mechanism which is independent of the workers, who are incorporated into it as its living appendages' (1990, 548). Hammett's very style is an attempted adequation with this systematic inversion of the relationship between 'man' and 'machine'; the uninflected, brutally direct and indicative language maps a cultural topography deprived of critical distance or reserve. The narrator/protagonist rattles off a kind of machine prose, in keeping with the element he inhabits.

Eugene O'Neill's great play, *The Hairy Ape* (1922), partly set in the mechanical bowels of a transatlantic liner, meditates similarly on the limits to subjectivity set by the technical horizons of modernity. Yank, trying to 't'ink' amid the ruckus of working-class revelry below deck, is met with predictable scorn:

> ALL – [*Repeating the word after him as one with same cynical amused mockery.*]
> Think! [*The chorused word has a brazen metallic quality as if their throats were phonograph horns.*] (O'Neill, 2007, 216)

The ship itself is an allegory for the new industrial conditions whose technological 'enframing' has inverted the traditional metabolism between nature and human labour, as Paddy tells Yank:

> Twas them days men belonged to ships, not now. 'Twas them days a ship was part of the sea, and a man was part of a ship, and the sea joined all together and made it one. [*Scornfully.*] Is it one wid *this* you'd be, Yank – black smoke from the funnels smudging the sea, smudging the decks – the bloody engines pounding and throbbing and shaking – wid divil a sight of sun or a breath of clean air – choking our lungs wid coal dust – breaking our backs and hearts in the hell of the stokehole – feeding the bloody furnace – feeding our lives along wid the coal, I'm thinking – caged in by steel from a sight of the sky like bloody apes in the Zoo! [*With a harsh laugh.*] Ho-ho, divil mend you! Is it to belong to that you're wishing? Is it a flesh and blood wheel of the engines you'd be? (O'Neill, 2007, 221)

Yank responds in the jubilant affirmative, effectively declaring the euphoria of his having become 'standing-reserve', the mindless source of energy for the whole industrial behemoth.

Harry Braverman has documented, with reference to the works of F. W. Taylor, the irreversible decline of workers' intellectual input to the labour process due to the rise of 'scientific management' in modern industrial relations, and the alienation of expertise from increasingly rationalized, efficient movements in the workforce. The splintering of once organic processes on the shop floor into micromanaged sub-gestures and biorhythms spells an absolute loss of control over the working day for workers and the rise of a specialist class of managers whose technical expertise is theoretical rather than practical. Yank's open declaration of his objective status as unskilled labour is delivered in the ironic accents of class pride, but the governing parallelism between himself and a caged gorilla, which comes to a grisly conclusion in the final scene, is underwritten by Taylor's quip that 'This work [pig-iron handling] is so crude and elementary in its nature that the writer firmly believes that it would be possible to train an intelligent gorilla so as to become a more efficient pig-iron handler than any man can be' (Taylor, 2008, 22).

The techno-capitalist social horizon was thus one in which the working class, traditionally imbued with all the various forms of expertise specific to each craft and branch of manufacture, was progressively reduced to merely physical functions. As Antonio Gramsci put it, the new technical division of labour worked by 'developing in the worker to the highest degree automatic and mechanical attitudes, breaking up the old psycho-physical nexus of qualified professional work, which demands a certain active participation of intelligence, fantasy and initiative on the part of the worker, and reducing productive operations exclusively to the mechanical, physical aspect' (Gramsci, 1971, 302). This paradox was the source of a rich vein of 'techno-primitivism' in the modern period (Trotter, 2014, 86–119), but could also be extrapolated in the literary imagination to scenarios of radical species devolution. In H. G. Wells's *The Time Machine*, the surface-dwelling Eloi, in the year AD 802,701, have their care- and toil-free lives paid for by the troglodytic race of subterranean workers, the Morlocks. The Morlocks dwell among technology as apes in a lightless jungle; the traveller's nightmarish descent into their underground world is accompanied by 'the throb-and-hum of machinery' Cyclopean in its intuited scale: 'Great shapes like big machines rose out of the dimness, and cast grotesque black shadows, in which dim spectral Morlocks sheltered from the glare' (Wells, 1963, 44). It is yet another speculative development of Marx's vision of factory labour, where the industrial proletariat is already a virtual race of Morlocks, blinded and stunted by the machinery they tend as servile biomechanical appendages. By the time we reach Allen Ginsberg's 'Howl' in 1955, this ruthless industrial division of labour has spread to the entire workforce under the auspices of a military-industrial complex that can be characterized in terms provided by Ammonite mythology:

> Moloch! Moloch! Robot apartments! invisible suburbs! skeleton treasuries! blind capitals! demonic industries! spectral nations! invincible madhouses! granite cocks! monstrous bombs! (Ginsberg, 2006, 27)

In all, it can be asserted beyond any question that technology was – as gadget, as system and as horizon of being – the most typical 'content' on which modern literary aesthetics went to work: enframing it, in turn, as a material to be challenged and made to declare its own 'standing-reserve' as so much potential artistic energy. Fredric Jameson is hardly overstating the case when he reports modernism's constitutive 'excitement' over machinery, which should be related directly to the unique 'capacity for representation' possessed by the technology that shaped it on all sides: 'the turbine, [...] Sheeler's grain elevators [and] smokestacks, [...] the baroque elaboration of pipes and conveyor belts, [...] the streamlined profile of the railroad train' (Jameson, 1991, 36–7), *ad infinitum*. That excitement knew variable valences and inflections, but it provided an entire cultural dominant with a palpable sign language. 'If everything means something else', Jameson notes of the allegorical situation of modernity, 'then so does technology' (1992, 11). And what technology means is capital.

Technique: The Technology of Form

One could go on indefinitely, notching up the innumerable ways in which modern literature absorbed the system of technology as a 'content' – phenomenological, psychological, political or economic. But perhaps the more interesting question is to what extent the modern technological infrastructure issued challenges to the technical substrate of literature itself. Walter Benjamin once put it this way:

> Rather than asking, 'What is the attitude of a work *to* the relations of production of its time' I would like to ask, 'What is its position *in* them?' This question directly concerns the function the work has within the literary relations of production of its time. It is concerned, in other words, directly with the literary *technique* of works. (Benjamin, 2008, 81)

Benjamin's remarkable 1934 lecture, 'The Author as Producer', adduces the instance of the Russian literary agitator Tretyakov in order to indicate

> how comprehensive the horizon is within which we have to rethink our conceptions of literary forms or genres, in view of the technical factors affecting our present situation [...]. There were not always novels in the past, and there will not always have to be; there have not always been tragedies or great epics. [...] All this is to accustom you to the thought that we are in the midst of a mighty recasting of literary forms, a melting down in which many of the opposites in which we have been used to thinking may lose their force. (Benjamin, 2008, 82)

This radical way of perceiving the problem, which makes vital sense of the many formal revolutions that characterized modernism, hearkens back to Marx's musings on the fate of myth in the techno-modern; the mortality of aesthetic forms is here recast explicitly as a matter of technical competition and redundancy.

For Benjamin, technology challenges literature in its essence; above all it calls forth literature's *own* technical materiality and forces serious verbal artists to assess the pertinence and tendency of all the available tropes, figures, styles, genres, modes, voices, and so on, in relation to the current state of the cultural productive forces. Brecht's theatre provides one sterling example of a 'theatre that, instead of competing with newer instruments of publication, seeks to use and learn from them – in short, to enter into debate with them. This debate the Epic Theatre has made its own affair. It is, measured by the present state of development of film and radio, the contemporary form' (Benjamin, 2008, 90). And indeed, the technologies most openly competitive with the institutionalized practices of literature were those assembled under the all-purpose modern concept of 'media'. In these industrial forms, technology assumed explicitly cultural guises, but transformed the logic of cultural production and distribution, from a condition of 'scarcity' (unique paintings and sculptures in faraway places, limited performance venues for orchestral music and theatrical productions, small print runs for little magazines, etc.) to one of oversupply, thanks to the logistics of mechanical reproducibility. These new media also challenged literature in a more specifically technical way. As Friedrich Kittler puts it, 'The ability to record sense data technologically shifted the entire discourse network circa 1900. For the first time in history, writing ceased to be synonymous with the serial storage of data. The technological recording of the real entered into competition with the symbolic registration of the Symbolic' (Kittler, 1990, 229–30). Writing's monopoly over information not only collapsed, but the very authority of discourse itself looked diseased alongside these indexical traces of the non-symbolizable 'Real'.

Paradoxically, however, it was generally the case that these extraordinary new means of communication and representation lagged aesthetically behind the older media, like literature, now thrown into crisis by their irresistible ascendancy. Rather than pursue their own technical consequences in a conscious reinvention of the senses and affects, cinema and radio adapted their forms to already exhausted materials from the literary archive: adapting melodramatic scenarios and narratives from the Victorian sentimental tradition. Bolter and Grusin (2000) call this process remediation, a constant law in media revolution whereby newer technologies, in order to establish their legitimacy, tend to masquerade in the guise of already consecrated media. As Marshall McLuhan put it, 'the "content" of any medium is always another medium' (McLuhan, 2001, 8). But if that is the case, then Benjamin's provocations raise the problem from the other side: while cinema, say, was busy cannibalizing the back-catalogue of the literary archive – 'The cinema', cried Virginia Woolf, 'fell upon its prey with immense rapacity, and to the moment largely subsists upon the body of its unfortunate victim' (Woolf, 1994, 349) – could literature not learn to return the favour, precisely by making cinema (or radio or the gramophone) its own media 'content'? To measure literary technique 'by the present state of development of film and radio' (Benjamin, 2008, 90) means attending closely to the transference of technical capacities lying dormant in the new media, to the verbal forms of the new literature. Modernism can in part be defined by this tendency: 'in a kind of circular flight, the various arts – better still, the media of the various arts – affirm their absolute quality only by borrowing representational features from the next' (Jameson, 2002, 173).

Gertrude Stein understood her own most radical breaks in literary technique as attempted 'borrowings' from the cinema and the technical horizon of mass production more generally. In her 1930s lectures to bemused American audiences, she explained that her pioneering portraits from the early 1910s were themselves remediations of the modern media: 'I was doing what the cinema was doing. [...] Each time that I said the somebody whose portrait I was writing was something that something was just that much different from what I had just said that somebody was and little by little in this way a whole portrait came into being' (Stein, 1998, 294), just as on the filmstrip one photogram differs 'that much' from the previous one, giving rise to the projected illusion of movement. Treating sentences as though they were photograms, Stein obliged the literary text to behave in an entirely distinct manner:

> Some said he was not clearly expressing what he was expressing and some of such of them said that the greatness of struggling which was not clear expression made of him one being a completely great one.
>
> Some said of him that he was greatly expressing something struggling. Some said of him that he was not greatly expressing something struggling.
>
> He certainly was clearly expressing something, certainly sometime any one might come to know that of him. Very many did come to know it of him that he was clearly expressing what he was expressing. (Stein, 1993, 139)

The brutal reduction in the variety of lexical units allows the prose to withdraw from the function of expressivity (which it is ironically celebrating) and experiment instead with patterns of variation and repetition that derive not from the archive, but from the assembly line. And it could well be said that this prose is more 'faithful' to the essence of technology than the melodramas of D. W. Griffith, given how radically it confronts us with the technical consequences that Griffith drowns in gallons of sentiment.

André Bazin reflected in the 1950s that 'the American novel belongs not so much to the age of cinema as to a certain vision of the world, a vision influenced doubtless by man's relations with a technical civilization, but whose influence upon the cinema, which is a fruit of this civilization, has been less than on the novel', leading to the perverse situation that 'it would seem as if the cinema was fifty years behind the novel' (Bazin, 1967, 63). Adorno wrote that 'Modern works [...] must show themselves to be the equal of high industrialism, not simply make it a topic. Their own comportment and formal language must react spontaneously to the objective situation' (Adorno, 2004, 42–3), and there was a fruitful paradox in the freedom to do so enjoyed by literary forms, relative to their compromised cinematic competitors. Ranging more widely across the arts, Adorno suggests that 'To still paint a picture or write a quartet may lag behind the division of labor and the experimental setup in film production, but the objective technical form of the painting and the quartet safeguards the potential of film that is thwarted by the mode of its production. The "rationality" of the painting and the quartet, however chimerically sealed in on itself and problematic in its uncommunicativeness, stands higher than the rationalization of film production' (Adorno, 2006, 88–9).

The avant-garde was a protected experimental and quasi-institutional space in which such 'rationality' could be transferred, via subterranean aesthetic channels, from high industrialism and the modern division of labour to artworks that 'safeguarded' the technical potential of cinema and radio currently being stymied by capitalist relations of production. Adorno's argument is that there is a utopian dimension to industrial efficiency and rationalization (above all, the objective fact that today, thanks to technology, nobody should go hungry) that cannot be nurtured in media whose rationale is the generation of profit or 'production as an end in itself' (Adorno, 1978, 156), and which therefore engenders irrationality and mystification. Avant-garde literary forms, on the other hand, can foster the utopian kernel of industrialization that the technological media foreclose.

This leads Adorno to one of the crowning formulations of modernism in general, as a ruthless technical adjustment to the technological conditions of industrial modernity:

The substantive element of artistic modernism draws its power from the fact that the most advanced procedures of material production and organization are not limited to the sphere in which they originate. In a manner scarcely analyzed yet by sociology, they radiate out into areas of life far removed from them, deep into the zones of subjective experience, which does not notice this and guards the sanctity of its reserves. Art is modern when, by its mode of experience and as the expression of the crisis of experience, it absorbs what industrialization has developed under the given relations of production. This involves a negative canon, a set of prohibitions against what the modern has disavowed in experience and technique; and such determinate negation is virtually the canon of what is to be done. (Adorno, 2004, 43)

For literature to absorb what is good in technology entails decommissioning all those technical elements that have been rendered redundant by the spread of technology under capitalism. Modernism thus harbours the utopian dimension of technology as the avant-garde, the way that capitalism harbours the utopian dimension of modern industrial relations as socialism.

Did any writer feel this as radiantly as Vladimir Mayakovsky, who wrote of Brooklyn Bridge that, precisely as a Communist,

> I am proud
> > of just this
> > > mile of steel;
> upon it,
> > my visions come to life, erect –
> here's a flight
> > > for construction
> > > > instead of style,
> an austere disposition
> > > of bolts
> > > > and steel.
> If
> > the end of the world
> > > > Befall –
> and chaos
> > > smash our planet
> > > > to bits,
> and what remains
> > > > will be
> > > > > this
> bridge, rearing above the dust of destruction;

then,
      as huge ancient lizards
                are rebuilt
from bones
        finer than needles,
                to tower in museums,
so,
    from this bridge,
           a geologist of the centuries
will succeed
      in recreating
           our contemporary world.
                    (Mayakovsky, 1975, 177–9)

Explicitly nominating the technological fossil record as the best available key for decoding capitalism itself, Mayakovsky goes on to argue that the 'geologist of the centuries' will be able to extrapolate from the bridge that:

here
    men
        had ranted
              on radio.
Here
    men
        had ascended
            in planes.
For some,
      life
        here
           had no worries;
for others,
      it was a prolonged
           and hungry howl.
                    (Mayakovsky, 1975, 179–81)

His form predicating itself both syntactically and spatially on the rearing engineering genius that had inspired Whitman and Hart Crane before him, and allowing the spill of lexical molecules across a ferociously jagged enjambment to perform the industrial status quo's reifying post-humanism, Mayakovky shows how literary form can 'safeguard' what lies dormant and unexpressed in the technical form of a bridge that, on its own, only expresses a violent social inequality. Lyric form is here subjected to a new division of labour: the 'experiential' elements are rigorously parcelled out on the page as so many inexpressive lexical *quanta*. Mayakovsky's 'cubo-futurist' poetic form experiment imagines, from a future transformed by the destructive event now confronting the capitalist mode of production, how a single 'rib' of the bridge might be used to reconstruct the very 'essence of technology' as capitalism itself. Yet it is the bridge, in its turn, that makes this experiment possible in the first place; for somewhere in its cathedral-like projection of technology's *modus operandi* lurks capitalism's utopian corrective, its rational promise of egalitarian distribution and social justice. The paradox is that only modern works of art, and above all literary ones, can make this promise visible, in the 'future anterior' tense of their political archaeologies.

Bibliography

Adorno, T. W. (1978), *Minima Moralia: Reflections from Damaged Life*, E. F. N. Jephcott (transl.). London and New York: Verso.

Adorno, T. W. (1991), 'In Memory of Eichendorff', in R. Tiedemann (ed.), S. W. Nicholsen (transl.). *Notes to Literature*, vol. 1, New York: Columbia University Press, pp. 55–79.

Adorno, T. W. (2004), *Aesthetic Theory*, G. Adorno and R. Tiedemann (eds), R. Hullot-Kentor (transl.). London & New York: Continuum.

Adorno, T. W. (2006), *Philosophy of New Music*, R. Hullot-Kentor (transl.). Minneapolis: University of Minnesota Press.

Adorno, T. W. and Horkheimer, M. (1997), *Dialectic of Enlightenment*. London and New York: Verso.

Agamben, G. (1993), *Infancy and History: Essays on the Destruction of Experience*, L. Heron (transl.). London: Verso.

Bazin, A. (1967), *What Is Cinema?*, vol. 1, H. Gray (transl.). Berkeley and Los Angeles: University of California Press.

Benjamin, W. (1999), 'Experience and Poverty' (*c.* 1933), in M. W. Jennings, H. Eiland, and G. Smith (eds), R. Livingstone (transl.), *Selected Writings, Vol. 2: 1927–1934*. Cambridge, MA: Harvard University Press, pp. 731–6.

Benjamin, W. (2008), 'The Author as Producer', in M. W. Jennings, B. Doherty and T. Y. Levin (eds), E. Jephcott (transl.), *The Work of Art in the Age of Its Technological Reproducibility, and Other Writings on Media*. Cambridge, MA: Harvard University Press, pp. 79–95.

Berman, M. (1983), *All That Is Solid Melts into Air: The Experience of Modernity*. London: Verso.

Bolter, J. D. and Grusin, R. (2000), *Remediation: Understanding New Media*. Cambridge, MA: MIT Press.

Eliot, T. S. (1969), *Complete Poems and Plays*. London: Faber.

Fearing, K. (2004), *Selected Poems*, R. Polito (ed.). New York: Library of America.

Ginsberg, A. (2006), 'Howl: For Carl Solomon', in B. Morgan and N. J. Peters (eds), *Howl on Trial: The Battle for Free Expression*. San Francisco: City Lights Books.

Goethe, J. W. (1990), *Faust: Part I and Sections from Part II*, W. Kaufman (transl.). New York: Doubleday.

Gramsci, A. (1971), *Selections from the Prison Notebooks*, Q. Hoare and G. N. Smith (eds and transl.). London: Lawrence & Wishart.

Hammett, D. (2010), *Red Harvest*. New York: Knopf Doubleday.

Heidegger, M. (1977), *The Question Concerning Technology and Other Essays*, W. Lovitt (transl.). New York: Harper & Row.

Jameson, F. (1991), *Postmodernism, or, the Cultural Logic of Late Capitalism*. London: Verso.

Jameson, F. (1992), *The Geopolitical Aesthetic: Cinema and Space in the World System*. London: BFI.

Jameson, F. (2002), *A Singular Modernity: Essay on the Ontology of the Present*. London & New York: Verso.

Kenner, H. (1987), *The Mechanic Muse*. Oxford: Oxford University Press.

Kittler, F. (1990), *Discourse Networks: 1800/1900*, M. Meteer and C. Cullens (transl.). Stanford: Stanford University Press.

Lambert, C. (1934), *Music Ho!: A Study of Music in Decline*. New York: Scribner.

Lovecraft, H. P. (1984), 'The Whisperer in Darkness', in A. Derleth and S. T. Joshi (eds), *The Dunwich Horror and Others*. Sauk City, WI: Arkham House, pp. 208–71.

MacNeice, L. (2007), 'Autumn Journal', in P. McDonald (ed.), *Collected Poems*. London: Faber.

Marcuse, H. (1982), 'Some Social Implications of Modern Technology', in A. Arato and E. Gebhardt (eds), *The Essential Frankfurt School Reader*. New York: Continuum, pp. 138–62.

Marx, K. (1990), *Capital, Vol. 1*, B. Fowkes (transl.). London: Penguin.

Marx, K. (1993), *Grundrisse: Foundations of the Critique of Political Economy*, M. Nicolaus (transl.). London: Penguin.

Marx, K. and Engels, F. (1978), 'Manifesto of the Communist Party', in R. C. Tucker (ed.), *The Marx-Engels Reader*, 2nd edn. New York and London: W. W. Norton, pp. 469–500.

Mayakovsky, V. (1975), *The Bedbug and Selected Poetry*, P. Blake (ed.), M. Hayward and G. Reavey (transl.). Bloomington and Indianapolis: Indiana University Press.

McLuhan, M. (2001), *Understanding Media*, 2nd edn. London: Routledge Classics.

Milton, J. (1969), 'Paradise Lost', Book VI, in *Poetical Works*. Oxford: Oxford University Press, pp. 319–39.

O'Neill, E. (2007), *Collected Shorter Plays*. New Haven: Yale University Press.

Stein, G. (1993), 'Matisse', in U. E. Dydo (ed.), *A Stein Reader*. Evanston, IL: Northwestern University Press, pp. 139–43.

Stein, G. (1998), *Writings: 1932–1946*. New York: Library of America.

Suárez, J. A. (2007), *Pop Modernism: Noise and the Reinvention of the Everyday*. Urbana and Chicago: University of Illinois Press.

Taylor, F. W. (2008), *The Principles of Scientific Management*. Stilwell, KS: Digireads.

Trotter, D. (2014), *Literature in the First Media Age: Britain between the Wars*. Cambridge, MA: Harvard University Press.

Veblen, T. (1922), *The Instinct of Workmanship and the State of Industrial Arts*. New York: Cosimo.

Villiers De l'Isle-Adam, A. (1981), *Eve of the Future Eden: L'Eve future*. Lawrence, KS: Coronado Press.

Wells, H. G. (1963), *Three Novels*. London: Companion Books Club.

Woolf, V. (1994), 'The Cinema', in A. McNeville (ed.), *The Essays of Virginia Woolf, Vol. 4: 1925–1928*. London: Hogarth Press.

Zukofsky, L. (1981), *'A'*. Berkeley and Los Angeles: University of California Press.

The Geopolitics and
Economics of Modernism

18

Can There Be a Global Modernism?

Emily Hayman and Pericles Lewis

Robert Graves and Laura Riding published *A Survey of Modernist Poetry*, a study of contemporary American and British poets, in 1927. In the field of literature in English, the term 'modernist' referred at first primarily to what Wyndham Lewis called the 'Men of 1914' – T. S. Eliot, James Joyce, Ezra Pound and Lewis himself. Over the past century, its meaning has expanded to encompass (at times) literature from the middle of the nineteenth century to the present in many languages, as well as modern tendencies in the other arts. To the extent that such usages share any common theme, modernist refers to the sense of a crisis of representation in the arts and a concomitant need for a renewal of the arts, which is closely related to the phenomena of sociological modernization (industrialization, mass movements, mass communications) and in the broadest sense philosophical modernity (an even older concept, connected to a notion of the autonomous, rational individual which was crucial to the Enlightenment; see Gumbrecht, 1992 and, in philosophy, Habermas, 1987). Modernism may celebrate or criticize modernization or modernity, but it normally engages with them in some fashion, and those modernists who liked to write manifestoes (a large subset) tended to link their experiments in literary or artistic form with their analysis of the modern condition, or more recently the postmodern condition (Lyotard, 1984). In other European languages, related concepts such as the *avant-garde, modernismo* (initially a Latin American avant-garde movement) and *Expressionismus* have much narrower application, but the themes that inspire English literary modernism draw on the paradoxical 'modern tradition' that took shape in nineteenth-century Europe. This was a tradition that saw the role of art as oppositional to a conformist, materialistic society and often also to tradition itself. The modern artist must continually break or at least reinvent conventions to 'make it new', in the words of Ezra Pound. Although the artist typically arises out of the middle classes, he (or later she) is a sort of class traitor who must shock and amaze the middle classes, in the famous phrase attributed to Charles Baudelaire: 'Il faut épater les bourgeois'.[1]

Can there be a global modernism? In the field of architecture, the answer is obviously yes. In the wake of the post-war expansion of the International Style, which inspired severe and beautiful office towers around the world, a certain kind of global modernism (and post-modernism) transformed the skylines of many world cities. Today, a member of the global bourgeoisie dropped by a Martian spaceship in one of the nicer shopping centres in Kuala Lumpur, Hong Kong, Madrid, Buenos Aires, New York or Abu Dhabi might understandably have trouble guessing his or her location from the architecture with its universal, modernist-derived idiom; the bourgeois might be amazed but would probably not be shocked by the similarity of global brands in each shopping centre and by their use of modernist techniques in advertising their wares. But it would be a mistake to lament the loss of modernism's putative anti-commercial critique; even the most radical avant-gardists often used their oppositional attitude as part of a marketing campaign. The greatest works of modern art, like the great works of earlier periods, contain elements of a critique of existing society, but they cannot be easily lined up with any existing sociological critique of global capitalism. Rather, as Theodor W. Adorno wrote, 'great works of art give voice to what ideology hides' by 'giving form to the crucial contradictions in real existence' (1991, 39).

Literary modernism too was arguably global right from the start, giving form to the contradictions of an earlier age of globalization. Many postcolonial writers borrowed directly from the modernist poets they read as students in colonial institutions (for example, the title of one of the most famous postcolonial novels, Chinua Achebe's *Things Fall Apart* [1958], is drawn from Yeats's 'The Second Coming' [1920]). More importantly, writers from around the globe have used modernist techniques to explore the dislocations of identity in an age of constant change, change which is motivated by the expansion of global capitalism and by related political and social developments. These techniques, in turn, are refracted to depict the different senses of dislocated or double identity, alienation and loss that arise from different sites of modernism. Global modernism may seem by its deliberately iconoclastic and pluralistic nature to resist taxonomy, yet the six examples of modernists that we will present in this chapter demonstrate prevailing themes that we might, indeed, label as 'modernist'. These include the contingency of language (often exacerbated by conflicts between local and imperial languages); a fascination with unconscious motives and especially dreams; a sense of dislocation and awareness that the 'centre' is elsewhere; and a yearning for some cosmopolitan identity that would either transcend localisms or transfigure the local into something of global importance (Lewis, 2012). The following examples show that each modernist locus and perspective takes on these themes from a different vantage as a means by which to express and explore the entanglement of place, history, identity and literature within the broad forces of globalization. Three examples come from the canonical high point of modernism in the early twentieth century (in England, Turkey and Argentina), while the three more recent examples show how modernist techniques and themes have been repurposed in 'postcolonial' and 'postmodern' contexts (see Walkowitz, 2006).

Singapore, 1880

The steamship *Jeddah*, with over 800 Malay Muslim passengers bound on pilgrimage to Mecca, left Singapore in July 1880. The next month, in a gale, it was abandoned by its British crew, who made their way in a lifeboat to Aden. The crew told the authorities that they had seen the *Jeddah* sink behind them, but the next day the ship was towed into harbour by another steamship, the *Antenor* (Watt, 1979, 265–8; for a more detailed account, see Sherry, 1966, 41–170). During ensuing enquiries in Aden and Singapore, the incident became international news. Joseph Conrad, who was in London at the time, later visited Singapore and encountered or heard gossip about a number of figures involved in the *Jeddah* incident, notably Augustine Podmore Williams, who became one of the models for the anti-hero of his novel *Lord Jim* (1900). Conrad, a Polish nationalist who grew up under Russian occupation in what is today the Ukraine (and in exile in northeastern Russia) – and who left home at sixteen to work first on French and then British ships – became one of the great chroniclers of the major wave of globalization of the late nineteenth century. Intimately involved in international trade as a sailor and later captain of steamships, Conrad witnessed the encounters at the edges of the British, Dutch, Belgian and Spanish empires and made them the subject matter of works from *Heart of Darkness* (1899) to *Nostromo* (1904). His first novel, *Almayer's Folly* (1895), is set on Borneo, where he brings the techniques of French realism and naturalism to bear on an exploration of competing factions including the Dutch, British, Arabs, Malays, Dayaks, Balinese Brahmins, Chinese and 'half-castes'. He became an important figure for British and global modernism after he invented the alter-ego Marlow, in some ways a British version of Conrad himself, and a form of *mise-en-abyme* narration that dramatized the moral horror of Europeans' encounter with colonized others.

In *Lord Jim*, Conrad transforms the story of the *Jeddah* into that of the *Patna*. He makes the British crew international, with an unforgettably vulgar German captain who views his human cargo as so many 'cattle' (Conrad, 2002, 11). Focusing the moral problem of the abandonment of duty on a single character, Jim, he makes Jim's abandonment of his ship both understandable (by subjecting him to the influence of the vile crew) and more mysterious (by having the incident take place in fine weather rather than a gale). One of the most memorable features of the novel is the way Conrad fractures chronology (something he would do again, for example, in *The Secret Agent*, 1907), having the alter-ego Marlow piece together the events of the plot through a series of enquiries that anticipate one of the most famous films of the twentieth century, Orson Welles's 1941 masterpiece *Citizen Kane* (Schotter, 2013). The result is a technique described by critic Ian Watt as 'delayed decoding', whereby the reader remains in suspense about the meaning of certain details throughout the narrative; some of these details are eventually explained, but the moral problem of the novel remains essentially unresolved (Watt, 1979, 175–9, 270–3). How could a respectable young sailor, son of a parson, seemingly 'one of us' (white, British, middle class, responsible) so abandon his sense of duty and ignore the humanity of the 800 pilgrims he is meant to have under his care? It is a more intimate form of the problem in Conrad's earlier *Heart of Darkness*, where Kurtz's savagery can be understood as a kind of madness. Jim, however, does not seem mad; rather, he seems perfectly normal, and it is this normality that troubles Marlow – and Conrad. Jim later becomes one of Conrad's characters on the edge of empire and of globalization, a ship chandler's clerk supplying goods to sailors but himself unable to go back to sea. Eventually, too ashamed to face his kind, he takes refuge in the interior of one of the islands of the Dutch East Indies where he becomes the ruler of a native state, 'Lord Jim', the spiritual epigone of Stamford Raffles, founder of modern Singapore, and James Brooke, the white Rajah of Sarawak, until he is finally undone by the forces of globalization in the person of the pirate and swindler 'Gentleman Brown'.

In an exchange that would echo through the history of English modernism, the German merchant Stein eventually advises Marlow on Jim's failed struggle to escape from his own self-delusions.[2] Marlow observes the impossibility of telling a story fully: 'Are not our lives too short for that full utterance which through all our stammerings is of course our only and abiding intention?' (Conrad, 2002, 163).[3] Concerned with trying to explain and express Jim's motivations, Marlow consults Stein, who compares life to a dream. A man, Stein says, 'wants to be a saint, and he wants to be a devil – and every time he shuts his eyes he sees himself as a very fine fellow – so fine as he can never be ... In a dream ...'. For Stein, it is a mistake to imagine that one can escape from such a dream; one must submit to it:

> Yes! Very funny this terrible thing is. A man that is born falls into a dream like a man who falls into the sea. If he tries to climb out into the air as inexperienced people endeavour to do, he drowns – *nicht wahr?* ... No! I tell you! The way is to the destructive element submit yourself, and with the exertions of your hands and feet in the water make the deep, deep sea keep you up. (153–4)

Conrad became a touchstone for T. S. Eliot, who frequently alluded to him in his poems (Ezra Pound dissuaded him from using Kurtz's famous last words from *Heart of Darkness* – 'The horror! The horror!' – as the epigraph to *The Waste Land*; see Eliot, 1974). The literary critic I. A. Richards, in an important essay that helped to make *The Waste Land* the most influential poem of the twentieth century, quoted Conrad on 'the destructive element', and Stephen Spender took the phrase as the title for a collection of essays on modern literature and politics (Richards, 1925, 511–28; Spender, 1936; Watt, 1979, 322–31). For these later modernists, Stein's speech signified the impossibility of arriving at a fully commanding view of the culture that surrounded them and that they perceived as being in crisis. It also meant that their literary forms, rather than attempting to arrive at formal perfection, reflected the partial and fragmentary nature of their understanding of their culture. Modernism sought to incorporate the destructive element into the work of art by making their fragmented forms reflect the crisis they perceived in the broader culture (see also Lewis, 2010). *Lord Jim* traces the moral isolation of the individual at sea in a world driven by motives of profit and domination. While Jim seeks a moral community that would allow him to overcome his shame and that would transcend the cash nexus, he ultimately becomes a victim not only of the forces of globalization but also of his own exaggerated ideals. Like his more perverse counterpart Kurtz, he stands at the leading edge of nineteenth-century globalization and at the origins of twentieth-century modernism.

Istanbul, 1939

Forty years after *Lord Jim*, as Europe teeters on the brink of the Second World War, a young writer, Mümtaz, wanders through Istanbul thinking about his lost love. His path through the city's tangled streets and clamorous markets provides a scaffolding and amplification for his memories of their passionate, failed affair, as Istanbul's neighbourhoods reflect the layering of modern forms and ideas upon an enduring topography of family and politics, of loyalty, passion and jealousy. In *Huzur* (*A Mind at Peace*, 1949), Ahmet Hamdi Tanpınar chronicles Mümtaz's experience of devotion, ideological uncertainty and loss as a reflection of the crises of identity occasioned by Turkey's abrupt transition into a modernity fashioned after a European model. As Tanpınar suggests in this *roman à clef*, the failure of Mümtaz's relationship with the modern, beautiful Nuran signals the tenuousness of Turkish attempts to tread the narrow path between Eastern and Western influences and to synthesize the many competing forms of Turkish modernity.

Tanpınar (1901–62), a born-and-bred *İstanbullu* and member of the literary circle centred around the journal *Dergâh*,[4] wrote *A Mind at Peace* and other works (most notably *The Time Regulation Institute*, 1962; see Ertürk, 2011a) from the charismatic perspective of the 1923 creation of the Turkish Republic. In response to the Republic's radical westernization under Mustafa Kemal Atatürk, Tanpınar used his novels to explore the place of Turkey – and especially its transcontinental epicentre, Istanbul – as the embattled geographic and cultural 'copula' linking Europe and the Middle East, a position made all the more tenuous by the suspension of modern Turkey between the rich cultural heritage of the Ottoman Empire and its effacement by the succeeding Republic (Ertürk, 2011b, 247). Following the Republic's establishment, Atatürk instituted the synonymy of 'modernity' and 'Europe' via sweeping decrees that refashioned nearly every aspect of Turkish life and culture according to a European model, including replacing Ottoman Turkish's Perso-Arabic script and diction with a Latin alphabet and secular vocabulary (Lewis, 1999). Although Tanpınar and his associates embraced modern literary forms and wrote in the 'new' Turkish, they also critiqued the unilateral brashness with which Atatürk sought to cover over Turkey's Ottoman past with a Republican, European present. Instead of embracing an 'internalized Orientalism' or reacting defensively against Western influences, Turkish writers of Tanpınar's generation sought to comprehend and implement a Turkish identity that imbricated East and West, past and present, and in so doing troubled these binaries themselves (Ertürk, 2011b; Seyhan, 2008).

A Mind at Peace, the novel that has been hailed as the 'apogee of Turkish modernism',[5] reflects directly upon what it means to be not just 'modern' but a modern Turk. The problem for Tanpınar's protagonist, Mümtaz, is the combination of his 'yearn[ing] for different ideas' – his desire for the modern – and his discomfort with the 'reactionary' reforms that strive to implement this difference via an effacement of the old. As Mümtaz explains, the result is a society whose cultural identity is self-abasingly, generationally striated:

> This is precisely what I see as the impasse; because [...] the past has no legs upon which to stand. Today in Turkey we wouldn't be able to name five books that consecutive generations read together. [...] We despise ourselves. Our heads are full of comparisons and contrasts: We don't appreciate Dede because he's no Wagner; Yunus Emre, because we haven't been able to cast him as a Verlaine; or Bâkî, because he can't be a Goethe or a Gide. Despite being the most well-appointed country nestled amid the opulence of immeasurable Asia, we're living naked and exposed. Geography, culture, and all the rest expect a new synthesis from us, and we're not even aware of our historic mission. Instead, we're trying to relive the experiences of other countries. (Tanpınar, 2008, 367, 289)

Tanpınar presents an ambiguous solution in what he terms 'exegesis' (*tefsir*[6]), or 'experienc[ing] ideas and emotions as living, breathing things' (Tanpınar, 2008, 290; Tanpınar, 1970, 228). As his novels illustrate, this means incorporating the global and the European in the local (the Ottoman, the Turkish), embracing the task of continuous re-evaluation and repurposing of ideas, culture and even time itself.

Tanpınar explores the possibilities for this synthesis through the story of Mümtaz's doomed love for Nuran, a young divorcée. As he demonstrates, the relationship between East and West, old and new, is as indecipherable, unresolvable and ineluctable as love itself, and the synthetic Turkish identity that arises out of such dialectics is as exhilarating and potentially damaging as this interpersonal congress. As Tanpınar suggests through the novel's central love story, the modern Turkish identity is always in the process of coalescing, yet this synthesis is never complete. This gives rise to a fruitful yet painfully protracted state of desire and uncertainty. 'Amalgam and synthesis only occurred at unendurable temperatures', Tanpınar explains, 'short of which he'd be relegated to the peripheries of a pilfered language' (Tanpınar, 2008, 318), be it the language of intimacy or the Latinized Turkish characters in which he inscribes its words.

Tanpınar's novels feature a recognizably modernist style, marked by a self-conscious use of language and self-reflexive exploration of his characters' consciousness within the modern metropolis. In these attributes, his work hearkens immediately to European models of modernist form, including that of Conrad, whose deliberately written English (his fourth language) resembles Tanpınar's self-conscious mixture of 'old' and 'new' Turkish diction (Göknar, 2013; Morzinski et al., 2009).[7] In addition, the immersive, pseudo-memoir style of Tanpınar's satirical novel *The Time Regulation Institute* is reminiscent of Joyce's *Portrait of the Artist as a Young Man* (1916), Proust's *Remembrance of Things Past* (1913–27) or Gertrude Stein's *Autobiography of Alice B. Toklas* (1933), and *A Mind at Peace* has frequently been described as the 'Turkish *Ulysses*', referring to James Joyce's modernist masterpiece *Ulysses* (1922).[8] Certainly Tanpınar's Istanbul novel shares much with Joyce's exploration of Dublin, from its map-like, *flâneurial* perspective and stream-of-consciousness style to its flashback-driven narrative set in a single day. And yet what is crucial in understanding Tanpınar's own position as an author as well as his influence over subsequent Turkish writers – chief among these was Orhan Pamuk – is that this resemblance is no crib on European forms, but rather a synthesis of these elements with decidedly Turkish concerns, a distinctively Turkish setting and a vocabulary forged from the hybrid Turkish language. Tanpınar's Istanbul is not Joyce's Dublin, and to make this claim would be to reduce the impact of both of these novels as commentaries on the site-specific repercussions of modernity. As Tanpınar demonstrates, 'modernity' need not conform only to the Republican regime's reductive, Euro-centric schema, but might take on a more organic, Turk- and Turkish-focused form.

Buenos Aires, 1939

Twelve thousand kilometres away from Istanbul, a librarian, recently released from a sanitarium where he was being treated for septicemia, rides the train south from Buenos Aires. As he heads south, he feels that he is entering 'a more ancient and sterner world' (Borges, 1967, 18). Although he is of mixed German and Spanish heritage, Juan Dahlmann embraces a 'voluntary, but never ostentatious nationalism' and romanticizes the Argentine *pampas* (plains) and the *gauchos* (cowboys) who live there (16). His trip south, however, seems no pure return to an original Argentine reality; rather, it has a dreamlike quality mediated perhaps by the fact that Dahlmann is reading *The Thousand and One Nights* on the train.[9] As he reads the stories that Scheherazade tells to keep herself alive, Dahlmann suddenly feels 'as if he was two men at a time: the man who traveled through the autumn day and across the geography of the fatherland, and the other one, locked up in a sanitarium and subject to methodical servitude' (19). The reader may suspect that the entire story is a dream taking place in the hospital room of the suffering Dahlmann, but while Jorge Luis Borges frequently glances at this possibility he never makes it explicit (see Frisch, 2004).

In the very brief space of this short story, 'The South' (1953), which Borges considered his best (Borges, 1998, 8), the southbound train takes on symbolic significance: 'The solitude was perfect, perhaps hostile, and it might have occurred to Dahlmann that he was traveling into the past and not merely south' (Borges, 1967, 20). When he arrives at the general store near his family's ranch, Dahlmann encounters some *peones* (labourers) and an ancient *gaucho* who seems 'situated in eternity' (21). Suddenly the dreamlike story becomes nightmarish. One of the labourers (who has Chinese features) spits at him, then curses him and threatens him with a knife. The *gaucho* throws Dahlmann a dagger, and as he is about to fight and likely die it occurs to him:

> As he crossed the threshold, he felt that to die in a knife fight, under the open sky, and going forward to the attack, would have been a liberation, a joy, and a festive occasion, on the first night in the sanitarium, when they stuck him with the needle. He felt that if he had been able to choose, then, or to dream his death, this would have been the death he would have chosen or dreamt. (23)

Although in some ways not characteristic of Borges's most famous, more fantastical or intellectually puzzling works, 'The South' has an uncanny quality that may explain its appeal to Borges, who placed many autobiographical elements in this dreamlike work. The story particularly recalls the short fiction of Kafka and anticipates the works of the magical realists who would combine sociological commentary with fantastic plots. What social commentary there is in 'The South' is muted (and this differentiates it from most of the works we address in this chapter), but is directed mainly towards a critique of the dream of a 'pure' identity. Dahlmann's own background is decidedly modern and hybrid – even his name is caught between German and Argentinian Spanish – and it contrasts with the supposed (but problematic and doubtful) 'purity' of the Argentine south. Dahlmann travels south, in part, to search for an original meaning or identity that always eludes him, and the story's ending seems to offer a caveat against the recourse to senseless violence – a sort of 'purification' – as a solution to the problem of modern anomie and hybridity. In addition, Dahlmann's experience of his world is mediated and mixed with the literature he reads and the dreams it provokes. The 'imperfect copy of Weil's edition of *The Thousand and One Nights*' that accompanies him on his trip south is itself hybrid (16) – Arabic stories collected and published in French and then edited and translated by a German Jew – and suggests Dahlmann's ineluctable participation in a 'world republic of letters', even on a train to the isolated *pampas*.[10] Indeed, Dahlmann's own existence seems to become part of his reading of this book;

perhaps his story is not just a dream, but another tale of *The Thousand and One Nights* that he invents for himself.

Like Dahlmann, Borges was multinational, one-quarter English and educated largely in Europe. Arriving a little after the high point of English modernist, he was aware of the works of Wilde, Woolf, Joyce, Lawrence and Kafka, and he and his mother translated several of these into Spanish. His preference for the condensed miniature – he would write a story about a world that could be the basis of an entire novel, but he had no use for writing novels – and his fascination with imaginary and alternative universes point the way to post-modernism as well as magical realism. In addition, and as we will see in the second half of this chapter, the problem that Borges dramatizes in his work and especially in 'The South' – Dahlmann's search for identity, the impossibility of disentangling purity from impurity, the 'more ancient and sterner world' of an imagined 'elsewhere' apart from the metropolitan centre – are themes which will form the through line from modernism to post-modernism.

Singapore, 1980

Two mothers gossip in the playground of their public housing complex. Each one-ups the other with tales of her son's successes and subtle criticism of the other's child. Each finds a way to brag discreetly about her recent acquisitions: a television set, a newly tiled floor, a sewing machine, a car, a sofa ('nearly two thousand dollars, sure must be good'). They have Chinese names and speak English but throw in the occasional word from Bahasa Melayu or the Hokkien dialect. In fact, they are speaking Singlish, a dialect that the Singaporean government has often campaigned against but that the people of this island stubbornly cling to, as it seems to express both the strengths and weaknesses of the national character:

> ah beng is so smart,
> already he can watch tv & know the whole story.
> your kim cheong is also quite smart,
> what boy is he in the exam?
> this playground is not too bad, but i'm always
> so worried, car here, car there. (Yap, 2013, 126–7)

The Singaporean poet Arthur Yap captures the strains of Singlish and the strain of lower middle-class existence in the fierce competition to keep up with the

Joneses that Singaporeans call *kiasu* ('fear of losing'). While his poetry draws on dialect and dialogue, it is notable for its stylization and compression of syntax. A professional linguist, Yap plays frequently with the interaction of 'standard' and 'non-standard' English in the everyday spoken language (Patke, 1999). Having studied at the University of Singapore under the poet D. J. Enright, Yap spent a year in Leeds and then returned to Singapore, where he earned his PhD and taught linguistics for most of his career; he was also a prolific painter and an author of several short stories marked by a concision of description reminiscent of Maupassant.

Yap's poems and stories often represent the modernization and effacement of a traditional Chinese culture (defined mostly by the immigrant Chinese who came to Singapore in the early twentieth century, but sometimes by the older Peranakan elites). He notes with detached irony the vestiges of the colonial city being transformed by the newly independent state's insistence on industrialization and progress. This new period of modernization, a century after the sinking of the *Jeddah*, might seem quite detached from Conrad's concerns, but Singapore remains a multinational entrepôt, and Yap casts an eye as jaded and humane as Conrad's on the human powers laid waste by getting and spending. In a poem about an old maid, he comments: 'vaguely, there is this thing called modernity,/the multiplicity of all hardship' (Yap, 2013, 141). Many of his poems chronicle decay and the planned obsolescence of the modern economy. Conrad's 'destructive element' has become identified for Yap with the workings of global capitalism, as in the poem 'there is no future in nostalgia':

> & certainly no nostalgia in the future of the past.
> now, the corner cigarette-seller is gone, is perhaps dead.
> no, definitely dead, he would not otherwise have gone.
> he is replaced by a stamp-machine,
> the old cook by a pressure-cooker,
> the old trishaw-rider's stand by a fire hydrant,
> the washer-woman by a spin-dryer. (154)

Thus, Yap explores his consciousness of historical transformation regarded with ironic distance in poems that are descriptive, often dialogic, but seldom personal. They represent small dramas of modernization, and though they are intensely local, relatively unaffected by the major British poets, and sometimes described as postmodern, they surely belong and contribute to global modernism.[11]

Others of Yap's poems are more philosophical and abstract, sometimes stretching the bounds of comprehensibility. His short fiction, written in straightforward prose, nonetheless has some of the ambiguity of his poems in the understated character of its endings. Even the death of the Chinese opera actor Wong Loo in the dramatic denouement of 'The Story of a Mask', one of his most characteristic prose works, leaves the reader nonplussed. The story turns on the Chinese actor's animistic belief that 'each night, when a person is sleeping, the soul departs from the body to return again when dawn arrives' (Yap, 2014, 42–6).[12] In the course of a few pages, Wong Loo leaves China and experiences the growing prosperity of Singapore and the rise and decline of an audience for Chinese opera. On New Year's Eve, he shares a grand dinner with his troupe, gives one of the best performances of his career, and, the next morning, does not wake up; it seems that his soul, wandering at night, fails to recognize his masked, sleeping body. One is tempted to read the story allegorically: the Chinese immigrant wears an actor's traditional mask; his soul, which leaves his body, seems connected still to his Chinese homeland; on the Chinese New Year, his soul is reconnected with his homeland, but his body has been degraded by the modernizing forces of Singapore. But in fact, Yap's immigrants to the *Nanyang* or 'Southern Ocean' (a traditional name for Singapore and Malaysia) do not expect to regain an authentic culture; they accept that 'change was inevitable and it was inevitable also for opera actors' (42). This may mark the shift that Yap and other authors like Orhan Pamuk and Roberto Bolaño make in moving from modernism to post-modernism, from a conscious reaction to the 'destructive element' of modernity to an ironic acceptance of its omnipresence.

Istanbul, 1980

Simultaneous with Yap's Singlish poetry but about 8,000 kilometres away, a young man, Galip, wanders through Istanbul searching for clues to the whereabouts of his journalist cousin Celâl and his wife Rüya. Much as in Tanpınar's fiction, the city he traverses is laden with resonances both Eastern and Western (from Dante to Borges to Rumi), yet in the days leading up to Turkey's 1980 military coup (its third in twenty years), these artistic influences are layered onto a more sinister cityscape. Galip's Istanbul is one that resists certainty or safety, and his quest for truth ends only with the discovery of echoes, dreams and refractions of himself, and at their core, the tragic recognition that his wife and cousin exist only in his mind and memories. The Turkish Nobel laureate Orhan Pamuk presents this most modernist of his novels, *The Black Book* (1990), as a detective story, but this categorization is misleading, as Galip's efforts to find Celâl and Rüya end only in nihilistic destruction – they have been murdered by an obsessive reader (perhaps an ex-military colonel, perhaps Galip himself) – and the true feat of 'detection' here is Galip's discovery of himself amidst the confusion of modernity, a byzantine journey that is, as in Tanpınar's novel, mirrored in the streets of the city (Almond, 2003). With its chapter-by-chapter alternation between Galip's third-person narrative and Celâl's shrewd, *feuilleton*-like articles, and with its reflection on the porousness of narrative voice, authenticity and identity, *The Black Book* might easily qualify as a 'postmodern' novel. Yet it is steeped in modernism, representing the political world through the consciousness of a self-conscious protagonist who is a stand-in for the author and responding to earlier manifestations of Turkish modernism.[13]

More than any other of Pamuk's novels, *The Black Book* serves as the author's response to the enduring legacy of Tanpınar's vision of Istanbul and Turkish modernism, demonstrating the persistence of East/West friction within Galip and Celâl's identities while also reflecting ironically on the meaninglessness of this binary in the context of a country so inextricably yet incompletely aligned with either pole. Pamuk recasts Tanpınar's East/West tension as a sort of historical red herring, a potent narrative that stands in for what Pamuk terms the untranslatable *İstanbullu hüzün*, the melancholic recognition of the division between past and present, the unknowability of other people or even of oneself (Pamuk, 2006b, 90–107).[14] If Tanpınar offered the love story of *A Mind at Peace* as a vision of a modern Turkish identity suspended between East and West, in *The Black Book* Pamuk presents this suspension itself as an endemic and unavoidable state, one whose shadow reaches far beyond the bounds of Turkey.

Tanpınar is one of Pamuk's dominant interlocutors in *The Black Book*, represented through Celâl's archly Tanpınar-ian voice in his articles. Galip's search for his own writerly and personal identity in relation to his older cousin might be read as Pamuk's 'anxiety of influence' in the wake of this formidable forebear, as well as his response to Tanpınar's vision of an Istanbul-based modernism. Celâl, like Tanpınar, traverses uneasy ground between East and West, and his columns explore questions of Western influence, as in his depiction of the mannequin-maker Bedii Usta, whose figures are rejected because they do not resemble the 'European models' to which Turks aspire, but instead look too much 'like us' (Pamuk, 2006a, 61). In the chapters that focus on Galip in novelistic 'real time', Pamuk revises and expands upon Celâl's version of modernity.[15] Questions of East and West still exist for Galip, yet they are treated as background rather than foreground: a radio that mixes Turkish and Western music, a disagreement between his parents over whether to call an accessory a 'necktie' (*gıravat*) or to 'put on Western airs' and name it a *'cravatte'* (*kravat*; that both terms come from the French is taken for granted; Pamuk, 1990, 13; Pamuk, 2006a, 5–6). As in Pamuk's description of modern *hüzün*, Galip's melancholy is predicated on the East/West division explored by Celâl or Tanpınar's protagonists, but it is not a direct response to it; instead, it arises out of the far more pervasive yet equally modern difficulty of discovering one's identity and making sense of the world, of forging a present in relation to an estranged, lost past. His concerns are Celâl's concerns, but at a further remove. Visiting Bedii Usta's mannequins, for instance, Galip focuses not on their distinctive, problematically un-European Turkishness but on the mannequin figure of Celâl himself: 'It's thanks to you I can't be myself! [...] It's because of you that I believed all those stories that turned me into you' (Pamuk, 2006a, 190). The West isn't the problem here; the culprit is instead Celâl and all that he represents: the power of stories, of the past, of others' minds and influence.

Galip returns to these issues again and again, wishing to inhabit 'a world where things meant themselves and nothing else' (282). These problems are fundamentally problems of imitation – both too much (as in Galip's imitation of Celâl) and not enough (as in his failed understanding of Rüya), and they are larger than the question of East versus West since this, too, is only one tenacious form of imitative anxiety (the anxiety of both too much imitation and not enough). *The Black Book* is rife with images of repetition and imitation, by which Pamuk seems to suggest that repetition itself repeats in a sort of cultural and coincidental *mise-en-abyme*, pointing to the failure of language to fully represent this deeper pattern but also language's facility in allowing us to make sense of such patterns at all. This tension is manifested in the seemingly allegorical names that Pamuk gives his protagonists – *galip* means 'hero', *rüya* means 'dream' – that attest to the symbolism of language and also undercut it with fundamental questions about the nature of reality and identity: Is Galip always a hero? Is Rüya entirely a dream? Such a consideration of authorship and identity seems to point back towards a European modernism of Joyce's Stephen Dedalus or Proust's Marcel, yet like Tanpınar's fiction, it arrives at these similarities by a non-European route, one which passes through the distinctive territory of Istanbul and the legacy of a tenuous, hybrid Turkish modernity. Pamuk's contribution to this tradition and to global modernism is to dig deeper into the question of what we term 'imitation'. As *The Black Book* indicates, modernist techniques in world literature may not just be a matter of Istanbul (or Singapore or Buenos Aires) aping the West, but instead may be the product of a convergent thinking that arises out of a complex interaction between East and West, yet arrives at modernism by a different road.

Buenos Aires, 2001

During a financial crisis, as riots rage in the capital, an Argentine lawyer and former judge retraces the southward journey of Juan Dahlmann to the *pampas*. Héctor Pereda, father of a writer named Bebe (whom he considers the best Argentine writer since Borges) and owner of a nice house in Buenos Aires, tells his maid and cook that he has made his mind to go back to his ranch in the south. While the political realm falls apart – 'In the space of a few days, Argentina had three different Presidents' – Pereda seems intent on returning to a more authentic rural Argentina (Bolaño, 2007, 80). *En route*, the scenes at the train station remind him of the film *Doctor Zhivago* (1965), but also of Borges's story 'The South'. When he reaches his ranch, he adopts the persona of a *gaucho*, but the *pampas* turn out to be deserted by their traditional cattle and horses and full instead of particularly vicious rabbits.[16] Momentarily, it seems that he will relive the ending of Borges's story by meeting violent death in a corner store. Later, when his writer son comes to visit, life returns to something a little closer to normal, and eventually the judge decides to return to Buenos Aires, only to confront there a sort of inverse parody of the ending of the Borges story that has obsessed him. The story 'The Insufferable Gaucho', by Roberto Bolaño, displays its author's characteristic reflexivity and playfulness, even as it suggests that the themes of global modernism remain pertinent to a relatively recent crisis of global capitalism and democracy.

Like Galip in Pamuk's *Black Book*, Pereda's experience of his life, and of his country, seems even more mediated by stories than did that of Dahlmann in Borges's tale. The narrative that most haunts him, however, is the idea that also appealed to Borges of an authentic Argentine identity to be found on the *pampas*. Bolaño's story lacks the uncanny frisson of the Borges original, but then part of its purpose is perhaps to question the notion of an original. In fact, Bolaño often compared himself to the 'inexhaustible' Argentine modernist, saying at one time, 'I could live under a table reading Borges', but also boasting: 'My life has been infinitely more savage than Borges's' (Bolaño, 2004, 187; Goldman, 2007). The *pampas*, as imagined by the Chilean novelist, seems more the product of literary reading than actual experience, although Bolaño did live for a time in Argentina. The author seems amazed that the countryside continues to coexist with the city even in the twenty-first century. He also gently satirizes the pretension of South American cities to resemble European capitals: 'It's hard not to be happy, he used to say, in Buenos Aires, which is a perfect blend of Paris and Berlin, although if you look closely it's more like a perfect blend of Lyons and Prague' (79). Even as the economy and government collapse, the citizens in the story are more concerned about Argentina's chances in the World Cup than about the future of their country. Pereda's writer son works in a university in the Midwestern United States, presumably not the ideal location for expressing the soul of his nation, while in any case Pereda himself considers that 'Argentina's shame or the shame of Latin America had turned [the *gauchos*] into tame cats' (86). The dream of an authentic Argentine identity, already undermined in Borges's fiction, becomes here a subject for humorous metaphysical speculation. The political world, largely excluded from Borges, plays a more direct role in Bolaño but still seems to exist on the periphery of his characters' concerns. Certainly there is no hope for collective political action; Bolaño alludes to the errors of Peronism and notes that in the middle of the political crisis, 'It didn't occur to anyone to start a revolution or mount a military coup' (80). What could be seen as the strength of Argentina's belated democratic institutions seems instead to signify the lack of a capacity for dramatic or world-changing action in a society tightly constrained by the international debt market. If Borges's Dahlmann despairs of a pure, forceful individual identity, Bolaño's Pereda suspects (perhaps reassuringly) that this might be impossible even on the level of the nation.

The Persistence of Modernism

Modernism is a capacious category. By the narrow definition of an English literary movement of the 1920s, none of the works analysed here would qualify as 'modernist' – they would be precursors, successors, echoes of modernism. A broader understanding of a global modernism, however, allows us to see the persistence of certain themes and challenges through the advanced literature of the past century and a quarter. The crisis of representation, explored in French poetry of the nineteenth century and in the European embrace of abstract art in the years before the First World War, motivates all six of these authors, who make the method of representing reality – its very representability – central to their narratives (see Auerbach, 1953). More or less directly, all the texts engage with the problem of modernization, seen in most cases as closely linked to globalization. Rather than making explicit political statements in favour of or opposed to global capital flows, the works explored here record the impact of trade and empire on local communities and on the very notion of community. They tend to pursue these challenges by examining the individual consciousness that registers the impact of historic events through intimate encounters and to abjure the omniscience of earlier novelistic traditions. This attention to consciousness extends to a concern with language, translatability and the inextricability of a character's thoughts from the language in which they are expressed. More broadly, the obsession with language tends to emphasize a certain distance between the artist and the world as represented in the literary work; in the works of all six authors discussed here, the challenges of globalization are seen at an oblique angle.

It would be risky to draw too many conclusions about the trajectory of global modernism from six examples. We have focused mainly on fiction; poetry is probably less susceptible to globalization (although the example of Arthur Yap shows that poetry often registers its effects), and drama may be more closely linked to global capital, given its dependence on audiences and markets. Likewise, we have focused on six male authors, but female counterparts do exist, from Virginia Woolf or Clarice Lispector to the Singaporean Lee Tzu Pheng or Turkish Halide Edib Adıvar. Nonetheless, the consistent themes of the works examined here point to modernism's ongoing engagement with the process of modernization, which it views warily but not always antagonistically. Conrad's Stein embraces 'the destructive element' that might allow art or the individual to grasp historical forces, or the human condition, and to escape from mere fatalism. Tanpınar and Borges explore the productive, tenuous and at times dangerous hybridities that modernity entails. Yap, Pamuk and Bolaño, writing decades after their forebears, dream nostalgically of a less alienated identity or authentic past, even as they recognize that 'there is no future in nostalgia'.

Notes

1   For more detailed discussion, see Lewis, 2007. On the paradoxical concept of a 'Modern Tradition', see Ellmann et al., 1965.
2   Stein was based at least in part on the important naturalist, and co-discoverer of evolution, Alfred Russell Wallace. That Stein, the moral compass of the novel, is German balances the fact that Conrad made the captain of the *Patna* German too and mitigates his well-known anti-German prejudice.
3   The passage is cited by Peter Brooks as the epigraph to his *Reading for the Plot* (1992).
4   Characteristically, *Dergâh* – which signifies a Sufi 'convent' or 'lodge' – hearkens back to the Ottoman past.
5   This is the title of Beatrix Caner's biography of Tanpınar and analysis of *A Mind at Peace*. Caner offers the additional, apt description of Tanpınar as 'the child of a world in transformation' (Caner, 2009, 19).

6   This is a significant word choice, since *tefsir* is the older, Arabic-derived term and thus religiously tinged, used especially in relation to reading the Quran (it is similar to the Greek-derived English 'exegesis', which was originally used for biblical reading). Like many other such loanwords, *tefsir* was replaced during Atatürk's language reforms with a more Turkic and secular term, *yorum*. As Seyhan discusses, another related term in Tanpınar's writing is *terkip*, signifying a 'composition' or 'synthesis' for which Tanpınar envisioned Istanbul as a template (Seyhan, 2008, 141–2).

7   Erdağ Göknar argues that Tanpınar's writing is itself a 'palimpsest in mixed registers of contemporary Turkish and "pre-revolutionary" Ottoman Turkish' (Göknar, 2013, 116).

8   See, for instance, the description of the novel on the cover of Archipelago Books' English translation.

9   Borges himself was much interested in this Arabic masterpiece and its translations, as he discusses in 'The Translators of *The One Thousand and One Nights*' (Borges, 2012).

10 On the 'world republic of letters', see Casanova, 2004.

11 For analysis of Yap as a post-modernist, see Patke et al., 2010, 118–23, 206–7.

12 For discussion, see Whitehead et al., 2014, 151–90.

13 On Pamuk's Turkish adaptation of the 'metaphysical detective story' genre, see Göknar, 2013, 217.

14 Seyhan (2008) summarizes this relationship with the past as a condition for contemporary Turkish fiction itself.

15 The contrast between Celâl and Galip's chapters extends even to the distinct styles of their language. See Baştuğ, 2009, 75–6.

16 On Bolaño's surprising humour, see Andrews, 2014, 90–1.

Bibliography

Adorno, T. W. (1991), *Notes to Literature*, vol. 1, S. W. Nicholsen (transl.). New York: Columbia University Press.

Almond, I. (2003), 'Islam, Melancholy, and Sad, Concrete Minarets: The Futility of Narratives in Orhan Pamuk's *The Black Book*'. *New Literary History*, 34, (1), 75–90.

Andrews, C. (2014), *Roberto Bolaño's Fiction: An Expanding Universe*. New York: Columbia University Press.

Auerbach, E. (1953), *Mimesis: The Representation of Reality in Western Literature*, W. Trask (transl.). Princeton: Princeton University Press.

Baştuğ, M. Y. (2009), *A Translational Journey: Orhan Pamuk in English*. Saarbrücken: VDM Verlag Dr. Müller.

Bolaño, R. (2004), 'Borges and Paracelsus', in I. Echevarría (ed.), N. Wimmer (transl.), *Between Parentheses: Essays, Articles, and Speeches, 1998–2003*. New York: New Directions.

Bolaño, R. (2007), *The Insufferable Gaucho*, C. Andrews (transl.). *The New Yorker* (1 October), 78–87.

Borges, J. L. (1967), 'The South', in A. Kerrigan (ed.) and (transl.), *A Personal Anthology*. New York: Grove, pp. 16–23.

Borges, J. L. (1998), '1966 Interview with Richard Stern', in R. Burgin (ed.), *Jorge Luis Borges: Conversations*. Jackson: University Press of Mississippi.

Borges, J. L. (2012), 'The Translators of *The One Thousand and One Nights*', in L. Venuti (ed.), E. Allen (transl.), *The Translation Studies Reader*, 3rd edn. New York: Routledge, pp. 92–106.

Brooks, P. (1992), *Reading for the Plot*. Cambridge, MA: Harvard University Press.

Caner, B. (2009), *Tanpınars Harmonie: Der Höhepunkt der türkischen Moderne*. Frankfurt: Selbstverlag.

Casanova, P. (2004), *The World Republic of Letters*, M. B. De Bevoise (transl.). Cambridge, MA: Harvard University Press.

Conrad, J. (2002), *Lord Jim*, Jacques Berthoud (ed.). New York: Oxford University Press.

Eliot, V. (ed.) (1974), *The Waste Land: A Facsimile and Transcript of the Original Drafts, Including the Annotations of Ezra Pound*. New York: Harcourt Brace Jovanovich.

Ellmann, R. and Feidelson, C. Jr. (eds) (1965), *The Modern Tradition: Backgrounds of Modern Literature*. Oxford: Oxford University Press.

Ertürk, N. (2011a), *Grammatology and Literary Modernity in Turkey*. New York: Oxford University Press.

Ertürk, N. (2011b), 'Turkey', in Pericles Lewis (ed.), *The Cambridge Companion to European Modernism*. New York: Cambridge, pp. 247–59.

Frisch, M. (2004), *You Might Be Able to Get There from Here: Reconsidering Borges and the Postmodern*. Madison, WI: Fairleigh Dickinson University Press.

Goh, I. (2013), 'Realia: A Short Introduction to the Poetry of Arthur Yap', in J. Yap and I. Goh (eds), *Collected Poems of Arthur Yap*. Singapore: NUS Press, pp. 1–15.

Göknar, E. (2013), *Orhan Pamuk, Secularism and Blasphemy: The Politics of the Turkish Novel*. London: Routledge.

Goldman, F. (2007), 'The Great Bolaño', *The New York Review of Books* (19 July).

Gumbrecht, H. U. (1992), 'A History of the Concept "Modern"', in Glen Burns (transl.), *Making Sense in Life and Literature*. Minneapolis: University of Minnesota Press, pp. 79–110.

Habermas, J. (1987), *The Philosophical Discourse of Modernity*, F. G. Lawrence (transl.). Cambridge, MA: MIT Press.

Lewis, G. (1999), *The Turkish Language Reform: A Catastrophic Success*. New York: Oxford University Press.

Lewis, P. (2007), Introduction, in P. Lewis (ed.), *The Cambridge Introduction to Modernism*. Cambridge: Cambridge University Press, pp. xiv–xix.

Lewis, P. (2010), 'Inventing Literary Modernism During the Great War', in M. Walsh (ed.), *London, Modernism and 1914*. Cambridge: Cambridge University Press, pp. 148–64.

Lewis, P. (2012), Introduction, in P. Lewis (ed.), *Cambridge Companion to European Modernism*. Cambridge: Cambridge University Press, pp. 1–9.

Lyotard, J.-F. (1984), *The Postmodern Condition: A Report on Knowledge*, G. Bennington and B. Massumi (transl.). Minneapolis: University of Minnesota Press.

Morzinski, M. and Pauly, V. (2009), 'Language', in A. H. Simmons (ed.), *Joseph Conrad in Context*. Cambridge: Cambridge University Press, pp. 18–25.

Pamuk, O. (1990), *Kara Kitap*. Istanbul: İletişim.

Pamuk, O. (2006a), *The Black Book*, M. Freely (transl.). New York: Vintage.

Pamuk, O. (2006b), *İstanbul: Memories and the City*, M. Freely (transl.). New York: Vintage.

Patke, R. S. (1999), 'Voice and Authority in English Poetry from Singapore', in K. Singh (ed.), *Interlogue: Essays on Singapore Literature in English, Volume II: Poetry*. Singapore: Ethos Books, pp. 85–103.

Patke, R. S. and Holden, P. (2010), *The Routledge Concise History of Southeast Asian Writing in English*. Oxford: Routledge.

Richards, I. A. (1925), 'A Background for Contemporary Poetry'. *Criterion*, 3, 511–28.

Schotter, J. (2013), 'Eye=I: Conrad, Welles, and Narrative Form'. *Literature/Film Quarterly*, 14, 39–51.

Seyhan, A. (2008), *Tales of Crossed Destinies: The Modern Turkish Novel in a Comparative Context*. New York: Modern Language Association.

Sherry, N. (1966), *Conrad's Eastern World*. Cambridge: Cambridge University Press.

Spender, S. (1936), *The Destructive Element: A Study of Modern Writers and Beliefs*. London: Houghton Mifflin.

Tanpınar, A. H. (1970), *Huzur*. Istanbul: Tercüman.

Tanpınar, A. H. (2008), *A Mind at Peace*, Erdağ Göknar (transl.). New York: Archipelago.

Walkowitz, R. (2006), *Cosmopolitan Style: Modernism Beyond the Nation*. New York: Columbia University Press.

Watt, I. (1979), *Conrad in the Nineteenth Century*. Berkeley: University of California Press.

Whitehead, A. and Gwynne, J. (2014), '"A Long Way from What"?: Folkways and Social Commentary in Arthur Yap's Short Stories', in G. Weihsin (ed.), *Common Lines and City Spaces: A Critical Anthology on Arthur Yap*. Singapore: Institute of Southeast Asian Studies, pp. 151–90.

Yap, A. (2013), *The Collected Poems of Arthur Yap*, J. Yap and I. Goh (eds). Singapore: NUS Press.

Yap, A. (2014), *Noon at Five O'Clock: The Collected Short Stories of Arthur Yap*, A. Whitehead (ed.). Singapore: NUS Press.

19

A Departure from Modernism: Stylistic Strategies in Modern Peripheral Literatures as Symptom, Mediation and Critique of Modernity

Benita Parry

It is well known that although modernist studies had from the outset assimilated writings from Ireland and the Austro-Hungarian empire into the canon (Joyce, Beckett, Kafka, Musil), modernism was subsequently institutionalized as the aesthetic invention of an avant-garde from Western Europe writing during the late nineteenth and earlier decades of the twentieth century.[1] Specifying the distinctive features of modernism as a literature of the city, radically innovative in style, autotelic and self-referential, discontinuous and ironic, eminent scholars acclaimed its achievement in mapping the psychic and emotional horizons of the new metropolitan middle-class subject and devising a typology of its tormented self- and inner consciousness. As is also common knowledge, this model has been charged with canonizing a selective tradition excluding writings that in continuing the tradition of social realism devised new vocabularies and narrative strategies to transfigure the unprecedented social forms generated by modernity, and more, to construe a critique of 'the real' (Williams, 1989, 32).

Of late, critics have questioned whether modernism's metropolitan location is as exclusive, its aesthetic as individualistic, its ideology as detached from

This chapter draws on the researches and writings of the Warwick Research Collective (WReC) within the English and Comparative Literature Department at Warwick University. A publication *Combined and Uneven Development: Towards a New Theory of World Literature* was published by Liverpool University Press in 2015.

My thanks to Keya Ganguly and Timothy Brennan for their suggestions and critical comments, and for sharing with me their work in progress.

the social world and its preoccupation with stylistic departures as uniquely an expression of a new and fractured urban sensibility as has been assumed. This current interest in modernism's 'global engagements' and wider vistas has stimulated those engaged in the revision to detect a transnational genealogy, a longer temporal span and a larger geopolitical space within which a greatly enhanced corpus of writing has been produced.[2] Adam Barrows, for instance, situates modernism's preoccupation with temporality in the context of the political and legislative arguments over world standard time, a contest he shows to be part of the globalization of imperial processes and policies. In examining how this stimulated writers to experiment with new ways of representing human time, Barrows cites Victorian adventure novels (Rider Haggard, Bram Stoker and Rudyard Kipling), early English-language South Asian novels as well as high modernist texts (Joyce, Woolf and Conrad), suggesting that these 'indicate an engagement with questions of paramount public concern rather than a philosophical retreat into bourgeois, private interiority' (Barrows, 2010, 4).[3]

In a wide-ranging study *1913: The Cradle of Modernism*, Jean-Michel Rabaté has proposed that modernism be understood 'as the inception of our modern period of globalization' covering manifestations in societies beyond Western Europe, a view he goes on to contradict when itemizing its essential features as those noticeably to the fore in its metropolitan incarnations (Rabaté, 2007, 1).[4] Previously, William Everdell had also located 1913 as modernism's *annus mirabilis*, adding Vienna and St Petersburg to the capital cities of Paris and London, and Mississippi to its geography, while also embracing art, music, film, physics, mathematics and philosophy as articulations sharing an 'assumption of ontological discontinuity' (Everdell, 1997, 347). The Russian Futurists alluded to above are also included in Peter Nicholls's study *Modernisms: A Literary Guide*,[5] serving as a reminder that this group was a precursor to the kaleidoscopic creativity of the short-lived Soviet avant-garde, whose participants had incorporated experimentation in poetry and novels, painting, film, architecture and the design of artefacts, the whole animated by, and often aligned with, the ideas and ideals of the Revolution. The genesis, political affiliations and radical inventiveness of this movement which have been discussed in depth by Paul Wood in a brilliant and neglected essay ('The Politics of the Avant-Garde') remains to be allotted its proper place in the discussion of the modern vanguard and is central to any consideration of its manifestations in peripheral locations, as well as in the larger discussion about the ingenuity of 'committed' art.

Still more recently and in line with what they call the current tendency of 'New Modernist Studies', Douglas Mao and Rebecca Walkowitz (2008), when observing how the enlargement of the field has challenged the notion of modernism as a product of 'the West', have promoted the study of literatures beyond Europe and North America, as well as that from marginalized communities within the metropoles.[6] As editors of *Bad Modernisms* (2006), they argue for extending its borders to include novels from the Harlem Renaissance and the Philippines, together with manifestos, philosophical treatises, movie musicals, anthropological essays and advertising campaigns, their aim being to demonstrate modernism's aesthetic to be inherently socially aware and subversive. The dissident credentials of modernism have also been asserted by Vicki Mahaffey (2007), who discusses the 'high' modernists such as Eliot, Joyce, Pound and Yeats alongside women, gay writers and participants in the Harlem Renaissance. She relates the modernist impulse to broader cultural and historical crises and movements, and claims for the field a special political and ethical relevance.

In a related vein, Jessica Berman examines the articulations of modernism comparatively in Britain, the Caribbean, India, Ireland, Spain and the United States, maintaining that 'reading modernism transnationally shifts our perspective on the forms and commitments of modernism' to reveal 'the continuum of political engagement that undergirds its world-wide emergence' (2012, 9). By understanding modernism as 'a constellation of rhetorical actions, attitudes, or aesthetic occasions motivated by the particular and varied situations of economic, social, and cultural modernity worldwide and shaped by the ethical and political demands of those situations', she pursues a connection between the narrative ethics and the literary politics of modernism, designating modernism as a player in anti-colonial discourse and maintaining that modernist narrative acts to help us 'imagine justice' (2012, 7).

Common to the above studies is the determination to redraw modernism's landscape so as to include the peripheries and semi-peripheries, rather than to focus on how the aesthetic strategies of such writing deviated from the normative criteria allotted to the modernist project. This tendency is amplified by those critics interested in identifying the specific character of peripheral modernism, even when this is not named as such. In an 'Afterword' to *The Oxford Handbook of Global Modernisms*, Laura Doyle chides 'the notion of borrowing [that] deforms and haunts all consideration of the relation between canonical modernism and other literatures, especially postcolonial literatures', and goes on to fault this position for 'a blindness to dialectical co-formations' (2012, 671). For Doyle, two clusters of words signify the opposing tendencies discernible in the discussion, both of which she rejects: on the one hand, 'belated', 'third world', 'expropriated', 'appropriated' 'derive' and 'revise'; on the other, 'original', 'metropole', 'first world', 'generate' and 'innovate' (2012, 671), a schema that I find registers allied and not contesting stances.

Instead of relegating belatedness, borrowing and extensive assimilation as categorically negative, Doyle proposes that we acknowledge the 'coproduction of cultures' (2012, 678) as the proper source of creativity. Hence her assumption that influences from core to periphery and peripheries to core constitutes a joint venture conducted by equivalently placed participants within a global space. Since this emerges as unencumbered by a history of dispossession and violence, there are, in her account, no traces of force and aggression for the critic to find and map onto its past and contemporary topography. Indeed, this infers an arena within which the 'European' and 'non-European' cultures, cognitive traditions and literatures had interacted cordially as equals and continue to do so in amicable transnational exchanges (Doyle, 2012, 682) – an astonishingly cosmetic portrait of imperialism's historic face.

If Doyle offers the conceit of 'dialectical co-formations' as the mainspring of modernism everywhere, then Andreas Huyssen, while setting out to 'de-westernize modernism', proceeds to undermine his own rejection of a geography confined to the metropolitan cities of Europe and North America. This he does by confining the ingenuity of writing in the colonial and postcolonial countries to its 'transformative negotiation with the modern of the metropolis' (Huyssen, 2005, 6), whereby metropolitan culture was 'translated, appropriated and creatively mimicked' (9). Another critic, Susan Stanford Friedman, who protests at the 'curse of presumed derivativeness' attached to colonial and postcolonial modernisms, intends to redress the silencing of 'the creative energies of colonial and postcolonial subjects as producers of modernism', but succeeds in restoring 'Western' aesthetics as its fount and origin by ascribing this vitality to the 'indigenization' and 'cannibalism' of cultural traditions from the West, transmitted through 'contact zones' and emerging as 'alternative' modernisms (2006, 431–43).[7] These efforts to expand the extent of modernism signally fail to address that which is stylistically novel in peripheral writings, which, as I go on to propose, always exceeds a metamorphosis of extant configurations and transcends the normative modes attributed to modernist literature.

Because my concern is with writing from the peripheries of capitalism's world-system, I must emphasize that in discussions on globalization, modernity and world literature, the use of core and peripheries/semi-peripheries signifies not a civilization hierarchy or a cultural ordering, but the geopolitical locations of pre- or nascently capitalist societies co-opted or coerced into world capitalism.

As well as the colonized worlds, these include Russia before and since the Revolution, the now disintegrated Austro-Hungarian empire, pre- and modern China, Japan, Eastern and Southern Europe, and the deprived and marginalized populations within the core. This accounts for the paradoxical beginning conditions of modern cultural forms among peoples who seemed, and may still seem, to inhabit multiple histories and temporalities, to be both modern and traditional.[8] When interpreting this historic process as it had unfolded in China and pre-revolutionary Russia, Leon Trotsky proposed a theory of combined and uneven development delineating a contradictory amalgam of pre-existing local structures of social life and external sociopolitical and cultural influences. These insights into the coexistence of antiquated modes and modern social formations and institutions were derived from observing that the imperialist powers had introduced into the non-capitalist world the most advanced means of commodity production accompanied by capitalist relationships while also safeguarding the continuation of 'archaic forms of economic life' and the maintenance of feudal social arrangements: 'The most primitive beginnings and the latest European endings', modern capitalist industry in an environment of economic backwardness; 'the Belgian or American factory, and round about it settlements, villages of wood and straw, burning up every year', a proletariat 'thrown into the factory cauldron snatched directly from the plough' (Trotsky, 1965, 476).

Whereas some critics have spoken of modernity as marking a ruthless break with preceding historical conditions, Perry Anderson has emphasized that its historic time accommodates eras discontinuous from each other and heterogeneous within themselves (1984, 101). In the same vein Fredric Jameson, echoing Trotsky, has argued that modernity uniquely corresponds 'to an uneven moment of social development' when realities from radically different moments of history coexist – 'handicrafts alongside the great cartels, peasant field with the Krupp factories or the Ford plant in the distance' (1991, 307). Elsewhere, in the essay 'The End of Temporality' (2003), Jameson writes of modernity as a culture of incomplete modernization in the metropoles as well as the peripheries, because of which, he maintains, we have to explain the emergence of various modernisms in areas of only partially industrialized and partially defeudalized social orders, and where the first modernists in their own lived experience had to negotiate two socio-economic temporalities.

It is true that residual traces of archaic ideologies and customs can be found in contemporary Western Europe and North America, where the capital cities remain contemporaneous with peasant or agrarian societies – about which

John Berger has written with empathy and critical distance in *Pig Earth* (1979) and which William Faulkner encrypts in fictions located in the Deep South of twentieth-century United States – even if these most commonly exist as vestiges. However in the zone of the semi-periphery, the synchronicity of disjunctive temporalities and discrepant types of social and economic organization persisted and continues to do so. Where lands were seized and colonized for their natural and labour resources, and expropriation and precipitate, selective modernization were imposed with memorable violence,[9] the survival of pre-existing forms of social life and culture interrupted/ disrupted by the arrival of capitalism ensured that anomalies remained and continue to remain structural.

This does not mean that the peripheries were latecomers to or existed/exist outside of modernity, as this can be conceived as the temporal condition of people everywhere since transformation was propelled by the same mode of production, even if at different speeds and to varying degrees. Paradoxically, some postcolonial critics have considered major modernist concerns such as consciousness, temporality and the experience of modernity as being markedly 'Western' preoccupations, rather than coextensive with capitalism's worldwide consolidation, and as a consequence have proposed that peripheral modernities be perceived as 'translations' of, or counters to, the Eurocentric prototype.[10] A strong case against 'transmuting a temporal lag into a qualitative difference' has been made by Harry Harootunian (2000a, 23). Acknowledging that modern forms were introduced into societies outside of Europe through imperial expansion, the export of capital and colonial deterritorialization, he emphasizes its consequences in creating a world where 'all societies shared a common reference provided by global capital and its requirements' (Harootunian, 2000a, 62–3). He thus directs attention to the disparate but simultaneous experiences of change and upheaval precipitated transnationally by capitalism, these generating 'differing inflections of the modern' and promising not alternative, divergent, competing and retroactive modernities – which imply 'the existence of an "original" that was formulated in Europe followed by a series of "copies" and lesser inflections' – but 'coeval ... modernities or, better yet, peripheral modernities' (62–3).[11]

Similarly, Samir Amir (1974) maintains that conditions in the peripheries represent not an earlier stage of development, but an equally modern consequence of the continuous alterations to which these societies have been subjected by capitalism.[12] This argument implies that metropolitan and colonial populations, whatever the profound material and cultural differences between and among them, were hurled into modernity at the same moment,[13] a perspective registered in Peter Osborne's designation of modernity as 'our primary secular category of historical totalization' (1995, 29)[14] and a description which brings its global reach into proper focus, serving as a reminder that modernity and modern times cannot be abstracted from the universalizing tendencies of capitalism. This concept of a singular capitalist modernity has been elaborated by Fredric Jameson: it is singular because worldwide, and because it is global, it is necessarily of infinite variety (2002).

The resituating of literary modernism within wider spatial and temporal perspectives has not been matched by a revaluation of modernism's status as the proper and only articulation of modernity. In a conjunctural model, modernity has been described as a consciousness, sensibility or time-space sensorium consistent with capitalism's economic and technological modernization, and aesthetic modernism perceived as generating a style adequate to mediating the lived experience of this historical transformation. But since modernity is one and many, is modernism its sole voice? The need to uncouple modernity from modernism so as to account for all literary forms born of modernity has been persuasively made by the editors and contributors to a special issue on 'Peripheral Realisms' in the *Modern Language Quarterly* (2002). In the introduction, Jed Esty and Colleen Lye write of an 'accustomed habit of reading against realism' which selects for canonization 'works that stylize global capitalism rather than describe its effects', thereby enabling 'North American scholars of the contemporary period to produce interconnected atlases of alternative, late, and global modernisms while ignoring a world of peripheral realisms' and consequently forgoing 'the possibility [...] of representing the world-system rather than thematizing its unrepresentability' (2012, 17).

However, it is an essay written by the Marxist theorist Theodor Adorno that has done much within radical circles to relegate realism. In an impassioned response to an article by Lukács – certainly one that appears as uncharacteristically inflexible – Adorno accused Lukács of projecting a dogmatic sclerosis of content, of art imitating reality, as if content is 'real' in the same sense as social reality. Claiming modernism as the singular source of a critical perspective on modernity, Adorno ascribed to it an intrinsic negative critique, whether delivered from the left or the right, directed at capitalism's intensification of dehumanization, while categorizing realism as formally anachronistic because unable to grasp, assimilate and transfigure the trauma of modernity. Lukács's indignation at the 'worldlessness of interior monologue' within modernist writing is met by Adorno's insistence that this mode is 'both the truth and the appearance of a free-floating subjectivity – it is truth, because in the universal atomistic state of the world, alienation rules over men', and it is 'appearance [...] inasmuch as, objectively, the social totality has precedence over the individual, a totality which is created and reproduces itself through alienation and through the contradictions of society' (Adorno, 1977, 160).[15] Adorno goes on to name Joyce and Kafka as exemplars of modernism, before rebuking Lukács with the reminder that Balzac and Dickens – writers Lukács held in high esteem – are 'by no means as realistic as all that', since Balzac's novels were 'an imaginative reconstruction of the alienated world, that is, of a reality no longer experienced by individual subject' (Adorno, 1977, 163). In suggesting that 'the difference between this individual subject and the modernist version is not that great', and implying the artificiality of containing realism and modernism within a rigid and exclusionary temporal framework, Adorno defuses some of the explosive rhetoric in his polemic (1977, 163). Concerning Dickens, Adorno elsewhere observed that he created characters who failed to internalize the domination of society, because of which – as the bearers and not the agents of objective factors – they remained experientially separated from the conditions determining their existence.[16]

After exposure to Adorno's scorn, it is necessary that the interested reader look at Lukács's more characteristically nuanced essay on Dostoevsky, written in 1943 and first published in 1949. He begins by observing that there is 'nothing unusual in the fact that a backward country produces powerful works', since locations deemed underdeveloped in terms of modernization were all the same the contemporaries of the metropolitan centres within the totality of world capitalism (1973, 146). In Dostoevsky he sees 'the first and greatest poet of the modern capitalist metropolis', the first to draw 'the mental deformations that are brought about as a social necessity in the life of the city' and the first to recognize and represent 'the dynamics of a future social, moral and psychological evolution from germs of something barely begun' (1961, 153). The journalist Dostoevsky, writes Lukács, spoke consolingly and as a conservative; only in his poetic writings does his social answer triumph and assert itself over political intentions: 'It is a revolt against the moral and psychic deformations of man which is caused by the evolution of capitalism', the experimentation of his character being 'a desperate attempt to break through the barriers which deform the soul and maim, distort, and dismember life' (1961, 156).

Lukács's reading disarrays any attempt to contrive a time frame for periodizing realism and modernism, since both have their source in the impulse to invent forms able to grasp and transfigure changing social and psychic landscapes.

Indeed, scholars of Japanese literature claim that the construction of bourgeois everyday life in the realist moment took place simultaneously and in conversation with its modernist moment. Following on the convincing argument made for recognizing that within the body of peripheral literatures are fictions that cannot be accommodated under modernism, including the recently expanded versions, I go on to suggest that such writing is better served by other terms. One such is 'irrealism', a literary form identified by Michael Löwy, and to which I will return; another is 'Homiletic Realism', proposed by Timothy Brennan, who argues that: 'Instead of reclaiming modernism for the periphery, my view is that we [...] explicitly depart from it' (2014a, 10). By grounding writings scored by linguistic polyphony and disjunctive narrative modes in the worldly conditions they also critically address, such suggestions open the way to show that the reconfiguration of what is incommensurable and absurd in institutional structures and social forms (cf. Jameson, 1986a) is not confined to theme, but is embedded in the peculiarities of its stylistic mannerisms.

There have been many attempts at identifying the characteristics of peripheral literatures, such as the overused category of the marvellous real, or magic realism,[17] before which there were definitions of Caribbean aesthetics that are arresting in their perceptions of a heritage of historical admixture and temporal and spatial unevenness. Such situations, critics argued, made for cultural métissage or creolization,[18] described by Wilson Harris as a heady mix 'bearing traces of the pre-Columbian, the rubble of the extinct Carib past, Arawak icons, vestiges of Amerindians' fable and legend, practices stemming from African vodun and limbo born on the slave ships of the Middle Passage' (1970, 30). The broken histories of the islands were also to the fore in the writings of the Martinican novelist and critic Édouard Glissant, who cited the subjugation, alienation and ultimately extermination of indigenous peoples by early colonial conquest, African slaves sold to the new world and the dehumanizing conditions endured by East Indian and Chinese indentured labour on the plantations (Glissant, 1989, 221–2, 260). Long before these observations, the Cuban novelist and musicologist Alejo Carpentier had noted the improbable coexistence of the ancestral and the contemporaneous in Latin America. Designating surrealism as the expression of the First World's subjective craving for heterogeneity and dereification, he attributed the superficially similar trend in the literature and art of Latin America in the 1920s and 1930s as springing from the fact of combined and uneven development in the object world itself, where 'stages of civilization known to humans throughout history can be witnessed in the present' (1995, 88).[19]

A different understanding of the stylistic mismatches and improbable contiguities in the formal features of the imported novel form in the peripheries is offered by the Brazilian critic Roberto Schwarz, who accounts for the fictions' 'originality' in the inappropriate affirmation of European ideas within conditions of historical backwardness (1992, 3, 29).[20] By locating the literary devices of the peripheral novel in its social ground, Schwarz finds that these, whether realist, fabulist, modernist or avant-garde, can be read as transfiguring and estranging the incommensurable material, cultural, social and existential conditions of an emergent capitalist modernity, where a system of ambiguities grows 'out of the local use of bourgeois ideas' (3, 29). Expanding on these observations in his study on the nineteenth-century novel in Brazil, Schwarz suggests that when the ideas and ideals of European liberalism were asserted in a society where social relationships were based on latifundia and the unfree labour of slaves, these reveal themselves as displaced, as not fitting the circumstances of Brazilian life. However, as he writes of Machado de Assis's *The Posthumous Memoirs of Brás Cubas* (1889), it is in 'their quality of being improper' that the ideology, through a Brechtian process of reproducing and estranging, becomes 'material and a problem for literature' (Schwarz, 2001, 47). What Schwarz finds is that the incompatibilities and improbable juxtapositions in narrative form and style – which he calls a 'Babel of literary mannerisms' (17) and a 'bazaar of classical and realist registers' (15) – correspond to an implausible society, slave-owning and bourgeois at the same time.

The question of what critical discourses authorize as exemplary, and how these instruct us to read, impinges on the classification of literary form. During the last decades, prominent tendencies in postcolonial studies had privileged writings from the once-colonized peripheries which stylistically inscribe hybridity, pastiche, irony and defamiliarization. The outcome, as Neil Lazarus contends in his book *The Postcolonial Unconscious* (2011), is that realist-associated conceptual categories such as mode of production, historical transition, nation and nationalism, class and class consciousness, land and environment are excluded (2011, 22). As to the first question about what we are directed to read, Lazarus refers us to a vast body of 'realist' writing from the peripheries that has been programmatically ignored. As to the approved reading practices, we can observe how critical commentary has determined the ways fiction is put into circulation and fixed in an allotted category. Consider Yambo Ouologuem's once notorious novel *Bound to Violence* (1968), earlier hailed by Kwame Anthony Appiah as a political novel that 'seeks to delegitimate' nationalism and the nationalist project of the postcolonial national bourgeoisie

(1991, 352). Republished in 2008 as *The Duty of Violence*, its excesses could now be recuperated as a chronicle of the harrowing transition to capitalism in an African state.[21]

Or consider Sharae Deckard's 'Peripheral Realism, Millennial Capitalism' (2012) and Nicholas Lawrence's essay on Roberto Bolaño's *2666*, where against the grain of its designation as a postmodern novel, both read its narrative arc as encompassing capitalism's global system, its consciousness incorporating the ubiquitous ramifications of world imperialism and its destiny a critique of a system that engenders moral and psychological deformation. As Lawrence writes:

> The global 'lit-system' thus forms not just the context but the content of a work such as Roberto Bolaño's novel *2666*, which is concerned to trace the imbrication of literary unevenness with the starkest manifestations of inequality in the social and economic realm – the 'deathworld' epitomized by the serial killings of female workers in the maquiladoras of Ciudad Juárez on the US-Mexican border. (2015, 68)

There was a time when commentators on peripheral literatures sought signs of synthesis, symbiosis and negotiation between the contradictions attendant on using a narrative form privileging the values of a liberal ideology and individual choice, when representing a tradition-bound society where life was mapped by family, community and the maintenance of social order. These glosses were intent on detecting the *marriage* of two cultures – the fables, myths and folktales of the native tradition *blended* with the traditions of the novel found in the literatures of the ruling empires (see Bahri, 2003).[22] Whereas Christopher Prendergast has generalized this mode when claiming the 'amalgamation' of different traditions as the source of cultural originality, Franco Moretti (2006) argues that this does not monopolize the process of change and suggests instead that major transformations occur when a device or genre enters a new cultural habitat.[23]

In the habitat of the peripheries, the intensity of the social and political disjunctions suggests that among the appropriate and productive designations of its literary domain is what Brennan names as 'Homiletic Realism', which 'exhorts its reader first to have faith in, and second to engage with, a totality that lies *behind* appearance' (Kent and Tomski, 2017, 265).

To substantiate the methodology I have argued is adequate to disclosing the singularities of modern peripheral writing, I will propose a reading of *Xala* (1974), a novella by the Senegalese writer and film-maker Ousmane Sembéne (earlier transcribed as Sembéne Ousmane). Born in 1923, Sembéne had little schooling and was in turn fisherman, bricklayer, plumber and apprentice-mechanic before being drafted into the French army during the Second World War. After moving to France, he was docker, trade union activist, member of the French Communist Party and a conscious internationalist. Without any affinity with Négritude, a cultural and political movement of the 1930s, in which Senegal's long-serving post-independence president Léopold Sédar Senghor was a founding member, Sembéne was critical of Senghor's policies which he accused of fostering the French connection as the agency of metropolitan capitalism's continued domination over Senegal. His commitment to Communism was further marked by his choosing to learn his skills as a film-maker in the Soviet Union during the 1950s, unlike other Francophone African film-makers, especially those from Burkina Faso, who apprenticed themselves to the French.

Initially intended as a film script, *Xala* was published as a book in 1974 and two years later it was again revised for cinema. Both versions dramatize the coercive modernization of a pre-capitalist African society and the consequent trauma of immersion in conditions of uneven development. It was Sembéne's intention that his writings and films should reach as many as possible within a largely illiterate population. Since *Xala* was written in a mixture of standard French, its vernacular form and the native Wolof (nuances that are lost in translation), its narrative is marked by unsettling shifts in genre, and its address encompasses the accents of both oral delivery and modern narration. It is thus uncertain that his ambition was fulfilled – which may have prompted Sembéne's return to the more accessible medium of cinema in order to tell his story to a wider audience. Although positioning himself within the tradition of the *griot* (the bards of West Africa considered to be the keepers of folk stories and indigenous systems of knowledge), Sembéne also understood the role of the artist as giving voice to the 'inner screams' of the people,[24] while his admonitory intercessions on colonialism, corrupt post-independence regimes and the persistence of deleterious tradition characterize a writer who accepted a responsibility to admonish and persuade his readers. If these positions suggest, as some commentators have claimed, that Sembéne worked within a functional aesthetics,[25] his expressionist style, which others have compared to that of Brecht,[26] frustrates transparent readings of narrative content.

The improbable juxtapositions of the recognizable and the fantastic in *Xala* are generated by the absurdities and incongruities of a society adhering simultaneously to the socialities, cultural forms, cognitive traditions and ethical sensibilities of both the ancestral and the nascent, evoking a locale inhabited by holy men in scanty robes and slickly suited entrepreneurs; where the journeys of the Mercedes are thwarted by unpassable roads and the antique sounds of the *kora* are drowned by the tango and rock music; in which the villages and shanty towns lack sanitation and the African urban elite drink only imported bottled water; where both seers and psychiatrists practice their crafts; and where a French-speaking African business class anxious to be seen as belonging to the modern world seeks the ministrations of traditional healers, is in fear of spells and curses, consumes holy liquids and initiates ceremonies where 'ancient custom was being more than just respected, it was being revived' (Sembéne, 1976, 4).

The satirical evocation of these bizarre concurrences is further and appropriately augmented by allusions to both the fetishism of pre-capitalist societies and modern commodity fetishism, both mysterious attachments transfixing those who while still immersed in past tradition are subject to the traumas of capitalism's intrusions. A victim seeking to dispel the curse of impotence wears 'esoteric writings [...] like fetishes around his waist'– in the film an actual fetish object is displayed[27] – while the marabout's services awaken in him 'the ancestral atavism of fetishism' (Sembéne, 1976, 42, 55). The new African business class, through a distortion of consciousness wrought by their indeterminate social and cultural positions, experience the perceptible artefacts made in Europe – the gold wristwatch, the Mercedes, the tailored suit, the bottled water – as actively 'thinglike', possessing an independent existence disconnected from their original context as products of human labour and their material properties, to be coveted for the imperceptible power they hold.[28]

It is therefore fitting that in such a society, a crime of material dispossession is punished by a metaphysically delivered and potent affliction. The doubleness in the speech of an African registrar in a hospital practising modern medicine, who modifies his affirmation that science 'is never powerless', by immediately adding 'we are in Africa, where you can't explain or resolve everything in biomedical terms' (Sembéne, 1976, 47), is not a corroboration of the irrational as characteristic of a continent, but a gesture to the continuing power of a received belief system (53). El Hadj, one-time primary school teacher and activist in the independence movement, a member of the Chamber of Commerce and Industry under a self-serving post-independence regime where nationalist rhetoric is still invoked, is presented as a figure of the incomplete fusion of two cultures (4): one a senescent feudalism, the other a pubescent capitalism. His crime has been the theft of communal land from his clan and its conversion into private property – a symbolic act of an individualist money economy replacing pre-capitalist community ownership; his penalty is the 'Xala', the curse of sexual impotence – which is also an allusion to a post-independence regime still reliant on metropolitan capitalism.

Without any sentimentality about premodern consciousness and tradition – patriarchy, polygamy and genital mutilation, the worship of spirits and the belief in gnomes and jinns, seers and saints – the novel unravels the injurious effects of the precipitate arrival of a money economy on pre-capitalist social relationships. Within a substantial body of commentary,[29] I find the most discerning reading of *Xala* to be that of Fredric Jameson, who detected that

> this tale raises the issue of what must finally be one of the key problems in any analysis of Ousmane's [*sic*] work, namely the ambiguous role played in it by archaic or tribal elements [...] The same double historical perspective – archaic customs radically transformed and denatured by the superposition of capitalist relations – seems to me demonstrable in *Xala*. (Jameson, 1986b, 80)[30]

The paradox of Sembéne's reflections on damaged, no-longer-intact indigenous social formations is that unblinking criticism of anachronistic practices coexists with an appreciation of the qualities in older forms of communal life and regret at their disruption. As Frederic Jameson writes: 'Thus the primordial crime of capitalism is exposed: not so much wage labor as such, or the ravages of the money form, or the remorseless and impersonal rhythms of the market, but rather this primal displacement of the older forms of collective life from a land now seized and privatized. It is the oldest of modern tragedies' (Jameson, 1986b, 84). A refusal to scant the commonality that had sustained earlier ways of living, together with a cool-eyed recognition of its accompanying deprivations, is condensed in an abrupt shift of sentiment in this remark: 'The village had neither shop, nor school nor dispensary; there was nothing at all attractive about it in fact. Its life was based on the principles of community interdependence' (Sembéne, 1976, 69).

This demonstration of affection and respect for pre-capitalist ways of life is anticipated by scenes of a landscape inaccessible to modern transport, 'marked by a grandiose, calm austerity and harmony'; in demonstrations of 'the customary courtesy' of its inhabitants; and in giving voice to a peasant's recoil from the nearby town, Dakar, overtaken by machines and a 'rhythm of madness' (Sembéne, 1976, 67–9). *Xala*, then, fashions a world in which the residual and the emergent intersect and clash, but where the agents of political revolution are not yet centre stage, as they are in Sembéne's *God's Bits of Wood* (1960). The venal African compradors, beneficiaries of independence and servants of metropolitan capitalism are agitating for greater economic power; the urban and rural women subject to their husbands and fathers are chafing at patriarchy; and the maimed and diseased beggars, the redundant men and women who can no longer be harboured in the impoverished villages and are surplus to the towns, rebel against their immediate and visible oppressors. Only in the medical student Rama, principled daughter of the corrupt businessman El Hadj, and who despises polygamy, scorns the pretentions of the French-speaking African elite and promotes the use of Wolof, do we see a radical political consciousness in the making.

The choreographed revenge of the dispossessed against the deprivations and injustices they had endured is reminiscent of the gang rape in Luis Buñuel's film *Viridiana* (1961) and is as allegorical.[31] If the surplus of physical affliction among the procession invading El Hadj's villa, overfilled with ostentatious and gaudy commodities, is a symptom of a diseased social order that would engender and tolerate such degradation, it also appears calculated to evoke fear and loathing in the reader: a leper, a human trunk on a roller, a 'cripple with a degenerates' head and runny eyes', another whose maggoty face has 'a hole where his nose had been', a woman with 'a cloven heel and stunted toes', a hunchback, a young man with 'an infected sore on his shin, covered with a zinc plate held in place by a piece of string [giving] off a smell of rotting flesh' (Sembéne, 1976, 108–10). It is noticeable that neither these adverse descriptions nor the beggars' obscene gestures and indecent conduct – causing Rama, who 'was always ready with the words "revolution" and "new social order"', to recoil (1976, 111–12) – are transcribed into cinematic language. Instead, and preceding the assault on property and person, the film visualizes a tableau of crippled beggars in colourful robes, their dignity intact as they make an arduous progress across a bleak landscape, before sharing an austere meal and lamenting the loss of communal funds to a thief who graduates from pickpocket to membership of the Chamber of Commerce.

Moreover, neither sight nor sound of the beggars' banquet in the film betrays a view of the vile and monstrous cohort that emerges from the book's surplus of inimical language. It could be argued that the vitriolic rhetoric is in part mitigated by the recurrent presence and refrain of the dignified beggar from whose community El Hadj had stolen and who in retaliation had laid the curse. Sitting cross-legged on a worn-out sheepskin, as if 'part of the décor' outside the office of the disconcerted businessman who does not recognize him, he is a figure of statuesque poise: hunchbacked with prominent ears and a skinny neck, chanting a never-changing holy complaint 'in a carefully modulated voice'

(Sembéne, 1976, 79) and always 'keeping a proud, distant pose' (101), in making his continuous passive protest.

The book also articulates the anger and contempt of the outcastes when in idioms not elegant but eloquent, they castigate the perfidious African elite: 'People like you live on theft. And exploit the poor [...] All your past wealth [...] was acquired by cheating [...] I am a leper! I am a leper to myself alone. To no one else. But you, you are a disease that is infectious to everyone. The virus is a collective leprosy' (Sembene, 1976, 111). All the same the hostile representation of the despised and rejected in the novella stands as a sign of deformed bodies incapable of the rational exercise of violence. Whereas the film ends with the ritual abasement of the miscreant by righteous enemies, this in the book is followed by the inevitable defeat of the haphazard rebellion and the restoration of the existing regime's fragile order – '[O]utside the forces of order raised their weapons into the firing position' (114) – intimating that the insurgents are not yet in possession of a class consciousness and the organizational skills needed to challenge entrenched power.

It was my intention to recuperate the novel's world as one where earlier forms of economic and social existence disrupted by capitalist expansion coexisted with antecedent modes of labour, belief systems and customs that defied the pervasive presence of the new. The density in the representation of social conditions in permanent crisis places *Xala* in the tradition of realism from which it also departs by accommodating formal and vernacular linguistic registers, bardic and impersonal address, drama and exegesis, sarcasm and exhortation, naturalism and the prodigious. Such stylistic ingenuity surpasses the imitation or adaptation of entrenched novelistic modes, to emerge as the metamorphosis of an historical moment into aesthetic form that, in turn, allows readers access to the material ground of traumatic existential states and the intimacy of their materialization.

Notes

1   See Joe Cleary: 'Twentieth-century modernism, as Franco Moretti writes, emerged with the greatest violence and brilliance not at the center of the modern literary world-system but on the semiperipheries of that system (in the United States, Germany, Ireland, the Scandinavian countries, Bolshevik Russia), and it was from the semiperipheries too (Germany, Hungary, the early USSR) that the most astonishing histories of realism were to be penned, all amid "the ruin of all

space, shattered glass and toppling masonry." [...] some of the semiperipheral modernisms emerged in countries in the throes of imperial collapse (Austria, Russia, Germany, Ottoman Turkey), others in countries emerging as major new world powers (the United States, the USSR, Japan, Germany), others still in largely agrarian colonies proximate to imperial metropoles and undergoing their own revolutionary independence struggles (Ireland, Mexico), others again in radicalized ethnic enclaves within the metropolis that had links to peripheral cultures beyond the metropole (Harlem)' (Cleary, 2012, 257–8, 260–1).

2   A glance at the discussions in the journal *Modernism/modernity* during the past five years shows the inclusion of Edward Upward and J. B. Priestley, both socially aware 'realist' British writers, as well as the avant-garde Soviet painter and architect Vladimir Tatlin and the experimental Portuguese author Fernando Pessoa. Topics range from art, sculpture, jazz, cinema, photography, cabaret and ballet, and themes from Futurism, Dada, the Harlem Renaissance, Fascism, queer and celebrity studies. The topographical expanse of articles covers China, Japan, Brazil, Mexico, Spain, Asia, Africa, the Pacific, Australia and South Africa. In a special issue of the journal *Modern Chinese Literature and Culture*, Eric Hayot presents a two-pronged attack on the notion that modernism began in the West, arguing first that 'at the so-called origin of European modernism, the foreign has already inserted itself', and second that 'it ought to be possible to reconceive a definition of modernism itself that [...] would consider the entire global output that has occurred under the name "modernism"'. This consideration, Hayot argues, 'would permit an understanding of "modernism" from a much larger historical and cultural perspective' (2006, 131). Seeking to expand modernism's locations and challenging its 'Europeanness', Hayot's work has examined the creation of a modernist tradition in Chinese literature (cf., for example, Hayot's *The Hypothetical Mandarin: Sympathy, Modernity, and Chinese Pain* (2009)).

3   Jed Esty, although very differently, also addresses modernism's sensibility of time when arguing that the English 'high' modernist writers and intellectuals sought, in the wake of imperial disintegration, refuge in an insular integrity, introducing 'a moment of shaped time from the resources of national culture', the narrowing of the spatial aperture of metropolitan perception leading to 'an increased focus on the national significance of time as opposed to its transformative, revolutionary potential, and marking them not as aesthetic dinosaurs, but as participants in the transition from metropolitan art to national culture' (Esty, 2004, 8, 50).

4   Rabaté's focus is on 'literary techniques [...] the use of free indirect speech tantamount to inner monologues [...] the numerous verbal leitmotifs and ironically repeated phrases and sentences, and the playfulness of the language that often engages in jokes, puns and double entendres. Modernist too is the overarching perspectivism that makes the point of view shift all the time, multiplying while integrating modern science so as to educate the reader' (2007, 154).

5   Nicholls too refuses to regard modernism as in the past.

6   As Douglas Mao and Rebecca Walkowitz note in their essay 'The New Modernist
    Studies', 'There can be no doubt that modernist studies is undergoing a transnational
    turn. This has produced at least three kinds of new work in the field: scholarship
    that widens the modernist archive by arguing for the inclusion of a variety of
    alternative traditions [...] scholarship that argues for the centrality of transnational
    circulation and translation in the production of modernist art and scholarship
    that examines how modernists responded to imperialism, engaged in projects of
    anticolonialism, and designed new models of transnational community' (2008, 738).
    The authors cite work on Brazil, Lebanon, India, China and Taiwan as well as the
    townships of Dublin and Native American communities in the United States (739).

7   See also Timothy Mitchell's introduction to *Questions of Modernity*, where he
    recognizes the significance of empire and the place of the 'non-West' in the rise
    of modernity (2000, 23). It is refreshing to come across an essay by the eminent
    architectural historian Gwendolyn Wright, which if sometimes lenient in her
    usage of the terminology circulating in the current discussion on modernity,
    imperialism and globalism holds that 'modernism came into being in a world
    framed by colonialism [...] The politics of space involved complex, asymmetrical
    assertions of power: domination, resistance, incorporation, and exclusion. It was
    an unstable calculus, both morally and practically [...] The fears and realities
    of inequality, instability, and extraneous control, all of which began under
    colonialism, have grown apace under the pressures of today's global economy
    [...] definitions of modernity tend to be inflexible, denying the multiple, even
    conflicting layers of conventions and change that shape any place or person. Ernst
    Bloch's term "nonsynchronicities" underscores the simultaneous but radically
    divergent experiences of "Now"' (2002, 125, 126 and 129).

8   As Neil Larsen has remarked, 'It has now in fact become something of an
    intellectual commonplace to remark on the distinctly Latin American and perhaps
    generally "postcolonial" of being both modern and traditional, both "ahead of"
    and yet "behind the times" at once, as if not one but two or multiple histories were
    being lived out in one and the same space' (2001, 139–40).

9   In 1919, Antonio Gramsci had written: 'The colonies were exploited to an
    unprecedented degree, using inflexible and inhuman methods such as can be
    conceived only in periods of civilization as marvellous as that of capitalism. The
    indigenous peoples of the colonies were not even left their eyes for weeping;
    foodstuffs, raw materials, everything possible was combed from the colonies to
    sustain the resistance of the warring metropolitan peoples' (1988, 112).

10 See, for example, Homi Bhabha's *The Location of Culture* (1994, 241). Some
    have theorized modernity as a *Western* phenomenon against which postcolonial
    thinking advances counter-discourses to its terms and truth-claims. See, for
    example, Tsenay Serequeberhan's 'The Critique of Eurocentrism' (1997, 142, 143).

11 See also endnote 4 (2000a, 163) and Harootunian's comment that 'whatever and however a society develops', its coeval modernity 'is simply taking place as the same time as other modernities' (2000b, xv).

12 For Enrique Dussel who rejects the developmentalist and Eurocentric position where modernity is conceptualized 'as an exclusively European phenomenon that expanded from the 17th century on throughout all the "backward" cultures', contending that the phenomenon should be understood as a global one within which Europe, through the discovery, conquest, colonization and integration of other spheres, attained centrality as the system's managers (Dussel, 1998, 18).

13 This scope is invoked in the opening lines of Marshall Berman's *All That Is Solid Melts into Air: The Experience of Modernity*: 'Modern environments and experiences cut across all boundaries of geography and ethnicity, of class and nationality, of religion and ideology: in this sense, modernity can be said to unite all mankind. There is a mode of vital experience – experience of space and time, of the self and others, of life's possibilities and perils – that is shared by men and women all over the world today. I will call this body of experience "modernity"' (2003, 1).

14 Osborne has suggested that there are 'three distinct but connected approaches to the concept of modernity: modernity as a *category of historical periodization, a quality of social experience and an (incomplete) project*' (1995, 5).

15 As Adorno also notes, 'There is no material content, no formal category of artistic creation, however mysteriously transmitted and itself unaware of the process, which did not originate the empirical reality from which it breaks free […] it is precisely as artefacts, as products of social labour, that they [artworks] also communicate with the empirical experience they reject and from which they draw' (Adorno, 1977, 190).

16 In a 1931 essay on *The Old Curiosity Shop* (1841), Adorno observes that 'the prebourgeois form of Dickens' novels becomes a means of dissolving the very bourgeois world they depict', adding that the novels of Dickens 'contain a fragment of the dispersed baroque that maintains a strange ghostly presence in the nineteenth century' (1991–92, 2: 171, 172).

17 See in this context Gabriel Garcia Marquez's comment: 'I am a realist writer because I believe that in Latin-America, everything is possible, everything is real – We live surrounded by these fantastic and extraordinary things […] I believe that we have to work, investigating language and the technical forms of narration so that the entire fantastic reality of Latin America might form part of our books, and so that Latin-American literature might in fact correspond to Latin-American life where the most extraordinary things happen every day […] I believe that what we should do is to promote it as a form of reality which can give something new to universal literature' (qtd. in Harris, 1967, 24–5).

18 See Thierry Bayle's 'Plea for Créolité' (1994) and Martin Munro's 'Chronicle of the Seven Sorrows (Review)' (2005).

19 The latter part of the essay 'On the Marvellous Real' first appeared as the Preface to
    Carpentier's novel *The Kingdom of this World* (1949), later expanded in 1967 and
    more recently published in *Magical Realism: Theory, History, Community* (1995).
    In Journey through the Labyrinth: Latin American Fiction in the Twentieth Century,
    Gerald Martin cites the following passage: 'After having felt the undeniable
    enchantment of this Haitian earth, after having discerned magical warnings on
    the red roads of the Central Plateau, after having heard the drums of Petro and
    Rada, I was moved to compare the marvelous reality I'd just experienced with
    the tiresome attempts to arouse the marvelous that has characterized certain
    European literatures for last thirty years' (1989, 171). For an analytic overview of
    the intellectual climate in which Carpentier was writing, see Timothy Brennan:
    'he was convinced that surrealism – laboriously constructed in the urban centers
    of Europe – already existed in the Americas [...] arguing that everything visually
    associated with surrealist discovery can already been found there' (2001, 18).

20 See also Roberto Schwarz's *A Master on the Periphery of Capitalism* (2001, 27). In
    'On Magic Realism in Film', Fredric Jameson refers to Cuban theoreticians of the
    1980s who, instead of decrying the technological underdevelopment of Cuban film,
    affirmed a 'Third World aesthetic politics' whereby 'its own "imperfect cinema"',
    consequent on economic constraints, is transformed 'into a strength and a choice, a
    sign of its own distinct origins and content' (1986a, 316).

21 See Yusufu Maiangwa's 'The Duty of Violence' (1979).

22 In proposing a postcolonial critical aesthetics, Bahri notes but without
    demonstrating that postcolonial literature provides glimpses of the contradictions
    and unevenness of global social development in the atonality of two time-schemes.
    Her interest is in formal innovation of traditional form that is in keeping with the
    preoccupation with hybridity in cultural studies where words like border-crossings
    abound. See also Stephen Heath's contribution to the debate on *World Literature*:
    'The very idea of the study now of world literature is involved in the hybrid:
    reading not merely comparatively and generically, this novel from here next to
    that one from there, but migrationally and impurely, writings intermingled with
    one another, against the grain of ready – legitimate – identities. To look at genre
    politically is to read with just such a migrant's-eye view, which is another definition
    of "world literature", the newness its study makes' (2004, 74). Here the new is
    conflated with the hybrid and the hybrid conceals the singularities marking the
    literatures of the peripheries.

23 Arguing for the correlation between space and style, Moretti refers to Ernst Mayr's
    theory of alopathic speciation predicting that 'all major transformations occur
    when the device enters a new cultural habitat', a concept which posits that 'a change
    in the environment encourages the spread of morphological novelties of which
    speciation is *the most significant* but not the only one' (2006, 78, 79).

24 See Samba Gadjigo, 'Ousmane Sembène: The Life of a Revolutionary Artist', an introductory outline of the forthcoming authorized biography of Ousmane Sembène of the same title (www.newsreel.org/articles/OusmaneSembene.htm).

25 See Sembène's novel *God's Bits of Wood* (1962 [1960]). Inspired by the strike of peasants recruited to work on the construction of the Dakar-Niger railway in 1947–48, the novel narrates the transformations in consciousness of those who, while still connected to pre-capitalist modes of production and attached to archaic social practices, are in the process of translating their experience of oppression and exploitation into organized resistance. Certainly the novel enacts a moment when agricultural workers pulled from the plough and women separated from their cooking pots discover their capacity for effective agency within a world in the throes of a form of modernization that would consign them to permanent servitude. The novel, however, is not only a reimagining of a new-found militancy: the kaleidoscopic protest march during which the forging of solidarity is interrupted by recurrent clashes between the traditionalists and those amenable to modernization estranges the real by staging the clash between the existent and the emergent.

26 See David Murphy, 'An African Brecht' (2002).

27 See Laura Mulvey, '*Xala*, Ousmene Sembène: The Carapace That Failed' (1991).

28 Marx: 'A commodity appears at first sight an extremely obvious, trivial thing. But its analysis brings out that it is a very strange thing, abounding in metaphysical subtleties and theological niceties.'

29 In addition to work cited in text and endnotes, see, for example, Ogundokun (2013), Messier (2011), Sorensen (2010) and Lynn (2003).

30 For a polemical and pedantic challenge to Jameson's reading, see Edwards (2004).

31 Since writing this I have come across an essay that makes this same point: see Marcia Landy, 'Political Allegory and "Engaged Cinema": Sembène's "Xala"' (1984).

Bibliography

Adorno, T. W. (1977), 'Reconciliation under Duress', in *Aesthetics and Politics*. London: New Left Books, pp. 151–76.

Adorno, T. W. (1991–92), *Notes to Literature*, 2 vols. W. W. Nicholsen (transl.), R. Tiedemann (ed.). New York: Columbia University Press.

Adorno, T. W. (1997), *Aesthetic Theory*, G. Adorno and R. Tiedemann (eds), R. Hullot-Kentor (new transl. and ed.). London: The Athlone Press.

Amin, S. (1974), *Accumulation on a World Scale*. New York: Monthly Review Press.

Anderson, P. (1984), 'Modernity and Revolution'. *New Left Review*, 144, (March–April), 96–113.

Appiah, K. A. (1991), 'Is the "Post" in "Postcolonial" the "Post" in "Postmodern"?'. *Critical Inquiry*, 17, (2), (Winter), 336–57.

Bahri, D. (2003), *Native Intelligence: Aesthetics, Politics and Postcolonial Literature*. Minneapolis: University of Minnesota Press.

Barrows, A. (2010), *The Cosmic Time of Empire: Modern Britain and World Literature*. Berkeley: University of California Press.

Berman, J. (2012), *Modernist Commitments: Ethics, Politics and Transnational Modernism*. New York: Columbia University Press.

Berman, M. (2003), *All That Is Solid Melts into Air: The Experience of Modernity*. London: Verso.

Bhabha, H. (1994), *The Location of Culture*. London: Routledge.

Brennan, T. (2001), 'Introduction', in A. Carpentier (ed.), *Music in Cuba*. Minneapolis: University of Minnesota Press.

Brennan, T. (2014a), 'Homiletic Realism', in E. Kent and T. Tomsky (eds), *Negative Cosmopolitanism*. Montreal: McGill/Queens University Press, pp. 24–39.

Brennan, T. (2014b), 'The Case against Irony', in B. Etherington and J. Zimbler (eds), 'The Crafts of World Literature', special issue of the *Journal of Commonwealth Literature*, 49, (Fall), 1–16.

Carpentier, A. (1995), 'On the Marvellous Real', in L. P. Zamora and W. B. Faris (eds), *Magical Realism: Theory, History, Community*. Durham and London: Duke University Press, pp. 75–88.

Cleary, J. (2012), 'Realism after Modernism and the Literary World-System'. *Modern Language Quarterly*, special issue 'Peripheral Realisms', 73, (3), (September), 255–68.

Deckard, S. (2012), 'Peripheral Realism, Millennial Capitalism'. *Modern Language Quarterly*, special issue 'Peripheral Realisms', 73, (3), (September), 351–72.

Doyle, L. (2012), 'Modernist Studies and Inter-Imperiality in the Longue Durée', in M. Wollaeger and M. Eatough (eds), *The Oxford Handbook of Global Modernisms*. Oxford: Oxford University Press, pp. 669–95.

Dussel, E. (1998), 'Beyond Eurocentrism: The World-System and the Limits of Modernity', in F. Jameson and M. Miyoshi (eds), *The Cultures of Globalization*. Durham, NC: Duke University Press, pp. 3–31.

Edwards, B. (2004), 'The Genres of Postcolonialism'. *Social Text*, 22, (1), 1–15.

Elliott, E., Caton, L. F. and Rhyne, J. (eds), *Aesthetics in a Multicultural Age*. Oxford: Oxford University Press.

Esty, J. (2004), *A Shrinking Island: Modernism and National Culture in England*. Princeton: Princeton University Press.

Esty, J. and Lye, C. (2012), 'Peripheral Realisms Now'. *Modern Language Quarterly*, special issue on 'Peripheral Realisms', 73, (3), (September), 269–88.

Everdell, W. (1997), *The First Moderns: Profiles in the Origins of Twentieth Century Thought*. Chicago: Chicago University Press.

Friedman, S. S. (2006), 'Periodizing Modernism: Postcolonial Modernities and the Space/Time Borders of Modernist Studies'. *Modernism/Modernity*, 13, (3), (September), 425–43.

Glissant, É. (1989), *Caribbean Discourse: Selected Essays*, M. Dash (ed.). Charlottesville: University of Virginia Press.

Gramsci, A. (1988), 'The War in the Colonies', in D. Forgacs (ed.), *A Gramsci Reader*. London: Lawrence and Wishart, pp. 112–13.

Harootunian, H. (2000a), *History's Disquiet: Modernity, Cultural Practice, and the Question of Everyday Life*. New York: Columbia University Press.

Harootunian, H. (2000b), *Overcome by Modernity: History, Culture, and Community in Interwar Japan*. Princeton: Princeton University Press.

Harris, W. (1967), 'Tradition and the West Indian Novel', in *Tradition, the Writer and Society*. London and Port of Spain: New Beacon Publications, pp. 28–47.

Harris, W. (1970), *History, Fable and Myth in the Caribbean and Guianas*. Georgetown, Guyana: The National History and Arts Council Ministry of Information and Culture.

Harvey, D. (1989), *The Condition of Postmodernity*. Oxford: Blackwell.

Hayot, E. (2009), *The Hypothetical Mandarin: Sympathy, Modernity, and Chinese Pain*. Oxford: Oxford University Press.

Heath, S. (2004), 'The Politics of Genre', in C. Prendergast (ed.), *Debating World Literature*. London: Verso, pp. 163–74.

Huyssen, A. (2005), 'Geographies of Modernism in a Globalizing World', in A. Thacker and P. Brooker (eds), *Geographies of Modernism: Literature, Culture, Places*. London: Routledge, pp. 6–18.

Jameson, F. (1986a), 'On Magic Realism in Film'. *Critical Inquiry*, 12, (Winter), 301–25.

Jameson, F. (1986b), 'Third-World Literature in the Era of Multinational Capitalism'. *Social Text*, 15, 65–88.

Jameson, F. (1991), *Postmodernism or the Cultural Logic of Late Capitalism*. London: Verso.

Jameson, F. (2002), *A Singular Modernity*. London: Verso.

Jameson, F. (2003), 'The End of Temporality'. *Critical Inquiry*, 29, (4), (Summer), 695–718.

Kent, E. and Tomsky, T. (2017), 'Introduction: Negative Cosmopolitanism', in E. Kent and T. Tomsky (eds), *Negative Cosmopolitanism: Cultures and Politics of World Citizenship after Globalization*. Montreal and Kingston: McGill-Queen University Press, pp. 263–82.

Landy, M. (1984), 'Political Allegory and "Engaged Cinema": Sembène's "Xala"'. *Cinema Journal*, 23, (3), (Spring), 31–46.

Larsen, N. (2001), *Determinations: Essays in Theory, Narrative and Nation in the Americas*. London: Verso.

Lawrence, N. (2015), 'The Question of Peripheral Realism', in S. Deckard, N. Lawrence, N. Lazarus, G. Macdonald, U. P. Mukherjee, B. Parry and S. Shapiro (eds), *Combined and Uneven Development: Towards a New Theory of World-Literature*. Liverpool: Liverpool University Press, pp. 49–80.

Lazarus, N. (2011), *The Postcolonial Unconscious*. Cambridge: Cambridge University Press.

Löwy, M. (2007), 'The Current of Critical Irrealism', in M. Beaumont (ed.), *Adventures in Realism*. Oxford: Blackwell, pp. 193–206.

Lukács, G. (1973 [1949]), *Dostoevsky, in Marxism and Human Liberation: Essays on History, Culture and Revolution by György Lukács*, R. Wellek (transl.). New York: Dell Publishing Company.

Lynn, T. J. (2003), 'Politics, Plunder, and Postcolonial Tricksters: Ousmane Sembène's *Xala*'. *International Journal of Francophone Studies*, 6, (3), (1 December), 183–96.

Mahaffey, V. (2007), *Modernist Literature: Challenging Fictions*. Oxford: Blackwell.

Maiangwa, Y. (1979), 'The Duty of Violence', in Kolawole Ogungbesan (ed.), *New West African Literature*. London: Heinemann, pp. 10–20.

Mao, D. and Walkowitz, R. (2008), 'The New Modernist Studies'. *PMLA*, 123, (3), 737–49.

Marcuse, H. (1977), 'Adorno on Brecht', in *Aesthetics and Politics*. London: New Left Books, pp. 178–95.

Martin, G. (1989), *In Journey through the Labyrinth: Latin American Fiction in the Twentieth Century*. London: Verso.

Messier, V. (2011), 'Decolonizing National Consciousness Redux: Ousmane Sembène's *Xala* as Transhistorical Critique'. *Postcolonial Text*, 6, (4), 1–21.

Mitchell, T. (2000), *Questions of Modernity*. Minneapolis: University of Minnesota Press.

Moretti, F. (2006), 'The End of the Beginning'. *New Left Review*, September/October, 41, 71–86.

Mulvey, L. (1991), '*Xala*, Ousmene Sembène: The Carapace That Failed'. *Third Text*, 16, (Autumn/Winter), 19–37.

Munro, M. (2005), 'Chronicle of the Seven Sorrows (Review)'. *Callaloo*, 28, (4), (Fall), 1103–05.

Murphy, D. (2002), 'An African Brecht'. *New Left Review*, 16, (July–August), 115–29.

Nicholls, P. (1995), *Modernisms: A Literary Guide*. Berkeley and Los Angeles: University of California Press.

Ogundokun, S. A. (2013), 'Cultural and Political Alienation in Sembène Ousmane's *Xala*'. *Global Journal of Human Social Science Research*, 13, (4-A), 27–31.

Osborne, P. (1995), *The Politics of Time: Modernity and Avant-Garde*. London: Verso.

Rabaté, J.-M. (2007), *1913: The Cradle of Modernism*. Oxford: Blackwell.

Radhakrishnan, R. (2003), *Theory in an Uneven World*. Oxford: Blackwell.

Schwarz, R. (1992), *Misplaced Ideas: Essays on Brazilian Culture*, J. Gledson (ed. with an intro.). London: Verso.

Schwarz, R. (2001), *A Master on the Periphery of Capitalism*, J. Gledson (transl.) Durham: Duke University Press.

Sembène, O. (1962 [1960]), *God's Bits of Wood*, F. Price (transl.). London: Heinemann.

Sembène, O. (1976), *Xala*, C. Wake (transl.). London: Heinemann.

Sembène, O. (2005), 'Interview with Ousmane Sembène'. *Socialist Worker Online*, 1955 (11 June).

Serequeberhan, T. (1997), 'The Critique of Eurocentrism', in E. C. Ez (ed.), *Postcolonial African Philosophy: A Critical Reader*. Oxford: Blackwell, pp. 141–61.

Sorensen, E. P. (2010), 'Naturalism and Temporality in Ousmane Sembène's *Xala*'. *Research in African Literatures*, 41, (2), (Summer), 222–43.

Trotsky, L. (1965), *History of the Russian Revolution*, vol. I. London: Gollanz.

Williams, R. (1989), *The Politics of Modernism*, T. Pinkey (ed. and intro.). London: Verso.

Wood, P. (1992), 'The Politics of the Avant-Garde', in *The Great Utopia: The Russian and Soviet Avant-Garde 1915–1932*. New York: Guggenheim Museum, pp. 1–23.

Wright, G. (2002), 'Building Global Modernisms'. *Grey Room*, 7, (Spring), 124–34.

20

Modernist Literature and Politics

Tyrus Miller

Preliminary Considerations

The relation of modernist literature to politics has been the subject of heated debate since modernism's emergence in the later nineteenth and early twentieth centuries. Claims for modernism's anticipation of new utopian human traits and social orders have been met with counterclaims of its portending of degeneration, social decline and collapse into sheer nihilism and anarchy. It has been seen as a rhetorical toolbox for individual and collective liberation, and, antithetically, as an oppressive instrument for aestheticizing power. For some it is an efficacious unshackling of mind and word from the chains of sterile tradition, for others a wanton destruction of the past and its values, without any affirmative compensation for them. Modernism has been aligned with such varying political tendencies as anarchism, socialism, fascism, revolutionary nationalism, the liberal defence of Western freedom against Eastern totalitarianism, pacifist internationalism, and even, in the recent 'culture wars' in journals like *The New Criterion*, with the politically conservative defence of quality, virtue and cultural tradition itself against liberal multiculturalism, post-modernism and political correctness. Strongly different ideological emphases, rhythms of development and national features are observable even within historical modernism's European 'core', and these differences become all the more pronounced when modernisms from colonial-imperial 'peripheries' and postcolonial independence cultures where complex appropriations of and resistances to metropolitan cultures come into play. Modernism has been viewed as a corollary of political internationalism, as an outgrowth of modern nationalism, as a product of complex transnational networks and exchanges, and as a reflection of distributed or utopian cultural geographies that do not neatly map onto the borders and categories of political geography but seem to place them, sometimes explicitly, in question. Depending on which language bases, which media and genres, which geographical units, which periods and time spans and which subcultural specifications (women writers, queer writers, exile writers, postcolonial writers and so on) one begins with, very different judgement about modernism's political valences will result. Consequentially, any attempt to formulate an inclusive theoretical and historiographic view of modernist literature's or modernist aesthetics' relation to politics seems quickly to verge towards the ambiguity, complexity and contradictoriness of a modernist artwork itself.

A further complication of the question of modernist literary politics is the relatively uncertain, even confused, relation between the several senses in which the two complex terms 'modernism' and 'politics' might be conjoined. What, for example, is the relation between the political commitments of the biographical modernist author and the 'politics' of his or her literary work? If an author professes support for Mussolini, for example, does the work that he writes automatically become, by virtue of that adherence or advocacy, 'fascist'? If an individual modernist writer's work (e.g. John Dos Passos) is associated with left-wing politics, or another with right-wing politics (e.g. T. S. Eliot), does either individual case tell us anything generalizable about 'modernism' as a broader literary tendency? What is the relation between the work's 'politics' understood as its internally represented ideological commitments and its 'politics' as its external, practical social commitments and effects (if any)? Must a modernist author or work have a manifest relationship to a state, a party or a political movement to be considered 'political'? If an author changes political affiliations – explicitly renouncing fascism as did, for example, Wyndham Lewis in the later 1930s or shifting from conservatism to democratic liberalism as did Thomas Mann after the First World War – does this affect only the 'politics' of the work subsequent to the ideological turn or the 'politics' of the whole corpus? Or, vice versa, does a previous political orientation continue to shadow the 'modernism' of the whole body of work? How can the futurist modernism of F. T. Marinetti be fascist, while the futurist modernism of Aldo Palezzeschi was anti-fascist? Were these both 'modernist' in the same way, or did their varying political directions also shape their aesthetics divergently? Insofar as Marinetti's and Pound's modernisms were ostensibly 'fascist' were they 'fascist' in the same way? And did the modernisms of Pound and Gottfried Benn relate to, respectively, Italian and German fascism in analogous or divergent ways? None of these questions, and many more we might pose, are trivial ones. They may offer directions for substantial, consequential historical and theoretical investigation by critics, theoreticians and historians. But our ability to proliferate such questions at will points to the great difficulty in making general statements about the relations of objects of such internal complexity as modernist literature and politics. It is easy to end up in a kind of exasperated scepticism, exclaiming of the whole issue of modernism's politics, as of Samuel Beckett's character Watt in the eponymous novel, 'I tell you nothing is known!' (Beckett, 1959, 21).

At the same time, however, mere scepticism towards generalizing precepts will not suffice either. Political meanings and ideological engagements manifestly accompany and in many cases drive modernist literature's linguistic, rhetorical and moral provocations, while this literature consistently and self-reflexively engages with the *question* of its own relation to politics, however variable the answers that it embraces may be. In fact, I wish to suggest, it may be precisely its singular combinations of political intention or interest and ideological indefiniteness that reveals an essential feature of modernism's literary politics: its 'representational' underdetermination, its speculative and inventive nature, its open adaptability to a variety of social-historical and ideological contexts. As Ferenc Fehér notes of modernist art and literature, it is 'thoroughly *free of ideology* (tolerating no interpretations, refuting all "ideal content" imposed on it), and at the same time it is thoroughly *ideological* (in so far as the "form", the formed world, is, so to speak, a sensualized theorem)' (Fehér, 1976, 185–6).

Modernist form may distance the work from any thesis-like formulation of a political position or argument, but it may at the same time open up a set of alternative possibilities for the modernist work to evoke political meanings and ideas. The paradoxically non-ideological/ideological 'sensualized theorem' of the singular modernist work stands in a charged hermeneutic tension with the actually existing world of the present. The modernist work resists decoding and interpretation; it is undetermined in its meaning, even nonsensical and incoherent in relation to the codes of 'normal', present reality. Yet it also, implicitly, urges towards a reorganization of that reality in a future in which its apparent difficulty or nonsensicality will be, at last, revealed to have been, all along, a higher form of clarity and sense. A piece of Russian futurist *zaum* poetry or a Gertrude Stein *Tender Buttons* does not expect immediate understanding from the present. Rather, it speculates on a future – occupied by, for instance, Malevich's transfigured 'Strong Men of the Future' – in which it might be *normal* to speak like the poetry of Khlebnikov or Kruchenykh, or in the cubist textures of Stein, and it ponders the conditions under which this future might come to exist. Insofar as the idioms and forms of the work project both a destruction of the present and a transfigured future, in which current indetermination is the typological anticipation of fulfilled meaning in a future *historical* order, there is a utopian 'politics' that inheres in much modernist writing, and certainly in its most radical, experimental instances.

In what remains, I will pursue this hypothesis further, exploring three distinct cases of modernist politics in which modernist writers deploy their works' utopian-critical tension with the present to point towards and imagine future, still-to-be-realized ideological meanings, a 'possible politics' that is evoked and indexed, if not fully represented or depicted by the work. The forms of possibility that different modernisms project, and the experimental literary means of producing them, are radically different across authors, contexts and periods. Yet, I will argue, together they share this common feature: they address and remotivate the gap between their own literary representations and actually existing politics, in order not simply to innovate in the form and content of the literary but also to imagine new shapes and expressions that politics might, in the present and future, take on. The three cases I will discuss relate in indicative ways to strong political background contexts; we may use them, however, to guide us in the interpretation of works for which the political background may be less intense, explicit or well defined. My cases are the politics of revolutionary messianism, of radical transfiguration latent in the present, in the poetics of the Dadaist Hugo Ball and the Hungarian avant-garde poet Lajos Kassák; a dystopian, demonic variant of this same, which represents a dystopian variant of this same modernist theo-political impulse in Wyndham Lewis's 1927 satirical novel *The Childermass*; and the 'Popular Front' modernism of John Dos Passos, who conceives of the modernist montage novel as the means to project the aesthetic image of 'the People', a popular political force with multiple cultural, racial-ethnic and geographical characteristics.

Revolutionary Messianism: Hugo Ball and Lajos Kassák

For those familiar with the name Hugo Ball, the first association is almost invariably with the costumed figure of 'the magic bishop' performing Dadaist sound poetry in the Cabaret Voltaire in wartime Zurich. The image of Ball reciting, in a priest-like liturgical voice, poems such as 'Gadji beri bimba' and 'Karawane', hoping to use words magically to heal the wounds inflicted by war and technical modernity, has become canonical. It is less observed that the Dadaist episode represents only a few months of Ball's career and that the dramatic theatricality of his Dada persona has obscured the erudite, restlessly intellectual and politically engaged character of his writings. The Dadaist phase was followed by important activity as a political journalist, cultural critic and religious writer, up to his premature death from cancer in 1927. Along with the messianic philosopher Ernst Bloch, he was one of the regular contributors to the progressive newspaper *Freie Zeitung* in Bern, where he also made the acquaintance of his neighbour Walter Benjamin, who was in Switzerland to flee the draft. After a conversion experience in which he embraced a monastic Catholicism, he wrote a book on Byzantine Christianity, which focused on three saints' lives, an important review of Carl Schmitt's Catholic juridical and political thought, the first literary critical treatment of his friend and benefactor Hermann Hesse and many other diverse works animated by his spiritual and political vision. What unites these various artistic, political and spiritual threads in Ball's work is the orientation of a fallen present towards an age of salvation, in which the apparent chaos of today, expressed in the extremities of Dadaist and expressionist verse, will be prophetically redeemed as portents of a higher sense to come.

Ball's relation with Ernst Bloch was warm and mutually influential, though eventually strained by intellectual and personal differences. In his diary entry of 18 November 1917, Ball wrote that 'I am often seen with a utopian friend, E. B., and he induces me to read More and Campanella, while he studies Münzer and the Eisenmenger' (Ball, 1996, 145). Already as early as 1914, Hugo Ball became interested in Thomas Münzer, one of the revolutionary religious inspirations and leaders of the peasant uprising in Germany in 1525, and worked with his picture hung above his work desk. The conclusion to the first chapter of Ball's 1919 book *Critique of the German Intelligentsia* pitted Thomas Münzer's connection of social freedom and religious belief against Martin Luther's attempt to appease the feudal princes. After publishing *Spirit of Utopia* in its first version in 1918, Bloch went on to publish a subsequent book *Thomas Münzer als Theologe der Revolution* in 1921; Ball encouraged Bloch to research the figure of Münzer. In turn, Walter Benjamin met Ernst Bloch through Hugo Ball. Gershom Scholem describes Benjamin's association with Ball as being both personal and intellectual (1981, 78–9).

Entries from Ball's diary, published late in his life as *Flight Out of Time*, exemplify the messianic dimension of his artistic thinking. A central dimension of his artistic, spiritual and political vision and the main axis linking them is the idea of incarnation. Already in an entry on 4 October 1915, Ball wrote:

> I tend to compare my own private experiences with the nation's. I see it almost as a matter of conscience to perceive a certain parallel there. It may be a whim, but I could not live without the conviction that my own personal fate is an abbreviated version of the fate of the whole nation. If I had to admit that I was surrounded by highwaymen, nothing in the world could convince me that they were not my fellow countrymen whom I live among. I bear the signature of my homeland, and I feel surrounded by it everywhere I go. (1996, 30)

This representative status would take on an explicitly 'passional' dimension in a note of 5 July 1919: 'I cannot make a fresh start in private and just for myself alone. All my ideas must go with me, the whole fabric that I grew up in and that my mind can grasp. That pulls and tears and bleeds from a hundred wounds. I want to fit in with the whole nation, or not to live' (176). And in a more general, philosophical way, in an entry dated 31 July 1920, Ball presents incarnation as the foundation of an alternative vision of history, which in turn motivates his salvational conception of the artist, occupying a position near the saint in a spiritual hierarchy of the capacity for suffering:

> The great, universal blow against rationalism and dialectics, against the cult of knowledge and abstractions, is: the incarnation. Ideas and symbols have become flesh in the divine-human person; they have suffered and bled in and with the person, they have been crucified. It is no longer just the intellect but the whole person that is the representative of the spiritual heaven. (192)

This incarnational poetics and politics also characterize the early messianic stance of the important Hungarian avant-garde poet, novelist, editor, artist group organizer and visual artist Lajos Kassák. Kassák, who came from a provincial city in the area of Greater Hungary now in Slovakia, went from a lower-middle-class family into work in workshops and factories, where he participated in the socialist labour struggles and demonstrations of pre–First World War Budapest. A dropout from school, he educated himself as a writer and founded a succession of journals – *A Tett* (The Act), *Ma* (Today), *Dokumentum* (Document), *Munka* (Work) – that established him as the incontestable centrepoint of the Hungarian avant-garde, which was characterized by both aesthetic and political radicalism. The journal *A Tett* was one of the central expressions of anti-war sentiment among the artistic intelligentsia and was banned by the authorities; its successor *Ma* spanned the end of the war and the Hungarian Soviet Republic of 1919, and Kassák managed to revive it in exile in Vienna and maintain it for another five years, while getting contributions from the most important avant-garde writers and artists from all over Europe. *Dokumentum* and *Munka* were path-breaking journals representing the political modernism that we associate with figures like Walter Benjamin and Bertolt Brecht, and, in fact, Benjamin published two articles in Hungarian translation in *Dokumentum* in 1926–27.

Kassák was a man of singular will and intelligence and his biography is an extraordinary one. Yet the cultural and political context of Hungary made it particularly ripe for the incarnation of the messianic idea in the figure of its artists and poets. Already in the 1848 independence struggle, the poet Sándor Petőfi set the tone for seeing the poet as the representative of the suffering and potential of the nation. In the first years of the war, the passionate apocalypticism of the influential modernist poet Endre Ady, whom Georg Lukács described at the time as a religious poet without God, was an important impetus towards the development of a revolutionary messianism (Lukács, 1998, 47–54). This climate of ideas was given what seemed practical confirmation with the declaration of the Hungarian Soviet Republic in March 1919, in which nearly all major modern intellectuals, from non-Communist modernists such as Béla Bartók to Communist converts like Lukács and Béla Balázs to utopian anarcho-communists such as Kassák, participated. During the first month of the Hungarian Soviet Republic (*Tanácsköztársaság*), on 10 April 1919, the avant-garde critic Iván Hevesy published an article in Kassák's journal *Ma* entitled 'Mass Culture, Mass Art', in which he took up Lukács's messianic impulse and situated the task of avant-garde art in fostering revolutionary, salvational impulses. Hevesy saw in the new mass culture an overcoming of individualism in a new epic representativeness, which provides the foundation for the unified belief of which great mass art requires. Typical of the cultural revolutionary viewpoint, Hevesy emphasized the spiritual dimension of the masses over their practical aims. 'It must be strongly emphasized', he writes, 'that the first and foremost precondition for the emergence of a social art is the emergence of a religion of the masses. The economic situation of the masses, their degree of liberation or exploitation can only play a secondary role' (Hevesy, 2002, 229). Seeing the essence of religion as 'belief in a perfected human life', Hevesy went on to argue that the 'new order', the Soviet Republic, 'brings a new religion [...] that demonstrates the perfect life right here on earth and does not defer to the goal of perfected life. [...] The new religion and the new society will form a new aesthetic culture and folk art of an inconceivably high order, next to which all that has gone before will shrink and vanish' (229).

Kassák added one further ingredient to Hevesy's millenarian conception of mass art, the 'incarnational' role of the avant-garde artist as the collectively representational figure. In his essay 'Activism', a lecture given on the eve of the declaration of the Soviet Republic and published in *Ma* in the same issue as Hevesy's article, Kassák argued that he and his avant-garde colleagues were fighting for the political goals of Communism, but also against the constraint of human liberation by politics, in favour of a permanent 'existential' revolution of life. They were fighting, in Kassák's coinage, for the 'collective individuum', which can be understood as a new epic monumentality and representativeness of the singular, individual artist as mass activist. Kassák saw 'activism' as an artistic and social movement 'toward individual revolution that will outlast all forms of government and party dictatorships'. Kassák formulated his goals – the task of the collective individuum and the avant-garde artist – as a revolution beyond Communism:

> The revolution of the political parties does not yet constitute the great all-consuming revolution of life [...]
> For us the meaning of life lies therefore beyond the speculative revolution of political parties, in the endlessness of existential revolution.
> ...
> With this conceptual definition we declare the rebirth of the human soul as the barely definable ultimate goal of the revolution – beyond Communism which is held by many to be the ultimate goal. (Kassák, 2002, 223)

The Hungarian Soviet Republic collapsed in July 1919, after a few, intense bloody months, and the response was a violent, repressive White Terror, with anti-semitic pogroms and a mobilization of Catholic conservative rhetoric to legitimate the militarist counter-revolutionary dictatorship of Admiral Horthy. After a period of imprisonment, Kassák managed to get across the border to Vienna, where he revived his journal *Ma* and provided a centre of avant-garde activity among the exiles from the terror. The avant-garde group around Kassák, however, began to polarize into those who remained aligned with him and those who more closely aligned themselves with the ultra-left of the Communist Party in the proletarian culture movement. Kassák's own writing in the three years after the collapse of the Hungarian Soviet Republic took on tragic shadings, but in no way lost their messianic tone, which, if anything, was heightened into a veritable passion of exilic suffering. Thus in his preface to his lyrical prose-poetic narrative of the revolution and reaction of 1919, *Máglyák Énekelnek* (The Bonfires Sing), Kassák explicitly takes on the role as the incarnated, crucified, Luciferian-Christ poet of that crushed revolution:

> When I place this, my book, before the reader, I feel that with my 34 years of life, I have passed the first station of my being a writer. [...] The sole indicator of value

is the artist's power and humanity, which as one is the measure of the world's level. Yet the world's totality is movement, eternal revolution in itself. Every artistic creation, however, as the world's expression, is a revolutionary demonstration in the face of limitation (the state, the conservative representative of society). Before viewers and listeners I want to make 'artistic traditions' collapse. And from this comes the book's apparent irreality and formal strangeness. (Kassák, 1920, n.p.)

Wavering between prose and poetry, between grimly realistic portrayals of pogroms and expressionistically abstracted representations of collective impulses, Kassák ends his 120-page text on a rhapsodic note of utopian hope:

> From our pure eyes the river-banks fall away.
> Beliefs bonfire.
> Bonfires sing.
> The goal! The goal!
> Above the city the organs incessantly rain red stars.
> By then, already no one believed in the saintliness of the regime.
> From somewhere the just man set out.
> And in the arms of the poor the pitiless power awakened anew.
> O my young, chance-found brothers! (Kassák, 1920, n.p.)

Satiric-Political Modernism in Wyndham Lewis's *The Childermass*

Wyndham Lewis's *The Childermass* constitutes my second case of how modernist politics is implicit in the tension between modernism's present context and its potential collective normalization in a future yet to be realized. Lewis's novel offers an allegorical vehicle for him to explore an open-ended set of historical, social, political and philosophical-theological ideas that together, in his view, constitute the larger, current modernist *zeitgeist*. *The Childermass* presents a limbo-like world of the dead spirits of young men, many of whom have been killed in the recent trench warfare of the First World War, though according to the fluidity of time in its heterocosmic setting, there are also incongruous mixes of historical period, cultures and races that are part of its world. This setting is a mixture of a military encampment, a concentration camp (a term that Lewis actually uses, though of course not with advance knowledge of what it would come to mean in the 1940s), a political rally and Roman bread-and-circuses festival – all forms of social space strongly marked by political connotations.

The camp is a holding area at one of the gates of the 'Magnetic City', where the souls will pass in and be moulded into a new collective mass. The Magnetic City, it is suggested, is a sort of neo-London, in which all the manifestations of modernity that Lewis also identified in cultural critical books such as *The Art of Being Ruled* (1926) and *Time and Western Man* (1927), from collective politics to the contemporary dedifferentiation of gender, will be manifest as a coherent, realized whole.

The *Childermass* camp is, as it were, the Magnetic City's *temporal* suburb – from which we are on the threshold of passing into the Magnetic City any day. The camp is thus largely a manifestation of time, a spatialized, allegorical dystopic exaggeration of tendencies in the extended present, pointing forward from recent history (First World War) to an imminent future (the coming age of political collectivism). This implication is reinforced by the opening 125 pages of the book – more than a third of its total length – in which the two dead ex-soldiers and schoolboy pals Pullman and Satters wander around in the 'time-flats' surrounding the camp, experiencing its strange phenomenology and manifestations. In these wanderings, Pullman has the tendency to take on traits and the idiom of James Joyce in the mode of *Work in Progress* (to become *Finnegans Wake*), which Lewis pilfered and parodied, while the corpulent, fleshy Satters can lapse into Gertrude Stein-like repetition.

The two young men return to camp from their wanderings in time for the daily proceedings of the camp's chief authority, the Bailiff, a Mephistopheles-like, Machiavellian 'Old Nick' stage devil and comic villain, who also bears traits of the hysterical Roman anarcho-tyrant like Heliogabalus or a brutal 'oriental despot'. In this latter two-thirds of the book, Pullman and Satters become essentially individualized members of a chorus that reacts in stereotyped fashion to a political and philosophical farce being staged by the Bailiff and his enemies in the camp, the hilariously ultra-Hellenic followers of the philosopher Hyperides. The Bailiff is a classic crowd-master, while Hyperides is a hyperbolic personification of resistance to everything the Bailiff represents – a parodic, polemical grotesque by which Lewis dramatizes his ideas, not unlike his persona of 'the Enemy', while also reflecting on the danger of satirical engagement: that the satirist becomes contaminated by the object of satire or appears disfigured by the negative imprint of that which he opposes.

In representing the fluctuating phenomenological fields of the time-flats around the camp, Lewis engages a relatively simple estrangement device, to which he nevertheless steadily accretes ideological, philosophical and aesthetic connotations: the substitution of time for space in the structuring of the object world, bodily motion, visual appearance and measures of proximity and distance. Thus, for example, at a certain point in their wandering, the two young men encounter an eighteenth-century English village full of miniature houses, cows the size of terriers, bush-like trees and diminutive villagers. Besides being a nod to his precursor in philosophical and political satire, Jonathan Swift, Lewis has taken painterly perspective as a metaphor for historical distance: in this world of the dead, being two centuries past from Pullman and Satters translates into being a third of their physical height and weight. More chaotic and deranging is a passage early in the book, in which Pullman and Satters pass through a time-vortex:

> The scene is redistributed, vamped from position to position intermittently at its boundaries. It revolves upon itself in a slow material maelstrom. Satters sickly clings to his strapping little champion: sounds rise on all hands like the sharp screech of ripping calico, the piercing alto of the slate-pencil, or the bassooning of imposing masses, frictioning each other as they slowly turn in concerted circles.
>
> Never before have there been so many objects of uncertain credentials or origin: as it grows more intricate Pullman whisks them forwards, peering into the sky for lost stars twirling about as he has to face two ways at once on the *qui vive* for the new setting, fearing above all reflections, on the look-out for optical traps, lynx-eyed for threatening ambushes of anomalous times behind the orderly furniture of Space or hidden in objects to confute the solid at the last moment, every inch a pilot. (Lewis, 1965, 42–3)

Lewis's implication is not just that his protagonists suffer from this disorganized time-scape. It is also that, in order to move and dwell in it, they need to *adapt* and *adjust* to it. Just as we in the modern present are adapting to new everyday experiences and phenomena, so too his characters Pullman and Satters, to an even more extreme degree, are becoming fluctuating time-beings, whose identity depends not on their physical, embodied, locational continuity, but rather on an asyntactical, futuristic chain of experiences and intensities 'in libertà', whose modernist literary expressions might be found in Marinetti's futurist ejaculations, Stein's continuous present, Joyce's multilingual punning, Proust's slowly thickening memories and Pound's transhistorical citational and stylistic montage.

Ultimately, it is the Bailiff who is the demonic figure who turns mastery of time into mastery of a new political principle, wielding his power over the mass of souls and guiding them on their pathway into the Magnetic City, where they will be the elements of the collectivist polis and a new post-liberal politics. While his alternatingly sinister and ridiculous camp spectacle nods towards modernist references such as Joseph Conrad's colonial outposts and D. H. Lawrence's *Kangaroo* and *The Plumed Serpent*, it is not accidental that the Bailiff deploys Stein and Joyce as touchpoints of his political rhetoric. The Bailiff is a kind of personified mask of modernist time as the continual metamorphoses, mimetism and the exchange of simulacra.

We need not imagine that Lewis's point is to morally castigate his modernist compatriots as the willing accomplices of the real devils who were looming up in the political landscape of the late 1920s. However, he was suggesting that modernist writing had an effective domain that was different from and separate from the direct space of political polemics and electoral campaigns. In the heterocosmic spaces of these texts, in their very distance from everyday life and their experimentation with new linguistic and narrative idioms, Lewis discerned a liquidation of social stabilities, boundaries and edges that could once have been taken for granted. Lewis believed that it was necessary to enter these liquid spaces and stage a polarizing set of confrontations that would harden the friend–enemy relations to a situation of *political* decision: either a final, irreversible capitulation to the forces of liquidation or a sovereign stand to reinstitute solidities and boundaries that had been effaced.

Acknowledging 'the People': Dos Passos's *U.S.A.* Trilogy

In his introductory prose to his *U.S.A.* trilogy, John Dos Passos evokes the meaning of 'USA' in a rhapsodic passage:

> USA is the slice of a continent. USA is a group of holding companies, some aggregations of trade unions, a set of laws bound in calf, a radio network, a chain of moving picture theatres, a column of stock quotations rubbed out and written in by a Western Union boy on a blackboard, a public-library full of old newspapers and dogeared historybooks with protests scrawled on the margins in pencil. USA is the world's greatest river valley fringed with mountains and hills, USA is a set of bigmouthed officials with too many bank accounts. USA is a lot of men buried in their uniforms in Arlington Cemetary. USA is the letters at the end of an address when you are away from home. But mostly USA is the speech of the people. (1996, 2–3)

Dos Passos asserts this at the outset of his more than 1000-page trilogy of novels *The 42nd Parallel*, *1919* and *The Big Money*. But we should not take this so much as a confident assertion that this 'speech of the people' has been achieved by his work, and rather as a designator of a struggle of this speech to be articulated and heard among the other elements Dos Passos names and gives space to in the interlocking narratives, biographical prose poems and 'Camera Eye' stream-of-consciousness elements montaged together in the whole of *U.S.A.* We can, in a sense, see the novel as a dramatization of a struggle for recognition and, to a great extent, that struggle's ultimate failure.

In his provocative *On Populist Reason*, the post-Marxist theoretician Ernesto Laclau formulates his notion of populism in a set of theses, which in turn can help us to explicate the political valences of Dos Passos's writing in *U.S.A.* First, he argues, 'the emergence of "the people" requires the passage – via equivalences – from isolated, heterogeneous demands to a "global" demand which involves the formation of political frontiers and the discursive construction of power as an antagonistic force' (Laclau, 2005, 110). Put in a somewhat more vernacular form, he means that 'the people' appears as a political agent when single particular demands begin to be linked up by their common opposition to some power and the unfulfillment of those demands is experienced as a common injury to a single community; latent in the chain of equivalent, unfulfilled demands is 'the people', ready to emerge onto the political scene. Second, however, there is a crucial step of 'nominating' this political agency as 'the people' and investing it with the feeling that a community may come to feel about its own bond of identity: 'Since, however, this passage [from isolated demands to single, "global" demand] does not follow from a mere analysis of the heterogeneous demands themselves [...] something qualitatively new has to intervene. This is why "naming" can have [a] retrospective effect. This qualitatively differentiated and irreducible moment is what I have called "radical investment." [...] If an entity becomes the object of an investment – as in being in love, or in hatred – the investment belongs necessarily to the order of *affect*' (110). Finally, because the chain of equivalences between demands entering into the political constitution of 'the people' remains, to some substantial degree, particular and irreducibly heterogeneous – composed of individuals and not a fused, uniform 'community' – the content of the name 'the people' and its political orientation is shifting, contestable and potentially unstable. Together, these three features – the movement towards linking particular demands as equivalents, the nomination of these linked equivalents by a collective name and the ambiguity of this name's meaning and reference – constitute the conceptual nodal points of Laclau's theory of populism.

Ironically, it is a strongly anti-modernist Popular Front thinker, Georg Lukács, who provides us with a critical link to understanding how Laclau's post-Marxist populism might illuminate the ambiguous, populist project of Dos

Passos's trilogy. Novels, Lukács consistently suggests, can be understood as a sort of rhetorical laboratory for constituting and nominating 'the people', exhibiting the conditions under which this succeeds or fails and with what social, political and existential results (see Lukács 1979, 1983). Lukács could see this clearly in relation to the realist novel, which, however, he took to be the exclusive and normative type of novel for which this was the case, in part because his theory of reification and ideological distortion was entwined with his particular version of 'populist reason'. Lukács required not only that the novel model the rhetorical articulation of equivalences between particulars and their summation into a collective narrative of an emerging 'people', but also that this model meet the demand for 'objective' social knowledge, as opposed to 'false consciousness' under the sway of reification.

Here, however, we must go beyond both Lukács's judgements of taste and his epistemology of reification, in order to embrace Laclau's idea that the heterogeneity and indefiniteness of the people is irreducible, which makes its identity unstable and the conflicts around its definition *inventive*. Not only, then, for the realist novel but also for a much vaster span of novels this logic of populism, this problem of constituting 'the people', would be at stake. Lukács's focus on the novel, including the realist novel, remains timely, insofar as the logic of populism increasingly defines the political and cultural horizon of our day. What is no longer timely, however, is his exclusive valorization of realism in the articulation of populist reason. 'Constituting the people', I would argue, is not only the underlying object of the great realist novels of Balzac, Tolstoy, Mann and Gorky, as Lukács believed; 'the people' – fulfilled in different ways – is also the object of the works of political modernist writers, such as John Dos Passos, whom Lukács spurned.

Lukács emphasized the question of 'perspective' in his criticism of modernism and defence of realism (1979, 33, 54–5). Ultimately, he implies that a kind of one-point perspective, taking in a temporally and spatially proportionate field of action in context, is the only proper norm that could correspond, mimetically, to the objective historical character of a 'people'. His notion of mimesis is not merely a crude reflection theory, a mirroring of a static, already existing entity. On the contrary, his theory of realism includes in it a pedagogical moment, in which the realist novel constitutes a kind of training ground for becoming, in a full sense, a people – and reflexively stages this emergence as part of its form-content unity. But if I may extend the analogy to painting, Lukács's realist theory rejects out of hand the various dimensions of agency, action, context and interrelationship that other perspectival systems might offer a people to learn from and to clarify its rhetorical articulations: the reversal of field and ground that reverse perspective might allow (Brechtian theatre and certain works of modernist film deliberately deployed this perspectival system); the highlighting of features against a flattened field that might come from a reduced perspectival system; the multiplication of aspects and ambiguities through multiple perspectival systems deployed at once; and so on. *Pace* Lukács, once we see 'the people' as a problematic entity – both epistemologically and as a performatively made and unmade unity – we cannot in advance prescribe what forms it should take. Constituting a people becomes a series of provisional ventures in form-giving, within which the novel may function as a kind of extended and multiple 'essayism', at once tentative in its construction and engaged with the range of social discourses and 'dispositions of the sensible' necessary to any potential popular sovereignty, from science and technology to religion, political ideology, experience of work and aesthetics.

Modernism and populism are thus structurally isomorphic within Popular Front culture, rather than being (as often thought) antinomies or at best mere chronological fellow-travellers, as 'residual' and 'emergent' but successive cultural formations. At the same time, however, 1930s modernist works such as Dos Passos's trilogy project a decisively different hermeneutic task for its readers, in which the accent falls not, first and foremost, on discovering and decoding a representational meaning rendered difficult by modernist form, but rather on fulfilling, through exemplary acts of reading, the emergence of a still-latent collectivity demanding recognition – a task of *acknowledgement* from which representational understanding will derive. Conventionally, critics see 1934 (possibly 1936) as the moment in which Dos Passos distanced himself from Communist politics, very quickly moving to hostility and eventually, after the Second World War, towards a far-right McCarthyist and Goldwater-supporting Republican Party affiliation. Not accidentally, 1934–36 was also the point at which the Communist Party itself made its turn towards the Popular Front. Dos Passos's *U.S.A.*, I would suggest, had already adumbrated the Popular Front's need, in the absence, still, of any reflection of it in the policy and actions of the Communist Party, which in the early 1930s was still characterizing Social Democrats and Socialists as social fascists and disrupting their rallies and demonstrations. *U.S.A.*, then, is a plea for recognition of the people and a testimony that such recognition was already compromised by the time it came. Dos Passos's trilogy is, in this regard, a monument of America's political failure to hear and respond to the 'speech of the people', a modernist work mourning a Popular Front that was too little, and too late.

Conclusion

Modernism encompasses a wide variety of ways in which the modernist text may relate to ideological 'content', from the text's apparently radical exclusion to its explicit treatment of ideologically motivated characters and events to its 'essayistic' disquisition on political ideas. Clearly, such different treatments of ideological and political materials have important implications for how we understand the 'politics' of modernist literature. In this chapter, however, I have stressed another vector of the politics of modernist writing: its 'politics of time', to use Peter Osborne's phrase (1995), its setting the present in which the work is received into a politically charged tension with a changed future that is implicitly or explicitly indexed by the work. Considering three different cases, with highly distinct ideological valences – the revolutionary messianism of Hugo Ball's and Lajos Kassák's avant-garde writing, the pessimistic dystopianism of Wyndham Lewis's futuristic satire and John Dos Passos's mournful montage-epic of a populist politics recognized too late – I have sought to suggest a mode of reading the politics of modernism different from that of interpreting it in light of the political commitments of its authors or the manifest ideological contents of the works. Such a mode of reading may extend to many other works of modernism beyond those of the specific cases discussed here. Although authorial political commitments and explicit ideological content are material to the question of modernism's politics, both of these dimensions are strongly inflected by this modernist 'politics of time'. It is thus in the multidimensional tensions generated between these dimensions, rather than in any single aspect of ideology or explicit engagement, in which the politics of modernism should be sought.

Bibliography

Ball, H. (1996), *Flight Out of Time: A Dada Diary*, John Elderfield (ed.), A. Raimes (transl.). Berkeley and Los Angeles: University of California Press.

Beckett, S. (1959), *Watt*. New York: Grove Press.

Dos Passos, J. (1996), *U.S.A. (The 42 Parallel, 1919, The Big Money)*. New York: Library of America.

Fehér, F. (1976), 'Ideology as Demiurge in Modern Art'. *Praxis*, 3, 184–95.

Hevesy, I. (2002 [1919]), 'Mass Culture, Mass Art', in T. O. Benson and E. Forgács (eds), *Between Worlds: A Sourcebook of Central European Avant-Gardes, 1910–1930*. Cambridge, MA: The MIT Press, pp. 227–9.

Kassák, L. (1920), *Máglyák Énekelnek*. Vienna: Bécsi Magyar Kiadó.

Kassák, L. (2002 [1919]), 'Activism', in T. O. Benson and E. Forgács (eds), *Between Worlds: A Sourcebook of Central European Avant-Gardes, 1910–1930*. Cambridge, MA: The MIT Press, pp. 219–24.

Laclau, E. (2005), *On Populist Reason*. London: Verso.

Lewis, W. (1965 [1928]), *The Childermass*. London: Jupiter Books.

Lukács, G. (1979), *The Meaning of Contemporary Realism*, J. and N. Mander (transl.). London: Merlin Press.

Lukács, G. (1983), *The Historical Novel*, H. and S. Mitchell (transl.). Lincoln, Nebraska: University of Nebraska Press.

Lukács, G. (1998 [1913]), 'Ady Endre', in *Esztétikai kultúra*. Budapest: Napvilág Kiadó, pp. 47–54.

Osborne, P. (1995), *The Politics of Time: Modernity and Avant-Garde*. London: Verso.

Scholem, G. (1981), *Walter Benjamin: The Story of a Friendship*, H. Zohn (transl.). Philadelphia: Jewish Publication Society of America.

21

A New Sense of Value:
Literary Modernism and Economics

Ronald Schleifer

A mere fifty years after [Jane Austen's] death, [her] world was altered beyond recognition. [...] The notion that man was a creature of his circumstance, and that those circumstances were not predetermined, immutable, or utterly impervious to human intervention is one of the most radical discoveries of all time. It called into question the existential truth that humanity was subject to the dictates of God and nature. It implied that, given new tools, humanity was ready to take charge of its own destiny. [...] Before 1870 economics was mostly about what you couldn't do. After 1870, it was mostly about what you could do.

– Sylvia Nasar, *Grand Pursuit: The Story of Economic Genius*
(Nasar, 2011, xiii–ix)

All types of societies are limited by economic factors. Nineteenth-century civilization alone was economic in a different and distinctive sense, for it chose to base itself on a motive only rarely acknowledged as valid in the history of human societies, and certainly never before raised to the level of a justification of action and behavior in everyday life, namely, gain. The self-regulating market system was uniquely derived from this principle.

– Karl Polanyi, *The Great Transformation:*
The Political and Economic Origins of Our Time (Polanyi, 2001, 31)

The Argument[1]

In this chapter, I examine our received ideas associated with twentieth-century modernism in relation to the transformations in economic practices and understanding in the late nineteenth and early twentieth centuries. My overall argument is that as well as situating post-classical economics – both neoclassical and institutional economics in the late nineteenth century – within the cultural formations of modernism, we can also rethink what we mean by modernism in relation to the re-evaluation of 'value' instituted by economics. In this, I am assuming that one can arguably define aesthetic modernism (1) in its engagement with the 'new' world of the nascent twentieth century and (2) in its challenge to the Enlightenment project in rethinking the autonomous and essentially conscious self-knowing individual subject of experience, the sovereignty of reason, the sense of (secular) truth transcending worldly experience, and the hegemonic assumption that the West and its cultural formations, including Western art, are the full realization of humanity (see Schleifer and Levy, 2016). In addition, economic concepts focused on intangible assets, institutional facts, ownership and the very notion of value itself allow us to see the workings of cultural modernism in new and historically determined ways. Many modernist artists – Yeats, Messiaen, Woolf, de Chirico, Schoenberg, Williams, Proust, Picasso, Stein – can be understood in new ways in the light of the reassessment of ownership, intangibility and value undertaken by modernist economics. At the beginning of his influential study, *The Struggle of the Modern*, Stephen Spender sets forth what has been a recurrent definition of the modern and modernism:

> The moderns are therefore those who start off by thinking that human nature has changed: or, if not human nature, then the relationship of the individual to the environment, forever being metamorphosized by science, which has altered so completely that there is an effective illusion of change which in fact causes human beings to behave as though they were different. This change, recorded by the seismographic senses of the artist, has also to change all the relations within arrangements of words or marks on canvas which make a poem or novel, or a painting. (Spender, 1963, xiii)

In 1924 Virginia Woolf, remembering the first Post-Impressionist exhibition organized by her friend Roger Fry, noticed the same thing in proclaiming that 'on or about December 1910 human character changed'. She goes on to note that 'all human relations have shifted – those between masters and servants, husbands and wives, parents and children. And when human relations change there is at the same time a change in religion, conduct, politics, and literature. Let us agree to place one of these changes about the year 1910' (Woolf, 1984, 194). While such experiences of change and 'newness' might be recorded by artists as sensitive to earth-changing events as a seismograph, economists studying value, human relations, conduct – and politics under the categories of political economy and economics – both recorded and shaped the unprecedented changes of human understanding and experience in the new twentieth century.

Modernism and the Second Industrial Revolution

The passage from Sylvia Nasar with which I begin illustrates the impulse in cultural modernism, as Ezra Pound notes, to 'make it new'. In fact, in the years around 1870 all kinds of newnesses were occurring: in the second half of the nineteenth century in Western Europe and the United States one of the greatest transformations of human life – in terms of knowledge, social relations, individual and collective experience, and the consumption of life-sustaining and life-fulfilling goods – took place. This transformation, as David Landes has argued, was comparable to the 'Neolithic [...] shift away from hunting and gathering [that] made possible towns and cities, with all that they yielded in cultural and technical exchange and enrichment' (Landes, 1999, 41). The phenomena of this period are sometimes described as 'the Second Industrial Revolution', a period, as I argue in *Modernism and Time* (2000) and *A Political Economy of Modernism* (2018), that in many ways conditioned and participated in what we call cultural modernism. During this historical moment, economists argue, a transformation from industrial to finance capitalism took place. In a remarkably titled book, *The Long Twentieth Century* – remarkable because it traces the twentieth century back to the fifteenth century – Giovanni Arrighi argues that 'the maturity of every major development of the capitalist world-economy is heralded by a particular switch from trade in commodities to trade in money' (Arrighi, 1994, 109). In the late nineteenth century, he notes, such a transformation took place in Britain and the United States, when there was a 'switch' of 'capital in increasing quantities from trade and production to financial intermediation and speculation [which redirected capital from reinvestment] in the material expansion of the world-economy [...] [to] a greater specialization in high finance' (215).[2] Moreover, the utilization of capital for financial power, rather than for the production –'the material expansion' – of goods is one of the impulses towards *intangible* assets, meanings and values in this period. The switch from trade in commodities to trade in finance coincided with the rise of impersonal corporations and trusts, particularly in the United States and Britain. Moreover, it gave rise to a new class of workers in the late nineteenth century, the lower middle class of 'information' workers (e.g. teachers, clerks, canvassers like Leopold Bloom), which had a signal effect on cultural modernism, both in terms of stimulating 'elitist' disdain in the arts and sciences towards this new, 'half-educated, self-educated' class (see Woolf 2015, 75) and in terms of making worldly pleasure as well as transcendental truth the goal of art (see Schleifer, 2011). The lower middle class, like corporations, is in an important way 'intangible': it is, as Arno Mayer says, 'a classless class or half-class of quasi workers and quasi bourgeois' (Mayer, 1975, 422). Finally, the emphasis on money – and really *credit* as opposed to tangible *species* – rather than commodities is consonant with a powerful strain in modernism that replaces things with forces, patterns and almost impalpable suggestions, what W. B. Yeats described in 1893 as the 'subtlety, obscurity, and intricate utterance [...] of our moods and feelings [which] are too fine, too subjective, too impalpable to find any clear expression in action or in speech tending towards action' (Yeats, 1970, 271). Thus, in his study of Yeats in *Quantum Poetics*, Daniel Albright notes that:

> most of us, when we read Yeats's poetry, pay close attention to the ravishing *images* – the Japanese sword, the bird made of gold, the old Norman tower. But in some ways the true subject of the poems consists not of these formal particulars, but of a hovering formlessness behind them: Yeats was less concerned with *images* than with the imagination itself, a shapeless matrix of shapes, a retina that could be knuckled into emanating waves of sparks and fields of intenser darkness. [...] Though critics once described Yeats's poems as perfected artifacts, urns of words, no poems are less iconic than Yeats's: they are histories of heaving imaginative processes, standing waves. (Albright, 1997, 31)

It is just this kind of *intangible* value – many years ago, Hugh Kenner (1971) described Ezra Pound and the writers of his 'era' in very similar terms to those of Albright – that infuses both aesthetic modernism and modernist economics at the very time, in Western Europe and in the United States that the sheer quantity of commodities produced and consumed created a culture of abundance. This seeming contradiction – the appearance of 'intangible assets' in art and economics *and* enormous quantities of tangible consumer goods in everyday life – is a contradiction that, in many ways, conditioned cultural and aesthetic modernism.

Modernism as a cultural movement itself can be understood in relation to the 'immediate history' of the turn of the twentieth century and especially to corporate economics I am describing here, and also in relation to the 'long history' of European culture from the 'early modern' Enlightenment of the seventeenth and eighteenth centuries. Karl Polanyi describes this long history of the 'great' European social transformation begun in the Enlightenment resulting in a self-regulating money/credit system that came to fruition in the late nineteenth century. In the coincidence of these historical engagements, the bourgeois culture of the nineteenth century can be understood as the culmination and fulfilment of Enlightenment secularization and, at the same time, as itself facing the crisis in world view and value in the arts, in the sciences, and in experience that we call 'modernism'. In this chapter, then, I study the phenomenon of re-evaluating the nature of wealth and value in the time of twentieth-century modernism in relation to *intangible* phenomena, such as Albright notices in Yeats and that I touch upon in Virginia Woolf, Ezra Pound and Edith Wharton. But examples of literary modernism could, with space, be neatly broadened: to the discourse of Henry James, constantly portending meanings that do not fully materialize; to the dark comedy of James Joyce; or to the probing questioning of the foundations of human experience in Samuel Beckett or Wallace Stevens.

'Modernist' Post-Classical Economics

In 1776 Adam Smith published *The Wealth of Nations*, a precise articulation of *classical economics* that encompasses and instantiates many of the assumptions of the European Enlightenment. It assumes that (1) there is a discoverable 'logic' within phenomena that can explain events; (2) this logic is recoverable by means of human reason (as opposed to divine revelation); (3) the active agent in historical events is the human individual (again, as opposed to divine intervention); (4) the world is essentially 'good' and compatible with human needs and well-being; and (5) progress and growth are natural and reasonably expected in human affairs, while regression is accidental and aberrant. One additional assumption at the centre of Smith's analysis is that (6) one can and should divorce wealth from other aspects of human and social life: that economics is a field of study that naturally distinguishes itself from wider senses of individual and social human existence. This last is a remarkable assumption, even though it seems so thoroughly self-evident for thinkers living in the nineteenth and twentieth centuries; it is an assumption that creates the situation in which a vast number of decisions made in the context of the market system of capitalism readily confine themselves to the narrow field of cost–benefit analysis. (The great articulator of such analysis is Jeremy Bentham, who, I shall note, laid the foundations for neoclassical economics.)

For Smith, the market system in which rational agents freely exchange items of value with strangers is the site where all of these assumptions about human life, work and well-being can be seen operating. For Smith, the market is the locus of self-interest which, almost miraculously, is transformed into social benefit. He articulates this under the metaphor of an 'invisible hand' that regulates the market: every agent within a system of political economy 'neither intends to promote the public interest, nor knows how much he is promoting it'. Nevertheless, 'by directing [his] industry in such a manner as its produce may be of the greatest value, he intends only his own gain, and he is in this, as in many other cases, led by an invisible hand to promote an end which was not part of his intention' (Smith, 1994, 485). In this statement – which Mark Blaug calls 'the central theme that inspires the *Wealth of Nations*' (Blaug, 1985, 60) – Smith is enacting one of the essential procedures of secular analysis as it developed in the Enlightenment, namely the combination of individual particulars and a general system. Such a combination is readily apprehensible in the Enlightenment negotiation of content and form, fact and law; and it is surely apprehensible in Smith's combination of individual intention and a general beneficial result.

The values of classical economics culminate in the high bourgeois society – replete with self-evident smugness – against which cultural modernism responded at the turn of the twentieth century (see Rainey, 1998; Lantham, 2003). Among the results of Enlightenment thinking are certain conceptions of knowledge, including that of the *scientific revolution* stemming from an understanding that careful observation of particulars can lead to 'laws' of nature that are at once simple and general; certain understandings of social life, including that of the *democratic revolutions* since the eighteenth century stemming from an understanding that individual men are 'equal'; and certain conceptions of well-being, including that of the *industrial revolution* stemming from an understanding that well-being is best measured in terms of material wealth. 'The Industrial Revolution [of eighteenth- and nineteenth-century England]', Polanyi argues, 'was merely the beginning of a revolution as extreme and radical as ever inflamed the minds of sectarians, but the new creed was utterly materialistic and believed that all human problems could be resolved given an unlimited amount of material commodities' (Polanyi, 2001, 42).

The key term here is 'commodity', which is central to Smith, Karl Marx and neoclassical economics as well as Polanyi. A commodity is a marketable item that is produced to satisfy a want or a need. (This is Marx's definition, but itself is derived from the work of Adam Smith and David Ricardo.) The commodification of all goods – including two categories of marketable items that Polanyi argues were *not* 'produced to satisfy a want or a need' (not produced to be sold), namely human labor and natural land – created the 'great transformation' of human life, as he entitled his study. At the heart of this transformation, he argues, was the institution of 'gain' rather than 'subsistence' as the motive of action, which in turn transformed all human transactions 'into money transactions' based upon 'a self-regulating system of markets' (Polanyi, 2001, 43–4). Such self-regulation is what Smith meant by an 'invisible hand', and with this, we have an understanding of how economics works – how value itself manifests itself in human life – that is at once human in a worldly sense and impersonally based upon transcendental laws, like those of physics, that are universal, immutable and – it turns out in the work of 'scientific' economics – powerfully simple.

The multiplication of both commodities and intangible assets in the Second Industrial Revolution of the late nineteenth century both fulfilled and transformed classical economics. The mass production of commodities transformed the seller's market of entrepreneurial capitalism into the buyer's market of corporate capitalism (Mills, 2001), while corporate capitalism instituted a host of intangible assets: trusts, economic good will, absentee ownership and common stocks, all kinds of financial 'instruments', the very abstractions of marginal economics itself. These intangible assets can be correlated with cultural impulses manifest in French symbolism, abstract (non-perspectival) painting, non-tonal music, fragmented narrative, psychoanalysis, post-Newtonian physics, and so on so that even 'realist' fiction writers like Theodore Dreiser or George Moore are caught up in fantastical digressions and a *rarefication* of substantiality (see Ermarth, 1983; Schleifer, 2000a, 155–78). Take, for instance, Virginia Woolf's *Mrs. Dalloway*, in which the novel makes the seeming 'experience' of intangibility a theme: 'But [Clarissa Dalloway] said, sitting on the bus going up Shaftesbury Avenue, she felt herself everywhere; not "here, here, here"; and she tapped the back of the seat; but everywhere [...] [In this way, she goes on to think] that since our apparitions, the part of us which appears, are so momentary compared with the other, the unseen part of us, which spreads wide, the unseen might survive, be recovered somehow attached to this person or that, or even haunting certain places, after death' (Woolf, 2015, 136–7). Like the technical economic category of 'good will', which as I note later, makes the simple *reputation* for wealth and power an economic asset, so Clarissa's experience of herself, spreading wide to airy thinness, even 'haunting certain places' (136), begins to feel almost 'intangible'.

In the new twentieth century, Thorstein Veblen in the United States called such intangible assets (i.e. trusts, good will, common stock, etc.) 'immaterial facts', and – unlike the contemporaneous neoclassical or 'marginal' economics, best represented by Alfred Marshall at Cambridge, which attempted to describe the 'normal' functioning of wealth in society at the time – Veblen attempted to describe the ways that 'immaterial facts' are 'turned to pecuniary account' (Veblen, 1969, 365) and thereby to social power. Nevertheless, despite their differences, both European neoclassical economics ('marginal' economics) and the American 'institutional' economics of Veblen at the turn of the twentieth century are conditioned by and responding to the same powerful transformations in human life and increases in Western wealth brought about by the market system and the Second Industrial Revolution. In fact, in the Preface to *The Theory of Business Enterprise* Veblen takes pains to note that he is responding to 'the same general range of facts' as other economists so that 'any unfamiliar conclusions are due to [his] choice of a point of view, rather than to any peculiarity in the facts, articles of theory, or method of argument employed' (Veblen, 1932, v). Ferdinand de Saussure's *Course in General Linguistics*, offered to students at almost the exact same moment that Veblen is writing in 1904, also begins by discussing the fact that in linguistics 'the viewpoint adopted [...] creates the object [of study]' (Saussure, 1986, 8). It is no accident, I think, that semiotic science emerged at the turn of the century in France and the United States – the very term, 'semiotics', was almost simultaneously coined by Saussure and Veblen's American contemporary and one-time teacher, Charles Sanders Peirce – because semiotics, like the 'intangible' economic structures that arose during the Second Industrial Revolution, is a tool designed to deal with abundance rather than dearth.[3]

Economists on either side of the Atlantic took different approaches to this situation of abundance. These approaches are best represented in the 'marginal' economics of Marshall at Cambridge – the great spokesman for neoclassical economics – and in the 'institutional economics' of Veblen in the United States.[4] Marshall's articulation of the economics of 'marginal utility' embodied ways that late nineteenth-century economics transformed the focus of political economy from *need* into an economics of *desire*, from an economics purportedly focused on the production of commodities understood to have 'value in use' to those that have 'value in exchange' (Smith, 1994, 31).[5] Veblen's institutional economics also focuses on desire rather than need, but the 'desire' towards which he is most attentive is the desire for social power rather than for individual pleasure: use-value for him is *social* value that manifests itself beyond subsistence and the particular 'uses' of a commodity. In both neoclassical economics and institutional economics, however, the *material necessities* of need are, as Veblen argues, superseded by the more or less 'intangible' phenomena of pleasure and power.

Marginal Economics

In the first edition of his *Principles of Economics* – a book initially published in 1890 that went through multiple editions up until the 1920s – Marshall succinctly describes the basis of marginal economics. 'It is an almost universal law', he writes,

> that each several want is limited, and that with every increase in the amount of a thing which a man has, the eagerness of his desire to obtain more of it diminishes; until it yields place to the desire for some other thing, of which perhaps he hardly thought, so long as his more urgent wants were still unsatisfied. There is an endless variety of wants, but there is a limit to each separate want. (Marshall, 1961, II 238; see also Gagnier, 2000)

Notable here are two things: the shift to 'desire' as the operative motive in economic activity and as a constant in experience, and Marshall's recourse (repeated throughout his work) to the concept of 'universal law'. These two gestures respond, respectively, to the 'immediate history' of the second Industrial Revolution that can be dated from 1870 to 1940 and to the 'long history' of the European Enlightenment.

In his analysis, Marshall takes up rather than challenges Enlightenment modes of understanding to offer *formal* (and mathematical) analyses of phenomena based upon the strict distinction between example/fact and principle/law in Enlightenment thinking.[6] The formal 'law' of economics manifests itself in mathematical analysis that Marshall's countryman, William Stanley Jevons, elaborated in *The Theory of Political Economy*, published in 1871 (which might have conditioned Nasar's choosing 1870 as a pivotal year in the history of economics). He creates a mathematical calculus of economics based upon the distinction between pain and pleasure set forth by the (laissez-faire) moral philosopher Jeremy Bentham in the early nineteenth century. But he does so in relation to economics rather than morality, at least in part, in order to address the enormous increase in the production of consumer goods – the buyer's market and the concomitant explosion of intangible assets – in the Second Industrial Revolution. Classical economics assumed that wealth is most accurately measured by use-value rather than exchange-value and that, because of this, the best account of wealth takes place from the point of view of production rather than consumption. Since the use-value of a pair of shoes is the general function of protecting the feet, use-value is best measured by the *first* pair of shoes a person has, without which she would walk barefoot. This definition assumes, with the Enlightenment, that wealth is a response to need: the *first* pair of shoes answers a general/universal need. But if classical political economy studies need as it is addressed in the first pair of shoes one obtains, then ('neoclassical') marginal economics studies desire as it is addressed in the *last* – or 'marginal' – pair of shoes one purchases.

This definition of value transforms the study of wealth and well-being from the study of *need* to the study of *desire*. Here is how Marshall describes it:

> The primitive housewife finding that she has a limited number of hanks of yarn from the year's shearing, considers all the domestic wants for clothing and tries to distribute the yarn between them in such a way as to contribute as much as possible to the family wellbeing. She will think she has failed if, when it is done, she has reason to regret that she did not apply more to making, say, socks, and less to vests. [...] But if, on the other hand, she hit on the right points to stop at, then she made just so many socks and vests that she got an equal amount of good out of the last bundle of yarn that she applied to socks, and the last she applied to vests. This illustrates a general principle, which may be expressed thus:–
>
> If a person has a thing which he can put to several uses, he will distribute it among these uses in such a way that it has the same marginal utility in all. (Marshall, 1961, I 117)

This analysis is significant in a variety of ways. First of all, it replaces money with an actual commodity in a way that makes well-being more fully the focus of economic activity. This is important because it is precisely the reality of money – functioning *intangibly* as credit – as a weapon of oppression that motivated American populism, including that of Erza Pound and William Carlos Williams, at the turn of the twentieth century.[7] Thus, one critic of Pound describes the central dialectical opposition in Pound's work as that between *Amor* and *Usura* (Surette, 1993), which is to say between the 'natural' fecundity of life and art and the artificial – and life-destroying – creation of something out of nothing in the credit system of 'usurious' banking. This is perhaps most clear in 'Canto XLV', one of Pound's most famous poems that rants against usury ('usura'):

> With usura hath no man a house of good stone
> each block cut smooth and well fitting
> that design might cover their face,
> with usura
> hath no man a painted paradise on his church wall
> *harpes et luz*
> or where virgin receiveth message

and halo projects from incision,

with usura

seeth no man Gonzaga his heirs and his concubines

no picture is made to endure nor to live with

but it is made to sell and sell quickly

with usura, sin against nature,

is thy bread ever more of stale rags

is thy bread dry as paper [...]

(Pound, 1989, ll. 1–15)

Usury, Pound goes on to say, is 'CONTRA NATURAM', against nature, because it raises the value of 'money' and transforms the life-sustaining production of housing ('of good stone'), of bread (turned into 'stale rags') and of artworks ('painted paradise', the music of harps and lutes, the imagined reception of the 'received' message of God) into things designed 'to sell and sell quickly', a 'sin against nature'. The interest of usury is literally an 'intangible' asset that is created by a bank lending out other people's money to accrue interest to itself. This creates what Hugh Kenner calls 'nonexistent values': 'cost amortized over and over again, but still carried on the books; and all waste; and all inefficiency; and all bank charges' (Kenner, 1971, 309). Throughout the *Cantos*, Pound makes the 'unnatural' value of money – its *intangible* power – visible.

In the passage from the *Principles of Economics* I cite above, however, Marshall does the opposite: by seemingly *erasing* money from his account, Marshall replaces the politics of power with the economics of utility. Second, Marshall's account creates a narrative that, more fully than abstractions, makes the representation and fulfilment of *desire* the goal of activity: the alternative to 'well-being' in Marshall's narrative is not destitution but inconvenience. Additionally – and notably – it makes the agent of economic activity female rather than male, erasing the opposition, embedded in classical economics and the 'two spheres' of nineteenth-century bourgeois life, between domestic economy and political economy. But perhaps most importantly this narrative – almost unconsciously, clearly unobtrusively – describes a world where the problem is not scarcity of yarn and the products to be produced and consumed, but where the problem is dealing with more than what is only necessary.

Marshall himself – unlike many marginalists who followed him, and some who preceded him – fully conceived the project of economics as one whose greatest purpose was to make lives better for the mass of people. He was the first to imagine that one 'economic function of the business firm [besides profits] ...

was to produce higher living standards for consumers and workers' (Nasar, 2011, 84), and throughout he clearly argues that *distribution* – the problem for a buyer's market – is indistinguishable from production (see Schleifer, 2003, 168–9). Thus, he argued – unlike other marginalist economists following what they took to be the mechanical logic of their 'science' – that economic activity takes place within larger social organizations. That is, he saw, at times, that the basic assumption of marginal economics – namely, that individuals making economic decisions are, first and foremost, self-interested rational agents divorced from any social context in their marketing, basically, with strangers – simply is not always, and often not significantly, true.[8] With this insight, Marshall situates himself within the modernist programme of questioning self-evident received truths about social relations, human well-being and value.

Institutional Economics

In 1909 Veblen published a critique of what he calls the 'bloodless' economics of 'marginal utility'. In a discussion of Marshall, he argues that contemporary economics 'postulated as immutable conditions precedent to economic life' (Veblen, 1969, 236) are particular *institutions* – such as private property, ownership, capital, 'natural rights', the 'primordial' oppositions between pleasure and pain, even taste – which require historical and cultural analysis. European neoclassical economics assumes that these institutions, Veblen writes, 'are part of the nature of things; so that there is no need of accounting for them or inquiring into them, as to how they have come to be such as they are, or how and why they have changed and are changing, or what effect all this may have on the relations of men who live by or under this cultural situation' (Veblen, 1969, 236). (I might add in the same way the self-evident 'truths' of Enlightenment experience – such as tonal music, perspectival painting, realism in literary narrative, the conscious autonomous self, etc. – do not call for inquiry.)[9] By making the pleasure of consumption the goal of economic activity, Veblen concludes, both classical and neoclassical economics leave out the vital issue of *cultural power*. 'Business men', he writes, 'habitually aspire to accumulate wealth in excess of the limits of practicable consumption, and the wealth so accumulated is not intended to be converted by a final transaction of purchase into consumable goods or sensations of consumption' (249).

Instead, as he argues throughout his career, such economic activity aims at the creation and maintenance of institutional social power. In place of what he calls the passive neoclassical 'hedonistic conception of man' understood as 'a lightning calculator of pleasures and pains, who oscillates like a homogeneous globule of desire of happiness under the impulse of stimuli that shift him about the area, but leave him intact' (Veblen, 1969, 73) – such 'globules' of desire can be seen in Dreiser's *Sister Carrie* and Joyce's *Dubliners* – Veblen argues that it 'is the characteristic of man to do something, not simply to suffer pleasures and pains'. 'All economic change', he concludes, 'is a change in the economic community – a change in the community's method of turning material things to account. The change is always in the last resort a change in habits of thought' (74–5). 'Turning things to account' is a ubiquitous phrase in Veblen and it is nicely contrasted with the impulse in marginal economics to create a scientific calculus of value. Thus, rather than Marshall's abstract and mathematical formulations found in the footnotes and appendices of *Principles of Economics*, Veblen responds to post-Civil War wealth with semiotics analyses. This is most telling, as John Patrick Diggins has argued, in the fact that Veblen was 'one of the first economists to perceive the implications of the emerging concept of intangible property', a concept that focused upon 'purely monetary estimates by businessmen of the strategic power of manipulation afforded by corporate securities, credit, monopolistic privileges, franchises, good will, advertising, [and] public relations' (Diggins, 1999, 56).

The 'strategic power' Diggins describes is the use of capital for social ends rather individual consumption. Veblen describes the *intangible* nature of such ends most fully in a discussion of the mobility of capital. 'The continuum', he writes,

> in which the 'abiding entity' of capital resides is a continuity of ownership, not a physical fact. The continuity, in fact, is of an immaterial nature, a matter of legal rights, of contract, of purchase and sale. [...] [That is,] 'capital' is a pecuniary fact, not a mechanical one; that it is an outcome of a valuation, depending immediately on the state of mind of the valuers; and that the specific marks of capital, by which it is distinguishable from other facts, are of an immaterial character. This would, of course, lead directly, to the admission of intangible assets; and this, in turn, would upset the law of the 'natural' remuneration of labor and capital. [...] It would also bring in the 'unnatural' phenomenon of monopoly as a normal outgrowth of business enterprise. (Veblen, 1969, 197)

For classical and neoclassical economics, profit-and-wages ('remuneration') is a natural rather than a social fact; since the market is likewise 'natural', monopoly (which, after all, destroys the free market) is an 'unnatural phenomenon'. In passages such as this, however, – and they recur regularly throughout his work –

Veblen is describing how what he calls 'institutional facts' (Veblen, 1969, 116) are naturalized and made to be seen as simply self-evident matters of fact. He does so, moreover, by *historicizing* economics, subjecting it to an understanding of its constant development without any 'teleological' goal.

In this way, the concept of intangible assets – closely connected, in Veblen, with the concept of a 'theory of value' (91) – is a function of process (rather than 'taxonomy') that construes 'human nature', not in 'inert terms' but rather 'in terms of functioning' (156–7). Such a *functional* notion of value is closely related to Saussure's notion of 'value' in linguistics as a function of the operating system of language rather than its 'inert' elements. Moreover, such a functional notion of value conditions the pronounced *conflation* of the Enlightenment distinction of form and content in modernist art: as Samuel Beckett put it in his essay on Joyce's *Work in Progress*, 'Here form *is* content, content *is* form' (Beckett, 1984, 27). Value, for Saussure, is a *relational* category opposed to self-evident meaning insofar as value designates signifying differences. His example is the different value of 'mutton' in English, as opposed to the French *mouton* in that the English term exists in relation to another English term, 'sheep' (Saussure, 1986, 114). That Saussure uses an example related to 'taste' – 'mutton', after all, is sheep under the category of food, which changes the *value* of its meaning – is, I think, not accidental in discussing value. Veblen includes taste among 'the institutions of society – customs, usages, traditions, conventions, canons of conduct, standards of life, of taste, or morality and religion, law and order' (Veblen, 1969, 180) – because he sees institutions are the result of shared, historical 'habits of thoughts', and in doing so he analyses the ways that 'institutional facts' are taken to be 'natural' (Veblen, 1969, 116).[10] It is habits of thought – communal, more or less conscious, creative of assumptions that govern 'attention' (see Veblen, 1969, 152) – that determine value. Veblen borrows the term 'habits of thought' from his teacher, Peirce, and in this he is describing and pursuing a semiotic understanding and analysis of what is taken to be self-evident truths in no need of analysis.

Perhaps, the most striking example is Veblen's discussion of the institution of ownership, a phenomenon that is simply assumed in the marginal economics of Marshall. In Marshall, ownership in the last instance is consumption, part of universal human nature; everywhere he argues 'consumption is the end of production' (Marshall, 1961, I 67). Veblen, on the other hand, historicizes ownership as we know it. 'It is not', he says, 'something given to begin with, as an item of the isolated individual's mental furniture. [...] It is a conventional fact and has to be learned; it is a cultural fact which has grown into an institution in the past through a long course of habituation, and which is transmitted from generation to generation' (Veblen, 1969, 42). More specifically, he argues that the greatest economic value to a community is its 'technological proficiency' or common-sense know-how – developed over generations, most generally maintained by women rather than men – that is available to all. That is, technological proficiency – what C. H. Douglas calls 'cultural inheritance'[11] – is like the 'immortal moods' in Yeats's poetry through which individuals pass or like Schoenberg's music, which according to Daniel Albright, citing Theodor Adorno, 'is not a simulation of passion [in a particular person], but passion itself' (Albright, 2000, 15). Cultural inheritance, the immortal moods and passion concomitant with art are not things to be *owned* but occasions for rethinking our relationship to the world and to experience itself – rethinking ownership itself. Capitalism, however, 'engrosses' (or appropriates) communal technological proficiency, and in his time of what he calls the 'inchoate new phase of capitalism' (Veblen, 1969, 384) Veblen saw the 'pecuniary magnates' of capital taking up this process of 'capitalization' to a whole new level. Just as the *historical* phenomenon of capitalism 'engrosses' the community's tangible and intangible wealth, so the magnates of the gilded age – Carnegie, Rockefeller, Morgan – engross, intangibly, the assets of capitalism itself. The magnate, Veblen says, 'in the measure in which he is a pecuniary magnate, and not simply a capitalist-employer, [...] engrosses the capitalistic efficiency of invested wealth; he turns to his own account the capitalist-employer's effectual engrossing of the community's industrial efficiency' (Veblen, 1969, 383). That is, he uses the capital of invested wealth not to create the 'material expansion' of consumer goods that Arrighi describes, but to assert personal control over existing and expanding wealth; by pursuing power rather than production, the magnate exists in what Veblen calls 'a higher degree of sublimation' (Veblen, 1932, 173).

Economic Engagements

Cultural and aesthetic modernism simultaneously results from and resists this phenomenon of corporate economic power in the new twentieth century. This phenomenon of power is, above all, *intangible* (as the term 'sublimation' suggests), and for this reason has no place in the calculations of pleasure and pain by marginal economics. Veblen describes such an intangible asset under the category of 'good will' in *The Theory of Business Enterprise* (1904). Good will is a traditional 'intangible asset' that was understood as far back as the sixteenth century as 'the privilege, granted by the seller of a business to the purchaser, of trading as his recognized successor' (*OED*). But in the late nineteenth century it became the underlying reality of common stocks, brand names, and the simple reputation for wealth and power of magnates like Rockefeller or Carnegie that seemed (as it did before 2008 in firms like AIG and Lehman Brothers) 'inexhaustible' (Veblen, 1932, 173). Such sublimation – like Freud's contemporaneous use of the term – exists in the very semiotic process of its formation, the very repetition of processes across 'new' facts, recursively, as those facts continue to be transformed.

I have already suggested that such sublimation, which entails engagements with *intangible* phenomena, is notable in Yeats's poetry. More generally, the crisis of the flood of commodities and the multiplication of 'intangible assets' participated in new and bewildering social formations and ways of experiencing the world at the turn of the twentieth century. As I have also already suggested, the transformation of need to desire accompanies the transformation of industrial capital to finance capital and the redefinition of the nature of intangible assets. Good will is no longer simply one businessman's ratification and recommendation of his successor; it becomes what Walter Benjamin calls in a different context the 'aura' of a commodity. This becomes clear when we look at the first chapter on Edith Wharton's *The Age of Innocence* (1921), a novel that explores the intricacies of intangible assets of personal and social life in fine detail. *The Age of Innocence* enacts an emphasis of the process of 'semiotic' depictions of intangible value within its discourse. The first chapter depicts the gathering of New York society at the opera in the late nineteenth century. Opera itself is the quintessential locus of spectacle, and from the very start of the novel, with the description of the convenience of hiring a 'Brown *coupé*' rather than one's own 'private broughams' (Wharton, 1987, 3), the novel emphasizes the culture of exchange that lies, submerged, within this society of conspicuous consumption.

The novel's main character, Newland Archer, arrives at the opera late for two reasons. One is the fact that 'in metropolises [like New York] it was "not the thing" to arrive early at the opera' (Wharton, 1987, 4), precisely because, as Veblen might say, the very wastefulness of consumption is a sign of power and importance. 'The second reason for his delay', Wharton tells us,

> was a personal one. He had dawdled over his cigar because he was at heart a dilettante, and thinking over a pleasure to come often gave him a subtler satisfaction than its realisation. This was especially the case when the pleasure was a delicate one, as his pleasures mostly were; and on this occasion the moment he looked forward to was so rare and exquisite in quality that – well,

if he had timed his arrival in accord with the prima donna's stage-manager he could not have entered the Academy at a more significant moment than just as she was singing: 'He loves me – he loves me not – *he loves me! –*' and sprinkling the falling daisy petals with notes as clear as dew. (Wharton, 1987, 4)

The pleasure Archer takes in the opera has less to do with the music and story than with a quality that is so rare and exquisite that the narrative breaks down in the face of it (at the moment that the 'quality' becomes unspeakable, represented by a dash): it possesses a subtlety beyond the resources of language so the very enactment – the *consumption* – of pleasure can only be marked as a 'significant moment' insofar as it is interrupted by an interjection, 'well'.

Although Archer can interpret the signs around him, Wharton does not – as a matter of fact, neither does Yeats, Eliot or notably Joyce, though Dreiser is constantly struggling to make sense of signs – and she leaves their possible meanings floating freely above Archer's discourse like the promise of some kind of intangible asset. In fact, Wharton enacts the function of such promises – the subtle satisfaction of 'thinking over a pleasure that comes' – by minutely describing a world of such abundance that the very delay of a gratification creates a satisfaction that is so subtle it needs no material accomplishment. Such an intangible asset is subject to semiotic science, the science of signs, so that the evidence at hand – the timing of his entrance, the words of the song, the meaning of gestures, the clarity of sound – can be taken as pointing to a meaning that is possible but not ratified by the narrator. 'Possible unratified meaning' is a useful working definition of desire altogether, just as 'possible unratified value' is a useful working definition of economic good will: these meanings are all 'unratified' because there is no positive fact corresponding to their meaning, no statement by the author, no absolute fulfilment. The great pleasure in reading Wharton is based on the precision of her vision and her continual hinting at the promise the image implies, just as the pleasure (and difficulty) in reading Henry James is a function of aurality, of the enormous prolixity of his convoluted sentences that also, continually, *promise* the fulfilment of a meaning that is subtler than its 'realization'. Such promises abound in modernist literature, as they abound in the new world of corporate capitalism at the turn of the twentieth century.

Conclusion

In the same way that Veblen historicizes ownership, we might historicize modernism: as a function of changing understandings of the meanings of value, property, ownership and even well-being itself. William Everdell does so when, at the beginning of *The First Moderns*, he notes that:

> the influence of structural steel on Sullivan, like that of standard time on Joyce, of the telephone on Proust, or the bicycle on Boccioni, or of electric streetlights on Delaunay, is real and not to be denied. […] It is hard to explain how Einstein could have imagined the equivalence of gravity and inertia in 1907 and come up with the general theory of relativity without an elevator [invented in 1854] to imagine himself in. As for the special theory of relativity, it was an answer to a question raised by the creation of standard time in the 1880s, and by the wireless telegraph of 1900. (Everdell, 1997, 9)

Everdell is suggesting, as I have in this chapter, that it is hard to explain aesthetic and cultural modernism without attending to the economic conditions and understandings that developed as people faced the new world of knowledge, social conditions and experience in the long turn of the twentieth century. Together these things – knowledge, social conditions, experience itself – conditioned new senses of well-being and new senses of value that imbue the institutions of modernism.

Notes

1   This chapter is based upon my recently published book, *A Political Economy of Modernism: Literature, Post-Classical Economics, and the Lower Middle-Class* (2018).

2   For an argument about how this turn to high finance manifests in the urban poetics of modernist novels, see Martin 2013. I want to thank Professor Martin for her careful reading of this chapter.

3   In fact, John Locke coined the term *semiotics* late in the seventeenth century, near the beginning of the First Industrial Revolution, though as far as I know neither Saussure nor Peirce knew about this. I examine this 'logic of abundance' in *Modernism and Time* (Schleifer, 2000).

4   Versions of marginal economics were also pursued in the United States, but for the purposes of this chapter, I distinguish between these two responses to the Second Industrial Revolution.

5   In *Cultural Capital*, John Guillory argues that Smith was also thinking in terms of desire, and he offers a strong argument of the relationship of *The Wealth of Nations* to Smith's work on moral philosophy (see Guillory, 1993, 294–320).

6   See Mirowski (1989) for a thorough examination of the parallels between mathematical laws governing 'energy' in nineteenth-century physics and 'utility' in neoclassical economics.

7   For a thorough-going account of the relation of Pound and Williams to Jeffersonian populism and the rethinking of economics, see Marsh (1998).

8   For an anthropological critique of the impersonal logic of neoclassical (and neoliberal) economics, see Graeber, 2011.

9   Lawrence Rainey (1998) specifically focuses on *institutions* of patronage in studying modernism in a gesture of historicization that nicely complements Veblen's institutional economics. For Veblen, however, as he says here, the institutions he describes are taken to be 'natural' rather than historical and call for the kind of *semiotic* analysis I describe in this chapter.

10   This is also clear in another 'semiotic' gesture, the way that speech-act theory describes in fine detail the nature of an 'institutional fact' (see Searle, 1969, 50–4).

11   Clifford Hugh Douglas, whose economic theories greatly influenced Ezra Pound and often informed Pound's poetry, emphasizes the ways that 'cultural inheritance' confers value (see Kenner, 1971, 311).

Bibliography

Albright, D. (1997), *Quantum Poetics: Yeats, Pound, Eliot, and the Science of Modernism*. New York: Cambridge University Press.

Albright, D. (2000), *Untwisting the Serpent: Modernism in Music, Literature, and Other Arts*. Chicago: University of Chicago Press.

Arrighi, G. (1994), *The Long Twentieth Century: Money, Power, and the Origins of Our Time*. London: Verso Books.

Beckett, S. (1984), *Disjecta*, R. Cohn (ed.). New York: Grove Press.

Blaug, M. (1985), *Economic Theory in Retrospect*, 4th edn. Cambridge: Cambridge University Press.

Diggins, J. P. (1999), *Thorstein Veblen: Theorist of the Leisure Class*. Princeton: Princeton University Press.

Ermarth, E. (1983), *Realism and Consensus in the English Novel*. Princeton: Princeton University Press.

Everdell, W. (1997), *The First Moderns*. Chicago: University of Chicago Press.

Gagnier, R. (2000), *The Insatiability of Human Wants: Economics and Aesthetics in Market Society*. Chicago: University of Chicago Press.

Graeber, D. (2011), *Debt: The First 5000 Years*. New York: Melville House.

Guillory, J. (1993), *Cultural Capital: The Problem of Literary Canon Formation*. Chicago: University of Chicago Press.

Kenner, H. (1971), *The Pound Era*. Berkeley: University of California Press.

Landes, D. (1999), *The Wealth and Poverty of Nations*. New York: Norton.

Latham, S. (2003), *'Am I a Snob?' Modernism and the Novel*. Ithaca: Cornell University Press.

Marsh, A. (1998), *Money and Modernity: Pound, Williams, and the Spirit of Jefferson.* Tuscaloosa: University of Alabama Press.

Marshall, A. (1961), *Principles of Economics*, 9th (Variorum) edn, 2 vols. C. W. Guillebaud (ed.). New York: Macmillan.

Martin, R. (2013), 'Finance Capitalism and the Creeping London of Howards End and Tono-Bungay'. *Criticism*, 55, 447–69.

Mayer, A. (1975), 'The Lower Middle Class as Historical Problem'. *Journal of Modern History*, 47, (3), 409–36.

Mills, C. W. (2001), *White Collar: The American Middle Classes.* New York: Oxford University Press.

Mirowski, P. (1989), *More Heat Than Light: Economics as Social Physics, Physics as Nature's Economics.* Cambridge: Cambridge University Press.

Nasar, S. (2011), *The Grand Pursuit: The Story of Economic Genius.* New York: Simon and Schuster.

Oxford English Dictionary, 2nd edn, (1989). 'Goodwill', 4. b. Oxford: Oxford University Press.

Polanyi, K. (2001), *The Great Transformation: The Political and Economic Origins of Our Time.* Boston: Beacon Press.

Pound, E. (1989), *The Cantos.* New York: New Directions.

Rainey, L. (1998), *The Institutions of Modernism: Literary Elites and Public Culture.* New Haven: Yale University Press.

De Saussure, F. (1986), *Course in General Linguistics*, R. Harris (transl.). La Salle: Open Court Press.

Schleifer, R. (2000), *Modernism and Time: The Logic of Abundance in Literature, Science, and Culture 1880–1930.* Cambridge: Cambridge University Press.

Schleifer, R. (2000a), *Analogical Thinking: Post-Enlightenment Thinking in Language, Collaboration, and Interpretation.* Ann Arbor: University of Michigan Press.

Schleifer, R. (2003), 'Narrative Discourse and a New Sense of Value: Meaning and Purpose in the Neoclassical Economics of Alfred Marshall', in C. Jacobs and H. Sussman (eds), *Rereading Narrative.* Stanford: Stanford University Press, pp. 157–73.

Schleifer, R. (2009), *Intangible Materialism: The Body, Scientific Knowledge, and the Power of Language.* Minneapolis: University of Minnesota Press.

Schleifer, R. (2011), *Modernism and Popular Music.* Cambridge: Cambridge University Press.

Schleifer, R. (2018), *A Political Economy of Modernism: Literature, Post-Classical Economics, and the Lower Middle-Class.* Cambridge: Cambridge University Press.

Schleifer, R. and Levy, B. (2016), '"The Condition of Music": Modernism and Music in the New Twentieth Century', in V. Sherry (ed.), *The Cambridge Companion to the History of Modernism.* Cambridge: Cambridge University Press, pp. 289–306.

Searle, J. (1969), *Speech Acts.* Cambridge: Cambridge University Press.

Smith, A. (1994), *The Wealth of Nations.* New York: Modern Library.

Spender, S. (1963), *The Struggle of the Modern*. Berkeley: University of California Press.

Surette, L. (1993), *The Birth of Modernism*. Montreal: McGill-Queens University Press.

Veblen, T. (1932), *The Theory of Business Enterprise*. New York: Charles Scribner's Sons.

Veblen, T. (1969), *The Place of Science in Modern Civilization and Other Essays*; published as *Veblen on Marx, Race, Science and Economics*. New York: Capricorn Books.

Wharton, E. (1987), *The Age of Innocence*. New York: Collier Books.

Woolf, V. (1984), Mr. Bennett and Mrs. Brown', in *The Virginia Woolf Reader*, ed. M. Leaska. New York: Harcourt Brace Jovanovich, pp. 192–212.

Woolf, V. (2015), *Mrs. Dalloway*, The Cambridge Edition of the Works of Virginia Woolf. A. E. Fernald (ed.). Cambridge: Cambridge University Press.

Yeats, W. B. (1970), *Uncollected Prose*, John Frayne (ed.). New York: Columbia University Press.

Part Two

Resources

22

A to Z of Key Terms

Alex Pestell and Sean Pryor

Avant-Garde

The military roots of the term 'avant-garde' give a deceptive precision to what is in fact a highly contested and ambiguous term. For Peter Bürger, author of the influential *Theory of the Avant-Garde* (1974), the avant-garde is a historically specific set of artistic movements, while for other critics, the avant-garde simply means 'the most extreme form of artistic negativism' (Calinescu, 1987, 140–1). This tension between historical and generic definitions of the avant-garde should not obscure certain common characteristics: a political radicalism, an implacable opposition to the institution of art and a critique of the artwork's autonomy. For some, like Bürger, this critique implies a clear-cut distinction between the avant-garde and modernism; for others, like Perloff, such distinctions are less obvious.

As Lawrence Rainey puts it, the quintessential avant-garde notion of a collectivity bound by certain social and aesthetic theories, and relying on 'publicity and spectacle' to broadcast its ideas, derives from Futurism (Rainey et al., 2009, 1). Futurism was launched in 1909, with F. T. Marinetti's 'The Founding and Manifesto of Futurism'. Here, Marinetti elatedly describes an automobile accident in which his car was flipped into a ditch, setting the scene for the constellation of technology, shock and delirium that would characterize the movement's work. By publishing his manifesto in *Le Figaro*, Marinetti signalled his group's desire to intervene in public affairs: as the authors of 'Futurist Painting: Technical Manifesto' (1910) put it, 'We desperately want to reenter into life' (Rainey et al., 2009, 65). Following this intervention, Futurism spread throughout Europe, affecting not just literature, but music, painting and photography.

The violent energy of the avant-garde dissipated with the First World War, which splintered and redirected its energies. Futurism was infatuated with technology, and that extended, notoriously, to the technologization of war. Writing in 1909, Marinetti proclaimed, 'We intend to glorify war – the only hygiene of the world' (Rainey et al., 2009, 51), and Futurism's patriotic, not to say nationalist, proclivities led to its later involvement with fascism. By contrast, Dada, emerging in 1916, viewed the war with contempt – unlike Futurism, it was fundamentally an internationalist movement, with centres in Zurich, Berlin and Paris. In formal terms, however, Dada artists inherited much from Futurism: Dada also sought to break through the barriers of institutionalized art. Its artworks, which incorporated chance sounds, photographs and newspaper cuttings, transgressed existing aesthetic categories. As Richard Huelsenbeck has argued, with Dada 'we can hardly speak of individual arts, music or literature' (Huelsenbeck, 1981, 25): its artworks were a mixture of poetry, music, photo-montage and found objects. Like the Italian and Russian Futurist movements, Dadaism immersed itself in the objects of technological and industrial modernity. In terms of literature, this led to the primacy of a constructivist over a representational approach to language. The *zaum* poetry of Velimir Khlebnikov, for example, subverted the traditional meanings of words to foreground their acoustic properties (Perloff, 2003, 121–2). Similarly, the Dadaist Huelsenbeck's poetry, Hugo Ball writes, 'is an attempt to capture [...] the totality of this unutterable age, [...] with all its noise and hollow din' (Ball, 1996, 56). In both cases, what is 'unutterable', or inconceivable in traditional forms of representation, becomes the formal principle, generating new, uncomfortable relations to the aesthetic.

One needs only to consider Dadaists like Francis Picabia and Baroness Elsa von Freytag-Loringhoven alongside modernists like Djuna Barnes and William Carlos Williams, to see that the role of the avant-garde in the modernist period is broader, and more diffuse, than Bürger claims. The historical avant-garde left a rich legacy of new aesthetic forms: the sound poem, the collage and the readymade. Yet 'avant-garde' still remains a much-prized epithet, one that is also vulnerable to an accusation that has dogged it since the Surrealists hurled it against Dada – that it is bound to become part of the institution it seeks to critique. The question remains whether the avant-garde's fundamental gesture (the critical undermining of art's institutionality) is repeatable: can the avant-garde stance recur or did it constitute a historic (and irrecuperable) moment?

Bibliography

Ball, H. (1996), *Flight Out of Time: A Dada Diary*, J. Elderfield (ed.), A. Raimes (transl.). Berkeley and Los Angeles, CA: University of California Press.

Breton, A. (1969), *Manifestoes of Surrealism*, R. Seaver and H. R. Lane (transl.). Ann Arbor: University of Michigan Press.

Bürger, P. (1984), *Theory of the Avant-Garde*, M. Shaw (transl.). Minneapolis: University of Minnesota Press.

Calinescu, M. (1987), *Five Faces of Modernity*. Durham: Duke University Press.

Huelsenbeck, R. (1981), 'En Avant Dada: A History of Dadaism', in R. Motherwell (ed.), R. Manheim (transl.), *The Dada Painters and Poets: An Anthology*. Boston, MA: G.K. Hall, pp. 21–48.

Murphy, R. (1999), *Theorizing the Avant-Garde*. Cambridge: Cambridge University Press.

Perloff, M. (2003), *The Futurist Moment*. Chicago: University of Chicago Press.

Rainey, L., Christine P. and Wittman, L. (eds) (2009), *Futurism: An Anthology*. New Haven: Yale University Press.

Consciousness

It was May Sinclair (1863–1946) who first used the term 'stream of consciousness' in a literary context. The idea is said to originate in William James's seminal study, *The Principles of Psychology* (1890), but Sinclair's philosophical works reveal the extent to which the question of consciousness occupied a far broader field. A philosopher, novelist and poet, Sinclair was well versed in the work of thinkers as diverse as William James, Henri Bergson, F. H. Bradley and Bertrand Russell. In *A Defence of Idealism* (1917), Sinclair considers the attitudes of these thinkers from the perspective of identity, and its correlate, consciousness. To what can we ascribe the apparent unity of the conscious self? Can we even posit such a unity without arresting the flow of thought? Sinclair was interested in the degree to which consciousness and reality could be conceived of as separate entities, and in *A Defence of Idealism*, she argued against pragmatists like James and 'new realists' like Russell on the grounds that one's perceptions and the world perceived could not be considered separate phenomena. Instead, building on a mix of Hegelian idealism and Vedic mysticism, Sinclair elaborated a theory of consciousness as an overarching force unifying the individual and its environment. If consciousness is indeed 'nothing but a stream', she argued, 'still the stream would not be a stream if it had not a certain unity' (Sinclair, 1917, 38).

Sinclair first used the term 'stream of consciousness' in a review of Dorothy Richardson's novel sequence *Pilgrimage* (1918). Although it is often used interchangeably with 'interior monologue', the key word here is *consciousness*: what is registered in the novels that deploy this technique is not merely an interior monologue, but the sense data that impinge on consciousness. Where 'interior monologue' suggests an inner chamber resounding with subjective thoughts, 'stream of consciousness' implies a blurring of perceptual categories and a connection between the world and the individual. Some have speculated that this change occurs as an 'epistemological shift' in our capacity to perceive our surroundings under modernity (Stevenson, 1992, 11), but the mysticism that informed Sinclair's thought, as well as that of many of her contemporaries, is an equally significant factor.

The first use of 'stream of consciousness' in literature is traditionally ascribed to Edouard Dujardin's novel *Les Lauriers sont coupés* (1888), though the most famous examples are James Joyce's *Ulysses* (1922) and Virginia Woolf's *Mrs Dalloway* (1925). Formally, 'stream of consciousness' is characterized by a general referential instability, in which pronouns melt into one another, fragments of overheard or remembered speech interrupt the narrative and psychological description is often indistinguishable from the sensory environment. The result is a disorientating and often exhilarating sense of immersion in a world rendered paradoxically more real by its dependence on these previously unfamiliar literary techniques. As such, while some critics see this quintessential modernist technique as a break with Realism (Majumdar, 2013, 10–11), one might argue that stream of consciousness is in fact one of its most powerful tools.

Some critics, most famously the Hungarian Marxist György Lukács, thought that the techniques of works such as *Ulysses* relied on a foregrounding of subjectivity that prevented any consideration of the larger historical environment or context. And certainly, the most famous use of stream of consciousness is possibly the final episode of *Ulysses*, 'Penelope', a long unpunctuated 'transcription' of Molly Bloom's interior monologue. But the political coordinates of modernist novels like Joyce's are often far more obvious than that Lukács suggests; moreover, the immersion in subjectivity has implications for political questions of identity and representation. The 'Penelope' episode, for instance, addresses questions of gender difference, for its lack of punctuation suggests that Molly's consciousness is more 'stream-like' than Leopold's. One legacy of this is the *écriture féminine* of Hélène Cixous, which posits a mode of writing, informed by Joyce's prose, that undermines phallocentric logic.

Bibliography

Cixous, H. (1976), 'The Laugh of the Medusa'. K. Cohen and P. Cohen (transl.). *Signs*, 1, (4), 875–93.

Lukács, G. (1964), *Realism in Our Time*, J. and N. Mander (transl.). New York: Harper & Row.

Majumdar, S. (2013), *Prose of the World*. New York: Columbia University Press.

Sinclair, M. (1917), *A Defence of Idealism*. New York: Macmillan.

Sinclair, M. (1918), 'The Novels of Dorothy Richardson'. *The Egoist*, 5, (4), 57–9.

Stevenson, R. (1992), *Modernist Fiction*. Hemel Hempstead: Harvester.

Difficulty

'[P]oets in our civilization, as it exists at present, must be *difficult*': Eliot's statement, dating from 1921, sees difficulty as an obligation, involving allusiveness and dislocation of language in order to reflect the 'variety and complexity' of civilization (Eliot, 1950, 248). Eliot's *The Waste Land* (1922) is perhaps the classic 'difficult' modernist poem, and its apparatus of explanatory notes testifies to the problems Eliot anticipated his readers would have with the poem's daunting range of reference. Yet the notes also raise difficult questions about modernist form: do the notes form part of the poem? What kind of ellipses are they designed to fill, if any, and what is their creative function? For the difficulty of modernist texts lies not so much in their allusions (which, after all, can now easily be traced) but in their novel relation to experience. It is tempting to modify Eliot's critical observation by suggesting that it is not civilization that has become more 'difficult' to decipher (is the world of *Paradise Lost* really less difficult than that of *The Waste Land*?), but the individual who lives in it, and whose relationship to it becomes ever more complex and enigmatic. After all, wittingly or not, Eliot said that 'poets', not 'poems', must be difficult, as if in the face of modernity the poet were obliged to be recalcitrant, unaccommodating.

This sense of duty, wearily attended to, is also present in a well-known poem by Yeats, alluding to his management of the Abbey Theatre in Dublin: 'The fascination of what's difficult/Has dried the sap out of my veins' (Yeats, 1996, 99). This 'fascination' delineates two kinds of difficulty: the technical labour of artistic creation, and the effort to negotiate the exigencies of 'Theatre business'. It is unclear which of the two has done more to destroy the speaker's 'Spontaneous joy'. Again, difficulty is associated with a complex relationship of the writer to the world, especially the world of 'business'. This imperceptible blending of two kinds of difficulty – commercial and technical/aesthetic – goes some way to explaining why these works of art retain an enigmatic allure for their readers.

For some critics, it has been easier to explain difficulty by reference to a putative snobbery that sought to distance literature from the tastes of the 'masses' (Carey, 1992). For others, 'difficulty' engages questions of economics, technique and professionalism – including that of the critics who specialize in modernist literature (Wexler, 1997). Joyce's famous quip about *Ulysses*, that he had 'put in so many enigmas and puzzles that it will keep the professors busy for centuries arguing over what I meant', anticipates the intellectual labour that the complexity of modernist literature brought into being (Ellmann, 1983, 521). This complexity also guaranteed a certain critical distance, imaginary or real, between the artist and society, endowing the artist with cultural, if not financial, capital; it became an essential component of canon formation (Guillory, 1993). By focusing on the institutions of modernism, some critics mitigate its aetherial autonomy (Rainey, 1998), and we might not be as willing now to accept Theodor Adorno's view that art that distanced itself from popular culture could be seen as resisting that culture's conformist assumptions. But when he wrote that modernist and popular art are 'torn halves of an integral freedom, to which however they do not add up' (Jameson, 1980, 123), Adorno testified to the utopian thought of an 'integral freedom' that glimmers behind the opacities and ellipses of modernist literature, and that has yet to be realized in spite of the attempts of postmodern art to blend 'high' and 'low' culture.

Bibliography

Carey, J. (1992), *The Intellectuals and the Masses: Pride and Prejudice among the Literary Intelligentsia, 1880–1939*. London: Faber and Faber.

Diepeveen, L. (2003), *The Difficulties of Modernism*. New York: Routledge.

Eliot, T. S. (1950), 'The Metaphysical Poets', in *Selected Essays*. New York: Harcourt, Brace.

Ellmann, R. (1983), *James Joyce*. Oxford: Oxford University Press.

Guillory, J. (1993), *Cultural Capital: The Problem of Literary Canon Formation*. Chicago: University of Chicago Press.

Jameson, F. (ed.) (1980), *Aesthetics and Politics*. London: Verso.

Rainey, L. (1998), *Institutions of Modernism: Literary. Elites and Public Culture*. New Haven: Yale University Press.

Wexler, J. P. (1997), *Who Paid for Modernism? Art, Money, and the Fiction of Conrad, Joyce, and Lawrence*. Fayetteville: University of Arkansas Press.
Yeats, W. B. (1996), *The Collected Poems of W. B. Yeats*, R. J. Finneran (ed.). New York: Macmillan.

Epic

If the epic poem, in Fredric Jameson's words, traditionally embodied a 'poetics of totality', modernity's social revolution cast considerable doubt over the ability of a literary text – the product of a single mind – to encompass, with any credibility, the range of reference the epic demanded (Jameson, 2007, 3). The new fragmentary, elliptical aesthetic, however, did not deter modernist authors from writing ambitious works on a grand scale. Indeed, James Joyce produced one of the defining epics of his time: *Ulysses* (1922). Where the unity of subject matter that characterizes the classical epic had been the founding myth of a nation, *Ulysses* took its unity from the duration of a single day, and found its epic breadth in the discovery of an intimacy hitherto considered to be beneath literature. Joyce was, in one sense, simply continuing the project of Victorian Realism, pushing the nineteenth-century novel's capaciousness to its logical extreme. Yet *Ulysses* was also 'epic' in its gathering of literary styles: a polyphony that is part delirious celebration, part satirical post-mortem.

Ulysses partook of the modernist vogue for anthropological studies of myth, but what Eliot called Joyce's 'mythic method' (Eliot, 1950, 175) (a form of unity in the absence of the reassuring categories of Realism) was also legible in H. D.'s *Trilogy* (1946), David Jones's *In Parenthesis* (1937) and Eliot's own *The Waste Land* (1922). The key text of anthropology in the period was James George Frazer's *The Golden Bough* (1890–1915). Frazer's 'comparative method' permitted the juxtaposition of evidence from quite disparate cultures and epochs, based on the universalist assumption that human culture always and everywhere obeys certain mythical impulses. We can see something of this eclectic approach in Ezra Pound's *Cantos*, the archetypal modernist 'poem including history' (Pound, 1968, 86), which arrayed figures and events from diverse historical periods into an 'ideogram': a constellation of disparate facts revealing hitherto unsuspected relationships. Other poems, like William Carlos Williams's epic *Paterson* (1958), were less confident in their ability to encompass vast tracts of history, and, as Jameson argues, incorporated their own failure to do so within their texts. But that did not stop Pound and Williams from inspiring other poets to create their own 'founding myths' of modernity, such as Louis Zukofsky's *A* (1978), Hart Crane's *The Bridge* (1930), Charles Reznikoff's *Testimony* (1934) and, later, Charles Olson's *Maximus Poems* (1953).

One crucial difference between the modernist epic and its classical counterpart is modernism's omission of a hero, since, as Terry Eagleton put it, 'the individual can no longer shape its own destiny. If *Ulysses* is an epic, it is one without agents' (2002, 126). For Franco Moretti, by contrast, the 'agents' of the modern epic are modes of generic representation rather than individual subjects: the epic as an encyclopaedic rag-bag of rhetorics and histories. Bertolt Brecht's 'epic theatre' sought to confound the expectations of classic Aristotelian poetics. Brecht's heroes are resolutely ordinary characters, shown to be at the mercy of a system too great in strength and scope for the individual to grasp. Through what he called the *Verfremdungseffekt*, Brecht aimed deliberately to erode the audience's suspension of disbelief, in order to stimulate an attitude of receptiveness to the *social*, rather than the *inner* life of the protagonists. The Brechtian epic, in this way, regains some of the genre's expansiveness. Brecht's openness to new technological forms of art, as Walter Benjamin recognized, also enabled an artistic response to the new forms of experience imposed by technological progress.

Bibliography

Benjamin, W. (1992), 'What Is Epic Theatre?', in H. Zohn (transl.), *Illuminations*. London: Fontana.

Eagleton, T. (2002), 'Capitalism and Form'. *New Left Review*, 14, 119–31.

Eliot, T. S. (1950), 'Ulysses, Order and Myth', in F. Kermode (ed.), *Selected Prose*. New York: Harcourt, Brace.

Jameson, F. (2007), *The Modernist Papers*. London: Verso.

Moretti, F. (1996), *The Modern Epic: The World System from Goethe to García Márquez*, Q. Hoare (transl.). London: Verso.

Pound, E. (1968), *Literary Essays of Ezra Pound*, T. S. Eliot (ed.). New York: New Directions.

Eugenics

The advance of eugenics – much like the construction of race and, to a degree, class – is inextricably bound up with the foundation of empire and nationalism:

indeed, eugenics might be said to have evolved as a 'science' designed to serve these other discourses. The atrocities of Nazi racial policy have rightly cast a shadow over it, but before the Second World War eugenics was seriously considered a viable solution to a range of social problems, and modernist writers such as Yeats, Lawrence, Eliot, Loy and Woolf were just a few of the figures to have enthusiastically embraced the idea. The term 'eugenics' was coined in 1833 by Francis Galton (1822–1911), Charles Darwin's cousin, who defined it as 'the study of agencies under social control that may improve or impair the racial qualities of future generations either physically or mentally' (Kühl, 2013, 193). As a supposedly scientific theory (deriving from a biological determinism influenced by Darwin), eugenics profited from the turn-of-the-century vogue for 'scientism' – the application of scientific methodologies and frameworks to the study of culture (Turda, 2010, 14).

In the face of a glaring disparity between the Victorian rhetoric of progress on the one hand and on the other the poor living conditions and associated social problems (including high rates of alcoholism, prostitution and violence) for millions of ordinary people, explanations were sought in race- and class-based theories. Prominent among these, the idea of 'degeneration' provided a seductive 'explanatory myth' that argued that hereditary transmission was a vehicle not only for the evolution of a species but also for the decline of a civilization (Greenslade, 1994, 15–16). The theory was popularized by the Hungarian-French journalist Max Nordau, in his study *Degeneration* (first published as *Entartung* in 1892). Nordau captured a commonly expressed fin-de-siècle anxiety, commenting that 'the prevalent feeling is that of imminent perdition and extinction' (Nordau, 1993, 3). In particular, for Nordau degeneration was associated with what he saw as a turn to sensationalism and moral corruption in the arts. Works of art and literature were read as symptoms of their authors' hereditary deficiencies – Baudelaire's poetry, for example, was taken as indisputable evidence of a diseased mind – and Nordau's theory found its most baleful echo in the Nazis' exhibition of degenerate art in Munich in 1937. And yet, despite his antipathy to modern literature and art, Nordau's theories influenced a range of modernist writers, including Conrad and Lawrence.

However crude Nordau's theory of degeneration was, its popularity points to a profound sense of unease that goes some way towards explaining the eagerness with which the 'science' of eugenics was received. David Trotter has shown that T. S. Eliot freely adopted themes from the discourse of eugenics for his poetry (Trotter, 1986), but the current, according to Donald Childs (2004), ran far deeper. Fabians like George Bernard Shaw and H. G. Wells saw the eradication of the degenerate masses as an indispensable step towards institutional reform, while the social analyses of Woolf, Eliot and Yeats owe much to debates about sterilization and 'breeding' that emerged from eugenicist 'research'. Eugenics was beginning to lose credibility in the late thirties, but Yeats chose this moment to publish his final prose work, *On the Boiler* (1939). In this essay, Yeats spoke of the need to place a check on the reproduction of the 'uneducable masses': 'the better stocks have not been replacing their numbers, while the stupider and less healthy have been more than replacing theirs', he comments (Childs, 2004, 149–50). In the context of debates about the alleged 'elitism' and difficulty of modernist literature and art, the persistent adherence of some of its most prominent practitioners to a vocabulary of 'uneducable masses' and 'degeneration' raises uncomfortable questions.

Bibliography

Childs, D. (2004), *Modernism and Eugenics: Woolf, Eliot, Yeats, and the Culture of Degeneration*. Cambridge: Cambridge University Press.

Greenslade, W. (1994), *Degeneration, Culture and the Novel: 1880–1940*. Cambridge: Cambridge University Press.

Kühl, S. (2013), *For the Betterment of the Race: The Rise and Fall of the International Movement for Eugenics and Racial Hygiene*, L. Schofer (transl.). New York: Palgrave Macmillan.

Nordau, M. (1993), *Degeneration*. Lincoln, NE and London: University of Nebraska Press.

Trotter, D. (1986), 'Modernism and Empire: Reading The Waste Land'. *Critical Quarterly*, 28, (1–2), 143–53.

Turda, M. (2010), *Modernism and Eugenics*. New York: Palgrave Macmillan.

Everyday

The range of concepts encompassed by the term 'everyday' – from art's focus on quotidian events and objects to the reorganization of experience by urban space – is dizzyingly broad. The everyday crosses disciplinary boundaries, with sociology, aesthetics, psychoanalysis, feminism, philosophy and politics all engaging in some way with the idea of the quotidian. In this sense, the 'everyday' seems impossibly all-inclusive. But the term also points to an ongoing theoretical concern that arguably originated in modernity, and that undoubtedly changed the course of modernist literature. Perhaps the ultimate theorist of the everyday is the French sociologist Henri Lefebvre, whose *Critique of Everyday Life* (1947–82) is a monument to a life's work studying the quotidian in modern society and culture. But everyday life is prominent in literature at least since the emergence of the novel as a major cultural form in the early eighteenth century and is increasingly important in nineteenth- and twentieth-century literature. The figure of the *flâneur* as an urban spectator of everyday life is the subject of Charles Baudelaire's *Les Fleurs du Mal* (1857), for example, and as Walter Benjamin argues, the disengagement suggested by the role can be understood to be bound up with the modern urban space. Benjamin argued that rather than the kind of experience that the individual has reflected on and has transformed into a rich personal narrative (*Erfahrung*), the technological and urban transformations of modernity mean that the *flâneur* merely receives experience as a series of unassimilated sense impressions or 'shocks' (*Erlebnis*) (Benjamin, 1992, 159).

The diffuseness of the everyday allows it to be freighted with both positive and negative connotations. On the one hand, the attentiveness of art to the everyday can be seen to 'recover the sensation of life': to restore what daily habit has ground into invisibility. As the Russian Formalist critic Victor Shklovsky argues in the mid-1920s, literature celebrates the ordinary and everyday by 'defamiliarizing' it and bringing it back to our attention (Shklovsky). On the other hand, the everyday can simply be seen as the pointless repetition, drudgery and boredom of modern life, as the Surrealists and Situationists conceived of it (Felski, 2002, 608–9). Crucial as the raw data of the documentary method underlying such projects as Mass Observation (q. v.) or the burgeoning practices of modernist film (Miller, 2002), a third way in which the modernists understood the everyday is as the radical other of high culture, the nonsignifying 'noise' of a popular culture towards which they held a variety of often ambivalent attitudes (Suárez, 2007).

Bibliography

Benjamin, W. (1992), 'Some Motifs in Baudelaire', in H. Zohn (transl.), *Illuminations*. London: Fontana.

De Certeau, M. (1984), *The Practice of Everyday Life*, S. Rendall (transl.). Berkeley: University of California Press.

Felski, R. (2002), 'Introduction'. *New Literary History*, 33, (4), 607–22.

Lefebvre, H. (1984), *Everyday Life in the Modern World*, S. Rabinovitch (transl.). New Brunswick: Transaction Publishers.

Miller, T. (2002), 'Documentary/Modernism: Convergence and Complementarity in the 1930s'. *Modernism/modernity*, 9, (2), 226–41.

Olson, L. (2009), *Modernism and the Ordinary*. Cambridge: Cambridge University Press.

Randall, B. (2008), *Modernism, Daily Time and Everyday Life*. Cambridge: Cambridge University Press.

Shklovsky, V. (1965), 'Art as Technique', in L. T. Lemon and M. J. Reis (eds and transl.), *Russian Formalist Criticism: Four Essays*. Lincoln and London: University of Nebraska Press.

Suárez, J. A. (2007), *Pop Modernism: Noise and the Reinvention of Everyday Life*. Urbana and Chicago: Illinois UP.

Fascism

The frequently cited description of fascism as 'political modernism' is a convenient if also somewhat misleading way of approaching the complex relationship between modernist art on the one hand and one of the dominant political movements of the early twentieth century on the other (Griffin, 2007). As Leon Surette has shown, Italian fascism was just one of a range of authoritarian political systems brought into being by a perceived failure of liberal economics in the years following the First World War (Surette, 2011). Like literary and artistic modernism, the political movement may be said to have arisen in part as a reaction against liberal theories of the Subject and of the State, and many modernists enthusiastically embraced its tenets. Nevertheless, as the Nazis' denunciation of modernist artworks shows, there are radical and indisputable differences between the ideology of fascism and many of the formal and conceptual challenges to and subversions of authority entailed by the artistic and literary movement.

During the interwar years there were various political movements that espoused Fascist tenets to a greater or lesser degree. In an attempt to define a 'generic fascism', Roger Griffin has identified a consistent core to its conceptions of social and political structure, revolving in particular around the idea of a mythic rebirth, and Jed Esty has uncovered a logic of nationalist mythopoeia in such works as Woolf's *Between the Acts*, Powys's *A Glastonbury Romance* and Eliot's *Four Quartets* (Esty, 2004). While pragmatic, analytical and empirical conceptions undoubtedly lie behind such works, it is nevertheless hard to dissociate them entirely from what one commentator refers to as 'a set of social forms which no longer exist, and perhaps never did, but which assume a mythic status and form the basis of emotional investment on a mass scale' (Neocleous, 1997, 61–2).

Walter Benjamin famously saw in fascism a broader impulse towards 'the aestheticisation of politics' and called, in response, for the politicization of the aesthetic (Benjamin, 1992, 242). Investment in culturally defined myths of nationhood has long been recognized in the works of high-modernist writers such as Eliot, Pound, Yeats and Wyndham Lewis, all of whom were attracted, to varying degrees, to the ideology of fascism (North, 1992). More recently, the extent of Gertrude Stein's collaboration with the Fascists has been the subject of controversy (Will, 2011). Evidence of anti-Fascist sentiment in modernist writers is less common, although it is notable that, according to Stephen Spender, it was reading *The Waste Land* that led him and Auden to join the Communist Party, and hence to support the struggle against fascism in Spain. Recent work has shown how other modernists – for example Djuna Barnes and Virginia Woolf – were vocal about the approaching threat of Nazism (Spiro, 2013), and there is a distinguished array of German and Austrian modernist writers – among them Hermann Broch, Thomas Mann, Robert Musil and Alfred Döblin – whose critique of fascism often put them in real danger. Rightly or wrongly, however, modernism still remains under the shadow of fascism, both on account of the very real allegiances and activities of some of its key figures and because of a general suspicion that the formalism with which it is associated cannot be extricated from an authoritarian (or indeed totalitarian) aesthetic.

Bibliography

Benjamin, W. (1992), 'The Work of Art in the Age of Mechanical Reproduction', in H. Zohn (transl.), *Illuminations*. London: Fontana.

Esty, J. (2004), *A Shrinking Island: Modernism and National Culture in England*. Princeton: Princeton UP.

Griffin, R. (2007), *Modernism and Fascism: The Sense of a Beginning under Mussolini and Hitler*. Basingstoke: Palgrave Macmillan.

Lacoue-Labarthe, P. and Nancy, J.-L. (1990), 'The Nazi Myth', B. Holmes (transl.). *Critical Inquiry*, 16, (2), 291–312.

Neocleous, M. (1997), *Fascism*. Buckingham: Open UP.

North, M. (1992), *The Political Aesthetic of Yeats, Eliot and Pound*. Berkeley: University of California Press.

Paxton, R. O. (2004), *The Anatomy of Fascism*. New York: Alfred A. Knopf.

Spiro, M. (2013), *Anti-Nazi Modernism: The Challenges of Resistance in 1930s Fiction*. St Evanston, IL: Northwestern UP.

Sternhell, Z. (1994), *The Birth of Fascist Ideology*, D. Maisel (transl.). Princeton: Princeton UP.

Surette, L. (2011), *Dreams of a Totalitarian Utopia: Literary Modernism and Politics*. Montreal and Kingston: McGill-Queen's UP.

Will, B. (2011), *Unlikely Collaboration: Gertrude Stein, Bernard Faÿ, and the Vichy Dilemma*. New York: Columbia UP.

High Modernism

Once a means of helping critics conceptualize a period in literary history, the notion of 'high modernism' has now become part of that history itself, to be read as much for what it reveals about the critics who establish the terms by which the movement is understood as for what it reveals about the movement itself. In this sense, the later generations of critics who enshrined 'high modernist' art are understood as reproducing the critical strictures of 'high modernist' poet-critics like T. S. Eliot. Along with theorists such as Clement Greenberg and Theodor Adorno, new criticism of the 1930s, 1940s and 1950s established such traits as parataxis, allusiveness, ellipsis and self-reflexivity as the distinctive stylistic features of the authentic modernist work of art.

It is sometimes argued that high modernism marks a divide between the intellectual products of an elite and the cultural products generated by and for a mass market. Yet as Andreas Huyssen argues, high modernism denotes not only the products of this elite, but this elite's insistence on the divide itself. Huyssen also proposes that this insistence conceals the extent to which their works were in fact dependent on the popular and commercial world that they rejected. Thus, while Lawrence Rainey has discussed the extent to which Joyce, Eliot, Pound and others relied on a network of patronage and deluxe editions to separate themselves from a contaminated mass culture, Aaron Jaffe has suggested that the cultural values generated by such practices in fact mirrored those of popular culture (Rainey, 1998; Jaffe, 2005).

High modernism has also come to be distinguished temporally from so-called 'late modernism' (q. v.). Critics have posited various dates for the division, but Jean-Michel Rabaté's designation for high modernism as 1917–29 is as good as any (Rabaté, 2007, 3). Its 'annus mirabilis' is usually considered to be 1922, the year in which Joyce's *Ulysses* and Eliot's *The Waste Land* and Woolf's *Jacob's*

Room were published, in which Woolf began to write *Mrs Dalloway*, and in which *The Great Gatsby* is set (see North, 1999, v–vi).

As a temporal marker, then, high modernism refers ambiguously to the activities of a set of writers who happened to be pursuing similar projects at the same time (in addition to those mentioned above, one might add Proust, Pound, Lawrence, Musil, Yeats and Rilke), or to a set of formal, technical and stylistic breakthroughs, or to both. 'High' also suggests the canonical stability of the 'High (Anglican) Church', the (ultimately racialist) conception of so-called high-, middle- and low-brow, and the idea of a purified, spiritual or quasi-religious notion of the category of the aesthetic (Cheeke, 2016). Some critics perceive an antagonism between high modernism and the avant-gardes that preceded and followed it; others posit a continuity of purpose. But if its ambiguity makes high modernism hard to pin down, it has also made it a persistent focus of critical interest. At stake in this interest is the realization that modernism is not a monolithic stylistic movement but – as the title of Peter Nicholls's book *Modernisms* suggests – a plural, international set of artistic practices. Revisionary critics have undermined the notion – perhaps best exemplified by Hugh Kenner's *The Pound Era* (1971) – that the most important literary work produced in the period was that accomplished by a select group of white heterosexual men. More antagonistic, but perhaps more transitory, were the practitioners and commentators of postmodernism, for whom high modernism tended to represent a phallocentric, elitist and history-eliding cultural phenomenon (Jameson, 1981). Yet despite its detractors and its lack of precise definition, 'high modernism' remains a current critical term, albeit one that is often nervously marked by quotation marks.

Bibliography

Cheeke, S. (2016), *Transfiguration: The Religion of Art in Nineteenth-Century Literature Before Aestheticism*. Oxford: Oxford University Press.

Huyssen, A. (1986), *After the Great Divide: Modernism, Mass Culture, Postmodernism*. Bloomington: Indiana University Press.

Jaffe, A. (2005), *Modernism and the Culture of Celebrity*. Cambridge: Cambridge University Press.

Jameson, F. (1981), *The Political Unconscious: Narrative as a Socially Symbolic Act*. Ithaca, Ny: Cornell University Press.

Kenner, H. (1971), *The Pound Era*. Berkeley: University of California Press.

Nicholls, P. (1995), *Modernisms: A Literary Guide*. London: Macmillan.

North, M. (1999), *Reading 1922: A Return to the Scene of the Modern*. New York: Oxford University Press.

Rabaté, J.-M. (2007), *1913: The Cradle of Modernism*. Malden, MA: Blackwell.

Rainey, L. (1998), *Institutions of Modernism: Literary. Elites and Public Culture*. New Haven: Yale University Press.

Image

'An "Image" is that which presents an intellectual and emotional complex in an instant of time', Ezra Pound declared in his groundbreaking essay, 'A Few Don'ts', published in March 1913 in Harriet Monroe's journal *Poetry: A Magazine of Verse* (Pound, 1968, 4). *Image* always meant more, for modernism, than something seen. On the one hand, Pound defined one major aspect of poetry as *phanopoeia*, the 'casting of images upon the visual imagination' (Pound, 1968, 25), while on the other, he praised Dante's *Paradiso* for being 'the most wonderful *image*', so that the long poem's manifold details are seen to cohere into a single, governing idea (Pound, 1970, 86). Pound's theories of the image shift, and Imagism, the movement which he inaugurated, together with H. D. and Richard Aldington, provided a banner for poets as diverse as Amy Lowell, D. H. Lawrence and F. S. Flint (Carr, 2009). Imagism was part marketing exercise, serving to launch careers and sell anthologies, and part revolution in poetic language, emphasizing the visual imagination but also enjoining verbal concision and rhythmic invention (Beasley, 2007; Thacker, 2006).

Beyond Imagism, the image was central to modernism because *image* (Latin *imitor*, to represent, copy, imitate) suggests not the thing itself but a representation, a likeness or sign. An image, in other words, requires reading, needs interpretation (Barthes, 1977; Mitchell, 1986). When T. S. Eliot presents the waste land of his famous poem, he places amongst the dead trees and dry stones a 'heap of broken images', suggesting that the ruin of civilization involves the breakdown of representation or signification (Eliot, 2006, 58). When Stephen Dedalus ponders the 'Ineluctable modality of the visible' in James Joyce's *Ulysses*, he reflects that the things he sees are 'Signatures [which] I am here to read'. Visible things are signs, and they entail interpretation: the modality of vision means 'thought through my eyes' (Joyce, 1998, 37). This association of seeing with thinking has a long tradition in Western culture. The task of fiction, wrote Joseph Conrad, is 'by the power of the written word to make you hear, to make you feel – it is, before all, to make you *see*' (Conrad, 1963, 13).

As this suggests, in Western culture the visual imagination is associated with understanding. Indeed, because *image* suggests representation, the word has long been used to refer to mental conceptions or ideas, while the word *idea* derives from the Greek verb ἰδεῖν, meaning 'to see'. Yet the 'image is not an idea', Pound insisted. The modernist image exceeds the single, stable concept because it presents an 'intellectual and emotional complex' (Pound, 1970, 92).

The relationship between seeing, thinking and feeling is complicated further when we consider the image's medium. The combination of word and image is evident in Pound's use of the Chinese ideogram, in the incorporation of text into Cubist collages, and in the lavish arrangement of words and illustrations in the productions of William Morris's Kelmscott Press in the late nineteenth century (McGann, 1993). Guillaume Apollinaire's calligrams and F. T. Marinetti's visual poetry offset the images which a text presents with the image of the text itself, arrayed on the page. Moreover, as Michael North has argued, modernism begins 'with the critical interrogation of the relationship between text and image, brought equally into literature and the visual arts by mechanical recording' such as in the new technologies of photography, film and gramophone (North, 2005, 12). Modernism enthusiastically explored the new possibilities of modern typography and printing technologies, and seized upon new technologies for recording and reproducing images. The advent of photography shaped the development of painting, while cinema may be understood to have decisively influenced conceptions of the literary image (Trotter, 2007; Murphet, 2009). Connor, for example, has shown that H. D.'s work charts a direct course from Imagism to cinema (Connor, 2004). Finally, the montage theory of Sergei Eisenstein, in which images edited in sequence become dialectical, again makes seeing a matter of thinking and feeling.

Bibliography

Barthes, R. (1977), 'The Rhetoric of the Image', in S. Heath (transl.), *Image Music Text*. London: Fontana, pp. 32–51.

Beasley, R. (2007), *Theorists of Modernist Poetry: T. S. Eliot, T. E. Hulme, Ezra Pound*. London: Routledge.

Carr, H. (2009), *The Verse Revolutionaries: Ezra Pound, H. D. and the Imagists*. London: Jonathan Cape.

Connor, R. (2004), *H. D. and the Image*. Manchester: Manchester University Press.

Conrad, J. (1963), *The Nigger of the 'Narcissus'*. Harmondsworth: Penguin.

Eliot, T. S. (2006), *The Annotated Waste Land with Eliot's Contemporary Prose*, 2nd edn, L. Rainey (ed.). New Haven: Yale University Press.

Joyce, J. (1998), *Ulysses*, J. Johnson (ed.). Oxford: Oxford University Press.

McGann, J. (1993), *Black Riders: The Visible Language of Modernism*. Princeton: Princeton University Press.

Mitchell, W. J. T. (1986), *Iconology: Image, Text, Ideology*. Chicago: University of Chicago Press.

Murphet, J. (2009), *Multimedia Modernism: Literature and the Anglo-American Avant-Garde*. Cambridge: Cambridge University Press.

North, M. (2005), *Camera Works: Photography and the Twentieth-Century Word*. New York: Oxford University Press.

Pound, E. (1968), *Literary Essays of Ezra Pound*, T. S. Eliot (ed.). New York: New Directions.

Pound, E. (1970), *Gaudier-Brzeska: A Memoir*. New York: New Directions.

Thacker, A. (2006), 'A Language of Concrete Things: Hulme, Imagism and Modernist Theories of Language', in E. Comentale and A. Gasiorek (eds), *T. E. Hulme and the Question of Modernism*. Aldershot: Ashgate, pp. 39–55.

Trotter, D. (2007), *Cinema and Modernism*. Oxford: Blackwell.

Late Modernism

There are broadly speaking two ways of conceiving late modernism. One is as a specific period, the other is as a set of aesthetic or ideological postures. In terms of periodization, 'late' suggests a belated, tired, perhaps defunct modernism, but also a mature, not to say ripe, modernism. Appropriately enough, then, the works that tend to be associated with late modernism by those critics who use the term in its temporal sense (Wilde, Miller), are characterized both by a world-weary morning-after feeling and by a bursting, last-gasp linguistic fecundity. For Tyrus Miller, late modernism begins around 1926 and ends around 1939, and as these dates indicate, late modernism arguably occupies a period whose dramatic historical events could no longer be (in Miller's words) 'view[ed] from the distance of a closed car, as part of a moving panorama of forms and colors' (1999, 13). The delirium of such works as Djuna Barnes's *Ryder* (1928), Samuel Beckett's *More Pricks than Kicks* (1934) and Malcolm Lowry's *Under the Volcano* (1947) speaks to these concerns, though they find their ultimate expression in Joyce's enigmatic *Finnegans Wake* (1939). Other late modernist works – Woolf's *Between the Acts* (1941), Eliot's *Four Quartets* (1943) – offer more elegiac assessments of the contemporary situation.

Given these circumstances, and the difficulty of defining modernism itself, even so brief a list as this is subject to debate. Should late modernism simply mean works produced in the 1930s and 1940s by former high modernists and their disciples? Or ought we to defend a particular aesthetic or ideological position, for example, an openness to politics that was arguably absent in high modernism? This would leave out the more elegiac, nostalgic texts of Woolf and Eliot (Esty, 2004), instead embracing the satirical edge of Beckett, Wyndham Lewis and Barnes (Miller, 1999). Alternatively, late modernism might be seen to embody a sceptical attitude to the formal extravagance of modernism, incorporating authors like George Orwell, Elizabeth Bowen and Christopher Isherwood (Maher, 2013). Whatever the position taken, once we have decided that late modernism is a style (or even an event) rather than a particular period, the way is open to designate texts from the 1940s to the present day as late modernist.

Such a position is not politically neutral: given the overwhelming popularity of the notion that postmodernism is the successor and corrective to an exhausted modernism (on modernism's death see, for example, Levin, 1962), to argue for the continuing presence of that modernism is to dispute this narrative, and the notions of authority, democracy and plurality that accompany it. In contrast to the argument that the 1950s and 1960s were best represented by a kind of social realism, for example, we can point to authors such as Anna Cavan, B. S. Johnson, Rayner Heppenstall and Brigid Brophy, all of whom took their bearings from the modernism of Joyce, Woolf and Beckett. Poets like Louis Zukofsky, Marianne Moore and Lorine Niedecker were quintessential modernists who carried on writing into the 1960s and 1970s. There are British and American poets writing today whose work has been described as modernist or late modernist (Mellors, 2005; Mengham and Kinsella, 2004). What these writers have in common is harder to define than what separates them. But despite their heterogeneity, one could hazard a broad definition by saying that while these writers recognize, with the post-modernists, the perilous connections between modernism and authoritarianism, unlike the post-modernists, the late (or contemporary) modernists have not relinquished the notion of author as privileged site of expression (though it is now hedged by an acute historical self-consciousness). The problems raised by modernism are to be solved, not by a recantation of modernism but (to paraphrase Mellors) by 'more modernism' (2005, 23).

Bibliography

Esty, J. (2004), *A Shrinking Island: Modernism and National Culture in England.* Princeton: Princeton UP.

Jameson, F. (2002), *A Singular Modernity*. London: Verso.

Levin, H. (1962), 'What Was Modernism?', in S. Burnshaw (ed.), *Varieties of Literary Experience*. New York: New York University Press, pp. 307–29.

Maher, A. (2013), '"Swastika Arms of Passage Leading to Nothing": Late Modernism and the "New" Britain'. *ELH*, 80, (1), 251–85.

Mellors, A. (2005), *Late Modernist Poetics: From Pound to Prynne*. Manchester: Manchester University Press.

Mengham, R. and Kinsella, J. (eds) (2004), *Vanishing Points: New Modernist Poems*. Cambridge: Salt.

Miller, T. (1999), *Late Modernism: Politics, Fiction, and the Arts between the World Wars*. Berkeley: University of California Press.

Wilde, A. (1981), *Horizons of Assent: Modernism, Postmodernism, and the Ironic Imagination*. Baltimore and London: Johns Hopkins University Press.

Manifesto

Buried within the now obsolete etymology of *manifesto* is the notion of proof or evidence (see *OED* 'manifesto', sb.1: 'A proof, a piece of evidence' (obs.)), and it is perhaps indicative of the mysterious character of modernist art that it is so often accompanied by explanatory documents attempting to offer some kind of proof that its existence is necessary, that it is not just another instance of the emperor's new clothes. Modernist manifestos carry within them the germ of the political manifesto, with the underlying assumption that the status quo requires a corrective: hence they offer both a diagnosis and a remedial programme. Sometimes, indeed, the two could overlap: the manifesto-prone Futurist movement, who gave us not only the founding Futurist manifesto (1909) but further manifestos on dance, theatre and electric signs, eventually became enthusiastic propagandists for Mussolini.

Manifestos were therefore a crucial tool for avant-garde movements, which saw themselves as staging incursions into decaying or obsolete institutions. In this respect, Marinetti's seminal 'The Founding and Manifesto of Futurism' set the stage for a series of documents proclaiming a radical break with existing attitudes and practices: these documents included Wyndham Lewis's vorticist 'Manifesto' (1914), Mina Loy's 'Feminist Manifesto' (1914), Tristan Tzara's 'Dada Manifesto' (1918) and André Breton's 'Manifesto of Surrealism' (1924). Standing somewhere between 'iconoclasm and iconography' (Lyon, 1999, 27), the manifesto figures a crisis, but also potential solutions, making it a quintessentially modernist document. It also helps to define groupings, with all the problems of identity that involves: who is excluded, who included, in the new vision? Its political associations reverberated in its use as a platform to denounce former adherents, the most notorious example being Breton's excommunication of dissident Surrealists in his 'Second Manifesto of Surrealism' (1930). The manifesto form as such reveals a series of contours abutting one another, illustrating the variety and heterogeneity of modernism.

Manifestos are formally various. Perhaps most familiar are the clamorous typography and outlandish exaggerations of the Futurist and Dada manifestos. But, as Mary Ann Caws notes, the manifesto encompasses the dialogue, bullet-pointed lists, poems, calligrammes and aphorisms (Caws, 2001, xxv–viii). Its poetics of the future can be traced back to Marx and Engels's *The Communist Manifesto* (1848) (Puchner, 2006), and if a less iconoclastic attitude is also discernible, in statements of poetics ranging from Wordsworth's 'Preface' to the *Lyrical Ballads* (1800) to Ezra Pound's more explicitly prescriptive Imagist manifesto, 'A Few Don'ts by an Imagiste' (1913), the form is most recognizable as a revolutionary document. Hence its appeal to movements seeking to move away from a marginal or culturally occluded position, often invoking explicitly utopian strategies. 'Manifesto for a Free Revolutionary Art' (1938), jointly authored by Trotsky, André Breton and Diego Rivera, is perhaps the best-known manifesto to have emerged from Latin America, but others – notably Chilean poet Vicente Huidobro's manifestos – similarly fuse the political and the aesthetic. And if manifestos have all too often set the terms by which literary criticism subsequently judges them, they also have the power to interrupt models of modernism as a unified narrative, often one founded on the exclusion of racial difference. On this reading, manifestos would include suffragette dramas, Nancy Cunard's anthology *Negro* (1934) and various texts by C. L. R. James and Suzanne and Aimé Césaire (Winkiel, 2008), as well as more explicitly political texts like W. E. B. Du Bois's *Manifesto of the Second Pan-African Congress* (1921).

Bibliography

Caws, M. A. (ed.) (2001), *Manifesto: A Century of Isms*. Lincoln: University of Nebraska Press.
Lyon, J. (1999), *Manifestoes: Provocations of the Modern*. Ithaca, NY: Cornell University Press.
Puchner, M. (2006), *Poetry of the Revolution: Marx, Manifestos, and the Avant-Gardes*. Princeton: Princeton University Press.

Rainey, L., Poggi, C. and Wittman, L. (eds) (2009), *Futurism: An Anthology*. New Haven: Yale University Press.

Somigli, L. (2003), *Legitimizing the Artist: Manifesto Writing and European Modernism, 1885–1915*. Toronto: University of Toronto Press.

Winkiel, L. (2008), *Modernism, Race, and Manifestos*. Cambridge: Cambridge University Press.

Mass-Observation

The Mass-Observation project was founded in 1937 by Tom Harrison, an anthropologist, and Charles Madge, a poet. Seeking to survey everyday life, it brought together disparate projects on which Harrison and Madge were already working. In its early years, Mass-Observation involved both paid investigators documenting behaviour and conversation at public events and in public spaces, and unpaid volunteers responding to questionnaires, keeping diaries and providing other materials. Mass-Observation emphasized a qualitative rather than quantitative approach to the sociology of contemporary life. Madge left the project in 1940, but it was given new impetus by the Second World War (including commissions from the Ministry for Information), and in 1949 it became a private firm specializing in market research; it was relaunched in 1981 and continues today. The rich and extensive Mass-Observation archive, much of which is now available online, is a major resource for historians of British society and for critics of modernism.

The phrase 'mass observation' speaks to the project's inherent epistemological and political tensions, and these have generated considerable controversy. The phrase suggests observation *of* the masses and observation *by* the masses (Hubble, 2006, 2), and it had in the period since the First World War already been used in both these senses (Anonymous, 1920; Bloomfield, 1935, 37–8). The implications of 'mass observation' therefore range from the panopticon or surveillance state to a new form of collective self-consciousness, though in practice Mass-Observation's various ventures fell somewhere between these extremes. The unstable relation between the terms *mass* and *observation* is complicated further by those terms' own ambiguities. *Mass* involves a democratic gesture towards all classes, an effort specifically to document the experiences of those conventionally excluded from notice or study, and condescension towards the 'mob' who represent or consume 'mass culture', 'mass media', and so forth (Williams, 1958, 316–32). This in turn raises the problem of personnel, of the groups who were to observe and represent the masses. In addition to well-known figures who assisted Harrison and Madge in their work, from Humphrey Jennings and William Empson to Kathleen Raine and Humphrey Spender, the volunteers were predominantly middle class, though by no means exclusively so (Hinton, 2013, 62). This further complicates the sense of the term *observation*, in which disinterested observation of oneself or of others shades into acting as a representative of one's own and others' interests, beliefs, values, and practices.

For these and other reasons, including the heterogeneity of the materials it collected, Mass-Observation has proved difficult to theorize and its archive difficult to analyse. Nevertheless, the project has been of increasing interest, enabling detailed study of the working class, society in war-time, television history, sexuality, food, dreams, and other areas. In 2013, an exhibition of photographs taken for the project was held at the Photographers' Gallery in London. Mass-Observation has also been productively compared with contemporary interest in 'the poetry of the everyday', including Jennings' and John Grierson's documentary film-making (Miller, 2002), and more broadly it invites comparison with the documentary photography of Walker Evans and Dorothea Lange, and with the documentary poetics of Charles Reznikoff and Muriel Rukeyser, not to mention Madge's own poetry.

Bibliography

Ano. (1920), 'Empiricism'. *Athenaeum*, 4689, (12 March 1920), 341–2.

Bloomfield, L. (1935), *Language*. London Allen and Unwin.

Buzard, J. (1997), 'Mass-Observation, Modernism, and Auto-ethnography'. *Modernism/modernity*, 4, (3), 93–122.

Groth, H. and Lusty, N. (2013), 'The Dream Archive: Mass-Observation and Everyday Life', in *Dreams and Modernity: A Cultural History*. London: Routledge, pp. 148–77.

Hinton, J. (2013), *The Mass Observers: A History, 1937–1949*. Oxford: Oxford University Press.

Hubble, N. (2006), *Mass Observation and Everyday Life: Culture, History, Theory*. Basingstoke: Palgrave Macmillan.

McCracken, S. (ed.) (2001), 'Mass-Observation as Poetics and Science'. Special issue of *New Formations*, 44.

Miller, T. (2002), 'Documentary/Modernism: Convergence and Complementarity in the 1930s'. *Modernism/modernity*, 9, (2), 226–41.

Williams, R. (1958), Culture and Society. London: Chatto and Windus.

Media

The early twentieth century gave broad currency to a new sense of the word *media*, meaning the collective means of mass communication. Whether the word was understood to be singular or plural, this sense nevertheless retained its relation to other usages of *media* and *medium*. Of these, in addition to the root sense of intermediary channel or intervening substance (Latin *medium*, middle, midst), the most important included the medium of exchange; a spiritualist medium; the raw materials of an art, especially of painting or drawing; and the material or technology used in mechanical reproduction (print, celluloid, the gramophone). Modernist writers and artists worked within and against this complicated constellation of meanings and practices. More recently, it has generated tremendous critical activity, both in documenting the history of the media and of mediums, and in theorizing the interplay of art, technology, mass culture and social practice.

One common approach has been to trace the influence of mass communication on aesthetic form, and in particular of print media on literature (Ardis and Collier, 2008; Wollaeger, 2006). From this perspective, modernism's relations with the broader channels of public discourse raise a series of important antagonisms: high and low, avant-garde and conservative, art and commerce. The rise of the little magazine, in opposition to major newspapers and popular journals, is a prominent example. Alternatively, some critics have examined the influence on modernist writing of new technologies, especially the cinema (Biers, 2013; Marcus, 2007; McCabe, 2005), while others have explored affinities between filmic and literary experimentation (Trotter, 2007). The widespread association of new technologies like the telegraph and the radio with mediations of the spirit world, with ghosts and with magic has been an especially fruitful area of research (Sconce, 2000; Thurschwell, 2001). A focus on media as technology has also allowed the materials of older art forms to be reconceived as technologies themselves, or at least in terms of technology. Criticism has thus sought to trace the relation between new media forms and, for instance, Wyndham Lewis's argument that modern artists ought to forego the 'medium' of oil paint and instead take up an 'orchestra of media' (Lewis, 1914). The challenge has been to understand how, when Ernest Fenollosa and Ezra Pound advocate the Chinese ideogram as an ideal 'medium' for poetry (Fenollosa and Pound, 2008), this development in an age-old art form is related to the rise of photography or film, as technologies and as arts (Bush, 2010).

This then poses a general question about modernism and mediation. By examining the reciprocal determinations of art and technology, some critics have theorized the broader 'media ecology' of modernism. The interactions of literature, photography, film, advertising, mechanical print and other artistic and media forms can thus be understood as complex competitions between the old and the new, the pre-modern and the modern, inherited prestige and radical innovation (Murphet, 2009). Finally, our newly enriched understanding of the constellated meanings of *medium* and *media* has meant that analysis can now move deftly between representations of communication technologies as social practices (telephone, radio) and representations of other new forms of connectivity and of the technological mediation of experience, from mass-transit systems to semi-synthetic plastics (Trotter, 2013).

Bibliography

Ardis, A. L. and Collier, P. (eds) (2008), *Transatlantic Print Culture, 1880–1940: Emerging Media, Emerging Modernisms*. Basingstoke: Palgrave Macmillan.

Biers, K. (2013), *Virtual Modernism: Writing and Technology in the Progressive Era*. Minneapolis: The University of Minnesota Press.

Bush, C. (2010), *Ideographic Modernism: China, Writing, Media*. New York: Oxford University Press.

Fenollosa, E. and Pound, E. (2008), *The Chinese Written Character as a Medium for Poetry*, H. Saussy, J. Stalling and L. Klein (eds). New York: Fordham University Press.

Lewis, W. (1914), 'Orchestra of Media'. *Blast*, 1, 142.

Marcus, L. (2007), *The Tenth Muse: Writing about Cinema in the Modernist Period*. Oxford: Oxford University Press.

McCabe, S. (2005), *Cinematic Modernism: Modernist Poetry and Film*. Cambridge: Cambridge University Press.

Murphet, J. (2009), *Multimedia Modernism: Literature and the Anglo-American Avant-Garde*. Cambridge: Cambridge University Press.

Sconce, J. (2000), *Haunted Media: Electronic Presence from Telegraphy to Television*. Durham: Duke University Press.

Thurschwell, P. (2001), *Literature, Technology and Magical Thinking, 1880–1920*. Cambridge: Cambridge University Press.

Trotter, D. (2007), *Cinema and Modernism*. Oxford: Blackwell.

Trotter, D. (2013), *Literature in the First Media Age: Britain Between the Wars*. Cambridge: Harvard University Press.

Wollaeger, M. A. (2006), *Modernism, Media, and Propaganda: British Narrative from 1900 to 1945*. Princeton: Princeton University Press.

New

It is nothing new to observe that when Ezra Pound published *Make It New* in 1934, giving to modernism one of its most enduring slogans, modernism was, if not old, certainly middle-aged. Pound's book dealt not only with Henry James and Remy de Gourmont but also with the Troubadours and the translation of classical Greek. Pound offered no Futurist injunction to celebrate the modern world's 'new beauty' by abandoning the monuments of the past (Marinetti, 2006, 13). Even James and Gourmont had been dead for almost two decades. But it is less often observed that, less than a fortnight later, Pound published *Eleven New Cantos*. The two titles suggest some of the competing senses with which modernists invested the term *new*. As a 'signifier for difference', the word was 'so widely adopted that the differences spread beyond distinction or accountability' (Rasula, 2010, 714). Pound's new cantos were his latest cantos; they formed the present instalment of an ongoing project. Those cantos then make it new when they incorporate extended prose passages from Jefferson's correspondence, and when they retell an episode from the *Odyssey* in a forbiddingly polyglot, seemingly fragmented evocation of sexuality and rebirth. The word *new* may be a temporal or a historical classification, and as evaluation it may praise the genuinely innovative or censure the merely novel. Indeed, the term's nuances emerge further in comparison with *novel*, which shades into the frivolous, trivial or transient, and with *modern*, opposed not to the old but to the ancient or to the past (Calinescu, 1987, 13–15).

Precisely because the word permits so many emphases, *new* had tremendous potency both within the arts and in society at large. *Make It New* appeared a year after Roosevelt instituted the New Deal, and Henry James, one of Pound's touchstones, helped to popularize the term New Woman. The Harlem Renaissance promoted the new social confidence and artistic success of African Americans under the banner of the New Negro, while new technologies of mass communication made it a new age for news (succeeded now by the age of new media). The sense of unprecedented social change and promise prompted A. R. Orage to call his first magazine the *New Age*, while the title of Orage's second journal, the *New English Weekly*, only specifies its position in the history of a format. The *New Masses* is ambiguous, alluding to the earlier socialist magazine *The Masses* and suggesting a new age for the working class. So, too, the mischievous title of Yeats's 1938 volume, *New Poems*, designates a simple successor to previous collections, and hints that the poems themselves, the works of a 73-year-old, may not be as obsolete or aesthetically conservative as they seem. The new has thus proved an enduring talisman for accounts of modernity and of modernism. With some irony, writing about the arts has itself been subject to the valencies of *new*, from New Criticism to the New Modernist Studies (Mao and Walkowitz, 2008).

Though modernism has been identified with 'the powerful and central presiding value of the New as such' (Jameson, 2012, 151–2), the identification is complicated by the long history of that value, stretching back to the pre-Socratics (North, 2013), and by its survival after modernism. Moreover, the modernist *new* risks becoming a fetish (Jameson, 2012, 157) and a commodity (Rosenquist, 2009). For this reason, Schoenberg remains sceptical in his 1923 essay, 'Neue Musik': 'apart from possible new ideas (new!)', the new music 'will be more a matter of relatively novel presentations of relatively novel ideas' (Schoenberg, 1984, 138). The new may merely advertise experiment for experiment's sake. Wyndham Lewis speaks contemptuously of jazz as 'a sort of *permanent novelty*' (Lewis, 1993, 123), and before him Matthew Arnold warned against the growing readiness to accept ideas 'simply because they are new' (Arnold, 1993, 61). And yet Proust praises a piece of music for seeming to have been composed after more recent pieces, for displaying an 'apparently contradictory and in fact deceptive character of enduring novelty' (Proust, 2002, 233). This 'durable nouveauté', cognate with *nouveau* or *new*, trumps historical sequence with an aesthetic quality, and this seems, if not a modernist achievement, at the least a characteristically modernist aspiration.

Bibliography

Arnold, M. (1993), *Culture and Anarchy and Other Writings*, S. Collini (ed.). Cambridge: Cambridge University Press.

Calinescu, M. (1987), *Five Faces of Modernity*. Durham: Duke University Press.

Jameson, F. (2012), *A Singular Modernity*. London: Verso.

Lewis, W. (1993), *Time and Western Man*, P. Edwards (ed.). Santa Rosa: Black Sparrow.

Mao, D. and Walkowitz, R. L. (2008), 'The New Modernist Studies'. *PMLA*, 123, (3), 737–48.

Marinetti, F. T. (2006), *Critical Writings*, G. Berghaus (ed.), D. Thompson (transl.). New York: Farrar, Straus and Giroux.

North, M. (2013), *Novelty: A History of the New*. Chicago: University of Chicago Press.

Pound, E. (1934), *Make It New: Essays by Ezra Pound*. London: Faber and Faber.

Proust, M. (2002), *The Prisoner and The Fugitive*, C. Clark and P. Collier (transl.). London: Penguin.

Rasula, J. (2010), 'Make It New'. *Modernism/modernity*, 17, (4), 713–33.

Rosenquist, R. (2009), *Modernism, the Market, and the Institution of the New*. Cambridge: Cambridge University Press.

Schoenberg, A. (1984), *Style and Idea*, L. Stein (ed.), L. Black (transl.). Berkeley: University of California Press.

Object

In 1934, Samuel Beckett announced that a 'new thing' had happened, 'namely the breakdown of the object, whether current, historical, mythical or spook' (Beckett, 1984, 70). If it did not quite lie in ruins, the noun *object* was certainly subject to forces pulling from disparate directions. The etymological sense of something thrown in the way or opposite (Latin *ob* + *iacio*, to throw) remains in the word's meaning as something presented to the senses or the understanding, and in its meaning as a goal or purpose. But this ordinary word also has a long and complex history in philosophy, and the philosophical opposition of *object* and *subject* has proved an enduring problem. More generally the term *object* has come to imply something material or physical, in opposition to the inner or metaphysical subject. From the Enlightenment onwards the concept of objectivity became increasingly influential, and its separation of the subject from a self-sufficient object was important for notions of an empirical or scientific gaze (Daston and Galison, 2007). For those who conducted experiments in spiritualism, even 'mythical or spook' objects were susceptible to this form of capture.

The *objets trouvés* or 'found objects' incorporated into Pablo Picasso's or Kurt Schwitters's collages clearly demonstrate modernism's fascination for the object as such, as do Marcel Duchamp's readymades. Though a poem like T. S. Eliot's 'The Love Song of J. Alfred Prufrock' may seem, in contrast, to be preoccupied with the isolated subject, with subjectivity or consciousness, Eliot himself proposed that art expresses emotion only by presenting an 'objective correlative': 'a set of objects, a situation, a chain of events' which serves as 'the formula of that *particular* emotion'. The 'external facts' must be adequate to the internal facts (Eliot, 1951, 145). Louis Zukofsky's Objectivist poetics advocated not a work which incorporates or deploys objects, but a work which is itself 'an object or affects the mind as such'. Through 'objectification' the work pursues the goal of 'rested totality', seemingly complete in and of itself (Zukofsky, 1931, 274). Cast before the mind, this particular object then sets itself against the other objects of modern life, so often merely means to an end or products to be exchanged for their equivalents. Similarly, Duchamp removes a standard-issue urinal from its ordinary context and makes of it a particular thing, an artwork whose meanings depend both on that former context and on cultures of artistic curation and appreciation.

By restoring the object and its meanings to social and political contexts, many modernists resist too crude a separation of object and subject (Mao, 1998; Siraganian, 2012). So, too, do philosophers who insist on the terms' dialectical interdependence, from Hegel to Heidegger. Approaching the problem from a historical perspective, dialectical materialists attribute the false alienation of subject from object to capitalism, which reduces objects to possessions and commodities. Following Marx, they urge that richer and more diverse relations to the object – 'within, in and through it' – allow the subject to 'enter into a complex network of human relations' (Lefebvre, 1991, 156). This dialectic means, as Beckett goes on to say, that the breakdown of the object could equally be called the breakdown of the subject: 'It comes to the same thing' (Beckett, 1984, 70).

Indeed, *object* should also be understood in relation to that other key term, *thing*. Combining Heidegger's notion of the thing (Heidegger, 1971) with the rise of material cultural studies (Hicks and Beaudry, 2010), recent theory has suggested that *thing* 'really names less an object than a particular subject-object relation' (Brown, 2001, 4). The thing is as much the matter at hand, the affair in question, as a material object. When Wallace Stevens titles a late poem 'Not Ideas About the Thing But the Thing Itself' (Stevens, 1997, 451–2), he seems to reject subjective ideas for a self-sufficient object, while insinuating that things themselves necessarily involve subjects and ideas. (Stevens's poem both describes and is that thing itself.) Thus, when a cubist painting of a woman or a violin, or a section from Gertrude Stein's *Tender Buttons*, breaks down the object in order to analyse and reconstitute it, at the same time it breaks down and reconstitutes the subject, and so reconstitutes the manifold relations of people and things. As Stein observes, 'the difference is spreading' (Stein, 1998, 313).

Bibliography

Beckett, S. (1984), *Disjecta: Miscellaneous Writings and a Dramatic Fragment*, R. Cohn (ed.). New York: Grove.

Brown, B. (2001), 'Thing Theory'. *Critical Inquiry*, 28, (1), 1–22.

Daston, L. J. and Galison, P. (2007), *Objectivity*. New York: Zone Books.

Eliot, T. S. (1951), *Selected Essays*. London: Faber and Faber.

Heidegger, M. (1971), 'The Thing', in *Poetry, Language, Thought*. New York: Harper & Row, pp. 163–84.

Hicks, D. and Beaudry, M. C. (eds) (2010), *The Oxford Handbook of Material Cultural Studies*. Oxford: Oxford University Press.

Lefebvre, H. (1991), *Critique of Everyday Life, Vol. 1: Introduction*, J. Moore (transl.). London: Verso.

Mao, D. (1998), *Solid Objects: Modernism and the Test of Production*. Princeton: Princeton University Press.

Siraganian, L. (2012), *Modernism's Other Work: The Art Object's Political Life*. New York: Oxford University Press.

Stein, G. (1998), *Gertrude Stein: Writings, 1903–1932*, C. R. Stimpson and H. Chessman (eds). New York: Library of America.

Stevens, W. (1997), *Wallace Stevens: Collected Poetry and Prose*, F. Kermode and J. Richardson (eds). New York: Library of America.

Primitivism

Primitivism has long been a controversial feature of modernist art and, more broadly, of the cultures of modernity (Barkar and Bush, 1995). The term makes the 'primitive' a vogue, thereby combining fascination and condescension, appreciation and prejudice. In particular, primitivism marshals a series of fraught oppositions as interpretative and evaluative categories: white and non-white, history and mythology, science and magic, civilized and uncivilized (barbaric, savage). As a set of intellectual and artistic practices, primitivism was deeply implicated in the colonial and nationalist projects of nineteenth- and twentieth-century Europe. Spurred by Edward Burnett Tylor's *Primitive Culture* (1871), many anthropologists and sociologists turned their attention to the study of non-European societies, and so to theorizing the difference between those societies and their own. Émile Durkheim, for instance, defined a primitive religion as a religion found in a society 'whose organization is of the utmost simplicity', and one which 'can be explained without introducing any element borrowed from an earlier religion' (Durkheim, 2001, 3). Though simplicity and aboriginality are ideological constructions, and though Durkheim focuses on the totemism of Australian Aborigines, more generally these same criteria allow an interest in the primitive 'without' to become an interest in the primitive 'within'. In this way, Jane Ellen Harrison explores the primitive roots of Greek civilization in *Prolegomena to the Study of Greek Religion* (1903), while in *The Golden Bough* (1890), James George Frazer frequently compares contemporary non-European societies to the earliest forms of European society. Primitivism thus represents a restless urge to identify and categorize the primitive across time and space. Condescension to the other may involve forms of identification, and narratives of evolution – from pre-modern to modern, from child to adult, from savagery to sophistication – may suggest the persistence of the primitive beneath the surface of civilized society.

In a further paradox, primitivism in the arts often generated avant-garde experimentation. Paul Gaugin's paintings of French Polynesia exaggerate and simplify shapes and colours, rejecting realism for post-Impressionism and anticipating abstraction. Pablo Picasso's groundbreaking *Les Demoiselles d'Avignon* (1907) famously depicts five prostitutes, two of whose faces are modelled on African masks (a primitive from 'without'), and three of whose faces are modelled on ancient Iberian art (the primitive 'within'). So, too, Stravinsky's 1913 ballet *Le Sacre du printemps* recasts the rituals of pagan Russia by combining traditional folk songs with experiments in bitonality and complex new rhythms. While Vaslav Nijinsky's choreography for *Le Sacre du printemps* substituted 'angular and earth-bound' movements for the grace and elegance of traditional ballet (Duffy and Atkinson, 2014, 95), Josephine Baker performed her 'Danse sauvage' in Paris wearing only a loincloth of pink feathers; in other performances she wore a skirt of fake bananas (Cheng, 2011, 41–5). From dance and jazz music to the writings of the Harlem Renaissance, African American culture provides many of the best examples of primitivism's vexed politics (Lemke, 1998; Winkiel, 2006). Working in quintessentially modern forms, artists like Josephine Baker and Louis Armstrong were both criticized for returning to humanity's 'savage' origins and celebrated for throwing off the shackles of a moribund, repressive civilization (Brothers, 2014).

Postcolonial theory has done much to deepen our understanding of primitivism's politics and aesthetics (Amselle, 2003; Li, 2012), and recent criticism has extended the concept into new areas. Scholars have, for example, traced a comparable dynamic in modernist Irish writing's use of Irish mythology and its representations of the Irish peasant (Mattar, 2004; McGarrity and Culleton, 2009). Others have proposed that primitivism provided models for the representation of homosexuality (Hackett, 2004), and that it promoted new ways of understanding and resisting capitalist economics (Willmott, 2008). Finally, a primitivist awareness and desire has been identified even in the modern experience of material substances, as for instance of rubber, a substance 'at once ancient and modern, exotic and mundane' (Trotter, 2013, 87).

Bibliography

Amselle, J.-L. (2003), 'Primitivism and Postcolonialism in the Arts'. N. Mellott and
J. Van Dam (transl.), *MLN*, 118, 974–88.

Barkar, E. and Bush, R. (eds) (1995), *Prehistories of the Future: The Primitivist Project
and the Culture of Modernism*. Stanford: Stanford University Press.

Brothers, T. (2014), *Louis Armstrong: Master of Modernism*. New York: W. W. Norton.

Cheng, A. A. (2011), *Second Skin: Josephine Baker and the Modern Surface*. New York:
Oxford University Press.

Duffy, M. and Atkinson, P. (2014), 'Unnatural Movements: Modernism's Shaping
of Intimate Relations in Stravinsky's Le Sacre du Printemps'. *Affirmations: of the
Modern*, 1, (2), 95–119.

Durkheim, É. (2001), *The Elementary Forms of Religious Life*. C. Cosman (transl.), M. S.
Cladis (ed.). Oxford: Oxford University Press.

Frazer, J. G. (2009), *The Golden Bough: A Study in Magic and Religion*. R. Frazer (ed.).
Oxford World's Classics. Oxford: Oxford University Press.

Hackett, R. (2004), *Sapphic Primitivism: Productions of Race, Class, and Sexuality in Key
Works of Modern Fiction*. New Brunswick, NJ: Rutgers University Press.

Lemke, S. (1998), *Primitivist Modernism: Black Culture and the Origins of Transatlantic
Modernism*. Oxford: Oxford University Press.

Li, V. (2012), 'Primitivism and Postcolonial Literature', in A. Quayson (ed.), *The
Cambridge History of Postcolonial Literature*. 2 vols. Cambridge: Cambridge
University Press, pp. 982–1005.

Mattar, S. G. (2004), *Primitivism, Science, and the Irish Revival*. Oxford: Oxford
University Press.

McGarrity, M. and Culleton, C. A. (eds) (2009), *Irish Modernism and the Global
Primitive*. New York: Palgrave Macmillan.

Trotter, D. (2013), *Literature in the First Media Age: Britain Between the Wars*.
Cambridge: Harvard University Press.

Tylor, E. B. (1871), *Primitive Culture: Researches into the Development of Mythology,
Philosophy, Religion, Art, and Custom*. London: Edward Murray.

Willmott, G. (2008), *Modernist Goods: Primitivism, the Market, and the Gift*. Toronto:
The University of Toronto Press.

Winkiel, L. A. (2006), 'Nancy Cunard's Negro and the Transnational Politics of Race'.
Modernism/modernity, 13, (3), 507–30.

Race

The recent turn in modernist studies towards global or transnational approaches
has generated new interest in the issue of race. Indeed, the category of race has

come under increasing scrutiny. We now have a much better understanding of the term's history, and in particular of nineteenth- and twentieth-century efforts to conceive race biologically, from the pseudo-science of phrenology to fascism's emphasis on racial purity. Though biological race was often distinguished from ethnicity, understood to be a social construction, the two concepts overlapped. In particular, biological theories were used to explain and to justify social structures and aesthetic practices. Reflecting upon this history, many contemporary critics and theorists understand race to be the historical product of political developments, cultural movements and intellectual disciplines, from fascism and Orientalism to biology and anthropology (Platt, 2011). The history of European colonialism, for instance, represents not simply a system of encounters between races, but the process of constructing race itself as a category. As Raymond Williams writes, the term *race* allowed physical, cultural and socio-economic differences to be 'taken up, projected and generalized' (Williams, 1983, 250), and so to be deployed for purposes of exclusion and expropriation.

Rather than framing specific races as fixed categories, scholarship tends now to conceive race as one element in a network of shifting constructions of identity, alongside class and gender in particular (Doyle and Winkiel, 2005; Forter, 2011). Critics have thus paid special attention to unstable or hybrid identities and their importance for literature and the arts. Recent work on the creole modernism of writers like Jean Rhys and Derek Walcott is an especially good example (GoGwilt, 2011; Mukherjee, 2013). It may be that the creole or the hybrid, though previously deemed aesthetically and politically marginal, actually offers better ways in which to understand the mixed and unstable identities of modernism in general.

This critique of the concept of race has accompanied an expansion in the scope of modernist studies (Mao and Walkowitz, 2008), and so an increase in the materials with which to consider modernism and race. The addition of a chapter on African American modernism to the second edition of Peter Nicholls's influential *Modernisms: A Literary Guide* (2009) indicates a broader movement beyond canonical works by white Europeans and Americans which, like Joseph Conrad's *Heart of Darkness* (1899) and Henri Rousseau's *Le Rêve* (1910), explicitly engage with race. Some of the most fruitful criticism has compared the modernisms of white and non-white writers and artists. While a Gertrude Stein or a William Carlos Williams mimics the dialects of African Americans, for example, a Claude McKay or a Zora Neale Hurston strives to escape the aesthetic and political confines of those same dialects (North, 1998). Others have examined the relation between the sciences of race and aesthetic form, as for instance the influence of phrenology on modernist poets' conceptions of rhythm (Golston, 2007). More generally, the critique of race, together with Postcolonial Studies and the rise of World Literature Studies, has allowed more sophisticated accounts of modernisms across the globe, from Chinese to Indian, Jewish to Caribbean (Doyle and Winkiel, 2005; Platt, 2011). At the same time, a historically informed understanding of race has offered new ways in which to read Irish modernism, whose major writers had previously been admitted into the modernist canon precisely because they were understood to be deracinated (Brannigan, 2009).

Bibliography

Brannigan, J. (2009), *Race in Modern Irish Literature and Culture*. Edinburgh: Edinburgh University Press.

Doyle, L. and Winkiel, L. (eds) (2005), *GeoModernisms: Race, Modernism, Modernity*. Bloomington: Indiana University Press.

Forter, G. (2011), *Gender, Race, and Mourning in American Modernism*. Cambridge: Cambridge University Press.

GoGwilt, C. (2011), *The Passage of Literature: Genealogies of Modernism in Conrad, Rhys, and Pramoedya*. Oxford: Oxford University Press.

Golston, M. (2007), *Rhythm and Race in Modernist Poetry and Science*. New York: Columbia University Press.

Mao, D. and Walkowitz, R. L. (2008), 'The New Modernist Studies'. *PMLA*, 123, (3), 737–48.

Mukherjee, A. (2013), *What Is a Classic? Postcolonial Rewriting and Invention of the Canon*. Stanford: Stanford University Press.

Nicholls, P. (2009), *Modernisms: A Literary Guide*. 2nd edn. Basingstoke: Palgrave Macmillan.

North, M. (1998), *The Dialect of Modernism: Race, Language, and Twentieth-Century Literature*. New York: Oxford University Press.

Platt, L. (ed.) (2011), *Modernism and Race*. Cambridge: Cambridge University Press.

Williams, R. (1983), *Keywords: A Vocabulary of Culture and Society*. Rev. edn. New York: Oxford University Press.

Sex

'If sex were all, then every trembling hand/Could make us squeak, like dolls, the wished-for-words' (Stevens, 1997, 14). Sometimes it seems that, for modernism, sex really was all. In 1905, Sigmund Freud published 'Three Essays on the Theory of Sexuality', first identifying the sexual object (*Sexualobjekt*) as the object of a need (*Bedürfnis*) or instinct (*Trieb*), and then arguing that adult sexuality is a late form of the need for gratification which, in infants, produces thumb-sucking (Freud, 2001). The term *sexual* seems thus to have slipped the grip of *sex*. How are the meanings of adjective and noun related in modern culture more broadly, and how are they related to that other noun, *sexuality*? In time, Freud came to posit a fundamental instinct or drive for life, and to call it the libido or Eros. If *sex* seems everywhere, partly it is because the word and the concept extend from a set of physical acts to so many other physiological and psychological experiences: diverse desires and pleasures, manifold satisfactions and dissatisfactions.

From the late nineteenth century, the burgeoning science of sexology sought to demonstrate that sex shapes our experience and our identity. Freud was accompanied in this by Richard Freiherr von Krafft-Ebing, whose *Psychopathia Sexualis* appeared in 1886, and by Havelock Ellis, whose *Sexual Inversion* (1897) was a pioneering study in homosexuality. Early sexology often focused on what were then considered aberrations or perversions, and this emphasis is shared by the literature of the period (Peppis, 2014; Schaffner, 2012). Novelists like Marcel Proust and Djuna Barnes played with conceptions of homosexuality as 'inversion', while Georges Bataille narrated a series of 'perverse' sexual encounters in *L'Histoire de l'oeil* (1928). Conversely, Wyndham Lewis's *Tarr* (1918) represented 'normal' heterosexual relations as casual, crude and sometimes quite brutal: 'Sex is a monstrosity' (Lewis, 1990, 26). Many modernists thus challenged the conventional morality which idealized some sexual practices and identities, and condemned others. Luis Buñuel's surrealist film, *L'Age d'or* (1930), in which a woman achieves satisfaction sucking the toe of a religious statue, is another excellent example. For writers as different as D. H. Lawrence and Mina Loy, sex meant liberation from societal repression. '[T]he realisation in defiance of superstition that there is *nothing impure in sex*', wrote Loy in her 'Feminist Manifesto' (1914), 'will constitute an incalculable & wider social regeneration than it is possible for our generation to imagine' (Loy, 1996, 156). Sex was political, whether associated with the freedoms of the jazz age (Ayers, 2004) or with fascism (Frost, 2001). Finally, sex had a profound influence on experiments in aesthetic form, from the extended arc of anticipation and release which structures Wagner's *Tristan und Isolde* (1865) to the way sexuality shapes the representation of consciousness in writings by Virginia Woolf and James Joyce (Boone, 1998).

In attacking the social codes that govern sex, and in linking sex to literary form, modernism paid new attention to the relation between sex and words, whether wished-for or wishful, liberating or oppressive. Long after Freud, Michel Foucault's *The History of Sexuality* (1976, 1984) considered sex not as an innate instinct or drive, but as formed by the set of discourses particular to a given moment in history. This shift is also important for that other major meaning of the word *sex*, the categorization of an organism as male or female (Latin *sexus*). Though *sex* and *gender* are often used synonymously, contemporary theorists usually distinguish between the former, as a biological category determined by an organism's anatomy, and the latter, as an identity determined by social discourses and practices. Both concepts are vital to modernism. They affected the arguments made by and against the Suffragette movement (Park, 2010), for instance, and they have been essential to recent work in modernist studies (Felski, 1995; Lusty and Murphet, 2014; Scott, 2007).

Bibliography

Ayers, D. (2004), *English Literature of the 1920s*. Edinburgh: Edinburgh University Press.

Boone, J. A. (1998), *Libidinal Currents: Sexuality and the Shaping of Modernism*. Chicago: University of Chicago Press.

Felski, R. (1995), *The Gender of Modernity*. Cambridge: Harvard University Press.

Foucault, M. (2008), *The History of Sexuality: The Will to Knowledge*. Volume I. R. Hurley (transl.). London: Penguin.

Freud, S. (2001), 'Three Essays on the Theory of Sexuality', in J. Strachey (ed. and transl.), *The Standard Edition of the Complete Psychological Works of Sigmund Freud, Vol. VII (1901–1905): A Case of Hysteria, Three Essays on Sexuality and Other Works*. London: Vintage Books, pp. 125–248.

Frost, L. (2001), *Sex Drives: Fantasies of Fascism in Literary Modernism*. Ithaca: Cornell University Press.

Lewis, W. (1990), *Tarr: The 1918 Version*, P. O'Keeffe (ed.). Santa Rosa: Black Sparrow.

Loy, M. (1996), *The Lost Lunar Baedeker*, R. Conover (ed.). New York: Farrar, Straus and Giroux.

Lusty, N. and Murphet, J. (eds) (2014), *Modernism and Masculinity*. Cambridge: Cambridge University Press.

Park, S. S. (2010), 'Political Activism and Women's Modernism', in M. T. Linett (ed.), *The Cambridge Companion to Modernist Women Writers*. Cambridge: Cambridge University Press, pp. 172–86.

Peppis, P. (2014), *Sciences of Modernism: Ethnography, Sexology, and Psychology*. Cambridge: Cambridge University Press.

Schaffner, A. K. (2012), *Modernism and Perversion: Sexual Deviance in Sexology and Literature, 1850–1930*. Basingstoke: Palgrave Macmillan.

Scott, B. K. (ed.) (2007), *Gender in Modernism: New Geographies, Complex Intersections*. Urbana: University Illinois Press.

Stevens, W. (1997), *Wallace Stevens: Collected Poetry and Prose*, F. Kermode and J. Richardson (eds). New York: Library of America.

Spiritualism

When Matthew Arnold praised the 'lofty spiritualism' of Jesus in *Literature and Dogma*, he did not mean that Jesus held séances or practiced automatic writing (Arnold, 1873, 246). By *spiritualism*, Arnold meant an advocacy of or emphasis on the spiritual rather than the material. But in the second half of the nineteenth century, a new sense of the term came to dominate: the belief that spiritual beings communicate with the living, especially through a medium, and that a set of practices – from table-rapping and table-turning to trance lectures and Ouija boards – enables those spirits to communicate or appear. (Some preferred the term *spiritism*, precisely because it seemed less ambiguous than *spiritualism*.)

Beginning in the United States and later moving to Britain, Spiritualism was a complex historical phenomenon. Some Spiritualists traced their beliefs and practices to the theories of Emanuel Swedenborg (Doyle, 1926), while others adopted Franz Mesmer's techniques of hypnotism (Lehman, 2009). Spiritualism was often aligned with Theosophy – and more broadly with the occult, with mysticism, and with other unorthodox or alternative belief systems – but the movement remained distinct. In response to rising secularism, Spiritualism offered support for belief in an afterlife. After both the American Civil War and the Great War, many of the bereaved turned to Spiritualism for comfort, looking to make contact with the dead. Arthur Conan Doyle famously became an adherent of Spiritualism after losing his son in 1918. The belief in access to a spirit world was also a response to materialism and rationalization, to what Max Weber, borrowing the phrase from Friedrich Schiller, called the 'disenchantment of the world' (Weber, 1946, 155). Seeking to reconcile this antagonism, some Spiritualists were members of the Society for Psychical Research, founded in London in 1882 in order to investigate paranormal phenomena by scientific methods. Many of these subsequently left the Society, angered by the way it exposed widespread fraudulent practices, but the vexed relation between Spiritualism, science and technology proved crucial for modernism (Armstrong,

2005, 122–9). Alternatively, because Spiritualism involved both private and public performance, it can be considered a kind of theatre, rather than a form of fraud. It allowed performers, many of whom were women, a new political voice and societal role (Lehman, 2009). Indeed, Spiritualism played an active part in supporting women's rights (Braude, 2001).

Spiritualism was frequently mocked as fad and as anachronism, by writers as diverse as George Eliot (Eliot, 1998, 50) and William Carlos Williams: 'Now it's spiritualism – again,//as if the certainty of a future life/were any solution to our dilemma' (Williams, 2001, 173). Yet its beliefs and practices influenced many modernists, especially women (Ingman, 2010). H. D.'s idiosyncratic Spiritualism, for instance, allowed her to resist established gender conventions (Connor, 2004). W. B. Yeats spent years turning the automatic writing scripts produced by his wife, George Yeats, into the philosophical system of *A Vision*, and this work decisively shaped his poetry. Surrealists like André Breton and Phillipe Soupault adopted automatic writing as a medium not for spirits but for the unconscious. The theatrical aspect of Spiritualism proved important, too. Yeats's late play, *The Words upon the Window-Pane* (1930), blurs the distinction between spirit medium and actor when, before a group of sceptics and believers, the medium at a séance channels – or seems to channel – the spirit of Jonathan Swift. Many modernists thus related the 'mediumistic discourse' of Spiritualism to aesthetic form, to the artwork as medium (Sword, 2002, 101). And while Spiritualists looked to technologies like photography to provide evidence of spirits, modernist photographers and film-makers exploited the association of new media with the spirit world for artistic ends (Sconce, 2000; Wilson, 2012).

Bibliography

Armstrong, T. (2005), 'The Vibrating World: Science, Spiritualism, Technology', in *Modernism: A Cultural History*. Cambridge: Polity, pp. 115–34.

Arnold, M. (1873), *Literature and Dogma: An Essay Towards a Better Appreciation of the Bible*. London: Smith, Elder, & Co.

Braude, A. (2001), *Radical Spirits: Spiritualism and Women's Rights in Nineteenth-Century America*. Bloomington: Indiana University Press.

Connor, R. (2004), 'Heterodox Visions: Spiritualism, Politics and Identity', in R. Connor (ed.), *H. D. and the Image*. Manchester: Manchester University Press, pp. 111–31.

Doyle, A. C. (1926), *The History of Spiritualism*. 2 vols. London: Cassell and Company.

Eliot, G. (1998), *Daniel Deronda*, G. Handley (ed.). Oxford: Oxford University Press.

Ingman, H. (2010), 'Religion and the Occult in Women's Modernism', in M. T. Linett (ed.), *The Cambridge Companion to Modernist Women Writers*, Cambridge: Cambridge University Press, pp. 187–202.

Lehman, A. (2009), *Victorian Women and the Theatre of Trance: Mediums, Spiritualists and Mesmerists in Performance*. Jefferson: McFarland and Company.

Sconce, J. (2000), *Haunted Media: Electronic Presence from Telegraphy to Television*. Durham: Duke University Press.

Weber, M. (1946), *From Max Weber: Essays in Sociology*, H. H. Gerth and C. Wright Mills (transl and ed.). New York: Oxford University Press.

Williams, W. C. (2001), *The Collected Poems of William Carlos Williams: Volume II, 1939–1962*, C. MacGowan (ed.). New York: New Directions.

Wilson, L. (2012), *Modernism and Magic: Experiments with Spiritualism, Theosophy and the Occult*. Edinburgh: Edinburgh University Press.

Suffragette

The concerted campaign for women's suffrage began in the second half of the nineteenth century. In Britain, the National Society for Women's Suffrage was founded in 1872, followed in 1897 by the National Union for Women's Suffrage Societies, while in the United States, the National American Women Suffrage Association was established in 1890. Women gained suffrage in New Zealand in 1893, but in Britain the campaign continued, its increasingly militant tactics spearheaded from 1903 by the Women's Social and Political Union. Many suffragettes were subsequently imprisoned and many, while in prison, engaged in hunger strikes; some were in turn subjected to force-feeding. In 1908, the movement gathered 250,000 people or more to a rally in Hyde Park (Pugh, 2000, 193). The Great War affected the role and status of women in British and American society to some degree, and in February 1918, the vote was granted to British women over thirty who met certain requirements of property or marriage, together with all British men over twenty-one; from November women could be elected to Parliament. Women in the United States were enfranchised in 1920, while British women finally joined them in 1928.

The suffrage movement sought a new role for women in public life, and it critiqued entrenched conventions of gender and sexuality (Howlett, 2000). Some opponents invoked those conventions with violence, reducing suffragettes to 'sexless creatures' and 'mad women': 'wild dishevelled sisters' who 'cry for votes' like parrots and foxes (Barlow, 1902–14). Other contemporaries laughed at the efforts of the suffragettes. In his one-act comedy, *Her Vote*, first performed in

1909, H. V. Esmond depicts a young suffragette who, in the end, blithely abandons the movement for a prosperous marriage. Virginia Woolf's *Night and Day* (1919) offers a more nuanced exploration, though its narrative denies to Mary Datchet, a suffragette, the romantic resolution allowed to its heroine, Katharine Hilbery. The representation of suffragettes thus involved many broader questions, from the nature of femininity to the rise of the New Woman, and it had consequences for literary form. Narrative resolution also conditions the account of the suffrage movement in H. G. Wells's *Ann Veronica*, for instance (1909). Many women writers were themselves active suffragettes, from Violet Hunt and May Sinclair to Alice Meynell and Ivy Compton-Burnett. In 1914, Djuna Barnes willingly submitted to force-feeding in order to describe, in an article for New York's *World Magazine*, the 'torture and outrage' suffered by suffragettes (Barnes, 1914, 17), while Rebecca West built on her experiences as a suffragette in her 1922 novel, *The Judge*.

The women's suffrage movement also prompted debates about the control of women's bodies, the legitimacy of political violence, the relation between discourse and action (Comentale, 2009), and the nature of democracy (Holton, 1986; Potter, 2006). Hostile to parliamentary democracy in general, Ezra Pound wrote condescendingly that suffragettes had swallowed 'the fiction that the *vote* is of some use' (von Helmholtz, 1914, 254). But many feminists opposed the suffragettes too, or sought to change the terms of the debate. The anarchist Emma Goldman urged women to refuse 'to be a servant to God, the State, society, the husband, the family': 'Only that, and not the ballot, will set women free' (Goldman, 1910, 217). But the anthropologist Jane Ellen Harrison argued that voting is no more 'unwomanly' that it is 'unmanly', for 'a vote has nothing whatever to do with either sex *qua* sex; it has everything to do with the humanity shared in common by two sexes' (Anonymous, no date, 4–5).

Finally, the suffrage movement had a major influence on the nature of public discourse and, specifically, on modernism (Chapman, 2014). 'Suffrage journals boomed in the Edwardian period' (Delap, 2007, 44), and the most remarkable instance of this, for modernist studies, is the evolution of the three journals edited by Dora Marsden: *The Freewoman* (1911–12), *The New Freewoman* (1913) and *The Egoist* (1914–19). Having split with the Women's Social and Political Union, Marsden addressed a range of feminist issues beyond suffrage, from free love to prostitution, and increasingly she moved between cultural politics, philosophy and avant-garde art. Thus, in *The Egoist*, she published Pound, Sinclair, H. D., Marianne Moore, T. S. Eliot, James Joyce and Wyndham Lewis. It was 'an evolution that metamorphosed a small feminist magazine into a very active organ of High Modernism' (Rabaté, 2009, 269).

Bibliography

Anon. [Jane Ellen Harrison] (no date), '*Homo Sum*': *Being a Letter to an Anti-Suffragist from an Anthropologist*. Uxbridge: Hillingdon.

Barlow, G. (1902–14), 'Sonnet XII Woman Suffrage', in *The Poetical Works of George Barlow*. 11 vols. London: H. J. Glaisher.

Barnes, D. (1914), 'How It Feels to Be Forcibly Fed'. *World Magazine* (6 September 1914), 5, 17.

Chapman, M. (2014), *Making Noise, Making News: Suffrage Print Culture and U. S. Modernism*. New York: Oxford University Press.

Commentale, E. P. (2009), 'Thesmophoria: Suffragettes, Sympathetic Magic, and Feminist Classicism', in *Modernism, Cultural Production, and the British Avant-Garde*. Cambridge: Cambridge University Press, pp. 199–238.

Delap, L. (2007), *The Feminist Avant-Garde: Transatlantic Encounters of the Early Twentieth Century*. Cambridge: Cambridge University Press.

Goldman, E. (1910), *Anarchism and Other Essays*. New York: Mother Earth Publishing Association.

Holton, S. S. (1986), *Feminism and Democracy: Women's Suffrage and Reform Politics in Britain, 1900–1918*. Cambridge: Cambridge University Press.

Howlett, C. (2000), 'Femininity Slashed: Suffragette Militancy, Modernism and Gender', in H. Stevens and C. Howlett (eds), *Modernist Sexualities*. Manchester: Manchester University Press, pp. 72–91.

Potter, R. (2006), *Modernism and Democracy: Literary Culture 1900–1930*. Cambridge: Cambridge University Press.

Pugh, M. (2000), *The March of Women: A Revisionist Analysis of the Campaign for Women's Suffrage, 1866–1914*. Oxford: Oxford University Press.

Rabaté, J.-M. (2009), 'Gender and Modernism: *The Freewoman* (1911–12), *The New Freewoman* (1913), and *The Egoist* (1914–19)', in P. Brooker and A. Thacker (eds), *The Oxford Critical And Cultural History of Modernist Magazines: Volume I, Britain and Ireland 1880–1955*. Oxford: Oxford University Press, pp. 269–89.

Von Helmholtz, B. [Ezra Pound] (1914), 'Suffragettes'. *Egoist*, 1, (13), (1 July 1914), 254–56.

Surrealism

Surrealism emerged from the French Dada circle led by André Breton in the early 1920s, but it swiftly became one of those terms that have escaped their originating circumstances. In Surrealism it might be argued that Dada's playful encounters with contingency and chance were definitively systematized, and yet the surreal has also come to mean that which stands outside of our organized, systematized lives, and reveals their oddness. Breton described Surrealism's procedures as being '[d]ictated by thought, in the absence of any control exercised by reason, exempt from any aesthetic or moral concern' (Breton, 1969, 26), and yet, a quite recognizable aesthetic was to emerge from its practitioners. This aesthetic was founded on Breton's 'discovery' of Freud's concept of the unconscious, a discovery which arguably gave a systematic inflection to the spontaneous assaults on the rational perpetrated by Dadaists. The continuity of sleep and waking, of image and word, are embodied in the dream, seen (in Freud's words) as the 'royal road to a knowledge of the unconscious activities of the mind' (Freud, 1953, 608). Consequently, the surrealists developed various ludic practices to approach or approximate the dream-state: automatic writing, games of chance and collages.

Critics have differed on the degree of freedom permitted by this approach. If for some it enables a dissolution of different 'kinds of thought and writing and creation' (Caws, 2001, xxx), others doubt the degree to which the rational can be prevented from guiding the creative process (Durozoi, 2002, 73), especially given the limits imposed by the fact that the Surrealist movement was run along the lines of a political party. The name first appeared in Apollinaire's play *Les Mamelles de Tirésias* (1917), and the movement was solidified by the publication in 1924 of Breton's *Manifesto of Surrealism*, the creation of the journal *La Révolution Surréaliste* and the establishment of a Central Bureau of Surrealist Research (Balakian, 1972, 144). In contrast to the Dadaists, the group developed close links with the international communist movement, including the French Communist Party (Short, 1966). As such it was a model for writers who sought to translate spiritual concerns into social movements. If the unconscious was an instrument for individual and collective emancipation, this meant that everyone potentially had access to its creative capacities.

Indeed, the question of Surrealism's affiliations is raised, not only because several members of the group were explicitly expelled by Breton, but by the more significant fact that its practices were appropriated by artists all over the world. Surrealism had a brief but vigorous moment in Britain, ushered in by David Gascoyne's *Short Survey of Surrealism* (1935), including the poets Hugh Sykes Davies and Humphrey Jennings, and arguably later issuing in the New Apocalypse poets, including Dylan Thomas. The anti-colonialist impulse of the Surrealists led Breton to form relationships with artists and writers in the Caribbean, particularly Haiti and Martinique. The poet Aimé Cesaire, along with his wife Suzanne and the philosopher Réne Ménil, published the important journal *Tropiques*: this, along with Cesaire's poem *Cahier d'un retour au pays natal* (1939), was instrumental in defining the radical ideology of 'négritude'

(Fijalkowski, 1996). Surrealism also spread to America, where a European emigration helped popularize its ideas among painters and poets.

Surrealism's focus on the unconscious has led some critics to attack it for an individualism that is at odds with its proclaimed communism. Such critiques came both during Surrealism's activity (Louis Aragon's turn from Surrealism to the Communist Party) and in retrospect. Adorno, for example, in 'Looking Back on Surrealism', argued that the isolated components of Surrealist montage were merely the subject's helpless reflection of contemporary commodity culture. In a similar vein, the situationist Raoul Vaneigem found Surrealism to be moored in a conception of the subject that renders it unable to assimilate the social and technological bases of any potential revolution in everyday life.

Bibliography

Adorno, T. (1991), 'Looking Back on Surrealism', in S. W. Nicholsen (transl.), *Notes to Literature I*. New York: Columbia University Press.

Balakian, A. (1972), *Surrealism: The Road to the Absolute*. London: George Allen & Unwin.

Breton, A. (1969), *Manifestoes of Surrealism*, R. Seaver and H. R. Lane (transl.). Ann Arbor: University of Michigan Press.

Caws, M. A. (2001), *Surrealist Painters and Poets*. Cambridge, MA: MIT Press.

Durozoi, G. (2002), *History of the Surrealist Movement*, A. Anderson (transl.). Chicago: University of Chicago Press.

Fijalkowski, K. (1996), *The Refusal of the Shadow: Surrealism and the Caribbean*. London: Verso.

Freud, S. (1953), *The Interpretation of Dreams*, in J. Strachey (transl and ed.), *The Standard Edition of the Complete Psychological Works of Sigmund Freud, Vol V*. London: Hogarth Press.

Short, R. (1966), 'The Politics of Surrealism'. *Journal of Contemporary History*, 1, (2), 3–25.

Vaneigem, R. (1999), *A Cavalier History of Surrealism*, D. Nicholson Smith (transl.). San Francisco: AK Press.

Theory of Relativity

Albert Einstein's Special Theory of Relativity was published in 1905, in a paper titled 'On the Electrodynamics of Moving Bodies', and was followed by his *General Theory of Relativity* in 1916. His work was part of a general dismantling of Newtonian physics: in contrast to the Newtonian model of reality, in which space and time are fixed, Einstein hypothesized that in fact it is the speed of light that is absolute, while space and time are actually relative, dependent on the observer's velocity. Einstein's General Theory posited a theory of gravitation quite different from Newton's assumption of a force exerted in Euclidean space. Instead, gravitation is to be understood as a distortion of space-time, a continuum that unifies what had previously been thought of as two separate entities.

Coming between Planck's quantum theory of energy and Heisenberg's Uncertainty Principle, Einstein's theories and the work of the high modernists equally occupied a period of epistemological uncertainty. If anything, Einstein's innovations came at a time when the very concept of scientific change was becoming something of a cause célèbre. Popular science books were hugely successful in the early twentieth century, a result partly of the increasing presence of newspapers and photography, and of the expansion of secondary education, as well as of the world-changing scientific discoveries then being made. The theory of relativity did not really capture the public imagination until 1919, however, when *The Times* reported on A. S. Eddington's expedition to observe the solar eclipse, the results of which went some way towards confirming Einstein's work. Einstein became a celebrity, invited to give public lectures all over the world (Friedman and Donley, 1989).

The interest of Einstein for literary scholars of the modernist period arguably lies less in the details of his scientific discoveries than in the sense of a transformed imaginative and intellectual space made possible by his thinking. This is not to say that writers were unfamiliar with his work: Betrand Russell wrote an introductory *ABC of Relativity* in 1925, and such authors as Muriel Rukeyser, Mary Butts, Wyndham Lewis and William Carlos Williams took an interest in this new celebrity. However, it was in questions of form that Einstein's work could be said to have had the greatest impact, or, since it is hard to delineate precise vectors of cause and effect, it is possibly more accurate to speak of a shared transformation of perception when it comes to the individual's relationship to space and time.

Correspondences exist between modernist form and the new contours given to perception by the theory of relativity. If it is not the case that 'everything is made relative' with the advent of Einstein's theory, nonetheless the loss of faith in an absolute model of time and space is everywhere legible in modernist texts and artworks. Cézanne and following him the Cubists introduced the depiction of heterogeneous, multiple spaces on a single canvas (Kern, 2003, 141). Mathematician Hermann Minkowski's four-dimensional 'space-time continuum' exerted a powerful influence over writers who sought a rival to contemporary forms of materialism (Bell, 2012). The worlds of Proust or Joyce are, arguably, ones of temporal simultaneity (in a letter about Einstein, Proust wrote that 'it seems we have analogous ways of deforming Time' [qtd Isaacson, 2007, 280]). More broadly, the sense of a dissolution of the traditional categories of time and space is reflected in metaphors of dissipation in writers like Conrad, Lawrence and Woolf (Whitworth, 2001), while metaphors of vortices and ideograms (where time is reconfigured according to a spatial trope) motivated the writings of Lewis, Pound and Yeats (Albright, 1997).

Bibliography

Albright, D. (1997), *Quantum Poetics: Yeats, Pound, Eliot, and the Science of Modernism*. Cambridge: Cambridge University Press.

Bell, I. (2012), 'Ezra Pound and the Materiality of the Fourth Dimension', in J. Holmes (ed.), *Science in Modern Poetry: New Directions*. Liverpool: Liverpool University Press.

Bowler. P. (2009), *Science for All: The Popularization of Science in Early Twentieth-Century Britain*. Chicago: University of Chicago Press.

Einstein, A. (1961), *Relativity: The Special and General Theory: A Popular Exposition*, R. W. Lawson (transl.). New York: Crown.

Friedman, A. J. and Donley, C. C. (1989), *Einstein as Myth and Muse*. Cambridge: Cambridge University Press.

Isaacson, W. (2007), *Einstein: His Life and Universe*. New York: Simon & Schuster.

Kern, S. (2003), *The Culture of Time and Space, 1880–1918*. Cambridge, MA: Harvard University Press.

Russell, B. (2009), *ABC of Relativity*. London: Routledge.

Whitworth, M. H. (2001), *Einstein's Wake: Relativity, Metaphor, and Modernist Literature*. Oxford: Oxford University Press.

Tradition

Mocking modernist experiment, Arthur Davison Ficke once suggested that 'there extends backwards from us an unbroken chain of distinguished *vers libre* tradition, through Whitman, Matthew Arnold, Southey, Shelley, Milton, and many others' (Ficke, 1914, 20). Gertrude Stein probably did not think of Shelley when she crafted her free verse. Yet, though *tradition* can mean a process of bestowing and inheriting a form or content (Latin *trado*, to hand over, to deliver), Stein's experiments engage tradition precisely by refusing the forms of Milton, and even of Whitman. In that case, as Clement Greenberg urged, modernism does not represent a break in the chain, 'a break with the past': 'It may mean a devolution, an unraveling, of tradition, but it also means its further evolution' (Greenberg, 1993, 92). Though Greenberg meant not to mock but to praise, he and Ficke both make tradition a value: art's success depends upon configuring the past and the present. Tradition, as T. S. Eliot famously put it, means an historical consciousness; it 'involves a perception, not only of the pastness of the past, but of its presence' (Eliot, 1951, 14). Though some portions of Eliot's work may seem traditional, others will not; they depend instead on alternative configurations of tradition. In fact, the term *traditional* is usually opposed to modernism, and one way to understand modernity is as a call for 'perpetual subversion of the past as the pre-condition of the future' (Friedman, 2001, 503). *Traditional* suggests moribund convention, blind adherence to tradition rather than radical innovation, when the tradition in question may record and recommend precisely that innovation. In this way, Picasso's late series of fifty-eight paintings, *Las Meninas*, configures the past anew by exhaustively analysing, reworking and reinventing Velázquez's masterpiece.

This raises the problem of *which* past, and *whose*. It is the problem of tradition as such, or in the abstract; of *the* tradition and of *a* tradition, one amongst many; of the value of tradition and of particular traditions; and of the slip which makes one tradition 'the' tradition, often with important social and political consequences. Eliot's use of Shakespeare is in this sense distinct from his use of the Bhagavad Gita and of music hall (Cianci and Harding, 2007), as is the appearance of African American folk traditions in the works of the Harlem Renaissance (Fernald, 2007). Tradition constructs groups of artists, audiences and critics across time and space, groups which include some and exclude others. In particular, tradition involves the problem of canon formation. (Ficke meant to mock by constructing so improbable a tradition, grouping Whitman with Arnold.) Though it often represents aesthetic duty and political authority, 'the' tradition is frequently a retrospective construction, and not 'an unbroken chain' of bestowal and inheritance. Indeed, an awareness of 'the' tradition might, quite paradoxically, 'come into existence only at the moment of rebellion against it' (Friedman, 2001, 503). That rebellion can involve actively unravelling a dominant tradition, or seeking instead an alternative tradition. The interest so many modernists showed in the occult, offering unorthodox spiritual and philosophical frameworks, is a good example (Surette and Tryphonopoulos, 1996).

In turn, many modernist works forge their own, idiosyncratic traditions. Louis Zukofsky's 'Mantis' (Zukofsky, 2011, 65–6), a sestina, borrows rhyme words from Dante's sestina, 'Al poco giorno e al gran cerchio d'ombra', and other materials from French Surrealism (Golston, 2006). 'Mantis' was preceded by Ezra Pound's 'Sestina: Altaforte', a major modernist example, and the verse-form also invokes Arnaut Daniel, its inventor; Philip Sidney, the first poet to write a sestina in English; and Swinburne, who gave the sestina a Victorian vogue. 'Mantis' adopts a traditional form, but constructs an entirely new 'tradition', necessarily partial and contingent. This is less an unbroken chain than a new 'order' of past and present, in which 'the relations, proportions, [and] values of each work of art toward the whole are readjusted' (Eliot, 1951, 15). And that, finally, has been the fate of modernism, too: Pound becomes a part of Zukofsky's tradition. Modernism is thus an inheritance to be rejected, embraced or developed further, from the anti-modernism of the Movement, through the late modernism of the British Poetry Revival or the Language poets, to the postmodernism of Thomas Pynchon and Don DeLillo.

Bibliography

Cianci, G. and Harding, J. (eds) (2007), *T. S. Eliot and the Concept of Tradition*. Cambridge: Cambridge University Press.

Eliot, T. S. (1951), 'Tradition and the Individual Talent', in *Selected Essays*, 3rd edn. London: Faber and Faber, pp. 13–22.

Fernald, A. E. (2007), 'Modernism and Tradition', in A. Eysteinsson and V. Liska (eds), *Modernism*. 2 vols. Amsterdam: Benjamins, vol. 1, pp. 157–71.

Ficke, A. D. (1914), 'In Defense of Vers Libre'. *The Little Review*, 1, (9), 19–22.

Friedman, S. S. (2001), 'Definitional Excursions: The Meanings of Modern/Modernity/Modernism'. *Modernism/modernity*, 8, (3), 493–513.

Golston, M. (2006), 'Petalbent Devils: Louis Zukofsky, Lorine Niedecker, and the Surrealist Praying Mantis'. *Modernism/modernity*, 13, (2), 325–47.

Greenberg, C. (1993), 'Modernist Painting', in J. O'Brian (ed), *The Collected Essays and Criticism*, 4 vols. Chicago: The University of Chicago Press, vol. 4, pp. 85–93.

Surette, L. and Tryphonopoulos, D. (1996), *Literary Modernism and the Occult Tradition*. Orono: National Poetry Foundation.

Zukofsky, L. (2011), *Anew: Complete Shorter Poetry*. New York: New Directions.

Unconscious

The adjective *unconscious* has for some time described those who are unaware or heedless of themselves or some other thing, actions which are performed unawares or without conscious attention, and thoughts or feelings which are not present to consciousness. Boredom, reflects a character in F. Scott Fitzgerald's *The Beautiful and the Damned* (1922), was 'the unconscious motive of all my acts' (Fitzgerald, 2000, 639). But in the second half of the nineteenth century, a grammatical switch redeployed these senses: the switch from adjective to noun. Late nineteenth- and early twentieth-century psychology seized upon *the unconscious* as a new concept. Eduard von Hartmann's influential *The Philosophy of the Unconscious* (1869) was followed by Sigmund Freud's studies of dreams and of jokes, which cemented the term's importance both for clinical psychology and for the broader cultural discourse. Though Freud experimented with *subconscious* (*das Unterbewusstsein*), he soon chose *unconscious* (*das Unbewusste*), preferring its prefix of negation (*un-*, *Un-*) to one which implies spatial array or subordination (*sub-*, *Unter-*, 'under'). He also distinguished the *unconscious* from the *preconscious* (*das Vorbewusste*). For Freud, the unconscious means more than thoughts, such as memories, of which we happen at a given moment not to be conscious. The unconscious 'designates not only latent ideas in general, but especially ideas with a certain dynamic character, ideas keeping apart from consciousness in spite of their intensity and activity' (Freud, 2001b, 262). The unconscious is the realm of thoughts and desires subject to active repression or censorship.

The social and political implications of this forceful repression – not least in Freud's use of the term *Zensur*, or Censor (Freud, 2001a, 142) – have given the unconscious currency in many other fields. For this reason, critics and theorists have subjected the noun to a series of specifying adjectives: the primitive unconscious (Foster, 1985), the material unconscious (Brown, 1996), the postcolonial unconscious (Lazarus, 2011), the mimetic unconscious (Lawtoo, 2013) and so forth. The 'optical unconscious' can thus designate a set of values which, though denied by accepted artistic and critical dicta, shape modern modes of seeing (Krauss, 1993). The 'political unconscious' names an occluded yet 'fundamental dimension of our collective thinking and our collective fantasies about history and reality' (Jameson, 1981, 34). This shift from an individual's unconscious to that of a society or culture in some ways resembles Carl Jung's theory of the collective unconscious. But much recent work, especially on cultural production and social relations, insists on the historical specificity of the structures regulating repression and expression.

The concept of the unconscious itself has a history. Some of Freud's contemporaries denied its existence; others remained wary. D. H. Lawrence was both fascinated and appalled by the discovery of thoughts and desires which, though previously unknown, nevertheless determine the subject: 'Gagged, bound, maniacal repressions, sexual complexes, faecal inhibitions, dream-monsters [...] horrid things that ate our souls and caused our helpless neuroses' (Lawrence, 2004, 9). Lawrence's struggle with Freud, and with the language of psychoanalysis, was crucial to his experimentation with literary language (Spitzer, 2014). In the later psychoanalytic theory of Jacques Lacan, the unconscious itself 'has the radical structure of language' (Lacan, 2006, 496). Alternatively, an array of modern writers explored the possibility that language, and especially literature, might, however obliquely, represent the unconscious (Marcus and Mukherjee, 2014). Thomas Mann, for instance, defines myth as 'the timeless schema [...] into which life flows when it reproduces its traits out of the unconscious' (Mann, 1959, 374). Henry James calls the writer's life 'the unconscious, the agitated, the struggling, floundering cause' from which literature is 'an objective, a projected result' (James, 1984, 119). Life is the unresolved complex out of which art emerges. So, too, the surreal imagery in Luis Buñuel's films or Salvador Dalí's paintings might, like dreams or jokes, offer access to the unconscious. But whose? While critics sometimes attempt to analyse an artist's unconscious by interpreting her work, James figures the author's life as the unconscious of the text itself, and other critics seek in turn to uncover, through texts, the repressed thoughts and desires of those texts' social and historical situations.

Bibliography

Brown, B. (1996), *The Material Unconscious: American Amusement, Stephen Crane, and the Economics of Play*. Cambridge: Harvard University Press.

Fitzgerald, F. S. (2000), *Novels and Stories, 1920–1922*. New York: Library of America.

Foster, H. (1985), 'The "Primitive" Unconscious of Modern Art'. *October*, 34, 45–70.

Freud, S. (2001a), *The Standard Edition of the Complete Psychological Works of Sigmund Freud, Vol. IV (1900): The Interpretation of Dreams (First Part)*, J. Strachey (ed. and transl.). London: Vintage Books.

Freud, S. (2001b), 'A Note on the Unconscious in Psycho-analysis', in J. Strachey (ed. and transl.). *The Standard Edition of the Complete Psychological Works of Sigmund Freud, Vol. XII (1911–1913): Case History of Schreber, Papers on Technique and Other Works*. London: Vintage Books, pp. 255–66.

James, H. (1984), *Literary Criticism, Vol. 2: French Writers, Other European Writers, The Prefaces to the New York Edition*. New York: Library of America.

Jameson, F. (1981), *The Political Unconscious: Narrative as a Socially Symbolic Act*. London: Methuen.

Krauss, R. E. (1993), *The Optical Unconscious*. Cambridge: The MIT Press.

Lacan, J. (2006), *Écrits: The First Complete Edition in English*, B. Fink (transl.). New York, W. W. Norton.

Lawrence, D. H. (2004), *Psychoanalysis and the Unconscious and Fantasia of the Unconscious*, Bruce Steele (ed.). Cambridge: Cambridge University Press.

Lawtoo, N. (2013), *The Phantom of the Ego: Modernism and the Mimetic Unconscious*. East Lansing: Michigan State University Press.

Lazarus, N. (2011), *The Postcolonial Unconscious*. Cambridge: Cambridge University Press.

Mann, T. (1959), 'Freud and the Future'. *Daedalus*, 88, (2), 374–8.

Marcus, L. and Mukherjee, A. (2014), *A Concise Companion to Psychoanalysis, Literature, and Culture*. Chichester: Wiley Blackwell.

Spitzer, J. (2014), 'On not Reading Freud: Amateurism, Expertise, and the "Pristine Unconscious" in D. H. Lawrence'. *Modernism/modernity*, 21, (1), 89–105.

Vers libre

Modernist free verse in English might be said to have had two commandments: 'break the pentameter' (Pound, 1996, 538), and 'no verse is free for the man who wants to do a good job' (Eliot, 1957, 37). The one enjoins freedom from constraint; the other insists on constraint's necessity, thereby invalidating the very term *free verse*. For the most part, Ezra Pound's free verse breaks the pentameter in order to generate new and independent rhythms, 'to compose in the sequence of the musical phrase, not in sequence of a metronome' (Pound, 1968, 3). But T. S. Eliot's free verse makes much of its meaning in relation to old and established metres: to break or bend or warp the pentameter is nevertheless to invoke that metre, and all its cultural and historical associations. Some subsequent studies of free verse in English discuss the former approach (Hartman, 1980), some discuss the latter (Finch, 1993; Kirby-Smith, 1996), and some consider both (Beyers, 2001). The poetics of French *vers libre* involves related issues (Scott, 1993). But modernist free verse, together with debates conducted by modernists and their contemporaries about the term and the practice, posed more fundamental questions about the nature of poetry itself.

First, there is the distinction between verse and prose. F. S. Flint argued that free verse is not actually verse since it has no measure, only rhythm. Instead he proposed the term 'cadence', which 'differs in no way from prose' (Flint, 1920, 18). Conversely, William Carlos Williams argued that even free verse 'must be governed by some measure, but not by the old measure' (Williams, 1969, 339), and so he proposed composition by the 'variable foot' (Williams, 1959, 154). But the trouble even with a flexible measure lies in justifying the unit of the line. The risk, as Amy Lowell protested, is that free verse – or bad free verse – is merely 'prose cut into arbitrary lines' (Lowell, 1930, 70). For A. R. Orage, the risk was that the 'mechanical devices' of free verse become 'largely typographical' ([Orage], 1917, 255). This judgement subordinates a poem's visual form to its aural form, but the typographical experiments of Mallarmé, e. e. cummings and others undo that hierarchy. So, second, the pertinent distinction may not be between metrical verse and free verse, but between lines determined aurally and lines determined aurally and visually, or even just visually (Attridge, 2013). Third, one could distinguish between poetry which adapts its materials to 'the exigencies of a prescribed form', whether visual or aural, and poetry which, with new 'self-consciousness', adapts its 'form to suit every special turn and item' of its materials (Bridges, 1922, 60). This liberation of poetic material might be compared to developments in modernist painting and music: freed from arbitrary and external convention, every element of the work must be necessary and integral.

As free verse developed, it gathered its own cultural and historical associations, and these have changed in time. Some critics have complained that, once free verse came to dominate modern poetry and so became a convention in itself, its lineation frequently served merely to signal literary 'elevation', disguising bad poetry as good (Perloff, 1981, 861). Yet Walt Whitman's wonderful long lines are inseparable from his materials, those expansive calls for freedom and inclusivity. The rejection of inherited traditions was often associated with the New World, historical progress or social emancipation. 'Does Poetry or does the Poet need to be disciplined?', asked Maxwell Bodenheim. 'Are they cringing slaves who cannot be trusted to walk alone and unbound?' (Bodenheim, 1914, 22). In America, free verse sometimes signalled political freedoms, whether in terms of democracy or individualism (Whalan 2014). More broadly, modernist free verse can be read, in its 'articulated structure of anticipation', as expressing the 'need to be situated in an open relation to futurity' (Patterson, 2011, 178). It thus gives a poetic form to the energies and anxieties of a new social and political experience.

Bibliography

Attridge, D. (2013), 'Poetry Unbound? Observations on Free Verse', in *Moving Words: Forms of English Poetry*. Oxford: Oxford University Press, pp. 203–21.

Beyers, C. (2001), *A History of Free Verse*. Fayetteville: The University of Arkansas Press.

Bodenheim, M. (1914), 'The Decorative Straight-Jacket: Rhymed Verse'. *Little Review*, 1, (9), 22–3.

Bridges, R. (1922), 'Humdrum and Harum-Scarum: A Paper on Free Verse'. *London Mercury*, 7, 54–63.

Eliot, T. S. (1957), *On Poetry and Poets*. London: Faber and Faber.

Finch, A. (1993), *The Ghost of Meter: Culture and Prosody in American Free Verse*. Ann Arbor: The University of Michigan Press.

Flint, F. S. (1920), 'Presentation: Notes on the Art of Writing; on the Artfulness of Some Writers; and on the Artlessness of Others'. *Chapbook*, 2, (9), 17–24.

Hartman, C. O. (1996), *Free Verse: An Essay on Prosody*. Evanston: Northwestern University Press.

Kirby-Smith, H. T. (1996), *The Origins of Free Verse*. Ann Arbor: The University of Michigan Press.

Lowell, A. (1930), *Poetry and Poets: Essays*. Boston: Houghton Mifflin.

R. H. C. [A. R. Orage] (1917), 'Readers and Writers'. *New Age*, 20, (11), 254–5.

Patterson, I. (2011), 'Time, Free Verse, and the Gods of Modernism', in J. Parker and T. Matthews (eds), *Tradition, Translation, Trauma: The Classic and the Modern*. Oxford: Oxford University Press, pp. 175–89.

Perloff, M. (1981), 'The Linear Fallacy'. *Georgia Review*, 4, (35), 855–69.

Pound, E. (1968), *Literary Essays of Ezra Pound*, T. S. Eliot (ed.). New York: New Directions.

Pound, E. (1996), *The Cantos*. New York: New Directions.

Scott, C. (1993), *Reading the Rhythm: The Poetics of French Free Verse, 1910–1930*. Oxford: Clarendon.

Whalan, M. (2014), 'Freeloading in Hobohemia: The Politics of Free Verse in American World War I Periodical Culture'. *Modernism/modernity*, 21, (3), 665–88.

Williams, W. C. (1959), 'Measure: A Loosely Assembled Essay on Poetic Measure'. *Spectrum*, 3, (3), 131–57.

Williams, W. C. (1969), *Selected Essays*. New York: New Directions.

23

Annotated Bibliography of Selected Criticism

Alexander Howard

Daniel Albright, *Quantum Poetics: Yeats, Pound, Eliot and the Science of Modernism* (Cambridge: Cambridge UP, 1997)

In this theoretically dextrous and wide-ranging study, Albright discusses the manner in which a number of prominent first-generation Anglo-American modernist writers responded to historical developments in scientific discourse. He seeks to demonstrate how major modernist writers such as W. B. Yeats (Chapter 1), Ezra Pound (Chapter 2) and T. S. Eliot (Chapter 3) sought to commandeer scientific metaphors as part of a more general attempt to reconceptualize poetry. *Quantum Poetics*, as Albright notes at the very start of his general introduction, is structured around three central propositions. The first of these propositions holds that canonical modernist writers such as Eliot, Pound and Yeats sought to uncover the preverbal roots of poetry. The second suggests that certain methods privileged by physicists such as Albert Einstein and Niels Bohr inspired these poets to search for the elementary particles of poetry, which Albright terms 'poememes'. Albright's third and final proposition foregrounds the decidedly elusive quality of such poememes. In the first section of *Quantum Poetics*, Albright examines the influential early modernism of W. B. Yeats, which, in the former's estimation, reveals a dialectical interplay between image and symbol. In the next section, Albright suggests that Pound's entire critical vocabulary can be viewed as a concerted effort to unify art and science. In the last section, Albright discusses Eliot's poetic and critical output in relation to poememes and wave particles. Here, among other things, Albright analyses the texture and rhythmic elements of Eliot's poetry, as well as the poet's fondness for geological and astrological metaphors.

Daniel Albright, *Untwisting the Serpent: Modernism in Music, Literature, and Other Arts* (Chicago: Chicago UP, 2000)

This unconventional, yet noteworthy, interdisciplinary treatise considers a number of collaborative, mixed-media modernist ventures, the majority of which engage with music in some shape or form. Traversing a number of different geographical sites (London, Paris, New York, Berlin, Vienna, Moscow), and discussing the work of a range of modernist writers, composers, dancers and artists such as W. B. Yeats, Ezra Pound, Pablo Picasso, André Breton, Vaslav Nijinsky, Samuel Beckett, Gertrude Stein, Paul Hindemith, Guillaume Apollinaire, Paul Hindemith, George Antheil, Sergei Prokofiev, Erik Satie, Igor Stravinsky, Kurt Weill and Bertolt Brecht, Albright's study explores some of the relationships that have developed between different cultural forms. Albright usefully situates his study in relation to the work of three influential aesthetic theoreticians: Gottfried Ephraim Lessing, Theodor W. Adorno and Clement Greenberg. Each of these three thinkers believed in the importance of aesthetic purism. This much becomes apparent when we read Albright's introduction, which discusses Lessing's *Laokoon*, Greenberg's 'Towards a Newer Laöcoon' and Adorno's *Philosophy of New Music*. Contrasting his interest in interdisciplinarity with the concern for formal purity expressed in these canonical texts, Albright lays the foundations for his subsequent enquiry into the field of aesthetic hybridity. Both historically and theoretically informed, Albright's study of the relationship between cultural modernism and musicality will appeal to a range of advanced students and scholars.

Tim Armstrong, *Modernism, Technology, and the Body: A Cultural Study* (Cambridge: Cambridge UP, 1998)

Armstrong's study is essential reading for students and scholars interested in the complex relationship between technology, the human body and the emergence of modern literature and aesthetics. Armstrong opens with the suggestion that the nineteenth century saw a revolution in attitudes concerning the human body. He notes that at the start of this century the human body was generally regarded as a machine in which the self resided, as a secure vessel that required conscious regulation and which, significantly, could not be penetrated. Armstrong also points out that this had all changed by the beginning of the twentieth century. Scientific, medical and technological advances ensured that the body, which had once seemed wholly impenetrable, now appeared decidedly permeable. Armstrong then turns his attention to modernism's response to this situation. He describes how many modernist practitioners had a fascination with the body, before detailing the many ways in which experimental texts can be said to have encoded, and then enacted certain experimental processes pertaining to trends in biology, psychophysics and a variety of popular bodily reform techniques. Comprised of four main sections, Armstrong's fascinating treatise considers how the interface between the human body and a rapidly changing technological landscape informs the work of notable modernists such as Henry James, W. B. Yeats, Ezra Pound, T. S. Eliot, Djuna Barnes, Mina Loy and Gertrude Stein.

John Attridge and Rod Rosenquist, *Incredible Modernism: Literature, Trust and Deception* (Farnham: Ashgate, 2013)

The twelve essays gathered in Attridge and Rosenquist's *Incredible Modernism* focus on the interwoven notions of trust and distrust. They examine the importance of these terms as defining influences on the literary output of a wide-ranging selection of influential first- and second-generation modernist writers including André Gide, Marcel Proust, Ford Madox Ford, Ezra Pound, Wyndham Lewis, Hilda Doolittle, James Joyce, Gertrude Stein, Wallace Stevens and Samuel Beckett, as well as later authors like Ralph Ellison. Attridge explains the critical impetus underpinning the collection in his general introduction. In it, he shows that trust played a crucial role in the understanding of modern society. Citing the influential views of self-defined sociologists such as Gabriel Tarde, H. G. Wells and George Simmel, Attridge notes that trust was, up until the start of twentieth century, regarded as a sort of social cohesive. In essence, a shared sense of trust helped to hold society together. But things changed. In Attridge's estimation, the emergence of cultural modernism was characterized by a profound sense of scepticism. It marked a decisive turning point in matters pertaining to categories of social trust. Recognizing this, the contributors in this collection accordingly consider how modernist interests in language, credulity, fictional truth and sincerity intersected with historically changing conceptions of trust and attendant notions of deception. Highlights include Paul Sheehan's treatment of Ellison and the mythology of deception (Chapter 4), and Sean Pryor's account of Pound's involvement with Italian Fascism (Chapter 10).

Houston A. Baker, Jr., *Modernism and the Harlem Renaissance* (Chicago: Chicago UP, 1989)

This is a helpful introductory account of the cultural moment of the 1920s commonly known as the Harlem Renaissance. It will appeal to students interested in the history of African American literature and aesthetics in the early stages of the twentieth century. In it, Baker takes umbrage at an earlier generation of critics and Afro-American analysts who tended to view the Harlem Renaissance in terms of its perceived collective 'failure' to produce instances of specifically 'modern' art and literature in the style of, say, a James Joyce or a T. S. Eliot. Baker is of the opinion that such critics get it badly wrong when it comes to the Harlem Renaissance. He suggests that critical attempts to unthinkingly equate the literary and aesthetic achievements of the Harlem Renaissance with established models of Anglo-American and European modernism are hopelessly misguided. Adopting an alternative approach, Baker repositions the literature produced by Harlem Renaissance writers, editors and affiliates such as Alain Locke, W. E. B. Du Bois, Countee Cullen and Zora Neale Hurston in relation to contemporaneous developments in African American musical forms, philosophy and art.

Rebecca Beasley, *Theorists of Modernist Poetry: T. S. Eliot, T. E. Hulme, Ezra Pound* (London: Routledge, 2007)

Students interested in the history and workings of early Anglo-American poetic modernism will find much of use in Beasley's refreshingly clear account of T. E. Hulme, T. S. Eliot and Ezra Pound. Comprising six chapters, Beasley's introductory study utilizes a broadly chronological approach to show how the literary experiments and theoretical speculations of these seminal modernist poet-critics developed over the course of time, and to demonstrate how the results of their investigations left an indelible imprint on twentieth-century poetry. In the first chapter, Beasley outlines the rapidly changing and fluctuating turn-of-the-century literary period in which these ambitious young men began to establish themselves as modernist writers of note. Beasley then turns her attention to developments in contemporary philosophy (as set forth in the work of diverse figures including Henri Bergson, F. H. Bradley and Bertrand Russell) and their influence on the thinking of the three poets. In the third chapter, Beasley discusses the problematic and, at times, overtly anti-democratic political attitudes underpinning the theories of literature espoused by Hulme, Eliot and, most notoriously, Pound. The fourth and fifth chapters detail the conceptual difficulties that Eliot and Pound encountered when composing their respective masterpieces, *The Waste Land* and *The Cantos*. The final chapter analyses the social criticism of these two major modernists in relation to their late literary output.

Joseph Allan Boone, *Libidinal Currents: Sexuality and the Shaping of Modernism* (Chicago: Chicago UP, 1998)

This is an impressive revisionary account of literary modernism. It will appeal to advanced students and scholars interested in the intersection between writing, desire and notions of sexuality. Boone draws on developments in the fields of feminist criticism, race studies and queer theory while engaging with an impressive range of canonical and lesser-known Anglo-American literary materials written between 1853 and 1962. He makes his critical intentions clear in the introduction of *Libidinal Currents*. In these illuminating opening pages, Boone writes of his desire to undertake a thoroughgoing investigation of the ways in which issues of sexuality, psychology, psychoanalysis and narrative can be said to have impacted on the trajectory of cultural, aesthetic and literary modernity as it developed during the nineteenth and twentieth centuries. To put it another way, Boone seeks, via detailed close readings of an expansive range of novelistic fictions, to describe how a number of broadly defined modernist writers and thinkers, such as Charlotte Brontë (Chapter 1), Kate Chopin, D. H. Lawrence, Sigmund Freud (Chapter 2), Virginia Woolf, James Joyce (Chapter 3), Bruce Nugent, Djuna Barnes, Charles Henri Ford, Parker Tyler, Blair Niles (Chapter 4), William Faulkner, Christina Stead (Chapter 5), Lawrence Durrell and Doris Lessing (Chapter 6), developed modes of literary expression which might better evoke the fluctuating conditions of subjective interiority and, in his own words, the erotics of mental activity. In this fashion, Boone seeks to revise our understanding of the literary and sexual politics of Anglo-American modernism.

Peter Boxall, *Since Beckett: Contemporary Writing in the Wake of Modernism* (London: Continuum, 2011)

Until recently, many literary critics tended to describe the major twentieth-century Irish writer Samuel Beckett as the 'last' true modernist. There are a number of reasons as to why this might have been so. As it happens, Peter Boxall touches upon some of these at the start of his wide-ranging and detailed *Since Beckett*, which will appeal to students and scholars interested in recent developments in American, European and South African writing. In Boxall's estimation, Beckett's formally uncompromising style of writing is a poetics of exhaustion, one which effectively signals the end of a whole gamut of literary and cultural possibilities. Hence the reductive critical tendency to characterize Beckett as some sort of terminal – perhaps even quasi-Beckettian – figure. In equal measure, however, Beckett's poetics of exhaustion is, as Boxall reminds us, also a poetics of persistence, one which aspires, paradoxically, to extend the various aesthetic possibilities it simultaneously seeks to foreclose. Recognizing this fact, Boxall notes that any attempt to inherit, or simply understand, Beckett's legacy has first to come to terms with this contradiction between a writing which is unable to go on, yet continues to go on. Grappling deftly with this insoluble contradiction, Boxall identifies, and then analyses, a discernibly Beckettian legacy which plays out across a diverse range of international contemporary writers such as Elizabeth Bowen, John Banville (Part 1), Thomas Bernhard, W. G. Sebald (Part 2), Saul Bellow, Don DeLillo and J. M. Coetzee (Part 3).

Malcolm Bradbury and James McFarlane (eds), *Modernism: A Guide to European Literature, 1890–1930* (London: Penguin, 1976)

Commonly regarded as a classic of early modernist scholarship, this anthology, which is notable for its range and scope, details the myriad cultural, philosophical, social and historical transformations that shaped the development of European literature in the period between 1890 and 1930. In 'The Name and Nature of Modernism', Bradbury and McFarlane discuss some of the nuances and contradictions in much literature produced in what was a particularly tumultuous era of European history. Then, having debated and contextualized the historical emergence of modernism at some considerable length, Bradbury and McFarlane turn their anthology over to a number of other critics. The second section of the collection examines the cultural and intellectual origins of modernism. The essays in this section find that while literary modernism was an art of an uncertain, rapidly modernizing world, it retained a curious sort of Victorian confidence in the certainty of progress. The third section focuses on the issue of geography. Eschewing comprehensiveness, the essays selected for inclusion here chart the development of literary modernism in a number of now familiar urban foci: Moscow, St Petersburg, Paros, Berlin, Vienna, Prague, New York, Chicago and London. The useful fourth section focuses on specific literary (and aesthetic) movements including Symbolism, Futurism, Imagism, Vorticism, German Expressionism, Dadaism and Surrealism. The fourth, fifth and sixth sections deal with lyric poetry, fiction and drama, respectively. In these highly informative chapters, sustained critical attention is paid to canonical modernist writers such as Paul Valéry, Rainer Maria Rilke, Thomas Mann, Italo Svevo, James Joyce, Joseph Conrad, Robert Musil, W. B. Yeats and August Strindberg.

Peter Brooker and Andrew Thacker (eds), *Geographies of Modernism* (London: Routledge, 2005)

This is an engaging collection of wide-ranging, cross-disciplinary essays, which, among other things, seeks to position modernist studies in relation to contemporary debates about postcolonialism and globalization. The editors set the scene for what is to follow in their useful co-authored introduction. In it, Brooker – the author of the equally geographically situated *Bohemia in London: The Social Scene of Early Modernism* (2007) – and Thacker suggest that students and scholars alike examine modernist literature and aesthetics within the spatial framework of geography. They then proceed to outline the reasons behind their desire to reread modernism in spatial terms, many of which have to do with relatively recent developments in the field of critical theory, most notably in the work of writers such as Fredric Jameson, Henri Lefebvre, David Harvey and Edward Soja. Of especial interest here is Jameson's spatially informed notion of 'cognitive mapping', which has been influential in discussions of the late modernism and post-modernism. They also refer to Homi K. Bhabha's theorization of the postcolonial, and to Harvey's work on cultural geography and contemporary capitalism, which responds to the ongoing changes wrought by globalization on our understanding of work, leisure, travel, information dissemination and cultural identity. Drawing on these and other assorted developments in literary and cultural theory, the essays featured in Brooker and Thacker's collection consider the relationship between literary and aesthetic modernism in the work of diverse writers, artists and architects such as Virginia Woolf (Chapter 2), Joseph Conrad (Chapter 5), Jean Rhys (Chapters 6 and 7),

Marcel Duchamp (Chapter 9), Le Corbusier (Chapter 12) and Rem Koolhaas (Chapter 13).

Brad Bucknell, *Literary Modernism and Musical Aesthetics: Pater, Pound, Joyce and Stein* (Cambridge: Cambridge UP, 2002)

Divided into five main chapters, this insightful interdisciplinary study considers the relationship between certain aesthetic and epistemological trends in music and literature during the modernist period. After furnishing the reader with a useful introductory account of the intricate and interwoven nature of the relationship between music and experimental literature (Chapter 1), Bucknell traces some of the various ways in which important proto- and canonical first-generation modernist figures such as Walter Pater (Chapter 2), Ezra Pound (Chapter 3), James Joyce (Chapter 4) and Gertrude Stein (Chapter 5) sought first to understand, and then engage with, contemporary developments in the fields of music composition and musical theory. Opening with a theoretically inflected comparative reading of Stéphane Mallarmé and Richard Wagner, Bucknell proceeds to demonstrate convincingly that his chosen writers were greatly interested in the expressive and specifically non-linguistic signifying potential of musical aesthetics. Developing his point, Bucknell considers Pound's opera *Le Testament de François Villon* (1923). Having done so, Bucknell then turns his attention to the 'Sirens' episode in Joyce's masterwork *Ulysses*. Finally, in the concluding chapter, Bucknell analyses Virgil Thompson's score for Stein's libretto *Four Scores in Three Acts* (1934). Lucid and measured in its assessments, Bucknell's account of musicality and modernism is of great use to students and scholars alike.

Christopher Butler, *Early Modernism: Literature, Music, and Painting in Europe, 1900–1916* (Oxford: Clarendon Press, 1994)

Butler engages with a variety of literary and aesthetic forms in this useful account of 'early' modernism, which will appeal to students interested in the formative stages of twentieth-century European avant-gardism. Butler's lavishly illustrated interdisciplinary study seeks to detail the manner in which highly influential (male) figures like Guillaume Apollinaire, Henri Matisse, Pablo Picasso, T. S. Eliot, Ezra Pound, Thomas Mann, Joseph Conrad, F. T. Marinetti, James Joyce, Igor Stravinsky and Arnold Schoenberg developed radically new conceptual frameworks and formal conventions for their respective arts in the decade before the First World War. Butler's theorization of early modernism depends on the idea that the artists and writers in question were in some shape or form reacting against the movements that came before them, such as Romanticism, Decadence, Realism, Naturalism, Aestheticism and Symbolism. Butler builds on this assertion in the first section of his study, which concerns early modernist scepticism about established artistic conventions and which describes how this questioning attitude precipitated an examination of the basic tenets of artistic language, such as harmony, perspective and logic. Having discussed these tenets in the second chapter of *Early Modernism*, Butler turns his attention to issues pertaining to subjective identity and the early modern interest in the primitive. In the fourth chapter, he discusses the relationship between modernism, the urban metropolis and rapid technological change. Butler's fifth chapter concerns the reception of early modernist ideas, which leads him to reflect on the nature of literary and aesthetic experimentalism in his conclusion.

Matei Calinescu, *Five Faces of Modernity: Modernism, Avant-Garde, Decadence, Kitsch, Postmodernism* (Durham: Duke UP, 1987)

This is a helpful historical and critical overview of key concepts pertaining to modernity, modernist literature and avant-garde aesthetics. It will appeal to students interested in the relationship between political modernity and aesthetic modernism. It also caters to those who wish to develop a clearer understanding of profound cultural shifts with roots stretching as far back as the late seventeenth century. Some of these cultural readjustments are discussed in the introduction to *Five Faces of Modernity*, where Calinescu outlines the various ways in which general conceptions of aesthetics changed over the course of the eighteenth century. He reminds the reader that what occurred during this period was nothing less than a collective rejection of previously established aesthetic notions of transcendence and permanence. The age of modernity, Calinescu points out, demanded an aesthetic model whose central values were primarily those of novelty, immanence and transitoriness. Calinescu then details the theoretical operations underpinning early, adversarial models of aesthetic modernism. Having explored the differences between classicism and modernism, Calinescu describes how the schism that emerged between the two terms paved the way for the subsequent emergence of the historical avant-garde, decadent and kitsch modes of aesthetic expression, as well as the twentieth-century cultural phenomenon that we have come to know as post-modernism. Despite showing some inevitable signs of age, Calinescu's theoretical and semantic treatise continues to resonate in today's ever-expanding field of modernist studies.

Donald J. Childs, *Modernism and Eugenics: Woolf, Eliot, Yeats and the Culture of Degeneration* (Cambridge: Cambridge UP, 2007)

This significant, well-researched and provocative study revisits the scene of early literary modernity. It will appeal to students and scholars interested in some of the more controversial aspects of canonical Anglo-American modernism. Childs discusses the ways in which three major first-generation literary modernists – W. B. Yeats, T. S. Eliot and Virginia Woolf – were very much influenced by the eugenics movement, the origins of which can be traced back to the early 1870s. This conflicted period in British history was, Childs notes, marked by a profound sense of cultural and societal anxiety. Preying on the fears of a hubristic imperialist society reeling from the psychological blows of early defeats in the Boer War, alarmists such as the early eugenist R. R. Rentoul invoked threatening visions of national degeneracy, physical collapse and collective race suicide. Responding to these apocalyptical predictions, and to the contemporaneous theories of natural selection and heredity espoused by Charles Darwin and his cousin Francis Golston, large swathes of the British public came to embrace the new 'science' of racial breeding. The early modernists proved no exception. Childs demonstrates convincingly the ways in which they were drawn to the discourse of eugenics. He then explains how this deep-seated interest in racial matters can be said to have impacted on modernist literary praxis. At times disquieting, Childs's readings (especially those concerning Eliot and Yeats) have much to tell us about the relationship between literary modernism and some of the more unpalatable aspects of what was in some ways a remarkably unpleasant period of history.

Peter Childs, *Modernism and the Post-Colonial* (London: Continuum, 2007)

This account of modernism and postcolonialism covers the period between 1885 and 1930. Childs considers the manner in which certain modern texts register cultural anxieties and personal ambivalences pertaining to powerful historical forces of empire and imperialism. He is particularly interested in the output of mainly British modernist writers whose work questioned the values of empire and which sought to move away from entrenched colonial perspectives and attitudes. In equal measure, Childs is keen to stress that modernism was not merely a response to colonialism. He proposes that a number of modernist practitioners sought, at least in part, to register in their literary and aesthetic experiments the complexities of what was a rapidly changing, increasingly globalized world. This much is evident in Childs's first chapter, where Joseph Conrad figures prominently. Here, Childs describes how modernists such as Conrad and Katherine Mansfield sought to distinguish their praxis from that of earlier Victorian writers such as H. R. Haggard. In the next chapter, Childs draws on the criticism of Edward Said in order to productively reread Rudyard Kipling's oeuvre. Childs broadens the terms of his discussion in the third and fourth chapters of his study, which situate modernism in relation to imperialistic conceptions of space, subjectivity and temporality. Finally, in a brief but intriguing conclusion, Childs describes how later writers like Virginia Woolf, Graham Greene and Malcolm Lowry oscillated between positions of ignorance and self-willed blindness when it came to matters of imperialism and empire in the 1930s.

Susan W. Churchill and Adam McKible (eds), *Little Magazines & Modernism: New Approaches* (Houndmills: Ashgate, 2007)

This invaluable collection of wide-ranging essays will appeal to students and scholars interested in understanding how the cultural phenomenon of the so-called 'little magazine' impacted on the development of Anglo-American modernism. It should be read alongside related volumes such as Morrison's *The Public Face of Modernism* (2001) and Scholes and Wulfman's *Modernism in the Magazines* (2010). In the co-authored introduction, Churchill and McKible highlight some of the ways in which the study of little magazine culture serves to strength our understanding of literary modernity. In their estimation, modernist little magazines offer us the critical means with which to recover the sometimes hidden connective lines of influence, identification, difference, conflict, commerce and resistance that underpin much, if not all, modernist literary production. Favouring what the editors describe as a conversational model for modernism, the contributors featured in this volume explore the vibrant historical origins of Anglo-American literary avant-gardism as fostered and documented in the pages of a number of important little magazines such as *Rhythm* (Chapter 1), *Poetry* (Chapter 5), *Epilogue* (Chapter 8) and *The Liberator* (Chapter 11). Reminding us of the simple, yet important, fact that many little magazines functioned as useful heterogeneous social forums for writers of different genders, ethnic backgrounds and nationalities, the essays gathered together in this collection put forth a compelling argument for the centrality of periodical culture in both modernism and contemporary modernist studies. Highlights include Jay Bochner's comparative account of *Rogue* and *The Soil*, Alan Golding's investigation of *The Dial* and *The Little Review* (Chapter 4), and Churchill's discussion of *Others* and the 'Great Spectra Hoax' of 1917 (Chapter 10).

Evelyn Cobley, *Modernism and the Culture of Efficacy: Ideology and Fiction* (Toronto: Toronto UP, 2007)

There are a number of things to admire about this engaging study, which will appeal to students and scholars interested in the development of canonical British modernist fiction during the first four decades of the twentieth century. Cobley's volume features detailed discussion of Joseph Conrad's *Heart of Darkness*, Ford Madox Ford's *The Good Solider*, D. H. Lawrence's *Women in Love*, E. M. Forster's *Howard's End* and Aldous Huxley's *Brave New World*. In particular, Cobley seeks to demonstrate some of the ways in which these texts and writers registered the presence of what she describes as a culture of efficacy. In Cobley's estimation, the roots of this ideologically charged culture have their basis in the profound series of socio-economic transformations brought about by the invention of the steam engine in 1794. In her useful historical introduction, Cobley describes how incremental improvements in locomotive construction and the coterminous growth of, and investment in, railroad networks during the nineteenth century laid the foundations for the emergence of the modern form of the technically efficient corporation and the concept of efficiency in its modern sense (as embodied in the theories and practices of Henry Ford and Winslow Taylor).

Having outlined the historical trajectory of the culture, Cobley draws on developments in game theory in order to highlight some of the more extreme – and extremely negative – aspects of a commitment to efficiency (as epitomized by the regimented brutality of Nazism). In turn, Cobley considers the various tensions that exist in modernist fiction regarding the rise of efficiency and the question of individual agency over the course of number of largely convincing close readings.

Sara Danius, *The Senses of Modernism: Technology, Perception and Aesthetics* (Ithaca and London: Cornell UP, 2002)

This is an important contribution to the field of modernist studies. It will be of great use to scholars and advanced students interested in the relationship between modernist literature and the technologies of production, reproduction and information dissemination. In *The Senses of Modernism*, Danius focuses on the literary output of three major European modernist writers working in the first half of the twentieth century: Marcel Proust, James Joyce and Thomas Mann. Comprising a series of detailed close readings focused on issues of narrative content and generic form in Mann's *The Magic Mountain*, stylistic inflection and the treatment of syntax in Joyce's *Ulysses*, and thematic structuring in Proust's *Remembrance of Things Past*, Danius's treatise demonstrates some of the ways in which specific procedures and technological innovations – such as the locomotive rail network, the mass produced automobile and the X-ray machine – can be said to have informed what we commonly understand as the aesthetics of high modernism. Emphasizing, as she does, the profound impact that technologies of cinematic, photographic and phonographic inscription had on the vital work of Proust, Joyce and Mann, Danius encourages us to reconsider historical and critical assumptions concerning issues of aesthetic autonomy, as well as challenging the long-standing presupposition that there exists an easily discerned line of demarcation between aesthetic and technological cultures.

Leonard Diepeveen, *The Difficulty of Modernism* (London: Routledge, 2003)

In this challenging, yet rewarding, treatise, Diepeveen makes a case for the continued relevance and persistence of modernistic ideas and practices.

Drawing on a range of historical, sociological and linguistic discourses, and featuring an impressive number of primary source materials, Diepeveen engages with the well-known – and long-debated – notion of modernist difficulty. Diepeveen suggests, quite rightly, that ideas of difficulty underpin our critical understanding of, and attitude towards, aesthetic and literary modernism. In order to better understand the ways in which we have come to conceptualize difficulty, Diepeveen revisits the historical scene of first-generation modernism. Diepeveen explains the reasoning behind this decision at the outset of his study. In his estimation, the specific sorts of difficulty associated with cultural modernism can only be understood if read alongside the various, often bewildered responses it elicited from its original audience. This belief underwrites Diepeveen's subsequent assertion that modernism's difficulty is not merely a classifiable set of (now readily identifiable) literary and aesthetic techniques. Examining the work of prominent Anglo-American writers including Ezra Pound, T. S. Eliot, William Faulkner, Virginia Woolf, James Joyce, Gertrude Stein and Marianne Moore, as well as charting the history of the reception of writers such as Willa Cather and Robert Frost, Diepeveen details how contemporary responses to modernist texts developed over the course of time. In turn, he productively considers the manner in which public debates about difficulty helped shape what we now recognize as the modernist canon.

Maud Ellmann, *The Poetics of Impersonality: The Question of the Subject in T.S. Eliot and Ezra Pound* (Edinburgh: Edinburgh UP, 2013)

This classic work of literary scholarship, which was originally published in 1987, discusses the output of T. S. Eliot and Ezra Pound. Ellmann's study focuses on the theory of poetic 'impersonality' as articulated in the literature and criticism of Eliot and Pound. The theory of impersonality, Ellmann suggests, existed long before Eliot placed it in the service of what we now recognize as first-generation Anglo-American literary modernism. Yet the impact that Eliot's resurrection of the term had on the trajectory of twentieth-century literature simply cannot be ignored. As is well known, Eliot's foray into the realms of literary impersonality can be traced all the way back to his seminal essay 'Tradition and the Individual Talent' (1919). In this difficult and occasionally paradoxical piece, Eliot proposes that the true writer submit to a process of continual self-suppression in order to gain his or her position along the literary immortals. Identifying a number of inconsistencies in this model of poetic impersonality, Ellmann finds that Eliot often seeks to 'smuggle' personality back into his poetry. Having unpacked the contradictions in Eliot's oeuvre, Ellmann then casts a deconstructive critical eye over Pound's poetry. Often startling, the fruits of Ellmann's perceptive enquiry will be of use to any serious student of modernism.

Mary Lou Emery, *Modernism, the Visual, and Caribbean Literature* (Cambridge: Cambridge UP, 2007)

Divided into four main sections, Emery's wide-ranging study considers the role played by vision in the work of a number of twentieth-century Anglophone Caribbean writers, artists and dramatists. Displaying a detailed engagement with theories of postcolonialism and transnationalism, Emery contends that the output of numerous figures such as Una Mason, Edna Manley, Jean Rhys, C. L. R. James, Derek Walcott, Wilson Harris and Michelle Cliff focuses on notions and acts of vision. In Emory's estimation, such acts, manifested in various works of Caribbean sculpture, criticism, drama, poetry and fiction, can refer either to social, collective acts of seeing inner visions or to reflections on matters of visual aesthetics. According to Emery, *all* such acts of vision are directly related to the experiences of mass migration wrought by the American, British and European colonization of the Caribbean (the personal and cultural effects of which are still being felt today). Emery concedes that this emphasis on the visual might strike some readers as surprising. From the outset of her study, Emery is upfront about the fact that her chosen topic of enquiry runs contrary to the majority of critical accounts concerning Caribbean culture, which emphasize the importance of sound, orality and musicality. Emery insists, convincingly, that the visual has just as much to tell us about Caribbean cultural production and conditions of diasporic subjectivity, especially when read in relation to, and against the grain of, the international field of mainstream Anglo-American and Continental literary modernism.

Astradur Eysteinsson, *The Concept of Modernism* (Cornell: Cornell UP, 1992)

In the introductory section of this theoretically informed study, Eysteinsson explains that he is interested in asking what the concept of modernism has been made to signify, and how. In order fully to appreciate what Eysteinsson is getting at here, we need first to place his treatise, with its myriad questions of definition and categories of signification, in historical context. Published in the early 1990s, Eysteinsson's study emerged at a time when productive scholarly discussion about modernist issues had, at least in the eyes of some critics, more or less come to a standstill. Suggesting that much modernist criticism had become unduly preoccupied with questions of institutionalization and assumptions about reactionary political stances, Eysteinsson moves to demonstrate some of the ways in which our often contradictory theoretical conceptions and terminological accounts of modernism have developed over time. In his first chapter, Eysteinsson examines a number of different theories of modernism. Attention is paid to diverse critical thinkers including Lionel Trilling, T. S. Eliot, Theodor W. Adorno, Viktor Shklovsky and Georg Lukács. Having completed his survey of modernist critics and critical paradigms, Eysteinsson then considers the significance of literary history in relation to canon formulation (Chapter 2), notions of post-modernism (Chapter 3) and the idea of the avant-garde (Chapter 4). In his concluding chapter, Eysteinsson proposes his own reconceptualization of modernism, which he views as a historically specific interruption of realist aesthetics.

Greg Forter, *Gender, Race, and Mourning in American Modernism* (Cambridge: Cambridge UP, 2011)

Forter's study will be of great use to students and scholars interested in understanding the way in which American modernism developed in the period between 1880 and 1920. Forter is, as the very title of his study suggests, interested in coming to terms with the complex relationship between systems of race, gender, sexuality and models of (literary) modernism in the United States. Opening with a broad historical overview, Forter argues that the arrival of disempowering nineteenth-century economic transformations wrought by monopoly capitalism had a profound impact on American society. Drawing on the work of contemporary historians and sociologists, Forter posits that American men responded to their economic disempowerment in a number of ways, some of which revealed an underlying desire to more carefully police the borders between traditional binary models of male and female identity. But this is not all. Forter also suggests that these disempowering processes impacted on conceptions of race in the United States. In his reckoning, reconfigurations within America's capitalist economic system subordinated what had been a predominately white workforce to new bureaucratic structures while concurrently fashioning a supplementary labour market comprised of African American freedmen and ethnic immigrants. Having presented his argument, Forter discusses how prominent writers such as F. Scott Fitzgerald, Ernest Hemingway, William Faulkner and Willa Cather registered (and sometimes mourned) these profound shifts in now-canonical works of American modernism including *The Great Gatsby, The Professor's House, The Sun Also Rises, Light in August* and *Absalom, Absalom!*

Abbie Garrington, *Haptic Modernism: Touch and the Tactile in Modernist Writing* (Edinburgh: Edinburgh UP, 2013)

Garrington's study of literary modernism deals with specific notions of non-verbal haptic perception. Broadly speaking, it will appeal to students and scholars interested primarily in the development of what we now describe as canonical twentieth-century British and Irish literature. In her helpful introduction, Garrington points out that the word 'haptic' is best understood as a general term which can refer to any, some or indeed all of the following bodily experiences: touch, proprioception, vestibular sense and kinaesthesis. In Garrington's estimation, the modernist period of literary history saw an increased interest in the last of these subcategories of sense perception, particularly in the reading and touching of human skin. In addition, she posits that the flowering of interest in all things haptic had much to do with rapid developments in the realm of technological innovation. Garrington argues that advances pertaining to the cinema and transport impacted on conceptions of human bodily experience and touch. Breaking with visually biased accounts of literary modernism, Garrington rewarding critical intervention proffers a series of detailed close readings of major writers like James Joyce (Chapter 2), Virginia Woolf (Chapter 3), Dorothy Richardson (Chapter 4) and D. H. Lawrence (Chapter 5), all of whom sought to document the shift towards the haptic in their work. Situating her study in relation to the work of critics such as Tim Armstrong and Santanu Das, Garrington encourages us to develop a new set of 'haptically attuned' critical reading strategies with which we might better understand the trajectory of first-generation literary modernity.

Jane Goldman, *Modernism, 1910–1945: Image to Apocalypse* (Houndmills: Palgrave Macmillan, 2003)

Goldman's handbook covers the main literary transitions that unfurled in the first half of the twentieth century. It will appeal to students of canonical Anglo-American and European modernism, to those interested in the intersection of gender, culture and art, and to researchers of vital first- and second-generation little magazines such as *transition, BLAST* and *The Egoist*. Goldman finds that the most interesting and energetic literary movements that emerged in the wake of the Edwardian Era were either modernistic or avant-gardist in nature, and that they are to be located between the loosely aligned grouping of Imagist poets writing in and around 1913 and the so-called Apocalypse movement of the early 1940s. Emphasizing the role that manifestos and periodicals played during the period in question (as well as the ways in which they have shaped the critical understanding of literary modernity), Goldman's account of modernism is divided into three main sections. In these sections, Goldman discusses the aesthetic and critical output of familiar major figures such as Virginia Woolf, Ezra Pound, T. S. Eliot, Wallace Stevens, James Joyce and Gertrude Stein, as well as lesser-known (but no less significant) figures including Nathanael West, John Rodker and David Gascoyne.

Michael Golston, *Rhythm and Race in Modernist Poetry and Poetics: Pound, Yeats, Williams, and Modern Sciences of Rhythm* (New York: Columbia UP, 2008)

This is a far-reaching and fascinating account of the relationship between modernism and science that developed in the first half of the twentieth century. Golston seeks to demonstrate how scientific advances in the late nineteenth and early twentieth centuries can be said to have directly influenced and motivated the formal innovations that we see in first-generation Anglo-American modernist poetry. In particular, Golston seeks to explain the role that the science of human physiology played in the development of modernism during the early stages of the twentieth century. Theories of 'rhythm' are important in this regard. Golston emphasizes as much in his introduction. He notes that, during the period in question, rhythm was thought to play a central role in a number of natural, social, psychological and physical processes. In equal measure, as rhythm was thought to serve as an important component in the workings of both body and mind, the various problematic, and often highly racialized, political roles to which it might serve also generated a significant amount of intense theoretical speculation (reaching an infamous culmination in the 'blood and soil' ideology of Nazism). Significantly, as Golston's study adroitly reveals, a number of prominent (and lesser known) modernists were heavily invested in these theoretical investigations. Charting the way in which notions of rhythm – or, to use Golston's terminology, *rhythmics* – informed the poetics and personal politics of canonical figures such as Ezra Pound (Chapters 1 and 2), W. B. Yeats (Chapters 3 and 4) and William Carlos Williams (Chapter 5), this study offers fresh insight into some of the ideological systems of thought underpinning Anglo-American literary modernism.

Alex Goody, *Modernist Articulations: A Cultural Study of Djuna Barnes, Mina Loy, and Gertrude Stein* (Houndmills: Palgrave 2007)

Goody challenges preconceived critical definitions of modernism in this theoretically informed account of literary experimentation. Featuring a detailed and useful introductory survey of recent developments in the related fields of literary studies, cultural studies and post-structuralist philosophy, Goody's revisionist study will appeal to students and scholars interested in the ongoing feminist reconsideration of Anglo-American modernism. Responding to the influential formulations of diverse critical theorists including Gilles Deleuze, Félix Guattari, Lawrence Grossberg and Stuart Hall, Goody proffers a series of original and detailed readings of three major female modernist writers: Gertrude Stein, Mina Loy and Djuna Barnes. Emphasizing what the author describes as the centrality of discontinuity, the various chapters of Goody's study meet Barnes, Loy and Stein at different stages in their respective literary careers. Among other things, Goody's *Modernist Articulations* features detailed discussions of Barnes's fiction and journalism, Loy's poetic engagement with artistic movements such as Dadaism and Futurism, and Stein's famous forays into linguistic experimentation and literary portraiture. Exploring issues of gender, sexuality, Jewishness, avant-gardism and transgressive potentiality in key texts such as Barnes's seminal document of queer modernism *Nightwood*, Stein's *Tender Buttons* and Loy's riotous *Lunar Baedeker*, Goody's study sheds important critical light on the challenging creative praxis of these three important Anglo-American experimentalists.

Roger Griffin, *Modernism and Fascism: The Sense of a Beginning under Mussolini and Hitler* (Houndmills: Palgrave MacMillan, 2007)

While not concerned with purely literary matters, this panoramic study has much to tell us about the ostensibly paradoxical relationship between cultural modernity and the political phenomenon of fascism. Drawing on the influential criticism of Frank Kermode and earlier literary studies such as Andrew Hewitt's *Fascist Modernism: Aesthetics, Politics, and the Avant-Garde* (1993), Griffin proposes a reconceptualization of modernism. He suggests that we define 'modernism' as a historical reaction against real and imagined threats of impending social collapse and cultural decadence between 1850 and 1945. In Griffin's estimation, modernism is best understood as an attempt to transform the various institutions, religious belief systems and general structures of society in response to the secularizing impact of Western modernization. Griffin defines two main types of modernist activity: 'epiphanic' (cultural) and 'programmatic' (political). According to Griffin, the first of these – 'epiphanic' – emphasizes spiritual rebirth, renewal and purification. The second – 'programmatic' – has more to do with societal practicalities. However, despite these significant differences, it soon becomes clear that both types of modernist activity were greatly preoccupied with the idea of overcoming, of *transcendence*. This is where the links between (conservative models of) modernism and purportedly anti-modern forms of fascism begin to be most clearly felt. A manifestation of what Griffin describes as programmatic modernity, fascism, in the eyes of its supporters, warded off the sense of existential terror generated by processes of secularization, to bring closure to the search for transcendence brought on by modernity's social, spiritual and political crisis, and to resolve humanity's primordial quest for wholeness. Griffin's historical study, which is divided into two main sections and features analysis of various literary works, will be of great interest to students and scholars of modernist culture and politics in the first half of the twentieth century.

Faye Hammill, *Women, Celebrity, and Literary Culture between the Wars* (Austin: Texas UP, 2007)

Hammill's comparative study of literary culture and celebrity considers the under-theorized relationship between modernism, popular culture and the middlebrow. As the title suggests, it has much to tell us about modernism and the interwar period. Hammill discusses a variety of famous and commercially successful women writers from America, Britain and Canada whose work and celebrity status serves to unsettle a number of conceptual categories and critical distinctions. Divided into seven sections, Hammill's study analyses the varied outputs of high-profile writers such as Dorothy Parker (Chapter 1), Anita Loos (Chapter 2), Mae West (Chapter 3), L. M. Montgomery (Chapter 4), Margaret Kennedy (Chapter 5), Stella Gibbons (Chapter 6) and E. M. Delafield (Chapter 7). In her own words, Hammill's primary goal is to reinscribe these critically marginalized writers into literary history and to reconsider their relationships with a number of canonical modernist writers (such as Wyndham Lewis, William Faulkner and James Joyce). However, there is more to *Women, Celebrity, and Literary Culture* than this. As well as highlighting the ways in which these writers sought to fashion their celebrity and literary personas via various strategies of public performance and tactics of cultural appropriation, Hammill reminds us of the fact that assumptions about literary value, commercial success and gender continue to inform critical judgements when it comes to the topic of literary modernism in the 1920s and 1930s.

Jaime Hovey, *A Thousand Words: Portraiture, Style, and Queer Modernism* (Ohio: Ohio State UP, 2006)

Hovey's study is an important contribution to the field of queer modernist studies. Engaging with conceptions of erotically charged literary and aesthetic portraiture, the self-conscious construction of 'personality' and theories of spectatorship in various instances of late nineteenth- and early twentieth-century experimentalism, Hovey's incisive account serves as a necessary corrective to established readings of modernistic 'impersonality'. Hovey begins by situating her study in relation to a number of works concerned with queer modernism, some of which feature elsewhere in this annotated bibliography. For example, she cites works of modernist literature such as Karen Jacob's *The Mind's Eye* (2001), studies of queer modernism including Anne Herrmann's *Queering the Moderns* (2000) and Colleen Lamos's *Deviant Modernism* (1998), and psychoanalytically informed treatments of avant-gardism like Judith Roof's *A Lure of Knowledge* (1991) and Joseph Allan Boone's *Libidinal Currents* (1998). Building on the critical advances made in these and other related studies, Hovey posits that a better understanding of queer performativity and self-consciousness serves to productively complicate our understanding of the (still) under-theorized relationships between concepts such as gender, sexuality, social behaviour, and modernist literary and aesthetic expression. Basing her argument around detailed readings of diverse canonical and non-canonical avant-gardists such as Oscar Wilde (Chapter 1), T. S. Eliot, Radclyffe Hall, Langston Hughes (Chapter 2), Djuna Barnes, Virginia Woolf, Compton Mackenzie (Chapter 3), Collette, Nella Larsen and Gertrude Stein (Chapter 4), Hovey provides the reader with a critical vantage point from which they might broach the topic of queer desire as pertains to literary modernism.

Ben Hutchinson, *Modernism and Style* (Houndmills: Palgrave Macmillan, 2011)

This is a clear and concise account of certain formal aspects of cultural modernism. Responding to ideas articulated by Fredric Jameson in 'Postmodernism and Consumer Society' (1983), and to questions posed by Bradbury and McFarlane in their introduction to *Modernism* (1976), Hutchinson contends that we cannot fully appreciate the nuances of modernism if we do not first understand the ways in which leading practitioners associated with the movement sought to interrogate notions of *style*. Hutchinson argues that modernist ideas about style were motivated by what he describes as an underlying double movement. He points out that the modernists tended to foreground style as a sort of subject matter in its own right, rather than simply as a formal means with which to view the purportedly objective, 'real' world. In equal measure, however, many tended to view that which Hutchinson characterizes as 'mere' style with a certain degree of suspicion, believing as they did that such formal exercises were representative of a secular realm stripped of any meaningful content. Navigating between these two positions, Hutchinson sets out to, in his own words, trace the development of modernism from 'pure' style to what one could call 'purely' style. Featuring discussions of canonical Anglo-American and Continental figures such as Arthur Schopenhauer and Friedrich Nietzsche (Chapter 1), Gustave Flaubert and Charles Baudelaire (Chapter 2), Marcel Proust, James Joyce and Thomas Mann (Chapter 3), Rainer Maria Rilke and T. S. Eliot (Chapter 4), and F. T. Marinetti, Tristan Tzara, Ezra Pound and Louis Aragon (Chapter 5), Hutchinson's study will appeal to students interested in the development of the modernist movement in the early twentieth century.

Aaron Jaffe, *Modernism and the Culture of Celebrity*
(Cambridge: Cambridge UP, 2005)

Jaffe's enlightening commentary is representative of a burgeoning branch of modernist studies that seeks to fashion an adequate critical vocabulary with which to describe the complex relationship that exists between aesthetic experimentalism and popular culture. Drawing on extensive archival research, Jaffe traces the ways in which the highly paradoxical, and often surprising, relationship between modernism and celebrity culture developed in the early decades of the twentieth century. He begins by pointing out that a substantial majority of modernist writers and artists were deeply concerned with the intricate and often bewildering workings of a continually fluctuating cultural marketplace. This interest stemmed from the simple fact that, like most other artistic producers, the modernists wanted to carve out a niche for themselves and their literary products and aesthetic commodities in what was an increasingly crowded cultural sphere. Jaffe's study accordingly describes how a number of prominent modernists and their assorted allies worked towards establishing and expanding a market for their literary works during the first half of the twentieth century. Issues of self-promotion and self-fashioning come into play at this point. For example, Jaffe details how prominent modernists such as Ezra Pound, James Joyce, T. S. Eliot and Wyndham Lewis sought *both* to publicize the modernist literary project *and* to cement their personal literary reputations. In so doing, Jaffe usefully demonstrates how these and other seemingly oppositional modernist practitioners promoted their individual and collective literary and aesthetics achievements via a skilled manipulation of the very same market forces that they so forcefully – and often disingenuously – claimed to reject.

David James (ed.), *The Legacies of Modernism:*
Historicizing Postwar and Contemporary Fiction
(Cambridge: Cambridge UP, 2012)

The essays grouped together in this volume insist that students and scholars need to recognize the continued relevance of literary modernism if they are to develop convincing accounts of the historical trajectory of the Anglo-American novel since 1945. When read together, the essays in this collection demonstrate the various ways in which contemporary and, for the main part, innovative writers working today continue to draw on the legacies of literary modernism. Divided into four main sections, *The Legacies of Modernism* considers questions of influence and adaptation, while also debating what the volume editor describes as the coexistence of tradition and invention in contemporary fiction. The first of these sections focuses on the ways in which the legacies of high modernist innovation impacted on literature produced in the years leading up to and the period following the Second World War. Following on from discussions of writers such as H. E. Bates (Chapter 2) and B. S. Johnson (Chapter 3), the second section considers post-war and postmodern contemporary authors including Michael Cunningham (Chapter 6) and Philip Roth (Chapter 7), who can be said to reappropriate – or rather 'reactivate' – particular modernist modes for their own ends. Featuring discussions of Iris Murdoch and Zadie Smith (Chapter 9) and A. S. Byatt (Chapter 10), the third section describes how post-war writers engage with ethical questions pertaining to morality and personal accountability. Engaging with recent theoretical developments in the field of transnational and global studies, the concluding section of *The Legacies of Modernism* features discussions of contemporary authors including Cormac McCarthy (Chapter 11), Chris Abani (Chapter 12) and J. M. Coetzee (Chapter 13).

Susan Jones, *Literature, Modernism, and Dance* (Oxford: Oxford UP, 2013)

Jones explores the complex, though surprisingly neglected, relationship between experimental literature and dance in this well-researched contribution to the field of modernist studies. In her introduction, Jones suggests that the scale of reciprocal interaction between these two particular modes of expression was simultaneously unique and striking – with dance drawing on modern literature and vice versa. Jones locates the origins of this productive aesthetic dialogue in the *fin de siècle* period of the nineteenth century. According to Jones, this era saw the emergence of enduringly mutual exchanges between influential dancers, choreographers, poets, philosophers and artists including Loïe Fuller, Stéphane Mallarmé, W. B. Yeats, Michio Ito, Arthur Symons and Isadora Duncan. Jones finds that this relationship continued to develop in the first half of the twentieth century. For Jones, the increasingly interwoven fields of dance and literature came also to exert a significant influence on a number of artistic movements associated with the rise of cultural modernism, such as symbolism, primitivism, expressionism, cubism and constructivism. Structured chronically, the interdisciplinary *Literature, Modernism, and Dance* will appeal to a wide range of critics and students, especially those interested in the aesthetic groupings listed above, as well as to scholars invested in the literary output of prominent Anglo-American authors such as T. S. Eliot, Virginia Woolf, D. H. Lawrence, Upton Sinclair, Ezra Pound and Samuel Beckett, the work of composers such as Igor Stravinsky and the cultural dealings of dance impresarios like Sergei Diaghilev, Léonide Massine and George Balanchine.

Daniel Katz, *American Modernism's Expatriate Scene: The Labour of Translation* (Edinburgh: Edinburgh UP, 2007)

Katz's absorbing study will appeal to advanced students interested in transatlantic cultural relations, cosmopolitanism, theories of translation, transnationalism and the overall development of American literary modernism. Katz proposes that we revisit the well-documented theme of expatriation. He argues that the widespread phenomenon of expatriation in American modernism should be viewed as a dialectical process. This leads Katz to propose a series of related questions. To begin with, he asks to what extent the dialectal act of expatriation might allow for a distanced and critical re-encounter with one's homeland? Further to this, Katz queries the impact that the condition of expatriatism has on one's relationship to language, one's 'native' tongue and the idea, indeed the very act, of translation. Pursuing these and other assorted questions, Katz's first chapter considers the figure of the 'cosmopolite', as defined in Henry James's 'Occasional Paris' and *The Portrait of a Lady*. James also features in the second chapter. Here, Katz explores issues of exoticism and multilingualism as found in *The Ambassadors*. Katz then explores Ezra Pound's sense of American cultural identity, as well as his indebtedness to the James of *The American Scene*. Katz's discussion of Pound carries over into the fourth chapter, which focuses on the poet's translations of Chinese poetry and Japanese drama. Gertrude Stein's dialectic of expatriate estrangement is the central focus of Katz's fifth chapter, which also touches on the work of Wyndham Lewis and Ernest Hemingway. Moving beyond the conventionally accepted historical bounds of modernism, Katz's final chapter and subsequent conclusion engage with the work of the post-war San Francisco Renaissance affiliate Jack Spicer and the New York School poet John Ashbery.

Vassiliki Kolocotroni, Jane Goldman, Olga Taxidou (eds), *Modernism: An Anthology of Sources and Documents* (Edinburgh: Edinburgh UP, 1998)

Performing a useful pedagogical function, this anthology brings together a wide range of modernist source materials and primary documents. To paraphrase the editors, this volume, which will primarily appeal to students and teachers, is driven by the need to present suitable interpretative strategies and critical tools with which to better understand some of the formal ambiguities and theoretical nuances of literary modernism, which is characterized here in terms of conflict and upheaval. Insisting that we remain cognisant of the fact that the broadly defined category of literary modernity was made up of a truly astonishing range of divergent, competing, and, more often than not, wholly contradictory theoretical formulations and critical practices, the editors of this anthology seek to present us, in their own words, a storehouse for continuing engagements with the modern. The anthology is structured thematically and comprises three main sections. The first section – 'The Emergence of the Modern' – opens with an extract from Karl Marx's correspondence and presents a variety of cultural, social, scientific and political documents alongside contemporaneous aesthetic treatises. The second section – 'The Avant-Garde' – contains an impressive selection of modernist literary manifestos and aesthetic declarations. The concluding section – 'Modernists on the Modern' – details the making (and subsequent remoulding) of modernist traditions in the first half of the twentieth century.

Frank Lentricchia, *Modernist Quartet* (Cambridge: Cambridge UP, 1994)

Comprising a series of textual and contextual readings, this historicist study focuses on the literary achievements of four major American modernist poets: Robert Frost, Wallace Stevens, Ezra Pound and T. S. Eliot. Remaining sceptical of the idealization of literary genius, Lentricchia proposes that we read the output of these canonical first-generation modernist poets in relation to a variety of historical, cultural and social factors. In particular, Lentricchia insists that attention needs to be paid to the ways in which the central poetic texts of his chosen modernist authors reflect and shape our knowledge of literary institutions and philosophical traditions, as well as our critical understanding of gender relations and systems of (capitalist) economic exchange. Lentricchia's examination of poetic modernism opens with an account of the landmark philosophical enquiries being conducted in the hallowed halls of Harvard University at the start of the twentieth century. In this introductory chapter, Lentricchia suggests that the work of three particular Harvard-based philosophers – George Santayana, William James and Josiah Royce – profoundly influenced what would subsequently come to be understood as modernism in the United States. In the second, Lentricchia considers the early literary careers of Pound and Frost. In addition, this chapter also touches on the important role of the cultural phenomenon of 'little magazines' in the development of literary modernism. The remaining chapters are given over to readings of Frost (3), Stevens (4), Pound (5) and Eliot (6). In these, Lentricchia seeks to evoke a sense of what he describes as the historical ground of culturally oppositional modernist experimentation.

Michael H. Levenson, *The Genealogy of Modernism: A Study of English Literary Doctrine 1908–1922* (Cambridge: Cambridge, 1984)

This major work of literary scholarship traces the historical and ideological development of modernism during the first two decades of the twentieth century. Specifically, *The Genealogy of Modernism* is concerned with the evolution of the various doctrinal literary ideologies developed by Ford Madox Ford, T. E. Hulme, T. S. Eliot, Ezra Pound and Wyndham Lewis between 1908 and 1922. Levenson seeks not to present us with a comprehensive account of the emergence of Anglo-American modernism, but rather, in his own words, to redeem certain lines of development which have been obscured or neglected, and which, once traced, may help restore modernity to history. Situating the literary advances and pronouncements made by his select band of first-generation writers and literary theorists in relation to contemporaneous ideas espoused by British and Continental thinkers such as Allen Upward, Hilaire Belloc, Wilhelm Worringer, Pierre Lasserre and Max Stirner, Levenson demonstrates accordingly, and in great detail, the manner in which early Anglo-American modernist thought often tended towards polarization and duality. By carefully analysing the often self-contradictory literary statements of his selected band of literary experimentalists in this exceptionally rigorous fashion, Levenson is better able to chart the trajectory of early Anglo-American modernism, from its initial emergence as a disruptive, radical force to its eventual return to a form of (Eliotic) classicism.

Pericles Lewis, *Religious Experience and the Modernist Novel* (Cambridge: Cambridge UP, 2010)

Lewis engages with well-known works of canonical high modernism in this impressive critical study, which will appeal to students and scholars interested in the transmutation of religious experience in early, ostensibly secular twentieth-century experimental literature. As the title of his study conveys, Lewis is primarily interested in one particular literary form: the novel. Lewis seeks to trace the development of the modern novel alongside what he perceives as a characteristically modernistic attempt to explain religious experience, and changing attitudes to religion, in primarily non-religious terms. He contends that major modernist novelists such as Henry James, Marcel Proust, Franz Kafka, James Joyce and Virginia Woolf sought in their prose to fashion oblique literary strategies that might permit them the opportunity to indirectly address issues pertaining to the spiritual and the sacred. So as to better illustrate his argument, Lewis reads the work of the aforementioned modernists alongside the theories of contemporaneous sociologists and psychologists including William James, Max Weber, Sigmund Freud and Emile Durkheim. Discussing weighty topics such as the transience of epiphany and the fragility of human communion, Lewis finds that the formal experimentation found in iconic modernist works of fiction like *Ulysses, The Golden Bowl, Remembrance of Things Past, To the Lighthouse* and *The Castle* was motivated, at least in part, by a continued interest in religious experience.

Jerome J. McGann, *Black Riders: The Visible Language of Modernism* (Princeton: Princeton UP, 1993)

There are a number of things to be said about this bibliographical study of literary modernism, which is made of up a highly informative introduction and two main sections. Students interested in the historical trajectory of early Anglo-American literature will find much to admire in McGann's introduction, which deals with modernism and the well-documented Renaissance of Printing. McGann's argument is that twentieth-century poetry written in English should be read both as a direct function and as an expression of the important historical developments in printing that began in the later stages of the nineteenth century. Unsurprisingly, the influential figure of William Morris looms large in this portion of *Black Riders*. McGann is especially interested in Morris's epochal Kelmscott Press. He contends that fine-press printing imprints like Kelmscott supplied key modernists such as W. B. Yeats, Emily Dickinson, Ezra Pound and Gertrude Stein with a number of new institutional and bibliographical possibilities, as well as affording them a wide range of hitherto unimagined typographical innovations. McGann builds on these assertions in the next section of *Black Riders*, which deals at great length with the impact and legacy of Morris's materialist aesthetics during the twentieth century. Divided into two subsections, the concluding section of McGann's study engages with the neglected praxis and criticism of Laura (Riding) Jackson and debates the supposed truth-value and function of poetry.

Douglas Mao and Rebecca L. Walkowitz (eds), *Bad Modernisms* (Durham: Duke UP, 2006)

This vibrant collection of essays will appeal to students and scholars interested in critical developments in the field of the so-called 'new modernist studies'. Among other things, the advocates of the new modernist studies – or 'new modernisms' – encourage us to challenge long-standing critical and methodological assumptions concerning the production of experimental literature, dance, architecture and aesthetics in the twentieth century. In essence, they broaden the definition of modernism. In their useful introduction, Mao and Walkowitz recognize an expanded modernism – whether in terms of global geography, cultural producers or periodization. They also embrace ideas of queerness and affect that have long been topics of psychoanalytic and theoretical discussion. In their own words, the new modernist studies has extended the designation 'modernist' beyond such familiar figures as Eliot, Pound, Joyce and Woolf. More critically inclusive and pluralistic, the new modernist studies has embraced – and analysed – the work of diverse writers and artists hitherto perceived as neglectful of, or even resistant to, the sorts of formal innovation traditionally associated with (predominantly Anglo-American) models of literary and aesthetic modernism. This critical shift is aptly reflected in *Bad Modernisms*. As well as reconsidering well-established figures, this volume engages with the work of lesser-known writers and visual artists such as Carlos

Bulosan and Len Lye. Read together, the eleven essays featured in this volume shed significant critical light on modernism's preoccupation with matters of transgression, nonsensicality, politics, affect, quietude, sexuality and elitism.

Laura Marcus, *The Tenth Muse: Writing about Cinema in the Modernist Period* (Oxford: Oxford UP, 2010)

This major work of criticism will be of great use to students and scholars of modernism, especially those interested in understanding the complex relationship between early cinema and twentieth-century Anglo-American literature. Marcus details how the very first writers who chose to engage with cinematic matters – be they critics, reviewers or theorists – strove to produce cultural and aesthetic categories that could be used to define and accommodate what was alternatively referred to as 'the seventh art' or 'the tenth muse'. *The Tenth Muse* opens with a detailed historical account of cinema's formative critical reception. Here, Marcus emphasizes that the earliest critical treatments of cinema discourse tended to read film in relation to other, far more established aesthetic categories such as drama, dance, opera, music and literature. At the same time, however, Marcus finds that many, if not all, of those who chose to write about film did so in an attempt to articulate new ideas about vision and identity in what was a rapidly changing, modernizing realm. Reading instances of early film criticism by figures such as Maxim Gorky and Sergei Eisenstein alongside contemporaneous literary texts by a diverse range of modern and modernist authors including H. G. Wells, Rudyard Kipling, John Rodker, D. H. Lawrence, Hilda Doolittle, Dorothy Richardson, James Joyce and Virginia Woolf, the subsequent chapters of *The Tenth Muse* – which also features detailed discussion of key periodicals such as *Close Up* – chart the various ways in which early developments in cinema necessitated a thoroughgoing recalibration of the relations between the literature and aesthetics.

Susan McCabe, *Cinematic Modernism: Modernist Poetry and Film* (Cambridge: Cambridge UP, 2005)

Students and scholars of poetry and film will find much of interest in *Cinematic Modernism*, which, among other things, features a series of readings of important texts such as William Carlos Williams's *Kora in Hell* and Gertrude Stein's *The*

Making of Americans. In particular, McCabe's study will appeal to those who are interested in the literary and visual application of psychoanalytical theory and experimental psychology, as well as to those whose critical expertise extends to the important, interwoven fields of racial, gender and queer studies. *Cinematic Modernism* considers the generative links that can be discerned between silent film and the poetic output of four major American modernist poets: Williams, Stein, Hilda Doolittle and Marianne Moore. In the five chapters of her study, McCabe pays special attention to the ways in which cinematic techniques such as montage can be said to approximate literary modernity's wider, contemporaneous fascination with notions of bodily fragmentation which rose to prominence in the wake of the First World War. In essence, McCabe's central contention is that particular formal and technical advances in experimental cinema afforded responsive modernist writers with a new critical vocabulary through which they might better explore – and subsequently rework – physical, metaphorical and figurative categories pertaining to the 'modern' body (such as the automaton, the femme fatale, the bisexual and the hysteric).

Gabrielle McIntire, *Modernism, Memory, and Desire: T. S. Eliot and Virginia Woolf* (Cambridge: Cambridge UP, 2012)

Divided into two main sections, McIntire's study focuses on the fictional, poetic, critical and autographical texts of two canonical first-generation Anglo-American modernists: Virginia Woolf and T. S. Eliot. McIntire proffers a detailed critical treatment of a profound, perhaps even insoluble, paradox residing at the heart of much, if not all, modernist literary production: the imbrication of memory and desire. As is well known, the numerous literary modernists were particularly effusive in their praise for, and equally demonstrative in their embrace of, innovation. At the same time, however, a number of the movement's leading lights were interested, sometimes obsessively so, in the way that present-day literature remained in constant dialogue with past works. Drawing on the ideas of diverse thinkers and theorists including Jean-Jacques Rousseau, Paul Ricoeur, Michel de Certeau, Homi K. Bhabha, Jacques Derrida, Julia Kristeva, Jacques Lacan, Sigmund Freud and Henri Bergson, McIntire considers the ways in which this interest in the mechanics of memory manifests itself in the work of Eliot and Woolf. Asserting that the act of remembrance is, in her own words, animated and preserved by eros, McIntire finds that in their writing the past functions as a never-fully-lost object that can always be revived in (and for) the present. Especially notable in its reassessment of Eliot, McIntire's study will appeal to students and scholars engaged in the study of high modernism, as well as those interested in critical theory and psychoanalytically inflected interpretations of largely familiar literary texts.

Tyrus Miller, *Late Modernism: Politics, Fiction and the Arts between the World Wars* (California: California UP, 1999)

Students and scholars interested in the development of second-generation or so-called late modernism will find much of use in Miller's influential contribution to the critical field, which focuses on the historical trajectory of experimental Anglo-American literature in the 1920s and 1930s. Miller opens his wide-ranging study with a useful account of the state of modernist criticism. Following the lead of influential writer-critics such as Ezra Pound and T. S. Eliot, the overwhelming majority of scholars have tended, in Miller's estimation, to define the movement in relation to evaluative and figurative underpinnings of modernism itself, and with the famous Poundian imperative to 'make it new'. Citing major studies of literary modernism such as Hugh Kenner's enduringly influential account of *The Pound Era* (1971), Miller also suggests that most traditional scholarship has focused on the formative origins and early stages of cultural modernism. Miller argues that this critical tendency does modernism something of a disservice. He suggests that we turn the chronological telescope around, so to speak. His revisionary *Late Modernism* is divided into two main sections and a coda. The first section contextualizes the literature of the late 1920s and 1930s. The second examines the late modernist output of important figures such as Wyndham Lewis, Djuna Barnes and Samuel Beckett. Miller's coda considers Mina Loy's posthumously published novel *Insel*.

Mark S. Morrison, *The Public Face of Modernism: Little Magazines, Audiences and Reception, 1905–1920* (Wisconsin: Wisconsin UP, 2001)

Providing detailed instances of textual and contextual analysis, this valuable contribution to the critical field challenges long-standing assumptions regarding Anglo-American modernism's supposed antipathy towards mass (commodity) culture. In it, Morrison seeks to document how literary modernity and mass culture existed in a sort of symbiotic relationship, developing in tandem, in the years between 1905 and 1920. The so-called 'little magazine' assumes a prominent position in Morrison's account of *The Public Face of Modernism*. Situating his intervention in relation to Jürgen Habermas's influential critical notion of the bourgeois public sphere, Morrison suggests that while many prominent modernists were more than happy to disparage the products of mass culture, their recourse to the literary support systems provided by periodical print culture productively complicates our understanding of the relationship between aesthetic autonomy and processes of commodification. Emphasizing the fact that the majority of ostensibly oppositional avant-garde periodicals draw on publicity and marketing strategies developed by the purveyors of commercialized media, Morrison explores the development and reception of a range of significant first-generation modernist little magazines including *The Little Review, The Freewoman* (later *The Egoist*), *Poetry and Drama, The English Review* and *The Masses*. This impressively researched study, which also includes discussions of canonical modernist writers such as James Joyce, George Bernard Shaw, T. S. Eliot, William Carlos Williams, Ford Madox Ford and Wyndham, will, among other things, appeal to students and scholars interested in interwoven issues of gender, race, class and the conflicted field of literary print culture in the early decades of the twentieth century.

Julian Murphet, *Multimedia Modernism: Literature and the Anglo-American Avant-Garde* (Cambridge: Cambridge UP, 2009)

This significant contribution to the field is informed in equal measure by developments in literary criticism, critical theory and media history. Murphet proffers a staunch materialist reading of first- and second-generation Anglo-American modernism. He seeks to detail the manner in which assorted developments in areas including photography, cinematography, advertising and media print technology impacted directly on the work of a number of early Anglo-American modernist writers. Specifically, Murphet endeavours to demonstrate the ways in which the formally innovative literary and aesthetic outputs of modernists such as Wyndham Lewis, Ezra Pound, Gertrude Stein and Louis Zukofsky were shaped by their imbrication in, and engagement with, what he characterizes as a rapidly changing media landscape or ecology.

First positioning his study in relation to the wider fields of modernist literary criticism and critical theory, Murphet then situates Stein's avant-gardism in relation to Alfred Stieglitz's ground-breaking photographic journal *Camera Work*. Murphet then reads Pound's early poetry alongside the cinema of D. W. Griffith, before turning his attention to Lewis's celebrated and confrontational Vorticist periodical *BLAST*. Then, in the last chapter of his study, Murphet establishes links between Zukofsky's poetry, the cinema of Charlie Chaplin and Marx's *Capital*. Encouraging us to reconsider our understanding of the relationship between modernism, media, technology and political economy, Murphet's study will appeal to those students and scholars who are interested in the field of new modernist studies (as set forth in the work of assorted critics such as Armstrong, Danius and Wollaeger).

Richard Murphy, *Theorizing the Avant-Garde: Modernism, Expressionism, and the Problem of Postmodernity* (Cambridge: Cambridge UP, 1999)

Murphy's study serves as a useful critical corrective and will appeal to students and scholars interested in the vexed relationship between modernism and the so-called historical avant-garde, as famously defined by the critic Peter Bürger. Murphy's introduction contains a detailed discussion of Bürger's seminal *Theory of the Avant-Garde* (1974). From the outset of his study, Murphy makes it clear that he has significant reservations about Bürger's classical theoretical overview of twentieth-century avant-gardism, which focuses almost exclusively on aesthetic formations such as Dadaism and Surrealism. Murphy's reservations have much to do with Bürger's now rather limited understanding of the relationship between the historical avant-garde and modernism. In Murphy's estimation, Bürger conspicuously fails to address the significant conceptual overlap between these two categories. In marked contrast, Murphy insists that we acknowledge the dialectical relationship underpinning modernism and the avant-garde. Drawing on the work of critical theorists such as Georg Lukács, Herbert Marcuse, Walter Benjamin and Theodor W. Adorno, and illustrating his revisionary account of avant-gardism with detailed close readings of German Expressionist literature and cinema, Murphy forces us to reconsider preconceived notions of the avant-garde and modernist literature and aesthetics. In turn, Murphy also seeks to reposition our understanding of the avant-garde in relation to contemporaneous conceptions of postmodernity.

Ira Nadel, *Modernism's Second Act: A Cultural Narrative* (Houndmills: Palgrave Macmillan, 2012)

Comprising three main sections and a coda, this study focuses on what is usually described as the late modernist period. Nadel makes this much clear in the preface, where he situates his study in relation to earlier treatments of modernism such as Samuel Hyne's *The Auden Generation* (1976) and Miller's influential *Late Modernism* (1999). In contrast to those accounts, which, broadly speaking, focus on Anglo-American literary and aesthetic avant-gardism, Nadel's study concentrates on the trajectory of European modernism as it developed between 1930 and 1960. Set against a historical backdrop blighted by Fascism, Nazism and Stalinism, and featuring analyses of figures such as Gertrude Stein, Pablo Picasso, Ezra Pound, Hermann Broch and Arthur Koestler, Nadel's study scrutinizes some of the troubling conceptual alignments and complicities between European modernism and systems of political totalitarianism which emerged in this period. To what extent, Nadel asks, did Continental modernism's continuation, indeed its very survival, depend on unsavoury political compromise with dominant forms of political authoritarianism? And what impact might this have had on the subsequent direction and shape of the post-war modernist project? These are some of the important questions that Nadel poses in his study, which demands that we revisit the past in order better to understand what the author describes as the cultural narrative of late modernism.

Peter Nicholls, *Modernisms: A Literary Guide, Second Edition* (Houndmills: Palgrave Macmillan, 2008)

This is an important and wide-ranging guide to a significant number of the literary and aesthetic movements which emerged between 1840 and 1940. It will appeal to modernist students and scholars alike. Nicholls proposes that we view modernism not as some sort of monolithic ideological formation, but rather as a series of discrete and often antithetical, yet sometimes interwoven, literary and aesthetic tendencies (hence the pluralized title of the volume). It is, according to Nicholls, emphatically *not* to be viewed as a comprehensive documentary survey of modernism. Nicholls makes this much clear in his preface, where he explains that his intention is to investigate the intersection of politics and style and to present a sort of conceptual map of competing modernist literary materials and movement. Nicholls's opening chapter focuses on what we might describe as the prehistory of modernism proper. In this chapter, Nicholls discusses the literary achievements of influential nineteenth-century writers such as Charles Baudelaire, Fyodor Dostoevsky and Herman Melville. Baudelaire also features in the next chapter, which focuses on the emergence of the Symbolism movement. In the third, Nicholls turns his attention to the decadent and philosophically inspired models of writing that came to prominence at the end of the nineteenth century. The remaining nine chapters cover the first three decades of the twentieth century. In these chapters, Nicholls analyses Italian and Russian Futurism, French Cubism, German Expressionism, Anglo-American modernism, the Harlem Renaissance, Dada, Neo-Classicism, 'high' modernism and Surrealism.

Michael North, *The Dialect of Modernism: Race, Language, and Twentieth Century Literature* (Oxford: Oxford UP, 1998)

The Dialect of Modernism is an irrefutably important contribution to the critical field. Serving as a useful and necessary corrective to the ethnically absolutist work of earlier critics like Houston A. Baker, North's study explores the contentious issue of race in relation to mainstream American literary modernism. North's central thesis is built around a troubling anomaly, which has much to do with language. North contends that ideas about race played a prominent, indeed central, role in the modernist preoccupation with the possibility of a specifically 'American' language. Specifically, North seeks to demonstrate the manner in which prominent American modernists including e. e. cummings, T. S. Eliot, Gertrude Stein, Ezra Pound and William Carlos Williams looked favourably, and problematically, upon representations of Afro-American dialect in poetry. According to North, American modernists such as those listed above equated their position as literary outsiders with the status of historically oppressed and marginalized racial subjects. In his estimation, American modernists tended to believe, unthinkingly, that the artist or writer occupied a role equivalent to that of a racial outsider because they sought recourse to a language opposed to the norm. This tendency, North suggests, accounts for the prominent use of dialect in much American modernist literature. North is critical of such an appropriation, and his account of the writers listed above demonstrates some of the ways in which modernism acted out a disquieting form of linguistic racial masquerade.

Michael North, *Machine-Age Comedy*
(Oxford: Oxford UP, 2009)

North's interdisciplinary study concerns the relationship between modernity and the comic form in literature, film, animation and the visual arts. It will appeal to students of literature and film, and to scholars interested in theories of technological reproduction, mechanization and the intersection of avant-gardism, fine art, and forms of popular culture. In it, North documents the manner in which the historic changes wrought by processes of industrialization have irrevocably changed the structure and content of the comic mode. Building on philosophical reflection, psychoanalytic speculation and literary criticism suggesting that certain characteristics associated with modernist aesthetics – such as fragmentation, repetition, paradox and incongruity – define the comic form, North puts forward a series of detailed close readings that engage with a wide range of popular and highbrow artworks. These readings reveal some of the creative – and often unconventional – ways that processes of industrial and societal routinization have been explored. Divided into three main sections, North's illuminating account of so-called 'machine-age comedy' describes how a wide range of modern and postmodern artists, film-makers, actors, writers, critical theorists and animators including Charlie Chaplin, Marcel Duchamp, Walt Disney, Henri Bergson, Dziga Vertov, Rube Goldberg, Wyndham Lewis, David Foster Wallace, Walter Benjamin, Samuel Beckett and Buster Keaton sought in their work to document, and respond to, the pressures exerted upon the individual in the twentieth century.

Deborah Parsons, *Theorists of the Modernist Novel:*
James Joyce, Dorothy Richardson and Virginia Woolf
(London: Routledge, 2006)

Complementing Beasley's *Theorists of Modernist Poetry* (2007), Parsons's informative introduction to the modernist novel is designed to appeal to students who are new to the field, as well as those who have an interest in the development of modernist narrative techniques such as so-called 'stream-of-consciousness' writing, and those who have a specific interest in understanding the finer nuances of the versions of literary modernism as practised by James Joyce, Virginia Woolf and Dorothy Richardson. Much like the aforementioned *Theorists of Modernist Poetry*, Parsons's account of the modernist novel is ordered chronologically. This study is divided into four main chapters. The first of these chapters situates the rise of the modernist novel in its proper historical and cultural context. Having done so, Parsons explores how Joyce, Richardson and Woolf each strove to formulate adequate narrative alternatives to pre-existing forms of literary realism in their early work. Having established a useful literary-historical framework with which to appreciate the conceptual and structural complexities of the modernist novel, concerned as it often was with the representation of subjective consciousness, Parsons proceeds to detail the different ways in which each writer sought to negotiate and limitations and possibilities of evermore self-reflexive modern fiction. The third chapter considers the issue of gender and the literary representation of a specifically female consciousness in major works such as Woolf's *Orlando*, Richardson's *Pilgrimage* and Joyce's *Ulysses*. As it happens, *Orlando* and *Ulysses* also feature at the start of the fourth and final chapter, which is given over to a helpful discussion of the treatment of temporality and the representation of history in the modernist novel.

Allison Pease, *Modernism, Feminism, and the Culture of Boredom* (Cambridge: Cambridge UP, 2012)

Engaging with ideas of affect, this critical study considers the representation of boredom among female literary characters in Britain modernist literature produced in the early decades of the twentieth century. Pease explores the manner in which changing conceptions and meanings of boredom inform (and reform) our understanding of modernist literature. In Pease's estimation, the presence of boredom in literary modernism should be read in the context of a number of wider cultural and social forces at play in early twentieth-century Britain, especially those pertaining to feminism, the Suffragist movement and the historical struggle for equal rights. Pease's central contention is that literary representations of boredom in modernist fiction form part of this broader feminist protest against the patriarchal strictures of early twentieth-century British society. Having first acknowledged the fact that this claim runs the risk of striking readers as counterintuitive, Pease proceeds to explore how the experiences of the indifferent and bored heroines which feature in the diverse works of British writers, such as May Sinclair, Virginia Woolf, D. H. Lawrence, E. M. Forster, Robert Hitchens, Arnold Bennett, H. G. Wells and Dorothy Richardson, can be said to reflect fluctuating cultural mores and changing social roles. In so doing, Peace finds that many of the male writers mentioned above effectively seek to shore up conservative societal structures, while their female counterparts refuse to acquiesce to the constrictive roles hitherto afforded them.

Allison Pease, *Modernism, Mass Culture, and the Aesthetics of Obscenity* (Cambridge: Cambridge UP, 2000)

Pease charts the development of distinctly modern conceptions of obscenity and pornography in this informative study, which will be of particular interest to students and researchers engaged in the analysis of canonical British and Irish literary modernism. According to Pease, the origins of modern pornographic discourse are to be found in the eighteenth century. She argues that the emergence of pornography coincided with the birth of modern aesthetics (as theorized by Immanuel Kant, Frances Hutcheson and the third Earl of Shaftesbury). Specifically, Pease suggests that pornography and aesthetics developed together, in a discernibly dialectical relationship. Pursuing the historical trajectory of this particular dialectic, Pease shows that many serious modern artists and writers were influenced by mass-cultural pornographic representations of sex, sexuality and the body. Moreover, as Pease convincingly demonstrates, these same artists and writers often sought to incorporate pornographic tropes and imagery into their highbrow creative projects. Over the course of five detailed chapters dealing with literary figures such as Charles Algernon Swinburne, D. H. Lawrence, Aubrey Beardsley and James Joyce, Pease considers the complex and conflicted consequences of such processes of aesthetic incorporation and textual accommodation. She finds that the impact of Victorian and Edwardian pornography on forms of sexual representation in modernist art and literature is much more substantial than one might first assume.

Marjorie Perloff, *The Futurist Moment: Avant-Garde, Avant Guerre, and the Language of Rupture* (Chicago: Chicago UP, 1986)

Emphatically not a standard survey of Italian or Russian Futurism, this major work of comparative and interdisciplinary criticism analyses the historical development and creative afterlife of a number of simultaneous developments in early twentieth-century European avant-gardism. Focusing on the tumultuous creative period leading up to the outbreak of global conflict in 1914, Perloff, who conceives of the avant-garde as a cultural force capable of transcending national, political and aesthetic boundaries, considers the impact and lasting significance of the various verbal and visual experiments carried out by a diverse range of writers and artists working against the historical backdrop of what she, following Renato Poggiolo, refers to as the 'futurist moment'. Perloff explores the myriad aesthetic, linguistic, generic and conceptual 'ruptures' in the work of influential avant-gardists such as Blaise Cendrars, F. T. Marinetti, Kasimir Malevich, Vladimir Mayakovsky, Tristan Tzara and Ezra Pound. Featuring richly detailed analysis of the poetry, prose, manifestos and artworks of these and other related avant-garde practitioners, Perloff's study, which serves as a synchronic companion piece to her equally useful treatise *The Poetics of Indeterminacy: Rimbaud to Cage* (1981), proposes that the creative ventures undertaken by these early twentieth-century figures anticipated subsequent developments in postmodern aesthetic and literary praxis.

Rachel Potter, *Modernism and Democracy: Literary Culture 1900–1930* (Oxford: Oxford UP, 2006)

This productive study, which will appeal to students and scholars interested in the political character of experimental literature, focuses on the interrelations between first-generation Anglo-American modernist writing and conceptions of democracy. Focusing almost exclusively on avant-garde poetry, Potter analyses the modernist response to the rise of mass democracy in the first three decades of the twentieth century. She begins by noting that the emergence of literary modernism coincided with the birth of what we recognize as the modern democratic state. Potter then proceeds to examine the interesting tension at the heart of the relationship between modernism and democracy. In the first chapter, Potter considers the intellectual context of the years before the outbreak of war in 1914. Potter's second chapter concerns the diverse range of modernist responses to the political environment of the 1910s and 1920s. In this chapter, Potter focuses on the shift in nature of the largely negative modernist response to the emergent forces of liberalism and democracy. The third, fourth and fifth chapters analyse in detail the literary output of three specific Anglo-American poets: Hilda Doolittle, T. S. Eliot and Mina Loy. In these chapters, Potter re-evaluates critical conceptions of the relationship between literary modernism, sexual differences and democracy. In so doing, Potter deftly accounts for male and female modernist unease with contemporaneous democratic political mechanisms.

Zhaoming Qian, *Orientalism and Modernism: The Legacy of China in Pound and Williams* (Durham: Duke UP, 1995)

Qian discusses a number of important issues in his helpful account of Orientalism and Anglo-American literary modernism. Drawing on – yet by no means dependent upon – the work of influential postcolonialist thinkers like Edward Said, Qian's critical study focuses primarily on the poetic praxis of Ezra Pound and William Carlos Williams. Qian begins by reminding us of the fact that these two poets shared a mutual, deep-seated interest in Chinese culture. Qian then demonstrates that Pound and Williams, like many of their modernist contemporaries (Eliot, Yeats, Stevens, Moore), cast their eyes to the Far East for literary inspiration. In Qian's estimation, modernists such as Williams and Pound responded positively to a long-standing cultural heritage that privileged intensity, objectivity, visual clarity, harmony and precision. Yet despite this widely accepted observation, much more in the way of sustained critical enquiry needs to be undertaken if we are to understand the profound manner in which certain styles of Anglo-American modernism were directly linked to a steadily growing affinity for Chinese literary ideals and practices. This is precisely what Qian sets out to do in his richly detailed account of *Orientalism and Modernism*. Using Pound and Williams as primary examples, Qian finds that literary modernism simply cannot be understood without first understanding something of the culture of the Far East, especially China.

Jean-Michel Rabaté, *The Ghosts of Modernity* (Florida: Florida UP, 1996)

This is a conceptually dense, yet rewarding reappraisal of canonical literary modernism. It will appeal to students and scholars who are interested in the workings of high modernism and in the historical legacy of literary modernity more generally. Rabaté discusses the achievements of high modernist progenitors such as T. S. Eliot, Ezra Pound, Paul Verlaine and Stéphane Mallarmé while making extended reference to critical discourses like Freudian psychoanalytic theory and post-structural philosophy. Rabaté posits that prominent high modernists such as Eliot and Pound were 'haunted' by a number of voices drawn from the long- and the not-so-distant past. In this sense, Rabaté's argument mirrors the one expounded by the influential literary critic Harold Bloom in *The Anxiety of Influence: A Theory of Poetry* (1973). In that volume, as is well known, Bloom famously posited that younger writers are hindered, or rather haunted, by their influential predecessors, with whom they maintain an ambiguous, often anxiety-ridden relationship. However, unlike Bloom, Rabaté does not view haunting in merely literary terms. Notions of *historical* haunting often supersede purely literary matters in Rabaté's rereading of high modernism. This much is evident in Rabaté's preface, which, among other things, considers Pound's problematic understanding of and relationship with history. Building on the critical framework established in his preface, subsequent chapters of Rabaté's treatise feature detailed analysis of the works of Marcel Proust, James Joyce, André Breton, Roland Barthes, Mallarmé, Verlaine, Hermann Broch, Gertrude Stein, Laura (Riding) Jackson and Samuel Beckett.

Lawrence Rainey, *Institutions of Modernism: Literary Elites and Public Culture* (New Haven: Yale UP, 1999)

This influential account of the various institutions and networks underpinning the development of literary modernism will appeal to students and scholars alike. Rainey is especially interested in issues pertaining to the production and transmission of literary modernism between 1912 and 1940. Drawing on a wealth of unearthed archival material, he proposes that we move away from more traditional modes of formal textual analysis in order to broach the topic of literary modernism's complex and often contradictory relationship with public culture. Literary modernism, Rainey suggests, was marked by a withdrawal from the public sphere as theorized by the French sociologist Pierre Bourdieu. Rainey argues that this retreat marked a crucial turning point in the historical trajectory of canonical modernism. Dismissing the common cultural sphere as hopelessly compromised, a number of prominent modernists sought solace in a far more specialized, rarefied realm of deluxe editions, little magazines and literary patronage. In Rainey's estimation, this willed retreat had a number of far-reaching and occasionally negative consequences, a number of which have to do with the critical reception and cultural status of modernism itself.

Interested parties will find much to admire and question in Rainey's accounts of F. T. Marinetti, Ezra Pound and the avant-garde (1), the marketing of James Joyce's masterwork *Ulysses* (2), the complex publication history of T. S. Eliot's *The Waste Land* (3), the development of Pound's *Cantos* (4) and the oeuvre of Hilda Doolittle (5).

Victoria Rosner, *Modernism and the Architecture of Private Life* (New York: Columbia UP, 2005)

Rosner brings significant critical attention to bear on the complex relationship between modernist literature, design, gender and that which she describes as the 'conceptual vocabulary' of architecture in this interdisciplinary study, which will appeal to students and scholars interested in canonical Anglo-American modernism. In particular, Rosner seeks to demonstrate some of the ways in which private and domestic spatial structures impacted on the developmental trajectory of British literary modernism. Drawing on a wide range of primary texts and related archival materials, Rosner discusses the work of a diverse collection of late nineteenth- and early twentieth-century writers, artists and interior designers including James McNeill Whistler, Robert Kerr, Radclyffe Hall, Robert Edis, Arthur Conan Doyle, Geoffrey Scott, E. M. Forster and Oscar Wilde, as well as Bloomsbury Group members such as Virginia Woolf, Roger Fry, Vanessa Bell, Duncan Grant and Lytton Strachey. Over the course of five chapters – 'Kitchen Table Modernism', 'Frames', 'Thresholds', 'Studies' and 'Interiors' – Rosner describes how the various treatments of domestic space contained in the literary and aesthetic works produced by these and other assorted practitioners sought collectively to refine symbolic and material forms of (middle-class) private life. In demonstrating this, Rosner also productively complicates conventionally accepted critical notions of modernistic *interiority*.

Stephen Ross (ed.), *Modernism and Theory: A Critical Debate* (London: Routledge, 2008)

This useful collection of essays, which, among others things, includes an afterword by Fredric Jameson, will appeal to students interested in the aesthetic and methodological links that exist between the fields of modernist literature and critical theory. Productively complicating our understanding of 'modernism' as a literary (and aesthetic) conceptual category, this volume strives, in Ross's editorial estimation, to achieve three main things. First and foremost, it seeks to respond to recent materialistic, historicist and archival-based developments in the critical field, particularly those concerning the phenomenon of the so-called new modernist studies. Secondly, it attempts to readdress certain misperceptions of modernism proposed by critical and cultural theorists during the latter half of the twentieth century. Finally, it seeks to contextualize and readdresses critical theory's marginalization within contemporary modernist studies. *Modernism and Theory* is divided into three main parts. The first two – 'Concrete Connections' and 'Abstract Affiliations' – propose a series of dialogue of critical encounters. In these sections, scholars such as Hilary Thompson, Roger Rothman, Ben Highmore, Martin Jay, Pam Caughie and Scott McCracken debate the work and ideas of a range of important critical theorists including Henri Lefebvre, Walter Benjamin, Jacques Derrida, Giorgio Agamben and Theodor W. Adorno. The third section – 'Forum' – features contributions from Charles Altieri, Jane Goldman, Bonnie Kime Scott and Melba Cuddy-Keane, and attends to critical issues arising from broader theoretical, ethical, historical and aesthetic concerns.

Robert Scholes and Clifford Wulfman, *Modernism in the Magazines: An Introduction* (New Haven: Yale UP, 2010)

This indispensable critical survey, which is co-authored by the founder of the online Modernist Journals Project (Scholes) and the coordinator of the Library Digital Initiatives at Princeton University (Wulfman), will appeal to a wide range of students and scholars, particularly those interested in understanding the complex and historically embedded literary networks underpinning experimental print culture in the early decades of the twentieth century. In chapters such as 'Modernism and the Rise of Modernism: A Review' (1) and 'How to Study a Modern Magazine' (6), Scholes and Wulfman illustrate why we need to read periodicals and 'little magazines' as primary modernist texts. Indeed, they go as far to suggest that periodicals and magazines were so integral to the development of what we perceive as literary and aesthetic modernism that it is practically impossible to imagine the movement with them. In their estimation, the archetypal modernist periodical is a fundamentally dialogic and heteroglossic text, featuring a wide range of competing and complementary literary voices and personas. Entertaining the notion of the modernist magazine as a coherent literary text, Scholes and Wulfman demonstrate some of the significant ways in which a practical and thoroughgoing assessment of avant-garde periodical culture (and the various archives in which such materials are often stored) can serve to strengthen our general critical understanding of modernism. It should be read alongside Churchill and McKible's *Little Magazines & Modernism: New Approaches* (2007) and all three volumes of *The Oxford Critical and Cultural History of Modernist Magazines*, which is edited by Peter Booker, Andrew Thacker, Sascha Bru and Christian Wiekop.

Bonnie Kime Scott (ed.), *The Gender of Modernism* (Bloomington and Indianapolis: Indiana UP, 1990)

Arranged alphabetically, this is an indispensable research tool for all students, especially those interested in understanding how issues of gender and sexuality impacted on the historical development of Anglo-American literary modernism. Challenging traditional – and predominantly masculine – critical assumptions concerning the (sexual) politics of literary production, this revisionary volume brings together a wide range of experimental and non-experimental authors whose work touches on the crisis in gender identification underlying much, if not all, modernist writing. Emphasizing the various ways in which men and women participate – actively and unconsciously – in gendered social and cultural systems, Scott's edited anthology features selections from, and includes useful scholarly introductions to, the work of the following modernist writers: Djuna Barnes, Willa Cather, Nancy Cunard, Hilda Doolittle, T. S. Eliot, Jessie Redmon Fauset, Zora Neale Hurston, James Joyce, Nella Larsen, D. H. Lawrence, Mina Loy, Rose Macaulay, Hugh MacDiarmid, Katherine Mansfield, Charlotte Mew, Marianne Moore, Ezra Pound, Jean Rhys, Dorothy Richardson, May Sinclair, Gertrude Stein, Sylvia Townsend Warner, Rebecca West, Antonia White, Anna Wickham and Virginia Woolf. It should be read alongside Scott's later edited collection, *Gender in Modernism: New Geographies, Complex Intersections* (Urbana and Chicago: Illinois UP, 2007).

Paul Sheehan, *Modernism and the Aesthetics of Violence* (Cambridge: Cambridge UP, 2013)

This panoramic critical study focuses on the ingrained, and always troubling, relationship between violence and experimental aesthetics. In particular,

Sheehan seeks to document the development of the widespread modernist fascination, and infatuation, with forms of violence and bellicose expression. Sheehan's account of modernism and violence opens in the middle decades of the nineteenth century. Sheehan notes that this was a period in literary history when those French and English writers associated with the Aesthetic movement began to celebrate transgressive sexualities and depict forms of stylized criminality. He explores the development of aestheticism on French and English shores in the first section of his study. In the opening chapter, Sheehan finds that writers such as Théophile Gautier, Charles Baudelaire, A. C. Swinburne and Walter Pater laid the groundwork for modernism's later interest in the aesthetics of violence. In the second chapter, Sheehan considers the question of sexual deviance as depicted in literary aestheticism. Here, Sheehan suggests that aestheticism afforded writers a means with which to channel transgressive agencies that, in his words, pit sensual delight and carnal pleasure against mimetic propriety. Then, in the third chapter, Sheehan describes how such processes of aesthetic admixture gave rise to subsequent forms of decadent writing. Sheehan develops this point in his fourth chapter, which concerns Oscar Wilde's proto-decadent *The Picture of Dorian Gray*. Inaugurating the second portion of Sheehan's study, the fifth chapter carries us across the historical threshold and into the early twentieth century. In this section, Sheehan analyses the ways in which modernism responded to the legacy of aestheticism. Here, attention is paid to a number of suitably transgressive (and aesthetically unruly) modernists including Ezra Pound (Chapter 5), Wyndham Lewis (Chapter 6), James Joyce, W. B. Yeats, T. S. Eliot (Chapter 7), T. E. Hulme, David Jones (Chapter 8) and Joseph Conrad (Chapter 9).

Paul Sheehan, *Modernism, Narrative and Humanism* (Cambridge: Cambridge, 2008)

Sheehan sheds critical light on modernism's critique of the fundamental presumptions of humanism in this valuable, and at times provocative, volume. At the outset, Sheehan highlights the fact that the decades since the Second World War have been notable for engendering a reappraisal of what it means to be human. In Sheehan's estimation, post-war theoretical discourse has profoundly altered our understanding of what was previously assumed to be a discrete, implicitly understood idea and conceptual category. Commenting upon this shift, Sheehan suggests that post-war theoretical advances effectively transformed the category of the human into a site of contention, where, to paraphrase the author, notions of hybridity, contradiction and dispersion tend now to circulate freely. Sheehan reminds us that the roots of this sceptical post-war shift have much to do with the cataclysmic events of the *Shoah*. As is well known, in the wake of the European Holocaust, hitherto stable humanistic principles and categories associated with the Enlightenment began to break apart. Sheehan acknowledges this in the introduction to his *Modernism, Narrative and Humanism*. However, having done so, Sheehan then sets out to show that the origins of the post-1945 reassessment of humanism and the human as a given category are to be found much earlier, in the first few decades of the twentieth century. Identifying discernible elements of antihumanistic thinking in the work of major modernist writers including Joseph Conrad (Chapter 1), D. H. Lawrence (Chapter 2), Virginia Woolf (Chapter 3) and Samuel Beckett (Chapter 4), Sheehan's study productively complicates our critical understanding of the literature produced in the last 150 years.

Vincent Sherry, *The Great War and the Language of Modernism* (Oxford: Oxford UP, 2004)

In this important contribution to the field of modernist studies, which will appeal to those interested in the development of canonical Anglo-American modernism, Sherry argues for a historically informed reading of the experimental literature produced in the aftermath of the World War of 1914–18. Drawing on the influential formulations of literary critics such as I. A. Richards, and responding to the important critical work undertaken by Paul Fussell in *The Great War and Modern Memory* (1975) and by Jay Winter in *Sites of Memory, Sites of Mourning: The Great War in European Cultural History* (1998), Sherry revisits one of the central locations of what we have now come to label as high modernism: London. Sherry reminds us that the London of the early twentieth century was a charged and intensely political environment. In his informative prologue, Sherry notes that a crisis internal to the governing party of Britain – the English Liberals – defined this highly emotive and divisive moment in local political time. He points out that the Liberal Party had come to support a war that they should – by convention and principle – ought to have opposed. Moreover, as the historical register shows, such support often came cloaked in an obfuscatory language of logic, political rationality and rhetorical abstraction. Sherry's study illustrates some of the ways in which key modernists such as T. S. Eliot, Virginia Woolf and Ezra Pound developed literary strategies that might effectively responded to, lampooned and combated what they collectively diagnosed as the spurious, disingenuous and highly destructive *il*logic underlying such purportedly rational political abstractions.

Juan A. Suárez, *Pop Modernism: Noise and the Reinvention of Everyday Life* (Urbana and Chicago: Illinois UP, 2007)

Juan A. Suárez attempts to refashion literary modernism in this study, which will appeal to scholars interested in queer studies, cinema, popular culture and theories of everyday life. Suárez disdains outmoded accounts of modernism that treat popular culture as something to be feared, or which deem it unworthy of critical enquiry. Self-consciously positioning his intervention on the periphery, Suárez proffers a reassessment of a wide array of canonical and overlooked American modernists who figured their praxis in relation to the pressures of the everyday. Divided into three sections, Suárez's study charts the trajectory of a pop-orientated American modernism from the start of the twentieth century until the advent of Pop Art. The key to understanding the structure of *Pop Modernism* resides in the subtitle. In Suárez's estimation, 'noise' designates nonsignifying matter in verbal, visual and aural guises. The presence of ungovernable noise in modernist art is, for Suárez, an indicator of radical alterity, of otherness. The first section of the study comprises studies of modernists – Vachel Lindsay, Paul Strand, Charles Sheeler, John Dos Passos – whose relationship with noise generated by popular culture and everyday life was characterized by profound anxiety. In the second, Suárez analyses the ambivalent treatment of nonsignifying matter in the work of T. S. Eliot and Joseph Cornell. In the last, Suárez considers a number of dissident modernists that embraced the murmur of otherness: Charles Henri Ford, Parker Tyler, Zora Neale Hurston, James Agee, Janice Loeb and Helen Levitt.

Juliette Taylor-Batty, *Multilingualism in Modernist Fiction* (Houndmills: Palgrave Macmillan, 2013)

This study analyses the phenomenon of multilingualism in canonical modernist literature. Situating her work in relation to earlier critics such as George Steiner, and drawing on the linguistically diverse theories of early modernist writers such as the French poet-critic Stéphane Mallarmé, Walter Benjamin and the influential Russian Formalist Viktor Shklovsky, Taylor-Batty explores that which she describes as an discernible 'multilingual turn' in twentieth-century Anglo-American experimental literature. In the opening chapter, having first reminded us of the fact that the modernist period was characterized by a profound ambivalence when it came to matters of linguistic plurality, Taylor-Batty scrutinizes the various ways in which seminal avant-garde texts such as T. S. Eliot's *The Waste Land* and Mallarmé's 'Crise de vers' seek to examine and represent notions of linguistic crisis. Moving forward chronologically, Taylor-Batty then examines some of the polarized critical responses to James Joyce's multilingual masterpiece, *Work in Progress* (later *Finnegans Wake*). In the second chapter, she turns her attention to the fiction of Dorothy Richardson, Katherine Mansfield and D. H. Lawrence. Here, Taylor-Batty considers the relationship between linguistic diversity and characteristically modern conditions of travel, exile and migration. The third section focuses on the work of Jean Rhys. In particular, Taylor-Batty discusses the finer nuances of Rhys's creolizing modernist fictional style, which is figured here in terms of hierarchical destabilization, and her work as a translator of French. In the fourth chapter, Taylor-Batty examines the anti-mimetic multilingualism of Joyce's seminal, heterogeneous text of modernist literature, *Ulysses*. In the concluding chapter, Taylor-Batty details how the mid-career fiction of Joyce's compatriot Samuel Beckett simultaneously undermines and represents what she terms the chaos of language.

David Trotter, *Cinema and Modernism* (Oxford: Blackwell Publishing, 2007)

Trotter's account of the interaction between late nineteenth- and early twentieth-century literary modernism and early cinema is an impressive and important contribution to the critical field. Students and scholars alike will find much to admire in Trotter's comprehensive study, which seeks to historicize the relationship between cinema and modernism. Eschewing what he perceives as overly simplistic comparative accounts of certain literary and filmic techniques (such as montage), Trotter considers modernism's mediation of, and convergence with, a range of cinematic forms. Drawing on the ideas of the influential French film critic and theorist André Bazin, Trotter finds that advances in cinema afforded Anglo-American literary modernists the opportunity to explore notions of automatism and representational neutrality. Following an initial discussion of the stereoscope, a nineteenth-century invention of significant interest for many prominent modernists, Trotter turns his attention to the way in which the dialectical tension between cinema's privileged engagement with the real ('immediacy') and its simultaneous tendency towards abstraction ('hypermediacy') impacted on the historical trajectory of literary modernity. Featuring compelling, chapter-length readings of writers and film-makers such as D. W. Griffith, Charlie Chaplin, James Joyce, T. S. Eliot and Virginia Woolf, Trotter's essential study finds that cinema and literature in the early decades of the twentieth century shared an interest in related – and quintessentially modern – ideas stemming from issues of reality, representation and impersonality.

David Trotter, *Paranoid Modernism: Literary Experiment, Psychosis, and the Professionalization of English Society* (Oxford: Oxford UP, 2001)

In this study, which focuses on the literary modernism of Joseph Conrad, Ford Madox Ford, D. H. Lawrence and Wyndham Lewis, Trotter explores the manner in which experimental writing of the late nineteenth and early twentieth century intersected with a number of related issues pertaining to questions of identity and insanity, subject formation, the fear of contingency (or randomness), gender anxiety, the spread of liberal democracy in the years leading up to the First World War, anti-mimetic aesthetic perspective, and the psychological impact and consequences of the professionalization of English society. In Trotter's estimation, the last of these – the issue of professionalization – is especially important, particularly when read in relation to contemporaneous psychoanalytic and psychiatric conceptions of paranoia. Trotter begins by reminding us that paranoia was, in the nineteenth century, one of the names given to a type of psychosis in which the patient typically developed an internally consistent, yet delusional system of beliefs based on the certainty that he or she was a person of great note. He then establishes a link between the condition of paranoia and certain anxieties exhibited by the members of the emergent professional class. Trotter suggests that there was more than a hint of madness in the average professional's understanding and pursuit of symbolic capital (represented here in terms of specialization, mastery and expertise). He reasons that the sense of disappointment arising from one's failure to secure adequate amounts of such symbolic capital could precipitate a slide into paranoia. Having thus established a working definition of professional paranoia, Trotter proceeds to detail the manner in which the work of modernists such as those mentioned above, all of whom wrote about madness and masculinity, sought to respond to the pressures of a highly pressurized, increasingly professionalized and potentially psychosis-inducing literary marketplace.

Raymond Williams, *Politics of Modernism: Against the New Conformists* (London: Verso, 1989)

In this posthumously published collection of polemical essays and fragmentary critical pieces, the important cultural materialist Raymond Williams seeks to move beyond what he regards as the unduly constrictive bounds of purely formal literary analysis. Instead, Williams proposes that we analyse modernism as a multifaceted cultural, social and historical phenomenon. We get a clear sense of Williams's intentions in the opening essay, 'When Was Modernism?' In this relatively brief, yet hugely influential instance of historicist criticism, Williams traces the origins of what we have come to understand as cultural modernism back into the middle decades of the nineteenth century. Having done so, Williams reminds us that the latter half of the nineteenth century was the occasion for the greatest series of developments ever witnessed in the apparatus of cultural production. Emphasizing the fact that such changes in the media of cultural production played a crucial role in the development of vital modernist movements such as Futurism, Cubism, Constructivism, Imagism and Surrealism, Williams then considers some of the reasons behind cultural modernism's subsequent integration into that which he describes as the new international capitalism. Ambitious in its scope, *The Politics of Modernism* is essential for any student interested in issues pertaining to modernism, post-modernism, avant-gardism and politics.

Mark Wollaeger, *Modernism, Media, and Propaganda: British Narrative from 1900 to 1945* (Princeton: Princeton UP, 2006)

This is an important historicist and intermedial reading of literary and aesthetic modernism. As the title of his study suggests, Wollaeger's interest concerns narrative modes of modernism – be they novelistic or cinematic – which were developed in Britain between 1900 and 1945. Supplementing a number of highly nuanced close readings with reference to contemporary media theory and freshly unearthed archival material, Wollaeger's impressively argued study reappraises the relationship between artistic experimentalism and modern propaganda. He suggests that both modernism and propaganda provided means with which to cope with increasingly dizzying flows of information which were threatening to outstrip the modern subject's mental processing capacity during the period in question. Wollaeger's central contention is that these two seemingly antithetical concepts were, in fact, mutually illuminating responses to the condition (and problem) of modernity. Having outlined his critical position, Wollaeger proceeds to consider a number of specific modernist responses to the emergence of propaganda in the first half of the twentieth century. In five detailed sections dealing with the literary and aesthetic praxis of Joseph Conrad and Alfred Hitchcock (Chapter 1), Leonard and Virginia Woolf (Chapter 2), Ford Madox Ford (Chapter 3), James Joyce (Chapter 4) and Orson Welles (Chapter 5), he reveals how the modernist response to the rise of propaganda could be antagonistic, markedly ambivalent or, at times, worryingly complicit.

Modernism – A Timeline

Date	Literary/Artistic Events	Other Events
1857	Charles Baudelaire: *Les fleurs du mal*	
1873	Arthur Rimbaud: *A Season in Hell*	
1876		Alexander Bell invents the telephone
1877		Thomas Edison invents the phonograph
1879	Henrik Ibsen: *A Doll's House*	Edison invents the light bulb
1880	Émile Zola: 'The Experimental Novel'	
1882		First Neurology Clinic founded at the Salpêtrière Hospital in Paris
1883		Friedrich Nietzsche: *Thus Spoke Zarathustra*
1885		Invention of internal combustion engine
1886	Jean Moréas: *The Symbolist Manifesto*	
1887		National Union of Women's Suffrage Societies founded
1888	August Strindberg: *Miss Julie*	George Eastman invents the box camera Proof of existence of electromagnetic waves
1889		Paris Exposition (Eiffel Tower)
1890	Knut Hamsun: *Hunger* Henrik Ibsen: *Hedda Gabler*	First automobile William James: *The Principles of Psychology*
1891	Oscar Wilde: *The Picture of Dorian Gray*	
1893	Edvard Munch's expressionist painting *The Cry*	
1894		Outbreak of Sino-Japanese War (1894–95)
1895		Discovery of X-rays Lumière Brothers show first projected moving pictures Guglielmo Marconi invents telegraphy Trial of Oscar Wilde

Date	Literary/Artistic Events	Other Events
1896	Anton Chekhov: *The Seagull*	
1897	H. G. Wells: *The Invisible Man*	Discovery of the electron
1898	Émile Zola: *J'accuse* H. G. Wells: *War of the Worlds*	Curies discover radium and plutonium
1899	Joseph Conrad: *Heart of Darkness*	Beginning of the Boer War (1899–1902) Peace Conference at The Hague Sigmund Freud *The Interpretation of Dreams* (psychoanalysis)
1900	Joseph Conrad: *Lord Jim* Anton Chekhov: *Three Sisters*	Max Planck introduces quantum physics
1901	Thomas Mann: *Buddenbrooks* August Strindberg: *Dance of Death* Picasso's pre-Cubist 'Blue Period'	Death of Queen Victoria First transmission of radio wave signals across the Atlantic
1902	André Gide: *The Immoralist* Hugo von Hoffmansthal: 'Lord Chandos Letter'	William James: *Varieties of Religious Experience*
1903	W. E. B. Du Bois: *The Souls of Black Folk* Henry James: *The Ambassadors* George Bernard Shaw: *Man and Superman*	Wright brothers' first successful airplane flight Women's Social and Political Union First narrative silent film (*The Great Train Robbery*)
1904	Anton Chekhov: *The Cherry Orchard* Joseph Conrad: *Nostromo* Opening of Abbey Theatre (Dublin)	Beginning of Russo-Japanese War (1904–05)
1905	Fauvism (Paris) Edith Wharton: *The House of Mirth* Oscar Wilde: *De Profundis*	Albert Einstein proposes special theory of relativity First electric bus in London Failed Revolution in Russia
1907	Pablo Picasso paints *Demoiselles d'Avignon*	
1908		Ford Motor Company begins mass production of cars
1909	Henri Matisse: *The Dance* Ezra Pound: *Personae* Filippo Marinetti: *The Futurist Manifesto* Gertrude Stein: *Three Lives* Serge Diaghilev founds the Ballets Russes	

Date	Literary/Artistic Events	Other Events
1910	First post-impressionist exhibition (London) E. M. Forster: *Howards End* Igor Stravinsky: *The Firebird*	
1911	Kandinsky and others found the Expressionist art group in Munich	
1912	Marcel Duchamp: *Nude Descending a Staircase* Arnold Schonberg: *Pierrot Lunaire* *A Slap in the Face of Public Taste* (Maiakovskii; Russian Futurist manifesto) Thomas Mann: *Death in Venice*	
1913	D. H. Lawrence: *Sons and Lovers* Marcel Proust: *A la recherche du temps perdu* (1913–27) Ezra Pound's Vorticist movement Kandinsky: *On the Spiritual in Art* Igor Stravinsky: *The Rite of Spring* (performed by the Ballets Russes in Paris) New York International Exhibition of Modern Art	Suffragette demonstrations in London
1914	James Joyce: *Dubliners* Franz Kafka: 'In the Penal Colony' Wyndham Lewis's magazine *Blast* first published (1914–15)	Assassination of Archduke Franz Ferdinand leads to outbreak of First World War (1914–19)
1915	Constantin Brancusi: *Princess X* Franz Kafka: *The Metamorphosis* D. H. Lawrence: *The Rainbow* Ford Madox Ford: *The Good Soldier* Ezra Pound: *Cathay* Dorothy Richardson: *Pilgrimage* (1915–67)	
1916	H. D.: *Sea Garden* James Joyce: *A Portrait of the Artist as a Young Man* Dadaism founded in Zurich	Albert Einstein's general theory of relativity Easter Rising in Dublin

Date	Literary/Artistic Events	Other Events
1917	Marcel Duchamp: *Fountain* T. S. Eliot: *Prufrock and Other Observations* Luigi Pirandello: *Right You Are, If You Think You Are* Paul Valéry: *La Jeune Parquet* Sergei Prokofiev: *'Classical' Symphony*	Russian Revolution Carl Jung: *The Unconscious*
1918		Women over thirty receive right to vote in the UK Oswald Spengler: *The Decline of the West* (1918–22)
1919	Pablo Picasso: *Pierrot and Harlequin* United Artists film studio founded in Hollywood	Treaty of Versailles; end of First World War Establishment of Weimar Republic First commercial flight (Paris to London) Women obtain right to vote in the United States
1920	D. H. Lawrence: *Women in Love* Ezra Pound: *Hugh Selwyn Mauberley*	Founding of the League of Nations Gandhi's non-violent campaign begins Prohibition in the United States (1920–23)
1921	Pablo Picasso: *Three Musicians* (Cubism) Luigi Pirandello: *Six Characters in Search of an Author* Arnold Schoenberg's twelve-tone method of musical composition	Irish Free State established Ludwig Wittgenstein: *Tractatus Logico-Philosophicus*
1922	Constantin Brancusi: *Bird in Space* James Joyce: *Ulysses* T. S. Eliot: *The Waste Land* Katherine Mansfield: *The Garden Party* Wallace Stevens: *Harmonium* Virginia Woolf: *Jacob's Room*	
1924	*First Surrealist Manifesto* E. M. Forster: *A Passage to India* Thomas Mann: *The Magic Mountain* Sean O'Casey: *Juno and the Paycock*	Death of Vladimir Ilyich Lenin

Date	Literary/Artistic Events	Other Events
1925	Sergei Eisenstein: *Battleship Potemkin* Franz Kafka: *The Trial* Alain Locke: *The New Negro* F. Scott Fitzgerald: *The Great Gatsby* Ezra Pound: *The Cantos* (1925–64) Gertrude Stein: *The Making of Americans* Virginia Woolf: *Mrs. Dalloway*	Adolf Hitler: *Mein Kampf* Werner Heisenberg's theory of quantum mechanics
1926	Alberto Giacometti: *The Couple; Spoon Woman* Ernest Hemingway: *The Sun Also Rises* Langston Hughes: *The Weary Blues* Franz Kafka: *The Trial* Fritz Lang: *Metropolis* Henry Moore: *Draped Reclining Figure* (sculpture) Frank Lloyd Wright's 'Graycliff Estate' (1926–29)	General Strike in the UK
1927	Launch of film magazine *Close Up* Virginia Woolf: *To the Lighthouse*	First cross-Atlantic flight (Charles Lindbergh) Werner Heisenberg's uncertainty principle BBC begins radio broadcasts
1928	Formation of CIAM (*Congrés Internationaux d'Architecture Moderne*) Bertolt Brecht: *The Threepenny Opera* D. H. Lawrence: *Lady Chatterley's Lover* Wyndham Lewis: *The Childermass* Claude McKay: *Home to Harlem* Virginia Woolf: *Orlando* W. B. Yeats: *The Tower*	Alexander Fleming discovers penicillin

Date	Literary/Artistic Events	Other Events
1929	Elizabeth Bowen: *The Last September* William Faulkner: *The Sound and the Fury* Luigi Pirandello: *Tonight We Improvise* Virginia Woolf: *A Room of One's Own* W. B. Yeats: *The Winding Stair* *Second Surrealist Manifesto* Museum of Modern Art opens in New York Luis Buñuel and Salvador Dalí's Surrealist film, *Un chien andalou*	Collapse of New York stock market; Great Depression
1930	Jean Cocteau: *The Blood of a Poet* Hart Crane: *The Bridge* Robert Musil: *The Man without Qualities* Luis Buñuel's film, *L'Age d'or*	Sigmund Freud: *Civilisation and Its Discontents*
1931	Fritz Lang's film, *M* Eugene O'Neill: *Morning Becomes Electra* Edmund Wilson: *Axel's Castle: A Study in the Imaginative Literature of 1870–1930* Virginia Woolf: *The Waves*	
1932	Foundation of journal *Légitime Défense*	
1933		Franklin Roosevelt becomes US President Adolf Hitler appointed Chancellor of Germany Dachau Concentration Camp opened
1934	Nancy Cunard edits *Negro: An Anthology*	
1935	Wallace Stevens: *Ideas of Order*	
1936	Djuna Barnes: *Nightwood* William Faulkner: *Absalom, Absalom!* T. S. Eliot: *Four Quartets* (1936–42)	Stalin's Great Purge (1936–38) Beginning of Spanish Civil War (1936–39) Assassination of Federico García Lorca

Date	Literary/Artistic Events	Other Events
1937	Zora Neale Hurston: *Their Eyes Were Watching God* Pablo Picasso: *Guernica* Wallace Stevens: *The Man with the Blue Guitar and Other Poems* Nazi 'Degenerate Art' Exhibition (Munich)	
1938	Samuel Beckett: *Murphy*	
1939	James Joyce: *Finnegans Wake* Jean Rhys: *Good Morning, Midnight*	Death of Sigmund Freud and W. B. Yeats Second World War (1939–45)
1940	Charlie Chaplin: *The Great Dictator* Ernest Hemingway: *For Whom the Bell Tolls*	
1941	Virginia Woolf: *Between the Acts*	Deaths of James Joyce and Virginia Woolf
1945		End of the Second World War

Index